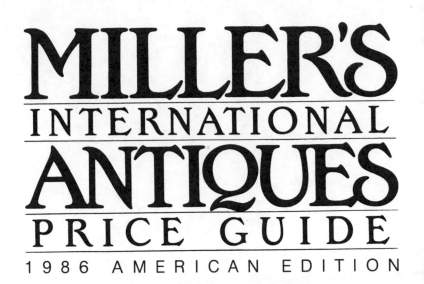

MILLER'S
INTERNATIONAL
ANTIQUES
PRICE GUIDE
1986 AMERICAN EDITION

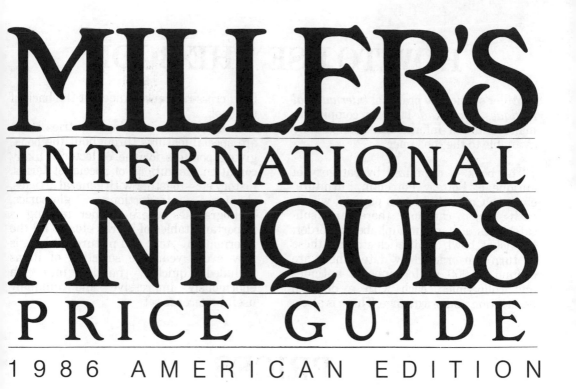

MILLER'S
INTERNATIONAL
ANTIQUES
PRICE GUIDE
1986 AMERICAN EDITION

COMPILED AND EDITED BY

JUDITH AND MARTIN MILLER

VIKING

HOW TO USE THE BOOK

Miller's uniquely practical *International Antiques Price Guide* has been compiled to make detailed information immediately available to the consumer.

The book is organized by category of antique: eg Pottery, Porcelain, Furniture, etc. (see Contents List on page 8); within each major category there are sub-categories of items in alphabetical order: eg basket, bowl, candlestick etc., and these in turn are ordered by date. There are around 10,000 photographs of antiques and collectibles, each with a detailed description and price range. There is also a fully cross-referenced index at the back of the book.

In addition to individual entries there are special features throughout the book, giving pointers for the collector – likely condition, definitions of specialist terms, history etc – together with general articles, chapter introductions, glossaries, bibliographies where further reading is important, tables of marks etc. As all the information – text and pictures alike – is new every year the selection of items included quickly builds into an enormously impressive and uniquely useful reference set.

PRICES

All the price ranges are based on actual prices of items bought and sold during the year prior to going to press. Thus the guide is fully up-to-date.

Prices are *not* estimates: because the value of an antique is what a willing buyer will pay to a willing seller, we have given not just one price per item but a range of prices to take into account regional differences and freak results.

This is the best way to give an idea of what an antique will *cost*, but should you wish to *sell* remember that the price you receive could be 25-30% less – antique dealers have to live too!!

Conditions
All items were in good merchantable condition when last sold unless damage is noted.

ACKNOWLEDGEMENTS

Judith and Martin Miller wish to thank a large number of International auctioneers, dealers and museums who have helped in the production of this edition. The auctioneers can be found in our specialist directory towards the back of this edition.

Copyright © M.J.M. Publications Ltd. 1986

**Viking Penguin Inc.,
40 West 23rd Street, New York,
New York 10010, U.S.A.
Penguin Books Canada Ltd.,
2801 John Street, Markham,
Ontario, Canada L3R 1B4**

**Designed and created by
M.J.M. Publications Ltd.
Sandway, Kent, England,
is association with
A.G.W. International Ltd.,
Chicago, Illinois.**

All rights reserved
First published in 1986 by Viking Penguin Inc.

Published simultaneously in Canada
Library of Congress Catalog
Card Number: 85-40714 (CIP Data Available)
ISBN: 0-670-810 36-3.

Printed in Great Britian
by William Clowes Ltd.
Set in Great Britain by Lin-Art Typesetters Ltd.,
Ashford, Kent.

Editors' Introduction

by

Martin and Judith Miller

We started *Miller's Antiques Price Guide* in 1979 as a small cottage industry. We believed that there was a great need for a guide that illustrated photographically a very large number of antiques and collectibles that had recently actually been on the market, and that gave good precise descriptions and realistic prices. We wanted to produce the book, because it was the book we wanted to buy and could not find. Obviously we were not alone, because the 1985 Edition of the guide, which we produced – as we did the previous five mainly for the British market, sold well over 100,000 copies and is now used daily not only by huge numbers of consumers but by major antique dealers and auction houses around the world as a standard reference work.

Last year we decided to produce a new edition especially for the US market. We have both travelled extensively and have always been convinced that, although there are obviously regional differences in the world of antiques, it is very much an *international* world and an *international* market – a fact borne out by the fact that the major auction houses in New York and London are the same companies. Dealers and collectors buy from all over the world directly or indirectly, and this makes a real impact upon the choice available everywhere. It really is a world without national barriers.

The first US edition followed the tradition of the original book. What we have produced was, we believe, by far the most comprehensive and practical book on the subject. Good, clear photographs of over 10,000 antiques and collectibles accompanied by detailed descriptions, masses of background detail, and researched price ranges made the book a standard reference for collector and professional alike.

The first U.S. edition of Miller's proved so successful in meeting the growing needs of the collector, dealer and enthusiast alike, to have a fully comprehensive International Antiques Price Guide, that we decided to follow up last years guide with this 1986 edition. As in last years guide, this 1986 edition includes 48 pages of colour photographs, illustrating a "Review of the Year" feature.

We constantly stress that *Miller's International Antiques Price Guide* is a GUIDE and not a LIST. There is no set price for an antique but *Miller's* will give you the best pictorial and descriptive guide there is, and a realistic price *range*. (See *How To Use the Book*, opposite).

We believe in a visual approach to the subject – how can you possibly judge the likely value of the item you wish to assess on the basis of comparative descriptions alone, except in the case of a few numbered collectibles? – so we change every photograph every year. This means that if you buy *Miller's* for a few years you will build up a fully comprehensive visual encyclopedia of every major category of antique and collectible with no repetitions from edition to edition.

We never use the standard photographs of museum pieces you will see in some guides. In any case these pieces are well covered in standard thematic reference books. All the items in *Miller's* are 'available' – they have actually been bought and sold during the past year. So we really do give a guide to the market, not just a theoretical survey.

Many people have helped us to compile the guide. However we could not possibly list everyone who has helped to make this book what it is, but their help has been invaluable. Because it is impossible for two people to have all the expertise to compile a general international price guide, we are in constant touch with salesrooms and dealers all over the world to check and recheck our facts. Catalogues from all over the world pour into our headquarters here in Kent, England, for assessment and sorting. Trends are predicted, anomalies resolved, final selections made. *Miller's* is a never ending task – but one which we find fascinating and personally rewarding.

We hope to show you something of the inside world of antiques and that you enjoy the book and find it a profitable companion throughout 1986 and beyond.

CONTENTS

A Doulton Lambeth Stoneware Exhibition ewer, shown at the 1893 Chicago Columbian World Fair, modelled by Mark V. Marshall, the slender ovoid form in two sections, the lower body carved in low relief with overlapping fronded leaves and acanthus glazed in tones of ochre, cobalt and green, the shoulders modelled in full relief with four mythical horses evolving from scrolling tendrils above a narrow band of formalised acanthus interspersed by four raised bosses pierced and carved, the upper body, handle and spout of similar organic form and predominant buff colour, 72 in (183 cm).
This piece realised $15,000 on the 7th December 1984 at Bonhams, London.

-A   B   C   D

A. A standing figure of Arthur Wellesley, first Duke of Wellington, 13in (32cm).
$300-400
B. A pair of figures in Eastern costume mounted on camels, some damage, 9in (22.5cm).
$700-900
C. The figure of Mary Campbell, otherwise known as Highland Mary, standing barefoot holding a garland of roses, brightly painted, 17in (43cm).
$300-400
D. A finely modelled figure of General Sir William Codrington, with a flag by his side and a cannon in the background, 13½in (33.5cm).
$1,100-1,300
E. A group depicting the Prince of Wales and Princess Royal, with a pony and cart, 8in (20cm).
$400-600
F. A pair of square based figures of reclining lions, each with a doleful expression, painted in naturalistic colours, 5in (12.5cm) long.
$700-900
G. A group depicting Jessie Brown, otherwise known as Highland Jessie, with a wounded soldier companion, 15in (37cm)
$300-400
H. A vase group, depicting the negro lion tamer Macomo holding the lion's paw in his lap, brightly painted, 8½in (21cm).
$600-700
I. A figure of the Irish politician Daniel O'Connell, dressed in a gold and black overcoat, 14in (34cm).
$400-600
J. A group depicting the eccentric young women known as The Alphington Ponies, each identically dressed with green shoes, hats and umbrellas, 4½in (11.5cm).
$400-600
K. A figure of Rubini the conjurer, dressed in a long blue cloak performing his well known beheading the lady trick, 10in (25.5cm).
$2,300-3,400
L. A group depicting the Queen and King of Sardinia, dressed in court costume, a dog at their feet, 14½in (34cm).
$300-400
M. A figure of Admiral Sir Charles Napier, standing with his hat in one hand and a cloak in the other, 9½in (23.5cm).
$400-600
N. A figure of Nelson, standing on a rocky cliff gazing on HMS Victory below, 6in (15cm).
$300-400
O. A figure of Benjamin Franklin, wearing a long blue coat, a tricorn hat in one hand and a manuscript in the other, 14in (35.5cm).
$500-700

The International Art Market – 1984-1985

It goes without saying, really, that the Dollar/Sterling exchange rate over the last year has had an enormous impact on trade of all kinds – from shopping weekends to the Harrods sale, to property, and by no means least, the art and antiques business.

English pottery continues to be in strong demand by American collectors, culminating in some spectacular prices paid for Staffordshire figures. None more so than the £21,000 bid by European Antiques, a US based firm, for _Wombwell's Menagerie_ in a Bonhams sale last November. The Menagerie group is based on the famous travelling circus of that name and dates from around 1830. Although considered exceptionally rare, the staggering price paid for this piece of pottery must have winkled more out of the woodwork, for Bonhams had another two to sell in February. European Antiques were again the buyers, at £12,000 and £6,000.

E   F   G   H

I   J   K   L   M   N   O

A Staffordshire figure of a cavalryman made from coloured clays and decorated with underglaze colours, Astbury type, c1745, 8¼in (21cm).
$12,000-17,000
Astbury type Staffordshire soldier figures were particularly popular at the time of the "45 Rebellion". For other examples see Collector's History of English Pottery – Lewis p76; Early English Earthenware – Burlington Fine Arts Club p142 No 32; Early English Figure Pottery – Mackintosh, p7 No 11.

A fine example of a 'Malling' jug, probably London, the silver mounts engraved TR, c1580, 7¼in (18.5cm).
$9,000-13,600
The term 'Malling' derives from West Malling Church, Kent, where one of these jugs was first identified and it is generally assumed that these represent some of the earliest delftware made in England. A similar jug is in the Victoria and Albert Museum.

A very rare Lambeth delftware plate decorated with a portrait of George III, c1761, 9in (22.5cm).
$6,000-8,500
The decoration is probably after the painted portrait by Jeremiah Meyer, from which many reproductions were taken. For a similar plate see Lipski, Part III, lot 572. A companion 'Queen Charlotte' plate is in the Mint Museum, English Pottery p23, No 21.

above left
A creamware teapot, dipped in green glaze and decorated with cold gilding, Swinton, Yorkshire, c1770, 6in (12cm).
$1,300-1,700
right
A creamware tea caddy, enamelled with the 'Miss Pitt' design, Cockpit Hill, Derby. c1765, 4in (10cm).
$1,300-1,700

A Staffordshire saltglazed stoneware bowl, with a very fine enamelled decoration of European figures in a landscape, with insects and a house on the reverse side, c1760, 8½in (21.5cm).
$1,500-2,200
The fashion for enamelling white saltglazed stoneware started in the late 1740's probably influenced by the London porcelain factories. The pots would have to be fired a second time at a very much lower temperature in order 'fix' the colours.

A Florentine famiglia gotica two-handled drug-jar, the shoulder with S Bernardino motif in blue, the rope-twist handles enriched in manganese and turquoise, crack in lower part, third quarter of the 15thC, 11½in (29cm).
$46,500-59,500

A delftware plaque, painted with Cupid aiming his bow at a lady, dated on the reverse in blue, 1708, 10in (25cm).
$3,000-5,100
Decorative plaques in English delftware are very rare. Those that are known all seem to fit within the first few years of the 18thC and to have been made in London.

Although not to everyone's taste, Minton maiolica has been dramatically gaining in value over the last few years, with the major impetus coming from American collectors. The early Minton wares, under the direction of the eponymous founder, were decorated with patterns similar to Derby, or with simple sprigs of flowers, but after the appointment in 1816 of a French potter, Leon Arnoux, lavish designs began to be used. Minton specialised in copying a wide range of historical styles and techniques, including Sèvres and 16th century Italian maiolica.

In the latter category there have been some notable results this season, headed by a pair of 6ft high Blackamoor figures which cost the New York collector, Linda Horn, £48,000 at Sotheby's sale in late February. Surprisingly perhaps, the English delftware did less well than expected, with the major lot being bought-in at a third of its top estimate. Generally though, English delftware, or tin-glazed earthenware as it is technically known, is a strong market.

A fine Dutch Delft blue and white garniture de cheminée, with bouquets of flowers, the upper borders with lambrequins reserved with bowls of fruit and régence scrolls, all with slight repairs to the upper parts, the centre vase with a monogram of Lambertus van Eenhoorn/25/0/DW, c1690, 20in (50cm).
$19,500-25,000

A Ralph Wood Toby Jug of Rodney's Sailor, c1775, 12½in (31cm).
$2,400-3,400

A Chelsea silver-shaped plate, finely painted in a pale palette with figures by a building on a quay-side, with pale blue clouds and birds in flight above, the border with a loose bouquet scattered flower-sprays and an insect, minute blemish to rim, c1752, 9in (22.5cm).
$9,000-13,600

A pair of 'Vienna' slender oviform vases, covers and waisted circular plinths, one finial repaired, signed Kreigsa, blue beehive marks, c1880, 45in (113cm).
$9,000-11,900

right

A Longton Hall circular melon tureen and cover, the underside of the cover with a firing crack disguised by foliage and a caterpillar, puce W mark, minor rim restorations to rim of cover, c1755, 4½in (11.5cm).
$16,500-24,000

At a sale of English ceramics at Christie's East in New York a charming Chelsea billing dove tureen from the red anchor period made two and a half times its estimate to sell for $17,000. English porcelain has done well this year, with a new found interest in Wedgwood and Worcester.

An area to watch for development is 18th century Italian maiolica which has been tipped for progress. At the moment prices are between £100-£300 for individual pieces. The top end of the Italian maiolica market is none too healthy though, with many important pieces failing to find buyers.

A pair of Chelsea artichoke-tureens and covers, naturally modelled with overlapping leaves enriched in tones of green and puce, the covers with finch finials, the finials repaired, three leaves with some minor restoration, red anchor marks, c1755, 6½in (16cm).
$27,000-34,000

A Royal Worcester vase by George Owen, signed and dated 1907, 5½in (14cm).
$3,000-4,300

A pair of Meissen figures of sparrow-hawks (Sperber), modelled by J J Kändler, perched on tree stumps and devouring their prey, one with a vole, the other with a bird, the tree-trunks with applied green foliage, insects and fungus, minor repairs, 1735-40, both about 11½in (28cm). high.
$33,000-42,000

A Meissen Augustus Rex coloured figure of a collared parakeet (Halsbandsittich) modelled by J J Kändler, naturally modelled and painted, broken through at the top of tree stump and the end of his tail, one small piece lacking, tip of the beak re-stuck, blue AR monogram mark, the porcelain 1731-34, 17in (42cm).
$12,000-17,000

A Chelsea figure of an ostler, standing before a tree stump on a circular base applied with flowers, minor restorations to flowers and hat, red anchor mark, c1755, 5½in (13cm) high.
$8,300-11,000

A very rare Chantilly white figure of a nodding Chinaman, standing beside a bowl formed of rockwork, his detachable head with turban-like top-knot, the right hand restuck, raised hunting horn mark at back 1725-35, 11½in (28cm) high.
$30,000-42,500

A Copeland blue-ground dessert service comprising: 2 cache-pots with gilt lion's mask and fixed ring handles 2 tall and 4 low lozenge shaped tazzas, 18 octagonal plates, green printed marks, restorations, c1870, in fitted oak chest.
$8,300-10,200

A Worcester, Barr, Flight and Barr, canary yellow ground part tea and coffee service, finely painted in purple camaieu, comprising; an oval teapot, cover and stand with a view of Barr Flight and Barr's Royal China Works; an oval two handled sugar bowl; an oval milk jug, a slop basin; a pair of saucer-dishes, 12 teacups, 11 saucers, 11 coffee cans, 10 saucers, incised B marks, repairs, c1805.
$12,000-15,300

Because of the trade links America had with China in the 18th and 19th centuries, it is natural that Chinese export armorial dinner services should be very popular, as indeed they are. An example of this was the huge sum of $6,500 paid in New York last November for only four pieces of a Qianlong service which Christie's had estimated at around $1,000. The rarest lot in this sale was a Qianlong ox-head tureen which was bought by the local trade for $26,000.

A Worcester, Flight, Barr & Barr, pale yellow ground part breakfast service, the borders painted with trailing wild roses, comprising 2 oval dishes, circular butter tub, cover and stand, 2 muffin dishes and covers, 9 plates, 2 slop basins, 7 breakfast cups, 8 saucers, 16 teacups, 18 saucers, 7 coffee cans, 14 saucers, 3 eggcups, some damage, rubbing to gilding, impressed and printed marks, c1820.
$3,000-5,100

A rare mottled powder blue glazed night light and detachable base, moulded in the form of a recumbent cat looking to its right with eyes, ears and mouth pierced to show the flickering glow of burning light issuing from the detachable oval hollow plinth inside, painted with lotus on a blue ground around the sides, c1640, 5½in (13cm) wide.
$18,000-23,000

Collectors of late Ming and Transitional porcelain have had much to interest them, after twenty thousand pieces had been recovered by Michael Hatcher in the South China Seas, where the ship had sunk in 1645. Both the vast numbers of items and the fact that many were minor and in bad condition meant that collectors, dealers and museums from all over the world could afford to buy, suiting the modest and extravagant pocket alike. The collection was divided into several sales, and after the last one had taken place in early 1985, every single lot was reported sold.

A large late Ming blue and white jar, the sides painted with a wide band of Buddhist lions amongst peony heads growing from scrolling stems with many curled leaves above a band of floral lappets, the shoulder with shaped panels of flowers and fruit reserved on a ground of diaper patterns, flowerhead sprays encircling the short waist neck, c1640, 16in (40cm).
$7,500-12,000

A late Ming blue and white octagonal box and cover, the slightly raised panel on top enclosing two phoenix in opposite directions, amongst the eight Buddhist symbols above eight panels of a central flowerhead and scrollwork repeated on the box, divided by zig-zag borders encircling the rims, mid 17thC, 8in (20cm).
$4,500-8,500

16

A blue and white double gourd vase, painted in 15thC Ming-style with a decoration of blue lappets reserved with white lotus heads above a border of rising flames, the upper bulb with leafy chrysanthemum heads issuing from trailing stems below a band of upright stiff leaves, c1640, 5½in (13cm).
$3,400-5,100

A blue and white urinal, the mottled blue handle in the form of a weasel with its head resting on the cup shaped mouth, the shoulder set with three monster masks, the body painted with fruiting gourd vine above a band of overlapping pointed leaves, footrim unglazed, c1640 8in (20cm).
$13,500-18,700

A Transitional blue and white bottle vase, painted on one side with a fan-shaped panel of a plump fantastic elephant seated on a fenced terrace, the other side with a panel of a mythical horse with partly scaled skin, divided by clusters of lotus, mid-17thC, 14½in (36.5cm).
$7,000-9,500

A large late Ming blue and white jar and cover, of shouldered ovoid form, the sides painted with densely scattered sprays of flowers amongst butterflies, precious objects and stylised flames above a band of flying horses above crested waves, c1640, 19½in (48cm).
$12,000-17,000

A large late Ming blue and white 'Kraak Porselein' dish, painted with a central barbed panel of a bird on rockwork, the well and everted rim with radiating panels of fruiting branches of peaches and Buddhist symbols divided by smaller panels of tasselled pearls, c1640, 19in (47cm).
$6,000-10,200

A painted grey pottery model of a bird in flight, the detachable bow shaped wings, fan-shaped tail and S-shaped neck slotting into a central boss, supported on a slender spreading column, column broken, chips, Warring States/Han Dynasty, 14in (35cm).
$27,000-34,000

A large Gansu painted pottery jar, the baluster body painted around the wide shoulder in black and red pigment with large looping waves forming whorls and points, the rim moulded with two small loop handles mirrored at the waist by two larger ones, some wear and damage, 3rd/2nd Millenium BC, 14½in (36.5cm).
$12,000-17,000

The focal point of the year for major Chinese collectors was the sale of the J.M. Hu collection in June, when a Jiajing five-colour wine jar sold for $1.1m to a Hong Kong collector. Mr. Hu was one of the founder members of the Min Chiu Society of porcelain collectors and was one of the most revered scholars in the field.

Some good prices were seen for Tang horses and figures, amongst which was $82,000 for a stoneware jar, but generally Tang and Han pottery has

An early Kakiemon baluster jar, with a continuous design of buildings among trees and a boat moored by rocks in a mountainous river landscape, the lower part undecorated except for two narrow iron-red lines above a tapered foot, base cracked, two small chips to neck rim, slight glaze bruising, c1670, 11½in (28cm).
$21,000-27,200

A rare Ko-Imari pear-shaped bottle vase, with tall neck and everted rim, boldly decorated in iron-red, turquoise and mustard-yellow enamels, the shoulder with a band of stiff leaves, neck rim repaired, Shoo-Kambun period (1652-1672), 9in (23cm).
$11,300-14,500

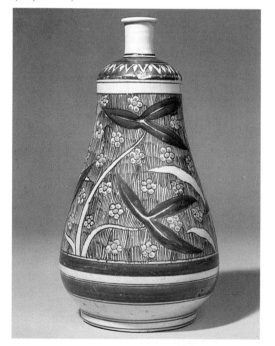

PRICES

The never-ending problem of fixing prices for antiques! A price can be affected by so many factors, for example:
- condition
- desirability
- rarity
- size
- colour
- provenance
- restoration
- the sale of a prestigious collection
- collection label
- appearance of a new reference book
- new specialist sale at major auction house
- mentioned on television
- the fact that two people present at auction are determined to have the piece
- where you buy it

One also has to contend with the fact that an antique is not only a 'thing of beauty' but a commodity. The price can again be affected by:–
- supply and demand
- international finance – currency fluctuation
- fashion
- inflation
- the fact that a museum has vast sums of money to spend

HOW TO USE MILLER'S

Unless otherwise stated, any description which refers to 'a set' or 'a pair' includes a valuation for the entire set or the pair, even though the illustration may show only a single item.

A very rare Chinese Imari helmet-shaped ewer and shell-shaped basin, each painted with long pendant leafy scrolls in iron red and blue, ewer handle restored edge frits, c1730, the ewer 12in (30.5cm) high, the basin 14½in (36cm) wide.
$12,000-17,000

A pair of richly enamelled 'famille rose' jardinieres, the spreading foot with bands of bamboo leaves, gilt scroll and floral lappets, the flat turquoise ground rim pencilled en grisaille with scale pattern and cloud scroll, enamels rubbed on the edge, c1790, 17½in (44.5cm).
$15,000-20,500

below left
An armorial dinner plate, Qianlong, c1745, 9in (23cm).
$2,300-3,400

below right
An armorial dinner plate, minute rim chips, Qianlong, c1790, 10in (25cm).
$3,800-6,000

A European subject dish, of unusually large size, painted in underglaze blue of good colour, the tones of sepia and rouge-de-fer heightened in gilding, the central scene depicting a European couple, the well and rim encircled by Precious Objects between leaf shaped panels in underglaze blue wash linked by a similarly painted band, c1725, 14in (36cm).
$7,000-9,500

bottom left
A pair of rare armorial Russian market plates, slight damage, late Qianlong, 9in (23cm).
$4,800-6,000

bottom right
A pair of rare armorial soup plates, for the Dutch market, some damage, Qianlong, c1755, 9in (23cm).
$3,000-4,300

A George II giltwood mirror, in the manner of Benjamin Goodison, with later oval plate, the massive cresting formed as 2 superimposed shells framed by acanthus scrolls and laurel swags and centered by a bearded mask wearing a triple plume head-dress encircled by a crown, 69½in (173cm) high.
$52,500-64,600

A giltwood overmantel, with later stepped triple plate in narrow frame with ribbon and pole ornament hung with flower swags and supporting 2 pairs of spirally twisting candle-branches, rising to a foliate wreath cresting framing birds, 54in (137cm).
$15,000-20,500

A pair of George III mirrors, with divided glazed borders and beaded slips, the moulded gadrooned frames with anthemion and urn cresting flanked by rams' masks and foliate and flowerhead loops, the bases with foliate sprays looped by bellflowers, 81in (202.5cm) high.
$39,000-47,600

A Queen Anne scarlet and gold lacquer toilet-mirror, with shaped cresting and turned uprights, the bureau base enclosing a tiered interior with pigeonholes and drawers above a drawer with divided interior containing 3 boxes and 2 brushes, on later feet, decorated in gilt and red with summer pavilions, birds and flowers, framed by silver lines; on later velvet-covered stand, 19in (48cm).
$30,000-40,000

not picked up its pre-1980 values. The lesser pieces are considered distinctly cheap at the moment.

One of the side effects of a strong Dollar has been a reluctance of the American trade to buy English furniture on their own soil when buying abroad has never been more favourable. Coupled with the fact that the New York auction houses have been setting very high estimates, the trade has felt inclined to give the cold shoulder when and where it feels like it. That is not to say that business has been slack but it has not been competitive either.

Probably the most popular period of furniture for the American market is good quality George III – a label which is wide enough to encompass fifty years of furniture design. One of the prize lots this season was a set of twelve carved mahogany armchairs made by Gillows of Lancaster which reached $160,000. Although the chairs had upholstery over the seat rails, they were in fact meant to have had drop-in seats.

Despite the unfavourable exchange rate, the London dealer Bernard Apter of Apter-Fredericks was able to successfully compete for a single George III armchair, virtually a duplicate of one in the V & A, for which he had to pay $25,000. While this chair was a little over the estimate, the American trade was astonished, and by no means delighted, to see a pair of

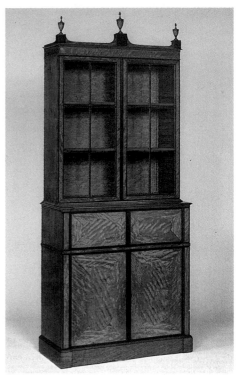

A George III satinwood and rosewood secretaire-cabinet, with shaped pediment mounted with turned vase finials, glazed cupboard doors enclosing a pair of shelves and a later cloth back, the baize lined secretaire drawer with 5 drawers and 11 pigeonholes, 37in (94cm) wide.
$19,500-25,000

A George III mahogany breakfront library bookcase, the broken dentilled triangular pediment carved with winged gryphons, with two pairs of Gothic pattern glazed cupboard doors, the base with two panelled cupboard doors enclosing shelves, the sides slightly adapted, framed each side by five small drawers, 72in (183cm) wide.
$33,000-40,800

A Regency brass-mounted mahogany and ebony dwarf bookcase, in the manner of S. Jamar, with double domed square top, each with pierced gallery and gadrooned edges, the frieze inlaid with key-pattern, above a pair of glazed cupboard doors flanked by a pair of panelled doors on open plinth base, 57in (145cm) wide.
$12,000-15,300

A fine Federal painted birch tilt-top stand, the top decorated with a polychrome painted landscape scene within a circular reserve framed by a floral garland tilting above an urn-turned pedestal, on floral-painted tripod sabre legs, signed 'Julia Pegram/1815/Susannah Todding/1816', Massachusetts 1805-1815, 22½in (55cm) wide (top).
$10,500-13,600

The Adams family Queen Anne mahogany high chest of drawers, in two sections: the upper part with a frieze of 3 drawers, above 4 graduated drawers each surrounded by cockbeaded dividers, the lower part with a long drawer over a frieze of 3 short drawers, Massachusetts, 1750-1770, 42in (105cm) wide.
$165,000-260,000

A fine Queen Anne tiger maple dressing table, the rectangular top with cusped corners and moulded edges above 4 short thumb-moulded drawers flanked by chamfered and fluted corners over a scalloped skirt centering a shaped pendant with a heart-shaped piercing, Delaware Valley, 1750-1770, 32½in (80cm) wide.
$90,000-120,000

A rare Chippendale mahogany tray-top tea table, with rectangular top with moulded edge and cusped corners above a convex moulded apron, on cabriole legs with shell carved knees and ball and claw feet, restoration to one foot, two mouldings pieced, New York, 1750-1780, 32in (80cm) wide.
$52,500-68,000

George III carved walnut side chairs sell for $60,000 when they had been estimated at a maximum of $20,000. The use of walnut was most favoured in the Queen Anne and George I periods, and thus to see it so late into the Georgian period is a rarity.

I think it is true to say that American buyers are particularly sensitive about condition and whether something has been seen on the market before. The condition factor puts a lot of people off giltwood furniture, so prone to damage and restoration, and on the occasions when the Trade is seen to give the thumbs down to a perfectly decent

A fine pair of Federal inlaid mahogany and gilt mirrors, with gilt urn finials with trailing gilt wheat sheaves and flowers suspended on wire, above a broken scrolled pediment with a gilt cornice centering an inlaid moth, the mirror plate flanked by pendant leaves suspended on wire, New Jersey or New York, 1790-1810, 27in (67.5cm).
$36,000-44,200

A fine small Chippendale mahogany blocked slant-front desk, the thumb moulded lid with a fitted interior of 2 vertical rows of 3 drawers, the top one fan-carved; the case with 4 blocked drawers with cock-beaded dividers above a conforming base moulding with a pendant fan, lid with pierced edge; prospect door restored, Massachusetts, 1760-1780, 43in (107.5cm).
$33,000-42,000

piece, it is as often as not because they have seen it before.

If the Americans are none too keen on giltwood furniture at the moment, this is not the case in England, according to Phillips' annual survey of the art and antiques market. Furniture experts were of the opinion that Regency, decorative period furniture such as lacquer, pedestal dining tables and sets of chairs were all in great demand. The articles they considered to be underpriced were large pieces of run-of-the-mill 'brown' furniture.

These observations were certainly borne out at a sale Christie's had in London in the beginning of the year, when a strong American presence in the rooms ensured high prices in all the above categories. A pair of satinwood side tables with inlaid decoration sold for £9,500 to New York

An important Chippendale carved mahogany scalloped-top tea table, with moulded elaborately scalloped single board top revolving and tilting above a birdcage support over a fluted, tapering columnar pedestal with meandering leafage-carved compressed ball and ribbon-and-flower-carved lower band, on cabriole legs carved with acanthus leafage centering a mirror-image C-scrolled reserve, Philadelphia, 1760-1775, 35in (87.5cm) diameter of top.   **$300,000+**

A set of four George III white-painted and parcel gilt open armchairs, with oval padded backs and bowed seats covered in pale yellow buttoned silk, the moulded frames with ribbon-tie crestings and centres to the seat-rails, the padded arms on moulded scrolled supports, on fluted tapering legs.
$21,000-27,200

A pair of George III giltwood open armchairs, in the manner of John Linnell, with cartouche-shaped padded backs and serpentine seats covered in striped velvet, the moulded frames crisply carved with foliage rising to shell and foliage swag crestings, the padded arms with down-curved supports carved with long leaves.
$19,500-25,000

dealers, as did a small pembroke table inlaid with peacock feathers and roses at £8,500.

Thomas Chippendale *lui-meme* is one of the most elusive names to attach authoritatively to a piece of furniture. Despite being the best-known English furniture maker of all time, none of his pieces was stamped, and much of the furniture he did make is not in the style associated with the name. However Christie's felt confident in attributing a pair of armchairs to Chippendale at their sale in New York in April. This was not reflected enthusiastically by the bidders though, as the pair sold below estimate at $75,000. By any standards not a high price compared with French or American furniture of a similar quality.

A Louis XV walnut fauteuil de bureau, by Etienne St George, with arched curved padded back and serpentine seat covered in brown leather in moulded frame carved with paired flowerhead cresting and centres to the seat-rails, on cabriole legs headed by single flowerheads, stamped ST GEORGE, 26in (66cm).
$10,500-13,600

An early George III mahogany open armchair, with slightly arched rectangular padded back and upholstered seat covered in freshly coloured floral gros- and petit-point framed by strapwork, the moulded down-scrolled arm-supports headed by foliate clasp finials, the waved seat-rail centred by C-scroll cabochons and shellwork, 28½in (72cm)
$31,500-39,100

A pair of George III giltwood open armchairs, the curved toprails painted, possibly later, with birds in colours on ivory and ebonised grounds above urn-pierced trellis-pattern splats, the arms carved with ropetwist on spirally turned supports, the bowed seats upholstered in yellow silk, on tapering fluted legs, 23in (59cm).
$15,000-20,500

A fine Regency brass mounted mahogany library armchair, with scrolled padded back and button-upholstered seat, the ribbed frame with scrolling arm supports on turned tapering feet, stamped ET.
$12,800-16,200

On the subject of the latter, American furniture has had a very good year, boosted by a handful of important private collections coming onto the market. The Federal period, so named after the establishment of the Federal government in 1789-c.1830, was very much in the limelight this season and some exceptionally high prices were paid. The main event was the private collection of the late Berry B. Tracy, who had been curator of the American Wing of the Metropolitan Museum of Art before he became a dealer in 1981. As one of the most respected scholars of American Federal and Classical furniture, it was hardly surprising that the contents of his home would be of the utmost interest to collectors. Foremost were a pair of barrel-back armchairs attributed to Duncan Phyfe which made $95,000, and a sofa of the same authorship followed at $75,000.

To my mind the most astonishing price in the field was the sum of $530,000 paid for a pair of mahogany dining tables made in Philadelphia in the 1780's.

An important pair of Regency mahogany and ebonised bergères, in the manner of Thomas Hope, the scrolling tub-shaped toprails inlaid with stylised tulipheads with leather upholstered backs and bowed seats and downscrolling arm supports ending in rams' heads on fluted tapering sabre legs headed by rosettes, one with a label inscribed 'Marqs of Clanricarde', 28in (71cm).
$82,500-100,000

But if new records were to be set in the furniture world then it is the French who have won hands down. I am referring to one piece of furniture, the collectors' cabinet, commissioned and personally used by Louis XVI, which was sold in Monaco last autumn for £1.3m, by far the highest price ever paid for a piece of 'utilitarian' art. The extraordinary thing about this cabinet is that it was mounted with panels of birds' feathers, insects and butterflies set in wax under glass. Although listed in a Versailles inventory as a 'medailler', it is not known whether it was intended for natural history specimens or medals.

After the excitements of the Wrightsman and Gould collections in the previous season, trade in New York was felt to be rather sluggish. At the highest levels, the French furniture market is dominated by a handful of individual collectors and this of course makes it highly volatile. However, the more routine furniture, particularly that sold in Europe, has again benefited from the strength of the Dollar, and business has been brisk.

A Charles II black and gold lacquer cabinet-on-stand, the doors decorated with a lakeside scene with a gondola, bathers, a pavilion and bamboo trees, with pierced giltmetal lockplate and hinges, the interior with 10 various sized drawers, the reconstructed giltwood stand with pierced foliate frieze with putti and flowerheads, 44in (112cm). **$13,500-17,000**

A large Tansu, the 2 outer doors enclosing 5 graduated drawers, entirely decorated in gold and silver hiramakie on a nashiji ground with Tokugawa (aoi) mon among flowering peony and foliage, on a matching stand similarly decorated, engraved silver kanagu, back slightly cracked, 19thC, 58in (146cm) high. **$39,000-47,600**

◄
A scarlet and gold lacquer cabinet-on-chest, with arched moulded cornice, 2 doors enclosing shelves and drawers, the base with 2 short and 2 long drawers decorated in raised gilt with Chinese scenes with figures, summer pavilions, birds and flowers on a sealing wax red ground, early 18thC, 44½in (113cm). **$18,000-24,000**

A George III satinwood and marquetry commode,
attributed to William Ince and John Mayhew, the top inlaid
in stained, shaded and engraved woods with a feather
lunette framed by ribbon-tied swags of summer flowers
hung from paterae, bordered with oval-framed flowerheads
and crossbanded with rosewood, edged with reeded ormolu
border threaded with ribbon, the sides inlaid with swagged
and spirally fluted urns, divided by bands of vases and
flowers, 40in (101.5cm) wide.
$69,000-85,000

A Régence ebony and boulle commode, the rectangular
top with moulded ormolu border inlaid in première
partie marquetry with Bérainesque designs of
interlaced scrolling strapwork and tendrils framing
dancing and music-making figures, fitted with drawers
framed by brass lines and mounted with espagnolette
mask lockplates and foliate handles, the brass-framed
coffered sides similarly inlaid between scrolled angles
ending in hoof sabots, 47½in (120.5cm).
$43,500-54,400

Returning briefly to American
furniture, two particularly
interesting long case clocks
appeared for sale in early
February. One was a miniature
Federal longcase made in New
Jersey in about 1800 and
standing 4ft 2ins high, which cost
a private collector more than
double the estimate at $140,000.
The second, sold on the following
day, was a mahogany lighthouse
clock marked *Simon Willard's
Patent*, and it was bought by
Richard and Gloria Manney for a
staggering $260,000. This rare
and unusual clock measured a
little over two feet high and was

An early George III lacquer commode, the cupboard
doors veneered with Chinese black and gold lacquer
decorated with birds and flowers, and bamboo nashiji
borders, the keeled angles decorated with nashiji
mounted with scrolled ormolu angles, 36½in (93cm).
$27,000-34,000

An early Louis XV amaranth and bois satine commode
attributed to Charles Cressent, with moulded griotte
marble top, the drawers sans traverse inlaid with
shaped panels à quatre faces, 50½in (128cm).
$60,000-85,000

A giltwood pier table, of Louis XV design, the
18thC top mirror-veneered with Sicilian jasper
edged with ormolu on gadrooned and foliate
frieze, stencilled 'From Wm Murray carver &
gilder to the Queen, 14 St Enoch Square,
Glasgow', mid-19thC, 57in (145cm).
$24,000-30,600

topped with a brown glass dome
which, remarkably, was the
original one. High quality
Federal clocks are in great
demand currently, especially
when signed.

French clocks of the mid to late
18th century, with their lavish
use of gilt bronze, appeal to a
certain taste – and pocket for that
matter. An early admirer was
Matthew Boulton who borrowed
many ideas from the French from
his Birmingham factory, and
indeed his use of ormolu received
reciprocal admiration in France.
His candelabra and *garnitures
de cheminee* are very valuable
when in good condition and can
on occasions surpass the classic
French versions of Chinese
porcelain and Louis XV ormolu.

A walnut and marquetry bureau plat, the ►
ormolu-bordered top inlaid in shaded woods
with flowers and birds, the frieze with 2 drawers
similarly inlaid, on cabriole legs headed by
rococo ormolu angles, c1830, incorporating
sections of Louis XIV marquetry, probably
from a bureau Mazarin, 50in (127cm).
$12,000-17,000

◄
A George III mahogany card table, with
serpentine baize-lined top edged with
cabochon-and-rosette ornament, the tablet-
centred frieze carved with a wheatsheaf crest
and a marquess' coronet framed by a laurel and
wheatear swag on moulded cabriole legs headed
by anthemions framed by husks, 37in (94cm).
$7,500-12,000

A pair of ormolu kingwood, burr-maple and ►
fruitwood centre tables, the tops inlaid with
parquetry panels, above 2 frieze drawers
centred by ribbon-tied arrows and trailing
vines flanked by key-pattern scrolls, on fluted
tapering legs with berried collars hung with
swags and beaded foliate feet, 55in (140cm).
$33,000-40,800

A George III burr-yew cylinder bureau, the raised top with 2 drawers banded with satinwood and inlaid with lines, with oval-inlaid solid cylinder operating a forward-sliding drawer with leather-lined easel, a well, pigeonholes and short drawers above 2 drawers framing the arched kneehole on square tapering legs, 36in (92cm).
$22,500-29,000

A Louis XV ormolu-mounted kingwood and tulipwood marquetry table à ouvrage by BVRB, the hinged top inlaid with a floral spray enclosing a fitted interior with one frieze drawer, the cabriole legs headed by S-scroll clasps joined by a rectangular gallery with C-scroll sabots, stamped BVRB JME, the drawer inscribed in ink on the underside '3 pieces argentes', the mounts struck with the C couronné poincon, 17in (42.5cm).
$49,500-61,200

A German gilt-gesso bureau de dame, the top and sloping flap carved with a central shell framed by foliate C-scrolls and strapwork surrounding shaped trellis- and ozier-work panels interspersed with flowerheads, enclosing a walnut interior with drawers and shelf, bearing a label inscribed Gerard, 38in (96.5cm).
$13,500-17,000

For some time now the American Arts & Crafts has been steadily gaining in respectability and value, to the extent that Christie's hold separate auctions of such things under the title of *architectural designs and commissions.* The two big names are Frank Lloyd Wright and Greene & Greene, but it was the latter who has dominated this past season. A Honduras mahogany fall-front desk designed by Greene & Greene sold recently in New York for $220,000. Charles Sumner Green and his brother, Henry Mather Greene were architects, and they undertook very detailed furniture commissions from affluent clients during the first decade of the century. This desk was made for the living room of the Charles M. Pratt House at Ojai, California.

As the twentieth century moves
towards its closing decade one
notices how the datelines creep
forward for collectible
decorative art. Hence the larger
sales are likely to include objects
made right up to the 1970's, but
the market for much post-war art
is still very flimsy. Italian glass of
the 1950's and 60's has been
promoted a few times but to no
apparent effect, but furniture by
the likes of Piero Fornasetti and
contemporaries is in great
demand. One lot that amused me
was a consumer non-durable of
the early 1970's – an inflatable
transparent plastic armchair
which sold for £230 in Monaco
last autumn.

To my mind a quite
extraordinary new record was
seen for a Tiffany floor lamp with
a poppy shade, hardly an item of

An Anglo-Indian ivory inlaid padoukwood bureau-
cabinet, with broken scrolled pediment pierced with
Gothic fretwork and moulded dentilled cornice above
geometrically-glazed cupboard doors, the base with
sloping flap enclosing a fitted interior, above 4
graduated long drawers mounted with silver handles
and hinges, Vizagapatam, late 18thC, 44in (112cm).
$66,000-81,600

A Queen Anne burr-walnut bureau-cabinet, with
moulded cornice above 2 arched mirrored panelled
doors enclosing 3 shelves, the centre with sloping
lid enclosing a fitted interior with a well above
3 long drawers with ring handles, the sides with 3
pairs of brass carrying-handles, 43½in (110cm).
$33,000-41,000

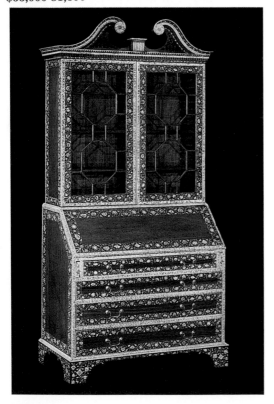

A Queen Anne walnut bureau bookcase, with
moulded double-domed cornice above a pair of
glazed cupboard doors enclosing an interior with 19
drawers around a pair of concave-fronted cupboard
doors, the fall-flap with a fitted interior, on later
feet, restorations, 31½in (80cm).
$25,000-32,300

A George III black and gold japanned cabinet-on-stand, with pierced fretwork gallery and 2 doors inset with 2 Chinese mirror paintings, delicately painted with elegantly dressed ladies on a rocky terrace in a mountain river landscape, enclosing 3 shells the reverse of the doors decorated with chinoiserie figures, the ebonised stand with pierced fretwork frieze and later arched cross-stretcher, 35in (88cm).
$37,500-51,000

A pair of Napoleon III ebony and polychrome boulle jewel cabinets in the Louis XIV style by Monbro, doors inlaid in contre partie marquetry, one cabinet enclosing velvet-lined drawers fitted for jewels and inscribed on mother-of-pearl plaques, 'Diamonds', etc one branded twice Monbro Aîné, one numbered 1209 and inscribed '18 mars 1851', the other branded 3 times and inscribed 'an 1851', 33½in (85cm).
$22,500-29,000

◄

An ormolu-mounted and tortoiseshell meuble d'appui, in the manner of A. C. Boulle, with stepped breakfront top and arched central door, framed by a matted channelled border and mounted with lambrequin and scrolled plaques, with 4 drawers each side inlaid in première partie marquetry with scrolling foliage and interlaced strapwork, the angles headed by blue-ground volutes, on toupie feet, 54½in (138cm).
$45,000-59,500

great rarity, which sold for nearly £430,000 in New York. By comparison, less than half of that sum bought a superb Koloman Moser symbolist cabinet inlaid with woods and metal. It was bought by an American collector in Monaco for £179,500. Kolo Moser was a founder of the Vienna Secession, and with Joseph Hofmann, of the Wiener Werkstatte.

In the same Monaco sale, which Sotheby's held in the autumn of 1984, was an Eileen Gray reticulated screen which did very well, selling to an American buyer for just over £34,000. This was a particularly high price, considering the screen had been sold here only four years ago, for less than a quarter of the sum.

◄
A pair of George III satinwood side tables, each with semi-elliptical top banded with rosewood and painted with a fan lunette and ribbon-tied medallions of rustic children framed by swags of summer flowers and foliage-bordered entwined ribbon, the plain frieze and square tapering legs decorated with laurel foliage, 54in (137cm).
$27,000-34,000

It has long been established that the most fervent collectors of French Art Nouveau glass have been the Japanese. Nonetheless, one of the most important creations by Galle to appear on the market was secured by a Swiss buyer. It was *Les Coprins,* one of only five mushroom lamps made by Galle in 1904, the year of his death, and it was auctioned by Christie's Geneva for just under £320,000.

While most sales of antiquities contain a number of pieces of ancient glass, single owner collections are not exactly thick on the ground. So when Christie's sold the Kofler-Truniger collection in March buyers from Europe, America and the Middle East flocked to attend, but it was the London trade who dominated the affair. The most extraordinary piece in the sale would have looked more at home in a sale of Wedgwood. It was a 3inch high cobalt blue flask cameo carved in white with a scene of putti, and is said to have come from Eskischehir in Turkey within a 25 year leeway of the birth of Christ. The bidding started at £80,000 but within seconds rose to £300,000 and was knocked down to Robin Symes, the St. James's dealer.

An ormolu-mounted rosewood bureau plat, of Louis XV design, attributed to Henri Dasson, with shaped leather-lined top edged with rockwork and scrolling foliage, the serpentine frieze with 3 drawers each side mounted with mask and scroll handles and curving plaques on inscrolled legs mounted with acanthus, cabochons and scrolls, mid-19thC, 88in (224cm).
$28,500-35,700

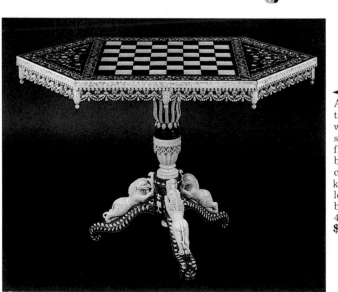

◄
An Anglo-Indian ivory and ebony games table, with trapezoidal-shaped top inlaid with chess squares framed by bands of scrolling foliage, the ends with sprays of flowers with elaborately pierced foliate border on baluster shaft framed by crisply carved leaves and urn-shaped knop, on scrolled tripod base inlaid with leafy sprays and mounted with mythical beasts eating fruit, early 19thC, 45in (112.5cm).
$31,500-39,100

A George III tulipwood bonheur du jour, the superstructure with a waved three-quarter gallery bordered with rosewood, crossbanded with satinwood and framed by chequered lines, the base with a leather lined hinged flap, and cedar lined frieze drawer fitted with inkwells, the sides inlaid with pollard-yew on sycamore grounds, 25in (63cm) wide. **$9,000-11,900**

◄

A Louis XV kingwood coiffeuse, with lifting top and hinged sloping flap and front, the interior fitted with blue silk-lined compartments containing St. Cloud porcelain and vernis Martin boxes, the lower part with a silk-lined drawer on one side and two on the other, one with a fitted interior, stamped B PERIDIEZ, 31in (79cm) wide.   **$45,000-59,500**

A Regency rosewood secretaire cabinet, attributed to John McLean with raised mirror-backed superstructure, the base with eared reeded border and panelled secretaire drawer mounted with flower swags and lion mask and ring handles enclosing a well fitted interior, with pigeonholes and cedar-lined drawers, 36in (93cm) wide. **$33,000-41,000**

Otherwise, the later periods of glass is still a surprisingly indiginous market. English 18th century glass is really only bought by the English, and to a large extent the same pattern applies to the various countries in Europe. I can't imagine why the sort of foreign collector who buys English furniture is not similarly interested in English glass.

The market for jade is extremely selective and therefore difficult to make generalisations about. For one thing the name jade is a mineralogically imprecise term for various kinds of hardstone, covering nephrite, and the superficially similar but structurally different

A Regency mahogany partners' desk, with concave-centred rounded rectangular leather-lined top fitted each side with nine drawers surrounding a central kneehole divided by reeded columns with foliate capitals, the ends mounted with carrying-handles, the turned feet ending in brass casters, 72in (183cm) wide. **$39,000-47,600**

►

A Louis XV ormolu-mounted corne verte bracket clock and bracket, with striking movement engraved on back plate 'Farine et Rade a Paris' in cartouche-shaped case mounted with scrolling foliate ormolu borders, central pierced plaque of a vase of flowers and flowerhead cresting, the bracket with central cartouche and flowers, bearing the trade label of Town & Emanuel, 105 New Bond St., 50½in (151cm).
$10,500-15,300

A burr walnut, brass and gilt metal bracket clock, the brass dial having silvered chapter ring with chime/silent and slow/fast subsidiary dials, gilt foliate spandrels flanked by Corinthian columns, the arched pediment having cone finials, German movement, late 19thC, 23½in (58cm).
$2,700-3,400

A George I walnut longcase clock, with arched trunk door, the unusual hood with finial to broken pediment, the brass dial with date ring in the arch, seconds ring and chapter ring signed 'Windmills London', later hands, the 8-day movement with anchor escapement and rack strike and 5 ringed pillars, 95in (244cm).
$12,800-16,200

dark green or emerald jadeite. Nephrite is native to Chinese Turkestan and central America, where it has been worked into amulets and ceremonial objects since pre-historic times. It is ice-cold to the touch, translucent and ranges in colour from white, known as Mutton Fat jade and the most highly prized, to shades of brown and green.

Nephrite jades are notoriously difficult to date, but on a very basic level, the more elaborate the later. Jadeite, on the other hand, presents fewer problems, as it was not worked in China until the 18th century.

A Meissen porcelain and Louis XV ormolu mantel clock, signed on the dial and striking movement 'Etienne Lenoir a Paris', in asymmetric cartouche-shaped case modelled with a seated figure of Flora and putti among flowerheads, the support painted with flowers, on pierced scrolled ormolu base, the porcelain c1745, 18in (46cm).
$6,000-10,200

A fine and rare 18ct. gold hunter cased minute repeating, perpetual calendar, grande sonnerie clockwatch, with chronograph by Sir John Bennett, London, No. 12679, the enamel dial by Willis, in a substantial case by Thoms, with double joints and thief-proof pendant, the chronograph button and repeating slide mounted in the band, the case marked London 1909, 2½in (6cm).
$40,500-51,000

left
An important early longcase regulator, by Geo. Graham, London, trunk door twice stamped 631, with some alterations and restorations, 1720-1727, 80¼in (204cm).
$22,500-29,000

centre
A fine mahogany longcase clock, by Matt. Dutton, London; 332, signed by Matthew Dutton London in the arch, repeated signature on the backplate with the number 332, slight restorations, 88in (224cm).
$16,500-22,100

right
A fine walnut longcase clock, the 12-inch dial signed Geo. Graham London, both below VI and on an oval silvered plaque, backplate and case numbered 657, 90in (229cm).
$30,000-39,000

There has been one outstanding piece of nephrite on the market this season; a Han dynasty Mutton Fat carving of bear which was so keenly sought after that it made six times the estimate, selling to a New York dealer for $80,000.

It is probably no more than coincidence but in the year which marked the 300th anniversary of the Revocation of the Edict of Nantes, Huguenot silversmiths in general and Paul de Lamerie in particular have been spectacularly successful. The British should be grateful to Louis XIV, without whose persecution of the Huguenots, English decorative art would have been a great deal the poorer.

left
An early Georgian mirror-veneered musical bracket clock, the dial signed Wm. Webster Exchange Alley London, some alterations and restoration 20½in (52cm).
$37,500-47,600

right
A highly important Augsburg ivory clock, with silver gilt mounts, the ivory ascribed to Ferdinand Murmann, the silver gilt mounts by David I. Schwestermüller and Daniel Zech, some damage mid-17thC, 26½in (66cm).
$120,000-160,000

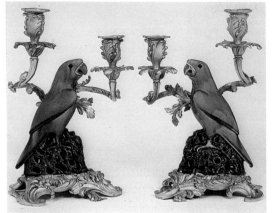

A pair of Louis XV ormolu and Chinese porcelain candelabra, each with a turquoise and aubergine-glazed model of a parrot framed by 2 scrolling foliate branches on asymmetric bases cast with C-scrolls and foliage, the porcelain Qing, 13½in (34.5cm) high. **$9,800-12,800**

A pair of George III ormolu and white marble twin-branch candelabra, by Matthew Boulton, each with urn stem mounted with entrelac and flowered collar and twin handles joined by bellflower swags, the scrolled foliate branches ending in chased and fluted nozzles, on spreading socles and circular swagged plinths, 12½in (32cm). **$27,000-34,000**

The pinnacle of de Lamerie's posthumous career was the sale of the 110-piece dinner service commissioned by the 7th Earl of Thanet, which reached a staggering £825,000 at Sotheby's in London. On a more modest level, a handsome George II period coffee pot sold recently in New York fetched $60,000. Only modest by comparison though, because this price was actually twice the expected sum.

In general the market for English silver is a very competitive one, fuelled by the enormous spending power of one London dealer, Koopman, whose keenness to buy does not appear to have been dampened by the exchange rate. There are of course many other influential dealers and collectors in the field but none dominate the top end of business in such a relentless manner as Koopman.

One of the most magnificent lots to be sold this season was the Bramham Moor Cup, a massive wine cistern dating from the early George II period and made by Thomas Folkingham of London. Indeed it is a prime example of Huguenot influence on silver design, with its heavy architectural form and cut card decoration. Offered at Sotheby's New York in April, the cistern was bought by a trio of London dealers working in partnership for $250,000.

A rare and important pair of Irish George III glass chandelier mirrors, each with oval plate in faceted stud frame with an arched brass hook suspending a faceted shaft supporting 2 faceted scrolled candle-branches and a central branch hung with loops of faceted beads, 34in by 21in (86 by 53cm). **$72,600-85,000**

A rare and important George II giltwood chandelier, with open frame formed of 8 combined double C-scrolls carved with acanthus fitted with 2 tiers of 8 later ribbed giltmetal branches, the upper spiralling, the lower outscrolled, applied with giltmetal leaves, the tapering base ending in a giltmetal ring, fitted for electricity, 58in (147.5cm) high.
$49,500-59,500

As always, Paul Storr has a strong following both sides of the Atlantic, but especially the American side. He worked in quite a wide variety of styles encompassing everything from rococo to Victorian, and so could be considered to be a silversmith for all tastes – all except the austere that is.

One cannot consider bronzes as a subject by itself for obvious enough reasons. It is the medium of many subjects, from Asiatic sculpture, to Egyptian art, Greek and Roman antiquities, Renaissance and Baroque art, and 19th century decorative art. While the latter has the least claim to art historical 'importance', it is by far the most saleable. The difficulties of attribution and dating make the market for Renaissance bronzes an erratic one, but one outstanding success was achieved for a late Renaissance figure of a prancing horse by Adrien de Vries which sold for £836,000 in France.

An early George III giltwood girandole, with asymmetric divided plate, the deep frame carved with broad scrolls, acanthus and gadrooning, with 2 scrolling foliate branches framing a seated figure of a Chinaman the mirrored cresting with acanthus foliage canopy of pagoda form, the waisted base outlined with C-scrolls, and another en suite of later date, 58 by 26in (147 by 66cm).
$27,000-34,000

A pair of good bronze and ormolu figural candelabra, in the manner of Clodion, the scantily clad maidens in classical drapery, holding cornucopia, with 3 reeded foliate branches, all on marble half columns, with applied swags, 28½in (71cm).
$5,300-7,700

In the early 19th century a group of French sculptors called *Les Animaliers* had departed from the conventions of equestrian sculpture, to pursue an anatomical approach to their art. The best known of them is Antoine-Louis Barye and his bronze studies of animals are remarkable for their quality and realism. He studied intensively in the zoological gardens, and followed up his observations by dissecting dead animals.

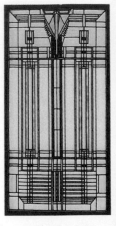

A rare leaded glass skylight, designed by Frank Lloyd Wright for the B.H. Bradley House, Kankakee, Illinois, leaded in a stylised American Indian motif, the glass in white, green, gold and tortoiseshell with various degrees of translucency, unsigned, in the original oak frame, c1900, 37¼in (94.5cm).
$24,000-32,300

A beechwood 'Sitzmachine' deck chair, designed by Joseph Hoffmann, the back pierced in 2 rows and adjusting with the use of a bar, the sides with parallel vertical slits, unsigned, c1905, 42in (106.5cm) high.
$22,500-29,000

An oak side chair, designed by Frank Lloyd Wright for the Hillside Home School, Spring Green, Wisconsin, the back a single oak plank running diagonally from crest rail to floor stretcher, the upper terminals surmounted by rectangular blocks, unsigned, 1887-1903, 40in (100cm) high.
$16,500-22,100

A fine earthenware vase, by Jean Lurcat, balustered with formed handles, the body decorated with highly stylised black portraits on a yellow ground bordered in black on a matt blue ground, the black-bordered white neck with a black abstract design, 19in (48cm).
$4,500-7,000

A mahogany, ebony and glass wall lantern, designed by Charles and Henry Greene for the James Culbertson House, Pasadena, California, executed in the workshop of Peter Hall, probably in conjunction with Emile Lang, of rare double lantern form, with a mahogany frame with square ebony pegs, unsigned, c1907, 17½in (43cm) high.
$33,000-41,000

At two summer sales in London of works of art Animalier bronzes proved the most successful category, after disappointing results in the medieval and Renaissance periods. Sotheby's had a single owner collection to sell, *The Troubadour Collection*, formed by a French industralist over the past ten years. His collection was made up entirely of horse studies, which together with dogs, are the most sought after. The top price was £21,000 for a pair of *Cheval Turc* figures.

It takes no more than a stroll round a fashionable garden centre and perusal of the personal columns of two national papers to see that we are in the grips of garden statuary mania. I found myself walking round the Bond Street premises of the advertiser in said personal columns, and the most breathtaking escape into grandiose fantasy it was. Putti fountains, a small temple or two, or a chinoiserie gazebo, all at a price that one would have to sell one's house for, mind you.

A very fine laburnum leaded glass and bronze table lamp, by Tiffany Studios, the large shade with yellow-gold flower clusters amongst green leaves on a brilliant blue ground shading to pale below, impressed by Tiffany Studios N.Y.; the freeform base impressed Tiffany Studios New York 553, the shade with gilt patina, 31in (78.7cm) high.
$55,500-70,000

A Tiffany vase, on original bronze base.
$4,500-6,000

A silver Liberty clock, with enamel face.
$4,500-7,000

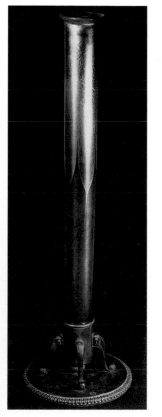

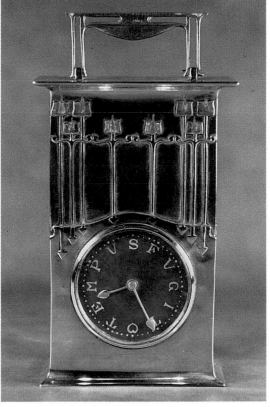

There are now specialist auctions of garden furniture, statuary and architectural antiques, and prices can be extremely competitive. Victorian cast iron seats and tables are deservedly popular, and anything in good condition will sell for at least £200. Antique architectural fittings such as fireplaces range from £300-1,000 depending on the elaboration and quality of material, and stone ornaments or statuary for the garden come very expensive indeed. One recent instance was the sale of two of a set of seven Saxon gods, comissioned by Lord Cobham for his gardens at Stowe which sold for £68,000 and £48,400.

A colourless glass 'snake-thread' flask, the ▶ ovoid body decorated with corrugated trails, with spiral threads wound around the top of the neck, on short stemmed base, intact except for small chip in rim, early 3rd Century AD, 7½in (19.1cm).
$27,000-37,400

A rare Facon-de-Venise filigree goblet, in vetro a retorti, the widely flared bowl decorated with vertical bands of pale blue ribbon, slightly twisted at the rim, alternating with opaque-white latticinio corkscrew ribbon, supported on a clear gadrooned cushion knop with traces of gilding, Low Countries, late 16thC, 5½in (13.5cm) high.
$12,800-16,200

A Fichtelgebirge dated Stagenglas, for the Bayreuther Hof, the slender bowl divided into 5 sections by white lines, painted with the arms of Georg Wilhelm Markgraf zu Brandenburg-Bayreuth (1712-1726), flanked by tied palm branches beneath an Elector's Cap and the initials G.W.M.Z.B., and with the date 1717 below, 10½in (26cm).
$3,800-5,100

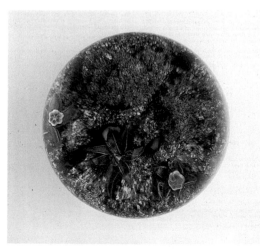

◄ A French magnum snake weight, by Pantin, the ochre and dark brown mottled reptile emerging from rocky mounds and gliding beneath a pink flower, the foliage edged in pale pink, flanked by 2 smaller blue periwinkle-type flowers with similar foliage, the sandy ground partially covered in green lichen, 4¼in (10.8cm) diam.
$7,500-10,200

A white jade bowl, Qianlong, with upright sides, the flattened base well carved on the interior in crisp relief with sprays of chrysanthemum and lingzhi fungus, 6¼in (15.5cm). wood stand.
$6,000-8,500

A large spinach jade vase and cover, Qianlong, the vessel of canted rectangular section crisply carved in low relief with a frieze of taotie masks interspersed by stylised dragons, all on an incised ground of leiwen, above a band of pendant cicada scrolls, a narrow band of stylised dragons on the neck, side handles issuing from horned dragons' heads, suspending loose rings, the stone of uniform rich colour, cloisonne enamel stand, 12½in (31cm).
$16,500-24,000

Chinese decorative art, including export porcelain and enamels, is currently enjoying great popularity in America, where the interior decorator market is nowhere more prosperous. The technique of pouring enamel into compartments came from Byzantium to China in the 14th century, and reached its height in the Qianlong period. Japanese cloisonné dates from the 19th century onwards and first came to the attention of the West at the Paris Exhibition of 1867.

At a sale in New York in April, a pair of large cloisonné rams standing nearly three feet high sold for $21,000, but a pair of massive and elaborate elephants did not find a buyer. A pair of rare vases in the form of double gourds fetched $8,800, and a duo of cranes standing on one leg brought $17,000.

A very pale celadon jade two-handled bowl and cover, the compressed body carved with 3 lobes on each side, the central lobe broader than the others and carved with a crisp shallow relief shou character, the 3 equal lobes on the back with tasselled musical stone, the large loose-ring handles with mythical bats forming the broad upper terminal, the domed cover with a thin band of archaistic dragons at the rim below a deeply pierced finial formed as a recumbent deer with a large spray of fruiting lingzhi held around its sides, 18thC, 7½in (18cm) wide.
$10,500-15,300

41

By virtue of their nature, gold boxes are a luxury market for collectors, starting at an absolute minimum in the four figure price range. Most gold boxes were made as containers for snuff, and it was not until the middle of the 18th century that the habit became socially acceptable for the middle and upper classes. Louis XIV had positively discouraged snuffing but by the time his successors were on the throne it was the most fashionable profession to have in high society. Lavish materials and exemplary craftmanship were employed in the making of boxes and they were justifiably seen as a potent status symbol. People of consequence owned several, for seasons and moods; Frederick the Great is reputed to have owned 1500, and Madame Pompadour had one for every day of the year.

An important English silver statuette, 'Perseus Arming', cast from a model by Sir Alfred Gilbert, R.A., standing on naturalistic circular moulded socle, sword strap replaced, late 19thC, 14½in (36cm).
$28,500-35,700

A George III circular two-handled soup-tureen, cover and stand, the stand with gadrooned border and scrolling foliage handles, chased within with a band of flutes, the tureen on a gadrooned spreading foot, with a band of palmettes beneath the border, with reeded handles springing from lions' masks, engraved twice with a coat-of-arms and with an inscription, by Paul Storr, 1806, 19½in (49.5cm), 290ozs.
$78,000-100,000

A porringer, by Paul Revere II, Boston, 1760-1800 circular, with curved sides and everted brim, the keyhold-type pierced handle with contemporary engraved initials 'HAD' mark struck on back of handle and inside bowl, with scratch weights on bottom, few small bruises, 5¼in (13cm), 8oz.
$19,500-25,000

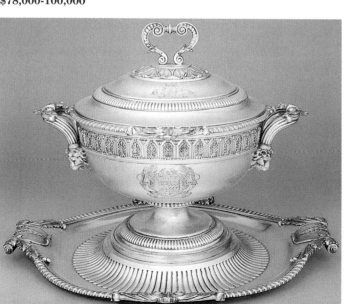

A bronze figure of a hunchback slave crouching, wearing a short chiton, partly slipping off his right shoulder, his right arm tucked inside his tunic, his hair pulled back and tied in a top-knot, the sensitively and strongly modelled face showing articulated pupils, on wooden base, Graeco-Roman, B.C. 1st Century/A.D., from Alexandria, 3¼in (8.4cm) high.
$12,800-16,200

A bronze figure of a seated cat, alert, with tail curled around paws, the ears and whiskers with lightly chased decoration, mounted, Dynasty XXVI, 8½in (21.5cm) high.
$43,500-52,700

By and large the French can claim to have been the greatest makers of snuff boxes. Many types of materials were used, including porcelain, painted and guilloche enamel, and hardstones, mounted with diamonds and other precious stones. Oval and rectangular were the most favoured shapes but there were several variations. The best of the German boxes are those mounted

A fine English bronze group known as 'The Kiss of Victory', by Sir Alfred Gilbert, the allegorical winged female figure of Victory supporting a naked hero with a shield strapped to his left arm, on a naturalistic base and bolted to a separately cast socle, late 19thC, 22½in (56cm) high.
$22,500-25,500

A French bronze equestrian group, known as 'Charles VII, Victorious', cast from a model by Antoine-Louis Barye, the armoured king astride his prancing steed and wearing a laurel wreath, signed Barye and inscribed F. Barbedienne, Fondeur, the underside inscribed 29, stamped Z and inscribed in ink 4908 etc, leaf tip on wreath missing, fitted wood base, rich green patina, 19thC, 15½in (38.6cm) high.
$5,300-7,700

A highly important French marble bust of Manon Lescaut, by Auguste Rodin, looking half-left, wearing a mob cap and open gown with frilly borders, a posy of roses attached to her gown over her left breast, her hair hanging loosely over her shoulders, signed on the under-edge of her right shoulder Rodin, on a separately carved square and moulded socle inscribed on the front Manon Lescaut and signed on the side Rodin, A, veined grey marble plinth, late 19thC, 24in (59cm) high.
$105,000+

in Meissen porcelain, and a mosaic of hardstones, the latter being particularly esteemed if by Johann-Christian Neuber.

The top end of the market is based on the biannual auctions in Geneva, and the most recent session in the spring included a number of important pieces which sold well. Foremost was a large Russian box presented to Count Esterhazy by the Empress Elizabeth Petrovna, and it sold to a private collector for £219,500. An oval Dresden gold box set with specimens of different polished hardstones in a fish scale pattern bordered by diamonds was the best of its kind in this sale, selling for £100,315. The names of all the stones used were catalogued in a little printed book which was still in its secret compartment.

A turquoise and dark blue glazed composition statuette of Isis and Harpocrates, her throne decorated with feather and border pattern on either side and the sign of the unification of the Two Lands on the back, the seated goddess wearing uraeus and throne sign, suckling Harpocrates, his sidelock and the tripartite wig and collar of Isis in cobalt blue glaze, repaired at waist and left hand, mounted, Ptolemaic, circa 3rd-2nd Century, B.C., 5½in (14cm) high.
$13,500-17,000

A marble cult statue of the goddess Cybele, seated on a high-backed throne, her wavy hair swept back under a low polos with ringlets escaping over her shoulders, wearing a chiton girdled high under her breasts, a lion seated on her lap, her left hand holding a tympanon, her right arm raised, phiale missing, Greek, Hellenistic, 15in (38cm) high.
$22,500-29,000

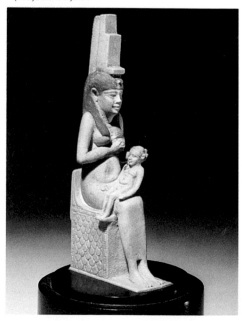

A rare pair of cloisonné enamel ewers, Qianlong, each modelled in the form of a duck with a long sleek body, the head gilded open beak, the back supporting a tapering neck, surmounted by a tall angular handle, 6 character marks of the period incised on the rims, 12¼in (31.1cm).
$58,500-71,400

Compared to gold boxes, textiles is a young and developing collectors' field, and therefore one which spans a price range to suit all pockets. The top end is dominated by the 17th and 18th century fabrics, early English chintzes being highly sought after in England, while in America indiginous samplers and quilts are naturally highly prized. American textiles are more often to be found in large sales of 'Americana', where the nationality rather than the type of object is the focal point. An unusually fine and early example can sell for stunning sums, for instance the $21,000 paid for a Rhode Island sampler dated 1769 at a sale by the Skinner Gallery in Bolton, Massachusetts. The

A massive cloisonné enamel and gilt bronze vase, assembled from 3 sections with broad baluster body, tall flaring trumpet neck set with 2 large gilt dragon handles and spreading foot, decorated on turquoise grounds with lotus-headed foliage in tight meanders divided by narrower bands of daisy scroll above the shoulder, 17thC, 25½in (63cm) high.
$7,500-10,200

An unusual pair of cloisonné enamel figures of zebra, each naturalistically modelled standing four-square, the hide alternately striped in black and white enamels inlaid with gilt wire scrolls to simulate the hair, a hinged oval cover on the back, 19thC, 25 by 31in (62.5 by 77.5cm).
$93,000+

auctioneers had estimated the sampler to sell between $7,000-$10,000. A late 18th century needlework family tree from Portland, chronicling the families of Moses Davis and Mercy Caldwell, was also highly sought after in this sale, selling at $11,500.

Antique costume has been gaining in respectability as a collectors' market over the last few years, to the extent that people are now buying old clothes with a view to forming a collection rather than as an extension of their wardrobe. The famous names of haute couture are obviously the most desirable, such as Fortuny, Schiaparelli, Poiret, Vionnet and Chanel. Chanel are actively collecting fine specimens of their founder's designs; they recently bought back a charming summer evening dress in white silk organza printed with red and blue flowers from Christie's South Kensington, at a cost of £2,200.

A Louis XVI gold snuff-box, inset with Japanese lacquer panels in gold hiramakie and okibirame with flowering chrysanthemums, by A. J. M. Vachette, Paris, 1787, with the poinçons of Henri Clavel, 3in (7.6cm).
$50,000-61,200

A French Empire gold snuff-box, enamelled en camaieu rose by Adrien-Maximilien Vachette, Paris, with second standard mark (20ct.) for 1795-97 (or later) and warranty marks for 1809-19, in fitted case, 3in (7.6cm).
$38,000-48,000

A Meissen Bergleute rectangular snuff-box, painted by Bonaventura Gottlieb Hauer with a figure probably intended as Augustus the Strong, each exterior surface painted with miners at various pursuits, one surface with a Hauptbergmann beside a miner carrying a tray of cups, the interior of the cover painted with a lady, 2 men and a child in a workshop interior, c1745, 3¼in (8cm).
$33,000-42,500

A Louis XVI oval gold snuff-box, the body with oyster-pink opalescent enamel panels painted in mauve, by Louis-Joachin Colmet de Courty, Paris, 1778, with the poinçons of J. B. Fouache, in leather case, 3¼in (8cm).
$22,500-25,500

An important early Swiss gold and enamel singing-bird box, the signed oval movement by Jaquet-Droz, London, with articulated bird, fusee chain and circular bellows, the lid painted with a shepherd and shepherdess, the deep blue guilloche enamel panels edged in gold foliage paillons, with draped vases around the sides, the hinged base with shallow key compartment and key, enamel chipped and restored, the box with the maker's mark of Georges Rémond, Geneva, c1780, 3½in (9cm).
$28,500-35,700

 is actually the sampler at top.

A fine needlework sampler, by Catherine Miller, New England, finely worked in silk and wool threads in a variety of stitches on a linen ground, depicting Adam and Eve in the Garden of Eden with the serpent, animals and an angel under an embroidered sky with the sun, moon, and stars centering 2 angels, inscribed 'Catherine Miller work done in the year 1791', framed, minor losses and discolourations, 21in (52.5cm).
$8,300-11,000

Although tapestries are strictly speaking textiles, they are firmly in the luxury bracket as a collectors' item, somewhere between fine and decorative art. Of all the areas in the 'works of art' market, tapestries are probably the most buoyant. While Renaissance bronzes and medieval wood sculpture have been proving sticky sellers, there is a good solid demand for tapestries from both sides of the Atlantic.

The least popular, and therefore expensive, are the 18th century verdure tapestries which were made in prolific numbers, with many versions produced from the same cartoon. That being said, this type of tapestry forms the staple diet of the goods sold at auction in France and Belgium, usually a handful are tacked on to the end of a furniture sale. They vary between £3,000-£10,000 depending on quality, condition, size and attractiveness.

A very rare William and Mary military cap, front flap of blue velvet with hessian stiffening, red front embroidered with crown above an intertwined W M cypher between thistles and interspersed with sequins, the band, front and flap with gold lace border, some wear to edge and one minor patch of mothing, c1690.
$11,300-13,600

A Chinese coat of terracotta silk, designed with dragons, flowers, and cosmic symbols in mainly green, blue, red and ivory silks and gold thread, worked in Pekin knot and satin stitch, the whole applied with gold thread in a key pattern design, having deep sleeves, relined, early 19thC.
$800-1,100

A French fan, the carved, pierced silvered and gilt ivory sticks decorated with cartouches of fashionably dressed ladies and gentlemen, the ivory silk leaf worked with gilt and coloured spangles and tamboured gold thread and painted with lovers gathered round a cupid on an altar and playing with flower chains, the reserves with love trophies, late 18thC, 10½in (27cm).
$1,000-1,200

◀
An important Flemish tapestry, woven in silk and wool with Hercules, the bearded hero poised to cut the throat of an enemy soldier with his scimitar with other armour-clad figures in the mêlée and dead men in the foreground with onlookers beyond standing on the ramparts of a walled city, Hercules again depicted in the top left hand corner untying a bleeding semi-clad figure from a tree, fairly extensive areas of restoration and repair, early 16thC, 133in (332cm) wide.
$81,500+

The rarer and much more desirable tapestries are those which date from the 16th and 17th centuries, particularly the 'choux-fleur', romance and historical types. There was one outstanding work on the market this season, a Franco-Flemish mille fleurs tapestry woven in the first quarter of the 16th century, possibly at Tournai. It was included in Sotheby's spring auction of European work of art in New York, with a pre-sale estimate of $40,000-$60,000, but competition was such that the American dealer, Edward R. Lubin, had to go to $200,000, bidding on behalf of an unnamed institution. Another rare work was a 16th century memorial tapestry of Baron von Khevenhuller, which was secured by a European collector for $80,000.

A Flemish verdure tapestry, woven in wool and silk in fresh colours with a stag seated in an allee of trees, woods to the left and an exotic bird and a formal garden on the right, the broad border woven with clusters of fruit and flowers, 17thC, 110in (275cm) wide.
$13,500-17,000

A fine Brussels tapestry, depicting the family of Darius before Alexander, the conqueror standing between the daughters of Darius offering his hand to raise the kneeling Sisygambis, Bucephalus held by a Nubian groom, cavalry nearby with figures and a city in the distance, the outer border with trophies of arms, fruit and foliage, signed B + B, Jan van Rottom, top left border restored, 17thC, 172in (430cm) wide.
$10,500-13,600

A fine South Caucasian rug, the royal blue field divided into panels, containing stylised human figures and animals, in a broad ivory cusped plant motif border between royal blue flowerhead and linked 'S'-motif stripes, ends slight damage, 35in (89cm) wide.
$5,300-7,700

A fine antique silk Chinese pictorial carpet, the ivory field with a series of temples, mountains, trees and lakes, in a gold flowering vine border between key-pattern and plain outer stripe, 73in (185cm) wide.
$10,500-14,000

A rare Imperial silk and copper thread rug, boldly decorated with a central leaping dragon, enclosed by 8 smaller matching dragons chasing 'flaming pearls', amidst cloud scrolls, all reserved on a copper thread field encircled by a border of blue crested waves divided by rockwork, inscribed 'Baohedian beiyong', 19thC, 61in (393.5cm) wide.
$15,000-25,500

A fine antique Heriz carpet, the salmon-pink field with palmettes and flowering vine around a large ivory serrated panel with brick-red floral medallion with indigo pendants, in a shaded brick-red turtle palmette and stylised vine border between light blue flowering vine and mill pattern stripes, 112in (285cm) wide.
$24,000-30,600

Since the collapse of Middle Eastern buyers in the carpet market a few years ago, auctioneers all over the world have had to work hard to rehabilitate the trade. It has been a symptom of carpet sales to be left with up to fifty per cent unsold, due to a number of reasons from sluggish demand, to greedy reserves, to the ring in operation. It was correctly perceived that auctions would do better if they were smaller and more specialised, both in terms of types of carpet and quality, and this is now generally the way business is done.

One of the results has been to encourage more private collectors into the salerooms which has made for better results than in the immediate past, but there is still a larger than average proportion of lots which do not sell.

George Engleheart
Lieutenant Colonel Thomas Hanmer facing right in dark blue coat, white waistcoat and cravat, signed with initial, gold frame with glass reverse, fitted red leather case, 3½in (8.5cm).
$6,000-8,500

At a sale in New York in May, a surprisingly high price of $47,000 was recorded for a silk Heriz rug from the last quarter of the 19th century which had been estimated at around half this sum. On the other hand a Mohtashem Kashan estimated at up to $60,000 did not sell, as was the case with several other of the more valuable carpets. An elegant Tabriz carpet did well to reach $40,000, as did another Tabriz at $23,000, in both cases well over the estimates.

The mother of God Troyeruchica, the icon covered with a repoussé and chased silver gilt riza, the robes of filigree, applied with vari-colour cloisonné enamel haloes and spandrels, maker's mark Cyrillic IF, Moscow 1894, 11in (25.5cm) wide.
$3,800-5,100

A Doulton Lambeth terracotta plaque, 'The Wheelwright Shop', by George Tinworth, modelled as a young man carving a face on a piece of wood in his father's wheelwright shop, inscribed with the title and signed with 'GT' monogram and 'H. Doulton & Co., Lambeth', 8in (20cm).
$2,400-3,400

◄
A lacquered wood panel, by Jean Dunand, a golden complexioned girl, stretched along the floor and propped up on her elbows, contemplates a double profile portrait, in dark red, tan and gold on black and grey ground, framed, signed Jean Dunand, 24½in (63cm).
$8,300-11,000

A fine Chinese mirror picture, delicately painted with a richly dressed lady in a blue robe and a servant seated by a river with pavilions and rocky outcrops opposite, a boy and a white horse on the left; in giltwood frame of George III design, the mirror picture 18thC, 30½in (77.5cm) wide.
$14,000-17,000

Carpets currently considered undervalued by Phillips' experts are run-of-mill Turkoman and medium quality Caucasus rugs from the turn of the century. At the lower end of the trade kelims are gaining in popularity.

Collectors of miniatures, like those of glass, are generally a patriotic bunch – English miniatures sell better in England and Continental ones do likewise on the Continent. Sotheby's two most recent sales in Geneva confirmed this pattern, especially where the property of

A rare Charles II stumpwork picture, worked in high relief in coloured silks on an ivory ground with Abraham banishing Hagar and Ishmael, with figures emblematic of the Seasons in the corners, richly dressed, among trees and flowers, buildings, a lion and a leopard, in ebonised parcel-gilt frame, 28in (71cm) wide.
$6,000-10,200

A Savona tile picture, emblematic of the Vintage with a Bacchic procession led by a nymph with a cup and a faun blowing pipes with satyrs bearing baskets of nuts and grapes in an extensive landscape within a rococo frame painted with flowers, one tile and one border tile damaged, blue shield mark in lower left-hand corner, c1750, 60½in (151cm) wide.
$7,500-12,000

The Crucifixion, with the Virgin and St. John, St. Mary Magdalena and Longinus, flanked by 2 angels, the sun and the moon, painted on gold ground, the basma frame chased with scrolling foliage and applied with an engraved plaque with the initials of Christ, Moscow School, 17thC, 12½in (31cm).
$10,500-14,000

51

An important Italian violin, by Antonio Stradivari, labelled Antonius Stradiuarius Cremonensis/Faciebat anno 1684; the two-piece back of faint small curl, the ribs cut on the slab, the scroll medium, the two-piece table of even fine grain, the varnish of a golden colour, the length of back 14in (35.5cm).
$135,000+

the late King Umberto II of Italy was concerned. Having reigned for only one month and spent the remainder of his life in exile, the late King amassed a comprehensive collection of portraits of his ancestors from the House of Savoy. It was formed with painstaking research and provides an interesting pictorial record of the major powers of central Europe of the 18th and 19th centuries.

The sale was a great success with Italian and Swiss buyers, headed by a portrait of the Duke of Chablais which went to a Swiss dealer for £12,260.

Miniatures are a small but flourishing market in Switzerland. In May this year a carnival scene by van Blarenberghe was bid to three times the estimate by a Belgian collector

An important Italian violin , by Carlo Tononi, labelled Carlo Tononi Bolognese/Fece in Venezia l'Anno 1725; the one-piece back of handsome small curl, the ribs similar, the scroll of fainter figure, the two-piece table of even medium grain, the varnish of a golden-orange colour, the length of back 14in (35.5cm), in shaped oak case by W. E. Hill & Sons.
$52,500-68,000

A fine Italian violin, of the Cremonese school, labelled Antonius & Hieronymus Fr. Amati/Cremonen Andrea fil F.16; the one-piece back of handsome wood cut on the slab, the ribs similar, the scroll plain, the two-piece table of fine to medium grain, the varnish of reddish-amber colour, the length of the back 14in (35.5cm).
$24,000-30,600

Icons are a particularly difficult art form, to penetrate by an outsider, by which I mean someone who is neither Greek or Russian. More than any other form of Western religious painting, they are pure symbols of ecclesiastical doctrine. It was the subject not the artist which was important, and this can still be seen today in the way religion is taught in small Greek communities.

Thus the icon market is an extremely small one, the Greek side being much more prosperous than the Russian, because, no doubt, there are more wealthy expatriate Greeks than there are Russians. Still, the bidding was sluggish at summer sales held by Sotheby's and Christie's, and poor results were seen for the early Cretan school which is usually the most desirable. It must be indicative of the market for musical instruments in New York that Sotheby's have decided to switch these sales permanently to London.

Their last musical instrument sale scheduled for New York took place in June, and it was marred by the fact that the most important lot failed to sell. This was the Gudgeon Stradivari violin, made in Cremona in about 1672. In all areas of the art world provenance is a crucial matter, and the fact that this violin had once belonged to George Gudgeon, a noted late 19th century collector, should have made it all the more desirable. Professional musicians are the most active buyers of antique musical instruments, and the more famous the soloist, the more famous the instrument he or she will want to own. There are many more violins with a Stradivarius label than could ever have been made by the man himself, and so authenticity and condition are of the greatest importance. Some Stradivarius instruments are thought to be beyond their best now. There is something fairly unpleasant about a 19th century surgical kit, knives,

An ivory azimuth diptych dial, signed Fait Par Charles Bloud Dieppe on the calender volvelle, the cover signed C. Bloud A. Dieppe engraved with a dial and all surfaces with scrolls, foliage and wheatear decoration, late 17th/early 18thC, 3½ by 4in (8.4 by 9.5cm).
$6,000-8,000

A brass Butterfield-type, signed Lordelle A Paris and dated 1738, the octagonal based engraved on the underside with the latitudes of 10 European cities and decorated with shells, scrolls and flowers, the upper surface engraved with hour scales for 43°, 45° and 48°, in the original lined, fitted leather covered case, 7in (17.5cm).
$7,500-10,200

◄

A rare silver quadrant dial with horizontal plate, vertical 45° triangular gnomon hinged to one side and held upright by a catch and cut-away for plumb-bob, now missing and 2 hinge pins replaced, signed Humfray Colle, c1570, the plate 3 by 3in (7.5 by 7.5cm).
$94,300+

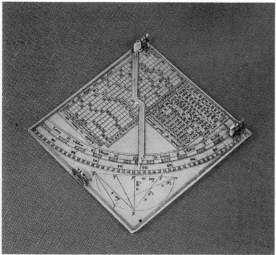

scalpels, and bone saws, and this was much the impression American collectors had when Sotheby's and Christie's offered medical instruments for the first time in New York. They were included in a sale of scientific instruments, clocks and watches, and did not meet with enthusiasm. However, this is a more established collectors' market in Europe, and it may take some time before American interest is properly penetrated.

Generally, the instrument market is not very buoyant in the USA, and is prone to erratic fits and starts. At Christie's sale in April prices fluctuated above and below the estimates, but more often the former. Indeed, their top lot which had been estimated at a maximum of $5,000, sold for $10,000. It was a late 16th century Spanish gilt brass and silver universal equatorial dial.

Dolls continue to sell well on both sides of the Atlantic, with probably the

A fine Bru Jeune bisque doll, French, with open/closed mouth, fixed brown glass eyes, pierced ears, blonde mohair wig over cork pate and the kid body with wooden lower legs and bisque forearms, paper label on the abdomen, white underclothes, impressed BRU Jne 3 on head and both shoulders, c1880, 14in (36cm). **$4,500-7,000**

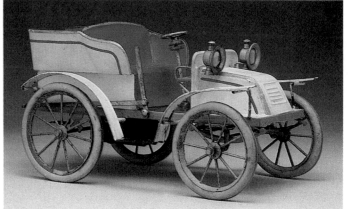

A fine large and scarce Bing tinplate Tonneau, German, finished in hand painted cream lined scarlet, gold and green, with simulated padded front seats, opening rear door to passenger compartment with small step below, on rubber-tyred spoked wheels, with original front lamps and steering wheel operating front axle, the clockwork mechanism driving the rear axle, c1903, 11½in (28cm). **$11,300-14,600**

greatest appetite coming from American collectors. Indeed the field is so popular that it supports a firm of auctioneers called Theriault who specialise in nothing but dolls. The top price in the dolls section of Sotheby's June Collectors' Carousel auction was a Jumeau bisque-head *bebe*, wearing original wig, clothes and shoes, and she sold to a private collector for $8,025. This was roughly twice the expected sum. A Bru swivel-head *bebe* made its target price of $5,500, but the buyer of another Bru *bebe* had to offer nearly double the estimate, or $4,400, to secure the lot.

A rare Vichy 'Pierrot Serenading the Moon' musical automaton, French, the seated figure with papier-mâché head, fixed brown glass eyes, black silk pate over black mohair, the metal arms playing a mandolin, the papier-mâché moon with brown glass eye which rolls to the music, the base containing mechanism activating Pierrot to play the mandolin, base distressed, mechanism in need of slight attention, c1870, 21in (53cm). **$16,500-22,100**

A Marklin tinplate clockwork
model of H.M.S. Terrible,
29in (72.5cm) long.
$12,000-15,300

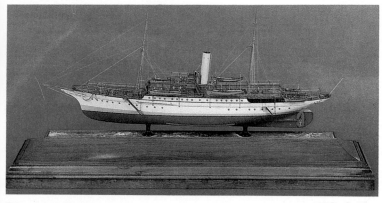

A shipbuilder's model of Lord
Ashburton's steam yacht
'Venetia', with white and blue
painted wooden hull and single
brass screw, 5 ship's boats and
a steam launch, all mounted on
davits, supported on 2 turned
ebony columns on velvet
covered base under glazed
mahogany case, Scottish,
1893, 67½in (171cm) long.
$11,300-14,500

The highlight of the toy collectors' market was the sale of the collection of
Raymond E. Holland, auctioned by Sotheby's in April. Holland's speciality was
automata, but despite the huge interest and publicity the sale generated, prices
were on the whole disappointing.

Teddy bears are in the throes of great popularity at the moment. To date the
record stands at £1,900 for a 1905 blond bear sold at Phillips.

The world of arms and armour is divided between East and West, with Middle
Eastern and Oriental artefacts catalogued as specialist subjects rather than
being thrown in to general sales as they were in the past.

In particular Middle Eastern arms have been upgraded into Islamic works of
art, as private buyers and museum authorities in that area show increased
awareness of their heritage.

Christie's New York sold important Japanese armour as part of their Japanese
works of art week in March, and prices were extremely competitive with not a
single lot unsold. The top price was $23,000 for a Myochin

A prisoner-of-war bone model
of a British frigate, the pinned
and planked solid hull with
baleen strakes presenting 48
guns on 2 decks, on shaped
pine base veneered with
mahogany, boxwood and
kingwood with turned bone
finials and 2 toggles for
operating the gun retraction, in
glazed wooden case, early
19thC, 15 by 19in (38 by
48cm).
$9,000-11,900

School suit of armour which had been expected to sell at around $10,000. It was bought by an American private collector.

In general the market for arms and armour could best be described as steady. There is a good solid demand for antique pistols, swords and other European arms, but the biggest growth area is in the field of specialist interests such as Islamic and Japanese arms. All types of Islamic art have been given a boost by the newly opened museum in Kuwait which has received a great deal of publicity around the world.

Victorian armour has seen a surprising surge in popularity this season, when Sotheby's took a price of £4,000 for what their department described as a suit of 'interior decorators armour'. These large cumbersome things that once lined baronial halls fell from favour by the late 19th century, and it is only in the very recent past that collectors have taken a fresh look at them.

Not surprisingly, American buyers are most keen on top quality indiginous items, such as Kentucky and Colt firearms, and this season has produced good steady results with few peaks or troughs.

Fenella Rowse

A fine gold-lacquered moyegi-ito-odoshi tatami-do, the kabuto with a sugake-laced folding hachi and five-lame shikoro, the mabizashi and munaita of black lacquer decorated in hiramakie with mon and karakusa, the manju-gote with gold-lacquered tekko, the o-sode fitted with shakudo kogai-kanamono, the black-lacquered mempo with kebiki-laced yodarekake, and with a kebiki-laced haidate.
$3,500-5,000

An exceptional French all-steel percussion target pistol, with three-stage octagonal polygroove rifled sighted barrel entirely chiselled with panels of running foliage and signed 'Le Page Moutier Arq. er Br. té à Paris', barrel bolt and fore-sight damaged, some light pitting and scratches on the stock and barrel, minor damage to gold work, No. 937, dated 1849 under the barrel, with the barrel maker's mark of Leopold Bernard, 16in (40cm).
$30,000-34,000

An exceptionally fine and rare Colt Hartford Dragoon Percussion cap revolver, 7½in (19cm) part round and octagonal barrel with London proof marks, top flat inscribed Address Sam Colt New York City, 1855-1857, 13½in (34cm).
$15,000-25,000

56

ENGLISH POTTERY

There has been a fair amount of good quality English delft available and prices for the best pieces often exceeding expectations.

The demand for English pottery has been particularly strong in almost all areas of the market. Run-of-the-mill pieces have held steady while anything slightly unusual or of academic interest has had a consistent and determined following. Some high prices, particularly for rare, early wares in good condition have reflected a powerful American interest.

The trend towards higher price levels has been shown throughout the range of English pottery with top flight examples of saltglaze, early slipware, creamware and Staffordshire figure groups all keenly sought.

It is unlikely that there will be any lessening of demand for good English pottery in the coming year particularly as American interest appears to be strengthening.

CONTINENTAL POTTERY

Demand in many areas continues to be relatively weak. Only exceptional pieces created the degree of competition amongst buyers necessary for above average prices.

The very finest examples of Dutch Delft stimulated some interest but more ordinary wares produced a patchy response, in general buyers being prepared to hold off in anticipation of a reduction in prices.

Good majolica has remained steady during the year with the demand for the finest early pieces occasionally exceeding expectations. This pattern was repeated for other types of pottery, rare German stonewares and good quality French and German faience being eagerly sought whilst more ordinary pieces failed to stimulate competition amongst buyers.

Baskets

A Leeds pottery basket, decorated in various shades of translucent green glazes, crossed marks, marked Leeds, c1790, 10¼ in (25.25 cm) wide. **$400-600**

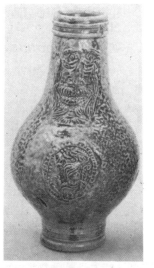

A Niderviller (Custine) basket and stand, the basketwork edged in puce, the interior of the basket with a landscape vignette, minor chip and crack to edge of stand, c1775, 12 in (30 cm) wide. **$1,300-1,700**

Bellarmine

A Rhenish stoneware Bellarmine (Bartmann krug) applied with crisply moulded birds among meandering oak leaves and acorns, the short neck carved in relief with a bearded mask of almost oriental appearance, the vessel is entirely covered in a pale honey-coloured saltglaze, Frechen or Cologne (incipient crackle), second quarter 16thC, 7 in (18 cm). **$4,500-7,000**

For a Bartmannkrug with oak-leaf and bird decoration and a comparable mask see Reineking von Bock, Steinzeug no 260.

A Frechen Bellarmine, covered in a brown tigerware glaze and applied with a crisply modelled mask above an oval medallion including a stylised animal, with grooved handle, chip to footrim, 17thC, 8¾ in (21.3 cm). **$500-600**

Miller's is a price GUIDE not a price LIST

A German stoneware Bellarmin the neck decorated with the usu bearded face, covered in a mottle light brown glaze, 16th/17thC, 9¾ in (24.5 cm). **$400-600**

Bottles

◄

A Southwark delft blue and white small sack bottle, the body with three panels of stylised flowers divided by double wavy bands, minor glaze flaking, c1640, 5 in (12.5 cm) high. **$2,500-3,500**

Cf Ivor Noel Hume, Early English Delftware from London and Virginia, pl 25 where he illustrates a manganese stippled bottle of similar form and relates it to biscuit fragments from the Pickleherring site.

A delft 'sack' bottle, probably London, dated 1651, 6 in (15 cm) high. **$4,000-5,000**

Bowls

An Ansbach blue and white bowl, with rope twist handles, painted in bright blue, flower-heads and C-scrolls, cracked, minor rim chips, c1745, 11 in (27.5 cm) wide. **$600-700**

A Castelli bowl, painted by Carlo Antonio Grue with the battle between Darius and Alexander, the border with four putti among scrolling, flowering foliage, cracked, c1715, 12¾ in (32 cm) diam. **$4,500-7,000**

A spongeware bowl, with blue markings, 11 by 3½ in (27.5 by 8.5 cm) deep. **$100-200**

A Wedgwood fairyland lustre bowl, painted with fairies, elves and pixies in a wooded landscape in pink, green, blue and gilt, 13 in (32.5 cm) diam. **$1,000-1,400**

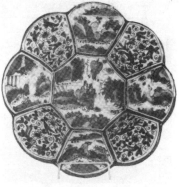

A Dutch Delft shallow bowl, with blue and white chinoiserie decoration of figures in landscapes and arabesques and foliates, mid 18thC, 12½ in (31.5 cm) diam. **$400-600**

A Caffaggiolo blue-ground fruit bowl, with everted rim, the interior painted with fruit, and the blue borders reserved with white foliage and chrysanthemum, rim repaired, first half of the 16thC, 12½ in (31.5 cm) diam. **$3,000-4,000**

►

A St Clement faience bleeding bowl, first half of the 19thC, 11 in (28 cm) wide. **$300-500**

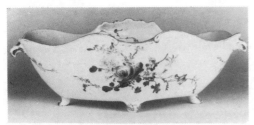

A Marseilles shaped bowl, on four branch feet, painted with trailing flower-sprays and with insects, the borders, handles and feet edged in puce, cracked, rim chips, c1760, 15 in (37.5 cm) wide.
$300-500

A Wedgwood pearlware foot-bath, transfer-printed in blue with The Tower of London pattern, the interior with ships on a river beside a castle, impressed mark, c1840, 18 in (45 cm) wide.
$1,700-2,500

A Minton majolica bowl, painted in typical pale enamel colours, impressed marks, mid 19thC, 23½ in (43.5 cm) long.
$1,700-2,500

A Wedgwood 'Boat Race' bowl, designed by Eric Ravilious, transfer-printed in black on white with a central scene of Piccadilly Circus, the exterior with panels of the race and other nautical scenes, and the 'Mermaid' device, 'Wedgwood, Made in England' and impressed 'Wedgwood', 12 in (30.50 cm) diam. **$700-1,000**

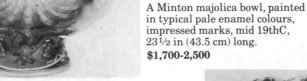

A Berlin lacquered faience bowl, the inside painted with blue stylised scrolling shells, the exterior with flowers and landscapes in Japanese style, in red, green and ochre, all beneath a scroll and trellis border and on a black ground, minor chips, c1720, 10½ in (26.2 cm). **$1,000-1,200**

Busts

An Alcora faience bust of a blackmoor, dressed as a hussar, wearing a blue cloak with purple border, white tunic and white hat with yellow cockade, his face coloured in manganese-purple, minor chips, 5 in (12.3 cm).
$2,000-3,000

A Copeland & Garrett white glazed stoneware library bust of Horatio, Lord Nelson, named on the reverse, impressed and green printed marks, hair crack to socle, and minute chip to collar, c1840, 9¼ in (23 cm) high. **$800-1,200**

A Deruta bust of the Virgin Mary her head with a blue shawl and a crown, her bodice moulded and painted with blue scrolls on an ochre ground, minor damage to the crown, mid 17thC, 12½ in (31.5 cm) high. **$600-900**

l A Wedgwood & Bentley black basalt miniature bust of Ariadne, small chips to socle, impressed lower-case marks to bust and socle, c1775, 4 in (10.5 cm) high. **$1,700-2,500**
Recorded in Wedgwood & Bentley's 1779 catalogue Class XII, Section 1.

c A Wedgwood & Bentley black basalt miniature bust of Aristophanes, impressed lower-case marks to bust and socle, c1775, 3¾ in (9.5 cm) high. **$1,500-2,200**
Recorded in Wedgwood & Bentley's 1779 catalogue Class XII, Section 1.

r A Wedgwood & Bentley black basalt miniature bust of David Garrick, chip to socle, impressed lower-case marks to bust and socle, c1780, 4 in (10.5 cm) high. **$2,000-3,000**
Perhaps taken from moulds supplied by Hoskins & Grant in 1779.

A Staffordshire pearlware portrait bust, perhaps of Admiral Duncan, in orange coat and yellow frogging and sash, the socle enriched in orange and yellow, restored, c1800, 9 in (22.5 cm) high. **$300-500**

An 'Enoch Wood' bust of George Washington, in enamel colours, 8 in (20 cm). **$500-600**

A Ralph Wood bust of Milton, his hair enriched in brown, draped in a pale-mauve cloak and brown jacket, crack restored to shoulder, impressed Ra Wood 81 mark, c1790, 8¾ in (22 cm) high. **$700-1,000**

A pearlware portrait bust of Admiral Duncan, in red coat with gold frogging and a white sash, on a socle moulded with naval trophies, chip to nose, perhaps Herculaneum, c1800, 8½ in (21.5 cm) high. **$1,700-2,500**

A bust of Shakespeare, probably by Enoch Wood, in multi coloured enamels, c1810, 11 in (27.5 cm). **$500-600**

A matched pair of Wedgwood black basalt library busts of Milton and Shakespeare, one impressed MILTON and Wedgwood in small caps, the other unnamed and impressed Wedgwood in larger caps, 14½ in and 15 in 36 cm and 37 cm. **$800-1,200**

A Herculaneum bust of Admiral Earl St Vincent, in blue jacket, yellow frogging and purple sash, the socle moulded with naval trophies, chips, restoration to nose and socle, impressed mark, c1800, 8¾ in (22 cm) high. **$1,000-1,200**

◄

Two Staffordshire busts: l Sir Robert Peel, c1830, 7½ in (17.5 cm) high. **$600-700.** r Lord Byron, c1840, 10 in (25 cm) high by 5½ in (17.5 cm) wide. **$500-600**

Commemorative

A commemorative bowl, of King George III and Queen Charlotte, 1793, 10½ in (26.5 cm). **$600-800**

A spill vase, to commemorate the coronation of King George IV, 4 in (10 cm). **$1,300-1,700**

A Davenport commemorative blue printed plate, of George III, normally called "The Farmer George" service, 10 in (25 cm). **$600-700**

A commemorative jug, 'God save Queen Caroline', in copper lustre, 6 in (15 cm). **$500-600**

A commemorative 'death' plate, made for the Lancastrian School Movement, c1820, 6¼ in (15.5 cm) **$700-900**

A lustre plaque, Queen Caroline 1820, 5½ in (13.5 cm). **$500-600**

A commemorative jug, of the Prince of Wales and Princess Alexandra, marked J. & M.P.B. & Co., 8 in (20 cm). **$200-300**

A saltglaze two-handled cup, of Prince Albert and Queen Victoria, c1840, 5¾ in (15 cm). **$300-400**

A commemorative mug, commemorating the coronation of Queen Victoria, 1837, printed in green, 3½ in (8.75 cm). **$800-1,200**

A commemorative jug, of the death of King George IV, marked G.B.H., 1830, 6 in (15 cm). **$300-600**

A plate, commemorating the death of Queen Caroline, 7½ in (18.75 cm). **$500-600**

A commemorative lustre jug, of the marriage of Prince Leopold and Charlotte, 1816, 6 in (15 cm). **$600-800**

A commemorative accession plate, to commemorate the coronation of Queen Victoria, 1837, 6 in (15 cm). **$500-700**

A commemorative lustre cup and saucer, of the Princess Charlotte. **$300-400**

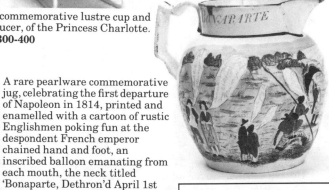

A rare pearlware commemorative jug, celebrating the first departure of Napoleon in 1814, printed and enamelled with a cartoon of rustic Englishmen poking fun at the despondent French emperor chained hand and foot, an inscribed balloon emanating from each mouth, the neck titled 'Bonaparte, Dethron'd April 1st 1814', some wear, c1814. **$300-500**

MAKE THE MOST OF MILLER'S

Every care has been taken to ensure the accuracy of descriptions and estimated valuations. Where an attribution is made within inverted commas (e.g. 'Chippendale') or is followed by the word 'style' (e.g. early Georgian style) it is intended to convey that, in the opinion of the publishers, the piece concerned is a later – though probably still antique – reproduction of the style so designated. Unless otherwise stated, any description which refers to 'a set', or 'a pair' includes a valuation for the entire set or the pair, even though the illustration may show only a single item.

A commemorative plate of Queen Caroline, printed in blue, 7¼ in (18 cm). **$300-400**

A commemorative jug with cover, showing the Death of Albert, in white parian ware, c1861, 10½ in (26.5 cm). **$300-400**

A commemorative jug, of the Princess Royal and the Prince of Prussia, 6 in (15 cm). **$100-150**

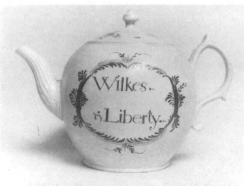

A commemorative Leeds creamware tea pot, in the manner of David Rhodes, 6 in (15 cm). **$2,000-3,000**

An English pottery mug, printed in brown with a portrait of Lady Elizabeth Bowes-Lyon and decorated in gilt, to commemorate the Royal Wedding, 1922. **$400-600**

A rare marriage of Victoria and Albert earthenware loving cup, printed in blue with the half length portrait of the royal couple, restored, c1840, 4½ in (12 cm). **$400-600**

A rare commemorative Leeds ▶ creamware jug, decorated in slate blue, iron-red and grey with a bell above an inscription, the reverse with a butcher at work above the inscription 'I will lay 18 to a Guniea (sic) this is Best Beef In OTLEY MARKET' flanking the name John Ibbotson 1802, impressed mark LEEDS POTTERY, repaired, 6½ in (16.2 cm). **$1,000-1,400**

◀ A Bourne saltglazed stoneware spirit flask, moulded as 'Daniel O'Connell Esq', holding a scroll impressed 'Irish Reform Cordial', impressed title and 'Denby and Codnor Park, Bourne' mid 1830s, 20.4 cm. **$500-700**

A plate, commemorating the death of Wellington, 7 in (17.5 cm). **$200-300**

A Staffordshire earthenware jug, moulded on each side with Mr Van Amburgh the Liontamer flanked by his animals, all picked out in coloured enamels and copper lustre, on a pale yellow ground, the handle in the form of a lioness, lip restored, c1820, 6¼ in (16 cm) high. **$300-400**

A pair of Staffordshire commemorative plaques, of The Two Boxers 'Spring' and 'Langan', 1824, 7½ in (17.5 cm). **$1,200-1,500**

An English pottery nursery plate, the centre printed in black, with a scene from the Incidents of the War, entitled 'The Naval Brigade News From Home', 6¼ in (16 cm). **$300-500**

A commemorative mug, of Earl Grey, leader of the 1832 Reform Act, Baron Brougham and Vaux, Champions of Reform, printed in pink, 3 in (7.5 cm). **$200-300**

A commemorative mug of Gladstone and Bright 3¾ in (9.5 cm). **$200-300**

A commemorative mug, of King William and Queen Adelaide, printed in purple, 4 in (10 cm). **$500-700**

A Dissolution of Parliament plate, 1831, 9 in (22.5 cm). **$400-600**

A Crimean war commemorative jug, showing Sebastopol, and Sir George Brown, 8 in (20 cm). **$400-600**

A Crimean war commemorative jug, showing the Light Cavalry Charge at Balaclava, 1858 and the Sebastopol attack and capture of the Malakhoff by the French, by G F Bowers. **$400-600**

PRICE

Prices vary from auction to auction – from dealer to dealer. The price paid in a dealer's shop will depend on
1) *what he paid for the item*
2) *what he thinks he can get for it*
3) *the extent of his knowledge*
4) *awareness of market trends*

It is a mistake to think that you will automatically pay more in a specialist dealer's shop. He is more likely to know the 'right' price for a piece. A general dealer may undercharge but he could also overcharge.

A commemorative jug, on yellow ground, A 'Napoleonic cartoon' jug, c1814, 8 in (20 cm). **$1,400-1,700**

A documentary lustre ware jug, decorated with two coaching scenes and inscribed 'The Hero Coach from the Fountain Inn, High Street, Portsmouth to the Spread Eagle, Gracechurch Street and Golden Cross, Charing Cross, London' by Mr Morris, Mr Horn, Thos. Voyce and P Russel etc, 19thC, 8 in (20 cm) high. **$1,000-1,400**

A jug, commemorating the death of Nelson, 1805, 4½ in (11.5 cm). **$400-600**

A Minton commemorative jug, of William and Adelaide, 8 in (20 cm). **$400-600**

A commemorative jug, of Sir Robert Peel Bart, with a print of Drayton Manor on the reverse, 7½ in (18.75 cm). **$200-300**

A rare commemorative Wedgwood creamware jug, painted one side with a medallion of an amusing rustic scene, the reverse with a spray of coloured flowers, divided by the inscription 'C Barker 1790', within blue-line borders, slight chips, impressed WEDGWOOD, 8½ in (22 cm). **$1,700-2,500**

An English creamware jug, painted on one side with "Signals at Portland Observatory", the tall building flying pennants and flanked by the flag symbols for the Western and Eastern Staffs, reversed with a group of sailing ships, including 'The Washington', 9 in (22.5 cm) high. **$700-1,000**

Cottages

A large Staffordshire pottery cottage pastille-burner, with two frontages, c1840, 5 in (12.5 cm) high. **$500-700**

A rare pastille-burner, modelled as a house with four central chimneys above gilt-lined windows and four pierced bay windows, the detachable mound base modelled with flowers on a green ground – 11¼ in (28 cm) high. **$2,000-3,000**

A pastille-burner, in the form of a Chinese pagoda, with detachable roof covered in gilt-edged scalloped slates and with four scroll finial, with open scroll-moulded windows and doors picked out in pink, grey and gilt between apricot pillars, base hairlined, cover chipped, 6 in (14.5 cm). **$400-600**

Use the Index!
Because certain items might fit easily into any of a number of categories, the quickest and surest method of locating any entry is by reference to the index at the back of the book.
This has been fully cross-referenced for absolute simplicity.

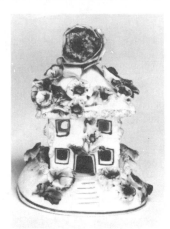

A pastille-burner, in the form of a thatched cottage with gabled roof, the building with pale orange walls, open gilt-edged windows and white door, the whole encrusted with flowers around the edges and on the base. **$300-500**

A pottery flower encrusted cottage pastille-burner, c1830, 7 in (17.5 cm) **$500-600**

A pastille-burner, with detachable mound base, cone-shaped roof and open doors and windows applied with large flowerheads and foliage and with gigantic flowerhead finial, roof with hairline crack, minor chips, 4¾ in (12 cm) high. **$500-600**

A pottery Staffordshire castle, c1845, (16.5 cm). **$100-200**

A Gothic garden pottery gazebo pastille-burner, c1850, 7 in (17.5 cm). **$300-500**

A Staffordshire pottery Windsor Castle, c1845, 6½ in (16.5 cm). **$200-300**

Cow Creamers

A Prattware cow creamer, sponged in brown, ochre and green, with additional blue on milkmaid, c1785, 6 in (15 cm). **$800-1,200**

A large cow creamer, possibly Newcastle, mainly black with touches of yellow, blue and green, c1815, 8 (20 cm) by 6 in (15 cm). **$600-900**

A Swansea cow creamer, decorated in red-brown enamels, c1830, 5½ in (14 cm). **$400-600**
Enamel decoration is much rarer than usual purple-lustre types.

A Newcastle-type cow creamer with milkmaid, in white and black with ochre and green base, c1810, 6 in (15 cm). **$700-1,000**

An early cow creamer, in splashed glazes, mainly brown, grey and green, c1785, 5 in (12.5 cm). **$700-1,000**

A brown glazed pottery cow creamer, probably Brameld, c1825, 5 in (12.5 cm). **$500-600**

A Yorkshire brown glazed pottery cow creamer, probably Brameld, c1825, 5½ in (14 cm). **$500-700**

A Yorkshire cow creamer sponged in red and ochre, with maid and base in green, cow with hobbled hind legs, c1790, 5½ in (14cm). **$600-900**

A Yorkshire cow group, with lady attendant and calf, in brilliant Pratt underglaze colours, c1790-1800. **$1,200-1,500**

A Swansea cow creamer, early 19thC. **$300-500**

A Yorkshire cow creamer in typical 'Pratt' colours of blue, ochre and green, c1790, 5½ in (14 cm). **$600-900**

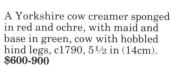

A Yorkshire cow creamer and cover, with black and brown markings, a milkmaid kneeling at its side on oval brightly coloured yellow and blue base, 6 in (15 cm). **$800-1,200**

◄ A cow creamer of large size, probably Newcastle, with head turned to side, white with black patches, c1810, 8½ in (21.5 cm) long. **$600-900**

A Yorkshire cow creamer with hobbled back legs, sponged in black and red, c1790, 5 in (12.5 cm). **$600-900**

Cups

A Staffordshire cow creamer, decorated in underglaze Pratt sponged colours, hobbling to hind legs, c1790, 5¼ in (14 cm). **$600-900**

A dated blue and white delftware stem cup painted with birds among magnolia between line borders, the interior scattered with flowers about the inscription 'T L/August. ye 30/1717', restored stem, chipped rim, 1717, 3¾ in (8 cm). **$2,000-3,000**

A Netherland majolica blue and white quaich, the cavetto painted in the 'Wanli' manner, the underside covered in a straw coloured glaze, 17thC, 9¼ in (23 cm) wide. **$1,700-2,500**

A similar bowl is illustrated in Delft Ceramics by C H de Jonge, colour plate 1.

A Wiltshire inscribed and dated glazed earthenware loving-cup and cover, the inscription 'Be Mery All Drink of the Best and Leef The Small' (sic) and with the date 1703, covered in a dark brown glaze chips, 28½ in (29.5 cm) high. **$2,500-3,500**

An Ansbach teacup and saucer, rim chips, c1740. **$300-600**

A Shorthose tea bowl and saucer, printed in colours with the Tea Party, the saucer marked 'Shorthose & Co'. **$200-300**

A pair of Bayreuth teabowls and saucers, in brown glazed red stoneware, gilt with figures with dogs and altars, gilding worn, c1730. **$600-900**

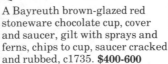

A Wedgwood 'three-colour' cup, cover and stand, sprigged with ochre coloured florettes on a black and white chequered ground, impressed WEDGWOOD, early 19thC. **$800-1,200**

A Bayreuth brown-glazed red stoneware chocolate cup, cover and saucer, gilt with sprays and ferns, chips to cup, saucer cracked and rubbed, c1735. **$400-600**

Miller's price ranges

The price ranges reflect what one should expect to pay for an item in similar condition to that illustrated. If you're selling you may be offered 30% less. Dealers have to make a profit too! However if the market has moved upwards, or your piece is a particularly good example – you could be offered more.

A rare Staffordshire deer's head stirrup-cup, the upper half picked out in a light brown glaze, its antlers picked out in yellow, one antler chipped, late 18th/early 19thC, 5 in (12.7 cm). **$1,700-2,500**

69

A pair of figures of greyhounds, standing facing to the right and left and holding hares in their mouths, on coloured gilt lined bases 8 in (20 cm) high. **$300-600**

A Victorian Staffordshire dalmation, on a blue base, c1860, 5 (12.5 cm) by 3½ in (9 cm). **$100-200**

A Pratt ware pug dog, cracked, c1800, 3 in (7.5 cm) high. **$300-400**

An early English pottery poodle, c1790, 3 (7.5 cm) by 2½ in (6.5 cm). **$200-300**

A pair of groups of poodles, with gilt collars, and puppies recumbent at their feet, on blue and gilt bases, 5½ in (14 cm) high. **$200-300**

A pair of figures of poodles, wearing gilt collars, 4½ in (11.5 cm) high. **$100-150**

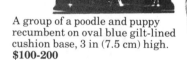

A group of a poodle and puppy recumbent on oval blue gilt-lined cushion base, 3 in (7.5 cm) high. **$100-200**

A Staffordshire model of a King Charles spaniel, decorated in green, with brown eyes, collar, and cushion tassels, c1800, 3¼ in (8 cm). **$600-700**

A rare model of a King Charles spaniel, 8½ in (21.5 cm) high. **$300-400**

A pair of well modelled spaniels, with black markings seated facing right and left and wearing gilt collars, 6¼ in (16 cm) high. **$60-100**

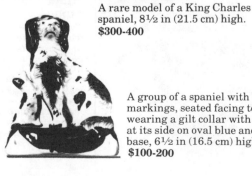

A group of a spaniel with brown markings, seated facing to the left wearing a gilt collar with a puppy at its side on oval blue and gilt base, 6½ in (16.5 cm) high. **$100-200**

A model of a spaniel, with black markings, on yellow and gilt-lined base, 3¼ in (8 cm) high. $100-150

A figure of a spaniel, with black markings seated on raised rectangular base, 5½ in (14 cm) high. $50-70

A pair of Victorian Staffordshire mantel dogs, c1860/1865, 10 (25 cm) by 6½ in (16.5 cm). $300-400

An early Pratt hollow based lion, c1770, 2¼ (5.5 cm) by 2 in (5 cm). $300-500

A Ralph Wood figure of a lion, crisply modelled and covered in a pale olive glaze, the base moulded with leaves and enriched in green, c1770, 13 in (33.5 cm) wide. $10,500-14,000

Ralph Wood Pottery, Mr Frank Partridge's Collection, no 20

Sir Harold Mackintosh, Bt. Early English Figure Pottery, pl 29, no 101.

A Staffordshire pottery lion, by Enoch Wood, c1790, 9½ (21 cm) by 12 in (30 cm). $1,400-1,700

A Pratt figure of a lion , with head turned to one side, its mane and features picked out in Pratt-type colouring, the plinth with stiff leaf moulded border and inscribed in yellow ochre 'A Lion', hairline crack, late 18thC, 7¼ in (18.4 cm). $2,000-3,000

A rare figure of a lion, standing facing to the left on oval coloured base, 6¾ in (17 cm) high. $500-600

A Yorkshire figure of a lion, its paw resting on a ball in brightly coloured brown-spotted yellow coat and with brown mane, tail and paws, on a green and yellow base with ochre rim, restoration to base, c1810, 7½ in (18.5 cm) wide. $4,500-7,000

A Staffordshire lion, with some repairs, early 19thC, 6 in (15 cm). $1,000-1,200

A pair of Staffordshire lions 'passant', after Ralph Wood originals, glazed in translucent brown on a rectangular green-edged plinth, one with piece missing from tail, c1840, 14½ in (36.3 cm). $1,700-2,500

A fine pair of terracotta models of lions, each standing on a vine decorated sloping plinth, covered in a thick brown glaze, slight chipping, early 19thC, 12 in (30 cm) long. $600-900

A Staffordshire figure of a ferocious lion, with reddish brown coat and shaggy liver-coloured mane, his forepaw resting on a yellow globe, his tongue curled out through enormous fangs to lick his nose, the base 'sponged' in brown, yellow, black and blue, minor hair cracks and chips to base, early 19thC, 12½ in (5 cm). **$2,000-3,000**

A pair of Walton figures of the Lion and the Unicorn, each of the Royal supporters resting on a mound base before a bocage and wearing a crown, the unicorn with a chain and a collar, chips and repairs, impressed label mark, early 19thC, 6 in (15 cm) and 6¼ in (16 cm). **$5,500-7,000**

A Ralph Wood figure of a ram, recumbent on mottled green and ochre rockwork, his horns enriched in brown, c1780, 7½ in (18.5 cm) wide. **$3,000-4,000**

Cf Mr Frank Partridge's collection of Ralph Wood Pottery no 29.

A Victorian Staffordshire lion spill vase, c1850, 6 (15 cm) by 4 in (10 cm). **$300-500**

A rare Yorkshire group of a ram with lamb, sponged with ochre and brown on a shaped green lined base, c1790, 3 in (7.5 cm). **$600-700**

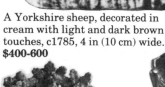

A Yorkshire sheep, decorated in cream with light and dark brown touches, c1785, 4 in (10 cm) wide. **$400-600**

A pair of Walton figures of a ram and a ewe, c1820, 7 (17.5 cm) by 4 in (10 cm). **$1,000-1,400**

A pair of Walton spill vases, with sheep in attendance, early 19thC, 7½ in (18.5 cm). **$500-700**

A pair of early Portobello figures, of a ram and a ewe, c1785. **$800-1,200**

A pair of figures of a recumbent ram and ewe, with pink sponged markings on oval green mound bases, 4 in high (10 cm). **$600-700**

A Victorian Staffordshire stag and fawn, c1850, 10 (25 cm) by 7 in (17.5 cm). **$300-400**

A Walton type standing doe, with bocage support, c1825, 6½ in (16 cm). **$300-400**

A Walton type Staffordshire figure of a doe and bocage, on grass encrusted and blue scroll decorated base, repaired, early 19thC, 8 in (20 cm) high. **$500-600**

A Staffordshire saltglaze white figure of a monkey wearing a collar and enriched with dark brown dots, his ears and eyes similarly enriched, tassel to collar restored, c1750, 5¾ in (14.5 cm) high. **$4,000-5,000**

An early English pottery cat, with hollow base, c1790, 2 (5 cm) by 2 in (5 cm). **$300-400**

A Victorian Staffordshire monkey, with a hat, c1860-65, 3½ in (9 cm) high. **$200-300**

A Staffordshire saltglaze solid agate figure of a seated cat, his body marbled in brown and enriched with patches of blue, minute chips to ear and paw, c1755, 5 in (12.5 cm) high. **$1,500-2,200**

A Ralph Wood squirrel, seated eating a nut, on a rockwork base covered in streaked ochre, brown and green glazes, restoration to ears, tail and base, c1775, 7 in (17.5 cm) high. **$1,300-1,700**

A Staffordshire figure of a squirrel, his coat in pale brown and his tail, collar and the base enriched in streaked dark brown glazes, ears restored, c1800, 7½ in (18.5 cm) high. **$600-900**

A Staffordshire model of a cockerel, the cream body decorated in various shades of brown, c1780, 3½ in (8 cm). **$300-500**

A Staffordshire figure of an eagle, c1825, 8 in (20 cm) high.
$300-500

A rare brightly coloured figure of a cockerel, standing on circular raised base, 7½ in (18 cm) high.
$800-1,200

A Victorian Staffordshire bird with nest and eggs, c1845, 9 (22.5 cm) by 5 in (12.5 cm).
$200-300

A Staffordshire fox spill vase, c1860, 6 (15 cm) by 5 in (12.5 cm). **$400-600**

A Ralph Wood group of Cupid on a panther, enriched in pale tones of brown and yellow, Cupid restuck, c1770, 8¼ in (21 cm) high.
$1,400-1,700

A pair of vases, each in the form of a giraffe reaching up to the foliage of a tree, brightly painted, 12½ i[n] (31.5 cm). **$2,500-3,500**

A Victorian Staffordshire zebra, c1860, 6 (15 cm) by 5 in (12.5 cm).
$100-150

A Victorian Staffordshire goat with sleeping child, c1850, 12½ (31 cm) by 7 in (17.5 cm).
$200-300

A Victorian Staffordshire zebra, c1860, 9 (22.5 cm) by 9 in (22.5 cm). **$100-200**

A Victorian Staffordshire table cigarette or cheroot holder, c1880, 7 (17.5 cm) by 7 in (17.5 cm).
$200-300

A Staffordshire pottery rabbit, c1860, 2 (5 cm) by 3 in (7.5 cm).
$200-300

Figures – People

A bull-beating group by Obadiah Sherratt, entitled "Bull" and "Now Captin Lad" in enamel colours, c1830, 10 (25 cm) by 14 in (35 cm). **$3,000-4,500**

A Reading Boy by Sherratt, in coloured enamels, c1825, 5½ in 14 cm). **$300-600**

A Sherratt figure of The Widow, with unusual wreath bocage, in well coloured enamels, c1825, 11½ in (27 cm). **$500-600**

An Obadiah Sherratt 'Bull baiting group', early 19thC, 13 in (32.5 cm) long. **$5,500-7,000**
The small size examples are later copies

An Obadiah Sherratt 'Gretna Green' runaway marriage group, of rare form, in coloured enamels, c1825, 6 in (15 cm). **$2,000-3,000**
This group is made more interesting by the unusual spelling on the tablet, 'GRATNAL GRERN'.

A Sherratt type Savoyard and Dancing Bear group, in coloured enamels, on shaped base, c1820, 8 in (20 cm). **$2,000-3,000**

A Staffordshire group of the Dandies, well decorated in enamels, c1825, 7½ in (18 cm). **$400-600**

An Obadiah Sherratt ale bench group, modelled as a wife berating her inebriated husband, restorations, c1830, 8¾ in (22 cm) wide. **$6,000-8,000**

An Obadiah Sherratt figure of a sweep riding a mule, the negro with a sack and holding the accoutrements of his trade astride a brown mule, some restoration, c1835, 6½ in (16 cm) high. **$1,700-2,500**

Cf Jonathan Horne, A Collection of English Pottery, Part IV, no 102 for a pair of these hitherto unrecorded figures.

The 'Politos Menagerie' by Obadiah Sherratt, this interesting and rare group usually seen in smaller form without two outer figures, c1830, 12½ (31.5 cm) by 12½ in (31.5 cm). **$1,300-1,700**

A Staffordshire Tithe-Pig group, with unusually large bocage, c1810, 7½ in (19 cm).
$700-1,000

A Tithe-Pig group, c1810, 7½ in (19 cm) by 5 in (12.5 cm).
$700-1,000

A Staffordshire Tithe-Pig group, with enamel decoration, some restoration, c1825, 8 in (20 cm).
$600-900
This is perhaps the most popular of all the 'early' Staffordshire pieces.

A pair of Staffordshire groups of the Sailor's Departure and the Sailor's Return, the hero in blue with striped waistcoat, her clothes in green and pink, on grassy mound, 'Departure' damaged, c1800, 8½ in (21.5 cm) high.
$500-600

A pair of Staffordshire groups, Flight and Return from Egypt, in coloured enamels, c1820, 7½ in (19 cm). **$1,300-1,700**

A well coloured Staffordshire group entitled 'Village Group', with rustic musicians on a mound base, c1825, 9 in (22.5 cm) high.
$600-700

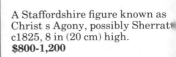

A rare Staffordshire figure of street musician Billy Waters, in coloured enamels, wooden leg a replacement, c1825, 8½ in (21.5 cm). **$500-700**

A Staffordshire 'Costume Group' the woman wearing a bonnet and holding a parasol and a book, a small dog at their feet, scroll moulded base, some repair, c181 7¾ in (19.7 cm).
$2,000-3,000

A Staffordshire figure known as Christ s Agony, possibly Sherrat c1825, 8 in (20 cm) high.
$800-1,200

An early Staffordshire square base figure, 7 in high. $300-400

A Staffordshire group of the Vicar & Moses, after R Wood, c1820, 8½ in (21.5 cm) high. $300-400

A Staffordshire figure of a rustic holding a pipe, with wreath type bocage, c1820, 6½ in (16.5 cm). $300-600

A figure of a hurdy-gurdy player, possibly Liverpool, decorated in enamel colours, c1810, 9 in 22.5 cm) high. $400-600

l A 'Cottage Girl' with book, c1815, 7 in (17.5 cm) high. $300-500
r A 'Crying Schoolboy', c1810, 8 in (20 cm) high. $300-400

A Victorian Staffordshire figure of a blacksmith, c1860, 12 in (30 cm) high. $200-300

A pair of white and gilt figures of cherubs, seated on the backs of swans on oval gilt leaf-moulded bases, 8¾ in (22 cm) high. $300-400

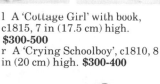

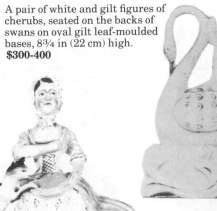

A figure of a young lady, seated with a cat and basket at her side, on coloured gilt-lined base, 8¾ in 22 cm) high. $400-600

A Ralph Wood group Vicar and Moses, in translucent glaze colours, being mostly brown, blue and lemon, restored, c1780, 9¾ in (24.5 cm). $500-700

A pair of Victorian Staffordshire Babes in the Wood group spill vases, c1845, 8 (20 cm) by 6 in (15 cm). $300-500

A Yorkshire group of Saint George and the Dragon, the Saint in bright yellow helmet and blue sash, on an ochre horse, the base and dragon enriched with green, restored, c1780, 11¾ in (28 cm) high. **$1,000-1,200**

l An early English pottery loving couple bocage group, c1815, 8½ (21.5 cm) by 5½ (18 cm). **$600-900**
r An early square base figure of a boy with eggs and dog, c1810, 6 (15 cm) by 3 in (7.5 cm).
  $300-600

A Ralph Wood group of St. George & Dragon, in semi-translucent coloured glazes, with minor restorations, c1785, 10½ in (26.5 cm) high. **$2,000-3,000**

A Ralph Wood figure of Venus, i translucent colour glazes, c1775 8¼ in (21 cm). **$800-1,200**

A pair of figures of a young boy and milkmaid, standing before cows beside streams on coloured gilt-lined bases, 6¾ in (16 cm) high. **$700-1,000**

A Ralph Wood Jr group 'Contest in underglaze enamels, c1795, 8 i (20 cm) high. **$500-600**

An R Wood Jr figure of 'Virgin Mary', in underglaze enamels, c1790, 9½ in (24 cm).
$500-600

A late Staffordshire figure of a man, seated holding a tankard.
$100-200

A Ralph Wood Jr group of 'Rural Pastime', in underglaze enamels, c1795, 8½in (21.5 cm).
$500-600

An Enoch Wood group entitled 'Vicar & Moses', well coloured in enamels and on raised plinth base, c1810, 11 in (27.5 cm) high. **$600-700**
This group is usually known as the Parson and Clerk.

l An early Staffordshire figure of a boy with a looking glass, c1810, 7 in (17.5 cm) high. **$300-400**
r A Staffordshire figure of a bagpiper, by Enoch Wood, c1800, 8½ in (21.5 cm) high. **$500-600**

A Ralph Wood Jr figure, entitled 'Bag Piper', c1795, 9 in (22.5 cm) high. **$300-500**

An early Walton figure of a gardener in enamel colours, c1820, 5 in (12.5cm) high. **$300-500**

An Enoch Wood pair Elijah and The Widow, decorated in over and underglaze enamels, c1800, 10 in (25 cm) high. **$600-800**
These figures are hollow and taken from earlier moulds by Ralph Wood.

An Enoch Wood figure, of The Lost Sheep, decorated in overglaze enamels, c1800, 9 in (22.5 cm) high. **$500-600**

MAKE THE MOST OF MILLER'S

Every care has been taken to ensure the accuracy of descriptions and estimated valuations. Where an attribution is made within inverted commas (e.g. 'Chippendale') or is followed by the word 'style' (e.g. early Georgian style) it is intended to convey that, in the opinion of the publishers, the piece concerned is a later – though probably still antique – reproduction of the style so designated. Unless otherwise stated, any description which refers to 'a set', or 'a pair' includes a valuation for the entire set or the pair, even though the illustration may show only a single item.

An Enoch Wood creamware figure of Spring, slight damage to garland, c1790, 13¼ in (19.5 cm) high. **$400-600**

A Walton figure 'Widow', with rare bocage, with enamel finish, marked WALTON, c1820, 12 in (30 cm) high. **$500-600**

79

A Walton type group of 'Tenderness', replacement bocage, c1825, 7½ in (19 cm). **$600-800**

An early Walton group of harvesters, with implements and cider barrel, c1820, 6 in (15 cm) high. **$600-700**

A Walton group 'Tenderness', decorated in blue, green, yellow and pink enamels, c1820, 6½ in (16.5 cm). **$1,000-1,200**

A Walton figure, modelled as a young girl, impressed mark, 7 in (17.5 cm) high. **$300-500**

A pair of Walton shepherds, with enamel decorations, on high rocky bases, bocage on one restored, marked WALTON, c1825, 5½ in (14 cm) and 6 in (15 cm). **$600-800**

A rare early Walton type Family group, in alfresco setting with dog and cat on grassy shaped base, c1820, 8 in (20 cm) high. **$1,200-1,500**

◀ A Staffordshire Walton-type group of 'St Peter' with cockerel, early 19thC, 10 in (25 cm). **$600-900**

A pair of marked Walton Apostles, bocage restored on St Mark, c1825, 8 in (20 cm). **$600-900**

l A Walton figure of a gardener, with part bocage, 6 in (15 cm) high. **$100-200**
r A Walton figure of a girl, with lamb, bocage missing, 9 in (22.5 cm) high. **$200-300**

A pair of marked Dixon, Austin & Co, seasons, 'Autumn' and 'Spring', decorated profusely with purple lustre with enamel details c1820, 8½ in (21.5 cm) high. **$1,000-1,400**

-SUMMER- -AUTUMN-

A set of four Dixon, Austin & Co figures of the Seasons, after models by Ralph Wood, 'Spring' with flowers, 'Summer' with fruits, 'Autumn' with wheat and Winter' wrapped in a cloak, the details in green, blue, orange and ochre, one repaired, c1825, 8½ in (21.5 cm) to 9 in (22.5 cm). $1,700-2,500

A Pratt figure of a Sportsman's Companion, in typical brilliant palette, some restoration, c1790, 7½ in (17.5 cm) high. $300-400

A Pratt figure of a boy, after the model by Cyfflé, wearing ochre coat, yellow hat and breeches and brown shoes, the base with sponged green and yellow decoration, 6¾ in (17 cm) high. $300-400

A Pratt figure depicting Winter, in ochre, yellow, blue and olive underglaze, with hollow unglazed base, c1790, 8 in (20 cm) high. $300-500

An early Yorkshire type classical figure, c1785, 7½ in (19 cm) high. $500-700

A Salt type figure of a gardener, on shaped mound base, in good enamel colours, c1825, 6 in (15 cm). $300-500

A Wedgwood white jasper group of Venus and Cupid, on a solid pale-blue jasper cylindrical pedestal moulded in white relief with swags of flowers and trophies suspended from rams' masks, Cupid with left leg lacking, chip to dolphin's tail, some cracks and staining to figure, both with impressed marks, c1785, the figure 7¼ in (16 cm) high, the pedestal 3½ in (8.5 cm) high. $3,000-4,000

This and the companion figure of Mars were most probably made as reductions from figures supplied by John Bacon in 1769. Bacon was awarded a gold medal by The Society of Arts, for his models of Mars and Venus in 1778; although there is documentary evidence to the effect that Bacon worked for Wedgwood, his work cannot be attributed definitively.
Cf Robin Reilly and George Savage, The Dictionary of Wedgwood, p233

Neale & Co figure marked 'APOLLO', c1790, 6¼ in (15.5 cm) high. $300-600

A rare pair of Wedgwood 'black basaltes' classical figures of Apollo and Mercury, restoration to Mercury, one impressed 'Wedgwood', c1780, 10¾ in (28 cm) high. $1,400-1,700

Four Bayreuth figures of Putti, emblematic of the seasons, painted predominantly in green and manganese and with some blue and ochre, manganese B:P marks of probably Pfeiffer, late 18thC, all about 9½ in (24 cm) high. **$1,000-1,200**

An Eastern European faience figure of a monkey, seated on a manganese base holding a blue, purple and yellow tulip, the blue/green stem outlined in manganese, possibly Holitsch, restoration to left arm and leaves, third quarter 18thC, 5½ in (13.6 cm) high. **$800-1,200**

A Brussels (Fabrique de la Montagne) blue and white figure of a Putto-Flautist, after the model by Duquesnoy, the flute missing, minor chips, c1760, 11¼ in (29 cm) high. **$1,500-2,200**

Cf George Dansaert: Les Anciennes Faiences de Bruxelles, pl XLVII for similar examples in the period of Jeanne Van der Bergue (1755-1783)

Victorian Staffordshire   A. British and Foreign Royalty

A pair of Victorian Staffordshire figures of Queen Victoria and King Louis Phillipe of France, c1845, 9 in (22.5 cm) high. (A15/34, A15/35). **$300-600**

A pair of Victorian Staffordshire figures of Albert and the Prince of Wales and Victoria and the Princess Royal, 7½ in (19 cm) high. (A20/56,57). **$600-700**

A Victorian Staffordshire figure of Victoria, standing wearing a top-hat draped with a spotted scarf and a full-length riding skirt on oval gilt-lined base, 7¼ in (18.5 cm) high, (A34/92). **$300-400**

A pair of well coloured Victorian Staffordshire figures, of Victoria and Albert both seated in high-backed thrones, with edged cloaks, their feet resting on cushions, 6¼ in (15.5 cm) high, (A20/55, 54a). **$300-500**

A spill vase modelled as Windsor Castle, with three turrets and gilt clock face above an iron-red doorway on shaped gilt-lined base, 5¼ in (13 cm) high, (A41A/119). **$300-600**

A pair of rare white and gilt
Victorian Staffordshire figures of
the Prince and Princess Royal, on
oval coloured gilt-lined bases,
8¾ in (21 cm) high, (A54/160,161).
$500-700

A Victorian portrait figure of the
Prince of Wales, restored, 14½ in
(36.5 cm) by 8 in (20 cm),
(A60/186). **$300-400**

Victorian Staffordshire figure of
he Prince of Wales, standing in
ll military uniform, holding a
umed cocked hat in his left hand,
a shaped oval base named in
lt capitals, 10½ in (26.5 cm)
gh, (A61/189).
00-400

A Victorian portrait figure of the
Prince and Princess, 9½ in
(24 cm) high, (A74/222).
$200-300

A pair of Victorian Staffordshire
figures of the Marquess of Lorne –
Princess Louise, one repaired, 13
in (32.5 cm) high, (A77/227/228).
$150-200

B. Statesmen & Politicians

A Victorian Staffordshire figure of
Wellington, small restoration on
head, 13 in (32.5 cm) by 5 in
(12.5 cm) (B3/23). **$300-500**

Victorian Staffordshire figure of
ichard Cobden, the English
conomist and politican, 7½ in
9 cm) high, (B1/6). **$300-500**

A rare Victorian Staffordshire
equestrian figure of the Duke of
Wellington, on Copenhagen,
wearing a black cocked hat and
full military uniform, the oval
coloured base printed in black 'Up
Guards and At Them', 12½ in
(31.5 cm) high, (B3/21).
$1,200-1,500
*Cf Anthony Oliver, The Victorian
Staffordshire Figure pl 65.*

rare, well modelled Victorian
affordshire bust of Sir Robert
el, wearing a pink jacket and
llow waistcoat on circular gilt
ed socle, 7¾ in (18 cm) high,
8/32A). **$400-600**

A Victorian Staffordshire figure of
Wellington, restored, 13 in (32.5
cm) high, (B2/17). **$150-200**

A late Victorian Staffordshire figure of Wellington on Copenhagen, 12¼ (31 cm) high, (B3/21). **$600-900**

A very rare Victorian Staffordshire figure of Sir Robert Peel, wearing a black top hat and dark blue riding jacket, pink and blue waistcoat and pink trousers, the oval coloured base modelled with brightly coloured flowers and named in gilt script, 13½ in (34 cm) high. **$6,000-8,000**
Cf Anthony Oliver, The Tribal Art of England cl pl VI.

A Victorian Staffordshire figure of Benjamin Franklin, standing beside rockwork, on oval base entitled 'The Old English Gentleman' in gilt script, 16 in (40 cm) high, (B21/67). **$600-700**

A Victorian Staffordshire figure Kossuth, the Hungarian Patriot 9 in (22.5 cm) high, (B20/64). **$200-300**

A Victorian Staffordshire figure of Benjamin Franklin, standing wearing a knee length blue coat, the oval base entitled 'Washington' in gilt-script, 15½ in (39 cm) high, (B21/68). **$800-1,200**

A Staffordshire figure of Thomas Sexton, standing in a knee length overcoat, outlined in brown on oval base, 15¼ in (38 cm) high, (B17A/58). **$200-300**

C. Naval, Military and Exploration

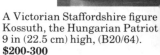

A group of the 'Death of Nelson', the dying Admiral supported by an Officer and civilian, the reverse moulded in the shape of the Victory, on oval gilt lined base, 8½ in (21.5 cm) high, (C8/6). **$200-300**

A group of Victoria, Napoleon III and Victor Emmanuel II, on oval coloured base entitled 'The Allied Powers', in gilt moulded capitals, 12¼ in high, (C32/74). **$1,300-1,700**
Cf Anthony Oliver, The Tribal Art of England pl 182.

A very rare large Victorian Staffordshire figure of Napoleon standing before a wall, in black cocked hat and blue great coat, wearing full military uniform, rectangular green canted cornered gilt-lined base named "Napoleon Bonaparte" in gilt script, 24 in (60 cm) high, (C23/61). **$4,500-7,000**
Cf Anthony Oliver, The Victoria Staffordshire Figure pl 130.

A group of Victoria standing crowned flanked by Abd-ul-Medjid and Napoleon III, the shaped rectangular base entitled 'Turkey, England, France' in gilt moulded capitals, 11¼ in high, (C32/75). **$300-500**

A Victorian Staffordshire group of Napoleon III and Empress Eugenie, the shaped oval gilt-lined base entitled 'Emperor and Empress' in gilt moulded capitals, 12 in high, (C39/95). **$800-1,200**

A Victorian Staffordshire figure of General Codrington, standing wearing a plumed cocked hat and full military uniform, the oval base named in gilt moulded capitals, 14 in high, (C43/107). **$1,500-2,200**

Victorian Staffordshire figure of ...e Empress of France, restored, ...½ in high (C37/87). ...30-150

A well modelled Victorian Staffordshire figure of Abd-ul-Medjid, Sultan of Turkey, the base named in yellow capitals, 13 in high, (C53/131). **$400-600**

A very rare equestrian figure of Lord Raglan, seated facing to the right, in iron-red military frock coat, holding a telescope in his left hand, on oval coloured base, 12¼ in high. **$3,500-5,000**

Cf Anthony Oliver, The Tribal Art of England pl 184. One of two examples known.

Victorian Staffordshire figure of ...mar Pasha, wearing a blue ...ilitary frock coat and iron-red ...z, named in gilt script, 12½ in ...gh, (C53/130). **$600-900**

...f Anthony Oliver, The Victorian ...affordshire Figure pl 88.

A Victorian Staffordshire figure of Colonel Sir George de Lacy Evans, on shaped-rectangular base named in gilt moulded capitals, 12¾ in high, (C54/135). **$1,700-2,500**

Cf Anthony Oliver, The Victorian Staffordshire Figure pl 158.

An equestrian figure of General Canrobert, the oval gilt-lined base named in ochre moulded capitals, 11½ in high, (C52/128). **$1,000-1,200**

A Victorian Staffordshire group of Florence Nightingale, and a wounded officer, the former standing to the right, wearing a blue veil and full length dress, the latter seated at her side, the oval base entitled 'Miss Nightingale', 10½ in high, (C55/143).
$1,200-1,500
Cf Anthony Oliver, The Tribal Art of England, pl 179.

A pair of equestrian figures of General Brown and General Simpson, the oval coloured bases modelled with cannons and named in gilt moulded capitals, 13¼ in high, (C56/149, 150).
$1,300-1,700
Cf Anthony Oliver, The Victorian Staffordshire Figure pl 153.

A figure of General Pelissier, standing in plumed cocked ha and blue military frock coat before shells, the oval gilt-line base named in gilt moulded capitals, 12¾ in high (C54/13&
$1,500-2,200

A Victorian Staffordshire equestrian figure of Marshal Arnaud, in full military uniform holding a plumed cocked hat in his right hand, the oval gilt-lined base named in black moulded capitals, 10¼ in high, (C64/164).
$600-700

A Victorian Staffordshire figure of Sir Colin Campbell, 11 in (28 cm) high, (C56/146). **$300-400**

A Victorian Staffordshire figure Omar Pasha, wearing an iron-re fez and military frock coat, the oval white-glazed rockwork base named in gilt script, 10 in high, (C62A/163). **$1,000-1,200**

A Victorian Staffordshire equestrian figure of Sir George Brown, the oval coloured gilt-lined base named in black moulded capitals, 8¾ in high, (C67/172). **$600-800**

Miller's is a price GUIDE not a price LIST

The price ranges given reflect the average price a purchaser should pay for similar items. Condition, rarity of design or pattern, size, colour, provenance, restoration and many other factors must be taken into account when assessing values.
When buying or selling, it must always be remembered that prices can be greatly affected by the condition of any piece. Unless otherwise stated, all goods shown in Miller's are of good merchantable quality, and the valuations given reflect this fact. Pieces offered for sale in exceptionally fine condition or in poor condition may reasonably be expected to be priced considerably higher or lower respectively than the estimates given herein.

A Victorian Staffordshire equestrian figure of Omar Pash in iron-red fez and blue military frock coat, the oval coloured bas printed in black 'Omar Pasha, Success to Turkey' 11 in high, (C63/163A). **$700-1,000**
Cf Anthony Oliver, The Victori Staffordshire Figure, pl 72.

A Victorian Staffordshire
equestrian figure of Sir Colin
Campbell, holding a plumed Scots
bonnet in his right hand, the oval
coloured base named in black
moulded capitals, 9½ in high,
(C67/176). **$1,000-1,200**

A figure of General Sir Colin
Campbell, standing before
rockwork and a flag wearing dark
blue military tunic and tartan
trousers, the oval gilt-lined base
named in moulded capitals, 10½
in high. **$1,500-2,200**

*This figure is unrecorded.
*some collectors collect only those
figures illustrated in Pugh even
though many figures exist which
Pugh does not record*

A Victorian Staffordshire
equestrian figure of General
Pelissier, the oval coloured gilt-
lined base named in black
moulded capitals, 9 in high,
(C67/173). **$600-900**

Victorian Staffordshire figure of
n English sailor, standing with
is legs crossed before a cannon,
he shaped oval base entitled
Ready and Willing' in gilt script,
2 in high, (C70A/191).
1,200-1,500

*f Anthony Oliver, The Tribal Art
of England, p1204.*

A rare Victorian Staffordshire
group of Victory, modelled as an
English sailor seated on a cannon,
with a goblet raised in his left
hand, before flags, flanked by a
Turkish soldier to the left, and a
French soldier to the right, the
oval coloured base named in gilt
capitals, 14¼ in high, (C69/185).
$3,000-4,500

*Cf Anthony Oliver, The Victorian
Staffordshire Figure cl pl IV.*

A Victorian Staffordshire
equestrian figure of Abd-ul-
Medjid, in a yellow circular hat
with pink plume and dark blue
ermine-edged cape, on oval gilt-
lined base, 8½ in high, (C68/179).
$500-700

Victorian Staffordshire group of
n English soldier and a
Highlander, seated on a large
rum, the former holding a bottle,
he latter a mug, the shaped oval
ase entitled 'Hears to the
asses', 11 in high, (C71/192).
700-1,000

A Victorian Staffordshire group of
'The Soldiers Return' modelled as
an officer wearing full military
uniform hugging a young woman
wearing a colourful full length
skirt, the oval gilt lined base
named in gilt capitals, 8¾ in
high, (C71/196). **$300-400**

A Victorian Staffordshire watch holder modelled as an English sailor and girl both standing holding high a banner entitled 'Peace', commemorating the end of the Crimean war, on coloured gilt-lined base, 11½ in high, (C73/207). **$400-600**

A well modelled Victorian Staffordshire group of Napoleon III and Albert, on coloured gilt-lined base, 12¼ in high, (C77/223). **$300-500**

A rare Victorian Staffordshire equestrian figure of Napoleon the Third, before him stands a woman carrying a barrel and wearing an apron, the oval coloured base entitled 'The Vivandiere' in gilt capitals, 12¾ in high, (C83/237). **$400-600**

A Victorian Staffordshire figure of Garibaldi, 9 in high, (C97/282). **$300-500**

A Staffordshire group, depicting Lady Hester Stanhope seated on a camel, being offered a cup of water by Doctor Meryon, picked out in pale colours, c 1850, 7¼ in (18.5 cm). **$500-700**

Compare with a similar figure in Pugh (C95A 279(a))

A Victorian Staffordshire figure of Sir Henry Havelock, 13½ in (34 cm), (C90/267). **$300-400**

A figure of General Napier, standing in full military uniform before a horse, the coloured base named in printed black capitals, 9 in high, (C104/283). **$500-700**

A Staffordshire pottery figure of Kitchener, c1885, 15 by 11½ in, (C128/355). **$300-400**

A Staffordshire figure of General Gordon, c1880, 17½ in high, (C119B/339). **$400-600**

A Victorian Staffordshire figure of Garibaldi, not restored, 12½ in high, (C98B/286). **$200-300**

A Victorian Staffordshire figure, Hackett in the role of Falstaff, 9½ in (24 cm) high, (E1B/3). **$300-400**

E. Theatre, Opera, Ballet and Circus

A Victorian Staffordshire figure group, Lorenzo and Jessica, in bower, 10 by 7 in, (E13/36). **$100-150**

A figure of Jenny Lind, standing wearing a green necklace and full length dress holding a music sheet in her right hand, the shaped base named in gilt capitals, 8 in high. **$500-700**

Cf John Hall, Staffordshire portrait figures pl 43. Compare with similar figures in Pugh E81 160, E82 160.

A very rare figure of Maria Malibran, seated on a brown sofa, wearing a blue and pink full length dress, on rectangular canted cornered gilt-lined base, 7½ in high, (E149/308). **$2,500-3,500**
This figure is unrecorded in underglaze blue.

F. Sport

A Victorian Staffordshire figure of an unidentified batsman, 14 in high, (F7/14). **$500-700**

A rare brown and green glazed figure of Jumbo standing on oval raised base, named in moulded capitals, 11½ in high, (E103/211). **$700-1,000**

G. Crime

A Victorian Staffordshire figure of Jemmy Wood, 7½ in (19 cm) high, (G16/33). **$300-400**

A Victorian Staffordshire figure of Dick Turpin, restored, 9¼ in high, (G4/11). **$60-90**

A Victorian Staffordshire figure of Tom King, restored, 8½ in high, (G4/12). **$60-90**

A Staffordshire model of Palmer's House, picked out in iron-red, grey and apricot, the base decorated with four moss sprigs above a moulded title, one chimney glued, c1856, 9 in (23 cm) high. **$400-600**

A Staffordshire portrait figure of William Palmer, the murderer standing in puce patterned waistcoat, black coat and white trousers, c1856, 12 in (31 cm) high, and the Illustrated Life and Career of William Palmer (2). (G18a/42). **$1,200-1,500**

A Staffordshire model of Stanfield Hall, restored, 5½ by 5 in, (G24/46(a)). **$150-200**

A Staffordshire model of Palmer House, picked out in iron-red, yellow and green beneath a coba blue roof, moulded and gilt title, one chimney glued, one missing, base cracked, c1856, 9 in (23 cm) high, (G18b/43). **$400-600**

A Victorian Staffordshire figure William Smith O'Brian, the Irish Nationalist, 7 in high, (G17/36). **$600-900**

H. Authors, Poets, Composers etc.

A Victorian Staffordshire figure of Lord Byron, 7½ in (19 cm) high, (H7/17). **$300-400**

A Victorian Staffordshire figure of three gentlemen seated around the table drinking, the oval base entitled 'Auld Lang Syne' in gilt script, 8½ in high, (H21/68). **$200-300**

A Victorian Staffordshire group John Anderson and wife, on shaped rectangular base inscrib 'John Anderson my Jo' in gilt script, 10½ in high, (H21/65). **$500-600**

A Victorian Staffordshire figure of Lochinvar, restored, 10 in high, (H27/78). **$150-200**

A Victorian Staffordshire figure Don Quixote, 9¾ in high, (H26/77). **$300-500**

I. Miscellaneous

rare watch holder group of
elert and Prince Llewelyn's son,
e dead wolf on oval coloured
ound base, 10¼ in high, (I21/
)A). **$300-500**

A Victorian Staffordshire figure of
Wallace, 15 in high, (I6/13).
$100-200

A Victorian Staffordshire figure of
Will Watch, the legendary
privateer and Sussex smuggler,
(I14/29). **$300-400**

A Victorian Staffordshire figure of
Jenny Jones, unrecorded, 10½ in.
$300-400

A figure of John Bull, c1845,
8½ in high, (I27/63). **$300-400**

Flasks

n Urbino armorial pilgrim flask,
n a blue and yellow ground, the
ody painted with classical
arriors, the reverse with Apollo
nd other classical figures
arrying off a scantily-clad
oddess, ebonised wood stand,
epairs to the shoulder, foot and
eck, c1538, 34 cm high.
,500-7,000

An early Pratt flask, with the
Duke of York on one side and the
French royal family on the other
side, c1795, 5 by 4½ in.
$600-900

A rare pair of North German or
Dutch faience flasks, modelled as
a naiad with human torso and
scrolled piscine tail which forms
the spout, all executed in cobalt
blue and yellow, late 17th or early
18thC, 16 cm high. **$600-900**

*The form would appear to be
based on a North German or
Dutch bronze door knocker of a
late 16th or early 17thC date in
turn derived from an earlier
Italian type.*

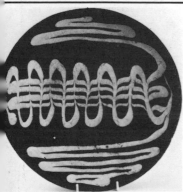

A slipware dish, the interior
trailed in cream on the chocolate-
brown ground, within a notched
rim, 18thC, 27.5 cm.
$1,200-1,500
◄

Flatware

►
A dated slipware dish, boldly
trailed in cream slip on a dark
brown ground, notched rim, dated
1795, 13¼ in. **$2,500-3,500**

A Staffordshire saltglaze plate, finely enamelled, in excellent condition, quality and colours, 8½ in. **$2,000-3,000**

A white saltglazed stoneware leaf dish attributed to Thomas Wedgwood, 24 cm. **$1,000-1,200**

Greatbach supplied Wedgwood with several moulds for leaf dishes including a 'Redpoll leaf dish'.

A Whieldon plate of octagonal shape, glazed in brown, ochre and green, c1765, 9 in diam. **$300-400**

A Brislington delft royalist portrait charger, the centre painted in blue and yellow with the crowned head and shoulders of Charles II, flanked by the initials CR2, the border with tulip sprays within a blue line rim, riveted, c1680, 34 cm diam. **$15,000-20,500**

Cf Frank Britton, English Delftware in the Bristol Collection, no 3.40 for an example dated 1682.

A Bristol polychrome delft dish, painted in green, blue, red and yellow in a panel with barbed outline in blue, 34 cm. **$500-700**

A Bristol dish, painted in blue, grey-green, iron-red and bright yellow with a parrot perched in a flowering oriental shrub, typical chipping to rim, 1730-1740 13 in. **$500-700**

A creamware miniature dish, se with a fish head painted with dark green scales and outlined red, c1790, 3 in wide. **$800-1,200**

A Bristol delft blue-dash Adam and Eve charger, painted in blue and enriched with yellow, Eve taking an apple from the serpent and offering it to Adam, with further sponged trees in the distance bearing yellow fruit, cracked chips to rim, c1700, 38 cm diam. **$4,500-7,000**

A Bristol delft farmyard plate, painted with a bright yellow and blue cockerel standing between sponged manganese trees, chips to rim, c1730, 22.5 cm diam. **$1,200-1,500**

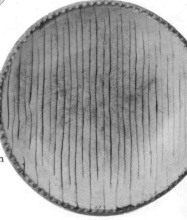

An English slipware dish, the cream coloured ground finely combed with close parallel lines in chocolate-brown within the notched rim, late 18th/early 19thC, 34 cm. **$800-1,200**

Two Bristol delft powdered-manganese-ground woolsack-pattern plates, rim chips, c1740, 12.5 diam. **$800-1,200**

A delft polychrome charger, painted floral centre and leafage border, 13 in diam. **$300-500**

An English delft tulip charger, painted in bright yellow, brown, green and blue with sponged blue rim, 17thC, 32 cm. **$1,700-2,500**

A Bristol delft tulip charger, painted with a blue tulip flanked by two other flowers within a border of green and yellow leaves and with sponged blue rim, c1700, 13in diam. **$800-1,200**

A Lambeth delft William and Mary polychrome plate, late 17thC, 8¼ in (21 cm). **$3,500-5,000**

A pair of English delft polychrome chargers, painted central garden scene and floral border, 11½ in diam. **$500-600**

An English delft blue and white charger, painted Oriental landscape with figures, 13½ in. **$500-600**

A Lambeth polychrome plate, with an exotic bird c1760. **$200-300**

An English delft polychrome charger, painted floral centre and zigzag border with ochre rim, 8½ in diam. **$200-300**

A Lambeth blue and white delft dish, with polychrome balloon, c1784, 14 in (35 cm). **$1,200-1,500**

A Lambeth delft polychrome plate, with bamboo design, c1760. **$400-600**
Bamboo design is most unusual.

A Lambeth delft polychrome plate, with powdered manganese ground, with scratched yellow design. **$500-700**

A Liverpool delft polychrome plate, 8 in (20 cm). **$500-700**

A London delft portrait charger, painted in blue, manganese and yellow with a half-length portrait of King William, with the initials KW to either side, the reverse with a grey lead glaze, triangular crack at 9 o'clock, minor chips and glaze flaking to rim, c1690, 14 in (35 cm) diam. **$4,000-5,000**

A rare Liverpool delft pill-tile, painted in blue with the arms of the Worshipful Society of Apothecaries with unicorn supporters, inscription in manganese-purple, pierced for suspension, hair-crack, chips, 2nd half 18thC, 10 in (25 cm). **$2,500-3,500**

A London delft blue and white Merryman plate, the centre with part five of the verse inscribed 'But if his Wife do Frown' and with the date 1752 within a circular leaf cartouche, cracked across and repaired, c1752, 8 in (20 cm) diam. **$500-700**

Cf Louis L Lipski and Michael Archer, op cit, pl 557E for a Merryman plate also dated 1752 with part 6 of the verse

◄ A blue and white Dutch Delft dish, the centre painted with David receiving the holy bread from Ahimelech the priest, the cavetto inscribed I SAM:XXI-6, second or third quarter 18thC, 13½ in (34 cm). **$600-900**

A Dutch Delft plate, painted in dark tones of blue with Christ walking on the waves (Matt. 14:22-33), Roos. in blue, De Roos, Arendt Jacobsz Cosyn factory mark, chips to rim, 1680-1700, 9 in (22.5 cm). **$1,300-1,700**

A Liverpool delft polychrome plate with insect. **$500-700**

A London delft blue-dash royalist portrait charger, boldly painted in blue, green, manganese and yellow with William III on a rearing charger, extensively cracked, c169 14¼ in (35.5 cm) diam. **$2,500-3,500**

A pair of Wincanton delft plate with manganese decoration, 1740's, 13½ in (34 cm). **$2,500-3,500**

Dillwyn plate, printed in black with a ship in full sail above martial trophies, impressed mark, 1840, 8¼ in (21 cm) diam. $100-200

l A Davenport pearlware small plate of dished circular form, decorated with chinoiseries within a foliate border. impressed Davenport over an anchor, 7 in (17.5 cm) diam.
r A Davenport stone china plate of dished circular form, the central panel printed with a bird of paradise pattern within a pierced border, printed stone china mark in underglaze blue, 10 in (25 cm) diam. $300-400   the two

A rare Davenport pottery plate, with a central panel painted with a chinoiserie landscape with two figures in a garden in colours, inscribed Longport over an anchor in red, 9½ in (24 cm) diam. $300-400

An ironstone meat-dish printed and painted in iron-red and blue flower sprays, 21 in (52.5 cm) wide. $400-600

A pair of delft plates, each painted in blue with the coat of arms of Baillic above the motto 'In Calgine Lucet', within a spearhead border, rim chips, late 18thC, 9 in (22.5 cm). $800-1,200

James Heath blue and white meat plate, the centre transfer printed with sealion and stork, with bearded hunter, slight chips to rim, early 19thC, 18 in (45 cm). 60-100

A Spode blue and white rectangular meat dish printed with the Principal Entrance to the Harbour of Cacamo, 14½ in (36.5 cm) wide. $300-400
A Spode blue and white oval meat drainer printed with the Principal entrance at the Harbour of Cacamo, 11¼ in (26 cm) wide. $300-400

A Spode blue and white rectangular meat dish printed with the tiger hunt, 20¾ in (52 cm) wide. $700-1,000

A pair of Don blue and white soup plates printed with the Tomb of Theron at Aggorgentum, one impressed Don Pottery, c1830, 9 in (22.5 cm). $100-200

Two ironstone meat-dishes printed and painted with a green parrot seated on a branch, 20½ in (51.5 cm) wide. $300-400

A Glamorgan pottery nursery plate, 19thC, 4½ in (11.5 cm). **$60-90**

A Don plate printed and brightly coloured with a large spray of garden flowers within a border of trailing leaves, impressed Don and Lion mark, c1820, 8½ in (21.5 cm). **$300-400**

A Glamorgan pottery nursery plate, transfer printed with chess players, with hair crack, 19thC, 7½ in (19 cm). **$60-90**

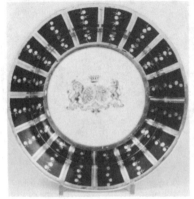

A pair of ironstone armorial plates, the centres printed with the royal arms of William IV and Queen Adelaide, within a wide blue border divided by ochre and gilt bands and trailing berries, the reverses with printed inscription Angel Hotel, Oxford on an entwined ribbon cartouche, c1835. **$400-600**

It is recorded that Queen Adelaide stayed at the Angel Hotel together with the Duke of Wellington, then Chancellor of the University, in 1835.

A pair of Marseilles faience plates, fauchier neveu, the yellow glazed body embellished with flowers in grand feu colours, damage to one, c1750-1760, 11½ in (28 cm). **$1,500-2,200**

A Dutch majolica dish, painted i ochre, cobalt blue and green on a white ground, the reverse washe with a thin dressing of lead glaze over a coarse pinkish buff body, first quarter 17thC, 9¾ in (24.3 cm). **$10,000-13,000**

A Wedgwood creamware diamond-shaped dish, painted by Emile Lessore with The Young Anglers named on the reverse within an ochre line rim, signed, impressed mark and date code for 1862, 12½ in (31.5 cm) wide. **$600-800**

A majolica wall plaque with centre roundel, depicting sea nymphs, dolphins and other mythical figures, marked on ba crown M, 24 in (60 cm). **$300-500**

A pair of Aprey plates, painted in a bright palette with birds beside a pond and perched on a tree-stump, with iron-red and gilt rims, black AP monogram marks, minor rim chips, c1780, 9½ in (23.5 cm) diam. **$1,000-1,200**

A French faience plate, in manganese with an oriental in fancy dress, mark in manganese, probably Luneville, c1770, 10 in (25 cm). **$500-600**

Two Moustiers plates, painted in blue with a central flower spray heightened in manganese, yellow and green, one cracked the other with minor chips, c1770, 10 in (25 cm). **$500-600**

A Fresian faience charger, painted in blue and yellow with a straw-haired gentleman, with a rim painted with a band of blue whorls alternating with yellow arrowheads, lead glazed back, late 17th-early 18thC, 13½ in (34.3 cm). **$1,300-1,700**

A Rouen plate, painted in bright colours with exotic birds, with a dragon to the right, rim chips, c1750, 9¾ in (24.5 cm) diam. **$600-700**

A St. Jean Du Désert large dish, the centre with four Chinese figures in a schematic landscape, rim chips, c1690, 19 in (47.5 cm) diam. **$800-1,200**

A large Rouen faience dish, decorated in polychrome 'a la double-corne', painted in blue, manganese, iron-red, yellow and green, the rim with an iron-red and blue border, painter's monogram S AR in iron-red, c1760, minor chips to rim, 20 in (50 cm). **$1,500-2,200**

A Frankfurt tin glazed dish, painted in blue in Chinese-style, c1700, 15½ in (39 cm). **$600-900**

A Frankfurt blue and white dish, ➤ painted with Chinese figures, rim chips, first half of the 18thC, 16 in (39.5 cm) diam. **$600-700**

A Caffaggiolo Istoriato dish, the centre painted in blue monochrome with Joseph and Potiphar's wife, cracked and rim chips, c1540, 15¼ in (41 cm) diam. **$10,500-14,000**
William Ridout collection no 28 Derived from an engraving by Marcantonio after Raphael's painting in the Logge.

A German faience plate, painted with flowers and chocolate rim, blue Z mark, perhaps Zurich, chip to glaze, c1760, 9¾ in (24 cm) diam. **$700-1,000**

A Holics yellow-ground dish, painted with a Chinoiserie figure, minor rim glaze chips, manganese H mark, c1760, 14 in (34 cm) wide. **$3,500-5,000**

A late Istoriato dish, painted with Jupiter casting down the giants with his thunderbolts, the reverse inscribed in blue Roman letters ISTORA DE IOVE CH/I FILUMINA IGIGATE, probably Faenza, cracked, mid-17thC, 15 in (37 cm) diam. **$3,000-4,500**

A Savona blue and white large dish, the centre painted with Diana and Actaeon, blue shield of arms of Savona mark, minor glaze chips, late 17thC, 17¾ in (44.5 cm) diam. **$1,700-2,500**

A Montelupo dish, boldly painted in typical style in yellow, cobalt, manganese, green and ochre, early 17thC, 13 in (32 cm). **$1,700-2,500**

A Faenza crespina, the central boss painted with a putto, the fluted well showing scrolling leaves on ochre and blue grounds, one chip and crack restored, 1540-60, 11½ in (23 cm). **$3,000-4,500**

A Faenza maiolica crespina, painted in cobalt blue, green, ochre, yellow and manganese, 1550-60, 11 in (27.5 cm). **$2,500-3,500**

A Gubbio lustred Istoriato dish, decorated at Castel Durante with the Rape of Proserpine and lustred at Gubbio by Maestro Giorgio Andreoli, with Pluto, Proserpine and nymphs in a landscape in blue, turquoise and yellow and green enriched in gold, copper and pink lustre, the reverse with scrolls in pink and copper lustre, 1533 MoGo mark in lustre, extensively damaged and with metal rim, 11 in (27.5 cm) diam. **$6,000-8,000**

An Urbino Istoriato crespina, painted in cobalt, ochre, green, manganese and white with the serpent, which has a winged human torso and head, tempting Adam and Eve, the base inscribed Adam e Eva, minor chips on rim, c1560-70, 11 in (27 cm). **$5,500-7,000**

A rare dated Urbino Istoriato tazza, painted with Cadmus slaying the dragon, showing the founder of Thebes with his companions following the cow and fighting the dragon, inscribed 'cadammo mise el serpe/al fonte p.d. liberar Li/con pagi' in blue, minor chips to rim, crack, 1539, 11 in (27.5 cm). **$9,000-13,000**

A Montelupo dish, painted with a portrait bust of a woman before an extensive landscape with trees, broken in two and repaired, rim chips, 17thC, 13½ in (33.5 cm) diam. **$800-1,200**

A Lodi (Rossetti) blue and white dish, the centre painted with a Roman aqueduct within a formal symmetrical foliage cartouche, blue GR monogram of Giorgio Giacinto Rossetti, minor rim chips, c1735 14 in (35 cm) wide. **$3,500-5,000**

These finely potted wares of Rossetti's are rare. Other examples, some inscribed and dated 1735, are illustrated in Maioliche di Lodi, Milano e Pavia nos 13 and 14.

An Urbino Istoriato dish, painted with Bacchantes being turned into trees, executed in cobalt, ochre, white, black, manganese and various tones of green, repaired, c1540-50, 11 in (27.3 cm). **$3,500-5,000**

An Urbino Istoriato deep dish, painted with the Story of Joseph, the rim reduced, c1550-60, 10½ in (26.5 cm). **$2,000-3,000**

A Savona dish, decorated in blue and manganese, with buildings and radiating flowers and fruit, rim chips repaired, mid 17thC, 16 in (39 cm) diam. **$800-1,200**

A Venice Istoriato circular dish, painted with Muzio Scaevola, minor rim chips, c1540, 9 in (24 cm) diam. **$2,500-3,500**

A pair of Venice Istoriato small dishes, painted with cupids standing in landscapes holding bows and arrows and shields, c1575, 6 in (15 cm) diam. **$2,000-3,000**

An Urbino Istoriato dish, painted with the judgement of Paris, in an extensive river landscape with distant mountains in blue, the reverse inscribed in blue 'De le tre ignude dee giudica Paris', workshop of Orazio Fontano, rim chips, c1560, 11 in (27.5 cm). **$7,500-10,500**

An Urbino Istoriato dish, painted with the story of Cadmus and the Serpent, the rim reduced and bound in pewter, the reverse inscribed in blue, Chadmo Va Contra il ser/pente altiero vedi ouidi 1548, 10 in (25 cm) diam. **$2,500-3,500**

When Camdus founded Thebes he had to kill the dragon to get water. Athene advised him to sow its teeth, and up came a harvest of armed men.

A fine Giustiniani saucer dish, the cream coloured body decorated in Etruscan-style surrounded by a broad iron-red border with formal decoration in black, late 18th-early 19thC, 7 in (18 cm). **$800-1,200**

An Hispano-Moresque copper lustre dish, with raised central boss, the well with pseudo inscription, rim chips, 15th-16thC, 16 in (40 cm) diam. **$1,000-1,200**

An Hispano-Moresque armorial dish, painted in copper lustre, the raised central boss with a shield charged with an eagle, symbolic of Sicily, probably Valencia, chipped and cracked, first half 16thC, 16 in (39 cm). **$1,700-2,500**

An Hispano-Moresque dish, painted in an iridescent gold lustre, cracked, late 15th or early 16thC, 13 in (32.5 cm). **$1,000-1,400**

Jars

An 'Ironstone' baluster jar and cover, colourfully enamelled and gilt with oriental flowers under a blue ruyi collared shoulder, all heightened in burnished gilding, possibly Spode, hair cracks, early-19thC, 19 in (46 cm). **$800-1,200**

A Minton pate-sur-pate jar and cover, with gilt lined rim and base and on a deep blue ground, 5 in (12 cm). **$400-600**

A Dutch Delft tobacco jar, painted in blue with an elaborate scrollwork panel enclosing the name 'Marteniek', slight crack, glaze chips, late-18thC, 11 in (29 cm). **$600-900**

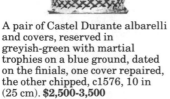

A pair of Castel Durante albarelli and covers, reserved in greyish-green with martial trophies on a blue ground, dated on the finials, one cover repaired, the other chipped, c1576, 10 in (25 cm). **$2,500-3,500**

A Faenza albarello, painted in yellow, blue, ochre and green with scrolling foliage and a label inscribed 'Il Prunus Fo', repaired, mid-16thC, 10 in (26 cm). **$2,500-3,500**

A Montelupo wet-drug jar, painted in ochre and green with a blank ribbon cartouche on a ground of scrolling, flowering foliage, the green strap handle painted wiith M.T. and G.T. below, rim chips, 17thC, 9½ in (22.5 cm). **$800-1,200**

A salt-glazed stoneware one gallon jar, by Clarkson Crolius, Manhattan, 1794-1838, 11in (27.5cm). **$900-1,000**

A salt-glazed stoneware two gallon crock and a salt-glazed stoneware two gallon jar, by Nicholas A. White & Co., Utica, NY., 1865-1877, 10½in (26cm). **$1,100-1,300**

A salt-glazed stoneware two gallon jar and a salt-glazed stoneware two gallon crock, the first by Nichols & Boynton, Burlington, VT., 1856-1859, with impressed mark and 2, 11in (27.5cm); the second by Nicholas A. White & Co., Ithaca, NY., 1865-1877, with impressed mark and 2, 10in (25cm). **$900-1,000**

A salt-glazed stoneware two gallon crock and a salt-glazed stoneware one gallon jar, the first impressed mark and '2', rim chips, by Charles N. White and George H. Wood, Binghamton, 1882-88, 9½in (23.5cm); the second impressed mark, by Nicholas A. White & Co., Utica, 1877-82, 10½in (26cm). **$500-600**

A salt-glazed stoneware one and one-half gallon crock, with a band of cobalt-blue floral decoration, impressed mark and '1½' on shoulder, by John Bell, Waynesboro, Pennsylvania, 1833-1880, 11in (27.5cm). **$500-600**

Two jars, the first stoneware, with green lead glaze decoration, impressed mark on shoulder; the second redware, with brown glaze decoration, impressed mark on body, rim chip, each by John Bell, Waynesboro, Pennsylvania, 1833-1870, 6in (15cm). **$250-350**

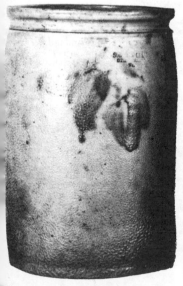

A salt-glazed stoneware three gallon jar, impressed mark, one handle missing, rim chips, by Paul Cushman, Albany 1807-1833, 13½in (33.5cm). **$500-600**

A salt-glazed stoneware one and one-half gallon crock, impressed mark on shoulder, by Samuel and Solomon Bell, Strasberg, Virginia, 1834-1882, 11½in (28.5cm). **$250-350**

A salt-glazed stoneware three gallon jar, painted with a cobalt slip bird on branch, impressed mark and '3', by Phillip Riedinger and Adam Caire, Poughkeepsie, N.Y., 1857-1878, 13½in (33cm). **$650-750**

A Faenza armorial albarello, painted in cobalt blue, ochre, yellow and green on a white ground, with the arms of the Salviati family below a scroll label inscribed in gothic script with the name of the drug, probably Lenitivum Electuarium, early-16thC, 10 in (24.5 cm). **$600-900**

A Palermo albarello, painted in bright colours with a standing figure of a saint, the reverse with highly stylised military trophies in yellow and grey on a blue sgraffito ground, one piece inscribed 'SPQR', the borders painted with beads and yellow chains on a blue ground, c1600, 9 in (22.5 cm). **$1,200-1,500**

A Palermo albarello, the reverse panel with the inscription 'SPQR', c1600, 9½ in (22.5 cm). **$1,000-1,400**

A Faenza tapered albarello, the contents E.de Sebesten r. on a ribbon scroll on a ground of flower-heads and foliage, cracks repaired, c1550, 7 in (17 cm). **$500-600**

Two Sicilian waisted albarelli, painted in ochre, green and blue with an armorial escutcheon set within a wreath on a ground of loose scrolling foliage, probably Trapani, worn, 17thC, 11 in (27 cm). **$1,000-1,200**

A documentary Puglia maiolica albarello, painted in a subdued polychrome palette including sage green, ochre, blue and manganese, the lower bulb inscribed 'Puglia' above the name of the drug 'Oximell.Absinth', rim chipped, 17th/18thC, 8½ in (21 cm). **$1,000-1,400**

A Montelupo oviform wet-drug jar, the reverse dated 1577 and with the pharmacy mark P, small crack in spout, chip to foot, 12 in (31 cm). **$1,200-1,500**

A Talavera de la Reina oviform jar, boldly painted with a continuous scene of deer hunters, executed in cobalt, manganese, yellow and ochre, probably after Johannes Stradanus, mid-17thC, 19 in (47 cm). **$2,500-3,500**

A Venice squat albarello, the contents u.d. betonica named in Gothic script, repaired, c1550, 6 in high (15.5 cm). **$600-900**

A Savona blue and white waisted albarello, the contents Vng:Martiaton named on a ribbon scroll and beneath pharmacy mark F.R., rim glaze chips, c1700, 9 in (22 cm). **$400-600**

A pair of Venice jars, c1560, 11 in (28 cm). **$10,000-13,000**

A pair of Turin polychrome albarelli, decorated in ochre, cobalt, manganese, green, yellow and iron-red, the upper bulb painted with a woman and two children, symbolising Charity, within an inscription 'Hosp.mai.char.civ. nov.', Rossetti's factory, the rims reduced, mid-18thC, 7 in (18 cm). **$2,000-3,000**

A Tuscan albarello, painted in cobalt blue, ochre, manganese and green on a white ground with pine cones between linear borders, 16thC, 8 in (21.5 cm). **$1,000-1,200**

Jugs

An English medieval oviform jug, the body incised with lines, the handle, rim and spout covered with an apron of glaze, spout and rim chipped, 14thC, 15½ in (38.5 cm). **$600-700**

An English medieval globular jug, the coarse pottery body with strap handle, piece missing to base and side, chips to rim, 14th/15thC, 9½ in (22.5 cm). **$300-500**

A Yorkshire Darlington town hall jug, dated 1800, 5½ in (13 cm). **$400-600**

A Bristol delft blue and white puzzle jug, painted with two panels of birds flanking the inscription 'Here gentlemen come try your skill I'll hold a wager if you will that you don't drink this liquor all without you spill or let some fall', c1750, 7½ in high (19.5 cm). **$1,000-1,400**

A Sunderland creamware large jug, printed and enamelled a view of the cast iron bridge, Sunderland, a shipping scene and a verse, 7½ in (19 cm). **$400-600**

A salt-glazed stoneware butter crock, with impressed mark and 'D' on shoulder, one repaired crack, one hairline crack, by Samuel and Solomon Bell, Strasberg, Virginia, 1834-1882, 6in (15cm). **$250-300**

A salt-glazed stoneware three gallon jug and a salt-glazed stoneware three gallon crock, the first by Nicholas A. White & Co., Utica, NY., 1865-1877, 14½in (36cm); the second by A.K. Haxstun & Co., Fort Edward, NY., 1875-1882, rim chip, hairline crack, 10½in (26cm). **$500-600**

A glazed redware quart jug, with a pale green lead glaze, impressed mark on shoulder, by John Bell, Waynesboro, Pennsylvania, 1833-1880, 7½in (18.5cm). **$250-300**

A fine salt-glazed stoneware harvest jug, inscribed in cobalt Deuer & Adrian, the reverse with a rose, rim chip to spout, probably New York State, mid-19thC, 10in (25cm). **$2,000-2,300**

A salt-glazed stoneware jug, impressed mark on shoulder, by Samuel and Solomon Bell, Strasberg, Virginia, 1834-1882, 9in (22.5cm). **$250-300**

A salt-glazed stoneware two gallon jug, impressed Brandy and '2', early 19thC, 14½in (36cm). **$450-500**

A salt-glazed stoneware three gallon jug and a salt-glazed stoneware one and one-half gallon jar, the first by C.E. Pharris & Co., Geddes, N.Y., 1864-1867, with '3', impressed mark, rim chips, 16in (40cm); the second, unmarked, possibly Pennsylvania, 1850-1880, '1½', rim chips, 9in (22.5cm). **$500-600**

A salt-glazed stoneware two gallon crock and a salt-glazed two gallon jug, the first with impressed 2 and 9lbs, unmarked, rim chips, probably by Adam Caire, Poughkeepsie, NY., 1878-1896, 9½in (23.5cm); the second with impressed mark and 2 by Thomas D. Chollar and Joseph Darby, Cortland, NY., 1835-1839, 13½in (33.5cm). **$500-600**

A salt-glazed stoneware six gallon crock, impressed mark and '6', chips to rim and handles, by Nicholas A. White & Co., Utica, N.Y., 1865-1877, 13½in (33cm). **$350-400**

A pink lustre jug, moulded with birds and landscape painted in polychrome, 6 in (15 cm). **$200-300**

l. A Pratt jug, with a hunting scene, with hairline crack, c1780, 6½ by 6 in (16 by 15 cm). **$300-400**
r. A Pratt pheasant jug, c1790, 6 by 7½ in (15 by 19 cm). **$300-400**

l. A Sunderland lustre jug, with coarse hunting scene, c1840, 6½ in (16 cm). **$200-300**
r. A Sunderland lustre jug, with stag and doe design, c1840, 5½ in (13 cm). **$200-300**

An Annaberg 'Birnkrug', the brown-glazed stoneware body applied on the front with a portrait of a lady, picked out in red, blue and white and painted with stylised fruit and yellow scrolls, the later pewter cover with acorn-shaped knop incised with the initials 'M.H. 1736' within a laurel wreath, 1660-1670, 8 in (20 cm). **$1,500-2,200**

A massive brown stoneware silver mounted harvest jug, decorated with applied and moulded scenes including huntsman and hounds, beer drinkers, hallmarked London 1870, 15 in (37.5 cm). **$600-700**

A North Country Tythe pig jug, moulded on each side with a poxed cleric surmounted by a pig, military trophies and crossed keys, impressed on a label 'tythe', the base with an impressed inscription 'His Grease The Reverend shepherd of his Flock, the Lord Bishop of shearemclean', stained around rim, nose chipped on one side, 9 in (23.5 cm). **$300-600**

An earthenware pitcher, covered in a yellow, brown and green mottled glaze, by Bell Pottery, Strasberg, Virginia, mid-19thC, 9in (22.5cm). **$450-550**

A Minton majolica tapering jug, well modelled with drinking and dancing figures below a border of stylised leaves, impressed marks date cypher 1873, 10 in (25 cm). **$2,000-3,000**

A Frankfurt/Hanau faience jug, painted in shades of blue with various chinoiserie scenes in landscapes, damage to spout, chips to footrim, early-18thC, 11 in (27 cm). **$1,200-1,500**

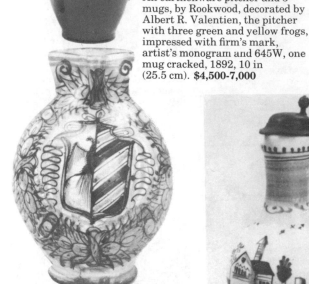

An earthenware pitcher and 3 mugs, by Rookwood, decorated by Albert R. Valentien, the pitcher with three green and yellow frogs, impressed with firm's mark, artist's monogram and 645W, one mug cracked, 1892, 10 in (25.5 cm). **$4,500-7,000**

A Deruta maiolica jug, painted in blue, ochre and green with a variation of the Nuremberg coat-of-arms, restored, 16thC, 11 in (28 cm). **$1,500-2,200**

A rare Westerwald stoneware jug (Sternkanne), applied with medallion incorporating the coat-of-arms of Louis XIV, the initials IB and the date 1668 within a manganese band, with pewter hinged lid, 10 in (26 cm). **$1,500-2,200**

A Hanau faience pewter-mounted jug (Enghalskrug), painted in cobalt blue with a landscape with a turreted building set among trees, the tall neck washed in blue early-18thC, 10½ in (26.5 cm). **$1,200-1,500**

Toby Jugs

A 'Collier' Toby Jug, with dark brown face, florette base, possibly Leeds origin, restored hat, c1785, 10 in (25 cm). **$800-1,200**

A squire Toby Jug, in Delft ware, probably Dutch, well coloured, mostly red, green and yellow, 1810-20, 12 in (30 cm). **$600-800**

This is a remarkably faithful copy of a Ralph Wood original.

A black-faced so called 'Collier' Toby Jug, possibly Davenport, in heavy overglaze enamels, c1830 9 in (22.5 cm). **$400-600**

glazed Toby Jug, blue sponged
ecoration, probably Leeds, 10 in
9.5 cm). **$700-900**

A Minton majolica Toby Jug,
painted in typical palette,
impressed marks, date code for
1865, 12 in (29 cm).
$1,700-2,500

A Pratt ware Toby Jug, in multi
coloured palette, c1800, 9 in
(22.5 cm). **$600-900**
*Note the typical decoration to jug,
stockings and base.*

n American sailor Toby Jug,
obably by Walton, inscribed
OLLARS' on sea chest, in
nglaze enamels, c1815, 12 in
9.5 cm). **$600-700**

A rare 'Martha Gunn' Toby Jug by
Obadiah Sherratt, decorated in
bright multi-coloured enamels,
c1830, 9 in (22.5 cm).
$1,000-1,200

A Pratt Toby Jug, well decorated
in typical multi-coloured
underglaze hues, c1790, 9½ in
(27 cm). **$700-900**

A Staffordshire Toby Jug, with
black coat, orange base and
unusual handle, c1815, 8 in
(20 cm). **$600-700**

◄ A Pratt Toby Jug, in manganese
hat, brown hair, sponged
manganese and ochre coat, striped
waistcoat, yellow breeches and
manganese shoes, chip to hat, late
18thC, 9¾ in (23.5 cm).
$1,000-1,200

A Ralph Wood Toby Jug, in mostly ►
brown and grey tones, glazed base,
c1780, 9½ in (27 cm).
$800-1,200

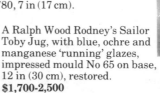

A Ralph Wood Toby Jug, wearing a brown glazed tricorn hat and knee-length blue jacket, 10½ in (26.5 cm). **$600-900**

A rare miniature Ralph Wood Toby Jug, in translucent glazes, mainly blue and manganese, with unglazed base, c1780, 7 in (17 cm). **$1,000-1,200**

A fine Ralph Wood Toby Jug, decorated in many coloured translucent glazes, with unusually deep manganese on face, c1770, 10 in (25 cm). **$1,200-1,500**

A Ralph Wood Rodney's Sailor Toby Jug, with blue, ochre and manganese 'running' glazes, impressed mould No 65 on base, 12 in (30 cm), restored. **$1,700-2,500**
This is the early type with rounded hat and white trousers.

A Ralph Wood Toby Jug, of conventional form with manganese hat and hair, trousers and shoes sponged blue coat and yellow ribbon and waistcoat and with ruddy complexion, chip to hat, c1770, 10 in (25 cm). **$1,300-1,700**

A Whieldon 'long face' Toby Jug, in brown tortoiseshell glazes, mostly brown and pale manganese, c1780, 12 in (30 cm). **$700-1,000**

A Ralph Wood Toby Jug, of standard type, decorated in translucent glazes of rich chestnut, green, yellow and beige, c1775, 9½ in (27 cm). **$1,000-1,200**

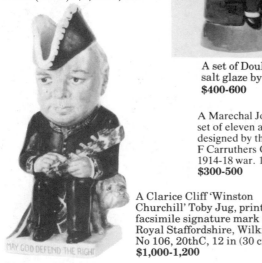

A set of Doulton Toby Jugs, the salt glaze by Harry Simeon. **$400-600**

A Marechal Joffre Toby Jug, from a set of eleven allied commanders, designed by the cartoonist F Carruthers Gould during the 1914-18 war. 10 in (26 cm). **$300-500**

A Clarice Cliff 'Winston Churchill' Toby Jug, printed facsimile signature mark and Royal Staffordshire, Wilkinson No 106, 20thC, 12 in (30 cm). **$1,000-1,200**

A Yorkshire standing Toby Jug, possibly portraying a barrister, c1820, 9½ in (24 cm). **$600-700**

TOBY

A Royal Doulton Charrington's Toby Jug, of a seated gentleman, wearing a green jacket and black tricorn hat, 'Charrington's Toby Charrington's', transfer inscription to base, 9 in (24 cm). **$300-400**

A Whieldon Toby Jug, with 'step' under base, some restoration, c1770, 9 in (22 cm). **$800-1,200**

The pear-shaped jug is unique to Whieldon.

A Yorkshire Toby Jug, decorated in Pratt underglaze colours, with a caryatid handle of female form, Crown impressed in base, c1810, 10 in (25 cm). **$1,000-1,400**

Mugs

A rare London mug, crack in base, chips, early 18thC, 7 in (17 cm). **$1,500-2,200**

A London delft dated blue and white broad cylindrical mug, painted with birds among flowering shrubs, the initials H/I.A and the date 1698 to the left of the handle, extensive crack to one side and base, rim chips, c1698, 5½ in (14 cm). **$3,000-4,000**

Cf Frank Britton, English Delftware in the Bristol Collection, no 6·6 for an example of similar form and decoration with the initials I.D.

A Dawson & Co Low Ford creamware cylindrical mug, transfer printed with a man-of-war flanked by Peace and Plenty with a rhyme below, c1810, 5 in (12 cm). **$500-700**

A Liverpool cylindrical mug, transfer printed in black by J. Johnson with 'The Sailor's Return', signed, chip to rim, cracks to base, c1800, 6 in (14.5 cm). **$800-1,200**

A cylindrical mug with strap handle, covered in marbled ochre, yellow and blue slip with an incised line to the rim and flared foot, perhaps Newcastle-under-Lyme, crack and minor chips to rim, c1745, 5½ in (13 cm). **$1,500-2,200**

A Cologne saltglaze stoneware pewter-mounted mug (Pinte), the sides moulded with three panels depicting 'The Fall' after an engraving by Virgilius Solis, the glaze of a pale honey colour, the slightly concave base with a 'thumb-print' impression, second quarter 16thC, 4½ in (11 cm). **$2,500-3,500**

A Staffordshire frog mug, in brown glazed treacleware, c1830. **$100-200**

A Ralph Wood plaque of Patricia, moulded and coloured in tones of green, brown and yellow, pierced for hanging, c1775, 11½ in (29 cm). **$2,500-3,500**

The design for this plaque is drawn from the series of mezzotints entitled Jack on a Cruise, published in 1780 by R Sayer and J Bennett, this particular illustration entitled 'Avast, there! Back your mainsail.'

Plaques

A pair of pottery plaques, green ground painted in green, brown and orange of Revolutionaries seated at pub, titled 'an Evening at Ye Lion Inn', D, by Buffalo Pottery, 1908, artist signed by Streissel, 13½in (33.5cm). **$450-550**

A Ralph Wood plaque, moulded and coloured with a profile portrait of a woman, perhaps Charlotte Corday, within a green self-moulded frame, pierced for hanging, minor crack to rim, c1780, 8 in (20 cm). **$1,000-1,200**

A Doulton Lambeth stoneware 'Greene King' advertising plaque, designed by G E Kruger-Gray, impressed 'Doulton Lambeth', incised 'M W' iniitials, 25 in (57 cm). **$600-900**

A Wedgwood green jasper dip plaque, applied in white with the 'Sacrifice to Love', impressed Wedgwood, 10½ in by 23 in (26 by 57 cm). **$3,000-4,000**

A rare Wedgwood and Bentley blue jasperware plaque of 'Capt Cook', impressed title, impressed mark, framed, rim chip, c1775, 3¼ in (8 cm). **$1,700-2,500**

A Wedgwood black basalt portrait medallion of the Prince of Wales, modelled by John Flaxman, impressed lower-case mark, c1785, 4½ in (10.5 cm). **$700-1,000**

A Dutch Delft plaque, painted in blue with Christ and the woman of Samaria, mid 18thC, 8½ by 10¼ in (21 by 25.5 cm). $800-1,200

Two rare Minton majolica wall plaques modelled as squirrels perched on leafy branches, impressed marks. $7,000-9,000

A Castelli maiolica plaque, painted in the Grue workshops probably after Antonio Tempesta, first half 18thC, 11½ in by 8½ in (28.7 by 21.5 cm). $3,500-5,000

A pair of Castelli plaques, painted in the Grue workshop, gilt frames, minor rim chips, 1st quarter of the 18thC, 8 by 10½ in (20 by 26 cm). $2,500-3,500

A rare Wedgwood fairyland lustre plaque, decorated in mother-of-pearl, black and gold, of the Elfin Palace, by Daisy Makeig-Jones, initialled, pattern no Z5292, printed Portland vase mark, c1920, 10 in by 7 in (23 by 17.5 cm). $2,000-3,000

A similar plaque is illustrated by Una des Fontaines in Wedgwood Fairyland Lustre, p194, p142. The author notes that this plaque is the only Fairyland pattern recorded as being decorated in mother-of-pearl, black and gold. The procedure of decoration was unusual in that the glazed white china was first lustred in mother-of-pearl, then the design was printed in gold, and finally printed again in black.

An important signed Urbino plaque, by Francesco Xanto Avelli da Rovigo, painted with Darius the Great getting married to Attusa, cracked, 1530-1540, 12 by 11½ in (30.3 by 28 cm). $22,500-25,500

A blue and white Dutch Delft plaque, painted in 'outline and wash' technique, probably after an engraving by Nicolaas Berchem, early 18thC, 6 by 8 in (15 by 20 cm). $800-1,200

A blue and white English Delft plaque, painted with 'trekked' rustic figures in a wooden dune landscape, the decorated surface applied with a thin lead glaze, enclosed within a contemporary 'japanned' black lacquer frame, early 18thC, 10 by 12½ in (25 by 32 cm). $4,500-7,000

Pots

A dated Makkum blue and white two handled posset-pot and cover, painted with religious figure panels, dated on the base 1718 and inscribed on the interior to the cover TH, cover repaired, minor chips, 10½ in (26 cm) wide. $2,500-3,500

An Ashworth Bros. real ironstone china part dinner-service in the Imari style, comprising: 2 vegetable-dishes and covers, 6 serving-dishes, 4 dishes, 24 soup-plates, 114 plates, some damages, puce printed, pattern No. B/3194, many pieces with impressed date code for 1908. **$3,500-5,000**

A pearlware blue printed dinner service, comprising: 4 vegetable tureens and 3 covers, 17 serving dishes, drainer, 12 soup plates, 41 meat plates, some damage, c1820. **$600-800**

A Mason's ironstone dinner service, printed, painted and gilt in 'famille-rose' style, comprising soup tureen, cover and stand, sauce tureen, cover and stand, 3 vegetable dishes and 1 cover, salad bowl, mazareen, 13 meat dishes, 18 soup plates, 49 meat plates, 15 pudding plates and 10 cheese plates, and 1 odd cover, impressed mark Mason's Patent Ironstone China. **$6,000-8,500**

A Mason's ironstone composite dessert-service, printed and painted with iron-red, blue and gilt foliage, comprising 2 sauce tureens and covers and stands, 6 dishes, a dinner plate, 17 dessert-plates and a milk jug. **$1,200-1,500**

A Mason's ironstone service, 22 pieces. **$1,300-1,700**

A Mason's ironstone part dessert service, 30 pieces, each piece in under-glaze blue and enamelled with 'the Locust Pattern', various marks, one riveted, early 19thC. **$4,500-7,000**

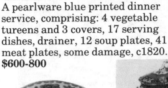

A Spode ironstone part dinner-service, comprising: 5 tureens, covers and stands, a bowl, 9 meat-plates, 10 soup-plates, 25 dinner plates and 5 dessert plates. **$1,200-1,500**

A Ridgway composite ironstone part dinner-service, comprising 5 tureens and covers, 3 bowls, 6 meat-dishes, 12 soup-plates, 56 dinner-plates and 24 dessert-plates, printed mark and retailers stamp of Ducroz and Milledge. **$3,000-4,500**

A Spode Felspar and composite yellow ground part dessert-service, comprising two sauce-tureens and covers, a pedestal-dish, 11 shaped dishes and 18 plates, printed marks, c1820. **$1,000-1,200**

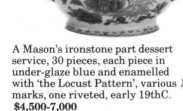

A Staffordshire part dinner service, printed with bright colours, comprising 6 tureens and covers, 2 gravy boats and stands, 10 meat dishes, 12 soup plates, 24 dinner plates, 12 dessert plates and 12 side plates. **$500-700**

A Spode blue and white part dinner service, printed with the 'Lucano' pattern, comprising: 1 sauce tureen, cover stand and ladle, 2 vegetable dishes and covers, 1 sauce boat, 1 straining dish, 6 dishes, 12 plates, impressed and printed marks, slight damage, mid-19thC.
$1,500-2,200

A Staffordshire part tea service, edged in purple lustre and bat printed with panels depicting Faith, Hope and Charity, comprising tea pot and cover , slop basin, 9 tea cups, 12 saucers, 2 plates, some damage, 19thC.
$300-500

A Spode dinner service, printed with 13 views from Aesops Fables in black, each plate titled, comprising: 5 meat dishes, 1 with drainer, 1 vegetable dish and cover, 1 sauce tureen, cover and stand, 8 soup, 15 large, 11 medium, 5 small plates and an odd drainer, some damage.
$600-700

A Wedgwood dessert service, comprising: 2 sauce tureens and covers, stand and ladle, comport, 10 dishes, a stand and 12 plates, pattern no. 1472, some damage, late 18thC. **$4,000-5,000**

A Staffordshire 'Anti-Slavery Movement' tea service, bat-printed in sepia with the vignette of a negro slave, comprising: a tea pot and cover, a sugar bowl and cover, a milk jug, a cake plate, a bread and butter plate, 5 cups and 5 saucers, some chips, cracks and staining, 1820-1830. **$600-900**

A Wedgwood black basalt encaustic-decorated part tea-service, comprising: a sugar bowl and cover, a milk-jug, a slop-basin, 10 teacups and saucers, 2 teacups and 3 saucers with lower-case marks, the remainder with upper-case marks and numeral 2, some damage, c1800. **$10,000-13,000**

A dinner service by H. & R. Daniel, decorated in Chinese style in sepia and gold in panels of puce on a black ground, comprising: 8 soup plates, 46 meat plates, 6 pudding plates, 14 meat dishes, a stand, 3 vegetable dishes and two covers, 2 sauce tureens and 1 stand, salad bowl, the main pieces with printed mark in blue, Oriental Vases Ne Plus Ultra D.
$1,000-1,200

A Staffordshire creamware toy tea service, painted in pink and green within pink line borders, comprising tea pot and cover, sugar basin and cover, milk jug, 5 tea bowls and saucers.
$400-600

A Dutch Delft polychrome tankard, glaze chips to rim, early 18thC, 7 in (18 cm). **$600-700**

A Wedgwood pearlware dessert service, printed in underglaze-blue and heightened in gilding, comprising: comport, 10 dishes and 17 plates, impressed Wedgwood, slight damage, early 19thC. **$3,000-4,500**

Tankards

A Bayreuth pewter-mounted faience tankard (Walzenkrug), painted in pale manganese and cobalt, B.K. mark in blue, Knolle period (1728-44), the pewter lid engraved 'G.H.', minor rim chips, stress fractures on upper and lower handle terminals, 10 in (24 cm). **$1,000-1,200**

A rare London tankard, the white tin-glaze crazed overall and showing a pink hue, minor glaze chips, second half 17thC, 8 in (21 cm). **$15,000-20,500**

A saltglazed stoneware silver-mounted armorial tankard, the upper half covered in a brown glaze and painted in bright enamels with a central coat-of-arms, the lower part in a pale-grey-brown with a reeded foot, the mount with London hallmark for 1824, the body and decoration, c1710, 8½ in (21.5 cm). **$10,500-14,000**

A Crailsheim pewter-mounted tankard, the pewter cover inscribed Johann Christian Pech 1732, painted in colours, blue P mark, hair crack, rim chips, 1st half of 18thC, 10 in (25 cm). **$800-1,200**

A Bunzlau faience spirally moulded tankard, covered in a green glaze, with contemporary pewter mounts, c1730, 8 in (21 cm). **$1,300-1,700**

An Austrian faience tankard, of metal form, the strap handle terminating in a mask covered in a deep lapis lazuli tin-glaze, the hinged pewter lid engraved with the sacred monogram IHS, interior chip, slight wear, 18thC, 9½ in (23.5 cm). **$1,000-1,200**
The form derives from a pewter tankard (Stitze) in common use in South Germany throughout the 18th and early 19thC.

A Bayreuth glazed red stoneware pewter-mounted cylindrical tankard, with traces of an elaborate rococo motif in gilding, slight losses to glaze on handle, c1745, 7½ in (18.5 cm). **$1,500-2,200**

A Hannoversch-Munden Walzenkrug, with manganese ground, painted with the rearing horse of Hanover in manganese, green and ochre within a blue bordered quatrefoil panel, pewter lid inscribed Conr. Haar Bergedorf 1866 , three C marks in manganese, 6 in (15.5 cm). **$600-900**

A Nuremberg white Enghalskrug, with contemporary pewter-mounted cover and foot-rim, minor glaze chips, c1750, 11½ in (28.5 cm). **$1,200-1,500**

A Haffner-ware pewter-mounted baluster tankard, decorated in the Westerwald manner, covered in blue, yellow and white glazes, 17thC, 8 in (21 cm). **$1,400-1,700**

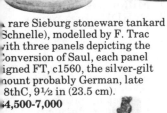

A rare Sieburg stoneware tankard (Schnelle), modelled by F. Trac with three panels depicting the Conversion of Saul, each panel signed FT, c1560, the silver-gilt mount probably German, late 18thC, 9½ in (23.5 cm). **$4,500-7,000**

A Westerwald pale-grey stoneware tankard, the pewter cover inscribed B.C.S. 1788, 2nd half 18thC, 11 in (27.5 cm). **$600-900**

A Nuremberg faience blue and white Enghalskrug, the pewter cover with a medallion portrait of Charles VI, Holy Roman Emperor, blue T or J mark, handle repaired, first quarter 18thC, 13 in (32 cm). **$2,500-3,500**

A Mettlach stein, picked out in colours between beige and green borders, the hinged pewter bound cover decorated with cats, impressed marks including pattern number 1053, 20thC, 10½ in (26.7 cm). **$600-900**

A dated Raeren or Westerwald Kurfürstenkanne, probably from the Mennicken workshop, in grey salt-glazed stoneware washed in cobalt blue, the final panel dated 1603, mounted with a pewter foot and hinged cover with double acorn finial, 1603, 8½ in (21.5 cm). **$600-700**

A Thuringian faience tankard with pewter mounts, in manganese, blue, yellow and green enamels, painted under the base with the initials B.P., mid-18thC, 10 in (25 cm). **$1,000-1,200**

A Nuremberg armorial tankard (Walzenkrug), painted in greyish cobalt on a pale blue ground, the hinged pewter lid with ball thumb-piece, the cover struck with the touch mark of Johann Mehlin (Mehli or Mehling), a Bamberg (Wurzburg) pewterer who became master in 1757 and died in 1787, third quarter 18thC 8 in (21 cm). **$2,000-3,000**

Tea, Coffee Pots

A Cockpit Hill creamware tea pot, decorated with roses and cherries, slight damage to lid, c1765, 5½ in (13 cm). **$600-700**

A creamware baluster coffee-jug and cover, transfer-printed in iron-red with exotic birds among trees, probably Wedgwood, restoration to the foot and cover, c1770, 9 in (22 cm). **$800-1,200**

A salt-glaze coffee-pot, painted in enamels, c1755, 8 in (20 cm). **$300-400**

A Derbyshire creamware tea pot, c1765, 5½ in (13 cm). **$1,200-1,500**

A Leeds creamware teapot, decorated with bands of cherries and leaves, c 1800, 5 in (12.5 cm). **$400-600**

Miller's is a price GUIDE not a price LIST

The price ranges given reflect the average price a purchaser should pay for similar items. Condition, rarity of design or pattern, size, colour, provenance, restoration and many other factors must be taken into account when assessing values.
When buying or selling, it must always be remembered that prices can be greatly affected by the condition of any piece. Unless otherwise stated, all goods shown in Miller's are of good merchantable quality, and the valuations given reflect this fact. Pieces offered for sale in exceptionally fine condition or in poor condition may reasonably be expected to be priced considerably higher or lower respectively than the estimates given herein.

A Cockpit Hill creamware teapot and cover, with entwined handle and curved spout with slight foliage-moulding, minute chip to cover, c1770, 5½ in (13 cm). $1,200-1,500

A Cockpit Hill teapot and cover, with crabstock spout and handle painted in the manner of David Rhodes, slight flaking to enamels, minute chip to spout, c1770, 5 in (12 cm). $800-1,200

A Staffordshire pearlware tea pot and cover, printed in blue with conventional flower sprays, scrolls and diaper pattern, 6 in (15 cm). $100-200

A Staffordshire tea pot and cover, painted with flowers in pink and green, with pink diaper and scroll borders, 6 in (15 cm). $150-200

A Staffordshire tea pot, painted with flowers beneath turquoise borders with berried foliage in black, 6 in (15 cm). $150-200

A pearlware punch pot and cover, printed in black and painted in yellow and green with Oriental figures and buffalo, probably Liverpool, c1810, 12 in wide (30 cm). $800-1,200

A pottery teapot, in the form of a monkey and a baby monkey holding a nut, with cover, 19thC, 7½ in (18.5 cm). $300-400

A Yorkshire teapot, in underglaze colours, impressed 'John Bull', lid missing, c1815, 8½ in (21 cm). $400-600

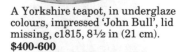

A creamware teapot and cover, with entwined reeded handle and plain curved spout transfer-printed in iron-red with three anglers, probably Leeds, minute flaking to rim, c1780, 6 in (14 cm). $600-900

A majolica teapot and cover, in the form of a crouching cockerel, 11 in wide (27.5 cm). $1,700-2,500

A Marseilles baluster jug and cover, with flower finial and puce foliage handle, painted in a bright palette, hair crack, minor chips, c1760, 9½ in (23.5 cm). $1,300-1,700

A South German yellow ground teapot and cover, enamelled in manganese, green, cobalt and black, 'K' mark in manganese, possibly Göppingen, c1770-80, 5½ in (13.5 cm). **$500-600**

The tentative attribution to Göppingen is primarily based upon the flower design. Whilst it is recognised that the South German factories of Durlach, Mosbach, Ludwigsburg and Göppingen borrowed each other's flower patterns, the present type would appear to be recorded only on Göppingen. Note particularly the distinctive bifurcated tendril emerging from the head of the carnation and the straggly flower spray on the domed cover.

A barge teapot, c1870, 13½ in (33 cm). **$300-500**

An unusual Mintons majolica tea-pot and cover, in the form of secretary-bird ensnared by a lar[ge] green snake, enamelled in typica[l] colours, impressed year symbol f[or] 1874, 9 in (22.5 cm). **$2,000-3,000**

Tiles

A Bristol delft blue and white tile, 1750's. **$30-45**

A Lambeth delft blue and white tile. **$30-60**

A Lambeth delft blue and white tile. **$30-45**

A Dutch Delft blue and white tile, with a windmill, 18thC. **$30-45**

A delft blue and white tile: a Lambeth ship. **$100-150**

A Bristol delft blue and white tile with European scene. **$60-100**

A Bristol delft blue and white ti[le] with European scene. **$60-100**

18th CENTURY DELFT TILES

★ *difficult to distinguish between some Dutch and English tiles*
★ *Dutch tiles are generally a little larger than English examples, roughly 132 mm square*
★ *Dutch tiles are generally made from a more sandy body*
★ *the Dutch glaze is generally dry and thin with a metallic glitter*
★ *Dutch tiles are usually neatly painted but often lack the spontaneity of English examples*
★ *tile designs are seldom taken from designs on domestic wares*
★ *as with other pottery, damage has considerable effect on value*
★ *designs depicting animals are scarce*

A Staffordshire tile picture, painted with a circular plaque of the Gulf of Venice, with a yellow scroll border surrounded by scrolling yellow, green and brown foliage, 57 by 74 in (145 by 188 cm). **$300-400**

A set of six Mintons glazed ceramic tiles, painted in polychrome enamels in the 'Arts and Crafts' taste, impressed mark to underside, slight chipping, 19thC, 20in (51 cm) wide. **$1,000-1,200**

A South German stove tile, covered in a moss-green glaze and depicting St. Paul, probably Salzburg, 16thC, 25 by 19 in (62 by 44 cm). **$1,700-2,500**

Tureens

A Staffordshire tureen and cover, modelled as a duck and duckling on oval basket outlined in gilt, and another tureen and cover modelled as a duckling on oval coloured basket base, 5 in (12.5 cm). **$1,200-1,500**

A rare well-coloured Staffordshire hen tureen and cover, the hen seated on a yellow basket painted with flowerheads, 5 in (12.5 cm). **$600-900**

A pair of rare Staffordshire tureens and cover, modelled as doves with brown and white markings, seated on oval coloured nests, 6 in (15 cm). **$1,300-1,700**

A rare Brussels tureen and cover, in the shape of a turkey, its feathers painted in shades of manganese, its neck, head and feet in pale green and yellow, very slight damage, late 18thC, 14 in (36 cm). **$4,500-7,000**

A Brussels boar's-head tureen and cover, naturally modelled and painted with sponged manganese and with green eyebrows, cover repaired, c1800, 12 in wide (29.5 cm). **$1,400-1,700**

A pair of Dutch Delft polychrome duck-tureens and covers, naturally modelled with orange beaks and blue and manganese markings on green mound bases, blue G:v:S marks to the bases of each tureen, one cover extensively repaired, the base cracked, both tureens with rim chips, c1760, 12 in (31 cm). **$15,000-20,500**

A Strasbourg tureen and cover, Paul Hannong period, crack to bowl, minor chips, c1760, 12 in (30 cm). **$1,500-2,200**

A Staffordshire tureen, printed with a figure seated on a camel before an Eastern building, 4 in diam. (10 cm). **$1,000-1,200**

A Proskau duck tureen and cover, its beak and feet painted in yellow, its feathers in manganese, manganese DP mark of the Dietrichstein period, minor chip to edge of cover and tail, c1775, 9 in (22.5 cm). **$4,000-5,000**

A Faenza faience tureen and cover, Ferniani period, modelled after a silver original and painted in blue, green, yellow, iron-red and manganese, three chips to cover, c1765, 14 in (35 cm). **$1,000-1,200**

Vases

A Ralph Wood triple spill vase, modelled as two entwined dolphins, enriched in green and manganese, impressed Ra Wood Burslem mark, minute chip to rim and slight cracks to foot, c1775, 8 in (20 cm). **$1,700-2,500**

A large Enoch Wood type spill vase, with sheep on rocky base, applied with flowers and moss, c1800, 8½ in (20 cm). **$400-600**

A pair of Enoch Wood spill vases, depicting boys birds-nesting, c1800, 8 in (20 cm). **$600-900**

A spill vase, depicting Bird-Nesting by Ralph Wood Jr, decorated in underglaze enamels, tree restored, c1790, 9 in (23 cm). **$600-700**

A Yorkshire spill vase, with sheep, goat and owl, decorated in semi-translucent glazes, c1800, 7 in (17 cm). **$600-900**

n Obadiah Sherratt spill vase,
ith rural musicians, and
nimals, c1825, 8 in (20 cm).
00-700

A pair of Staffordshire quatrefoil
spill vases, moulded with masks
and flanked by boys and girls in
classical dress, sparsely decorated
in manganese glazes and outlined
in blue, 10 in (25 cm).
$1,300-1,700

A William Ridgway ironstone
vase and cover, with blue and gilt
dolphin handles, printed and
coloured with flowering branches
on a green ground between gilt
line rims, the cover with minor
crack to underside, c1840, 20 in
(49 cm). **$600-900**

Mason's ironstone vase and
ver, applied with dragon
andles, printed in black and
cked out in colours, reserved on
blue ground, cracked, c1820,
½ in (69.7 cm). **$600-700**

A pair of Mason's ironstone Imari
vases and covers, decorated with
growing peonies, divided by
blooms and gilt foliage on a rich
blue ground, some repair, c1825,
19 in (48.3 cm). **$2,500-3,500**

A massive ironstone vase and
cover, attributed to Mason's,
painted in Imari style with panels
of flowering plants in blue, red,
orange and gold, the neck and foot
with blue enamel dragons
heightened with white dots, slight
repair to cover, 28 in (69 cm).
$1,300-1,700

*Probably Mason's, and may well
correspond to the 'Pagoda Vase,
Japan' included in the 1822
Mason's sale catalogue*

A pair of Minton majolica vases,
icked out in brightly coloured
lazes, one vase restored
mpressed Minton, c1870, 14 in
35.5 cm). **$1,300-1,700**

An unusual Mintons majolica
vase, modelled as a yellow glazed
bamboo section with two apes,
glazed in aubergine, involved in a
playful encounter, the reverse
with a scarab beetle climbing a
green shoot impressed mark and
year cypher for 1882.
$1,700-2,500

USE THE INDEX!

*Because certain items
might fit easily into any of a
number of categories, the
quickest and surest method
of locating any entry is by
reference to the fully
cross-referenced index at
the back of the book. This is
particularly true this year
when certain sections, e.g.
Liverpool Porcelain and
Oak Furniture have been
featured in isolation.*

A pair of Wedgwood and Bentley porphyry vases, each speckled in greenish/blue and moulded with gilt flowers, moulded marks, 1770's, 9 in (23 cm).
$4,500-7,000

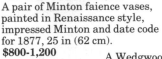

A pair of Minton faience vases, painted in Renaissance style, impressed Minton and date code for 1877, 25 in (62 cm).
$800-1,200

A Wedgwood black and white jasper copy of the Portland or Barberini vase, the rim with impressed mark and 1, c1900, 10 in (26 cm). **$800-1,200**

A pair of early Wedgwo granite vases, with cov impressed mark, 13½ (32.5 cm). **$2,000-3,00**

A Wedgwood 'three colour' jasperware vase and cover, the white body sprigged in green and lilac, impressed mark, slight damage, late 19thC, 14 in (36.2 cm). **$1,400-1,700**

A pair of Wedgwood & Bentley black basaltes vases, applied with Bacchic mask handles, pendant swags between broad engine-turned bands, impressed wafer mark, some repair, c1770, 10 in (25.3 cm). **$1,700-2,500**

A Wedgwood black basaltes va and cover, applied with close-fitting loop handles issuir from Bacchic masks, pedestal base, knop damaged, early 19th 13 in (35 cm). **$800-1,200**

A pair of Wedgwood lustre vases, gilt with dragons, on a lustred powdered blue ground between gilt brick-pattern borders, printed Portland vase mark in gold, pattern no. Z4829, c1925, 7 in (21.5 cm). **$600-700**

A Wedgwood fairyland lustre flared vase, outline-printed in gold and coloured with two fairies, on a mottled blue and purple ground, the interior with pixies, bats and insects, printed Portland vase mark in gold, pattern no. Z4968, c1925, 9 in (23.5 cm). **$800-1,200**

A Wemyss mug, painted with wild roses, impressed WEMYSS, 5½ in (13.5 cm). **$100-200**

A large Wemyss bulb bowl, painted with roses, impressed WEMYSS, R.H. & S., 14½ in wide (36 cm). **$200-300**

A small Wemyss tyg, three-handled mug, painted with an iris, impressed WEMYSS Thomas Goode, 5 in (13 cm). **$300-400**

A Wemyss heart-shaped tray, painted with red Jubilee ribbons and monograms, 12 in (30 in). **$400-600**

A rare Wemyss goblet, commemorating Queen Victoria's Jubilee, 1837-1897, with yellow foot, 6 in. (14.5 cm). **$300-400**

Miscellaneous

A Prattware duck sauceboat, in blue, yellow and green, restored beak, c1785, 7 in wide (17.5 cm). **$400-600**

A Staffordshire saltglaze sauceboat, the sides moulded with vine leaves enriched in green and reserved and painted with flower sprays within pink-line cartouches, handle restored, c1760, 8 in (20 cm) wide. **$1,200-1,500**

Two Victorian Staffordshire watch-holders, c1850:
l. With cherubs, 11½ (29 cm).
r. With castle, 10½ in (27 cm). **$200-300 each**

A Staffordshire stick stand, restored, c1870, 36 in (90 cm). **$150-200**

A Victorian Staffordshire St. George and the Dragon watch-holder, 11 in (27.5 cm). **$200-300**

A Prattware cradle, depicting a distraught man in panel, female bust on reverse panel, with ochre and green decoration, c1790, 5½ in wide (13.5 cm). **$400-600**

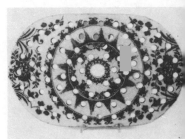

A Staffordshire blue and white foot bath, printed with ladies and gentlemen before castles and buildings, 19½ in wide (49 cm). **$1,300-1,700**

A delft drainer, decorated in cobalt blue with concentric bands of stylised flowers enclosed by sprays at each end, probably Liverpool, c1765, 14 in (35 cm). **$300-400**

A Davenport stone china ice pail, liner, fruit dish and cover, decorated with birds of paradise in underglaze blue, iron red, green, pink and gilt, printed Davenport Stone China in blue, cover restored, 12 in (30.5 cm). **$1,000-1,200**

A Minton majolica jardiniere, applied with double putti handles divided by lion masks, picked out in brightly coloured glazes, impressed mark including date cypher for 1870, 10½ in (27 cm). **$1,000-1,200**

A delft blue and white flower brick, pierced with six holes, probably London, c1740, 6 in long (15 cm). **$300-500**

A Minton majolica garden seat, impressed mark and date code for 1870, slight damage, 19 in (47 cm). **$1,700-2,500**

A rare pair of Kellinghusen faience shoes, coloured yellow with manganese piping and blue bows, the manganese sole incised through the glaze in script G.H., both restored, c1800 8 in (19.5 cm). **$600-900**

A pair of Dutch Delft blue and white tazzas, in the Chinese style with gilt metal mounts, both with blue AK monograms of Adriaenu Koeks, one with rim repair, c1690 9½ in diam. (23.5 cm). **$1,400-1,700**

A pair of Minton majolica garden seats, painted in typical enamel colours, unmarked, one with firing crack in base and crack in cushion, 19 in (47 cm). **$18,000-24,000**

A Dutch Delft blue and white sweetmeat dish, minor chips, first half of the 18thC, 9 in diam. (22 cm). **$1,200-1,500**

A Pair of Dutch Delft shoes, painted and 'trekked' in blue with flower sprays, some chipping and hairline cracks, third quarter of the 18thC, 5 in (21 cm). $1,700-2,500

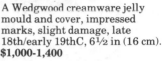

A Wedgwood creamware jelly mould and cover, impressed marks, slight damage, late 18th/early 19thC, 6½ in (16 cm). $1,000-1,400

A Yorkshire clock-case money box, the buff body with puce, black, blue and yellow decoration, with unusually small figures at sides, c1800, 8½ in (21 cm). $1,200-1,500

A rare pair of Minton's earthenware 'Renaissance' candlesticks, in the St. Porchaire style by C. Toft, decorated in brown, ochre, green and blue glazes on cream grounds, the bases signed in brown C. Toft Mintons, c1878, 13 in (33 cm). $4,500-7,000

A pair of Wedgwood black basaltes candlesticks, with bronzed and gilt details, impressed mark, Z3793 in gilding, one stem repaired, c1900, 5 in (13 cm). $1,200-1,500

A pair of rare massive Minton majolica stick stands, modelled as herons, both with impressed marks, model numbers 1916/1917, 40 in (100 cm). $10,000-13,000

English Porcelain

The popularity of early blue and white porcelain has shown no sign of waning during the year. Particularly sought after are rare shapes or unusual examples from the first few years of the production of individual factories. This is especially true of Lowestoft, Worcester and the earlier Liverpool factories.

Minor damage is increasingly accepted by collectors on rare or early pieces of blue and white, less so on polychrome wares.

With the notable exceptions of pre-1756 Worcester, pre-1754 Chelsea and some rare later wares from these and other factories, the anticipated rise in the price of polychrome wares has not yet got under way. Polychrome wares and

later blue and white wares in good condition now seem excellent value as do the majority of English porcelain figures.

CONTINENTAL PORCELAIN

As last year the market for fine quality pieces in perfect condition is strong but demand for more ordinary wares is, at best, patchy.

As in many other areas of collecting the price differential between extremes of quality is increasing.

Meissen

Continuing strong demand for the finest quality pieces, particularly from the early 18th Century. More modest examples have held relatively steady but price ranges have

been difficult to determine due to the uneven demand for these wares.

Price levels for other German factories have shown similar variations with top quality pieces exceeding expectations in comparison with the performance of more run-of-the-mill wares.

French Porcelain

The most noticeable trend towards higher price levels has been for French porcelain. This has been evident in the keen competition for chinoiserie decorated pieces from the factories of St. Cloud, Mennecy and Chantilly. The traditional American interest in French porcelain has, undoubtedly influenced the trend, especially when fine pieces of Sèvres have been available.

A pair of Fürstenberg baskets, the interiors well painted in the manner of Pascha Weitsch, with landscape vignettes, the exteriors picked out in turquoise and applied at the intersections with pink florets, script F mark in underglaze blue, c1775, 8 in (19 cm). **$3,000-4,500**

A rare Worcester pierced oval butter-cooler and cover painted with scattered flower-sprays between moulded pale-yellow rope-twist bands, the cover with cherry finial, minute crack to cover, c1758, 4½ in (14 cm). **$3,000-4,500**

A pair of Marcolini Meissen pierced baskets and covers, the sides pierced and painted with woodland birds, the covers surmounted by a carrot and chestnut knop, crossed swords and star marks, 1780-1790, 7 in (17 cm). **$1,500-2,200**

A Worcester yellow ground pierced basket, the brown twig handles with flower terminals, the exterior applied with pink flowerheads, c1770, 11½ in (28 cm). **$1,500-2,200**

Yellow ground Worcester is keenly collected and commands a high price. This form of basket was made in three sizes and can be found with a wide range of decoration including underglaze blue.

A pair of Worcester quatrefoil chestnut-baskets, pierced covers and stands, the brown twig handles with applied flower terminals on a ground of pink and yellow moulded flowerheads, the centre of the stands painted with bouquets and scattered flower-sprays, one basket and one stand cracked, some chipping to flower terminals, c1770, the stands 11 in (23 cm) wide. **$4,000-5,000**

Baskets complete with covers and stands command a premium.

A Meissen basket on three feet, applied with gilt and blue rosettes with baroque shell scroll and paw handles in white and gold, blue crossed swords mark, some restorations, c1740, 8½ in (21 cm). **$600-900**

A Worcester yellow ground chestnut basket, with twig handles, the exterior with moulded pink florets. the interior enamelled with a large spray of English garden flowers, minor chips, 9 in (22 cm). **$1,500-2,200**

A pair of Derby baskets, painted with cherries, moths and an insect, the exterior moulded with turquoise and yellow flowerheads puce crown, crossed batons mark, c1780, 9 in (23 cm). **$600-700**

ORDER
The English and Continental porcelain section is ordered in alphabetical category order. Each category is then divided into alphabetical factory order and each factory is chronologically ordered.

A very rare dated Worcester pierced oval basket, printed in the centre with the 'pine cone' pattern, the latticed sides applied with florets, the double rope-twist handles with flowering terminals, the base incised '1772', script W mark, 8 in (20 cm). **$1,400-1,700**

A Worcester pierced circular basket, transfer-printed with L'Amour, the exterior with purple flowerheads at the intersections, c1760, 5 in (13 cm). **$1,500-2,200**

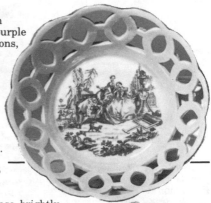

A garniture of three Derby eel baskets, the bases modelled with two ducks in naturally coloured plumage, gold anchor marks, Wm. Duesbury & Co. some minor restoration, c1775, 9 to 10 in (21.5 to 24 cm). **$2,000-3,000**

Bottles

An early Worcester vase, brightly painted with the figure of a Chinaman standing in a fenced garden, c1753, 4½ in (11.3 cm). **$3,000-4,500**

Though rare, this is the most commonly found of early Worcester vase forms. A rarer variant has handles applied to the neck.

early Worcester vase of xagonal section, painted in ght enamel colours, on one side th a Kakiemon design of wers, blossom and grasses and the other with a single plant, 753, 4½ in (11.2 cm). **,000-4,500**

milar vases with overglaze ansfer printing are known. No ue and white examples are corded.

A pair of Royal Worcester covered bottles, with pierced neck, painted and gilt with berry sprigs, flanked by gilt foliate handles, raised on shaped feet, late 19thC, 15½ in (38 cm). **$1,200-1,500**

A pair of Paris (Jacob Petit) bottles and stoppers, with applied yellow-centred white mayblossom grounds, the rims gilt, one with blue JP mark, minor damages to foliage and to one bird, c1840, 14 in (37 cm). **$1,200-1,500**

Bowls

rare Lund's Bristol bowl and ver, painted in smudgy derglaze blue with a pavilion ongst oriental islands, a mpan and 'three-dot' type rocks the reverse, small hair crack to ver, chip to rim of bowl, c1750, wl 5 in (12.5 cm). **,000-4,500**

ly the second recorded example this shape, which was copied m a Chinese original.

Kakiemon style

The Kakiemon family worked at the Japanese Arita factory towards the end of the seventeenth century. Their patterns are executed in a distinctive palette of iron red, pale yellow, turquoise and green. The Meissen factory copied from the Japanese originals and the patterns became fashionable in Europe.

A Chantilly bowl, well painted in Kakiemon style, brilliant enamels with flowering sprigs behind a blue rock, scattered flowers and banded wheat-sheaves, brown rim, horn mark in iron red, c1740, 8 in (20.5 cm). **$3,000-4,500**

Kakiemon and Chinoiserie decoration on Chantilly wares is highly saleable.

A rare Bow 'Partridge' or 'Quail' pattern bowl and cover, painted in Kakiemon style, with plump birds and flowering shrubs within iron-red and gilt borders, c1755, 4 in (10 cm) **$3,000-4,500**

A rare and collectable example of Bow porcelain. A combination of perfect condition, brilliant painting and good provenance could lead to a slightly higher value. Conversely, any form of damage or imperfection would reduce the value considerably. Interest in unusual Bow wares has been stimulated by two recent books.

Two Chelsea pierced bowls and stands painted with bouquets of flowers within moulded cartouches, chocolate line rims, one bowl and stand with red anchor mark, both bowls and one stand cracked, 1756-58, the stands 9 in (22 cm). **$1,000-1,400**
A similar example is illustrated by Mackenna, Chelsea, The Red Anchor Wares, fig 24.

A circular bowl, the interior painted with Oriental figures, the border en camaieu rose with fenced gardens, perhaps Minton, c1820, 12 in (30 cm). **$800-1,200**

A New Hall bowl, printed and painted with the Boy at the Window pattern, patt 425, c1810, 12 in (30 cm). **$400-600**

A rare Lowestoft blue and white bowl, painted with a central circular panel of waterfowl within flowering oriental shrubbery, further birds and winged insects divided by naive scrolling border, small chips on rim, slight wear, c1759-60, 8½ in (21 cm). **$3,000-4,500**

This exceptional bowl embodies a the motifs used on early Lowestof Because of this it represents a unique reference piece against which to assess other early wares Until recently the bowl was used a a fruit bowl by its owner. For similar decoration see Godden, The Illustrated Guide to Lowesto, Porcelain; Watney, English Blue and White Porcelain of the 18th Century; Spencer, Early Lowestof

A Meissen quatrefoil bowl, decorated in the Japanese manner with figures at various pastimes, birds and flowering plants, the interior painted with three iron red birds, chocolate rim, two hair cracks, c1730, 6½ in (16 cm). **$1,000-1,400**

A Meissen bowl, painted in reserves with merchants and galleys on a river estuary, the reverse with a caparisoned elephant and dressed ship on a foreshore with Turkish figures, the interior with a Chinoiserie figure holding a fan on a terrace within a similar elaborate cartouche, the rims with gilt , c1725, 7 in (16.5 cm). **$14,000-17,000**
Both the quality of the decoration and the attractive shape of the bowl contribute to a high value.

A Meissen slop bowl, painted in puce, the exterior with two pane. of estuary scenes in colour, the centre with a similar panel painted in red monochrome, crossed swords mark, gilt numera. 31 impressed former's mark of a five-pointed star, 1725-1728, 6 i (15.5 cm). **$8,500-11,000**

A Meissen Kakiemon bowl, painted with snarling tiger, prunus and bamboo issuing from hedges and chocolate rim, blue crossed swords mark, impressed 24, c1740, 7 in (18.5 cm). **$4,500-7,000**

Use the Index!
Because certain items might fit easily into any of a number of categories, the quickest and surest method of locating any entry is by reference to the index at the back of the book.
This has been fully cross-referenced for absolute simplicity.

MEISSEN

★ in 1709 J. F. Böttger produced a white hard paste porcelain

★ wares often decorated by outside decorators (Hausmaler)

★ in 1720 kilnmaster Stozel came back to Meissen bringing with him J. G. Herold

★ from 1720-50 the enamelling on Meissen was unsurpassed – starting with the wares of *Lowenfinck* – bold, flamboyant chinoiserie or Japonnaise subjects, often derived from the engravings of Petruschenk, particularly on Augustus Rex wares, *J. G. Herold* – specialised in elaborate miniature chinoiserie figure subjects, *C. F. Herold* – noted for European and Levantine quay scenes

★ crossed swords factory mark started in 1723

★ marks, shapes and styles much copied

★ underside of wares on later body has somewhat greyish chalky appearance

★ in late 1720's a somewhat glassier, harder looking paste was introduced, different from the early ivory tones of the Böttger period

★ finest Meissen figures modelled by J. J. Kändler from 1731

★ best figures late 1730's and early 1740's – especially the great Commedia dell'Arte figures and groups

★ other distinguished modellers who often worked in association with Kändler were Paul Reinicke and J. F. Eberlein

★ cut-flower decoration (Schnittblumen) often associated with J. G. Klinger. The naturalistic flower subjects of the 1740's, epitomised by Klinger, gradually became less realistic and moved towards the so-called 'manier Blumen' of the 1750's and 1760's.

★ early models had been mounted on simple flat pad bases, whereas from 1750's bases were lightly moulded rococo scrolls

A Meissen yellow-ground bowl, blue crossed swords mark, impressed 9, c1745, 7 in (17 cm). **$600-900**
The painting is slightly less attractive than usual.

A Meissen pale powdered lilac ground bowl, the exterior with two estuary panels, the interior with a similar subject en camaieu rose surrounded by floral sprays, blue crossed swords mark and V impressed, c1740, 28 in (15.5 cm). **$4,000-5,000**
en camaieu rose: pink enamel colours

A Meissen circular bowl, painted with huntsmen and dogs in a landscape vignette, scattered Kakiemon flowersprays, chocolate rim, blue crossed swords mark, impressed 20, c1745, 6½ in (16.5 cm). **$600-900**

A Meissen bowl, moulded with sprays of prunus and painted with scattered insects and butterflies, blue crossed swords mark and impressed 3, c1750, 6½ in (16.5 cm) **$1,000-1,400**

A Meissen quatrefoil bowl, painted with birds within raised pink-scroll cartouches and with gilt rim, blue crossed swords mark, c1750, 8½ in (21 cm). **$1,000-1,200**

A pair of Meissen cachepots, with mask handles, painted with a continuous landscape on panels separated by gilt bands, 19thC, 4in (10 cm). **$600-900**

A pair of Paris pâte-sur-pâte cache pots, decorated in diaphanous white reliefs with riverscapes against a mushroom ground between blue and gilt-line borders, foliate handles, hair cracks, c1870, 6½ in (16.7 cm). **$1,000-1,200**

A St Cloud white pot-pourri bowl and cover, formed as a basket, the basketwork body with flower sprays in relief and with Louis XV ormolu handles, chips to leaves, the base drilled, the porcelain c1735, 11 in (29 cm). **$2,000-3,000**

A large Sèvres punch bowl, painted in bright enamels by Chabry fils, with three ovals of putti flying, emblems of peace and war and baskets of flowers by Bouillat père, within gilt bands joined by berried laurel wreaths below a bright blue band gilt with leaves, gilt dentil rim and lined foot, interlaced Ls, painters marks and dated letter u for 1773, 13 in (32.4 cm). **$2,000-3,000**

Etienne-Jean Chabry, working 1765-1787
Edme-François Bouillat working 1758-1810
This bowl conforms in date and in all elements of the painted decoration, with the exception of the crowned CL monogram, to the service ordered by Louis XV as a gift to Marie Caroline Louise Josephe Johanna Antonie, sister of Marie Antoinette, wife of Ferdinand IV, King of Naples, when Louis became godfather to one of her daughters.

A gilt bronze mounted 'Sèvres' centre bowl, with gilt scroll borders against a bleu celeste ground, mounted with a pierced rim, scrolling branch handles, a circular foot and shaped square base, late 19thC, 16½ in (46.5 cm). **$1,300-1,700**

A Wedgwood 'Fairyland Lustre' bowl, painted in rich colours and with gilding on the exterior 'Woodland Elves part VII' and on the interior 'Fairy in a Cage', printed Portland Vase mark in gilding, inscribed Z4968 in black, 1920s, 9 in (23 cm). **$800-1,200**

Similar bowls were made by Carltonware and Rosenthal. Although less valuable these are becoming increasingly collectable.

An unusual Wedgwood flame Fairyland Lustre bowl, decorated with the 'Bridge' design within a wide border of lush foliage and little folk, the exterior with the 'Spring bok' border against a vivid shaded-orange ground, printed urn mark Z5445, 1927-1929, 8 in (20 cm). **$3,000-4,500**

A Worcester bowl, painted in a delicate 'famille rose' palette with an Oriental lady holding a fan by a pine-tree and a plant, the interior with a shrubby river island in iron red, incised line mark, crack to base, rim chip, c1754, 5½ in (13 cm). **$400-600**

A Wedgwood Fairyland Lustre bowl, printed urn mark in gilding '2 No 5125', c1930. 11 in (23 cm). **$1,200-1,500**

A pair of Worcester blue printed salad bowls, the interiors crisply moulded with scallop shell panels, printed and painted in bright underglaze blue with flower and fruit sprays within a dentil border, hatched crescent marks in underglaze blue, 1770-1775, 10 in (25 cm). **$1,000-1,200**

A Worcester bowl, from the Stormont service, painted with pink swags of drapery edged in gilding, suspended from a gilt dentil rim, minute rim chip and slight rubbing to gilding, c1765, 7 in (17.5 cm). **$1,300-1,700**

The 7th Viscount Stormont was born in 1727 and died in 1796. The pattern also occurs in turquoise.

Boxes

A Chantilly yellow-ground snuff box, painted with chinoiserie figures in landscapes, contemporary copper-gilt mounts c1740, 3½ in (8 cm). **$1,500-2,200**

A particularly saleable box because of the chinoiserie subject.

A Meissen counter box, painted with playing cards, deutsche Blumen and the arms of Saxony, the interior painted with a basket of flowers, minor damage to interior, c1750, 7 in (17 cm). **$4,000-5,000**

Originally sold with inner boxes and counters.

A Meissen snuff box, painted with figures on harbour and river foreshores, the interior painted with figures in a formal garden, contemporary gold mounts, c1745, 3½ in (8 cm). **$5,500-7,000**

A German oviform bonbonniere, painted with figures in landscape vignettes and with scattered flower sprays with engraved contemporary silver-gilt mount, probably Fürstenberg, c1770, ½ in (8 cm). **$1,000-1,200**

A Ludwigsburg snuff box, painted with landscape panels between borders of osier moulding, the base with a flower-spray and the interior of the cover with a turbanned figure smoking a pipe, gilt metal mounts, base repaired, c1770, 3½ in (8 cm). **$1,300-1,700**

A Fürstenberg snuff-box, the base painted with putti, in landscapes within cartouches, the cover with horsemen approaching buildings, the hinged silver mount engraved on the interior with foliage, 18thC, 3½ in (8 cm). **$1,500-2,200**

A rare Meissen artichoke box and cover, naturalistically modelled and coloured, swords mark in blue, some repair, 1760-1770, 6 in (15 cm). **$2,000-3,000**

A Meissen box and cover, painted en camaieu rose with equestrian figures and wayfarers on paths supported by rococo brown and gilt C scroll and foliage supports, two chips to foot ground down, c1750, 6 in (15 cm). **$1,300-1,700**

A Mennecy snuff box, with contemporary silver mounts painted with bouquets of garden flowers and moulded with basket-work, hair crack, minor chip to base, c1740, 2½ in (6 cm). **$600-700**

A Mennecy snuff box, modelled as a recumbent cat suckling a kitten, the cat with manganese fur markings, the kitten with brown fur, the interior with a flower spray, contemporary silver mounts, with Paris décharge marks of the Fermier Général Eloi Brichard, 1756-1762. **$2,500-3,500**

A Mennecy hen snuff box, with silver-gilt mounts, her plumage in shades of buff, brown and purple, the contemporary mounts with décharge mark of Eloy Brichard, Paris, 1756-1762, 2 in (5 cm). **$1,700-2,500**

A porcelain bonbonnière, c1770.
$300-500

A 'Sèvres' casket, of bombé shape, gilt metal mounts, the cover painted with a lady seated in her boudoir, her lover escaping through a window, mazarine blue ground, blue crossed L mark, 19thC, 6½ in (16 cm).
$600-900

A St Cloud snuff box and cover, modelled as a seated rotund Chinese man, contemporary silver mount bearing décharge marks, c1740, 2½ in (5.5 cm).
$1,700-2,500

Caddies

An Ansbach tea caddy, painted with river landscapes within gilt C-scroll cartouches, later English silver cover, blue A mark, c1770, 4 in (9.5 cm). **$1,000-1,400**

A rare Boettger tea caddy and a cover, painted in Schwarzlot and gilding probably by Ignaz Preissler, with Orientals in landscapes, impressed repairer's mark for Wildenstein, cover modern replacement, 1715-1720 4 in (10 cm). **$3,000-4,500**

A Ludwigsburg tea caddy and cover, the simulated wooden ground reserved with en grisaille paintings in the style of etchings, the picture on one side inscribed beneath, Hoffman peinter and Tomann gr:, the reverse with Hes pen X and Fogt ge:, finial repaired, small chip to shoulder and base, c1775, 5½ in (13.5 cm).
$600-900

A Höchst tea caddy, painted with a sailing vessel approaching harbour, blue wheel mark and incised 14NI, c1760, 4 in (11 cm).
$1,300-1,700

A Meissen tea caddy and cover, painted in puce, the sides edged with gold lines, the shoulder and cover in solid gold, the four panels painted with estuary scenes and a figure crossing a stream in a wooded valley, 1725-1728, 4 in (9.5 cm). **$3,000-4,500**
Though well painted the lack of a cartouche around the scene reduces the attractiveness of the piece as a whole.

A Meissen tea caddy and cover, painted in puce, the shoulder brightly gilt, the flat cover with a formal star pattern in puce and gold, crossed swords mark, gilt numerals 31 on cover and base, impressed former's mark of three dots, 1725-1728, 4 in (9.5 cm).
$6,000-8,000

MAKE THE MOST OF MILLER'S
Price ranges in this book reflect what one should expect to pay for a similar example. When selling one can obviously expect a figure below. This will fluctuate according to a dealer's stock, saleability at a particular time, etc. It is always advisable to approach a reputable specialist dealer or an auction house which has specialist sales.

A Meissen Hausmalerei armorial tea caddy and cover, the coat of arms painted in blue, puce and gilt and surmounted by a helmet and a coronet, the reverse and cover with Chinoiserie figures, blue enamelled crossed swords mark, c1735, 4½ in (11.5 cm).
$6,000-8,000

Accurate identification of the coat of arms would enhance the value considerably.

A Meissen yellow-ground tea caddy and later cover, impressed 26, blue crossed swords mark, c1745, 5½ in (13.5 cm).
$1,000-1,400

A Meissen tea caddy and cover, painted with merchants on quaysides, blue crossed swords mark and gilder's number 64, cover repaired, c1740, 4 in (11 cm).
$1,500-2,200

A rare Sèvres tea caddy and cover, painted by Taillandier with swags of summer flowers on an apple green ground gilt with diaper, feathery leaves and stylised grapes, interlaced Ls mark, c1780, 3 in (8 cm). **$4,500-5,000**

Vincent Taillandier, working 1753-1790.

A pair of Worcester tea caddies, painted in the atelier of James Giles, with puce flowering branches divided by pale orange bands gilt with trellis-pattern and reserved with mons, c1770, 5 in (13 cm). **$1,200-1,500**

In 1767 the Worcester factory entered into an agreement with an outside decorator, James Giles, whereby the factory was to supply him with white porcelain for decoration in his London workshop.

A Schrezheim tea caddy, painted with buildings and landscapes, chips to rims, c1775, 4 in (10·5 cm).
$1,200-1,500

Examples of wares from the Schrezheim factory are rare.

Candelabra

A pair of Bow candlestick figures, enriched in vivid enamels, on four-footed scroll-moulded bases enriched in blue and puce, one nozzle with impressed T mark, one branch repaired, some minor chipping to flowers and one nozzle, c1762, 8 in (19.5 cm).
$600-900

A Worcester fluted tea caddy and cover, of Lord Henry Thynne type, painted with a river landscape within a turquoise cartouche flanked by wreaths of flowers and foliage, blue border gilt with C-scrolls, the cover with flower finial, blue crescent mark, restored, c1775, 7 in (16.5 cm).
$1,200-1,500

The loss of the cover would reduce the value considerably. Though the type is popularly termed 'Lord Henry Thynne', the association between the individual and the pattern is unclear. Lord Henry Thynne (1797-1837) was the second son of the second Marquess of Bath.

A pair of German porcelain four-light candelabra, on shaped oval scroll-mounted bases enriched with gilding, blue cross marks, chips, restorations and part of one wax pan lacking, c1880, 15 in (38 cm). **$1,200-1,500**

A Derby candleholder, with floral design, damaged, 1758-1760. **$400-600**

A Capodimonte (Carlo III) white chinoiserie candelabrum, formed as a lady seated between two cornucopiae set with fluted candle nozzles, rococo scroll base, chips to leaves, c1755, 8 in (19 cm). **$2,000-3,000**

A coloured example of this model, in the Museo Arquelogico Nacional, Madrid, is illustrated by Arthur Lane: Italian Porcelain pl 82.

A pair of Bow 'Birds in Branches' chamber candlestick groups, on shaped oval bases enriched in puce and applied with a dog, the tôle peint branches terminating in petal-moulded nozzles enriched in a bright palette, incised S marks, some restoration, firing crack to one base, c1762, 9 in (22.5 cm). **$2,000-3,000**

A pair of Derby candlestick figures, each modelled as a putto holding a bird in his left hand and a floral sprig in his right, base heightened in turquoise, c1765, 7 in (17 cm). **$300-500**

A Derby candlestick group, in the form of a seated piper with his dog at his side, painted in bright enamel colours, slight damage, c1770, 9 in (22 cm). **$300-400**

Some rather poor 20thC copies of Derby candlestick groups occasionally confuse the market.

A Dresden three light candelabrum, formed as two revelling drinking cherubs, the base with scrolls, painted birds and insects, candle branches encrusted with coloured flowers, underglaze blue crossed swords, incised H196, damaged. **$300-400**

A pair of Dresden candelabra, the scroll columns with figures of children with emblems symbolic of the four Seasons, crossed sword marks in underglaze blue, 20 in (50 cm). **$1,000-1,200**

A pair of Thuringian candelabra, by Schierholz of Plaue, marked in underglaze blue, 6 in (15.5 cm). **$1,000-1,200**

A pair of Meissen candelabra, formed as children and adults birds nesting, the flowering trees supporting foliage candle nozzles, blue crossed swords mark at back, minor chips to foliage, c1750, 9½ in (23.5 cm). **$3,500-5,000**

Models were re-issued over a long period. Early examples are generally considerably more valuable than their 19thC counterparts.

A pair of Meissen blue and white onion-pattern baluster candlesticks, blue crossed swords and dot marks and painter's marks R and MO Möbius, c1765, 10 in (24.5 cm). **$2,000-3,000**

Centrepieces

A Bow three-tier shell centrepiece, painted in a 'famille rose' palette, the exterior of the shells enriched in puce, resting on pierced rockwork applied with coloured shells and seaweed, some chipping to shells, c1755, 8 in (19.5 cm). **$1,000-1,400**

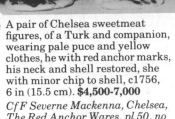

A pair of Chelsea sweetmeat figures, of a Turk and companion, wearing pale puce and yellow clothes, he with red anchor marks, his neck and shell restored, she with minor chip to shell, c1756, 6 in (15.5 cm). **$4,500-7,000**

Cf F Severne Mackenna, Chelsea, The Red Anchor Wares, pl 50, no 99.

A Derby kingfisher centrepiece, enamelled with winged insects and a moth, some restoration, c1765, 7 in (17 cm). **$1,400-1,700**

A fine Meissen centrepiece, painted and encrusted with flowers in delicate shades of pink, green and gold mounted with cherubs representing the harvest, crossed swords mark in underglaze blue, c1870, 20½ in (50.5 cm). **$1,500-2,200**

A Kerr and Binns Worcester Grecian flower bowl and pierced cover, decorated in Raphaelesque colours and gilding, printed shield mark including the date 1862, minor restoration, 9 in (22.5 cm). **$800-1,200**

A Sèvres pattern centre-dish, reserved on a turquoise ground and decorated with soldiers within a foliage cartouche, the reverse with a castle in a misty river landscape, with imitation Sèvres and Chateau des Tuileries marks to the interior of the bowl, last quarter of the 19th C, 23in (58.5 cm). **$3,000-4,500**

A Meissen centre-dish, with coloured flowers and with figures supporting a flared shell-moulded basket, blue crossed swords marks, impressed and incised numerals, c1880, 20 in (49 cm). **$1,500-2,200**

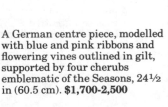

A pair of Worcester sweetmeat dishes, after Kate Greenaway and signed Hadley, 8½ in (21 cm). **$600-700**

A German centre piece, modelled with blue and pink ribbons and flowering vines outlined in gilt, supported by four cherubs emblematic of the Seasons, 24½ in (60.5 cm). **$1,700-2,500**

A pair of Royal Worcester sweetmeat dishes, one containing a girl playing a banjo, the other a boy with a tambourine, probably decorated by George Topham Roberts, the features in enamel colours and other details in gold, printed and impressed marks with date code for 1884, 9 in (22 cm). **$800-1,200**

A porcelain centrepiece, modelled as a neo-classical temple, the gilt dome moulded with fruit swags in the white over six eagles surmounting twin column supports 'marbled' in colours over the cylindrical base, probably Paris, mid 19thC, lacking one column, minor repairs, 15 in (38.5 cm). **$1,000-1,400**

A German porcelain centrepiece, the bowl applied with flowers supported on tree trunk pedestal, the base surmounted by a pair of rustic lovers, 19thC, 19½ in (45 cm). **$500-700**

Clock Cases

A Meissen rococo clock and stand, moulded with scrolls in white and gold, the movement within rococo gilt-metal surround, the enamel dial marked Chabrier, London, blue crossed swords mark on each piece, the crest restored, other minor damages, c1750, 13 in (32 cm). **$4,000-5,000**

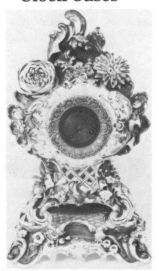

A French porcelain mantel clock, the movement signed Vanson à Paris, the case modelled in relief with flowerheads and sprays on a royal-blue ground, mid 19thC, 13 in (28 cm). **$700-1,000**

A Meissen rococo mantel clock, surmounted by Venus with a cupid attendant, the case moulde with pink-edged shell scrolls and green gilt scrolling foliage, the front and side panels painted wit hunting figures, the gilt metal clock movement inscribed on the enamel dial L Leroy & Cie 13 Palais Royal 15 Paris, blue crosse sword and impressed 28, some repairs, c1750. 16½ in (41 cm). **$3,500-5,000**

MAKE THE MOST OF MILLER'S

Miller's is completely different each year. Each edition contains completely NEW photographs. This is not an updated publication. We never repeat the same photograph.

A Vienna (Du Paquier) architectural clock case, painted en camaieu rose in the manner of J P Dannhofer, the upper part with a portrait of Emperor Franz Stephan, some damages, c1730, 15 in (37 cm). **$2,000-3,000**

A mantel clock in French porcelain case, painted with sprays of flowers in bright enamel colours and gold, late 19thC, 18 in (42.5 cm). **$600-700**

A large Dresden bracket clockcase, encrusted with bright coloured flowers, shells and cora blue crossed swords and star marks, restorations to Time and minor restorations and chips to flowers and foliage, c1880, 37 in (93 cm). **$4,500-7,000**

A Samuel Alcock tea cup and saucer, the centres painted with a castle in landscape within ornate gilt borders, pattern no 7705, in gold, c1840, 6 in (15 cm). **$100-200**

Cups

A pair of Berlin green-ground cabinet cups, covers and stands, reserved and painted with views in Berlin named on the bases Die Domkirche zu Berlin and Strasse unter den Linden mit Zeughaus, blue sceptre marks, c1880. **$1,700-2,500**

An Ansbach teacup and saucer, painted with vegetables, fruit and flowers, gilt dentil rims, blue A mark to each piece, minor chip to cup, c1770. **$500-700**

A Bow miniature cup and saucer, with red flower and green leaf, saucer cracked, 1762-65. **$500-600**

A Chelsea blue ground teabowl and saucer, from the Gladstone service, painted with exotic birds between gilt dentil rims, gold anchor marks, slight rubbing to gilding on teabowl, minor crazing to reverse of saucer, c1760. **$800-1,200**

A Chelsea decagonal teabowl and saucer of large size, painted in iron red with two dragons divided by emblems within a barbed rim, the saucer with raised anchor mark, c1750. **$3,500-5,000**

A fine Doccia teabowl, decorated with chinoiserie figures in rocky landscapes within an elaborate gilt scrollwork border enriched with purple and iron red, gilt rim, 1770-1780, 3½ in (8 cm). **$600-900**

A Bow tea cup and saucer, c1752. **$200-300**

l A Davenport cup and saucer, painted with cabbage roses in pink and gilt, printed marks in brown and numbered 730 in gilt, printed marks in puce. **$60-100**

c A Davenport porcelain trio, painted with acanthus leaves and wriggle work in gilt on an orange ground, printed registration mark in underglaze blue, numbered 2144 in red. **$80-150**

r A Davenport cup and saucer, panels of acanthus leaves alternating with diapering on a scaled ground, in underglaze blue, iron red, salmon pink and gilt, standard printed mark in red, numbered 3590 in red. **$60-90**

A pair of Doccia chinoiserie beakers and two saucers, painted with chinoiserie after Heroldt within iron red, puce, lustre and gold Laub-und-Bandelwerk cartouches, one saucer chipped, c1755. **$2,500-3,500**

These pieces were copied directly from a Meissen original.

A very rare Longton Hall loving cup, amusingly painted in lime green, bright yellow, greyish-blue and raspberry-pink, with Chinese 'magician' figures, minor chip and hair crack to rim, c1755, 4½ in (10.5 cm). **$2,500-3,500**

No other Longton Hall loving cup is recorded. Polychrome wares with Chinese figures are, in any case, rare on Longton wares. The handle form is typical.

A Frankenthal coffee cup and saucer, with panels painted in puce camaieu, within rococo gilt C-scroll cartouches, the cup and saucer with flowers in puce, and gilt husk and dot borders, blue crowned CT monogram marks, the cup incised H 10, the saucer with V.11.0, slight glaze crack to saucer, c1765. **$1,200-1,500**

A Frankenthal coffee cup and saucer, painted with nymphs an Cupid in landscapes, gilt rims, blue crowned CT monogram marks and the date 1779, variou incised marks. **$500-600**

A Ludwigsburg teacup and saucer, painted with landscape vignettes after Riedel, crowned interlaced C's marks in underglaze blue, 1765-1770. **$700-1,000**

A pair of early Höchst chinoiserie teacups and saucers, painted in puce and gold, iron red wheel marks and N 1 incised, c 1755. **$1,700-2,500**

An early Meissen teabowl, in the Kakiemon style, blue enamel crossed swords mark and incised Johaneum mark N=363W, c1728. **$600-900**

A Meissen beaker and a saucer, painted with merchants and merchandise in shore landscape with shipping, within quatrefoil lustre, gold, iron red, and puce Laub-und-Bandelwerk cartouches, crossed swords in bl and puce, gilder's marks 7 and T chips to beaker repaired, c1726. **$1,500-2,200**

A pair of Meissen tischenmuster cups and saucers, painted in the Imari style, with flowering plants around a table, blue crossed swords and painter's marks, c1730. **$800-1,200**

A pair of Meissen teabowls and saucers, the centres of the bowls and undersides of the saucers with sprays of indianische Blumen, crossed swords marks, gilt numerals 31, impressed former's marks of five pointed stars. **$3,500-5,000**

A pair of Böttger teabowls and saucers, with shaped rims painted in Holland in the Kakiemon palette, c1735. **$1,000-1,400**

A pair of Meissen teabowls and saucers, painted in puce with figures in wooded landscapes, the teabowls with caduceus marks, the saucers with crossed swords marks. **$3,000-4,500**

A pair of Meissen chinoiserie teabowls and saucers, painted by C F Herold, blue crossed swords and gilt H marks, the saucers with Pressnummer 64, and the teabowls with Pressnummer 65, c1735. **$4,500-7,000**

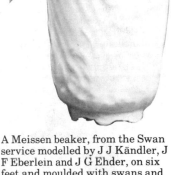

A Meissen octagonal teacup and saucer, painted with scattered insects and with gilt rim, blue crossed swords marks and Pressnummer 23 on each piece, chip to rim of cup, c1740. **$600-800**

A Meissen yellow ground beaker and saucer, with gilt cartouches flanked by scrolls and puce cell-pattern and with elaborate gilt borders, blue crossed swords marks and gilder's letter F to each piece, c1740. **$3,000-4,500**

A Meissen cup and saucer, with double scroll handles, the cup painted with a portrait bust of a Saxon Hussar, the saucer with soldiers in blue and red uniforms, blue crossed swords marks and Pressnummer 2 and 6, c1745. **$6,000-8,500**

A Meissen beaker, from the Swan service modelled by J J Kändler, J F Eberlein and J G Ehder, on six feet and moulded with swans and storks, the arms of Bruhl and his wife and sprays of Kakiemon flowers below the gilt rim, blue crossed swords mark, c1740, 4 in (9 cm). **$9,000-13,000**

This is an unusual shape from this well known service, it was presumably intended for fruit juice.

Six Meissen coffee cups and saucers, painted with birds perched on branches and scattered insects, blue crossed swords mark and various Pressnummern, two handles repaired, two saucers chipped, c1750. **$1,400-1,700**

A fluted St Cloud blue and white cup and trembleuse saucer, lambrequin borders, blue St CT and F marks, c1730. **$400-600**

A St Cloud white cup and trembleuse saucer moulded with flowers in relief, minor hair cracks to cup, c1725. **$600-900**

A pair of Meissen yellow ground coffee cups and saucers, blue crossed swords marks, c1745. **$1,000-1,400**

NYMPHENBURG

★ factory founded in the late 1740's but the main production started in 1753
★ J. J. Ringler was employed as arcanist
★ from 1757 a fine milky-white porcelain was produced
★ the porcelain is of great quality and virtually flawless
★ F. A. Bustelli modelled some excellent figures from 1754-63 which perfectly expressed the German rococo movement
★ the models are the epitome of movement and crispness and are invariably set on sparingly moulded rococo pad bases
★ note light construction of the slip-cast figures
★ J. P. Melchior, previously at Frankenthal and Höchst, was chief modeller from 1797-1810
★ on finest pieces the mark is often incorporated as part of the design
★ the factory still exists

A Nymphenburg cabinet cup and saucer, painted with Maximilian Joseph Platz, as inscribed on the base in black, in the centre the Nationaltheater, on the left the south front of the Residenz, impressed shield and incised marks, 1835-1840. **$2,000-3,000**

The Nationaltheater was designed by Karl von Fischer. The foundation stone was laid on 20 October 1811, the theatre opened in 1818, and was rebuilt after a disastrous fire in 1823.

A Sèvres coffee cup and cinquefoi saucer, painted with flowerheads in blue and gilt, blue shaped cell-pattern borders with gilt dentil rims, the cup with blue interlaced L marks enclosing date letter K for 1763 and painter's mark S for Pierre Antoine Méreau, the cup with incised ND, the saucer with 60. **$1,500-2,200**

A Sèvres brown ground coffee cup and saucer, moulded with trailing sprays of prunus with silver flowers and gilt stems, gilt crowned interlaced L marks and the letter L, minor chips to underside of saucer foot-rim, c1782. **$500-700**

A Sèvres turquoise ground chocolate cup, cover and trembleuse stand painted with birds in wooded landscapes, blue interlaced L marks enclosing the date letter Z for 1777 and painter's mark of Aloncle. **$1,700-2,500**

A Vincennes cup and saucer, painted with brightly coloured birds within a border of gilt flowers reserved on a bleu lapis ground, underglaze blue Ls and one dot (on saucer), two dots (on cup), blue enamel painter's mark, 1753-1754. **$2,500-3,500**

A very similar cup and saucer, also without a date letter and with the same unidentified painter's mark is in the Palazzo Pitti, cat no 11, marks 5 and 6, p 173.

A Sèvres verte pré coffee cup and saucer, painted with Turkish figures in landscapes with Classical ruins, the green ground reserved with scrolling gilt foliage and garlands, interlaced L marks in grey above the painter's mark of Claude Charles Gerard and the gilder's mark of Le Beljeune, c1775. **$2,500-3,500**

Two Spode teacups, coffee cups and saucers, pattern no 2947, marks in red. **$200-300**

A Tournai teacup and saucer, painted by Joseph Duvivier with exotic birds in landscape vignettes and with gilt rims, the saucer incised with JV, c1770. **$800-1,200**

A Spode trio, pattern 1250, c1810.
$200-300

A pair of Venice (Cozzi) teabowls and saucers, painted with scattered bouquets of flowers beneath green-scale rims edged in foliage, iron red anchor marks, c1765. **$600-900**

A Venice (Cozzi) teabowl and saucer, painted with cameo portrait medallions suspended from ribbon and foliage garlands, iron red rims, iron red anchor mark, c1765. **$400-600**

An early Worcester fluted coffee cup, painted in delicately coloured enamels with a butterfly, insects and scattered sprigs, small rim chip repaired, c1754, 2 in (5 cm). **$500-600**

A Vienna Empire style cup and saucer, painted with a named view 'Vue d'une partie du palais J:R: du cote de rempart, a Vienne', impressed date numeral for 1816 and 17, shield mark in underglaze blue. **$1,000-1,200**

A Worcester teabowl and saucer, transfer printed and coloured with the Red Cow pattern within a green diaper border reserved with flowerheads, c1755. **$3,000-4,500**

Two rare Worcester cups, each of flared beaker form, the sides painted in blue with a Long Eliza in a fenced garden, plain loop handles, painters marks, one rim hair cracked, one chipped, c1752. **$4,500-7,000**

An unusually high standard of potting and decoration was achieved early in the life of the Worcester factory. The pattern on these cups is known as 'the Willow Root' and was in use on both blue and white and polychrome wares from 1752-1755. A variant, lacking the figure, is also known.

A first period Worcester coffee cup and saucer, painted in underglaze blue with flower branches and insects on a moulded herringbone pattern ground, workmen's marks. **$300-600**

An early Worcester miniature tea bowl and saucer, painted with the Rock Warbler design, with painter's mark, cup 1 in (2.5 cm). **$1,500-2,200**

A Worcester coffee cup and saucer, painted in puce camaieu with a peacock perched on the branch of a tree, within a C-scroll cartouche, the border with scattered rose sprays in colours and with a puce C-scroll rim, c1760. **$2,500-3,500**

A Worcester teabowl and saucer, transfer printed in black by Robert Hancock with The King of Prussia, the reverse of the teabowl with martial trophies, the interior with Cupid holding a laurel wreath, signed 'Hancock fecit Worcester' and 'R H Worcester' with the rebus of an anchor, c1757. **$3,500-5,000**

A Worcester teacup and a saucer, painted in the atelier of James Giles, with pink berried vines and leaves in two tones of green joined by gilt tendrils, the cup with blue crossed swords and 9 mark, c1765. **$1,000-1,200**

A Worcester ribbed coffee cup and saucer, the gilt-enhanced border with turquoise shagreen panels and pink swags of flowers, c1768. **$600-700**

A Worcester ribbed teacup and saucer, painted in the 'famille verte' palette with The Dragon in Compartments Pattern, c1770. **$600-700**

18th Century Worcester Porcelain

★ founded in 1751
★ soft paste porcelain using soaprock (steatite)
★ circa 1751 to 1753 a short experimental period. Sometimes difficult to differentiate between Lund's Bristol and Worcester
★ both blue and white and 'famille-verte' polychrome wares produced
★ circa 1752-1754 some wares marked with an incised cross or line
★ circa 1755 to 1760 some finely painted and potted wares produced
★ painters marks, resembling Chinese letters, appear on base of wares
★ the underglaze blue is well controlled and of a good pale colour
★ polychrome decoration is crisp and clean
★ almost all patterns are based on Chinese prototypes
★ transfer printed wares appear circa 1754
★ from 1760-1776 a consistently high standard of potting and decorating achieved though lacking spontaneity of earlier wares
★ most blue and white pieces now marked with a crescent
★ 1776-1793 the Davis/Flight period
★ often difficult to differentiate from Caughley where open crescent mark also used

A Worcester fluted cup and saucer, decorated with polychrome enamels, centre with a ring of turquoise husks, the border with gros bleu with gilding, 1768-1770. **$500-600**

Two Worcester blue-ground teacups and saucers painted with 'famille rose' flowers within gilt cartouches, blue crescent and W marks, c1770. **$1,000-1,200**

A first period Worcester coffee cup and a saucer, painted with exotic birds among foliage, and with insects and flowers in panels outlined with gilt scrolls on a scale blue ground, the cup with script W mark, the saucer with W mark. **$500-600**

A Worcester blue-scale teacup and saucer painted with exotic birds and insects within gilt cartouches blue square seal marks, c1768. **$600-800**

Three types of underglaze blue ground were used at Worcester – scale blue, powder blue and gros bleu. Scale blue derives its name from the scale like pattern which produces an excellent deep coloured ground. Any form of damage or rubbing reduces the value considerably.

A Worcester fluted teacup and saucer, painted with an exotic bird, within a border of three green diaper panels suspending pink swags of flowers, gilt rims rubbed, c1775. **$1,300-1,700**

A Worcester fluted hop-trellis teabowl and saucer, with radiating trellis and berried foliage between turquoise shagreen and royal blue borders edged with gilt C-scrolls, the saucer with blue W mark, c1775. **$800-1,200**

Compare with the earlier example of this pattern.

A Worcester fluted coffee cup and saucer, painted with swags of flowers and red berried foliage suspended from a turquoise shagreen border within gilt line rims, chips to underside of saucer, c1775. **$600-900**

Two Royal Worcester teacups and saucers, painted and signed by Rice, Townsend and Ayrton, with various fruits, purple printed marks including date codes for 1926 and 1931. **$300-400**

A set of six Royal Worcester coffee cups and saucers, each painted by Stinton, signed, with highland cattle, the interior of the cups gilt, printed crowned circle mark, retailer's mark, date code, 1936, saucer 4 in (10 cm). **$1,400-1,700**

A Chamberlain's Worcester coffee cup and saucer, from the celebrated Horatio service, painted in a vivid Imari palette, with panels of flowering shrubs divided by Nelson's crest and motto, a baronial and ducal coronet, pattern no 240, 1802-1805. **$3,500-5,000**

The Horatio breakfast service, referred to by Lady Hamilton in her diary, was ordered on their visit to Chamberlain's factory on 26 August 1802.

◄
A continental ewer, possibly Herend or Sampson, of Persian inspiration, in early 18thC Chinese taste, painted with underglaze blue and overglaze 'famille rose' flowers dividing panels with impish children, crack in base, late 19thC, 14 in (35 cm). **$500-700**

Ewers

A pair of Belleek ewers, the lower parts applied with a spray of trailing coloured flowers and moulded with a band of flowerheads, with foliage-moulded scroll handles and shaped rims, black-printed marks, second period, 8 in (20 cm). **$800-1,200**

A Meissen pear shaped ewer, with beaded silver gilt mount, painted with lovers in landscapes within gilt scroll cartouches, blue crossed swords mark, foot chipped, minor chips to flowers, c1750, 10 in (24.5 cm). **$1,700-2,500**

Make the most of Miller's

Unless otherwise stated, any description which refers to 'a set' or 'a pair' includes a valuation for the entire set or the pair, even though the illustration may show only a single item.

A pair of 'Vienna' green ground oviform ewers, on fixed square plinths, the bodies decorated in colours, the apple green ground necks, spreading feet and plinths gilt with stylised ornament and with gilt foliage scroll handles, blue beehive marks, late 19thC, 27½ in (68 cm). **$1,700-2,500**

A Sèvres ewer and basin, painted by Thévenet père with shell and feather roundels within green wreaths and hung with pink ribbons, the rims with blue and gilt borders, gilt metal hinged cover, interlaced Ls, painter's mark and date letter K for 1763, gilding with some wear, ewer 8 in (19 cm). **$6,000-8,500**

Thévenet père working 1741-1777

Figures – animals

A rare Bow tawny owlet, perched on a stump splashed in two shades of green, an applied puce flowerhead between its claws, plumage picked out in shades of brown, the alert eyes in reddish brown and black, firing cracks and repair to base, beak restored, c1755, 8 in (15 cm). **$6,000-8,500**

Bird models, particularly those which are realistically modelled, are very desirable. The owlet, of which only very few are known, is arguably the most attractive of all Bow bird models.

A pair of early Derby squirrels, c1765, 3 in (7.5 cm). **$1,200-1,500**

A Derby porcelain setter, c1795, 5½ in (13 cm). **$600-700**

A Bow figure of a cat, with striped puce markings and yellow eyes, chips to base, back and ears, part of tail lacking, c1756, 2½ in (6,5 cm). **$1,500-2,200**

Cf Elizabeth Adams & David Redstone, Bow Porcelain pl 135 and Anton Gabszewicz & Geoffrey Freeman, Bow Porcelain pl 253

A group of thirteen Dresden 'Monkey Band' figures, on scroll bases outlined with gilding, two o the bases oulined in pink, and tw of the figures duplicated, crossed swords marks in underglaze blue 19thC, **$1,500-2,200**

Similar bands were produced by other continental factories.

A Derby figure of a peacock, enriched with gilding, blue crossed swords mark, chips to flowers, c1825, 6 in (15 cm). **$1,000-1,400**

A Royal Dux porcelain group lion, lioness and dead gazelle rustic base, No 1600, 19 in (47 cm) wide. **$400-600**

A Ludwigsburg group of a boar being attacked by three hounds, the hounds with black and and gold collars, blue interlaced C mark, repair to the forelegs of one hound, minor chips, c1763, 7 in (17 cm). **$1,500-2,200**

A Meissen miniature figure of a monkey, modelled by J J Kändler, naturally decorated with fur marks in pale brown on grasswork base, c1740, 23 in 4 cm). **$1,400-1,700**

A Rockingham figure of a white cat, gilt collar, features picked out in brown and red, impressed mark, incised No 104, painted Cl mark in red, ear chipped, c1830, 2½ in (6 cm). **$600-900**

BOW FIGURES

★ the earliest Bow figures had simple pad bases in common with Chelsea and Derby
★ many figures left in the white
★ figures tend to be less sophisticated than those from the Chelsea factory
★ from 1750-54 many figures were modelled by the 'Muses modeller'
★ these figures have quite thick glaze and low square bases
★ best period runs from 1750-59
★ the influence of Meissen can be seen in the figures from c1755 on
★ rococo bases appeared in late 1750's, earlier bases of c1760 in common with Chelsea are relatively restrained
★ by 1760 'C & S' scroll decoration was in great demand as were large shell bases, which are often thought of as a trade mark of Bow (although other factories did use them)
★ by 1760's typical colours used are blue, emerald-green, yellow and a good red
★ from c1765 greater use of underglaze blue as a ground colour, like contemporaries at Longton Hall
★ late 1760's figures elevated on more elaborate and pierced bases, generally applied with flowers
★ figures with elaborate bocage are typical
★ figures tend now to copy Chelsea gold anchor groups
★ figures with an underglaze blue crescent tend to be Bow (Worcester produced very few figures)

A Bow figure of Minerva, by The Muses Modeller, in black helmet, flowered pink and blue-lined dress and yellow cloak, chips to helmet, neck restuck, dagger damaged, c1752, 8½ in (21 cm). **$1,200-1,500**

A figure of a bagpiper, standing beside a spotted dog and wearing a puce-edged jacket enamelled with flowers, his yellow breeches trimmed with iron red, pockets and ribbons, probably Bow, repairs to jacket, bagpipe, hat and shoe, early 1750s, 6 in (15 cm). **$800-1,200**

The identical model was also produced at Derby.

A Bow set of the Seasons, left in the white, Summer cracked through waist and re-stuck, some chipping, c1755, 5 in (12.5 cm) to 5½ in (14 cm). **$3,000-4,500**

A Bow figure of a girl with sheep, left in the white, some damage, c1753, 6½ in (16.5 cm). **$800-1,200**

A Bow figure, of Ceres, goddess of Earth, sometimes called Una and the Lion, c1765, 8 in (20 cm). **$1,200-1,500**

A composite set of four Bow figures, emblematic of the Seasons, on scroll moulded turquoise, puce and gilt bases, c1765, 6½ in (16.5 cm). **$1,200-1,500**

A pair of Bow bocage groups, painted in bright enamel colours, some restoration, 8½ in (23 cm). **$700-900**

A Bow figure, allegorical of Autumn depicted by a man seated wearing a blue apron and flowered breeches holding a bunch of grapes over a goblet, some repair, c1760, 5½ in (14 cm). **$500-700**

A Capodimonte (Carlo III) white figure of Capitano Spavento, from the Commedia dell'Arte, modelled by Guiseppe Gricci, blue fleur-de-lys mark, chip to his snood and sword hilt, c1750, 6 in (14 cm). **$7,000-9,000**

This figure is not recorded in Stazzi.

A Chelsea figure of Cupid disguised as a beggar, wearing a black hat and eye-patch and scantily draped in yellow, red anchor mark, crack to base, chips to fingers, hat and one wing, the other wing lacking, c1765, 5 in (12.5 cm). **$800-1,200**

A Bristol figure emblematic of Air, draped in a flowered pink and green-lined robe, standing on a pink and yellow cloud base, Richard Champion's Factory, firing crack to base, some minor flaking to enamels, c1775, 11 in (27.5 cm). **$1,200-1,500**

A Chelsea white bust of William Augustus, Duke of Cumberland, minor restoration to nose, c1751, [?] in (13 cm). **$4,500-7,000**

Prince William Augustus (1721-1765) second son of George II, was patron of the Chelsea Porcelain Manufactory and Sir Everard Fawkener, his secretary, was the owner of the house in which Sprimont built up the business. It has been suggested that through Fawkener, Cumberland secretly subsidised the factory, though there is no evidence to support this view.

A Chelsea figure of Uranie, in a grey lined puce flowered cloak and yellow dress, inscribed 'Uranie 4', gold anchor mark, some minor chipping to figure and pedestal, c1760, 15½ in (39 cm). **$1,700-2,500**

A pair of Buen Retiro figures of Venus with Cupid and Diana, scantily draped in blue and gold and yellow flowered cloth, the bases enriched in pink and gold feuille-de-choux, restorations to extremities, 1765-1770, 7½ in (18 cm). **$1,500-2,200**

A Coalport figure, c1926. **$100-150**

This figure was made just before the works closed and the factory moved to Stoke (Cauldon).

PARIAN WARE
* ★ first produced by Copeland in 1844
* ★ it is a white porcelain with a granular surface
* ★ sometimes called 'statuary' porcelain
* ★ mainly used for figures and busts
* ★ in 1845 The Art Union of London commissioned Copeland to make figures taken from the works of contemporary sculptors

---

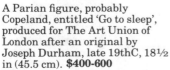

Two porcelain figures, white hard-paste porcelain with clear glaze, the first a figure of General Lafayette, the second a figure of George Washington, with scratchmark on bottom, chip to base, 19thC, each 11½in (28.5cm). **$700-900**

A Parian figure, probably Copeland, entitled 'Go to sleep', produced for The Art Union of London after an original by Joseph Durham, late 19thC, 18½ in (45.5 cm). **$400-600**

18thC. DERBY

* some early white jugs incised with the letter 'D' have been attributed to the Derby factory under the direction of John Heath and Andrew Planché, believed to start c1750
* early Derby is soft paste and is generally lighter than Bow and Chelsea
* very rare to find crazing on early Derby, the glaze was tight fitting and thinner than Chelsea
* glaze often kept away from the bottom edge or edge was trimmed, hence the term 'dry-edge' (particularly applied to figures)
* c1755, three (or more) pieces of clay put on bottom of figure to keep it clear of kiln furniture, giving 'patch' or 'pad' marks – which now have darker appearance

* Duesbury had joined Heath and Planché in 1756.
* Duesbury's early works display quite restrained decoration, with much of the body left plain, following the Meissen style
* Derby can be regarded as the English Meissen
* the porcelain of this period has an excellent body, sometimes with faintly bluish appearance
* 1770-84 known as the Chelsea-Derby period
* Chelsea-Derby figures almost always made at Derby
* 1770's saw the introduction of unglazed white biscuit Derby figures
* this points to the move away from the academic Meissen style towards the more fashionable French taste

* in 1770's a leading exponent of the neo-classical style, and comparable to contemporary wares of Champion's Bristol
* body of 1770's is frequently of silky appearance and of bluish-white tone
* 1780's Derby body very smooth and glaze white, the painting on such pieces was superb, particularly landscapes, Jockey Hill and Zachariah Boreman
* 1780's and 1790's noted for exceptional botanical painting of the period especially by 'Quaker' Pegg and John Brewer
* around 1800 the body degenerated, was somewhat thicker, the glaze tended to crackle and allow discolouration.

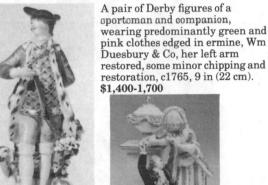

A pair of Derby figures of a sportsman and companion, wearing predominantly green and pink clothes edged in ermine, Wm Duesbury & Co, her left arm restored, some minor chipping and restoration, c1765, 9 in (22 cm). **$1,400-1,700**

A Derby bisque figure of a boy smelling flowers, c1770, 5½ in (13 cm). **$700-900**

Derby figure of a bagpiper, in le flowered clothes, Wm uesbury & Co, some chipping to wers, coat and foot, c1768, 8½ (21 cm). **$600-900**

A Dresden group, on oval base with gadrooned and gilt border, crossed swords mark in underglaze blue, 10 in (24.5 cm). **$800-1,200**

A group of three Derby figures allegorical of the Continents, picked out in coloured enamels, incised N 200, some damage, 1770's, 6 in (15 cm). **$600-700**

A rare Derby figure allegorical of Summer, his frock coat picked out in puce, scroll base, c1758, 4 in (10 cm). **$1,000-1,400**

A similar example is illustrated by Barrett and Thorpe, Derby Porcelain, fig 48.

A pair of 19thC Dresden porcelain maidens, one figure restored, 11 in (27.5 cm). **$800-1,200**

A rare Doccia Italian comedy figure, wearing a yellow hat and breeches, lilac jacket and black apron, indistinctly incised numeral, hand repaired, 1760-1770, 4 in (10.5 cm). **$1,400-1,700**

A pair of Dresden figures of a gallant and his lady, decorated in colours and gilt, blue painted mark, late 19thC, 17in (42 cm). **$600-900**

◄

A Doccia standing figure of a Turk, in tall iron red and gilt head dress, green striped cloak and flowered robes, iron red slippers on square base, some repair to the edge of his cloak and to fingers, c1760, 6½ in (16 cm). **$1,500-2,200**
Derived ultimately, via the Meissen model by Kändler and Reinicke, from the illustration by Hay to le Comte de Ferriol's : Les Cent Nations du Levant.

A pair of Royal Dux porcelain figures of an Arab man and a woman, on rocky circular bases, pink patch marks, damaged, 16½ in (41 cm). **$600-700**

A Royal Dux porcelain group, 'The Blacksmith, his wife and child', no 1944, 19 in (47.5 cm). **$800-1,200** ➤

A Royal Dux group of two maidens, one kneeling and ◄ bathing the other's foot, pink triangle mark, one foot restored, 21 in (54 cm). **$500-600**

A pair of Royal Dux figures of a goat herd and a shepherdess, pink triangle mark, 21½ in (61 cm). **$600-800**

A Frankenthal figure of Venus, modelled by Karl Gottlieb Lück, blue crowned CT monogram mark, mark of Adam Bergdoll and 6, gilder's number N., c1776, 9 in (22.5 cm). **$1,500-2,200**
Cf. F.H. Hofmann: Frankenthaler Porzellan, Taf.95, no. 414 for a similar group but with the addition of Cupid standing before Venus.

Frankenthal allegorical group
Peace and Harmony, modelled
/ J.W. Lanz, crowned CT
onogram in blue, and 6 in blue,
cised workman's marks SZ,
760, 6 in (14 cm). **$1,300-1,700**

A Frankenthal figure of a young
woman, modelled by K.G. Lück, in
puce and white head-scarf, white
bodice, flowered apron and striped
skirt on green base edged with gilt
rococo scrolls, blue crowned CT
mark, minor chips, c1775, 6 in (14
cm). **$1,000-1,200**

rare Kloster-Veilsdorf figure of
piter, from a set of the Seven
anets, modelled by Wenzel Neu,
e interior of the base marked in
derglaze blue with an 'S', some
storation, 1764-1765, 9 in (22
1). **$1,000-1,400**

A Limbach figure of a lady
musician, wearing a
floral-patterned skirt with pink
bodice and white apron, yellow hat
and green shoes, incised numerals
and letters, 1775-1780, 7 in (18
cm). **$800-1,200**

A pair of Höchst figures of
children, modelled by J.P.
Melchior, the girl in black apron
and pink-striped yellow dress, her
companion in yellow-lined pink
jacket and puce-striped grey
trousers, blue wheel marks and
incised N134M and N129R,
damage to his hat and through her
waist, c1770, 6 in (14 cm).
$1,300-1,700

A Ludwigsburg figure of the Muse
Clio, modelled by Joseph
Weinmüller, with yellow-lined
and gilt-trimmed white shawl,
spotted under-dress, restored at
neck and her right arm, c1770, 14
in (34 cm). **$700-1,000** ►

◄ A Böttger porcelain pagoda figure,
seated with Böttger lustre hat and
blue, green and puce floral robe on
mound base, neck repaired, chips
to foot, c1720, 4 in (9 cm).
$800-1,200

Meissen figure of Harlequin, in
ik hat, white shirt and pink and
low breeches, holding
g-pipes, blue crossed sword
irks at back, restoration to his
t, fingers, left leg and bag-pipes,
nor chips, c1742, 6 in (14 cm).
,300-1,700

▶ A Ludwigsburg figure of Mars,
modelled by J.C.W. Beyer, nude
save for iron-red cloak, his armour
in grey and gold on rock-work
base, blue crowned interlaced C
mark, painter's mark S in grey
and incised T 3 N 353, c1765, 6 in
(14 cm). **$800-1,200**

A Meissen pagoda figure, seated in
yellow and blue hat, puce-flowered
robe and feathered apron, blue
crossed swords mark, his head and
neck repaired, chips to base,
c1730, 4½ in (10.5 cm).
$1,000-1,200

LUDWIGSBURG

★ porcelain factory was
  founded in 1758
★ J.J. Ringler directed the
  factory from 1759-1799
★ best period was from 1765-
  1775
★ porcelain has a distinctly
  greyish tone which is
  generally poorer than
  contemporary German
  factories
★ specialised in producing
  figures
★ most desirable are the
  'Venetian fair groups'
  produced by Jean-Jacob
  Louis
★ in 1770's figures of a more
  classical nature were
  produced
★ the later figures were of a
  much poorer quality
★ quality of the flower
  painting is of a fairly
  undistinguished nature
★ the factory closed in 1824

149

◄ A Meissen group of an Oriental musician and companion, modelled by J.J. Kändler, the base with traces of blue crossed swords mark, restoration to their hands, necks and the tea table, minor chips, c1745, 4½ in (10.5 cm). **$2,500-3,500**

A Meissen figure of Scaramouche, from the Duke of Weissenfels series, modelled by J.J. Kändler and P. Reinicke, his right wrist and cuff restored, c1745, 5 in (3.5 cm). **$4,500-7,000** ►

A Meissen figure of a girl dancing, modelled by J.J. Kändler, in white hat and shirt, red and white bodice, yellow skirt and puce apron on tree-stump mound base, repair to both hands and edge of apron, c1745, 7 in (17.5 cm). **$700-1,000**

◄ A Meissen group of a peasant woman, modelled by P. Reinicke, their clothes in yellow, pink, green and blue on gilt scroll base, blue crossed swords mark, chip to boy's hat, c1745, 6 in (15 cm). **$1,700-2,500**

A Meissen Chinoiserie group, modelled by P.J. Reinicke, as a man in straw hat, yellow-lined flowered robe, puce pantaloons and yellow shoes, blue crossed swords mark, minor chip to the child's topknot, c1750, 7 in (16.5 cm). **$3,000-4,500** ►

A Meissen group of miners, modelled by J.J. Kändler and P. Reinicke, in green hats, orange-lined grey jackets and yellow trousers, traces of blue crossed swords mark on base, some damages and repairs, c1750, 8 in wide (20 cm). **$5,500-7,000**

A Meissen Turkish equestrian figure from a chess set, in green and white turban and jacket and puce tunic, mid-18thC, 3½ in (6.5 cm). **$1,200-1,500**

A Meissen figure of a river god, restoration to his cloak, his right foot and the fruit, c1750, 8 in w (19 cm). **$1,000-1,400**

A Meissen figure of a biscuit seller, from the Cris de St. Petersburg, modelled by J.J. Kändler, in a brown jacket tied with a pink sash and white breeches, blue crossed swords mark at back, repair to his hat a right arm, c1750, 7 in (17 cm). **$1,700-2,500**

A pair of Meissen figures of a lady and suitor, both attired in colourful 18th century garments, crossed swords mark, 19thC, 14 in (36 cm). **$1,700-2,500**

A Meissen figure of a lady ► gathering flowers in her puce over skirt, incised BZO and mark in blue at back of tree stump, and decoration initial P on base, mid-18thC, 5 in (12.5 cm). **$600-900**

Miller's price ranges

The price ranges reflect what one should expect to pay for an item in similar condition to that illustrated. If you're selling you may be offered 30% less. Dealers have to make profit too! However if the market has moved upwards, or your piece is a particularly good example – you could be offered mor

A Meissen figure of a tinker, entirely in the white, crossed swords in underglaze-blue, minor chips, mid-18thC, 6½ in (16 cm). $800-1,200

A Meissen figure of an itinerant street vendor, yellow-lined iron-red cape and lilac tunic, blue crossed swords mark, minute chip to bottle on base, c1755, 6 in (15 cm). $4,500-7,000

A Meissen figure of a young man, in puce and yellow jacket with gilt edges, black cape, breeches, tricorn hat and shoes, blue crossed swords mark on base, repair of the dog's near fore-leg, c1745, 5 in (12 cm). $3,000-4,000

A pair of Meissen figures of a lady and gallant, their attire picked out in coloured enamels and gilding standing on scroll moulded grassy bases, swords marks in blue incised and impressed numerals, some repair, 19thC, 20 in and 19 in (51 and 48 cm). $1,300-1,700

A Meissen group of the Triumph of Aphrodite, after the model by J.J. Kaendler, in three sections, blue crossed swords and incised No. 2 marks, chips, fire-cracks and minor restorations, c1860, 22 in wide (56 cm). $2,500-3,500

A Marcolini Meissen group of four children, on circular pedestal modelled in relief with husk festoons, in green crossed with pink ribbons, crossed swords and star mark in underglaze blue, some damage, 11 in (27.5 cm). $1,000-1,200

A pair of Meissen groups, decorated in colours and gilt, blue crossed swords, incised and impressed numeral marks, one repaired, 19thC, 6 in high (15 cm). $800-1,200

A Meissen figure of a small boy, attired in claret jacket with peppermint stripe breeches, the base with scroll moulding heightened in gilt, underglaze blue cross swords mark, late 19thC, 5 in (12.5 cm). $400-600

A large Meissen white figure of Augustus the Strong, after the model by J.J. Kaendler, wearing the Garter and Sash of the Golden Fleece, some chipping to flowers, mid-19thC, 30 in (75 cm). $1,500-2,200

Two Meissen figures of putti, after Acier, blue underglaze swords mark, "Felicite Couronnee". $1,400-1,700

A Meissen figure of a gardener's companion, wearing pink and green striped skirt, blue-lined yellow overskirt reserved with flowers and pink bodice, blue crossed swords and incised marks, slight chips to flowers, c1880, 18½ in (48.5 cm). $1,000-1,200

A pair of Meissen groups, emblematic of 'Summer' and 'Winter', each on scroll moulded square base, crossed swords in blue, incised numbers, late 19thC, 12 in and 11 in (30 and 28 cm). $1,000-1,200

A Meissen group depicting lovers, picked out in colours and gilding, swords in blue, incised numerals, slight damage, late 19thC, 8 in (20 cm). **$500-700**

A rare Mennecy white group of France, incised DV mark at back, chip to baton and flag, c1745, 5 in (14 cm). **$4,000-5,000**

The creator of this model has skilfully used the traditional pose and attributes of Europe to depict France, thus implying that France and Europe were one and the same. It is interesting to compare the Vincennes treatment of this theme in the Victoria & Albert museum.

A Naples (Ferdinand IV) figure of a dwarf, with gilt hat, black mask, white tunic with gilt dots, the tortoise gilt, on oval base, repair to his head and the tortoise, c1765, 3 in (7.5 cm). **$1,000-1,200** ►

A late Meissen group of a lady and gentleman, 9½ in wide (28.5 cm). **$600-700**

A Nymphenburg putto, emblematic of autumn modelled by F.A. Bustelli in pink and yellow hat, incised D3, minute chips to foliage, c1760, 3½ (9.5 cm). **$1,000-1,200**

A St. Petersburg figure of a peasant boy, wearing a blue shirt and striped trousers, incised cyrillic initials S.M. La, Imperial factory St. Petersburg, c1820, 10 in (26 cm). **$600-900**

A Gardner figure of a street vendor, wearing a brown hat, beige coat, and blue trousers, impressed St. George and factory mark, Moscow, c1840, 8 in (20 cm). **$800-1,200**

A female figure from the Guryevsky service, wearing national dress of dark blue with gold edging over a white blouse and a gold headdress, by the Imperial porcelain factory, St. Petersburg, with impressed factory mark, 19thC, 7 in (19 cm). **$800-1,200** ►

A documentary Naples (Ferdinand IV) figure of a Neapolitan, modelled by Aniell Ingaldi, his hand tucked into hi orange sash, in blue cap, puce striped kerchief, the base incise Aniello, c1790, 5 in (12.5 cm). **$4,000-5,000**

This model is not recorded in Angela Carolà's standard work. La Porcellane della real fabbric ferdinandea, though many germaine models by Ingaldi are illustrated.

◄ c. A pair of Samson porcelain figures, of boy and girl at foot of floral tree, 19thC, 10½ in (25 cm). **$500-600**
l.&r. A pair of Continental porcelain groups of boys, with tropical animals, 7 in (17.5 cm). **$500-600**

An early St. Cloud white figure of a seated chinaman, his round hat with stiff leaves, c1725, 6½ in (16 cm). **$2,000-3,000**

A Vincennes white group
emblematic of France, her left arm
repaired at the elbow, c1752, 8 in
(21 cm). **$14,000-17,000**
*These figures originally cost 20
livres.*

A large Sèvres biscuit bust of
Napoleon I, set on a blue and gilt
socle and a square gilt-metal base,
moulded 'Buste Officel Napoleon
Empereur 1805', firing cracks
overpainting, chips, 28 in
(69 cm) 19thC. **$1,500-2,200**

A Samson 'Gold Anchor' group,
depicting a seated musician and
his dog, gold anchor, impressed no.
273, some damage, late 19thC, 11
in (27.5 cm). **$400-600**

A Sèvres biscuit group, of la petite
acheteuse de gimblettes, modelled
by E.M. Falconet, incised B for the
repairer Brachard, c1757, 6 in (16
cm). **$2,000-3,000**
*Very few examples of this group
appear to have survived. The
Elisabeth Parke Firestone example
is illustrated by Ruth Berges:
Soft-paste biscuit figures from
Vincennes and Sevres, in
Connoisseur, November 1967, fig 5.*

A rare Thuringian equestrian
figure of a Roman warrior, holding
a baton, detailed in yellow, puce,
orange-red, cerulean, pale russet,
black and gilding, probably
Kloster Veilsdorf, reins missing
and base cracked, part of baton
missing, c1770, 8in (20 cm).
$2,000-3,000
*This figure, which appears to be
unrecorded, is loosely based on a
bronze figure of Marcus Aurelius
after the antique.*

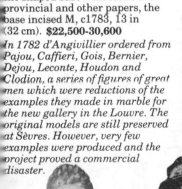

A Sèvres white biscuit figure of
Pascal, after the model by Pajou
from la serie des grands hommes,
the shaped base with lettre à un
provincial and other papers, the
base incised M, c1783, 13 in
(32 cm). **$22,500-30,600**
*In 1782 d'Angivillier ordered from
Pajou, Caffieri, Gois, Bernier,
Dejou, Leconte, Houdon and
Clodion, a series of figures of great
men which were reductions of the
examples they made in marble for
the new gallery in the Louvre. The
original models are still preserved
at Sèvres. However, very few
examples were produced and the
project proved a commercial
disaster.*

A Tournai white group, of a young
man and companion playing the
flute, minor chip to the back of his
hat, c1770, 6½ in (16 cm).
$600-900

A pair of Vienna figures of a
pretzel and vegetable-seller,
standing in pale-coloured clothes,
blue beehive marks, minor chips,
c1760, 8 in (20 cm). **$1,500-2,200**

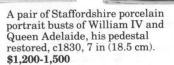

A pair of Staffordshire porcelain
portrait busts of William IV and
Queen Adelaide, his pedestal
restored, c1830, 7 in (18.5 cm).
$1,200-1,500

A Venice Cozzi white figure of a
girl, damages to her hat, the sheep
and her hands, c1775, 6 in (15 cm).
$300-500

A Royal Worcester figure, 'The
Bather Surprised' naked but for a
tasselled drape, coloured in pale
tones of green, yellow and apricot,
puce printed marks, No. 486 and
date code for 1897, right hand
restored, 25 in (64 cm).
$1,300-1,700

A pair of Royal Worcester
comports by James Hadley, one
known as the Queen Anne rustic
boy comport, the other as the
Queen Anne sleeping girl
comport, each with highlights in
gold and the features in enamel
colours, painters mark for George
Topham Roberts, impressed and
printed marks with the date code
for 1885, 9 in (23 cm).
$1,500-2,200

A Vienna figure of a trinket-seller,
standing in black hat, green-lined
puce cloak, red-lined yellow jacket
and orange breeches, blue beehive
mark, repair to his hat, left hand,
c1760, 8½ in (21 cm). **$800-1,200**

A pair of Royal Worcester figures,
depicting Cairo water carriers,
their attire picked out in pale
colours, and edged in gilding,
purple printed marks including
date code for 1895, 6 in (16 cm).
$600-900

A Royal Worcester figure of an
Arab water carrier, kneeling
wearing traditional dress,
decorated in shot enamels and
gilt, printed mark in red, 10 in
(25 cm). **$600-900**

A Zurich figure of a sportswoman,
in green suit and white waistcoat
with puce flowers, blue Z mark,
some restoration, c1770, 8½ in
(21 cm). **$1,700-2,500**
*Ducret illustrates this model, Die
Zürcher Porzellan manufaktur, fig
78, and dates it before 1768.*

A rare Zurich figure of a youth,
probably by the 'Master of the
dancing groups', wearing grey
breeches, and a light-blue
waistcoat with purple edges over
loose white shirt, white and gre
hat and black shoes, E,3/5 incis
c1785, 6 in (15 cm).
$3,000-4,500

A Royal Worcester figure of The
Violinist, standing wearing a red
and gilt trimmed cream frock coat,
printed mark in puce and
numbered 1487, damaged, 21 in
(52.5 cm). **$800-1,200**

Flatware

Twelve Berlin plates, with pierced
basketwork borders, the centres
painted with brightly coloured
flowers and scattered insects, the
green and chocolate borders
enriched with gilding, blue
sceptre marks, c1780, 10 in
(24 cm). **$4,500-7,000**

A Bow dish, with replacement
flower, c1758. **$400-600**

*Two books about Bow porcelain
have recently been published.
These have stimulated interest in
Bow wares.*

A rare Bow blue and white
circular dish, painted in a vibr
blue with two fishermen, with
border of stylised emblems an
diaper-pattern beneath a thick
lardy glaze, c1750, 11 in (27 cm
$2,500-3,500

*The illustrated dish bears a ra
early pattern.*

Bow Blue and White Wares

★ blue and white wares are divided into three periods which coincide roughly with changes in the appearance of the wares

★ *early period 1749-54*
  – wares often thickly potted, glaze can be blue/green in pools
  – many wares painted in a pale clear royal blue which sometimes blurs
  – some very well potted wares, often marked with an incised R also produced
  – 'in the white' wares with applied decoration also produced

★ *middle period 1755-65*
  – darker underglaze blue
  – wares more thinly potted but relatively heavy
  – body more porous and prone to staining
  – painter's numerals used on base and occasionally inside footrings as Lowestoft

★ *late period 1765-76*
  – translucency poor
  – marked deterioration in quality
  – can resemble earthenware

Bow polychrome wares

★ early period wares are decorated in vivid and distinctive 'famille rose' colours – pink and aubergine predominate

★ the patterns used usually include chrysanthemum and peony

★ earliest wares have a greyish body but by 1754 a good ivory tone was often achieved

★ on wares after 1760 the colours can appear dull and dirty and this has an adverse effect on value

★ in the late 1750's some attractive botanical plates were produced

★ after 1760 Meissen influenced floral decoration most commonly found

A Bow dish, with the quail pattern, c1760, 17 in (42 cm). **$600-900**

A Chelsea dish, painted in the Vincennes style with a bouquet, scattered flowers and insects, the reverse with raised anchor mark, slight rim chips, c1750, 10 in wide (24.5 cm). **$2,000-3,000**

A Chelsea silver-shaped dish, painted in a bright palette, the border with scattered flowersprays, the shell thumbpieces and border edged in chocolate, c1752, 10 in wide (24.5 cm). **$4,500-7,000**

Chelsea raised anchor period 1749-1752

★ paste now improved

★ shapes still derived from silver, although Meissen influence noticeable

★ mostly restrained decoration, either Kakiemon or sparse floral work (often to cover flaws)

★ often difficult to distinguish from rare 'Girl in a Swing' factory wares

★ the most collectable ware of this and the Red Anchor period was fable decoration by J.H. O'Neale

A Chelsea 'Hans Sloane' dish, painted in naturalistic colours, red anchor mark, small chip on rim, slight wear, c1757, 11 in (27 cm). **$2,000-3,000**

Quality of painting and condition is crucial to value. This is a dish of average quality.

A Caughley blue and white egg-drainer, printed with the Fisherman pattern, 1785-1790, 3 in (7.5 cm). **$500-700**

CAUGHLEY

★ factory ran from 1772-99, when it was purchased by the Coalport management

★ painted wares tend to be earlier than printed ones

★ Caughley body of the soapstone type

★ often shows orange to transmitted light, but in some cases can even show slightly greenish which adds to the confusion with Worcester

★ glaze is good and close fitting, although when gathered in pools may have greeny-blue tint

★ from 1780's many pieces heightened in gilding, some blue and white Chinese export wares were similarly gilded in England

★ main marks: impressed 'Salopian', 'S' was painted on hand-painted designs, 'S' was printed in blue printed designs, although an 'X' or an 'O' was sometimes hand-painted beside it, one of the most common marks was the capital C. Hatched crescents never appear on Caughley; they were purely a Worcester mark

★ Caughley is often confused with Worcester; they have many patterns in common, eg. 'The Cormorant and Fisherman' and 'Fence' patterns

A pair of Chelsea 'fruit painted' dishes, painted in the atelier of James Giles, brown anchor marks, 1758-1760, 10 in (25 cm). **$800-1,200**

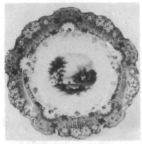

A Davenport porcelain plate, painted with figures in a landscape, printed mark in puce, numbered 315 in gilt, 10 in diam. (24 cm). **$100-200**

A Derby yellow-ground botanical plate, the centre painted by John Brewer, crown, crossed batons and D mark and pattern no.216 in blue, Wm. Duesbury & Co., c1790, 9½ in diam. (23 cm). **$1,000-1,200**

For a discussion concerning the various Derby botanical painters Cf. John Stanley Clarke, 'Curtis Botanical Magazine and the Derby Botanical Dessert Services', Antique Collecting, November 1983.

A set of four Duesbury Derby botanical specimen plates, in the manner of William 'Quaker' Pegg, painted in enamel colours, with gilt line borders, each titled to the reverse French Marigold and Double Lilac Primrose, Monks Hood and Indian Pink, Red Plumeria, and Articulate Vetch, Strawberry and Early Phlox, marked and inscribed in red, one damaged, 9 in diam. (22 cm). **$1,200-1,500**

A pair of Derby plates, painted in the manner of George Robertson with named views of Stonebyers seat of Daniel Vere Esqr. and Bothwell Castle, crown, crossed batons and D marks in iron red, Robert Bloor & Co., c1815, 9 in diam. (22 cm). **$800-1,200**

A pair of Davenport porcelain cabinet plates, painted with 'Bolton Abbey, Yorkshire' and 'View on the River Taner', the main apple green rim pierced and moulded, printed mark in underglaze blue, inscribed in red and numbered 1267, 9½ in (23.5 cm). **$400-600**

A Derby armorial dish, from the Duke of Hamilton service, the central arms with a shaped yellow cartouche below surrounded by pink and ermine mantling, crown, crossed batons and D mark in puce, Wm. Duesbury & Co., c1790, 15 in wide (36.5 cm). **$1,500-2,200**

A Derby plate, painted by George Robertson, with a fishing scene, with Isle of Wight named, c1810. **$300-500**

A Davenport porcelain plate, painted with a tulip in pink, yellow and green within a pale yellow and gilt border, printed mark in underglaze blue, numbered 607 in red, 10 in diam. (24 cm). **$80-150**

A Derby botanical plate, painted in the manner of John Brewer with Moss Rose, within a lobed gil line and berried foliage rim, crown, crossed batons and D mark in blue, Wm. Duesbury & Co., c1790, 9 in (22 cm). **$1,300-1,700**

A Derby gold-ground plate, painted with Vue d'une Partie de Palais J.R. a Vien; pris du cote de rempart, crown, cross batons and D mark in black, Duesbury & Kean, c1810, 10 in diam. (25 cm). **$700-900**

A Derby plate, painted with a view on the Dutch Coast, crown, crossed batons and D marks in red, c1820 9 in diam. (22 cm). **$100-200**

A Derby plate, the centre painted in the manner of Lucas with 'In Westmorland' named on the reverse, crown, crossed batons and D mark in iron red, Robert Bloor & Co., c1820, 9 in diam. (22.5 cm). **$300-600**

Two Derby plates, with named landscapes On the River Wye and Near Bakewell, the borders with green bands edged in gilding, crown, crossed batons and D marks in iron red, Robert Bloor & Co., c1815, 9 in diam. (22 cm). **$600-700**

A pair of Derby shell dishes, the centres painted by Richard Dodson with exotic birds, printed crown and Bloor Derby marks within a circle, Robert Bloor & Co, c1825, 10 in wide (25.5 cm). **$1,200-1,500**

A pair of Royal Crown Derby armorial soup plates, painted in iron red, blue and gold, with a coat-of-arms above the motto Semper Vigilans, iron red printed and impressed marks, date code for 1887, 10½ in diam. (26 cm). **$300-500**

A Royal Crown Derby plate, decorated and signed by Leroy, c1900. **$800-1,200**

An unusual and superbly executed subject leads to a higher than average price.

A Frankenthal chinoiserie plate, moulded with panels of flowers, incised JH monogram and 3, and underglaze blue JAH monogram and rampant lion, Joseph Adam Hannong, slight wear, 1759-1762, 9 in (23 cm). **$1,400-1,700**

A Fulda tray, painted en grisaille with figures beside Italianate ruins, the border with landscape vignettes within gilt foliage and C-scroll cartouches divided by basketwork and with gilt rims, blue crowned double F mark, repaired, c1780, 13 in wide (32.5 cm). **$1,400-1,700**

A pair of Furstenberg plates, the centres painted by C.G. Albert with water fowl, the silver-shaped rim decorated in a restrained manner by J.F.B. Wegener, script F mark in blue, various pressnummern, c1770, 12 in (30 cm). **$1,500-2,200**

A set of four Longton Hall dishes, each moulded as an open puce-coloured peony between pale green leaves, c1756, 7 in (18 cm). **$6,000-8,500**

A pair of Longton Hall peony dishes, the flower edged in bright yellow and pink, indecipherable incised marks, one with slight rim chip, c1755, 7 in wide (17 cm). **$5,500-7,000**

LONGTON HALL

- ★ factory founded by William Jenkinson in c1749
- ★ in 1751 he was joined by Wm. Littler and Wm. Nicklin
- ★ earliest pieces the 'Snowman' figures and some blue and white wares
- ★ there has been a re-attribution of some Longton wares to the West Pans factory started by Wm. Littler in the early 1760's
- ★ West Pans wares are usually decorated in a crude tone of blue, polychrome decoration is often badly rubbed
- ★ some West Pans wares are marked with 2 crossed L's with a tail of dots below
- ★ the figures, in particular, tend to have a stiff, lumpy appearance
- ★ the porcelain is of the glassy soft-paste type
- ★ the glaze can tend to have a greenish-grey appearance
- ★ pieces often thickly potted
- ★ Duesbury worked at Longton Hall before going to Derby
- ★ the 'middle period' of the factory from c1754-57 saw the best quality porcelain produced
- ★ specialised in wares of vegetable form, some of ungainly appearance, unlike the more sophisticated wares of Chelsea
- ★ much of the output of the middle period was moulded
- ★ two famous painters from the period are the 'Castle painter' and the 'trembly rose' painter
- ★ Sadler's black printed wares are extremely rare and sought after
- ★ the porcelain is generally unmarked
- ★ some Longton moulds purchased by Cookworthy for use at Plymouth
- ★ the factory closed in 1760 – all wares are now rare.

Six Meissen plates, painted with scattered deutsche Blumen, blue crossed swords marks, one with pressnummer 22, one with hairline crack, all with small rim chips, c1745. **$1,400-1,700**

A Ludwigsburg plate, blue crowned interlaced C mark and impressed RVI mark, c1760, 10 in diam. (24.5 cm). **$300-600**

The bird subjects are probably based upon G.F. Riedel's prints published in Augsburg.

A Meissen chinoiserie dish painted in the manner of J.G. Hoeroldt, with orientals, a wild dragon spitting fumes flying above, the rim decorated with four chinoiserie panels reserved on a ground of trellis in underglaze blue and gilding, crossed swords in underglaze blue, 1725, 13 in (32.5 cm). **$1,700-2,500**

An engraving by Hoeroldt showing elements of this scene is illustrated by S. Ducret, Meissener Porzellan bemalt in Augsburg.

A set of four Meissen soup plates, each painted in Kakiemon style, 'Der Fleigender Hund' utilising a Chinese 'femille verte' palette with a winged chimera, a flying crane, insects and grasses, shrubs and flowers, crossed swords marks in underglaze blue, two with an impressed workman's mark 'E' on the footrim, one with a pressnumber 16, c1740, 9 in (23 cm). **$2,500-3,500**

For a discussion of the origin of this pattern see Takeshi Nagatake, Kakiemon, chapter V 'Influences of the Kakiemon Ware on the Pottery of Europe'.

A Ludwigsburg dish, painted with wayfarers seated on a track beside a river estuary, gilt rims, blue crowned interlaced C mark and impressed 3N8, c1765, 12 in diam. (30 cm). **$1,200-1,500**

A Meissen Kakiemon saucer, blue enamelled crossed swords marks and incised Johanneum mark N=336W, c1728. **$800-1,200**

A Meissen plate, the centre painted in blue with a spray of flowers, within an iron red and white scroll surround and with brilliant flowers in the Oriental style, within a blue and white trellis surround and chocolate rim, blue crossed swords mark, c1730, 12 in (29.5 cm). **$2,000-3,000**

A pair of Meissen ornithological plates, blue crossed swords mark pressnummer 36, one with rim chip, c1745, 9½ in (24 cm). **$1,300-1,700**

A Meissen Hausmalerei plate, painted by J.F. Mayer von Pressnitz, with people seated at a table and another dancing in garden landscapes, inscribed Das gelicht, blue crossed swords mark, rim chip repairs, c1740, 9 in diam. (22 cm). **$1,000-1,400**

A Meissen Hausmalerei plate, ➤ painted in the workshop of J.F. Mayer of Pressnitz, with a Hussar and figures skirmishing within a gilt quatrefoil calligraphic surround, blue crossed swords mark, c1740, 8½ in diam. (21 cm). **$1,700-2,500**

Plates

A fine Meissen plate, from the Christie Miller service, painted with harbour scenes, a bag on a boat bearing the number 41, blue crossed swords mark, pressnummer 22, c1741, 9 in (22 cm). **$4,500-7,000**

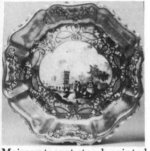

A Meissen teapot stand, painted with figures seated by a path, the reverse moulded with may blossom, puce crossed swords mark, minor chips to flowerheads, c1745, 6 in (15 cm) wide. **$2,500-3,500**

A pair of Meissen saucer dishes, painted with brightly coloured birds, insects and butterflies within spirally moulded borders, blue crossed swords marks and pressnummer 36, one with two minor rim chips, c1750, 10 in (25.5 cm). **$1,400-1,700**

A rare Meissen plate, decorated in underglaze blue after a contemporary Chinese original, by Peter Colmberger, crossed swords and K in underglaze blue, impressed and incised numerals and marks, c1745, 9½ in (23 cm). **$2,500-3,500**

This pattern seems to be unrecorded. Peter Colmberger (Kulmberger) was the head of the bluepainters and worked in the Meisen factory 1745-1779.

A Meissen Marcolini plate, painted in underglaze blue and gilt in the Herold style, blue crossed swords and star mark, pressnummer 12, c1775, 9½ in (23.5 cm). **$800-1,200**

A pair of Meissen blue and white onion-pattern dishes, blue crossed swords and dot marks and painter's marks R and three dots, c1780, 12 in (30 cm). **$1,000-1,200**

Six Meissen plates, painted in the manner of J.G. Klinger with flowers and insects, gilt rims, crossed swords in underglaze blue, minor wear, 1740-1745, 9½ in (23.5 cm). **$4,500-7,000**

The botanical flowers most likely derive exactly from Johann Wilhelm Weinmann's Phytanthoza-Iconographia oder Eigentliche Vorstellung etlicher Tausend, sowohl einheimisch als Ausländischer, aus allen vier Welten Theilein, Regensburg 1737-45.

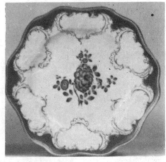

A Meissen plate, from the von Möllendorf service, painted in iron red and gilt and moulded with flowers and musical instruments, blue crossed swords mark and pressnummer 36, c1755, 10½ in (26 cm). **$1,000-1,400**

A large Meissen dish, the centre painted with a bouquet of Manierblumen with a spirally scalloped and osier moulded border, crossed swords marks, 1750-1760, 14 in (35 cm). **$800-1,200**

A Minton plate, painted and signed by J.E. Dean, named on the reverse within an ornate gilt border, printed crowned globe mark and retailer's name 'Tiffany & Co. New York', painted pattern no. B.8863 in puce, impressed marks including the date code for 1902, 9 in (22.5 cm). **$500-600**

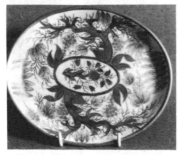

A Newhall teapot stand, pattern 446, c1800. **$80-150**

A Nantgarw plate, painted with four groups of pink roses within a shaped gilt dentil rim, impressed Nant-Garw C.W. mark, c1820, 9 in (22 cm). **$500-600**

A Minton armorial plate card tray, c1865. **$60-90**

A set of twelve Minton's dessert plates, the borders with a gilt band with berried foliage ciselé decoration, impressed and puce printed marks and various date codes, pattern no.G4266, one with rim chip, one repaired, c1885, 9½ in (24 cm). **$1,500-2,200**

A Nantgarw plate, from the Macintosh service, painted with a pheasant among foxgloves and grasses, the border with elaborate gilt feuille-de-choux cartouches enriched with scrolls, foliage and shells, impressed Nant-Garw C.W. mark, c1820, 9½ in (23.5 cm). **$1,700-2,500**

A Ridgway plate, painted with a fisherman in landscape within a blue and orange border with gilt foliate scrollwork, painted pattern no. 941 in iron red, c1815, 9 in (22 cm). **$300-400**

A Minton cabinet plate, decorated in pâte-sur-pâte by Lawrence Birks, artist's monogram in slip, impressed and puce printed mark, c1880, 9½ in (24 cm). **$600-900**

In England Minton were undoubtedly the masters of this technique. The quality of their pâte-sur-pâte (paste on paste) is often outstanding.

A set of six Mintons turquoise-ground plates, the gilt band rims with black zig-zag line, printed and impressed marks, pattern no.G865, one with small rim chip, c1875, 9½ in (24 cm) **$2,500-3,500**

RIDGWAY

★ one of the most important factories manufacturing English bone china

★ most of the early Ridgway porcelain from 1808-30 is unmarked; some, however, do have pattern numbers which are fractional, as did Coalport, with which it is often confused

★ the quality of the early porcelain is excellent, brilliant white and with no crazing in the glaze

★ there were many skilled flower painters employed at the Cauldon Place works including George Hancock, Thomas Brentnall, Joseph Bancroft

★ The development of the Ridgway factory is as follows:
John Ridgway & Company, 1830-55
Bates, Brown-Westhead & Moore, 1859-61
Brown-Westhead, Moore & Company, 1862-1905
Cauldon Ltd., 1906-20
Cauldon Potteries Ltd., 1920-62

l. and r. A pair of Rockingham plates, painted with named views of Swinton Church from the West and Woodnook, Wentworth Park, Yorkshire, the first with red griffin mark, 1826-1830, 9 in (22.5 cm). **$3,000-4,500**

No similar landscape decorated service would seem to have been recorded.

c. A Rockingham muffin dish and cover, the base with red griffin mark, 1826-1830, 9½ in (23.5 cm). **$800-1,200**

VINCENNES

★ production started in the late 1730s

★ early production was generally of indifferent quality

★ inferior to the contemporary productions of St. Cloud and Mennecy

★ towards end of 1740's probably influenced by Meissen introduced coloured grounds

★ 1750's lightly tooled gilding was used to heighten their reserve panels

★ coloured grounds:
'gros bleu' from the late 1740's
'bleu celeste' from 1752
'jaune jonquille' from 1753
'rose pompadour' from 1757

★ factory had moved from Vincennes to Sèvres in 1756

Two rare Vincennes cheese dish stands, with deep wells and everted rims painted in bleu camaieu with sprigs of flowers, the rims moulded with gilt scrolls, interlaced Ls, painter's marks, both chipped and worn, date letter C for 1755, both 8 in (20 cm). **$500-700**

A similar dish but with polychrome flowers and birds and its fromager (cover) is illustrated in Vincennes, no.93, and in Verlet, pl.14; a dish with similar painting is illustrated in Honey, pl.72A. The same form was used as a butter tub stand, see Vincennes, no.42.

The painter signing with a crown specialised in bleu camaieu but is as yet unidentified.

A Vincennes bleu lapis dish, painted with birds, blue interlaced L mark, minute rim chips, 11½ in (28.5 cm). **$1,000-1,200**

A Rockingham porcelain octagonal plate, decorated in 'famille verte' enamels, the border with panels of birds and insects on a green ground scattered with flowerheads, Royal Rockingham Works, Brameld, griffin mark printed in puce, 1831-1842, 14 in (35 cm). **$400-600**

A Sèvres tray, painted in colours with a garland of flowers, the blue and gilt border pierced with scrolls and harebells, blue interlaced L marks enclosing the date letter G for 1759 and with the painter's mark of Taillander and incised pc and 6c, 6 in square (15 cm). **$1,500-2,200**

SÈVRES

★ most decoration of these early years has a somewhat tentative appearance and few pieces show the sharpness of German contemporaries

★ the vases and other hollow wares including ice pails and flower holders epitomised the rococo style predominant at the court

★ Sèvres plaques were inset into furniture from 1760's

★ Sèvres managed to discover the secret of hard paste porcelain at the same time as Cookworthy at Plymouth in 1768

★ 'jewelled porcelain' was introduced in 1773, using a technique of fusing enamels over gilt or silver foil

A Vincennes ecuelle stand, painted with ducks in a pond, floriated Ls mark and seven dots in blue enamel, handle crack, minute chips, gilding worn, c1752, 11½ in (29 cm). **$6,000-8,500**

A stand of the same form, with its ecuelle, is illustrated in Tamara Préaud, Porcelaines de Vincennes, Paris 1977, fig. 80.

A pair of Sèvres oval dishes, painted in soft palette with exotic birds in parkland, blue trellis border enclosing coloured sprigs, interlaced Ls in blue, slight rubbing, 1765-1780, 10½ in (27 cm). **$800-1,200**

A Sèvres low stand, painted by Méreaud âiné with wreaths of flowers separated by panels of gilt diaper on the bleu nouveau ground, interlaced Ls, painter's mark S and date letter L for 1764, some wear, 9 in (23 cm). **$500-600**

A Sèvres plate, painted by Méreaud âiné, on a bleu nouveau ground, interlaced Ls, painter's mark S and date letter M for 1765, later gilded decoration, 10 in (25.5 cm). **$300-400**

Pierre-Antoine Méreaud, working 1754-1791.
The value is reduced by the later gilding.

A pair of Sèvres-pattern jewelled plates, the centres painted with portraits of Court Beauties, named on the reverses, within gilt, turquoise, white and ruby jewelled cartouches, enriched with gilding on royal blue grounds edged with gilt foliage and crowns, the borders with floral garlands, lobed gilt rims, imitation interlaced L marks, c1880, 10 in (24.5 cm). **$600-900**

A Spode armorial marriage plate, with relief floral border and good mark, c1820, 10 in (24.5 cm). **$150-200**

MAKE THE MOST OF MILLER'S

When a large specialist well-publicised collection comes on the market, it tends to increase prices. Immediately after this, prices can fall slightly due to the main buyers having large stocks and the market being 'flooded'. This is usually temporary and does not affect very high quality items.

A Sèvres soup plate, painted in bright enamels by Cornailles, interlaced Ls, painter's mark and date letter V for 1774, 9½ in (24 cm). **$300-400**

Antoine-Toussaint Cornailles working 1755-1800. ▼

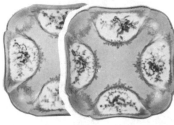

A pair of Sèvres pink-ground dishes, blue interlaced L marks enclosing the date letter V for 1774, painter's mark of Le Beljeune, gilder's mark of Bauduoin, 8½ in (21.5 cm) wide. **$3,000-4,500**

A Swansea plate, painted with wild flowers, impressed trident mark on base, gilding slightly rubbed, c1820, 9 in (22.5 cm). **$400-600**

A Swansea dessert plate, outline printed and coloured with a pheasant perched on pierced rockwork, with shaped green and gilt line rim, impressed mark, c1820, 9 in (22 cm). **$500-700**

A Sèvres tray, painted by Méreaud jeune, with scattered roses and forget-me-nots within the blue scalloped border, interlaced Ls, workmen's marks and date letter x for 1775, firing cracks and cracks to both handles some wear, 16 in (39 cm). **$1,200-1,500**

Charles-Louis Méreaud, working 1756-1779.
A tray of the same form also painted by Méreaud with similar rose sprays is in the Collection at Waddesdon Manor, illustrated by Eriksen no.84. The present tray has sprays of either single or a pair of roses, the only triple group has been painted to disguise a raised area of the ground.

SWANSEA PORCELAIN

★ factory produced high quality soft-paste porcelain from 1814-22
★ factory started by Dillwyn, Billingsley and Walker
★ superb translucent body, excellent glaze
★ in many ways one of the best porcelain bodies produced in the British Isles
★ also noted for delicacy of flower painting, usually attributed to Billingsley although much was obviously done by other decorators including Pollard and Morris
★ a close study of marked pieces will give one an idea of Billingsley's work but unless actually signed by him pieces should be marked 'possibly by Billingsley'
★ on pieces moulded with the floral cartouches the moulding can be detected on the other side of the rim, unlike the heavier Coalport wares which later utilised same moulds
★ especially notable are figure and bird paintings by T. Baxter
★ the Swansea mark often faked, particularly on French porcelain at the end of the 19th, beginning of the 20thC
★ in 1816 Billingsley left to start up again at Nantgarw
★ many pieces were decorated in London studios

A Vienna (Du Paquier) dish, painted with unusual chinoiserie leaf vignettes, c1730, 14 in (34.5 cm). **$4,500-7,000**

A pair of Tournai plates, the centres painted in colours, crossed swords and four stars in gilding, 1770, 9 in (24 cm). **$800-1,200**

A pair of Tournai spirally adrooned plates, painted en amaïeu rose, the rims gilt, gilt crossed swords and star marks, 1770, 9 in (23 cm). **$1,300-1,700**

A pair of Tournai plates, painted in colours, with puce rims, the footrim chipped, c1770, 9 in (23 cm). **$1,000-1,200**

A French dish, painted in puce with a seventeenth century battle scene entitled 'conguéte de la Hollande', possibly Tournai, crossed swords and crosses in gilt, underglaze 4G, late 19thC, 13 in (33 cm). **$300-600**

A rare pair of Vienna plates, enamelled with scattered bouquets and sprays of flowers, both impressed and painted underglaze blue shield marks, early State period, c1749, 9½ in (23.5 cm). **$600-900**

TOURNAI

★ founded in 1751 by F. J. Peterinck

★ produced soft-paste porcelain which is strongly reminiscent and difficult to distinguish from Mennecy

★ early body tends to be a little greyish becoming more yellow later

★ early wares were imitations of Meissen, then in the 1760's copied Sèvres

★ much porcelain sold 'in the white' and decorated elsewhere

★ as with many other European factories, the Louis XVI style was followed in the 1780's

★ amalgamated with the Saint-Amand-les-Eaux factory

★ closed in the mid 18thC

A Vienna rectangular tray, with pierced galleried sides painted en grisaille after an engraving, blue beehive mark, c1775, 14½ in (36.5 cm). **$1,700-2,500**

VIENNA

★ factory founded by C. I. du Paquier in 1719 with the help of Stolzel and Hunger from Meissen

★ the body of du Paquier wares has a distinctive smoky tone

★ decoration tends to cover much of the body and can be more elaborate than Meissen

★ extensive use of trellis work or 'gitterwerk'

★ the 'State' period of the factory ran from 1744-84

★ the style of this period was 'baroque', with scrollwork and lattice-like gilding

★ plain bases were used from mid 1760's

★ excellent figure modelling was undertaken by J. J. Niedermayer from 1747-84

★ Konrad von Sorgenthal became director from 1784-1804

★ the style became far less based on rococo and much simpler in taste, but with good strong colours and raised gilding

★ factory closed in 1864

A 'Vienna' circular dish, painted by Wilner with King Stephen of Hungary standing among his subjects, inscribed on the reverse, within a richly gilt border with raised crowns and sceptres, signed, blue beehive mark, c1880, 17 in (42 cm). **$1,000-1,200**

A Vienna plate, painted by Knoeller with an Egyptian courtyard scene, gilding slightly rubbed, late 19thC, 10 in (25 cm). **$300-500**

A 'Vienna' saucer dish, the centre painted in colours with a scene from classical mythology, the reverse inscribed Der Grazien Rache, the border gilt on shaped panels in apricot, claret, pale blue and mauve, the rim gilt, blue beehive and impressed Meissen marks, c1900, 11½ in (28.5 cm). **$500-600**

A German porcelain charger, in the Vienna style, the centre painted after Wouverman, the border gilt within puce, purple, pink and iron red panels beneath a gilt rim, overglaze blue KPM, Dresden marks, c1900, 15 in (37 cm). **$1,000-1,200**

A Worcester blue and white flared circular patty-pan, the centre painted in a pale blue with two fishermen by a wooded rocky outcrop and a river island in the distance, the reverse with three foliage sprays, two different painter's marks, c1754, 5½ in (1? cm). **$3,500-5,000**

A Worcester leaf-dish, of conventional type painted with The Valentine Pattern within a green border, rim chips and rubbing, c1758, 10½ in (26.5 cm) wide. **$500-600**

A Worcester circular plate, painted with brightly coloured birds, royal blue border edged with gilt scrolls and festooned with flowers, c1768, 9 in (22 cm). **$1,200-1,500**

A Worcester blue and white scallop-shell sweetmeat dish, painted with 'The two peony rock bird' pattern, painter's mark, slight rim chip, c1755, 6½ in (16 cm) wide. **$600-800**

This pattern was used 1754-1765 and is only recorded on shell dishes and leaf dishes. A number of similar patterns are known.

A pair of Worcester blue and white Blind Earl sweetmeat dishes, painted with scattered insects, the leaves and buds enriched in blue, blue crescent marks, one with minute rim chip, c1765, 6 in (15.5 cm) wide. **$2,500-3,500**

A Worcester blue and white, shallow saucer dish, painted with 'The Dragon Pattern', the reverse with cloud scrolls, blue crescent mark, c1760, 7½ in (18.5 cm). **$1,300-1,700**

The dragon pattern was used by the majority of 18th century English factories. Worcester examples are found on a wide range of shapes, including the full range of tea wares. The majority of Worcester examples are marked with a crescent but this was copied on the same pattern by Bow. Early Worcester examples c1756 to 1758 sometimes bear workmen's marks. Worcester examples are rarer and more valuable than their Bow or Lowestoft counterparts.

A Worcester dish, unmarked, slightly damaged, c1765. **$600-800**

A pair of Worcester gros-bleu ground small plates, the even blue borders with lobed gilt dentil rim, blue square seal marks, c1770, 8 in (19.5 cm). **$3,000-4,000**

A Worcester shell-moulded pickle dish, painted in a bright 'famille rose' palette, slight chip, c1754, 3 in (8 cm) wide. **$800-1,200**

Worcester polychrome Blind Earl plate, painted in the atelier of James Giles, c1768, 7½ in (19 cm). **$1,200-1,500**

A Worcester plate, moulded and painted with the Blind Earl design, in enamel colours and gold, slight chip to rim, mid-18thC, 8 in (19 cm). **$500-700**

A pair of Worcester Blind Earl sweetmeat dishes, moulded with rosebuds and painted in the Kakiemon manner with a dragon among turquoise and yellow cloud scrolls above two crabs by shrubs and grasses, within a border of iron red scrolling foliage and gilt flowerheads, c1765, 6½ in (16.5 cm) wide. **$2,500-3,500**

The pattern name derives from an association with the Earl of Coventry who was blinded following a hunting accident in 1780. He is reputed to have enjoyed feeling the moulded pattern and presumably the name was coined as a result.

A pair of Worcester plates, painted in the atelier of James Giles, the centres with a bouquet of fruit including a sliced apple and peach, the borders with fruit and insects, and with gilt line rim, minute flaking to gilt rim, c1770, 8 in (19.5 cm). **$4,500-7,000**

A Worcester lobed dish, painted in a vivid 'famille verte' palette, with the Bishop Sumner Pattern, within a brown line rim, gold crescent mark, c1775, 10 in (25 cm). **$3,000-4,500**

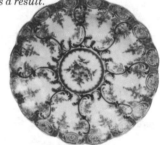

A Worcester lobed dish, from the Earl Manvers service, typically painted with berried foliage about puce C-scrolls, from a pink diaper and dot-pattern border, two minute rim chip repairs, c1770, 9 in (22.5 cm). **$1,000-1,200**

A Worcester plate, with the 100 Antiquities pattern, with scalloped edge, with pseudo Chinese character mark, c1770. **$500-600**

A Worcester foliage-moulded octafoil dish, painted with a central bouquet of flowers and leaves, edged in green and with puce veins, the border with puce C-scrolls, c1770, 11 in (27.5 cm) wide. **$3,500-5,000**

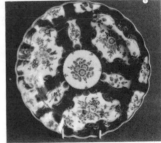

A pair of Worcester scalloped edged plates, with scale blue ground, decorated with flowers, with a square seal mark, c1770. **$1,200-1,500**

A Worcester kidney-shaped dish, painted in the 'famille verte' palette, with The Dragon in Compartments Pattern, lightly enriched in gilding, c1770, 10½ in (26.5 cm) wide. **$700-1,000**

A Worcester green-ground plate, c1775, 8½ in (21 cm). **$1,200-1,500**

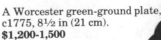

A Worcester kidney-shaped dish, painted in the manner of Duvivier, with spotted hounds in a landscape, c1775, 10½ in (26 cm) wide. **$2,500-3,500**

Duvivier worked as a decorator at several eighteenth century factories. His work is of excellent quality and fetches high prices.

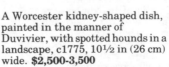

A Worcester armorial plate, decorated in colours, within a blue border suspending swags of fruit and foliage and enriched in gilding, blue crescent mark, rim chip, c1785, 9 in (22 cm). **$1,000-1,200**

The arms are those of Bostock with Rich in pretence. The service was perhaps commissioned by the Rev. Charles Bostock of Shirley House Co. Hants, who married in 1784 Mary Francis, only daughter and heir of Lt.-Gen. Sir Robert Rich of Rose Hall, Co. Suffolk.

A Worcester (Flight & Barr) botanical centre dish, the centre finely painted with Chinese Apple Tree within a green border reserved with panels of pink roses on a gold ground, script mark, c1810, 14½ in (36 cm) wide. **$1,000-1,200**

A set of fourteen Chamberlain's Worcester plates, enamelled in brilliant turquoise, blue, green and iron red and gilt, 'Chamberlain's Worcester' inscribed in puce script, five small rim cracks, chip, late 18th/early 19th C, 9½ in (24 cm). **$3,000-4,500**

A fine Flight Worcester 'Hope Service' soup plate, painted en grisaille by John Pennington with a figure of Hope seated on a rock near an anchor and gazing out to sea, a ship in full sail in the background, crowned Flight and crescent mark in underglaze blue 1790-1792, 10 in (25 cm). **$1,500-2,200**

John Flight's diary records that the Duke of Clarence chose 'Hope' as the theme for this service from three specimen patterns provided - 'Arabesque', 'Peace and Abundance' and 'Hope and Patience'.

A set of nine Chamberlain Worcester dessert plates, printed crowned 'Regent China' mark, three damaged, minor rubbing to gilding, c1820, 8½ in (21 cm). **$1,400-1,700**

A pair of Worcester (Flight, Barr & Barr) armorial plates, the central coat-of-arms in black and gold surrounded by a green border gilt, impressed mark of BFB and printed mark of FB&B, c1813, minor rubbing to gilding, 8½ in (21 cm). **$500-600**

A rare Kerr and Binns Worcester plate, painted with a classical scene within an ornate blue and gilt border, and bearing an indistinct signature amongst the foliage on the painting, impressed circle mark, c1855, 9 in (23 cm). **$800-1,200**

It is thought that pieces were allowed to be signed in this way only once; when the porcelain artist had completed his seven-year term of apprenticeship.

A Chamberlain's Worcester armorial dessert dish, painted by P. Bradley, the pale yellow ground reserved with the crest of a collared hind head surrounded by finely painted wild flowers, impressed 'Chamberlains', inscribed 'P. Bradley' in puce script, 13 in (35.5 cm). **$500-600**

A Flight, Barr & Barr dessert plate, with a scene of Grappen Hall, Cheshire, with triple gilding, 1820-1830, 10 in (25 cm). **$500-700**

A Worcester plate, painted with a butterfly, flowers and ferns, within a floral and gilt border, probably decorated outside the factory by Thomas Shaw, impressed circle and Worcester mark, painted initials and date 1876 on the reverse, 9 in (22.5 cm). **$300-400**

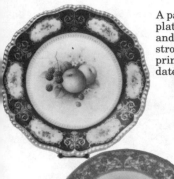

A pair of Royal Worcester dessert plates, painted with sprays of fruit and blossom in characteristic strong colours, signed A. Shuck, printed Royal Worcester marks, date codes for 1936. **$300-400**

A Royal Worcester plate, painted with fruit by George Cole, signed, within a blue and pink ground border with foliate scrollwork in raised gilding, printed crowned circle mark in puce, date code for 1912, 9 in (22.5 cm). **$400-600**

A Royal Worcester plate, decorated by Harry Davis with a view of Loch Fyne, in an atmospheric early morning light, signed H. Davis, script title, date code for 1903, 9½ in (23.5 cm). **$600-900**

A pair of Royal Worcester dessert plates, painted by R. Rushton with Ships Off Hastings and a View of Tours within gilt entwined fruiting vine borders, signed, puce printed marks and date code for 1914, pattern no.C/946, 9½ in (23.5 cm). **$600-900**

Icepails

A pair of Sèvres seaux-a-bouteilles, the shaped panels edged with cisele gilt and reserved on the bleu nouveau ground further enriched with symmetrical gilding, blue interlaced L marks and the letters p and u, and the gilders mark of Le Guay, c1768, 4 in (10.5 cm). **$2,000-3,000**

A rare Sèvres seau a bouteille, painted with X-form green scrolls picked out in gilding enclosing swags and rings of flowers, incised, floreated interlaced Ls, two dots above and two at apex, restored, c1757, 6½ in (16.5 cm). **$3,000-4,500**

Lazare Duvaux sold a service similarly painted with green scrolls to Madame de Pompadour in 1757 and the Maria Theresa service of the following year had similar decoration.

A pair of Marcolini Meissen ice pails, covers and liners enamelled with bouquets and sprays of Manierblumen within gilt-line borders, crossed swords marks in underglaze blue, c1780, 9 in (23 cm) wide. **$3,000-4,000**

A pair of Sèvres-pattern turquoise-ground jewelled seaux, with gilt band and white and ruby jewelled cartouches flanked by hatched and floral decoration, waved gilt rims, imitation interlaced L and initial marks, c1880, 7 in (17 cm) wide. **$1,000-1,400**

A pair of ice pails, liners and covers, painted by P. Bradley with cyclamen, iris, roses and other flowers, embellished in gilding and set with vine moulded handles with Pan masks, yellow-washed foot, simulated marble base, signed 'P. Bradley' in puce script, stress cracks to bases, c1830, 13 in (33 cm). **$14,000-17,000**

A pair of Paris royal blue ground ice pails, covers and liners, painted in colours with sprays of garden flowers, iron red stencilled Darte, Palais Royale No 21, marks, both liners chipped, one vase with small chip to stem and restoration to rim, c1823, 18 in (44 cm) high. **$3,000-4,000**

Ink Wells

A Meissen turquoise-ground inkpot and sander from an ink-stand, the turquoise ground reserved with panels enclosing figures in landscapes, traces of blue crossed swords marks, pressnummer 30, one corner repaired, c1745, 2½ in square (6 cm). **$600-900**

A Berlin desk set, modelled by Friedrich Elias Meyer, in the white, sceptre mark in underglaze blue, impressed and incised numerals and letters, damage to bell, a later replacement, c1763, 11½ in (28.5 cm).
$1,700-2,500

This model was made in two variations, differing in the presence of a figure of Mercury or a candlestick. The Furstenberg factory copied the shape of the inkwell and sandcaster.

A Minton pale blue-ground rectangular desk set, the ground painted with specimen feathers, some restoration to one foot, covers and by handle, c1830, 7 in wide (18 cm).
$600-900

A Flight & Barr inkstand, applied with a handle in the form of a serpent, covered with a gold decorated orange glaze and painted with a panel of colourful feathers, marked with an incised B, the knop on two of the covers, repaired, 7 in wide (17 cm).
$1,500-2,200

Jardinieres

A Derby bough pot and pierced domed cover, painted with a landscape at sunset, named on the base 'Treath Maur, Wales' in blue, and attributed to George Robertson, on a gilt vermicelli ground between bands of salmon pink and gilding with a continuous band of gilt rosebuds and leaves to the base, crown, crossed batons and D in blue, small hair crack to cover, 1797-1800, 8 by 12 in (20 by 30 cm). **$1,700-2,500**

A pair of Sèvres jardinières, each with gilt scroll handles and painted by Rosset and Leve with panels of flowers reserved on a gilt cailloute bleu nouveau ground, incised and interlaced Ls, painters marks and date letters N for 1766, firing faults, gilding worn, 12 in (29 cm) across handles.
$3,500-5,000

Comparison with the flower painting on other Rosset and Levé examples leaves little doubt that they are of the date indicated, but the gilding, and possibly the ground also, are of later date.

A Coalport jardinière, with gilt rams head handles, painted with river scenes by J. H. Plant within richly gilt borders, on a yellow and dark blue ground, printed mark, 15 in (37 cm) wide.
$1,200-1,500

A pair of Royal Worcester jardinières, painted in colours with pheasant and partridge in misty wooded landscape vignettes, green printed marks, c1882, 7 in wide (18 cm). **$600-900**

A pair of Pinxton D-shaped bough pots, painted with spiral pink bands edged in gilding dividing trailing flowers, between gilt line rims and gilt foliage and cherry borders, one extensively cracked one with small chip to base, c1800 7 in wide (17 cm). **$1,300-1,700**

◀ A pair of Sèvres jardinières, painted with the head and shoulders of a woman within a border of flowering vines outlined with gilt scrolls and flowers on a dark blue ground, gilt metal mounts, 4½ in (11 cm).
$1,000-1,400

Miller's is a price GUIDE not a price LIST

The price ranges given reflect the average price a purchaser should pay for similar items. Condition, rarity of design or pattern, size, colour, pedigree, restoration and many other factors must be taken into account when assessing values.

Jugs

Bow sparrow beak cream jug, with 'famille rose' pattern, 1752-1754. **$500-600**

Bow jug, 1760-1765. **300-400**

Coalport cream jug with sprig bouquet pattern , c1870, 4 in (10 cm). **$50-70**

Mennecy white jug and cover, with contemporary hinged silver mount, moulded with sprays of prunus in relief, incised DV mark, the silver with decharge mark of Julien Berthe, c1740, 4½ in (11.5 cm). **$2,000-3,000**

A porcelain pitcher, internal firing defect, by William Tucker's American China Manufactory, 1826-1838, 9in (22.5cm). **$1,300-1,500**

A Derby jug, the painting attributed to Mountford, red marked, hairline crack on spout, c1810. **$100-200**

A Coalport milk jug, c1891, 8 in (20 cm). **$60-90**

A Coalport hand painted jug, initialled 'W.P.' and dated 1825, 11 in (27 cm). **$300-400**

A Coalport milk jug, c1880, 6 in (15 cm). **$50-70**

A Lowestoft blue and white milk jug, painted with flowers and pierced rockwork in a fenced garden, 3 in (8 cm). **$300-400**

A Meissen hot-milk jug and cover, painted in puce, enriched with gilding, with contemporary hinged silver-gilt mount, blue crossed swords mark, c1745, 5½ in (14 cm).**$1,300-1,700**

LOWESTOFT

★ soft paste porcelain using bone ash
★ damage tends to stain brown
★ from 1757 to 1766 only blue and white painted wares produced
★ printed and coloured wares introduced c.1766
★ decoration of early wares is well detailed and less stylized than post 1765
★ collectors are interested in unusual shapes
★ coloured wares presently undervalued
★ no factory mark but many pieces pre-1775 numbered inside footrim or on base if no footrim
★ numbers are usually between 1 and 11

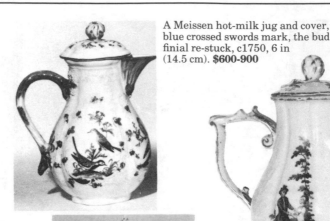

A Meissen hot-milk jug and cover, blue crossed swords mark, the bud finial re-stuck, c1750, 6 in (14.5 cm). **$600-900**

A Meissen (Augustus Rex) white jug, for the Japanese Palace, formed as a fabulous beast, blue AR marks, extensively fire-cracked and repaired, probably 18th century, 28 in (70 cm). **$7,500-10,500**

The 'Umtier Krug' was one of the earliest animal pieces conceived for the Japanese Palace. The model was worked on by Kirchner around 1730.
No examples of this model seem to have been fired successfully. Two variant types exist.
Although it is known approximately when these figures were first produced, there is no clear evidence as to when their manufacture was finally abandoned.

A Meissen jug and cover, painted in 'famille verte' style with the 'Vogelbaum' pattern, crossed swords in underglaze blue, repairer's mark oo incised, chip to handle, c1735, 6 in (15 cm). **$4,000-5,000**

A Meissen hot-milk jug, of Grune Watteau type, moulded with 'Gotzkowsky erhabene Blumen' and lovers in 'kupfergrun' and flesh tints in landscape vignettes, blue crossed swords and gilt 57 mark, glaze slightly worn, c1745 5½ in (14 cm). **$800-1,200**

A Meissen cream jug, painted with Chinese figures in a landscape, on a bright yellow ground, painted crossed swords mark within a double circle in underglaze blue, slight glaze scratch, c1735, 3 in (6 cm). **$4,500-7,000**

A Newhall clip handle jug, pattern no. 140, c1790. **$300-400**

A Newhall silver shaped jug, pattern no. 213, 1790-1795. **$100-200**

A Newhall London shaped jug, pattern no. 856, c1810. **$200-300**

A Newhall boat-shaped jug, pattern no. 455, slightly worn, 1795-1800. **$100-150**

A Sèvres milk jug, painted by Bouillat pere with loops of flowers hung between apple-green and gilt feathery scrolls, incised interlaced Ls, gilders mark IN and painter's mark y, date letters CC for 1780, 5 in (12.5 cm). **$1,000-1,200**

Etienne-Francois Bouillat, working 1758-1810.
Milk jugs of this form were made three sizes of which this example the largest.

A Sèvres milk jug, painted by Evans, gilt borders reserved on the bright blue ground, c1700, 4 in (9.5 cm). **$700-900**

A Vincennes bleu celeste milk jug and cover, painted with bouquets of garden flowers with gilt enrichment, blue interlaced L marks enclosing the date letter A for 1753 and painter's mark 4, 5½ in (14 cm). **$4,000-5,000**

A Worcester blue and white sparrow beak jug, printed on one side with a Chinese fenced garden scene and on the other with a Pagoda in a landscape, c1770, 4 in (10.5 cm). **$300-400**

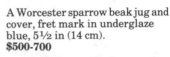

A Worcester sparrow beak jug and cover, fret mark in underglaze blue, 5½ in (14 cm). **$500-700**

A first period Worcester cream jug, with sparrow beak spout, painted with a spiral 'whorl' pattern in pink and iron red between dark blue bands, with scrolls in white and gold, square seal mark, 4 in (10 cm). **$500-700**

A Worcester pear-shaped milk jug and cover, transfer printed with 'The Milkmaids' the reverse with travellers in a landscape, c1770, 5 in (13 cm). **$1,000-1,200**

A Worcester mask-jug, gilded and painted, with flowers between blue borders, slight chip to lip, blue crescent mark, c1775, 7½ in (19 cm). **$1,200-1,500**

A Worcester blue and white cabbage-leaf mask jug, transfer printed with a parrot and fruit, c1775, 9 in (22.5cm). **$400-600**

A Worcester blue and white cabbage-leaf mask jug, printed with rare floral and fruit patterns, hatched crescent mark, 1770-1775, 11½ in (28.5 cm). **$1,300-1,700**

Mugs

A Bow mug, with grooved loop handle and heart-shaped terminal, painted in 'famille-rose' palette, brown edged rim, handle repaired, 1760-1765, 5 in (12.5 cm). **$400-600**

A fine Derby Porter mug, the border of gold scrollwork reserving the initials NB, painted in rich colours probably by Daniel Lucas, with a view of the City of Derby including the shot-tower built in 1809, crown, crossed batons and D mark in red, script title 'View of Derby', 5½ in (13.5 cm). **$1,500-2,200**

A rare Bow baluster-shaped 'Golfer and Caddy' pattern mug, painter's numeral 45, typical overall crazing, minor chips on rim, 1760-1765, 5 in (12.5 cm). **$1,700-2,500**

A Lowestoft mug, c1785, 4½ in (10.5 cm). **$700-900**

A Sèvres-pattern turquoise ground mug, reserved and decorated with a gallant and his companion, within white, ruby and turquoise jewelled and gilt oval cartouche, gilt dentil rim, imitation interlaced L mark, c1880, 4 in (10 cm). **$600-900**

A Worcester bell-shaped mug, naively painted in blue with three birds in branches, grooved strap handle chip, early 1750's 4 in (9 cm). **$1,400-1,700**

A Worcester blue and white flared mug, painted with The Root pattern extending over the rim to the interior, painter's mark, c1756, 2½ in high (6.5 cm). **$1,000-1,400**

A Worcester blue and white tankard, with strap handle, painted with The Root Pattern, painter's mark to base of handle, star crack to base, firing crack to top of handle, c1755, 6½ in (14 cm). **$1,300-1,700**

A Worcester blue and white small mug, painted with the Landslide pattern, painter's mark, c1758, 2 in (6 cm). **$1,200-1,500**

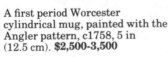

A first period Worcester cylindrical mug, painted with the Angler pattern, c1758, 5 in (12.5 cm). **$2,500-3,500**

A Worcester blue and white m[...] reserved on a cracked-ice grou[...] with stylised flowerheads, blue[...] crescent mark, crack to top of handle, c1765, 5 in (12 cm). **$1,200-1,500**

A Worcester yellow-ground mug, painted with two panels of river islands in puce, with an iron-red scroll-pattern border, rim chip, c1765, 3½ in (8.5 cm). **$1,500-2,200**

A Worcester blue and white mug, painter's mark, small rim restorations, c1758, 3½ in (8.5 cm). **$1,200-1,500**

MAKE THE MOST OF MILLER'S

Price ranges in this book reflect what one should expect to pay for a similar example. When selling one can obviously expect a figure below. This will fluctuate according to a dealer's stock, saleability at a particular time, etc. It is always advisable to approach a reputable specialist dealer or an auction house which has specialist sales.

A Worcester mug, painted in a bright famille rose palette with Oriental figures on a terrace by an iron-red fence, with iron-red foliage and bands of puce diaper-pattern, c1765, 6 in (14.5 cm). **$1,300-1,700**

A Worcester blue and white baluster mug, transfer printed with a loose bouquet containing a rose and a lily, a slight crack to rim, minute star crack to base, c1765, 5 in (12 cm). **$300-500**

A Worcester blue-scale mug, painted in a bright palette with birds and insects on a blue-scale ground, blue crescent mark, c1775, 5 in (12 cm). **$1,500-2,200**

A Worcester Imari-pattern bell-shaped mug, painted with Oriental flowering shrubs divided by orange bands gilt with diaper-pattern and reserved with mons, c1768, 6 in (15.5 cm). **$1,200-1,500**

A Worcester mug, of Lord Henry Thynne type, painted with a ruin on a river island within a turquoise and gilt scroll surround between bright blue borders gilt with diamond-pattern, blue crescent mark, c1775, 5 in (12.5 cm). **$2,000-3,000**

A Worcester mug, with the monogram WNA within an oval turquoise fishroe and gilt C-scroll cartouche, blue crescent mark, c1775, 5 in (12 cm). $1,000-1,200
Cf.H. Rissik Marshall, Coloured Worcester porcelain of the First Period, pl. 20, no. 365.

Plaques

A 'K.P.M.' Berlin plaque, painted with a Christian allegory of Jesus accompanied by the Holy Mother, children and angels, impressed K.P.M. and sceptre mark, gilt frame, mid-19thC, 12 by 10 in (31 by 25 cm). **$1,400-1,700**

A Berlin plaque, painted by E. Ens after F. Mieris with a portrait of a learned figure, giltwood frame, signed and dated 1860, 11 by 9 in (28 by 22 cm). **$1,000-1,400**

A Berlin plaque, painted with the portrait of a bearded old man, carved giltwood frame, impressed sceptre and K.P.M. marks, c1880, 7 by 6 in (18 by 15 cm). $600-900

A Berlin plaque, painted with a portrait of a young woman in Tudor dress, impressed sceptre and K.P.M. marks, c1880, 13 by 10 in (34 by 23 cm). $1,400-1,700

A Berlin K.P.M. oval plaque, painted in colours by Weigel signed with a portrait of Marie Antoinette, giltwood frame, impressed sceptre K.P.M., letters and numerals, c1840, 14 in by 11 (35 by 28 cm). **$1,400-1,700**

A pair of English porcelain floral plaques, perhaps Coalport, signed P. Scott and S. Baker, c1870, 6 in (15 cm). **$600-700**

A pair of Vienna plaques, signed Wagner, entitled Reflection and Blossom, giltwood frames, 13 in (34 cm). **$7,500-10,500**

A Royal Worcester plaque, with swans against a blue sky, green printed marks, impressed numerals, painted and signed by C. Baldwin, c1902, 12 in (30 cm). **$2,000-3,000**

An English porcelain floral and fruit plaque, c1820, 7 in (17 cm). **$600-700**

A pair of German porcelain plaques, painted with Psyche scantily draped, c1880, 12 by 9 in (30 by 22 cm). **$2,500-3,500**

A continental porcelain plaque, painted by Ed. Brochart, depicting the execution of Mary, Queen of Scots, in gilt frame, signed, 9 by 8 (22 by 19 cm). **$1,000-1,200**

A continental porcelain plaque, depicting a woman returning from a mask ball, in gilt frame, 9 by 7 in (22 by 16 cm). **$1,000-1,400**

Pots

A Crown Derby pot pourri vase and cover, decorated in raised gold and silver lustre on an ivory ground between elaborate claret, turquoise and gilt borders, red and sepia printed marks, cover cracked, c1880, 14 in (35 cm). **$500-600**

A Coalport posy pot with two gilded handles, c1880, 4 in (10 cm). **$150-200**

A Höchst yellow-ground chocolate-pot and cover, in the Meissen style, painted with harbour scenes en camaieu rose, metal fittings to the cover, gilt wheel mark, c1755, 7 in (17 cm). **$1,500-2,200**

A pot pourri and two covers, painted in underglaze blue, iron-red, puce, mauve, green, black and gilding, Derby mark on inner cover in iron-red, knop to inner cover glued, cover glued, 19 in (48 cm). **$1,300-1,700**

A Meissen chocolate pot and cover, the background in grey monochrome, the knop and handle in green-stained ivory, cover and base both with gilt A, impressed 23, spout damaged, c1745, 7 in (18 cm). $2,000-3,000

A pair of Ludwigsburg rococo pot pourri vases and pierced covers, in blue enamel and gold enclosing landscape panels en camaieu brun, blue interlaced C marks, minor damages, c1770, 11 in (28 cm). $3,000-4,500

This model was originally made at Frankenthal.

A 'Sèvres' ormolu mounted pot pourri vase and cover, with elaborate gilt foliate scroll borders on a rich blue ground, interlaced L's in blue, late 19thC, 19 in (49 cm). $3,000-4,000

HÖCHST

★ factory was founded in 1746 by the painter A.F. von Löwenfinck from Meissen
★ porcelain was produced from 1750
★ milk-white in colour, almost tin-glazed appearance
★ early wares tended to have poor translucency and be somewhat heavy
★ from 1758-65 the style reminiscent of the French 'Louis Seize' style came into fashion
★ this style was continued and developed by J.P. Melchior who was chief modeller 1767-79
★ the base of figures from 1765 tends to be in the form of a distinctive grassy mound, executed in dark café-au-lait and green stripes
★ the factory closed in 1796

A Minton jar and cover, painted with panels of peaches, grapes, blackberries and cherries on a flower-encrusted ground, star crack, 1830-1840, 12 in (30 cm). $600-900

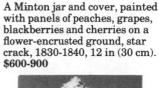

A Minton pot-pourri bowl, cover and stand, painted on one side with 'Carisbrook Castle' in tones of brown and green, blue crossed swords, minor hairline at rim, chips and enamel flaked, c1825-1830, 9 in (22 cm). $600-900

A St. Cloud gilt-metal mounted white pot-pourri vase and cover, the contemporary gilt-metal mounts with further porcelain flowers, the cover repaired, minor chips, c1740, 11 in (26 cm). $7,000-9,000

French soft-paste potiche and cover, decorated by Jean-Adam Mathieu, picked out in polychrome enamels on a solid gilt ground, the base signed Mathieu, gilding rubbed, knop reset, chips, 1745-1750, 3 in (7 cm). $4,500-7,000

Jean-Adam Mathieu, enameller to Louis XV, was in charge of the decoration at Vincennes from about 1745 to 1753.

A Royal Worcester pot pourri jar and cover, painted by C. Balwyn, the azure ground with pink, green, brown and gilt details, signed, printed crowned circle mark, shape number 1515, date code, c1902, 8 in (20 cm). $2,500-3,500

A Royal Worcester pot pourri bowl and cover, painted with highland cattle and mountainous landscape by James Stinton, 5 in (11 cm). $400-600

A Royal Worcester pot pourri, painted by Roberts, on a mottled blue/green ground, signed, puce printed mark and date code for 1907, shape no. 1428, knop glued, 13 in (33 cm). **$1,300-1,700**

A Royal Worcester pot pourri jar and pierced cover, painted in autumnal colours with highland cattle in a landscape by John Stinton jnr. printed mark and date code for 1923, 7 in (16 cm). **$400-600**

A Royal Worcester pot pourri vase, cover and liner, painted with spring and summer flowers, in colours in a shaded cream ground, printed marks in pink and numbered 1286, knop chipped, 10 in (25 cm). **$500-700**

Sauceboats

A pair of Derby blue and white sauceboats, printed with Oriental figures and buildings, c1765, 7 in wide (18 cm). **$300-400**

A pair of Bow sauceboats, modelled in high relief with flowers, and gilt both inside and out with flower branches and a scroll border, c 1750, 9 in (22 cm). **$1,700-2,500**

A similar sauceboat shape with a dragon handle is known. The shape is rare and is known in both polychrome and 'in the white'. No blue and white examples have been recorded.

A pair of Derby sauceboats of small size, each moulded with overlapping leaves, decorated in puce camaieu and gilding with flower sprays, slight chips, 5 in (12 cm). **$600-900**

A Lowestoft blue and white oval sauce-boat printed with flower sprays on a pleated ground, c177 6 in (15 cm). **$100-200**

The Lowestoft factory made something of a speciality of sauce-boats. This type is fairly common. Painted blue and white as opposed to printed, examples would be worth more. Polychrome examples are rare.

A Meissen chinoiserie cream-pot, painted in the manner of J.G. Herold, blue crossed sword mark and gilder's H, c1728, 6 in (16 cm). **$2,000-3,000**

A Worcester blue and white butter boat, with workman's mark of a cross within a circle below the handle, c1754, 4 in (10 cm). **$2,500-3,500**

An extremely rare pattern known as 'The Creamboat Warbler'. The name derives from the use of a bird motif below the lip of the creamboat. The pattern appears on only two shapes, the illustrated creamboat and a similar small sauceboat of more elongated form with a scroll handle.

A Worcester oval sauceboat, painted in a bright famille rose palette with an Oriental in a fenced garden, crack to rim and foot, c1754, 10 in (24 cm). **$800-1,200**

A Worcester blue and white fluted oval butter boat, painted with the twisted root pattern, painters mark, 4 in wide (10 cm).
$1,300-1,700

A Worcester pleated oval sauce-boat, painted with swags of flowers within shaped moulded cartouches enriched in green and puce, with vivid yellow-ground, c1765, 6 in (15 cm).
$3,000-4,500

A matched pair of first period Worcester sauce-boats, printed in underglaze blue with flowers with narrow blue diaper borders, open crescent marks, 7 in (19 cm).
$500-600

A Worcester spirally-moulded helmet-shaped cream-jug, painted in a famille rose palette, slight rim chip, c1770, 3 in (9 cm).
$1,300-1,700

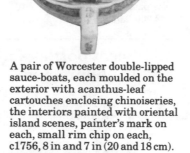

A pair of Worcester double-lipped sauce-boats, each moulded on the exterior with acanthus-leaf cartouches enclosing chinoiseries, the interiors painted with oriental island scenes, painter's mark on each, small rim chip on each, c1756, 8 in and 7 in (20 and 18 cm).
$1,700-2,500

These particularly well painted, early examples would fall at the upper end of the price range. The pattern is one associated with this type of sauceboat, c1756-1775 and the flair with which it is executed combined with condition and date of production, affects the value considerably.

A Worcester blue and white scale-moulded oval sauceboat painted with an Oriental in a garden and another fishing from a river island within moulded cartouches, blue crescent mark, c1760, 8 in (18 cm). **$800-1,200**

This uncommon pattern is called 'Man with a Bomb' by Branyan, French and Sandon in 'Worcester Blue and White Porcelain 1751-1790' P.74 IA31. The pattern is generally associated with this particular form of sauceboat.

A first period Worcester sauce-boat, painted in underglaze blue with Chinese river scenes, the inside painted with flowers and a panel of diaper pattern, scroll handle, 6 in (17 cm).
$600-800

A Worcester blue and white shell-moulded cream-boat, with lamprey handle and moulded entwined dolphins beneath the lip, painted with trailing flowers and insects, blue crescent mark, c1765, 3 in (9 cm).
$14,000-17,000

Similar cream-boats were made at Lowestoft, Derby and Liverpool. Worcester examples are rare. Derby examples are fairly common ($300-500)

A Worcester pear-shaped cream-jug, painted with flower-sprays, the interior with a gilt line and iron-red loop pattern border, c1765, 3 in (8 cm).
$700-900

A Worcester outside-decorated cream-jug painted with loose bouquets in a predominently pink, iron-red and blue palette, the interior border inscribed 'Desire the sincere milk of the word. Prov.' c1770, 4 in (10 cm).
$1,700-2,500

It is rare to find inscriptions on Worcester wares of this period. A similar jug, lacking the inscription, would be valued at $300-600

A Worcester flared cream-boat, painted with flowers, the interior rim with gilt and iron-red loop and dot-pattern, c1765, 5 in (11 cm). $2,000-3,000

A pair of Worcester sauce-boats, painted in coloured enamels with sprigs and insects, brown-edged rims, workmen's marks in sepia, c1760, 7 in (18 cm). $1,300-1,700

Scent bottles and bonbonnieres

◄ A Chelsea gold-mounted scent-bottle and stopper, c1765, 3 in (9 cm). $1,400-1,700

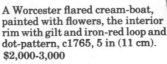

A Chelsea gold-mounted scent-bottle, modelled as the infant Bacchus giving Cupid a drink, inscribed 'J'Anime L'Amour', the gold cover with diamond and ruby inclusions, stained, quiver and bow damaged, c1765, the mounts c1830, 3 in (9 cm). $600-700

A Chelsea gold-mounted scent-bottle and stopper, naturally modelled as a pug-bitch, base cracked, c1755, 2 in (6 cm). $1,700-2,500

A Chelsea gold-mounted scent bottle and stopper, modelled as Cupid, damage to quiver, repair t base, c1755, 3 in (7 cm). $800-1,200

A 'Girl in a swing' gold-mounted scent-bottle and stopper, modelled as a girl in a flowered dress and apron and yellow hat, playing the hurdy-gurdy, slight crack to base, minor damage beneath neck mount, restoration to hat, 1751-1754, 3 in (8.5 cm). $2,500-3,500

Cf. George Savage, 18thC English Porcelain, pl. 19(b) and Kate Foster, 'Chelsea Scent Bottles-'Girl in a swing' and another Group', E.C.C. Transactions, Vol. 6, Pt. 3, pl. 208(b).

A Chelsea gold-mounted double scent-bottle, modelled as a nun in black and white habit holding a rosary, restoration to base and stoppers, c 1755, 4 in (10 cm). $1,500-2,200

A 'Girl in a swing' gold and enamel-mounted bonbonniere, the moss agate cover fitted with a mirror and with the motto 'Leurs Atteinte Est Mortelle', 1751-1754, 1 in (3 cm). $2,000-3,000

A Chelsea gilt-metal-mounted scent-bottle and stopper, modelle as Orpheus playing his lyre with lion, a fox, a dog, a bird and squirrel, restoration to instrument and right arm, c1765 4 in (10 cm). $1,500-2,200

A 'Girl in a swing' gold-mounted scent-bottle and stopper modelled as an oval vase of garden flowers painted with bouquets, the neck with gold and enamel collar and with butterfly stopper, minute chipping to stopper and flowers, 1750-1754, 3 in (9 cm).
$3,500-5,000

This rare scent bottle forms an interesting link between 'Girl in a Swing' domestic wares and the more ornamental pieces.

A gold-mounted scent-bottle and stopper, of 'Girl in a Swing', type, stopper restored, c1755, 4 in (10 cm). **$2,000-3,000**

A gilt-metal-mounted scent-bottle and a stopper, of a 'Girl in a Swing' type, some chipping and repair to base, c1755, 3½ in (8.5 cm).
$1,200-1,500
Cf. G.E. Bryant, op. cit., pl. 26. no. 6

Mennecy 'Chasseur' bonbonnière, the figure wearing a blue-spotted jacket, pink and yellow hat, pink breeches and yellow hose, his dog at his feet with silver-mounted hinged cover, the interior with floral sprays and sprigs, slight wear and small chips to hat, probably remounted, mid-18thC, 3 in (7 cm).
$1,300-1,700

A rare Rockingham scent sprinkler, with a lilac ground, encrusted with finely modelled and coloured flowers, marked CL2 in red, 5 in (11.5 cm). **$1,000-1,200**

A Saint-Cloud bonbonnière, modelled as a shepherd, the silver-mounted hinged cover also decorated inside and out with flowers, in Kakiemon style, the silver with French control mark, minor wear, mid-18thC, 3 in (7 cm). **$1,500-2,200**

A Grainger's Worcester scent bottle and stopper, painted with a scene of Worcester, named on the base, on a blue celeste ground with gilt borders, script mark Grainger Lee & Co. Worcester in iron-red, c1815, 5 in (11 cm).
$1,000-1,200

Services

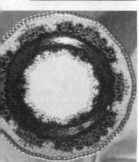

Coalport very heavy part dessert service, comprising: twelve plates, six dishes in three shapes and one comport.
$1,300-1,700

Various Belleck 'Neptune' and 'Tridacna' pattern tea wares, the majority 1891-1926, each piece tinted in pale green, pale blue or pink, comprising: two tea pots and covers, a sugar bowl, two milk jugs, twelve cups and saucers, five tea plates and two cake plates, printed dog and harp mark, several items cracked.
$800-1,200

A Coalport dessert service, decorated with gilt-edged panels of coloured flowers reserved on a 'gros-bleu' ground, comprising: sauce tureen, cover and stand, shaped rectangular centre dish, six dishes and eight plates, c1830.
$2,500-3,500

A Coalport part dessert service, painted in colours, comprising: four stands, thirteen plates, one with hair crack, pattern no. 5/684, c1845. $3,000-4,500

A Coalport dessert service, each piece painted with a different flower spray, the borders with reserves of flowers on a dark blue ground, comprising: five comports, four footed dishes, eighteen plates and one comport in two parts. $4,000-5,000

A Daniels part dessert service, with pink and gilt borders comprising: three dishes, and six plates, pattern 4021, c1830. $600-900

An early Derby part coffee service painted in 'famille-rose' enamels with chinoiserie figures, the chai link borders in iron red and gilding, comprising: coffee pot ar cover, six coffee cups, two coffee cups with stained foot rim, coffee pot slightly stained, cover with small hairline crack, 1758-1760. $2,500-3,500

A 19th century Davenport part amorial dessert service, with apple green borders, painted with central amorial crest against a white ground, comprising: twelve plates, three comports, two dishes, and two comports and covers. $4,000-5,000

A Doccia dessert service, comprising: two baskets and stands, nine bowls, and ten plates, some wear, one basket and stand, one bowl and two plates damaged, c1760. $2,000-3,000

DOCCIA

★ factory started by Carlo Ginori, near Florence in 1735
★ hybrid hard paste porcelain of pronounced greyish-white appearance
★ body liable to firecracks
★ often decorated with mythological, religious and hunting subjects
★ glaze can have a 'smudgy' look
★ used strong enamel colours
★ from 1757-91 the factory was directed by Lorenzo Ginori, glaze and body improved considerably
★ figures often in the white and sometimes decorated with an iron-red colour exclusive to the factory
★ porcelain often confused with Capodimonte, although Doccia is hard paste and Capodimonte soft-paste
★ around 1770 figures covered in a white tin-glaze, often firecracked
★ factory still exists

An extensive Royal Crown Derby dinner service, comprising: two vegetable tureens and cover, two sauce tureens, covers and stands, six oval serving dishes in sizes, eighteen soup plates, eighteen meat plates, eighteen dessert plates and eighteen cheese plates, red printed marks with date codes, 1905 and 1912. $3,500-5,000

Unless otherwise stated, any description which refers to 'a set' or 'a pair' includes a valuation for the entire set or the pair, even though the illustration may show only a single item.

A Derby breakfast, tea and coffee service, decorated with an Imari pattern, comprising: teapot, cover and stand, sucrier and cover, nine cups and saucers, twelve coffee cans and ten saucers, eight teacups and ten saucers, twelve plates, slop bowl and five egg cups, crown, cross batons and script D marks in iron-red, c1820. $1,700-2,500

Miller's is completely different each year. Each edition contains completely NEW photographs. This is not an updated publication. We never repeat the same photograph.

lateVictorian Crown Derby
reakfast service of 14 pieces
ith orange floral and inset
ansfer decoration.
00-400

A Mintons porcelain part dessert
service, with a bleu-celeste rim
embellished with gilding and
white enamel studs, comprising:
twelve plates and six comports,
printed retailer's mark and date
code for 1875, damaged, 10 in
(24 cm). $600-700

A Herculaneam part dessert
service, painted with a Chinese
scrolling lotus design in iron red
and gold, comprising: two tureens
and covers, a shell dish, six dishes
and eight plates, slight
discolouration and some gold
rubbed, early 19th century.
$1,700-2,500

Fulda part tea service,
mprising: a baluster jug and
ver, a sugar bowl and cover, a
acup, four saucers, damages,
owned FF mark and impressed
, c1775. $3,500-5,000

A 22 piece tea set,
commemorating the birth of
Princess Margaret, in Royal
Paragon China. $400-600

Rockingham tea-service,
mprising a teapot, cover and
nd, a milk jug, a sugar bowl and
ver, two bread-plates twelve
ffee cups, twelve teacups and
uccrs, puce griffin mark pattern
75, c1835. $1,500-2,200

An unusual porcelain tea service
by Machin & Company, Burslem,
comprising: teapot and cover,
sugar basin and cover, milk jug,
eight cups and six saucers, some
damage and restoration, early
19th century. $600-700

A Paris porcelain coffee set, green
and gilt bordered with panels of
hand painted flowers, in Empire
style, comprising: coffee pot and
cover, milk jug, four cups and five
saucers, one cup repaired, chips,
19th century. $700-900

Ridgway tea service,
mprising: teapot and cover,
gar basin and cover, milk jug,
a plate, slop bowl, ten saucers,
n tea cups, ten deep cups,
ttern no. 3/265.
00-800

A Spode Imari pattern part tea
and coffee service, comprising a
teapot, cover and stand, a sugar
bowl and cover, a milk jug, a slop
basin, two saucer dishes, ten
teacups, five coffee cups and ten
saucers, red mark, pattern no.
967, c1815. $2,500-3,500

A Spode botanical dessert service,
comprising: sauce tureen and
cover, a bowl, six dishes and
nineteen plates, pattern no. 1875
in black, 1815-1820.
$1,300-1,700

A 'Sèvres' pattern bleu celeste
ground tête-a-tête, comprising: a
chocolate-pot and cover, a
milk-jug, a sugar basin and cover,
two cups and saucers, one saucer
restored, on a lobed circular tray,
imitation interlaced L marks, in
fitted velvet lined case, c1880.
$2,000-3,000

A Swansea part dessert service,
comprising: twenty four plates,
four serving dishes, four deep
plates, two covered sauce tureens
and two basket form compotes,
mid 19th century.
$2,500-3,500

A cased Vienna solitaire se
various impressed date code
original tooled red leather b
chipping, c1795.
$1,500-2,200

A Vienna porcelain cabinet tea
set, on matching tray, decorated
with a French blue ground, each of
the sixteen pieces signed by the
artist 'Furst', oyster pink bands on
feet and around rim of tray,
further embellished with gilding.
$500-600

◄
A Royal Worcester miniature tea
service of four pieces, signed by
various artists, comprising: teapot
and cover, sucrier and cover,
cream jug and slop bowl.
$500-600

A Worcester dessert service, wi
gilt borders and peacock design
signed by Powell, Lewis &
Jarman, one comport, two dish
and six plates.
$700-900

Sucriers

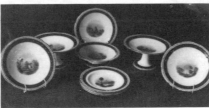

A dessert service, with blue and
gilt border, comprising: twelve
plates and six comports, 19th
century. **$300-500**

An English porcelain part dess
service, with pink borders gilt
with trailing leaves and shells,
comprising: four tazzas, two
pedestal dishes and twenty fou
plates. **$1,000-1,200**

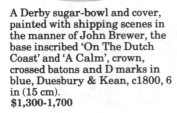

A Derby sugar-bowl and cover,
painted with shipping scenes in
the manner of John Brewer, the
base inscribed 'On The Dutch
Coast' and 'A Calm', crown,
crossed batons and D marks in
blue, Duesbury & Kean, c1800, 6
in (15 cm).
$1,300-1,700

A Meissen peach-shaped
sugar-bowl and cover, blue crossed
swords mark, minor chip to cover
and finial, base drilled for
mounting, c1750, 5 in (13 cm)
long. **$500-600**

A Meissen sugar box and cover,
painted in puce, with various
estuary scenes including figure
resting by unloaded cargo, cross
swords mark, 1725-1728, 4½ i
(11.5 cm). **$7,000-9,000**

Miller's price ranges

*The price ranges reflect
what one should expect to
pay for an item in similar
condition to that
illustrated. If you're sellin
you may be offered 30%
less. Dealers have to make
profit too! However if the
market has moved
upwards, or your piece is
particularly good example
– you could be offered mor*

Meissen Marcolini sugar-bowl
nd cover, blue crossed swords and
ar mark, c1780, 4 in diam.
1 cm). **$1,000-1,400**

A Newhall sucrier, with blue and
gold design pattern, 170, c1787.
$400-600

A Rockingham sugar-bowl and
cover, small crack to cover and
base, 1826-1830, 7 in (18 cm) wide.
$600-700

Sèvres sucrier and stand, with
arbled porphyry background
ainted with panels of fruit and
wers within ciselé gilt
rrounds on marbled grounds,
ue interlaced L's enclosing
egible date mark, chip to stand,
'65-1770. **$2,000-3,000**

*his ground colour seems
recorded.*

A Vincennes sugar-basin and
cover, ribbed in blue with gilt
ribbons and bouquets of flowers in
colours, blue interlaced L's
enclosing the date letter B for
1754, unidentified painter's mark,
4 in (10 cm) diam. **$1,000-1,200**

A Tournai sugar-bowl and cover,
on a deep blue ground, gilt crossed
swords and four cross marks, the
decoration probably Arras, c1780,
4 in (11 cm). **$400-600**

Worcester fluted sugar-bowl
d cover, with dry-blue and gilt
ellis and swags of berried foliage
tween shaped pink
aper-pattern borders, c1770, 5 in
2 cm). **$7,000-9,000**

A Worcester blue and white
documentary miniature Root
pattern saucer, the reverse
inscribed C+S 1758, 3½ in
(8.5 cm) diam, and a miniature
sugar-bowl and cover en suite,
painter's marks, c1758, 3½ in
(7 cm) diam. **$7,000-9,000**

Tankards

A Sèvres tankard, 'tasse litron'
enamelled by Tallandier with
sprays of bright summer flowers
including roses, within thin blue
lines, the mouth with gilt dentil,
interlaced Ls, painter's mark,
incised, c1760, 5 in (12 cm).
$1,700-2,500

*Vincent Taillandier, working
1753-1790.*

Bow baluster mug or tankard,
ainted with the Golfer and Caddy
ttern, c1758, 5 in by 3½ in (12.5
9 cm). **$2,000-3,000**

A silver gilt mounted Naples
tankard, late 19th century, 8 in
(20 cm). **$600-800**

183

A Vienna Du Paquier tankard, the scroll handle with foliage in iron-red and the body painted in the manner of Dannhofer with two Chinese figures beside a pagoda on a continuous terrace landscape, silvered rim to the interior, c1730, 4½ in (10.5 cm).
$5,500-7,000

Claudius Innocentius Du Paquier, started the Vienna porcelain factory in 1719. He managed to persuade two ex-Meissen employees, the arcanist C.C. Hunger and the kiln master Samuel Stolzel, to join him there. He employed many fine decorators — J.G. Herold, J.K.W. Anreiter, J.P. Dannhofer and A. Schultz.

A Worcester cylindrical tankard, painted in the workshop of James Giles with a bouquet of flowers, including a purple rose, carnation and purple and yellow tulip, c1770, 6 in (15 cm).
$1,700-2,500

A Worcester blue and white tankard, transfer printed with a building beneath a pine tree and bamboo at the side of a fence, c1770, 6 in (14.5 cm). **$200-300**

A Worcester blue and white tankard, transfer printed with a Chinese lady with a basket of flowers, blue crescent mark, c1775, 5 in (12 cm). **$600-700**

Tea and Coffee pot

A Coalport tea kettle, with Bamboo or Blue Bird pattern, c1880, 7 in (17 cm).
$200-300

A Caughley blue and white tea pot, with gilding, c1785.
$300-400

A Capodimonte Carlo III balust coffee pot and cover, painted in colours, blue fleur-de-lys mark, c1750, 10 in (25 cm).
$7,500-10,500

A Frankenthal lilac ground teapot and cover, decorated in the Meissen style, with harbour scenes within chocolate surrounds, the spout and handle enriched in gilding, blue crowned CT and AB monogram mark, c1770, 6 in (16 cm).
$4,500-7,000

A Derby tea pot, with floral decoration, c1750.
$1,000-1,200

One similar, illustrated in 'Dixon's English porcelain', pl: 33a,

A Coalport green coffee pot, c1891.
$200-300

A Derby coffee pot, with chinoiserie decoration, c1750, 1 in (25 cm). **$1,500-2,200**

A Meissen teapot and cover, painted with Chinoiserie figures brewing tea, gilder's number 44 to each piece, small chip to edge of cover and rim, some staining, 1725, 5 in (12 cm). **4,000-5,000**

A Höchst coffee pot and cover, minor damage to finial, crowned blue wheel mark and incised N, c1765, 12 in (29.5 cm). **$3,500-5,000**

The richness of the floral decoration on this piece is quite exceptional. Neither Röder nor the Mainz catalogue illustrate floral decoration of the quality.

A Ludwigsburg bullet shaped teapot and cover, painted with birds perched on branches in landscape vignettes, blue crowned interlaced C's mark and impressed ST I, minor chips to finial and rim, c1765, 6½ in (16.5 cm). **$1,200-1,500**

A Meissen teapot and cover, painted in puce, painted with merchants unloading a cargo of casks from a ship anchored in an estuary, crossed swords mark, 1725-1728, 5 in (12.5 cm). **$14,000-17,000**

This service, according to family tradition belonged to Frederick William, Duke of Brunswick. Known as the Black Duke, he was rescued during the Napoleonic wars by an English ship.

A Meissen coffee pot and cover, painted in puce with eastern merchants conversing while seamen unload casks, crossed swords mark, 1725-1728, 8 in (19.5 cm). **$7,500-10,500**

A Meissen coffee pot and a cover, painted with travellers in mountainous wooded landscapes, blue crossed swords mark and gilder's number 68, c1730, 8½ in (21.5 cm). **$3,000-4,500**

A Meissen cockerel teapot and cover, modelled by J.J. Kändler, some restoration to beak, crack to base, blue crossed swords mark, c1740, 6½ in (15.5 cm). **$2,500-3,500**

A Meissen pale powdered lilac round teapot, cover and stand, painted in the manner of B.G. Hauer with panels of harbour scenes, with bird's mask spout and shell and scroll handle enriched in iron red and gold, blue crossed swords marks, c1740, the teapot in (19 cm). **$4,000-5,000**

A Rockingham waisted coffee pot and cover, base and handle cracked, the base indistinctly inscribed, 1826-1830, 10 in (25.5 cm). **$1,200-1,500**

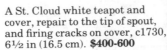

A St. Cloud white teapot and cover, repair to the tip of spout, and firing cracks on cover, c1730, 6½ in (16.5 cm). **$400-600**

185

A Worcester powder blue ground teapot and cover, minute chip to spout, iron red crescent mark to foot rim, c1765, 6 in (16 cm). **$2,000-3,000**

A Worcester teapot and cover, painted in a famille verte palette, with an Oriental by a pavilion in a shrubby landscape, the spout repaired, c1753, 4 in (11.5 cm). **$6,000-8,500**

A Worcester faceted teapot and cover, painted in a Kakiemon palette with the Jabberwocky pattern within shaped turquoise borders, chips to finial, blue square seal mark, c1770, 6 in (15.5 cm). **$3,000-4,500**

A Worcester blue scale teapot, cover and fluted stand, painted with iron red and gilt flowerheads, c1770, the teapot 6 in (15 cm) the stand 5½ in (14.5 cm) wide. **$2,000-3,000**

A Worcester Doctor Wall teapot, c1770. **$700-1,000**

A Worcester hop trellis fluted teapot, cover and stand, with pu and gilt trellis between turquois scale pattern borders enriched i gilding, the stand repaired, c177 the stand 6 in (15 cm) wide. **$3,000-4,500**

A Worcester barrel shaped teapot and cover, painted in the 'famille rose' palette, slight chip to spout and finial, c1770, 4½ in (11.5 cm). **$1,300-1,700**

A Royal Worcester teapot and cover, inscribed beneath 'Fearful consequences through the laws of natural selection and evolution of living up to one's teapot', repaired, various printed marks including factory and patent registration, patent registration 'Budge', date code for 1882, 6 in (15.2 cm). **$1,000-1,400**

A Worcester blue and white teapot, with gilding, 1775-178 5 in (12.5 cm). **$200-300**

Tureens

A Dresden ecuelle, cover and stand, blue AR mark, c1880, the stand 10 in (24.5 cm) wide. **$600-900**

A massive Capodimonte Carlo III white two-handled rococo tureen, cover and stand, the stand with impressed fleur-de-lys mark, one foot re-stuck, c1750, the stand 24 in (59 cm) wide. **$4,500-7,000**

A Derby sauce-tureen, cover an stand, painted in the manner of Steele, Crown crossed batons an D marks in iron-red, Robert Blo & Co., slight crack to stand, c181 the stand 8in (20 cm) diam. **$600-900**

A Derby butter tub, 1770-1775.
$700-1,000

A Meissen powdered-purple
ground ecuelle and cover, blue
crossed swords mark, finial
restored, c1740, 6 in diam. (15 cm).
$2,000-3,000

A pair of Meissen Kakiemon
soup-tureens and covers, painted
with birds perched on pink-lustre
branches of flowering
chrysanthemum and enriched
with gilding, blue crossed swords
marks, one handle repaired, one
finial re-stuck, hole in base
restored, chip to one cover, c1735,
11 in (28.5 cm) wide.
$3,000-4,500

A pair of Meissen
cabbage-tureens, covers and fixed
stands, the leaves naturally
modelled and coloured in green
and pink, traces of blue crossed
swords marks, Pressnummer 21,
one with minor chip to base, one
cover with minor rim chip, c1750,
9½ in (23.5 cm). $2,500-3,500
Cf. H. Morley-Fletcher: Meissen
Porcelain, pl. 80-81.

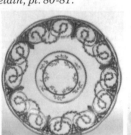

A Rockingham butter-tub, cover
and fixed stand, cracked base and
cover, 1826-1830, 8 in wide (21
cm). $800-1,200

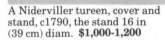

A Niderviller tureen, cover and
stand, c1790, the stand 16 in
(39 cm) diam. $1,000-1,200
Cf. Emile Tilmans: Porcelaines de
France, p. 122, for a similar tureen,
cover and stand called Strasbourg.

A Sèvres ecuelle, cover and stand,
the borders with shell motifs in
puce, pink and yellow, blue
interlaced L's enclosing date letter
for 1767 and painter's mark of
Chevenet, small chip to rim, the
lobed stand 8 in (20 cm) diam.
$3,000-4,500

A pair of Worcester
partridge-tureens and covers,
their plumage in tones of brown,
both covers extensively damaged,
c1765, 6 in (14.5 cm) diam.
$3,000-4,000

An ormolu-mounted Samson
tureen and cover, 13 in (33 cm)
diam. $3,000-4,500
The porcelain is a copy of
Chantilly.

A pair of Worcester quatrefoil
sauce tureens, covers and stands
and a ladle, painted with the
Jabberwocky pattern, handles
with minute chips, one finial
chipped one cover repaired, c1770,
the stands 10 in (24.5 cm) wide.
$4,500-7,000

A Worcester blue and white
butter-tub, cover and stand, blue
crescent mark, the stand with
extended firing cracks, c1765, the
stand 8 in (20.5 cm) wide.
$1,500-2,200

187

Vases

A Berlin commemorative vase, presented in 1844 to Carl Gottlieb Werner, the Royal Theatre Inspector on the celebration of his 50th year of service, sceptre, orb and K.P.M. marks, 19 in (46 cm). **$5,500-7,000**

A pair of Berlin urns, painted in Italian maiolica style, with emblems allegorical of 'Poetry', 'Music', 'Painting' and the 'Plastic Arts', sceptre and shield marks in underglaze-blue, 1860-1880, 11 in (27 cm). **$700-1,000**

A pair of Berlin pedestal vases and covers, relief moulded with branches and leaves, twin ram head handles, scaled pink and gilt panels, underglaze-blue sceptre mark, 19thC, 14 in (35 cm). **$800-1,200**

BERLIN

* first factory started by W.K. Wegely in 1752
* body hard to distinguish from Meissen
* particularly close are the Cupids in Disguise and the Commedia dell'Arte figures
* closed in 1757 at the start of Seven Years War
* a second factory was started in 1761 by J.E.Gotzkowsky
* many artists came from Meissen, including F.E.Meyer
* porcelain has a distinctly creamy tone
* painting was in the restrained rococo manner
* pieces with puce scale borders and delicate flower painting
* derived from fashion for Sèvres – in common with most major German factories
* from 1770 the porcelain has a much colder more brilliant white tone
* the factory became influenced by the neo-classical movement in common with Fürstenburg and Meissen
* figure modelling was perfected by the brothers Friedrich Elias Meyer and Wilhelm Christian Meyer – note the characteristic small heads and elongated bodies
* c1775 figure bases became more architectural in design, notably oval and square pedestals
* in the early 19thC the 'Empire' style of Sèvres and Vienna was copied
* as the 19thC progressed Berlin tended to follow the prevailing trends

A pair of Belleek vases, modelled as conch-shells, the rims and edges to the wings enriched in pink, black printed marks, first period, 5 in (11.5 cm). **$700-900**

A Belleek fish spill-vase, applied with coloured butterflies and caterpillars, enriched in pink and with gilding, on a stepped pink, yellow and brown rockwork base applied with lizards, black printed and impressed marks, c1880, 16 in (40.5 cm). **$1,500-2,200**

A Chelsea vase, painted with three birds in a tree, c1756, 7 in (16.5 cm). **$1,300-1,700**

A pair of scale blue Coalport vases painted by J. Randall, c1880, 6 in (15 cm). **$300-500**

A Coalport small vase, with Hawthorn patten, on gilded background decoration in red, black and green, c1880, 3 in (9 cm). **$60-100**

A pair of scale blue Coalport vases
with covers, with birds painted by
P. Simpson, c1891, 14 in (35 cm).
$1,000-1,200

A Coalport vase, signed by ➤
Chivers, c1891, 3½ in (9 cm).
$100-200

A pair of Coalport vases and
covers, an overall ground of cobalt
with pale yellow reliefs, printed
marks, finials restuck, c1890,
11 in (26 cm). **$600-700**

A pair of Coalport royal
blue-ground vases, reserved and
painted by E.O. Ball with named
views of Windermere and Loch
Arne, on pale yellow shaped
cartouches gilt with scrolls and
foliage, signed, green printed
marks, c1910, 5 in (13 cm).
$600-800

Coalport vase with a turquoise
round, 12 in (30 cm).
300-400

A Davenport garniture of three
vases, with a gros bleu ground, the
bases with marbled decoration,
standard printed marks in red,
complete with three eboniss
turned wooden stands, one vase
restored, central vase 19 in
(46.5 cm), outer vases 17½ in
(42 cm). **$4,500-7,000**

A Coalport vase, to commemorate
the Coronation of Edward VII,
with birds painted by Perry,
c1902. 9 in (21 cm).
$1,000-1,400

Coalport vase and cover,
ainted with the Weir Bridge,
illarney, on dark blue ground,
reen printed mark, numbered in
lt V.5327 and M/S 130, inscribed
tle, retailer's stamp of Townsend
Co., 25 Holmeside, Sunderland,
arly 20thC, 13½ in (31 cm).
500-600

A garniture of five Derby
Imari-pattern campana vases,
painted in underglaze-blue and in
overglaze iron-red and gilding,
crown, crossed batons and D
marks in iron-red, Robert Bloor &
Co., some chips, some rubbing to
gilding throughout, c1815, 5 in to
9 in (13 to 22 cm). **$1,500-2,200**

A pair of Crown Derby pink
ground vases, black printed
marks, 1877-1890, 12 in (29.5 cm).
$600-700

A Crown Derby vase and cover,
blue and gilt with a signed painted
scene. 6½ in (15 cm).
$1,300-1,700

189

A pair of Paris vases, modelled in relief with cattle, sheep and goats on a dark blue ground, in panels with gilt scroll outline and vermicular ornament, 17 in (43.5 cm). **$300-400**

A massive pair of Samson vases and covers, painted in Imari palette with the arms of France, late 19thC, 49 in (124.5 cm). **$9,000-13,000**

A pair of Paris porcelain vases, richly gilt with dolphin handles, painted with garden landscapes on reverse, black square bases, one with restored rim, 19thC, 21 in (27 cm). **$1,700-2,500**

A large Samson vase and cover, in Chinese style , decorated with famille-rose flowers, on a rich blue ground gilt with prunus and cracked ice , the cover with dog of fo finial, some damage and repair, late 19thC, 41 in (104 cm). **$1,700-2,500**

A pair of 'manufacture de Sèvres' ormolu-mounted turquoise-ground vases, the porcelain signed Ab:Schilt de Sèvres, adapted for electric light, c1875, 17 in (43 cm). **$3,500-5,000**

A Sèvres hard paste squat oviform vase, the coral-red lower half gilt with simulated jewelling and foliage, traces of gilt crowned interlaced L marks enclosing a date letter, c1790, 3 in (8.5 cm). **$2,000-3,000**

This ground colour occurs several times in the 1780s, frequently with the arabesque decoration to be found on the present piece. Though a 'pot-à-sucre étrusque' is recorded for 1785 its arabesque decoration is on a gold ground.

A garniture of three Spode spill-vases, painted in a bright palette with figures in costume, the bases inscribed Comic Lover in Harlequin in China, Inhabitants of Naxia, and Women of Argentiera, c1820, 5½ in and 6½ in (12 and 16.5 cm). **$1,300-1,700**

PRICES

The never-ending problem of fixing prices for antiques! A price can be affected by so many factors, for example:
- **condition**
- **desirability**
- **rarity**
- **size**
- **colour**
- **provenance**
- **restoration**
- **the sale of a prestigious collection**
- **collection label**
- **appearance of a new reference book**
- **new specialist sale at major auction house**
- **mentioned on television**
- **the fact that two people present at auction are determined to have the piece**
- **where you buy it**

One also has to contend with the fact that an antique is not only a 'thing of beauty' but a commodity. The price can again be affected by:–
- **supply and demand**
- **international finance – currency fluctuation**
- **fashion**
- **inflation**
- **the fact that a museum has vast sums of money to spend**

A pair of Sèvres-pattern royal-blue-ground vases, covers and detachable bases, the royal blue waisted necks and spreading feet gilt with berried foliage and scroll ornament, signed H. Desprez, Sèvres, the covers with mock interlaced L and initial marks, last quarter of the 19thC, 39 in (97 cm). **$7,500-10,500**

Unless otherwise stated, any description which refers to 'a set' or 'a pair' includes a valuation for the entire set or the pair, even though the illustration may show only a single item.

A Sèvres-pattern gilt-metal mounted vase and cover, on a royal blue ground, imitation interlaced L marks, signed A. Callot, neck repaired, c1880, 26 in (64 cm). **$700-900**

A Spode porcelain vase, with a deep-blue ground scaled in gilding, between a beaded foot and galleried rim, 'Spode 1166' inscribed in iron-red, c1820, 10 in (25.5 cm). **$3,000-4,500**

A pair of Spode stone china 'Chinese' vases, decorated in 'famille-verte' colours, pattern 3143 printed mark Spode and stone china, rims restored, 9½ in (24.5 cm). **$800-1,200**
(ref. 'Spode' Leonard Whiter pl. 294, pub., Barrie and Jenkins 1970).

A pair of 'Vienna' vases and covers, painted with 'Malerei' and 'Psyche am Wasser' or 'Musik' and 'Waldelfe', on a deep blue ground, blue shield, red painted mark, one cover chipped, late 19thC, 15½ in (38 cm). **$1,300-1,700**

A Vienna vase, painted in colours, with a scene entitled 'Venus', reserved against a pink and purple ground decorated in gilt with foliate scrolls, raised on a circular foot, slight damage, late 19thC, 15 in (38 cm). **$300-600**

A 'Vienna' green-ground vase and cover, reserved and decorated in colours with scenes from Classic mythology, with purple iron-red and yellow bands, late 19thC, 15 in (37 cm). **$700-1,000**

A pair of Worcester blue scale vases and covers, painted with exotic birds, blue square seal marks, one vase chipped and repaired, the cover with chip to underside of rim, c1768, 13½ in (34 cm). **$7,000-9,000**

A large Worcester Flight, Barr & Barr campana vase, painted with 'Buildwas Abbey Salop-View of the Nave East End & Looking N.E., The Property of W.M. Moseley Esqr. and Buildwas Abbey Salop, the Property of W.M. Mosley Esqr.' the base inscribed in iron-red and with Davenport Longport mark, c1820, 12½ in (32.5 cm). **$2,000-3,000**
Cf. Henry Sandon, Flight & Barr Worcester Porcelain 1783-1840, col. pl., p49.

A Worcester Barr, Flight & Barr vase, with a pink ground, impressed marks, one handle repaired, early 19thC, 6½ in (16.5 cm). **$1,300-1,700**

A Flight Barr & Barr vase, with landscape panel on blue-ground with gilt scrolls on square base, inscribed on base 'View of the Derwent near Matlock Bath, Derbyshire', 6 in (15 cm). **$300-500**

A Vienna blue ground vase and cover, blue bee hive and green printed marks, c1900, 31½ in (79 cm). **$600-900**

A pair of Kerr and Binns Worcester vases, painted with an owl and a sparrowhawk in mountainous landscapes by Luke Wells Snr., on a green ground with gilt foliate borders, printed shield mark including the date 1862, minor restoration to one lip, 9½ in (22.5 cm). **$1,500-2,200**

A Grainger's Worcester vase, with reticulated panels and neck and gilt borders, shape no. 1/1963 in iron-red, printed shield and Royal China Works Worcester mark, c1890, 7½ in (18.5 cm). **$300-500**

A Royal Worcester pot pourri vase, inner cover and pierced cover, painted with fruit signed Chivers, within rich gilt borders on gilt and royal blue ground, reg. no. 413250, pattern no. 2294, c1903, 11½ in (29.5 cm). **$1,200-1,500**

A pair of Royal Worcester vases printed shape no. 1573 and date code for 1894, one restored, 15 in (38 cm). **$600-800**

A Royal Worcester vase and cover, painted with six flying swans on a pale blue ground by Charles Henry Clifford Baldwyn, signed, shape no. 1572, 1902, 11 in (28 cm). **$1,700-2,500**

A rare vase and cover by Harry Davis, shaded in 'blush ivory' and gilt, painted with a scene of Haddon Hall, under a hazy yellow sunset, signed H. Davis, shape no.2160, date code for 1903, script title. **$600-700**

An early example of the artist's work, painted at the age of 18 and showing the considerable influence of Ted Salter's landscape style.

A Royal Worcester double-handled vase, painted and signed by C. Baldwyn with swans in flight within moulded and gilt borders, green painted mark, c1902, 11 in (28 cm). **$500-600**

A blue and gilt Worcester urn vase, with cover, 15 in (36 cm) **$600-800**

A large vase and cover, by John Stinton, shaded in 'blush ivory' and edged in gold, painted with two large highland cattle on a hillside, the reverse with a misty mountain scene, signed John Stinton, shape no. 1847, date code for 1912, 17 in (42 cm). **$1,700-2,500**

A Royal Worcester vase and cover, painted and signed by Harry Stinton with highland cattle in a misty mountain vignette, printed mark in puce including a date code, 1919, 14 in (36 cm). **$1,500-2,200**

A pair of Royal Worcester cabinet vases and covers, by George Owen, on pierced foot with bead border and square gilt base with re-entrant corners, with pierced knopped and cork lined stopper, printed gold crowned circle mark, shape number 2064, incised signature and date 1912 and 1913, one wing on each vase faulty, 10½ in (25.5 cm) overall height. $4,000-5,000

A Royal Worcester beaker vase, painted with blackberries and leaves in colours on a shaded cream ground by K. Blake, printed mark in pink and numbered G923, signed, 9 in (22 cm) high. $300-400

A Royal Worcester vase, painted sheep in landscape by Ernest Barker, printed crowned circle mark in puce including the date code for 1923, shape no. F106/H, 8 in (20 cm). $1,000-1,400

A Royal Worcester vase and cover, with gilt scroll handles, painted by J. Southall, puce printed marks and date code for 1913, pattern no. 2307, chip and hair crack to inner rim of cover, 12 in (30 cm). $600-700

A Royal Worcester lobed globular vase and cover, painted by H. Stinton with highland cattle, the pierced cover with spire finial similarly enriched, signed, puce printed mark, pattern no. 175/H date code for 1931, 5 in (12 cm). $600-900

Miscellaneous

A Bow powder blue ground egg-cup, mock Oriental four character mark, c1760, 2½ in (6.5 cm). $1,200-1,500
Cf. Anton Gabszewicz and Geoffrey Freeman, Bow porcelain no. 103.

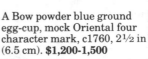

A Coalport egg cup, c1880. $15-30

A Worcester blue and white egg-cup, painted with trailing flowering branches beneath a cell pattern rim, crescent mark, repaired chip to foot, c1765, 2½ in (6.5 cm) high. $600-900
Egg cups are a rare form of 18thC English porcelain and tend to be highly valued by collectors.

A Derby pickle dish, with sticky blue floral design, c1765, 3 in (7.5 cm) long by 2½ in (5.5 cm) wide. $600-700

A Worcester pickle dish, with blue and white floral pattern, c1756, 4 in (10 cm) long by 3½ in (8.5 cm). $600-900

BOW PORCELAIN
c1745-1776

★ probably the first porcelain factory in England
★ early wares were mostly decorated in overglaze enamel colours
★ the body is of the phosphatic soft paste type as Lowestoft, early Chaffers and early Derby
★ it is sometimes difficult to differentiate between blue and white wares from Bow, Lowestoft, and Derby
★ painters numerals sometimes used on base or inside footrings as the Lowestoft (and occasionally Chaffer's, Liverpool)
★ body heavy for its size

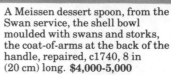

A Worcester blue and white sma[l]
sauce-spoon, slight rim chip to
bowl, c1770, 5 in (13 cm) long.
$400-600

A pair of Royal Worcester pilgrim
flasks, painted canine subjects
after Landseer by Robert Perling,
on a green ground with raised gilt
borders, and gilt base and handles,
shape no. 6/202, printed crowned
circle mark in red including the
date code for 1874, gilding
retouched, 11 in (27.5 cm).
$1,700-2,500

A Meissen dessert spoon, from the
Swan service, the shell bowl
moulded with swans and storks,
the coat-of-arms at the back of the
handle, repaired, c1740, 8 in
(20 cm) long. **$4,000-5,000**
*Very few pieces of this type seem to
have survived from the service.*

A German pipe bowl and hinged
silver gilt cover, painted with an
oval panel of a young girl with gilt
border, PFS mark in blue, c1870,
6½ in (15.5 cm) long.
$500-700

A rare Royal Worcester oil lamp,
fully fitted with metal burner,
glass dome and chimney, the base
painted with butterflies, flowers
and insects and monogrammed by
Edward Raby on an apricot
ground with gilding by John
Hopewell, together with the
restored oil reservoir, shape no.
1576, printed crowned circle mark
in puce including the date code for
1892. 24½ in (60.5 cm) high.
$2,000-3,000

A large Paragon loving cup, of
Edward VIII, printed in colours
and decorated in enamels and gi[lt]
with royal arms, trophies and
inscription, limited edition no.
252/500. **$300-500**

A Chantilly Kakiemon bourdalou,
iron red hunting horn mark,
c1735, 7½ in (18.5 cm) wide.
$1,700-2,500

A Chelsea needle case, modelled
in the form of a bunch of garden
flowers, applied with engraved
gold mounts, slight damage,
3½ in (8.3 cm). **$600-800**

A Tournai oval oil and vinegar
stand, re-decorated at Arras wi[th]
merchants on foreshores, on a
deep blue ground, gilt crossed
swords and four cross mark,
c1780, 9 in (23 cm) diam.
$500-700

A 'Sèvres' bourdalou, the bleu
celeste ground enriched with gilt
foliate sprays, interlaced L's,
script 'W' and 'CM' in overglaze
blue, 18thC and later, 9½ in
(24.5 cm). **$500-600**

A Worcester cornucopia wall
pocket, painted in underglaze blue
with flowers and trellis designs,
mid 19thC, 8½ in (21.8 cm).
$1,000-1,200

A pair of Derby London decorated
cornucopia shaped wall pockets,
painted with birds among berried
shrubs and foliage within
moulded rococo scroll cartouches
enriched in turquoise, puce and
gilding, Wm. Duesbury & Co.,
extended fire cracks to back and
sides, c1765, 10 in (24.5 cm).
$2,000-3,000

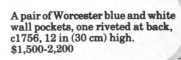

**A pair of Worcester blue and white
wall pockets, one riveted at back,
c1756, 12 in (30 cm) high.
$1,500-2,200**

Liverpool Porcelain – *General*
Introduction

The attribution of Liverpool porcelains to their various factories
has, for the most part, taken place within the last thirty years.
Previously Liverpool wares were grouped together and largely
disregarded. This attitude has now changed completely and
porcelain from the Liverpool factories is eagerly collected.

The process of forming theories about the attribution of output to
factories was based on several factors. Firstly insurance and
other records gave names, and in some instances date, of those
who manufactured china in Liverpool. These were:-

Samuel Gilbody	*c.1754 to 1761*
Richard Chaffers	*c.1754 to 1765*
William Ball	*c.1755 to 1769*
William Reid	*c.1755 to 1761*
Phillip Christian	*c.1765 to 1776*
James, John &	
Seth Pennington	*1763 to 1799*
Wolfe & Co	*1795 to 1800*

Having identified the manufacturers it was then a question of
dividing Liverpool wares into groups with similar visual
characteristics. Three groups which showed some common
characteristics and stylistic development were ascribed to the
factories of Chaffers, Christian and Seth Pennington as these
occupied the same premises – Christian taking over from
Chaffers in 1765 and Pennington from Christian in 1776.

The factories of Gilbody and Reid were short lived and so the
smallest surviving groups of wares were attributed partly on
that basis. This left a slightly more plentiful group of wares
which was attributed to the William Ball factory. These
attributions are now accepted by most authorities as largely
correct though research into the factories' history continues.

A Liverpool shallow bowl, painted
in underglaze blue and overglaze
coloured enamels with a boy
riding a buffalo, the reverse with a
huntsman and hound chasing a
stag, reserved on a
'bianco-sopra-bianco' ground of
flowers and scrolls, Samuel
Gilbody's factory, c1760, 6½ in
(16 cm) diam. **$1,200-1,500**
*This pattern, known as the
'Staghunt' pattern was also used
by Worcester. All examples of
Gilbody's porcelain are extremely
rare.*

A William Reid's, Liverpool leaf
dish, painted in pale underglaze
blue with a flowering shrub,
c1755, 7½ in (19 cm).
$1,200-1,500

A very similar Liverpool delft leaf
dish, raised on three low feet,
1750-1760, 5½ in (13 cm).
$1,000-1,200

A William Reid Liverpool pickle
dish, designed with vase and
feathers, c1758, 4 in (10 cm).
$1,000-1,200

A William Reid Liverpool pickle
dish, c1758, 3 in (7.5 cm) wide.
$1,200-1,500

The Factories

Samuel Gilbody *c.1754 to 1761*

Samuel Gilbody almost certainly purchased his father's factory from his mother in 1754. His father had died in 1752 leaving the Gilbody Pot Works to his wife but with the proviso that Samuel should have the option to purchase, "**$80** cheaper than anyone else," at the age of 21.

Between 1755 and 1758 Gilbody advertised, 'wholesale and retail at the lowest prices, china ware of all sorts, equal for service and beauty to any made in England'. Sadly by 1761 his factory had failed and he was made bankrupt. Williamson's Liverpool Advertiser announced, on July 3 1761, the sale of 'the large pot-house situate on Shaw's Brow late in the possession of Samuel Gilbody, a bankrupt, also china belonging to the assignees of the said Gilbody'.

The accuracy of the attribution of wares to Samuel Gilbody's factory was confirmed by the discovery of a large quantity of fragments of domestic porcelain near the factory site.

Among shapes so far discovered are teapots, mugs, jugs, coffee cups, bowls, plates, sauceboats and a spoontray. A number of coffee cans have been discovered both in underglaze blue and enamel colours and it is worth noting that some of the excavated shards include handles of complex form.

The Gilbody group is the rarest of all Liverpool groups. Blue and white pieces are especially scarce and are particularly difficult to identify correctly. The factory was adjacent to that of Richard Chaffers and some patterns and workpeople were common to both factories and it is not surprising, therefore, that Gilbody wares are occasionally incorrectly ascribed to Chaffers.

Samuel Gilbody's Factory

- an attractive, sometimes blurred greyish underglaze blue
- some blurred blue designs were then enamelled in iron red
- heavily potted early wares in blue and overglaze iron red can be confused with Bow porcelain
- enamel colours are often pale and sink into the glaze
- the typical Gilbody glaze is smooth and silky
- designs include the Jumping Boy pattern found and more commonly on Chaffers wares

---

William Reid and Partners *c.1755 to 1761*

The group of wares presently attributed to William Reid's factory forms one of the most academically interesting groups of English porcelain. William Reid and partners established the Liverpool China Manufactory about 1755 but Reid also had business connections in Shelton and a part of the factory's output may have been made there c. 1759 to 1761.

There is some conjecture that a link may exist between the Reid factory and an earlier factory at Newcastle-under-Lyme, indeed recent research suggests that the surviving output of the mysterious Limehouse factory may be contained within the group presently attributed to Reid. All this conjecture adds up to an interesting and highly collectable group of wares.

The group consists largely of shell shaped dishes, sauceboats, teapots and pickle leaves of various shapes. Other shapes are rare.

Though an advertisement of November 19th 1756 claimed the blue and white wares were, 'not inferior to any made in England', the earliest pieces are particularly primitive in appearance, crudely potted, grey in colour and sometimes sanded, blistered and mis-shaped. The normal test for porcelain, that of holding

These illustrations of Liverpool wares are not representative of the normal range or distribution wares available on the market. They include some of the more unusual pieces seen on the market over the past ten years.

A William Reid's Liverpool shell dish, decorated in tones of slate blue with ducks and a house on a river island, 4½ in (10.5 cm) wide **$1,000-1,200**

A rare William Reid's, Liverpool beaker, the decoration of a lady walking in a garden by the lakeside is especially attractive, c1758. **$4,000-5,000**
The high value comes from the combination of unusual form and attractive decoration.

A William Reid's Liverpool miniature bottle, decorated in blue with flowering plants, c175 3 in (7.5 cm). **$1,000-1,200**

he piece to the light to test for translucency, does not apply to these early wares – most pieces being almost opaque.

Some pieces probably produced in the latter half of the factory's life, contain steatite, are whiter in appearance, better potted and show a green translucency.

Reid became bankrupt in June 1761 and his factory was then occupied by William Ball and in 1763, by James Pennington and Company.

A rare William Reid's, Liverpool sauceboat, of primitive appearance, though well moulded and decorated with sophisticated landscapes and rose sprays, 8½ in (20.5 cm). **$4,000-5,000**

William Reid's Factory

- often a crude semi opaque body
- glaze opacified by the use of tin outside
- shell dishes and sauce boats are most commonly found
- mainly blue and white
- enamel colours are often vibrant and akin to saltglaze
- some good landscapes, also fruit and roses in underglaze blue
- identical motifs usually include imitation Chinese decoration – stylised peacock's feathers on handles and spouts
- body of early phosphatic wares is often grey in colour

A William Reid's, Liverpool hexagonal cream boat, painted in blue and white, with scenes of a lady in a garden within oval panels and moulded with scrolls and floral motifs, c1758, 5½ in (14.5 cm). **$1,700-2,500**

A rare William Reid's, Liverpool tea caddy in the form of a chubby faced boy's head, the cover modelled as a pointed hat, c1756, 5 in (13 cm) high. **$3,000-4,500**

A William Reid's, Liverpool blue and white sauceboat, the moulded body supported on lion-masked paw feet. Perfect **$3,000-4,500**

l. A William Reid's, Liverpool shell shaped pickle dish, painted in underglaze blue with bamboo behind a fence, 2½ in (7 cm). **$600-900**
c. A William Reid's, Liverpool cream boat, painted with landscapes and trellis pattern, 5½ in (14.5 cm). **$2,000-3,000**
r. A William Reid's Liverpool shell shaped pickle dish, painted with a vase and foliage. **$600-900**

William Ball c.1755 to 1769

William Ball wares are amongst the most eagerly collected of all English porcelains. Examples are less rare than contemporary Reid and Gilbody pieces but the wares are so charming that the market for well painted examples is particularly strong. As the group is more common than Reid and Gilbody wares the value is more affected by damage.

It is possible that William Ball migrated from Limehouse in London via Staffordshire before opening a pot house in Liverpool. From 1766 to 1769 he is recorded as a china maker in Ranleigh Street, Liverpool where a pot works is recorded in 1755. The existence of a jug belonging to this group of wares and dated 1756 fits in well with the theory.

The factory produced a large variety of shapes including tewares and more unusual and now scarce examples such as chamber candlesticks, flowerpots, mortars, goat and bee moulded jugs, knife and fork handles, trinket boxes, cornucopiae and vases.

A William Ball, Liverpool saucer, decorated in typical bright blue beneath a glossy glaze with a house on a river island, c1758.
Saucer only $200-300
Tea bowl and saucer $500-700

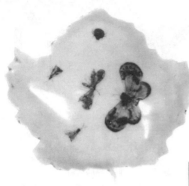

A William Ball Liverpool blue and white pickle leaf dish, c1758. **$1,300-1,700**

A rare William Ball, Liverpool vine leaf pickle dish, supported on three conical feet and painted in bright colours with winged insects, some damage, 4 in (10 cm). **$1,000-1,200**

Polychrome wares from the factories of William Ball, Samuel Gilbody and William Reid are scarce.

A William Ball, Liverpool teapot, decorated in bright underglaze blue with a chinoiserie of pagodas and willow trees on river islands, 1758-1760, 4½ in (10.5 cm). **$1,000-1,400**

A rare William Ball's, Liverpool shell sauceboat decorated in colours with moths and floral sprays. **$1,700-2,500**

A pair of rare William Ball's, Liverpool sauce boats, decorated in colours with flowering plants, the handles with monkey's head thumb rests, c1758, 7 in (17.5 cm). **$4,000-5,000**

A William Ball, Liverpool coloured creamer, c1756. **$600-900**

A rare William Ball's, Liverpool snuff box, of cylindrical form, painted in colours with sprays of flowers and insects. **$4,000-5,000**

A William Ball, Liverpool blue and white sauce boat, c1756. **$1,300-1,700**

A William Ball's, Liverpool cream boat, decorated in bright blue with a chinoiserie of Orientals in a garden. **$600-700**

A rare William Ball's, Liverpool covered vase, the cover moulded in relief with two putti and painted in coloured enamels with flower sprays, c1755, 5½ in (12.5 cm). **$1,000-1,400**

A William Ball's, Liverpool blue and white tea bowl and saucer. **$500-600**

A William Ball's, Liverpool small mug, painted in underglaze blue with a fenced garden. **$500-600**

A William Ball Liverpool blue and white sparrow beak cream jug, c1760. **$800-1,200**

A William Ball, Liverpool tea bowl and saucer, with a sticky blue river scene, with small chips, c1760. **$500-600**

A William Ball mug, painted in underglaze blue and overglaze iron red and gilt, c1758. **$500-600**

A 'William Ball', Liverpool bowl, painted with a pagoda and pine trees on an island, 1760-1762, 5 in (12.5 cm) diam. **$600-700**

A rare William Ball flared beaker, naively painted in bright underglaze blue with a figure in a sampan amongst islands, pseudo-character marks 3 in (9 cm). **$4,000-5,000**

This rare example of Liverpool porcelain might easily be mistaken for a Bow beaker c1752. Beakers are scarce in 18th century English porcelain and examples from all factories are highly prized

A William Ball Liverpool coloured bowl, c1756. **$300-400**

A rare and attractive William Ball, Liverpool bowl, painted in brilliant underglaze-blue with a girl in a rustic landscape with a church and an obelisk to one side, the interior with a solitary pointing figure, 1758-1760, 6 in (15 cm). **$1,700-2,500**

The William Ball factory produced a number of patterns of English, as opposed to Chinoiserie, landscapes and these are particularly collectable.

William Ball's Factory

- underglaze blue is often bright and the glaze 'wet' and 'sticky' in appearance
- shapes and style of decoration influenced by the bow factory
- decoration often resembles delft
- paste often shows small turning tears. These show up as lighter flecks when held up to the light
- polychrome wares are rare and collectable
- polychrome transfer prints overpainted with enamels are sought after
- elaborate rococo sauceboats were a factory speciality

Richard Chaffers and Partners *c.1754 to 1765*

Richard Chaffers and partners conducted an earthenware manufactory in Liverpool during the 1740's. In 1755 Chaffers signed an agreement with Robert Podmore, formerly a potter at Worcester, to engage him as factory manager in return for the secret, 'of making earthenware in imitation of or to resemble china ware'. Chaffers and Podmore sought to produce a steatitic porcelain body to the Worcester formula but it seems that they were unable to do so until 1756. The group of wares attributed to Chaffers includes a small group of phosphatic pieces and it is likely that these were produced between 1754 and 1756 prior to the introduction of the steatitic body.

The early phosphatic wares have a well potted greyish body and chinoiserie designs are painted in a greyish blue which can be quite dark in tone. Occasionally the bases are marked with painters numbers.

The later steatitic body continues to be well potted and is much whiter in appearance. Translucency is generally a clear green. A full range of teaware shapes was produced including a highly collectable group of octagonal cups, saucers and beakers most usually found with the attractive "jumping boy" pattern.

A rare William Ball 'King of Prussia' bowl, painted on the exterior in bright under-glaze blue with two Orientals by a fence, the interior inscribed, 'Succefs to the King of Prufsia' within a double-lined circle, wear, 7 in (17.5 cm). **$1,400-1,700**

Prussia fought on Britain's side in the Seven Years War. During the period 1757-1760 delftware was produced with the inscription 'Success to the King of Prussia' porcelain examples are, however, much rarer.

A Chaffer's Liverpool bowl, with willow and peony pattern, with sharp inward slope typical of Liverpool, c1765, 6 in (15 cm) diam. **$300-500**

A Liverpool Chaffer's bowl, decorated in brilliant enamels, 1760-1765, 9 in (22.5 cm) wide. **$500-600**

A Chaffer's Liverpool blue and white bowl, with chip to base. **$300-500**

◄ A Chaffer's Liverpool jug, with typical broad strap handle and painted in underglaze-blue, iron-red and gilding with an estuary scene including a terrace, pagoda and willow trees beneath a diaper band, 1758-1760, 7½ in (20 cm). **$600-700**
A higher price would be obtained for a similar jug decorated only in underglaze blue.

A Chaffer's, Liverpool jug, with ► fluted body and typical broad strap handle, decorated in underglaze blue with an estuary scene, c1758, 7½ in (20 cm). **$600-700**
The Chaffer's factory produced an excellent range of attractive large jugs.

A Chaffer's Liverpool cream jug, painted in underglaze blue with the 'Root' pattern, c1756, 3 in (7.5 cm). **$600-900**

A Chaffer's Liverpool blue and white tea bowl and saucer, c1755. **$300-500**

◄ A Liverpool mask mug, well moulded with flowers and ferns, the moulded reserves decorated in inky blue with Chinoiserie landscapes, c1765, 9½ in (25 cm). **$1,000-1,200**
Liverpool porcelain has undergone a number of reconsiderations of attribution since 1975. This jug is an excellent example of that process being catalogued as Pennington's in 1975 and Christian's in 1980.

l. A Chaffer's, Liverpool hexagonal tea bowl, painted in underglaze blue with the 'Jumping Boy' pattern, c1758. **$600-900**
r. A Chaffer's, Liverpool hexagonal tea bowl, painted in underglaze blue with stylized flowers. **$700-1,000**
This type of tea bowl usually bea[rs] pseudo Chinese character marks beneath the base.

A Chaffer's Liverpool tea bowl and saucer, with a Chinese river scene, the tea bowl straight sided, 1756-1758. **$500-600**

A Chaffer's Liverpool tea bowl and saucer, with chinoiserie design, c1760. **$500-600**

A Chaffer's Liverpool blue and white tea bowl and saucer, c1760. **$400-600**

A Chaffer's Liverpool coffee can, decorated in enamels, 1760-1765. **$600-700**

A Chaffer's Liverpool coffee can, with small chip, 1760-1762. **$100-150**

A Chaffer's Liverpool coffee can, with flat loop handle, with small chips, c1760, 2½ in (5 cm). **$800-1,200**

A Chaffer's Liverpool mug, painted in 'famille-rose' palette with a lady in a garden, c1756, 5 in (12.5 cm). **$1,000-1,400**

A Liverpool swelling mug with scroll handle, painted in an Imari palette with flowering shrubs issuing from pierced blue rockwork, Richard Chaffer's Factory, c1754, 5 in (12 cm). **$1,000-1,200**

A Chaffer's Liverpool tea pot, with two men on an island, indistinct, c1760. **$600-700**

A Chaffer's, Liverpool blue and white meat dish, painted in dark tones of blue with a pair of Chinamen in conversation on a bridge joining two islands, a pagoda to one side, diaper borders, 1760-1765, 14½ in (35 cm). **$600-800**

A Chaffer's Liverpool cylindrical mug, decorated in colours with sprays of flowers, c1760, 6 in (15.5 cm). **$600-900**

An unusual Chaffer's, Liverpool polychrome pipe stopper. **$800-1,200**

A rare bust of George II, in the white, the King wearing a large wig and loose cloak clasped at the front over an embossed cuirass and partly concealing the star of the Order of the Garter, his head turned to sinister, incised numeral 10, Chaffers Liverpool, replacement wooden socle, c1760, 13½ in (35 cm). **$6,000-8,000**

This model has previously been attributed to Plymouth, Chelsea, Bow, Longton Hall, Derby and even Worcester. In recent years a number of figures have been re attributed to Chaffers Liverpool.

Richard Chaffer's Factory
- early phosphatic wares have a greyish body
- some fine polychrome wares are decorated with carefully drawn Chinese figures
- attractive polychrome mugs are found in the phosphatic body
- later steatitic wares are noticeably whiter in appearance
- the underglaze blue of later wares is brighter and less grey
- the 'Jumping Boy' pattern is particularly collectable
- late chinoiseries are often peppered with dots. This decorative habit continues on Christians wares
- potting based on Worcester shapes

Philip Christian and Son *c.1765 to 1776*

Following the death of Richard Chaffers one of his partners, Philip Christian, took over the factory and continued to produce steatitic porcelain. Initially shapes and patterns continued unchanged as did the porcelain formula. It is difficult to differentiate between late Chaffers and early Christians pieces though late Christians wares lack the spontaneity and fluidity of decoration which typify Chaffers porcelain circa 1755 to 1760. By 1771 Christian had bought out Chaffers widow and children and in 1772 he renewed his licence to mine steatite at Predannak near Mullion in Cornwall. In 1776 Philip Christian and Son sold their interest in the mining operation to the Worcester proprietors and ceased manufacturing porcelain.

A full range of teaware shapes was produced but some shapes are quite scarce. These include sucriers, teapot stands, spoontrays and plates. Bowls were a speciality of the factory and some large examples are particularly attractive.

Christians Wares are less enthusiastically collected than those of the earlier factories but some very pleasing pieces, among them a number of well moulded pickle leaves, were produced and are still available at reasonable prices ($300 to 400) though these are less undervalued than some coloured wares which, even if of rare shape, command far less attention than might be expected.

A Chaffer's Liverpool pickle leaf decorated in tones of slate blue with moths in flight, c1763, 4 in (10 cm) wide. **$400-600**

Pickle leaves are attractive and eagerly sought by collectors. Few appear on the market at present than in recent years. The decoration on this leaf is more desirable than more usual floral designs.

A rare Christian's Liverpool bowl, transfer printed with an officer and two native attendants carrying spears, c1775, 8 in (19 cm). **$600-700**

A Christian's Liverpool bowl, moulded with trailing flowers and decorated in underglaze blue with chinoiseries within moulded panels, c1770, 5 in (12.5 cm). **$200-300**

This type of Liverpool bowl (also saucers and coffee cups) is sometimes mistaken for the similar Lowestoft type.

A Christian's Liverpool pickle leaf, decorated in dark tones of underglaze blue with the pattern most commonly found on leaves from the Christian factory, c1770. (if perfect) **$300-400**

This example is perfect and slightly unusual in shape. It would therefore command a higher price than average.

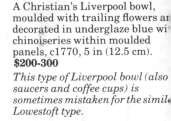

A Phillip Christian Liverpool bowl, with a typical Liverpool pattern of a bird on a branch, with tiny dots on the outline, c1775, 6 in (10 cm) diam. **$60-100**

A Liverpool teapot, by Phillip Christian, decorated in enamels, c1768. **$800-1,200**

A Christian's Liverpool coffee pot, painted in colours with flowers in the style of Meissen, c1772, 10 in (25 cm). **$800-1,200**

A Liverpool blue and white mug of cylindrical form, slightly spreading towards the base and applied with a strap handle, painted in underglaze blue with pagoda-like structure on an island below a scroll and trellis border, Phillip Christian's factory, tiny chips to rim, 1770-1775, 5 in (12.5 cm). **$500-600**

An unusual combination of borders.

Pennington's *c.1769 to 1799*

The Pennington family were extremely active in the ceramic industry of Liverpool. In 1763 James Pennington took over William Reid's factory following a short tenure by William Ball but so far these early Pennington wares remain unidentified. Some experts believe that his output is contained within The William Ball Group but these conjectures, though of interest, do not affect the collectability of that group of porcelain.

A large group of wares is attributed to Seth Pennington, youngest of the three Pennington brothers, who took over Christian's factory in 1776. This group of wares includes dated examples from 1771 and it is thereby confirmed that the company was engaged in porcelain manufacture before taking over from Christian in 1776. There is some evidence of co-operation between the Pennington brothers, James, John and Seth and it is possible that Pennington and Part was a continuation of the manufactory started by James in 1763. In the late 1790's Pennington and Part's china works were sold at auction and the partnership dissolved. Documentary evidence shows that the Pennington family continued to have interests in porcelain manufacture in Liverpool as late as 1805.

Pennington and Part continued to produce shapes and patterns previously used by Philip Christian. Transfer printed wares are commonly found and these are often poorer versions of Christian prints. The underglaze blue can be bright in tone but is often a shade of grey-blue and can be almost black. On the base of wares with a footring the blue-grey gathers in cloudy pools.

A complete range of teawares as well as more unusual shapes were produced. Most shapes are quite common and often carelessly made. Scarce pieces which are more eagerly collected include vases, and bowls and jugs painted with well detailed ships.

A Pennington's Liverpool blue and white baluster milk-jug, lightly moulded and painted in an inky tone of blue with scattered flowers, and scroll handle, c1785, 4 in (10 cm). **$200-300**
The handle of this type of jug is sometimes clearly modelled as a snake striking at the rim.

A rare Pennington Liverpool cream jug, HP marked, badly cracked, c1778. **$100-200**

A Pennington Liverpool blue and white sauce boat, 1775-1778. (Perfect). **$300-400**

A Pennington Liverpool sparrow beak cream jug, c1775, 3½ in (7.5 cm). (Perfect). **$400-600**

A Pennington Liverpool coloured jug, c1775, 3½ in (7.5 cm). **$200-300**

A Pennington Liverpool coloured tea pot, c1780, 6 in (10 cm). **$200-300**

A Pennington Liverpool blue and white coffee can, c1775. **$200-300**
By convention, the principal decorative feature on coffee cans faces the drinker. In this example, if the handle were held in the right hand, the design would face away from the drinker.

A Pennington Liverpool blue and white tea bowl and saucer, c1775. **$200-300**

A Pennington Liverpool coloure
tea bowl and saucer, 1770-1775.
$200-300

Pennington's Factory

● not as enthusiastically collected as the earlier factories
● in common with the earlier factories the majority of the output was blue and white
● some highly collectable ship painted dated jugs and bowls produced in the 1770's and 1780's
● a very dark underglaze blue was used in the 1770's and early 1780's
● the glaze is sometimes tinted blue/grey
● transfer prints often smudgy in appearance

A Pennington Liverpool coloured
sauce boat, repaired, c1775.
$60-100

Three Liverpool bowls:-
l. William Ball's factory blue a
white, c1760, 6 in (14.5 cm).
$300-400
c. Phillip Christian's factory, b
and white, c1765, 8 in (19.5 cm
$200-300
r. Richard Chaffer's factory,
underglaze blue and white wit
overglaze iron-red and gold,
c1758, 6 in (16 cm). **$300-400**

Wolfe and Co. *c.1795 to 1800*

In 1795 Thomas Wolfe and partners took over one of the Pennington family's factories. Unlike the other Liverpool factories the vast majority of their output was decorated in polychrome. Very few blue and white pieces have been identified. To date collectors have shown little interest in the wares produced by Wolfe and Co. though some of their wares are well potted and attractively painted.

Goss Cottages

Portman Lodge **$500**; Lloyd
Georges Home with Annexe**$2**
Dove Cottage **$600**.

Shakespeare's House: large
half-length, **$150** with separate
base, **$150** small full-length,
$80.

Newquay: Huers House **$150**
Look-Out House**$150** Thomas
Hardy's Birthplace **$500**; Dr.
Johnson's House **$300**.

Manx Cottage, small **$150** Burns
Nightlight **$300**; First and Last
House with annexe **$800**.

Oriental Ceramics

In producing an annual price guide we are constantly asked how we arrive at our price ranges. We do not use saleroom estimates – we judge what is a 'reasonable' range for a piece in consultation with one of our specialists.

As anyone involved in the antique trade will know, this is never exactly easy but it is certainly made exceedingly difficult when there is a dramatic change in the market as happened in 'The Bunker Hunt' silver explosion of 1980 . Over a four month period the scrap value of silver shot up from $5-7 an oz to $25-30 an oz. This was followed by the inevitable crash. Silver again levelled out but placing prices on pieces sold during that period was very difficult.

A similar but opposite phenomenon is upon us. The market for Chinese ceramics which has been very erratic for several months has now fallen dramatically, with most auctioneers reporting a large percentage unsold.

The sale at Christies, London on June 17 1985 reflected this collapse and reaffirmed that

prices have not yet reached rock bottom as the market is still very wary.

This has been caused by the massive amount of Chinese ceramics smuggled out from China. These pieces include more recent examples and a fair percentage of fakes. Many others have been discovered in recently opened tombs. This oversupply and market place fear has led to a drop in demand which will eventually lead to a diminishing supply – due to the poor prices realised.

An example of the type of problem faced by auctioneers was the good quality Cizhou jar which sold for $1,300 . The auctioneers' estimate of $4,000-6,000 would have been conservative last year. This sale had 48% unsold. And this in an otherwise buoyant, if slightly steadied, antiques market.

Of course, as one always has to say when making wide generalisations, very rare, unusual pieces continue to sell and seem somehow unaffected by the fluctuations below them!

Chinese export porcelain seems to have been relatively unaffected by this panic possibly due to the strong market in America. This has not helped the Chinese taste market which seems destined for a difficult year.

These great crests and troughs usually do level out in calmer times and for those with nerves of steel and a healthy bank balance – this could be the time to buy.

A green-glazed buff pottery pouring vessel, the exterior and thick rim all under a vivid glaze stopping irregularly above the deeply cut spreading foot, the interior under a deep straw glaze, Tang Dynasty, minor chips, 5 in (12.5 cm) wide. **$4,500-7,000**

A Longquan Guan Yao bowl and dish, under fine thick semi-translucent bluish-green glazes stopping around a circle of orange-fired biscuit on the uncut base, Southern Song Dynasty, minor chips, the dish 6 in (15 cm) wide, the bowl 4 in (9 cm) wide. **$8,500-11,000**

A Jun Yao tripod bulb bowl, the lavender glaze pooling to an opaque white and thinning to brown in some areas, impressed with a numeral er (two), Yuan Dynasty, crack and rim chip restored, 9 in (22.5 cm) diam. **$14,000-17,000**

Bowls

A Jizhou brown-glazed bowl, reserved on the interior in the streaky glaze, the dark brown exterior with pale splashes stopping around the shallowly cut buff stoneware foot, Song Dynasty, minute chips, 5 in (12 cm) diam. **$3,000-4,500**

A 'famille rose' oval barber's bowl, painted with the Tang poet Li Po recumbent against his wine vat, Yongzheng, corner of chin recess repaired, 12 in (31 cm) wide. **$2,000-3,000**

A blue and white and underglaze copper red bulb bowl, a flaming pearl, the rim washed in brown, Kangxi, 8 in (21 cm) diam. **$1,300-1,700**

A large 'famille rose' punch bowl, Yongzheng/early Qianlong, restored, 16 in (39 cm) diam. **$1,500-2,200**

A Chinese Qianlong period bowl, decorated in 'famille rose' enamels, with rare designs of Europeans, 18thC, 9½ in (25 cm) diam. **$1,300-1,700**

A 'famille rose' punch bowl, Qianlong, minute rim nicks, 14 in (35 cm) diam. **$3,000-4,500**

A large 'famille rose' punch bowl, Qianlong, restored, 16 in (39 cm) diam. **$800-1,200**

Use the Index!
Because certain items might fit easily into any of a number of categories, the quickest and surest method of locating any entry is by reference to the index at the back of the book.
This has been fully cross-referenced for absolute simplicity.

A Wucai dragon bowl, the exterior with two striding dragons in iron-red and green, Qianlong six-character seal mark and of the period, minute rim frits, 6 in (15 cm) diam. **$2,500-3,500**

A blue and white and underglaze-copper red bowl, Qianlong six-character seal mark and of the period, minute frits, 8 in (20 cm) diam. **$2,000-3,000**

A fine fish bowl, painted and enamelled with extensive river scenes, with figures in boats and on bridges, in lobed panels outlined in yellow on a black ground, with formal scrolling flower branches in rich enamel colours between bands of iron red floral ornament, the inside decorated with carp and crustaceans among lotus and aquatic plants, gilt kylin mask handles, on a wood fluted column stand painted brown and gilt, Ch'ien Lung, 20 in (48 cm). **$8,500-11,000**

A Cantonese punch bowl, painted in 'famille rose' palette, Daoguang, 16 in (40 cm). **$1,700-2,500**

A small Wucai flared bowl, Daoguang seal mark and of the period, 6 in (15 cm) diam. **$600-800**

1. A clair-de-lune glazed bowl, the glaze stopping above the slightly spreading foot, Qianlong six-character mark and of the period, minute glaze frit, 7 in (18 cm) diam. **$2,500-3,500**
r. A cafe-au-lait-glazed bowl with everted rim, the exterior washed pale brown, the interior plain, Qianlong seal mark and of the period, 7 in (18 cm) diam. **$1,000-1,200**

A 'famille-rose' bowl, Daoguang six-character seal mark and of the period, 5 in (13 cm) diam. **$1,000-1,400**

A turquoise-ground 'Empress Dowager' bowl, the exterior with a bird perched in further vine with rose sprays on the reverse, inscribed Daya Zhai (Studio of Great Culture) and a seal mark, the base marked 'Yong qing chang chun', (eternal prosperity and enduring spring,) Guanxu, 7 in (17.5 cm) diam. **$2,500-3,500**

A 'famille rose' bowl, painted with emblems, a horse and an elephant alternating with Buddhist figures, Daoguang six-character seal mark and of the period, 6 in (14.5 cm) diam. **$600-900**

A 'famille rose' sgraffiato red-ground bowl, Daoguang six-character seal mark and of the period, frit chips, 6 in (14.5 cm) diam. **$800-1,200**

A fine massive Canton 'famille
rose' punch bowl, restored, early
19thC, 24 in (58 cm) diam.
$4,000-5,000

A Canton basin, first half 19thC,
16 in (38 cm). **$1,200-1,500**

A massive Canton 'famille rose'
punch bowl, restored, early 19thC,
24 in (58 cm) diam. **$4,000-5,000**

Canton porcelain bowl, 19thC,
11½ in (27.5 cm) diam.
500-900

A pair of Cantonese fish bowls,
with blue background, 18 in
(45 cm) diam. **$1,300-1,700**

A Chinese circular fish bowl,
painted in coloured enamels, on a
yellow ground, 19thC, 18 in
(45 cm) diam. **$1,700-2,500**

A pair of 'famille noire' fish bowls,
Kangxi seal marks in iron red,
20thC, 16 in (40 cm). **$1,200-1,500**

An Imari bowl, painted in a
typical palette, on a solid iron red
ground, 16 in (40 cm) diam.
$1,300-1,700

An Imari barbers bowl, c1700,
11 in (28 cm) diam. **$600-900**

A Satsuma bowl, 5 in (12.5 cm).
$1,500-2,200

A Kutani bowl, with orange and
gold colouring, 14 in (36 cm) diam.
$2,500-3,500

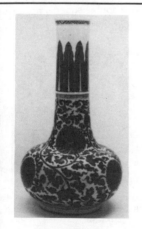

A Fukugawa bowl, painted in
underglaze blue and black, mark
in under-glaze blue, c1900,
15½ in (39.5 cm). **$700-900**

Bottles

blue and white bottle vase,
decorated in good tones of blue
with a broad stylised lotus scroll,
Kangxi, 18½ in (47 cm).
1,700-2,500

A rare pair of Imari slightly
tapering rectangular sake bottles,
Tokkuri, Genroku period, one
cracked, neck restored, both about
8 in (21 cm). **$3,000-4,500**

A liver-red glazed pear-shaped
bottle, under a minutely dimpled
rich bubbled glaze firing paler on
one side, encircled Yongzheng
six-character mark and of the
period, 8 in (20 cm). **$1,000-1,200**

207

A pair of Arita blue and white bottle vases, with tall garlic necks, each painted in the Chinese Transitional manner, late 17thC, both about 14 in (36 cm). **$3,000-4,500**

An Arita white glazed apothecary bottle, one side painted in underglaze cobalt blue with the initial M, within a laurel cartouche, lip restored, 1665-1685, 9 in (23 cm). **$1,300-1,700**

Cf. Soame Jenyns, Japanese Porcelain, pls. 10A and 10B, Martin Lerner, Catalogue of blue and white, Early Japanese Export Ware, pls. 39-46.

A large Arita blue and white bottle vase, late 17thC, 20 in (45 cm). **$2,500-3,500**

A large Satsuma koro and cover, very slight damage, 22½ in (57 cm). **$1,500-2,200**

Censers

A Japanese blue and white tripod koro and pierced domed cover, painted with prunus on a cracked-ice pattern ground, signed Makazu Kozan, 8 in (20 cm) diam. **$400-600**

A Dehua Blanc-De-Chine censer, cover and stand, some damage, 17th/18thC, the stand 6 in (16 cm) wide. **$300-500**

A late Ming blue and white stem-cup, Wanli, rim chipped and reduced, 6 in (14.5 cm) diam. **$1,000-1,400**

Cups

A pair of 'Trumpeter' teabowls and saucers, enamelled on a black ground, Qianlong. **$5,500-7,000**

A blue and white tea bowl, Chenghua six-character mark within a double square, Kangxi, 2 in (5 cm) diam. **$800-1,200**

A blue, pink and white wine cup, painted in pink enamel with three bats amongst under-glaze blue surrounds, Qianlong six-character seal mark and of the period, 2 in (6 cm) diam. **$1,000-1,200**

A pair of Chinese 'famille rose' tea bowls and saucers, some damage, 19thC. **$300-500**

A set of seven teabowls and saucers, decorated in 'famille-rose' enamels, stylised lotus sprig in the centre, Qianlong, **$1,200-1,500**

Ewers

A Transitional blue and white ➤ pear shaped ewer, handle base fritted, c1640, 9 in (22 cm). **$1,500-2,200**

Cf G. Lang, The Wrestling Boys, Chinese and Japanese ceramics in the collection at Burghley House, no. 148

n olive glazed ewer, the olive own glaze over a white slip opping short of the uncut buff oneware foot, neck restored, aze slightly degraded, early ing Dynasty, 6½ in (16.5 cm). 700-1,000

A pair of rare Kakiemon globular kendi or gorgelets, decorated in iron red, turquoise and blue enamels, the sides moulded in relief with figures of Hotei, spouts chipped, neck rims damaged, probably Empo/Tenwa period 1673-1683, both about 7½ in (19 cm). **$5,500-7,000**

An Arita blue and white broad oviform ewer, late 17thC, 11 in (27.3 cm). **$1,200-1,500**

A fine silver mounted blue and white Arita ewer, the porcelain handle partly with engraved mounts, by Adriaan Brandt, Delft, the porcelain Japan, c1660, 9 in (22.5 cm). **$3,500-5,000**

Figures – Animal

brown glazed red pottery anding dog, the glaze stopping regularly around the feet and e belly, ears restored, Han ynasty, 7 in (17cm) long. 3,000-4,000

A pair of white glazed cockerels, the combs, wattles and legs painted red and gilt, one body incised with feathers, both standing on pierced rockwork bases, gilding rubbed, one comb slightly chipped, 19thC, 18½ in (46 cm). **$2,000-3,000**

Two red painted grey pottery horse heads, one with traces of white, the other with traces of black, earth encrustation, chipped, Han Dynasty, 7 in (17 cm). **$6,000-8,000**

◄ A pair of Chinese cockerels, the combs coloured red, minor chips to comb, Qianlong, 14 in (34.5 cm). **$3,000-4,500**

An Imari model of a leaping carp, painted in underglaze blue, iron red, black and gilt, tail restored, c1700, 12 in (30 cm). **$1,400-1,700**

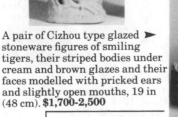

A pair of Cizhou type glazed ➤ stoneware figures of smiling tigers, their striped bodies under cream and brown glazes and their faces modelled with pricked ears and slightly open mouths, 19 in (48 cm). **$1,700-2,500**

pair of green glazed figures of rrots, standing on pierced bergine rockwork, their beaks d feet painted red, minor chips, ng Dynasty, 8 in (20 cm). ,300-1,700

HOW TO USE MILLER'S

Unless otherwise stated, any description which refers to 'a set' or 'a pair' includes a valuation for the entire set or the pair, even though the illustration may show only a single item.

A pair of Chinese turquoise glazed Buddhist lions, Yongzheng, 7 in (17.8 cm). **$600-900**

Figures – People

An unglazed buff pottery figure of a standing Western Asiatic merchant, with extensive black pigment remaining and his body with areas of red, neck restored, Tang Dynasty, 12 in (29 cm). **$1,500-2,200**

A straw glazed buff pottery figure of a standing soldier, traces of red pigment remaining on his garments and black on his belt over a partially degraded glaze, Sui/early Tang Dynasty, 14 in (35 cm). **$1,200-1,500**

A glazed tilemaker's figure of a horse and rider, the man with green robes wearing a black hat, the straw glazed horse with green mane, tail and caparisons, he with turquoise belt and turquoise bridle, restored, Ming Dynasty, 11 in (28 cm). **$2,000-3,000**

Two Sancai buff pottery figures of court officials, under green, ochre and straw glazes, their heads reserved in the biscuit and with red and black pigments remaining, restored, Tang Dynasty, 32 in (79.5 cm) and 31 in (77.5 cm). **$14,000-17,000**

Two unglazed buff pottery figures of standing ladies, with areas of red and black pigment remaining, one with traces of striped decoration on her robes, minor damage, Tang Dynasty, 10½ in (26.5 cm). **$2,500-3,500**

A large glazed stoneware standing figure of an Immortal, his robe chestnut brown with an aubergine band and moulded key pattern border, the face and hands straw glazed, restored late Ming Dynasty or later, 37 in (93 cm). **$6,000-8,000**

A blanc de chine figure, 18thC, 14 in (35 cm). **$1,000-1,400**

A pottery figure of a Daruma, with red glaze robe and biscuit body, mid 19thC, 15 in (37.5 cm). **$600-900**

A Dehua blanc de chine figure of a Bodhisattva, with a swastika pectoral on his open chest, the head with a beatific and impassive expression below a large knotted usnisa, one finger and lotus petal chipped, kiln elbow flaw polished, 18thC, 21½ in (49 cm). **$4,500-7,000**

A 'famille rose' export figure of a standing lady, with blue and green jacket, over a gilt and orange dress, restoration to sconce and hand, Qianlong, 12 in (29.1 cm) high. **$1,500-2,200**

An Imari figure of a standing man, his kimono painted in underglaze blue, iron red, coloured enamels and gilt, 16 in (39.2 cm), and another of a standing lady, cracked and hair piece restored, both Genroku period, 14 in (36 cm). **$1,700-2,500**

A pair of exportware figures of Guanyin, dressed in a heavy white cloak painted in grisaille, with pink cuffs and collar, over a bright turquoise robe strewn with flowers picked out in 'famille rose' palette, Qianlong, 13 in (33 cm). **$1,300-1,700**

> In the Ceramics section if there is only one measurement it refers to the height of the piece.

Flatware

An olive celadon glazed dragon dish, the centre moulded with a shallow relief four clawed dragon, the exterior petal moulded, 14thC, 14 in (35.5 cm). **$2,500-3,500**

A Jun Yao saucer dish, under an opaque pale lavender glaze with a large purple splash in the interior, Song/Yuan Dynasty, 16½ in (16.5 cm). **$700-1,000**

A Ming white glazed saucer dish, moulded in indistinct anhua around the interior of the side with dragons striding in mutual pursuit, the surface under an opaque thick glaze, 15th/16thC, 8½ in (21 cm). **$1,000-1,200**

A heavily potted celadon dish, under an olive glaze, scratches, 14th/15thC, 14 in (39 cm). **1,000-1,200**

A Ming imperial yellow dish, under a rich mustard yellow glaze, encircled Zhengde six character mark and of the period, cracks, 8½ in (21 cm). **$1,300-1,700**

A late Ming blue and white saucer dish, encircled Jiajing six character mark and of the period, chipped, 6 in (16.1 cm). **$1,400-1,700**

A large Ming blue and white kraak porselein dish, frit chips, Wanli, 20½ in (51.5 cm). **2,000-3,000**

A late Ming blue and white dish, fritted, base chip, Wanli, 17 in (43 cm). **$1,200-1,500**

A large late Ming blue and white kraak porselein dish, frit chips, early 17thC, 19 in (47 cm). **$2,000-3,000**

A pair of 'famille verte' dishes, painted in iron red, green and gilt, rims fritted, one dish with four corners restored, late Kangxi, 12 in (31 cm). **$2,000-3,000**

Chinese 'famille verte' deep dish, enamelled in iron red, green, yellow, manganese, Kangxi, 11 in (28 cm). **$1,300-1,700**

A Chinese Imari dish, Kangxi, 20 in (50.2 cm). **$2,000-3,000**

A pair of fine blue and white dishes, printed with figures, the border reserved on a key-pattern ground with eight radiating panels of alternate pairs of 'long Elizas' and foliage, rim frits, encircled Kangxi six character marks and of the period, 13 in (33.5 cm). **$3,000-4,500**

A 'famille verte' dish, painted with four ladies holding a book and bundles of scrolls on a pavilion terrace below a knotty tree issuing from rockwork, chipped, encircled leaf mark, Kangxi, 14 in (35 cm). **$1,500-2,200**

A 'famille rose' saucer dish, painted in the Chinese taste, engraved on the base and stained green with the Johanneum mark N176, Yongzheng, 9 in (22.2 cm). **$3,000-4,000**

A large 'famille verte' dish, painted with a phoenix standing on rockwork amongst peony at the centre, the trellis pattern border reserved with Buddhist emblems, rim fritted and chipped, Kangxi, 21 in (52 cm). **$7,500-10,500**

Two blue and white tureen stands, slight frits, Qianlong, 16 in (39.5 cm) and 15 in (37 cm). **$800-1,200**

A blue and white saucer dish, painted with a writhing four clawed dragon grasping a flaming pearl, foot rim chipped, encircled Yongzheng six-character mark and of the period, 8 in (20 cm). **$1,000-1,400**

An oval dish, decorated in 'famille rose' enamels with flowers with an iron red and gilt band in the cavetto, Ch'ien Lung, 12½ in (31.5 cm). **$600-900**

A rare pair of exportware dishes, following a Worcester or Longton Hall original, the centre white shading to vivid green on the sides and with overall veining delicately pencilled in puce enamel, Qianlong, 10 in (25.7 cm). **$1,000-1,200**

A pair of 'famille rose' dishes, painted with ladies on riverbanks beneath peony trees in river landscapes, the borders with flower sprays, Qianlong, 17 in (42.5 cm). **$1,500-2,200**

A circular dish, enamelled in 'famille rose' colours and gilt with two phoenix, Ch'ien Lung, 11 in (28.5 cm). **$500-600**

A rare 'famille rose' teapot stand, painted with a view in the Pearl River, one of the Dutch Folly fort in the background, the underglaze blue border reserved with small vignettes, enamels rubbed, Qianlong, 5 in (12.5 cm). **$800-1,200**

A pair of 'Compagnie-des-Indes' dishes, Qianlong, 13 in (32.4 cm). **$1,000-1,200**

Two large blue and white circular dishes, one border restored, Qianlong, 22 in (54.5 cm). **$1,300-1,700**

A Chinese export plate, painted with a scene of classical figures depicting 'The Judgment of Paris' within a scroll border in iron red and gilding, brown edged rim, slight rubbing, Qianlong, 9 in (22.8 cm). **$1,200-1,500**

Imari type serving dish, for the
tch market, enamelled in
ours and gilt and painted in
der-glaze blue with 'Governor
ff', minor restoration and chips,
730, 12½ in (31.5 cm).
,000-4,000

A blue and white Armorial dish,
enclosed by underglaze blue
butterflies, restored rim chips and
hair crack, Qianlong, 9 in
(22.5 cm). **$700-1,000**

A pair of unusual Armorial dinner
plates for the Dutch market,
enclosed by a gilt and iron red
scrolling foliage band, small rim
chips, Qianlong, 9 in (22 cm).
$2,000-3,000

'famille rose' plate for the
dian market enamelled in
ours and gilt, reserved in a
atrefoil panel on a dense floral
anco-sopra-bianco ground, rim
ips, c1770, 9 in (23.5 cm).
,300-1,700

Three blue and white shaped oval
meat dishes, one fritted, c1780,
14 in (35 cm) and 12 in (30.2 cm).
$600-900

A large 'famille rose' dish, the
centre painted in tones of sepia
enhanced in gilding, with
alternating pink and turquoise
diaper ground panels of lappet and
angular scroll outline centred
with demi-flowerheads in rich
pink, Qianlong, 15 in (36 cm).
$1,700-2,500

Chinese charger, painted in
mille verte' enamels, the
verse painted with flowering
unus branches, 18thC,
maged, 15 in (38.5 cm).
00-600

A Chinese porcelain charger,
18thC, 15 in (38.5 cm).
$600-800

A green dragon dish, painted in
the centre with a five clawed
dragon and flaming pearl, the
exterior in 'an hua', Daoguang six
character mark and of the period.
7½ in (18 cm). **$1,300-1,700**

hinese dish, the border painted
h 'famille rose' flower sprays
hin rows of ochre and gilt
ow heads, the central armorial
motto in black, gilt and
ours, slightly rubbed, 18thC,
in (36 cm). **$1,300-1,700**

A set of four Chinese 'famille
rose' plates, 9 in (23 cm).
$800-1,200

Unless otherwise stated,
any description which
refers to 'a set' or 'a pair'
includes a valuation for
the entire set or the pair,
even though the
illustration may show only
a single item.

A large 'famille rose' dragon dish,
painted with blue and pink
striding dragons around a central
iron red contorted dragon, the
reverse glazed pink, encircled
Yongzheng six character mark
late Qing Dynasty, 21 in (54 cm).
$1,300-1,700

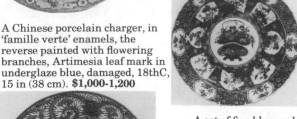

An unusual 'famille rose' oval platter, enamelled in colours and gilt, shaded grisaille and sepia with a central scene of Iberian inspiration, probably redecorated, late Qianlong, 14 in (37 cm). **$4,500-5,000**

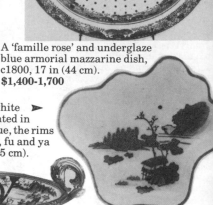

A Chinese porcelain charger, in 'famille verte' enamels, the reverse painted with flowering branches, Artimesia leaf mark in underglaze blue, damaged, 18thC, 15 in (38 cm). **$1,000-1,200**

A 'famille rose' and underglaze blue armorial mazzarine dish, c1800, 17 in (44 cm). **$1,400-1,700**

A set of five blue and white kosmetsuke trays, painted in purplish underglaze blue, the rims edged in a brown wash, fu and ya marks, 17thC, 7 in (17.5 cm). **$1,000-1,400**

A large Arita blue and white dish, base slightly cracked, late 17thC, 24 in (60.6 cm). **$1,400-1,700**

A pair of ormolu mounted Japanese Imari deep dishes, decorated in iron red, blue and gilt, the dishes late 17th/early 18thC, 21 in (53.5 cm). **$4,500-7,000**

A pair of Arita blue and white plates, each painted with long tailed birds, one with base rim chips, late 17thC, 8 in (21.5 cm). **$3,000-4,500**

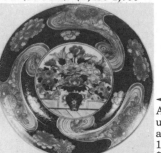

A large Imari dish, painted in underglaze blue, iron red, pale aubergine and gilt, late 17th/early 18thC, 22 in (55.5 cm). **$1,700-2,500**

A pair of unusual Imari dishes moulded in underglaze blue and gilt around the central floral panels, early 18thC, 11½ in (29 cm). **$4,500-7,000**

A Japanese Imari charger, decorated in typical palette, Meiji period, 23½ in (60.5 cm). **$1,000-1,400**

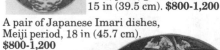

A pair of Japanese Ko Kutani earthenware chargers, in iron red, blue, pink, green, black and gilt, 15 in (39.5 cm). **$800-1,200**

A pair of Japanese Imari dishes, Meiji period, 18 in (45.7 cm). **$800-1,200**

An Imari dish, 19thC, 18 (46 cm). **$400-600**

A Japanese dish, with blue and flower decorated border, 18 in (46 cm). **$400-600**

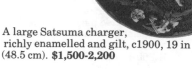

A large Satsuma charger, richly enamelled and gilt, c1900, 19 in (48.5 cm). **$1,500-2,200**

A set of five Kinkozan earthenware dishes, impressed square mark, 'Kinkozan tsuku' within gilt dragons, paper labels, minor rubbing, early 20thC, 8½ in (21.5 cm). **$3,000-4,000**

Garden Seats

A pair of Chinese blue and white garden seats, early 19thC, 18½ in (48 cm). **$4,500-5,000**

A pair of hexagonal garden seats, glazed in periwinkle blue and decorated in contrasting white slip with birds beside the Flowers of the Four Seasons, 18 in (47.3 cm). **$2,000-3,000**

pair of 'famille verte' garden ats, 19 in (49 cm). **$700-900**

A Chinese richly decorated garden seat, 19 in (49 cm). **$1,200-1,500**

Jardinieres

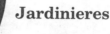

pair of blue and white diniéres and stands, small ps, late Qing Dynasty, e stand 9 in (22.8 cm). ,500-2,200

'amille rose' jardinière, orated on an opaque turquoise und, rim slightly chipped, 00, 12 in (31 cm). 500-2,200

A blue and white jardinière, Qianlong, 24 in (61 cm). **$3,500-5,000**

A pair of blue and white jardinières, one with base crack, late Qing Dynasty, 14 in (36.5 cm). **$2,500-3,500**

An Imari jardinière, 19thC. **$1,000-1,200**

A large Arita blue and white jardinière, late 19thC, 24½ in (62.8 cm). **$1,000-1,200**

A large Japanese Imari jardinière, decorated with coloured enamels and typical Imari colours, mid 19thC, 21 in (54 cm). **$3,000-4,000**

A blue and white close pattern jardinière, on hexagonal stand, damaged, early 19thC, 16 in (41 cm). **$1,400-1,700**

Jars

An ochre glazed red pottery jar, glazed in the interior and half way down the exterior over a white slip extending below the glaze, slight glaze frits, Tang Dynasty, 6½ in (16.5 cm). **$1,000-1,400**

Use the Index!

Because certain items might fit easily into any of a number of categories, the quickest and surest method of locating any entry is by reference to the index at the back of the book. This has been fully cross-referenced for absolute simplicity.

en glazed red pottery jar and r, chips, Han Dynasty, 9½ in 5 cm). **$2,500-3,500**

A grey stoneware jar, the body moulded with a dense cell pattern, with uncut foot, Warring States, 6 in (15.5 cm). **$1,000-1,200**

A large Chinese blue and white oviform jar, Transitional, c1660, 19 in (49 cm). **$3,000-4,500**

A Cizhou brown and white baluster jar, painted in dark chocolate brown on a creamy white ground, minor fritting, Jin/Yuan Dynasty, 5½ in (14 cm). **$1,400-1,700**

A large late Ming blue and white jar, painted in a strong colour with birds in flight between pine, prunus and bamboo, fritted, Wanli, 16½ in (42.5 cm). **$4,500-5,000**

◄ A pair of Chinese blue and white jars, both rims damaged, 19 in (49 cm). **$4,500-7,000**

A pair of Wucai baluster jars, painted with long tailed phoenix flying in pursuit of yellow scaly dragons grasping at blue flaming pearls above green waves, one neck hair crack, small rim chips, mid 17thC, 13 in (33 cm). **$1,700-2,500**

A 'famille verte' jar, on a seeded green ground band of lappet outline below a diaper border reserved with emblem vignettes encircling the shoulders, Kangxi, 8 in (20 cm). **$1,300-1,700**

A'famille rose' ginger jar and cover, the ovoid body painted and enamelled with flowers, late 18thC, 9½ in (24.5 cm). **$300-400**

A Kinkozan koro and cover, signed, 7 in (18 cm). **$1,500-2,200**

A large Imari baluster ► jar, painted in underglaze blue, iron red, coloured enamels and gilt, late 17th/early 18thC, 23 in (57.8 cm). **$2,000-3,000**

◄ A fine and rare large Imari octagonal baluster jar, painted in underglaze blue, iron red and gilt, the neck and foot mounted in European gilt metal, one pierced panel slightly damaged, Genroku period, 27 in (66.2 cm). **$4,500-7,000**

A large Imari jar and cover, slight damage, late 18th/early 19thC, 18 in (44 cm). **$4,500-5,000**

A large Arita blue and white baluster jar and domed cover, painted with scrolling karakusa and decorated in iroe hiramakie and takamakie, some of the lacquer chipped away, late 17th/early 18thC, the lacquer decoration probably of slightly later date, 36 in (90.5 cm). **$5,500-7,000**

An Arita blue and white jar, painted with panels of flowering chrysanthemum, late 17thC, 11½ in (29.8 cm). **$2,500-3,500**

A rare biscuit Cadogan winepot, the body washed in aubergine dappled in a richer tone, Kangxi, 7½ in (19 cm). **$1,700-2,500**

Tea & Coffee Pots

A silver mounted miniature blue and white teapot and domed cover, moulded with petal shaped panels of standing 'lange liezen', the porcelain Kangxi, the mounts probably contemporary European. **$1,000-1,200**

A Qianlong period Chinese mandarin coffee pot, c1760. **$700 900**

A puce decorated sauce tureen, cover and stand, late Qianlong, 7½ in (19 cm). **$1,000-1,400**

Tureens

An armorial tureen and cover with a matching dish, decorated in 'famille rose' enamels with the arms of Stephenson, further decorated in rich blue enamel heightened in gilding, Qianlong, tureen 12 in (30.4 cm). **$2,000-3,000**

A pair of 'famille rose' armorial vegetable tureens and covers, painted in iron red, pink enamel, blue enamel, grisaille and gilt, c1880, 11 in (27.5 cm). **$3,000-4,000**

A pair of 'famille rose' soup tureens and covers, Qianlong, 13 in (32.5 cm). **$3,500-5,000**

A blue and white tureen, cover and stand, Jiaqing, 15 in (37.4 cm). **$2,000-3,000**

A 'famille verte' rooster tureen and cover, the bird painted with grisaille details over the merging tones of yellow, green and light aubergine, the inside with a turquoise glaze now scratched, some restoration and repainting, early 19thC, 12 in (30.5 cm). **$1,700-2,500**

A green and gilt decorated bombé tureen, cover and stand, gilding rubbed on the finial, c1790, the stand 14½ in (36.5 cm). **$3,000-4,500**

Chinese Nankin blue and white tureen, cover and underdish. **$1,500-2,200**

A green glazed pottery vase, a translucent deep glaze thinning in the lower part, with some degradation, chipped, Han Dynasty, 15 in (38 cm). **$1,300-1,700**

Vases

A well potted northern white stoneware vessel, zhadou, the clear ivory glaze over an even white slip stopping neatly about the unglazed flat base, chipped, Tang Dynasty, 6 in (15.5 cm). **$3,000-4,500**

Cf. the very similar example at the Freer Gallery of Art, Washington, illustrated, Kodansha Series, vol 9, fig. 24, which is described as dating from the second half of the 9thC.

Two oviform funerary vases, under ivory white glazes pooling irregularly above the obliquely cut white feet, some restoration to extremities and one handle, Song Dynasty, both 15 in (37 cm). $2,000-3,000

A small brown glazed double gourd vase of Huang Dao type, the rich glaze thinning to pale brown at the rim and shoulder, the glaze stopping around the white stoneware footless base, c10thC, 3 in (8.8 cm). $1,300-1,700

A blue and white baluster vase, painted in blackish blue under a widely crackled glaze, probably from a South-Western kiln with Annamese influence, glaze bubble burst, rim fritted and possibly a rim crack, late 15thC, 15 in (37 cm). $1,500-2,200

A pair of late Ming blue and white vases, meiping, with widely crackled glazes, fired brown in areas, luting crack, late 16th/early 17thC, 9 in (23 cm). $1,500-2,200

A Transitional blue and white ➤ pear shaped vase, rim mounted in metal, rim reduced, c1640, 14 in (36 cm). $1,300-1,700

A Wucai baluster vase, decorated in 'famille verte' colours on iron red scale ground with birds, flowers and rocks, Transitional period, 15 in (37 cm). $600-900

A large late Ming blue and white gu-shaped vase Wanli, six character mark within a horizontal rectangle below the rim and of the period, damaged and repaired, 29 in (72.5 cm). $2,500-3,500

◄ A Chinese blue and white vase, Transitional, 14 in (35 cm). $1,300-1,700

A Transitional blue and white sleeve vase, c1650, 14 in (35 cm). $1,300-1,700

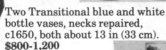

A Transitional blue and white bottle vase, rim crack and chips, mid-17thC, 15 in (37.5 cm). $1,500-2,200

Two blue and white octagonal vases, painted with exotic flowers, in the European style, chipped, one with large interior rim chip, early Kangxi, 18 in (46 cm). $2,500-3,500

Two Transitional blue and white bottle vases, necks repaired, c1650, both about 13 in (33 cm). $800-1,200

A dated Dehua blanc-de-chine ➤ sleeve vase, with Buddhistic lion mask handles carved on one side with a column of calligraphy under a milky white glaze, frit chips, dated guihai year, corresponding to AD 1683, and of the period, 18 in (45.5 cm). $1,700-2,500

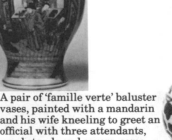

A pair of 'famille verte' baluster vases, painted with a mandarin and his wife kneeling to greet an official with three attendants, wood stands and covers, some repair to enamels, Kangxi, 14 in (34 cm). $5,500-7,000

Two blue and white baluster vases, chipped, Kangxi, 20½ in (51.5 cm). $3,000-4,000

A fine blue and white yanyan vase, small rim chips, Kangxi, 20 in (51 cm). $2,000-3,000

A pair of blue and white double gourd vases, Kangxi, 6½ in (16.5 cm). $1,500-2,200

A large 'famille verte' yanyan vase, neck restored and cracked, Kangxi, 34 in (69.5 cm). $3,000-4,000

A fine blue and white slender baluster vase, Kangxi, 18 in (44 cm). **$7,000-9,000**

◄ A good 'famille verte' triple gourd vase, decorated in enamels and underglaze blue, heightened in gilding, Kangxi, 14½ in (36.8 cm). **$4,500-7,000**

A blue and white gu-shaped beaker vase, fritted, rim underside chip, encircled leaf mark, Kangxi, 18 in (46.5 cm). **$1,700-2,500**

A Chinese blue and white yanyan vase, painted with figures in boats and before pagodas in mountainous river landscape, Kangxi, 18 in, (22.5 cm). **$1,000-1,200**

A pair of Chinese flower holders with pierced covers, painted in bright enamel colours and gold on a blue 'cracked ice' ground painted with flower heads, handles missing from cover, Qianlong, 7 in (17 cm). **$3,000-4,500**

A blue and white vase and cover, rosewood veneered stand, cracked, Kangxi, early 19thC, 24.7 in (61 cm). **$1,500-2,200**

A pair of 'famille rose' beaker vases, with pink ground shaped borders with lotus flowers at the necks and feet, damaged and restored, Yongzheng/early Qianlong, 14 in (35.3 cm). **$1,000-1,400**

Chinese 'famille rose' vase, with anels of birds and butterflies, anlong, c1820. **$400-600**

A 'famille rose' garniture of five vases, brightly decorated with vases of flowers within floral lappets above and below, Qianlong, 15 in (37 cm). **$5,500-7,000**

◄ A 'famille rose' baluster vase, painted with a gilt and iron red long tailed bird perched on rockwork beside peony, prunus and exotic flowers, Qianlong, 18½ in (46.5 cm). **$1,500-2,200**

pair of export reticulated vases, storation to foot and neck of one, e other minutely chipped, anlong, 12½ in (31.5 cm). **,500-2,200**

A pair of Canton hexagonal baluster jars and covers, covers glued or riveted, one jar cracked, Jiaqing, 25 in (63.5 cm). ► **$8,500-10,500**

A 'famille verte' vase, painted on each face with tall panels of two birds perched amongst lotus, rim crack, base chipped, Qing Dynasty, 20 in (50 cm). **$2,500-3,500**

A Chinese broad pear shaped vase, covered in an even sang-de-boeuf glaze, Qianlong seal and of the period, 12 in (30 cm). **$1,300-1,700**

A pair of 'famille rose' vases and covers, enamelled in colours and gilt with figures in palace landscapes, within gilt outlines on turquoise cell patterned grounds, restorations to handles and finials, Qianlong, 18 in (46 cm). **$8,500-11,000**

A pair of Chinese 'famille rose' vases and covers, covers damaged, Qianlong, 17½ in (44 cm). **$4,500-7,000**

A massive pair of 'famille noire' vases of yenyen form, the exterior decorated in 'famille verte' enamels on a lustrous black ground, with an overall scene depicting yellow breasted song birds amongst bamboo canes and blossoming prunus trees, the interior plain, 19thC, 35 in (88.9 cm). **$6,000-8,000**

A pair of Chinese blue and white porcelain baluster vases and covers, 19 in (47.5 cm). **$1,000-1,200**

A finely painted Canton 'famille rose' vase, the sides painted with Hundred Antiques beneath polychrome ruyi-sceptre handles, between a gilt ground mouth and foot strewn with butterflies and flowers, Jiaqing, 23½ in (60 cm). **$2,000-3,000**

An unusual 'famille rose' vase and cover, the salmon pink ground enriched in gilding with fruiting vines, reserved on one side with a panel of courtiers surrounding a dignitary, Jiaqing, 26½ in (67.3 cm). **$4,500-7,000**

A pair of Cantonese vases, painted in 'famille rose' palette with panels of birds and insects amongst flowers and figures in pavilions, Daoguang, 14 in (35.9 cm). **$1,200-1,500**

A Chinese porcelain vase, painted in blue with a scene of Orientals around a stall, 18 in (45 cm). **$300-500**

A Chinese porcelain vase and cover, neck repaired, 16 in (40 cm). **$500-700**

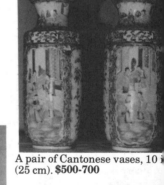

A pair of Cantonese vases, 10 in (25 cm). **$500-700**

A pair of Chinese vases, painted iron red, the body with a continuous scene of a fishing village with figures, painted various tones of green enamels, 19thC, 14 in (35 cm). **$400-600**

A Canontese vase, some damage, 18 in (45 cm). **$300-500**

A Cantonese cylindrical vase, with wooden stand, 18 in (45 cm). **$500-600**

A pair of Canton 'famille rose' vases, each vividly decorated with numerous panels enclosing dignitaries and attendants, reserved on a scroll filled gilt ground, wood stands, Guangxu, 24 in (60.7 cm). **$3,000-4,000**

A pair of Chinese blue and white pillar vases, each decorated with a pair of dragons among chrysanthemums, peony and other foliage, cracked, late 19thC, 24 in (60 cm). **$1,000-1,400**

A fine Arita blue and white bottle vase, painted with three sparrows among flowering chrysanthemum and rocks, a tiny figure of a fisherman running over waves in the foreground, late 17thC, 16 in (39.1 cm). **$10,000-13,000**

A Japanese porcelain vase, painted in blue, green, iron red and gilt with sprays of tree peonies, damaged, 17thC, 11½ in (29 cm). **$1,700-2,500**

pair of Chinese vases, on a black round, Kangxi marks in verglaze blue, Guangxu, 16½ in 42 cm). **$1,000-1,400**

A Japanese Imari vase, moulded and painted in blue, iron red, green and gilt with sprays of chrysanthemums, peonies and foliage on a white ground, 19thC, 20 in (49 cm). **$2,500-3,500**

A Japanese Imari vase and cover, repaired, late 17thC, 25½ in (64.7 cm). **$1,000-1,200**

A Satsuma trumpet shaped vase, painted in colours and gilt with a butterfly among flowering chrysanthemums before tsuitate between rows of lappets, 19thC, 7 in (17.8 cm). **$600-900**

A fine and rare Kyoto ware calendar vase, the buff stoneware body painted in coloured enamels and gilt over a finely crackled creamy glaze with the calendar for the year 1705 A.D. Kyoto, 19thC, 13½ in (33.9 cm). **$2,500-3,500**

The first page of the calendar is shown which provides correspondences between successive days and the Japanese cyclical system, with notes on other relevant matters. In the 18thC such calendars were sold under Government monopoly, and various devices were resorted to by vendors to publish them.

fine Hirado blue and white vase, ainted in underglaze cobalt blue nd moulded in low relief with two rge carp against a background of mountainous river landscape, 9thC, 16 in (39.7 cm). ,000-1,200

A pair of Japanese cream glazed earthenware vases, impressed mark to base, 13 in (32.5 cm). **$600-800**

A pair of large Satsuma pottery vases, painted in iron red, colours, richly gilt and moulded in relief with warriors in landscapes, 17 in (42.5 cm). **$4,000-5,000**

Satsuma oviform vase, corated in blue enamel on a ely crackled off white ground th an overall hanabishi design, ted with a silvered metal rim, erced silvered metal cover, thC. **$800-1,200**

A pair of Kutani vases, 14 in (36 cm). **$1,000-1,400**

An Ao-Kutani vase, enamelled in various shades of green, aubergine, yellow and black on a crackled ground, Fuku mark on the base, 19thC, 18 in (45.8 cm). **$1,400-1,700**

A Satsuma beaker vase, decorated in iron red, coloured enamels and gilt with shaped rectangular panels of Rakan and other figures, signed on the base Fukyuen, and Kao, 19thC, 18 in (47.7 cm). $1,500-2,200

A Fukagawa vase, decorated in underglaze blue, iron red, sumi and slight colour with three swimming carp, Meiji period, 8 in (20.3 cm). $600-900

A large Satsuma vase, with a gold painted foot and neck, 18 in (46 cm). $1,500-2,200

An Arita vase and domed cover with seated karashishi finial, painted in underglaze blue, iron red, coloured enamels and gilt, body with slight glaze cracks, signed on the base Fukagawa se late 19thC. $4,000-5,000

A Japanese Imari vase, moulde and painted in blue, iron red, green and gilt with sprays of chrysanthemums, peonies and foliage on a white ground, 19thC, 19½ in (49 cm). $2,500-3,500

A large Imari vase, painted in underglaze blue, iron red and gilt with cranes among pine, bamboo, berried foliage and rocks between shaped floral lappets, the inner rim with bamboo sprays, late 19thC, 37 in (92 cm). $2,000-3,000

A Japanese vase, painted in underglaze blue with bamboo, on a yellow ground, signed Makazu Kozan, 13 in (32.5 cm). $2,000-3,000

A Japanese Imari vase, Meiji period, 36 in (90 cm). $2,500-3,500

A pair of large Kutani vases, painted in iron red and gilding with a large eagle eyeing a small monkey, inscribed mark 'Dai Nihon, Kutani, Akako', c1900, 18 in (46.2 cm). $3,000-4,000

A Kinkozan earthenware vase, on a deep blue ground embellished with gilt and silvered panels of flowers, trelliswork and vine, c1900, 10 in (24.5 cm). $800-1,200

A Japanese Imari vase, decorated with cranes in flight on a diaper ground between stylised foliate borders, Meiji period, 15 in (38 cm). $1,300-1,700

An unusual Arita vase, painted in underglaze blue, colours and gilt with carp swimming in an iris pond, signed on the base Dai Nihon Arita cho Fukagawa sei above the words 'Nishikide Wara, Made in Japan', late Meiji period, 14½ in (36.4 cm). $800-1,200

A pair of Japanese Imari vases, Meiji period, 25 in (64.2 cm). $3,000-4,500

Miscellaneous

A Chinese blue and white basket, some damage, Qianlong, 15 in (38 cm). $300-600

A blue and white bidet, of keyhole shape, Qianlong, 24 in (61 cm). $1,500-2,200

A 'famille rose' bourdalou, the sides painted with sprays of peony and pomegranate under a gilt spearhead border, Qianlong, 9 in (22.5 cm). $600-800

A silver mounted 'famille rose' snuff box and cover, glaze slightly rubbed, the porcelain Qianlong, in (7 cm) $1,000-1,200

A large Doucai pillow, painted with four phoenix in flight amongst scrolling peony on a green quatrefoil panel, cracks and fritting, 18thC, 22½ in (56 cm). $1,500-2,200

A pair of 'famille verte' flasks, painted in bright enamels with arrangements of Precious Objects, Kangxi, 9 in (23.2 cm). 4,500-7,000

A Chinese stupor (shrine), in 'famille rose' colours, made for the Chinese market, Jiaqing, c1800. $1,700-2,500

A pair of Chinese blue and white altar sticks, in early Ming style, painted in rich underglaze blue with scrolling flowers showing 'heaped and piled' effect, between key fret borders, Guangxu, 21½ in (54.3 cm). $1,500-2,200

A Transitional blue and white candlestick, chipped, neck cracked, c1650, 10 in (25.5 cm). $1,700-2,500

A 'famille verte' biscuit shrine, on yellow and trellis pattern grounds, some restoration, fitted box, Kangxi, 4½ in (11.5 cm). $1,500-2,200

A pair of large blue and white carp, changing into dragons, the character Wang reserved on their foreheads, some restoration, late Qing Dynasty, 22 by 13 in (55 by 33 cm). $3,000-4,500

A pair of Chinese blue and white sauce boats, 18thC, Qianlong period. $500-600

A small Chinese Imari teacaddy, painted and moulded with panels of pagodas in mountainous river landscapes, wood cover, Kangxi, 3½ in (8.5 cm). $300-500

Chinese dynasties and marks

Earlier Dynasties

Shang Yin, c.1532-1027 B.C.
Western Zhou (Chou) 1027-770 B.C.
Spring and Autumn Annals 770-480 B.C.
Warring States 484-221 B.C.
Qin (Ch'in) 221-206 B.C.
Western Han 206 BC-24 AD
Eastern Han 25-220
Three Kingdoms 221-265
Six Dynasties 265-589
Wei 386-557

Sui 589-617
Tang (T'ang) 618-906
Five Dynasties 907-960
Liao 907-1125
Sung 960-1280
Chin 1115-1260
Yüan 1280-1368

Ming Dynasty

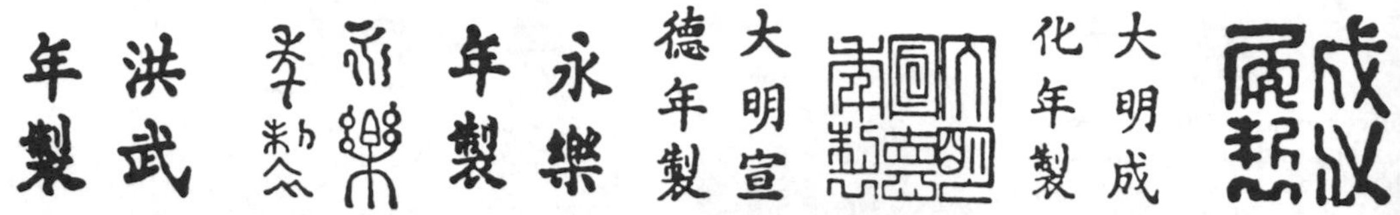

Hongwu (Hung Wu)
1368-1398

Yongle (Yung Lo)
1403-1424

Xuande (Hsüan Té)
1426-1435

Chenghua (Ch'éng Hua)
1465-1487

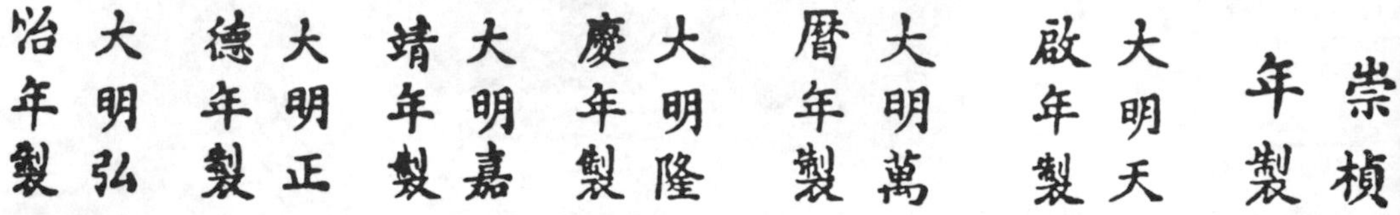

Hongzhi
(Hung Chih)
1488-1505)

Zhengde
(Chéng Té)
1506-1521

Jiajing
(Chia Ching)
1522-1566

Longqing
(Lung Ching)
1567-1572

Wanli (Wan Li)
1573-1620

Tianqi
(Tien Chi)
1621-1627

Chongzhen
(Ch'ung Chêng)
1628-1644

Qing (Ch'ing) Dynasty

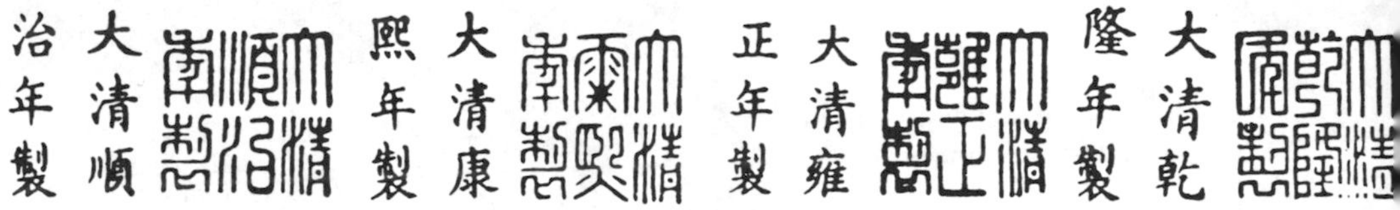

Shunzhi
(Shun Chih)
1644-1661

Kangxi (K'ang Hsi)
1662-1722

Yongzheng (Yung Chêng)
1723-1735

Qianlong (Ch'ien Lung)
1736-1795'

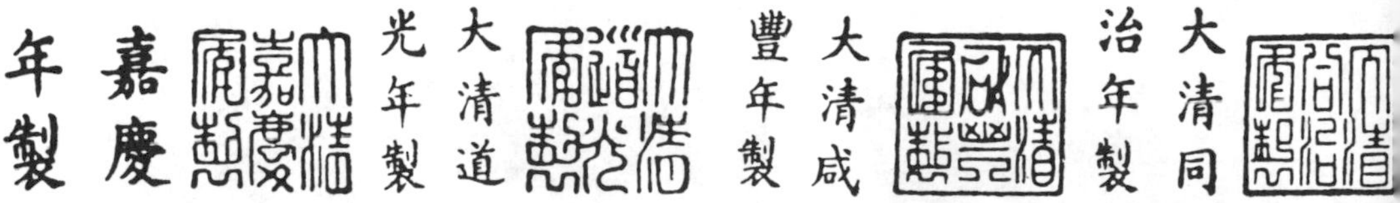

Jiaqing (Chia Ch'ing)
1796-1820

Daoguang (Tao Kuang)
1821-1850

Xianfeng (Hsien Féng)
1851-1861

Tongzhi (T'ung Chih)
1862-1874

Guangxu (Kuang Hsu)
1875-1908

Xuantong
(Hsuan T'ung)
1909-1911

Hongxian
(Hung Hsien)
1916

TURNED TABLE LEGS OF THE SEVENTEENTH CENTURY

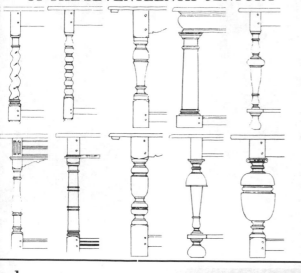

MONARCH CHRONOLOGY

Dates	Monarchs	Period
1558-1603	Elizabeth I	Elizabethan
1603-1625	James I	Jacobean
1625-1649	Charles I	Carolean
1649-1660	Commonwealth	Cromwellian
1660-1685	Charles II	Restoration
1685-1689	James II	Restoration
1689-1694	William & Mary	William & Mary
1694-1702	William III	William III
1702-1714	Anne	Queen Anne
1714-1727	George I	Early Georgian
1727-1760	George II	Georgian
1760-1812	George III	Late Georgian
1812-1820	George III	Regency
1820-1830	George IV	Late Regency
1830-1837	William IV	William IV
1837-1860	Victoria	Early Victorian
1860-1901	Victoria	Late Victorian
1901-1910	Edward VII	Edwardian

Beds

n oak cradle, with chamfered
ood and turned finials on ring
urned supports joined by a
nforming stretcher, 18thC, 36 in
1.5 cm). **$1,000-1,200**

An English panelled oak cradle,
18thC, 36 in (90 cm).
$1,000-1,400

A panelled oak cradle, with
shaped hood with carved knob
finials, on rockers, 18thC.
$1,000-1,400

An oak bed, the panelled tester
carved with flowerheads entrelacs
and arcades, the footrest with
geometric strapwork and central
mask with moulded sides, box
mattress, 17thC and later, 51½ in
(131 cm). **$2,500-3,500**

n oak four post bed, with some
storation, mid-17thC.
,500-11,000

An oak four poster, with
restorations, made up from 17th
and 18thC oak, 60 in (105 cm).
$4,500-7,000

Bureaux

A George I oak bureau, the fall
revealing small drawers, pigeon
holes and a well, above a dummy
long drawer, on later bracket feet,
35 in (87 cm). **$1,500-2,200**

A Queen Anne oak and
crossbanded bureau, the fall
revealing a stepped and fitted
interior, c1710, 36½ in (93 cm).
$2,000-3,000

A George III oak bureau bookcase, the lower part with a cleated flap enclosing a fitted interior, late 18thC, the bookcase section later, 36 in (92 cm) wide. **$3,000-4,500**

An Italian Renaissance walnut cabinet, c1600, Genoa, 36 in (90 cm) wide. **$10,500-14,000**

A George III oak bureau bookcas c1750. **$5,500-7,000**

Chairs

A carved oak box seat settle, dated 1664, 54 in (117 cm). **$4,000-5,000**

A settle in oak, 19thC, 76 in (118 cm). **$600-900**

An oak joined back wainscot armchair, the top rail inscribe John Cort, mid-17thC. **$1,000-1,200**

An oak and ash turned armchair, 17thC, 49 by 39 in (122 by 73 cm). **$1,500-2,200**

See Eric Mercer, Furniture 700-1,700. Illustration No. 46. Here benches of secular origin dating from the 12th-13th Centuries are shown, of very similar form.

An oak wainscot chair, with restored feet, mid-17thC, 25 in (62.5 cm) wide. **$1,000-1,400**

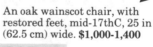

A composed set of eight joined back Farthingale dining chairs, some with restorations, 17thC. **$7,500-10,500**

An oak wainscot armchair, late 17thC. **$1,500-2,200**

An oak armchair, with carved top rail and carved with a motif to the centre of the back panel, 17thC. **$1,500-2,200**

A Commonwealth oak wainsc armchair, c1650. **$3,000-4,000**

A large wainscot chair, late 17thC, 29 in (72 cm) wide. **$5,500-7,000**

An oak chair, 17thC, 26 in (65 cm) wide. **$1,700-2,500**

A Charles II carved walnut armchair, c1680. **$1,500-2,200**

A rare Charles II oak child's chair, 1675. **$4,000-5,000**

A pair of Charles II style carved walnut and cane armchairs, c1880. **$1,300-1,700**

An oak Eisteddfod commemorative wainscot armchair, carved Eisteddfod, Gadeiriol, Meirioion Calan 1907, the back stamped Owen Tudor, Carver Bolgellau. **$600-900**

A Charles II upholstered oak armchair, lower part of back legs restored, c1660. **$3,500-5,000**

A set of 10 Lancashire carved panel-back oak chairs, harlequin set, 1660-1680. **$1,400-1,700**

One of a set of eight Commonwealth style oak chairs, including two carvers, the rectangular backs and stuffed seats covered in nailed hide, restored. **$4,000-5,000**

A Scottish oak armchair with gouge and floret carved top rail, lozenge and gouge carved panel back. **$1,500-2,200**

A set of six oak chairs, including two carvers in 17thC style. **$1,500-2,200**

A set of six oak dining chairs, with barley twist columns and stretchers. **$2,000-3,000**

A set of four Charles II beechwood side chairs, with restorations, late 17thC. **$1,700-2,500**

A set of eight William and Mary style oak framed armchairs. **$4,500-5,000**

A pair of limed oak thrones, the crestings carved with masks and pierced scrolling foliage, with later bun feet. **$1,700-2,500**

A pair of late Victorian architect designed Gothic oak armchairs. **$800-1,200**

A Charles II walnut chair, with spindle turned back within ball turned uprights with reserve blocks, c1675. **$1,400-1,700**

A pair of James II walnut and beechwood side chairs, one stamped I.T. **$2,000-3,000**

An oak chair, 17thC. **$300-400**

A William and Mary walnut side chair, the arched partly caned back with pierced strapwork splat scrolled gadrooned cresting, the frame carved with flowerheads, with later blocks. **$1,500-2,200**

A pair of James II oak, ash and fruitwood side chairs, the scroll carved toprails above moulded and convex slats within turned uprights, c1690. **$2,500-3,500**

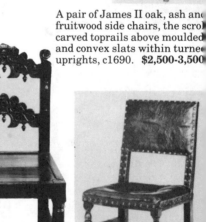

A set of four oak side chairs, three with spliced back legs, late 17thC. **$3,000-4,500**

A Harlequin set of five Derbyshire oak side chairs, two stamped RS, early 17thC. **$5,500-7,000**

An oak Yorkshire chair. **$800-1,200**

A Harlequin set of six oak and leather dining chairs, with restorations, c1700. **$3,000-4,500**

A set of eight George III ash, elm and fruitwood ladder back chairs, including a pair of armchairs. **$5,500-7,000**

A set of eight elm ladder back dining chairs, early 19thC. **$5,500-7,000**

A pair of yew and beech Windsor chairs. **$1,000-1,200**

An ash and elm ladder back elbow chair, 18thC. **$1,000-1,200**

A pair of yew and beechwood Windsor chairs, early 19thC, c1800. **$1,500-2,200**

A matched set of six Lancashire spindle back chairs, 19thC. **$3,000-4,500**

A yewwood, elm and beechwood Windsor armchair, early 19thC. **$1,500-2,200**

A pair of comb-back Windsor side chairs, 2 legs pieced, New England, late 19thC, 37in (92.5cm). **$1,500-1,800**

PRICES

The never-ending problem of fixing prices for antiques! A price can be affected by so many factors, for example:
- *condition*
- *desirability*
- *rarity*
- *size*
- *colour*
- *provenance*
- *restoration*
- *the sale of a prestigious collection*
- *collection label*
- *appearance of a new reference book*
- *new specialist sale at major auction house*
- *mentioned on television*
- *the fact that two people present at auction are determined to have the piece*
- *where you buy it*

One also has to contend with the fact that an antique is not only a 'thing of beauty' but a commodity. The price can again be affected by:–
- *supply and demand*
- *international finance – currency fluctuation*
- *fashion*
- *inflation*
- *the fact that a museum has vast sums of money to spend*

229

A maple slat-back chair, the turned finials above sausage-turned posts, rear legs pieced, one front stretcher restored, one slat repaired, New England, mid-18thC, 47in (117.5cm). **$300-400**

A William and Mary maple and ash bannister-back armchair, with ogee-shaped tablet crest flanked by baluster-turned finials, New England, 1720-1750, 48in (120cm). **$3,000-4,000**

A pair of William and Mary mapl and ash carved bannister-back side chairs, 3 finials restored, Nev England, 1720-1740, each 44½in (111cm). **$4,000-5,000**

A slat-back maple armchair, repairs to arm, Delaware Valley, 1750-1800, 44in (110cm). **$2,500-3,000**

An assembled set of 6 Chippendal maple side chairs, pieced feet, New England, 1760-1780, 40½in (101cm). **$2,600-3,000**

A black-painted slat-back armchair, Delaware River Valley, mid-18thC, 49in (122.5cm). **$2,000-2,500**

A Queen Anne painted maple armchair, with molded yoke crest above a solid vasiform splat, with baluster-turned legs, joined by a baluster-turned front stretcher with Spanish feet, feet pieced, New England, 1730-1750, 45½in (113.5cm). **$1,000-1,200**

A pair of fan-back Windsor side chairs, old black paint, New England, 1770-1790, 38in (95cm **$1,100-1,300**

A painted ash child's armchair, now upholstered in Victorian berlin work and painted black with gilt details, New England, 18thC, 25in (62.5cm). **$450-500**

A maple and ash slat-back side chair, Hackensack area, New Jersey, late 18thC, 38½in (96cm). **$500-600**

A Windsor fan-back armchair, arms restored, repair to one stile, Philadelphia, 1790-1800, 43in (107.5cm). **$3,500-4,000**

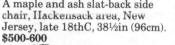

A Windsor style sack-back armchair, labelled on underside of seat, by the Fancy and Windsor Chair Manufactory, New York, 1923, 37in (92.5cm). **$450-550**

A Windsor armchair, on bamboo-turned legs joined by swelled H-stretcher, patch to seat, Philadelphia, 1790-1820, 37in (92.5cm). **$1,300-1,800**

A child's sack-back Windsor armchair, on bamboo-turned legs joined by swelled H-stretchers, New England, mid-19thC, 23in (57.5cm). **$800-1,000**

A comb-back Windsor armchair, on bamboo-turned legs joined by stretchers, repairs, 39½in (98.5cm). **$500-600**

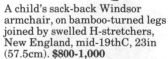

A set of four Macclesfield chairs. **$2,000-3,000**

231

A harlequin set of seven George IV elm and yewwood Windsor armchairs, two stamped Wheatland Rockley.
$7,500-10,500

William Wheatland is first recorded as a chair maker living and working at Beardsalls Row, East Retford, Notts, in 1822. In 1821 he was the Wesleyan leader in a small parish of Gamston which lies close to the hamlet of Rockley. By 1828 he is recorded as chair maker and Wesleyan Class leader in Rockley. By 1841 William Wheatland is no longer recorded as living in the parish.

An elm Windsor armchair, mid-19thC, **$300-600**

A set of six early 19thC. Windsor armchairs, stamped F. Walker ➤ Rockley. **$7,500-10,500**

Frederick Walker was born at Thornhill, near to Leeds in 1798. In 1823 he was a member of the Gamston Methodist Society and by 1828 he was a member of William Wheatland's class at Rockley. He became class leader himself in 1831, and remained so for at least 30 years. By 1851, he and his son Henry were the only remaining chair makers in the parish, where they were specifically called Windsor chairmakers.

A small elm rail back Windsor type armchair, c1850. **$300-400**

l. A low back Windsor armchair in yew with elm seat, late 18thC. **$600-900**
r. A low back Windsor armchair in elm and yew, early 19thC. **$1,000-1,200**

A small yew and elm Windsor elbow chair, with crinoline stretcher. **$600-900**

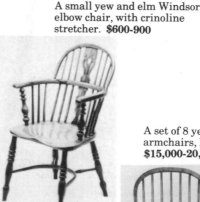

A set of 8 yew-wood low back armchairs, late 18thC. **$15,000-20,500**

A broad arm North country elm Windsor chair, c1860. **$500-700**

A set of five yew wood Windsor elbow chairs, with elm seats, early 19thC. **$5,500-7,000**

Two from a matched set of eight ➤ ash and elm Windsor armchairs, with stick backs and solid seats. **$4,500-5,000**

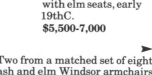

A set of eight Gothic Windsor dining chairs, principally of elm and beech, two carvers, six standard, 20thC. **$2,000-3,000**

A primitive elm cottage armchair, 19thC. **$500-700**

A rare Dutch oak child's chair, second half 17thC, 40½ in (102 cm). **$2,500-3,500**

A pair of baroque beechwood open armchairs, Low Countries, some restorations, late 17thC. **$2,000-3,000**

A pair of Italian walnut open armchairs, 17thC. **$3,000-4,500**

A pair of Roman walnut armchairs, partly 17thC. **$4,500-5,000**

A set of four Spanish oak and walnut armchairs, padded with embossed leather, with restorations, mid-18thC. **$4,500-7,000**

A pair of Italian walnut side chairs, late 17thC. **$700-1,000**

Chests

An oak chest, with Romayne heads, early 16thC, 67 in (170 cm). **$10,500-14,000**

A rare example of a studded velvet covered travelling chest, with original metalwork, 1580-1640, 37 in (92.5 cm). **$2,000-3,000**

A James I oak chest, the three front panels applied with diamond mouldings and two carved with roses, one corner of the top with an old break, lockplate replaced, c1620, 41½ in (106 cm) wide. **$3,000-4,500**

An oak coffer, with nulling motif to front, c1630, 40 in (100 cm) wide. **$700-1,000**

A James I oak boarded chest, the front plank carved with enriched nulling and simple diamonds, c1620, 41 in (104 cm) wide. **$2,000-3,000**

A Chippendale pine blanket chest, on bracket feet, restoration to side panelling and one segment of a top panel, Pennsylvania, late 18thC, 57in (142.5cm) wide. **$1,200-1,600**

A Chippendale grain-painted blanket chest, the top lifting above a compartment with a till, the surface with brown sponged decoration, the case with 3 arched panels of blue graining within white borders, the moldings painted red, the feet painted black, patch to top, black and white paint possibly restored, Pennsylvania, late 18thC, 49½in (123.5cm) wide. **$2,500-3,000**

A Chippendale sponge-painted pine miniature blanket chest, the top opening to a well with covered till, painted with yellow and red sponge decoration, repairs to feet, Pennsylvania, late 18thC, 17in (42.5cm) wide. **$700-1,000**

A Chippendale mahogany blanket chest, Pennsylvania, 1760-1790, 52in (130cm). **$1,300-1,600**
This chest had with it a complete genealogy. This can considerably increase the value.

A Chippendale pine blanket chest, the top with applied molded edge opening to a well with covered till, some restoration to feet, Pennsylvania, 1770-1800, 49in (122.5cm) wide. **$400-600**

A shaker box, the molded lid with self-locking mechanism, signed in red ink 'Made July 1843, New Lebanon', New Lebanon, New York, mid-19thC, 19in (47.5cm) long. **$500-700**

An oak bridal chest, with iron strap hinges and handles either side with original lock, with firm's logo, by Roycroft, c1912, 46in (116.8cm) wide. **$1,800-2,400**

A Federal grain-painted blanket chest, the top with applied molded edge opening to a well, the case elaborately grain-painted in black and red, on French feet, Pennsylvania, early 19thC, 44in (110cm) wide. **$600-700**

An oak six plank coffer, pegged throughout, c1630, 29½ in (73 cm) wide. **$700-1,000**

An oak coffer, West Country, early 17thC, 48 in (120 cm). **$1,000-1,400**

A James I oak coffer, the four panelled lid above a leaf and scroll carved frieze, the front centred by a panel carved with scrolls, fleur-de-lys, the initials IF and the date 1613, the carving and pellet mouldings retaining traces of the original black paint, 54 in (138 cm) wide. **$2,000-3,000**
cf. Victor Chinnery, The Oak Tradition, page 116.

A Charles I oak chest, the frieze carved with scrolling strapwork and leaves, Gloucestershire, c1630, lid later, 61 in (155 cm) wide. **$4,500-5,000**

A Jacobean oak chest, the drawers with moulded fronts and brass drop handles, 37 in (92.5 cm). **$2,000-3,000**

A Commonwealth oak chest of drawers, with a saw edged banding, with later bun feet and handles, c1650, 45 in (114 cm) wide. **$1,000-1,400**

A Charles I oak child's chest, c1640, 21 in (53 cm) wide. **$2,000-3,000**

A Charles II walnut chest of drawers, the drawers applied with geometric mouldings divided by a bead moulding, on bun feet, c1675, 37 in (94 cm). **$3,000-4,500**

A coffer, with inlaid panels, mid-17thC. **$3,000-4,500**

An oak chest, the two panels carved with flowers and fruit above a jewelled apron, the sides similarly carved, mid-17thC, 54 in (137 cm). **$1,500-2,200**

An oak plank chest, with carved floral decoration, 17thC, 51 in (127.5 cm). **$1,000-1,400**

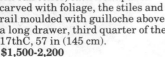

An oak coffer, each front panel carved with foliage, the stiles and rail moulded with guilloche above a long drawer, third quarter of the 17thC, 57 in (145 cm). **$1,500-2,200**

A fine oak dower chest, the front four panels each carved with a Tudor Rose and the top rail with arcaded carving and a lock, 17thC, 66 in (165 cm). **$1,400-1,700**

An early oak coffer, with carved frieze, 48 in (120 cm). **$800-1,200**

An oak boarded chest, c1660, 35 in (87.5 cm). **$600-700**

A Charles II oak chest, the later plank top above a panelled frieze drawer, 46 in (117 cm). **$2,500-3,500**

An early walnut and oak chest, drawers with geometric mouldings, raised on bun feet, 32 in (80 cm). **$3,000-4,500**

A Charles II oyster veneered walnut fruitwood and oak chest, on later bun feet, with later back, 41 in (104 cm) wide. **$1,700-2,500**

An oak chest, in two parts, the drawers with geometrically moulded panels, partially veneered in fruitwood, bun feet, mid-17thC, 40 in (100 cm). **$3,000-4,500**

An oak chest, with deep moulded panels, with original escutcheons, c1660, 40 in (100 cm) wide. **$1,700-2,500**

An oak linenfold coffer, 44 in (110 cm). **$1,700-2,500**

A Charles II oak chest on stand, the drawers with applied mouldings and bobbin turned borders, c1680, 39 in (100 cm) wide. **$4,500-7,000**

An oak coffer, the top with a moulded border above a frieze rail signed Thomas Moult, 1668, 51 in (130 cm). **$1,700-2,500**

A Charles II oak coffer, the central front panel inscribed J. Partrig, above a stylised bird, the top rail initialled and dated 1680, 51 in (130 cm) wide. **$1,700-2,500**

A Charles II walnut chest of drawers, c1680. **$4,500-5,000**

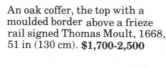

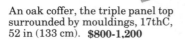

An oak coffer, the triple panel top surrounded by mouldings, 17thC, 52 in (133 cm). **$800-1,200**

A William and Mary fruitwood chest, the crossbanded planked rectangular top with a dentilled and corbelled frieze, 41½ in (102.5 cm). **$5,500-7,000**

237

An oak coffer, initialled I.B. dated 1699. **$3,000-4,500**

An oak chest on chest, with restorations, late 17thC, 58 in (148 cm). **$1,400-1,700**

A James II moulded oak chest of drawers with secret drawer, c1685. **$3,000-4,500**

A mid Georgian oak and mahogany banded dwarf linen chest, on ogee bracket feet, 62 in (155 cm). **$1,400-1,700**

A panelled oak coffer, dated 1700. **$1,500-2,200**

An oak mule chest, with geometrically moulded panelled front, 17thC, 48 in (120 cm). **$800-1,200**

A Gothic Revival carved oak chest, with painted Victorian wooden plinth, c1876, 61½ in (15. cm) wide. **$4,500-5,000**

The interior bearing the carved inscription Made from oak 160 years old from Salisbury Cathedral. Harry Hems carved Exeter England 1876. Medal awarded Philadelphia 1876, Honourable mention awarded Paris 1878, Gold medal Douglas Isle of Man 1892. Harry Hems (London 1842-Exeter 1916), work is found in different parts of England though he settled in Exeter, Devonshire, where he founded 'The Lucky Horse Shoe', 69, Paris Street, Exeter, and devoted the remainder of his life mainly to ecclesiastical wood carving and restoration.

A George III oak chest, with crossbanded top, 37 in (94 cm) wide. **$1,500-2,200**

A James I carved and inlaid mule chest. **$10,500-14,000**

An oak mule chest, with original lock, 17thC, 46 in (115 cm). **$1,400-1,700**

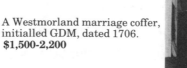

A small George III oak chest of drawer, with brushing slide and dressing mirror, c1775, 30 in (75 cm) wide. **$4,500-5,000**

A Westmorland marriage coffer, initialled GDM, dated 1706. **$1,500-2,200**

An oak mule chest, with scroll carved frieze, four parquetry and marquetry decorated front panels, on later stand, 18thC, 51 in (127.5 cm) wide. **$800-1,200**

A George III oak corn chest, the hinged cover with a shallow raised back and open tier, below are four fielded panels, four apron drawers and apertures, c1760, 63 in (161 cm) wide. **$1,000-1,200**

An oak mule chest, having applied geometric decoration, 17thC, 55 in (137.5 cm). **$1,400-1,700**

A George III oak mule chest, with hinged top over six dummy drawers and three small drawers to the base, 61 in (154 cm) wide. **$1,400-1,700**

A pair of Italian Renaissance walnut and parcel gilt cassones, 16thC, 63 in (161 cm) wide. **$15,000-20,500**

A yew wood mule chest, early 18thC, 48 in (120 cm) wide. **$3,000-4,500**

An Italian walnut cassone, the front panels carved in deep relief with Roman mythological scenes, 17thC, 70 in (160 cm). **$3,000-4,500**

A Italian Adige chest, the interior fitted a candle box, 17thC. **$800-1,200**

A Dutch oak commode, c1750, 49 in (123 cm) wide. **$4,500-7,000**

A Spanish walnut vargueno, with interior drawers, carved in the manner of Berrugnette, restoration to interior, c1550, 41 in (102.5 cm). **$1,400-1,700**

A Flemish oak coffer, the fielded panels carved with tracery divided by beaded and foliate pinnacled pilaster columns, on block feet, 19thC, 55 in (137.5 cm). **$2,000-3,000**

A German iron bound Gothic chest, 74 in (188 cm) wide. **$7,000-9,000**

Cupboards

A Charles II oak mural spice cupboard, enclosing an arrangement of four further drawers, the base renewed, c1680, 11½ in (30 cm) wide. **$1,500-2,200**

An Italian & Renaissance carved and inlaid walnut cassone, restorations, 80½ in (200 cm) wide. **$1,700-2,500**

An oak bow front corner cupboard with mahogany crossbanding column surmounted with boxwood inlay, interior fitted with unusual fretwork frieze, brasses original, c1780. **$800-1,200**

A small James II cedarwood spice cupboard, the plain plank door inlaid with a geometric pattern in fruitwood stringing, the interior with a series of eight oak drawers of varying size, c1690, 12 in (30 cm) wide. **$1,500-2,200**

Illustrated by Victor Chinnery, op. cit., p. 334, fig. 3.302.

A George III oak corner cupboard, c1780. **$800-1,200**

A standing oak corner cupboard, back partly replaced, 18thC, 48 in (122 cm). **$1,500-2,200**

A George III oak and mahogany banded standing corner cupboard, 40 in (100 cm). **$1,700-2,500**

A William and Mary oak court cupboard, the frieze incised with initials and date JE 1697, the cornice a later replacement, 56 in (142 cm). **$1,500-2,200**

A standing oak corner cupboard, back partly replaced, 18thC, 48 in (122 cm). **$1,500-2,200**

An oak tridarn, with restorations, c1680, 54½ in (136 cm). **$2,500-3,500**

A Welsh oak tridarn, carved later and dated 1724, wooden knobs, 18thC, 53 in (132.5 cm). **$1,500-2,200**

A small George I Welsh oak tridarn, initialed S.H. dated 1720. **$3,500-5,000**

An oak three tier court cupboard, 17thC, 48 in (120 cm). **$6,000-8,500**

An oak livery cupboard, the overhanging cornice carved with stylised foliage, early 17thC and later, 49½ in (125 cm) wide. **$4,500-7,000**

George I Welsh oak tridarn, 720. $3,500-5,000

An oak press cupboard, late 18thC, 59 in (150 cm) wide. $2,500-3,500

An English canted buffet, in oak and inlaid with other woods, from the 17thC. $1,400-1,700

fine oak press cupboard, with erhanging moulded cornice, the eze carved with flower heads, e doors inlaid with geometric arquetry within entrelac arches, rly 17thC, 61 in (155 cm) wide. ,000-8,500

A Charles I oak press cupboard, probably Gloucestershire, with restoration, c1640. $2,500-3,500

A Charles II oak Lancashire press cupboard, the cornice carved with meandering leaves and berries, above doors outlined with chevron banding carved Thomas Meller and Ellen Meller 1681, 55 in (140 cm). $3,500-5,000

A George II oak press cupboard, 53½ in (136 cm) wide. $2,000-3,000

A George II oak panelled wardrobe, c1740. $3,000-4,500

An oak clothes press with two moulded panel doors, inlaid with boxwood and ebony star motifs, 18thC, 52 in (130 cm) wide. $2,500-3,500

A small George III oak livery cupboard, original pegs to interior, iron 'H' hinges to panelled doors, c1750. $3,000-4,500

A Welsh oak press cupboard, c1790, 53 in (135 cm) wide. $2,000-3,000

oak hanging cupboard, with elled doors, 18thC, 60 in 0 cm) wide. $1,000-1,400

A George III Welsh oak cupboard, with rope twist canted corners, shaped panelled doors, c1820.
$2,500-3,500

A George III Welsh chestnut cupboard, with panelled doors and two drawers in the middle, c1820.
$2,000-3,000

Dressers

An oak low dresser, the drawers applied with geometric mouldings divided by split balusters, late 17thC, 82½ in (210 cm) wide.
$7,500-10,500

An oak dresser base, with geometrically moulded panelled drawers, late 17thC, 77½ in (195 cm) wide.
$4,500-7,000

An oak dresser, fitted with four moulded panelled drawers, late 17th/early 18thC, 85½ in (217 cm). **$3,000-4,500**

A yew-wood dresser base, good colour and patination, mid-18thC, 83 in (207.5 cm).
$14,000-17,000

A George II oak dresser base, c1730, 72½ in (185 cm) wide.
$3,500-5,000

A Georgian oak dresser, the moulded top cross banded with mahogany, with three cock beaded drawers similarly cross banded, 75 in (191 cm) wide.
$2,500-3,500

An oak moulded dresser base, with 4 drawers, 5 turned front legs, good colour and patination late 17thC, 102 in (260 cm).
$14,000-17,000

An early Georgian small oak and yew wood low dresser, the top and front inlaid with diamond and triangular panels of yew wood, some alterations, 54 in (137 cm).
$2,500-3,500

A George II oak dresser, with moulded terminals, with later top, 93 in (236 cm) wide.
$4,500-7,000

An oak dresser, formerly with a rack, mid-18thC, 71 in (181 cm) ...ide. **$2,500-3,500**

A George III oak dresser base, ...extensively restored, 83 in ...212 cm) wide. **$1,500-2,200**

An oak and elm dresser base, ...8thC, 68 in (170 cm) wide. **$2,000-3,000**

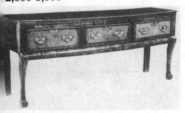

...n oak low dresser, minor ...estorations, 18thC, 54½ in ...194.5 cm) wide. **$5,500-7,000**

A George II oak and mahogany ...rossbanded dresser, c1740, 62 in ...158 cm) wide. **$3,000-4,500**

A George II oak dresser, the five drawers above an arched apron, the baluster turned supports above a pine platform base, c1750, 60½ in (154 cm). **$2,500-3,500**

An unusual Charles II oak dresser, restored and altered c1680, 55½ in (141 cm) wide. **$3,000-4,000**

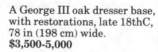

A small north Wales canopy oak dresser, c1740, 50 in (125 cm) wide. **$7,500-10,500**

A George III oak dresser base, with restorations, late 18thC, 78 in (198 cm) wide. **$3,500-5,000**

A George II oak and fruitwood dresser, c1750, 55½ in (141 cm) wide. **$3,500-5,000**

A George II mahogany crossbanded dresser base. **$9,000-13,000**

An oak dresser base, the shaped moulded top above 6 fielded drawers and a pair of arched fielded panel centre doors, good colour and patination, early 18thC, 83 in (207.5 cm). **$7,500-10,500**

A George III oak dresser, with mahogany crossbanding, 70 in (130 cm) wide. **$3,500-5,000**

A Lancashire crossbanded breakfront oak dresser base, mid-18thC. **$10,500-14,000**

An oak dresser, 18thC, 60 in (152 cm). **$3,500-5,000**

A rare North Wales oak dresser, with original lozenge carved panels, well-shaped rack, good colour and patina, late 17thC. **$14,000-17,000**

A good Denbighshire oak dresser, early 18thC, 60 in (150 cm) wide. **$9,000-13,000**

An oak dresser, North Wales, withoverhanging shaped rack, early 18thC, 50 in (125 cm) wide **$9,000-13,000**

A fine Montgomeryshire oak dresser and rack. **$10,500-14,000**

A Queen Anne walnut dresser, of good colour and patination, 62 in (115 cm). **$9,000-13,000**

A North Wales oak dresser and rack, with spice drawers, well-shaped rack, good colour an patination, early 18thC, 73 in (182.5 cm). **$10,500-14,000**

A North Wales oak dresser, the rack featuring arched fielded panel cupboards and spice drawers, good colour and patination, early 18thC, 60 in (150 cm). **$10,500-14,000**

A Denbighshire oak dresser and rack, early 18thC. **$14,000-17,000**

A North Wales oak dresser and rack, with raised fielded panels early 18thC. **$9,000-13,000**

An oak dresser, of good patina, the base with drawers and panelled cupboards with brass drop handles, 18thC.
$4,500-7,000

A small oak dresser, with alterations, 18thC, 54 in (138 cm).
$2,500-3,500

An oak Lancashire closed dresser, the rack with moulded cornice and pierced scrolling frieze above three shelves, crossbanded in mahogany, mid-18thC, 87 in (207.5 cm) wide.
$4,500-7,000

An oak dresser, the base with three inlaid drawers, 18thC, 73 in (185 cm) wide. $3,000-4,500

An oak Welsh dresser, mid-18thC, 71 in (180 cm) long.
$3,500-5,000

A Swansea Valley oak dresser, with original brasses, with an unusual arrangement of six dummy spice drawers with brass knob handles, mid-18thC, 72 in (180 cm) wide. $4,500-7,000

A mid-Georgian oak dresser, with five mahogany banded drawers on baluster supports with an undertier and block feet, 72 in (192.5 cm). $4,500-7,000

A George III oak dresser, c1760, 66 in (168 cm) wide.
$3,000-4,500

A George III oak dresser, restored, c1770, 67 in (170 cm) wide.
$3,000-4,500

An oak dresser, possibly Irish, height reduced at the feet, second half of the 18thC, 100 in (253 cm).
$3,500-5,000

An oak dresser, late 18thC, 63½ in (161 cm).
$2,500-3,500

A George III oak dresser, restored, c1770, 70½ in (178 cm) wide.
$4,500-7,000

A George III oak dresser, the projecting base with three crossbanded drawers and a pair of fielded cupboards with arched walnut crossbanded panels flanking a similar panel, c1785, 70½ in (180 cm) wide. **$7,500-10,500**

A late Georgian Welsh oak dresser, with mother of pearl inlaid turned wood knob handles, 68 in (172 cm) wide. **$4,000-5,000**

A small oak dresser, 18thC, 55½ in (139 cm). **$2,500-3,500**

An oak dresser, late 18thC, 72 in (180 cm) wide. **$3,000-4,500**

An early Victorian Welsh dresser, the stepped base with a bank of six dummy spice drawers, the frieze with three short drawers above an ogee-shaped apron, 60 in (150 cm) wide. **$2,500-3,500**

Stools

An oak joint stool, of unabused original patination and colour, mid-17thC, 17 in (42 cm) wide. **$2,000-3,000**

An oak box stool, mid-17thC. **$1,000-1,400**

An oak joint stool, with chipped decoration to frieze, top replaced. **$300-600**

A pair of Flemish or French walnut joint stools, c1700, 16 in (40.5 cm) wide. **$2,000-3,000**

Tables

An oak refectory table, the solid trestle ends joined by a flying stretcher on plinth bases, 17thC and later, 113 in (287 cm). **$7,000-9,000**

An oak draw-leaf dining table, with plain frieze and turned supports, 17thC and later, 105 in (267 cm) wide, fully extended. **$3,000-4,500**

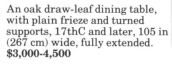

An oak refectory table, 17thC, 70 in (175 cm). **$3,000-4,500**

In the Furniture section if there is only one measurement it refers to the width of the piece.

A James I design oak refectory table, made-up 94 in (238 cm). **$1,500-2,200**

A James I oak refectory table, with 6 turned legs, carved frieze, original spandrels, good colour and patination, 180 in (450 cm). **$22,500-34,000**

A William and Mary pine and maple butterfly table, converted from a tavern table, feet restored, Massachusetts, 1700-1720, 37½in (93.5cm) wide. **$400-600**

An oak refectory table, with some restoration, late-17thC, 108 in (275 cm). **$4,500-7,000**

large oak Tudor style refectory ble, but incorporating some arlier elements, c1880, 120 in 05 cm). **$3,000-4,500**

An oak gateleg table, Spanish feet, with late-17thC, 56½ in (140 cm). **$800-1,200**

A James I oak refectory table, the plank top above six bulbous turned legs, 121 in (252 cm). **$7,500-10,500**

An oak gateleg table, late-17thC, 48 in (122 cm). **$1,000-1,400**

A Charles II oak gateleg table, on Braganza feet, c1675, 30½ in (78 cm). **$2,000-3,000**

William and Mary oak gateleg ble, the top possibly later, 50 in 27 cm). **$2,000-3,000**

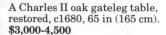

A Charles II oak gateleg table, restored, c1680, 65 in (165 cm). **$3,000-4,500**

A good Charles II oak gateleg table, 63 in (158 cm). **$3,500-5,000**

An oak gateleg table, with Spanish feet, square section stretchers, 17thC, 29½ in (72.5 cm). **$2,000-3,000**

A Charles II triangular oak gateleg table, c1685, 36 in (91 cm) wide. **$2,500-3,500**

An oak gateleg table, with restorations, late 17thC, 62 (158 cm). **$2,000-3,000**

A solid yew-wood 6 seater gateleg table, late 17thC. **$7,500-10,500**

A large oak gateleg table, early-18thC, 75½ in (192 cm). **$4,500-7,000**

A yew-wood gateleg table, the shaped frieze containing a sing drawer, c1720, 40 in (103 cm) wide. **$4,500-7,000**

An oak barley-twist gateleg tab 1930's, 45 in (112.5 cm). **$100-200**

A William and Mary maple gate-leg table, on ball feet, minor cracks to top, Pennsylvania, 1700-1725, 52¼in (130cm) long. **$4,500-5,500**

A William and Mary yew-wood side table, c1700, 36 in (90cm). **$4,500-7,000**

A William and Mary oak rectangular lowboy, 29½ in (71 cm). **$4,500-7,000**

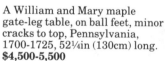

A small oak side table, 17th **$2,500-3,500**

A rare William and Mary curly walnut center table, Pennsylvania, 1720-1750, 60in (150cm) long. **$12,000-15,000**

A William and Mary oak and walnut tavern table, flaring ball feet, loss to one foot, Pennsylvania, 1720-1750, 27¼in (67.5cm) wide. **$4,000-4,500**

Georgian oak and pollard oak de table, with three crossbanded awers, 34½ in (87.5 cm) wide. ,000-8,500

A George II cherrywood lowboy, c1735. **$3,000-4,500**

A Georgian oak lowboy, mid-18thC, 33 in (84 cm). **$3,000-4,500**

Dutch oak draw-leaf dining ble, 18thC, 81 in (202 cm). ,000-4,000

A period oak lowboy with some later amendments, 30 in (75 cm). **$1,400-1,700**

A George III fruitwood lowboy with original brasses, c1790. **$1,500-2,200**

Flemish oak draw-leaf table, 3 in (261 cm). **$2,500-3,500**

A George I oak side table, c1720. **$1,000-1,400**

A Dutch oak refectory table, with ebonised banding, 17thC style, 59 in (150 cm). **$1,500-2,200**

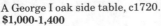

249

A Tuscan walnut writing desk, the hinged top and fall-front revealing two small drawers, the later testle supports with iron stretchers, restored, c1650, 34 in (86 cm). **$1,500-2,200**

A large Italian oak drawleaf table, early 17thC, 180 in (450 cm). **$10,500-14,000**

A Spanish walnut side table, 16thC, 57 in (145 cm). **$2,500-3,500**

An oak table desk, on a later stan with turned and tapered column mid-17thC, 31 in (79 cm). **$500-700**

A Georgian oak linen press, fitted with a turned screw and plates, above a drawer and a cupboard, mid-18thC, 65 in (165 cm). **$600-900**

Beds

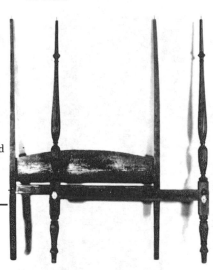

A fine mahogany four post bed, t waved giltwood cornice boldly carved with gadrooning and foliate clasps centred by quatrefoils, the angles headed b acanthus, the reeded spreading posts carved with entwined foliage, with later pine frame, printed valance, hangings and pelmet, 130 by 90 in (330 by 229 cm). **$33,000-42,600**

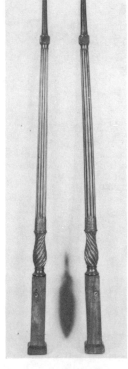

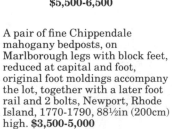

A late Federal mahogany four-post tester bedstead, the foot-posts each with reeded double balusters above baluster turned legs, the head posts each with square tapering legs centering an arched pine headboard with 4 old rails, North Shore, 1800-1820, foot posts, 87in (217.5cm) high. **$5,500-6,500**

A pair of fine Chippendale mahogany bedposts, on Marlborough legs with block feet, reduced at capital and foot, original foot moldings accompany the lot, together with a later foot rail and 2 bolts, Newport, Rhode Island, 1770-1790, 88½in (200cm) high. **$3,500-5,000**

An Empire mahogany lit en bateau, mounted with later anthemion and wreath plaques, with later canopy and matching curtains, 71½ in by 35 in (181 by 89 cm). **$4,000-5,000**

Bonheur du jour

A North Italian rococo style oak bedstead, extensively carved with foliate scroll borders and crested with flowers, the panels carved with C-scroll cartouches, 19thC, 7 in (207.5 cm). 3,000-4,000

A French carved and gilded bed of massive proportions, the scrolled headboard and foot elaborately decorated, the sides with strapwork moulding, c1860, 89 by 77 in (210 by 183 cm). **$10,500-14,000**

A George III satinwood harewood and rosewood bonheur du jour, the oval inlaid cupboard doors enclosing a well fitted interior of 8 drawers and 16 pigeonholes, the serpentine top with a drawer in the waved frieze enclosing a leather-lined slide and divided compartment, 48 by 36 in (122 by 91.5 cm). **$5,500-7,000**

A George III tulipwood and boxwood strung bonheur du jour, after a design by Thomas Sheraton, with elevating panel and having a leather lined top between stepped sides fitted with hinged drawers, containing a concave frieze drawer, 30 in 75 cm). **$8,500-10,500**

A George III satinwood bonheur du jour, the writing surface crossbanded and above a frieze drawer with leather lined writing slide, c1795, 39 by 33 in (99 by 84 cm). **$4,500-7,000**

A mahogany bonheur du jour, in the manner of Gillow, English, c1795, 48 by 31 in (120 by 77.5 cm). **$10,500-14,000**

◀ A Regency rosewood bonheur du jour, with grey marble galleried top, the base with a long drawer inlaid with interlocking ormolu rings, c1820, 49½ in by 37 in (137 by 92.5 cm). **$5,500-7,000**

A mahogany kingwood crossbanded and brass mounted bonheur du jour, inlaid with boxwood lines, possibly German, late 18th/early 19thC, 27 in 68 cm). **$5,500-7,000**

A Victorian ebonised bonheur du jour, decorated with walnut banding and floral scrolls, 42 in (105 cm). **$1,400-1,700**

A satinwood bonheur du jour, with ribbon tied frieze drawer with a fall front glazed panel enclosing a shelf, c1860, 50 in by 31 in (127 by 79 cm). **$2,500-3,500**

A French ebonised and boulle bonheur du jour, with serpentine drawer and pull out writing slide below, 19thC, 30 in (75 cm). **$1,700-2,500**

A French gilt metal mounted writing table, of rosewood and kingwood with 9 small drawers, leather writing surface and frieze drawer below, the base with mask mounts and ornate knees and sabots, 19thC, 39 in (97.5 cm). **$6,000-8,000**

A Victorian ormolu mounted figured walnut bonheur du jour, inlaid with floral and foliate marquetry, slant front enclosing well, 3 drawers and pigeon holes, 32 in (80 cm). **$3,000-4,000**

A Louis XVI style bonheur du jour, with painted porcelain panels, with folding writing section, standing on reeded tapered supports, veneered in a wide range of exotic woods with profuse inlay and ormolu mounted decoration, 52 by 19 in (110 by 40 cm). **$3,000-4,000**

A walnut and gilt bronze bonheur du jour, the outset base of serpentine outline fitted with a frieze drawer, on exaggerated cabriole supports, German, third quarter of the 19thC, 53 by 33 in (135 by 84 cm). **$1,400-1,700**

A Victorian walnut and marquetry bonheur du jour, applied with gilt brass foliate mounts and inlaid throughout with foliate arabesques, the sloping fall front enclosing pigeonholes, drawers and a well above a shaped apron and on cabriole legs, 55 by 34 in (137.5 85 cm). **$2,000-3,000**

Breakfront Bookcases

A French rosewood and ormolu mounted bonheur du jour, inlaid with floral sprays and stringing, the raised arched back with an open tier, c1890, 50 by 39 in (127 by 71 cm). **$1,400-1,700**

A burr walnut writing desk in Louis XV Revival style, crossbanded in tulipwood, the arbelette frieze containing three drawers, on cabriole legs with gilt bronze mounts, c1875, 46 in (117 cm). **$2,000-3,000**

A George III mahogany breakfront bookcase, with moulded dentilled cornice and later broken scrolled pediment pierced with fretwork, 92 in (234 cm). **$15,000-20,500**

George III mahogany library
breakfront bookcase, adapted,
in (229 cm). **$6,000-8,500**

A George III mahogany
breakfront library bookcase, 112
by 99 in (285 by 252 cm).
$6,000-8,500

George III mahogany
breakfront bookcase, the doors
laid with ovals, the left hand one
ted with 6 graduated
awers on plinth base, 102½ in
60.5 cm). **$6,000-8,500**

A George III mahogany
breakfront bookcase, the glazing
bars perhaps altered, 55 in
(140 cm). **$15,000-20,500**

George III mahogany
breakfront bookcase, with a fitted
iting drawer, c1800, 95 in
1 cm). **$5,500-7,000**

George IV mahogany
breakfront bookcase, inlaid with
ass medallions, c1825, 100 in
4 cm). **$6,000-8,500**

A late Georgian mahogany
breakfront library bookcase, 96 in
(244 cm). **$6,000-8,000**

A George III mahogany
breakfront bookcase, the base
with 4 frieze drawers and 2 pairs of
panelled cupboard doors on foliate
plinth base, 75 in (190.5 cm).
$6,000-8,000

Bookcases

★ Check that the glazing bars
match the rest of the
bookcase in quality, timber
and age. Breakfront
wardrobes of the mid to late
19th century can be turned
into bookcases by removing
the solid panels to the doors
and glazing the frames.

★ During the late 19th century
many old glazed door
cabinets were removed from
their bureau or cupboard
bases to have feet added and
the tops fitted in to make
'Georgian' display or
bookcases. This was not an
18th century form; the
correct version was much
taller and often had drawers
to the frieze base. The low
'dwarf' bookcases without
doors became popular during
the late 18th century.

★ The earliest form of
adjustable shelf on the better
quality bookcases was
achieved by cutting rabbets
into the sides of the cabinet
into which the shelves could
slide. Next came a toothed
ladder at each side, the
removable rungs forming the
shelf rests. Finally, by the
end of the 18th century, came
movable pegs fitting into
holes. Regency examples
were often made of gilt metal
or brass.

★ Check when a bookcase sits
on a bureau or cupboard base
that it is slightly smaller
than the base, and it is
preferable that the retaining
moulding is fixed to the base
not the top; also, it is
unlikely that the top surface
to such a base would have
been veneered originally.

★ A bureau made to take a
bookcase on top will have a
steeper angle to the fall front
to create a greater depth to
accommodate the case or
cabinet.

A William IV mahogany breakfront library bookcase, the lower part with three bolection drawers above three cupboard doors, outset scrolling pilasters, on a plinth base, c1840, 96 by 74 in (244 by 188 cm).
$2,500-3,500

A Victorian mahogany breakfront bookcase, with fluted frieze and scrolled cornice, 124 in (315 cm).
$15,000-20,500

An Edwardian mahogany bookcase, of breakfront outline, the moulded cornice inlaid with leafage and flowers, c1900, 91 by 163 in (231 by 414 cm).
$4,000-5,000

A mahogany breakfront library bookcase, in the Chippendale manner, the upper section with a moulded cornice and dog tooth and fluted frieze, the lower section with a carved gadrooned moulding, 118 in (299 cm).
$3,000-4,500

A George III style mahogany and satinwood breakfront bookcase, bearing trade label of Warings, Liverpool, c1910, 50 in (127 cm).
$2,500-3,500

A George III style yewwood breakfront bookcase, with 2 cockbeaded panel doors with roundel re-entrant corners, 53 i (132.5 cm). **$1,700-2,500**

A large Victorian mahogany breakfront bookcase, 102 by 120 in (258 by 305 cm). **$3,000-4,500**

Bureau Bookcases

A small Queen Anne oak bureau bookcase, 26 in (65 cm).
$8,500-10,500

A George III mahogany bureau and later bookcase top, sloping fall front enclosing drawers and pigeonholes, 43 in (107.5 cm).
$4,500-5,000

A Queen Anne walnut and featherbanded bureau bookcase, restored, later mirror panels, c1710, 78 by 36 in (198 by 91.5 cm). **$10,500-14,000**

A walnut double dome bureau ▶ bookcase, the upper part with a moulded cornice fitted with pigeonholes, shelves and drawers, fitted with candle slides below, the lower part having a crossbanded and featherstrung sloping fall enclosed fitted graduated interior, with later restorations, early 18thC, 41½ in (104 cm). **$14,000-17,000**

◀ A George III country made yew bureau bookcase, 33 in (84 cm). **$6,000-8,000**

A George I style walnut bureau ookcase, of small proportions, artly early 18thC but probably econstructed and with lterations, 23 in (59 cm). 8,500-10,500

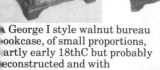

A walnut bureau bookcase, early 18thC, 40 in (100 cm). **$6,000-8,500**

A Georgian mahogany bureau bookcase, 42 in (105 cm). **$2,500-3,500**

mahogany bookcase, the shaped rnice with vase finial, lacking o, 42 in (107 cm). 5,500-7,000

A Chippendale walnut desk and bookcase, in two sections: the upper case with a scrolled pediment, the lower case with a thumb-molded slant lid opening to a fitted interior, top of scroll pediment pieced, small patch to writing surface, corner piece missing, probably Southern, 1760-1790, 92½in (230cm) high. **$6,500-7,500**

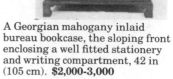

A Georgian mahogany inlaid bureau bookcase, the sloping front enclosing a well fitted stationery and writing compartment, 42 in (105 cm). **$2,000-3,000**

Georgian mahogany bureau ookcase, the sloping flap closing a fitted and later inlaid terior, associated and adapted, 4 in (110 cm). 4,500-5,000

A Chippendale mahogany bureau bookcase, the top with figured mahogany blind doors, original throughout except 2 handles, c1770. **$4,500-5,000**

A Georgian mahogany bureau bookcase, the bureau with fitted interior, restored, 84 by 39 in (214 by 99 cm). **$5,500-7,000**

A George III mahogany bureau bookcase, the associated upper section with a dentilled cornice and blind fret frieze, with fitted interior, c1770, 46½ in (118 cm). **$5,500-7,000**

A late Victorian mahogany bureau bookcase, in Sheraton Revival style, with satinwood line inlay, the base with a fall flap inlaid in marquetry, 30 in (75 cm). **$2,500-3,500**

A Dutch marquetry and mahogany bureau bookcase, in three sections, and with scroll carving, the interior with mahogany shelves and 3 small drawers above a pair of candle slides, c1760, 92 in (234 cm) high. **$15,000-20,500**

A mid Georgian provincial red walnut bureau bookcase, with a broken arched pediment centred by a gadrooned urn above a pair of arched fielded panelled doors, on ogee bracket feet, c1745, 91½ in (232 cm). **$6,000-8,500**

A Federal mahogany secretary, the upper case with shaped pediment centering 3 plinths above 2 glazed Gothic arch doors over 2 cockbeaded and veneered short drawers, the lower section with hinged writing flap, top restored, Massachusetts, 1790-1810, 72½in (180cm) high. **$1,400-2,000**

A George III mahogany open low bookcase, with a pair of drawers outlined in boxwood, 33 in (88 cm). **$4,500-5,000**

A Federal cherrywood desk and bookcase, the lower part with a thumb-molded slant lid opening to a row of 7 valanced pigeonholes over an open compartment flanked by 2 short drawers, New England, 76½in (191cm) high. **$4,000-5,000**

A mahogany breakfront dwarf bookcase, 73½ in (184 cm). **$1,500-2,200**

A pair of Victorian rosewood open bookcases, 22 in (55 cm). **$2,000-3,000**

pair of Regency mahogany and rossbanded open bookcases, with rass moulded borders and pine helf, on later brass bun feet, 810, 31½ in (80 cm). 2,000-3,000

An Edwardian mahogany revolving bookcase, 20 in (50 cm). **$500-600**

A pair of French Empire mahogany open bookcases, the rouge Royal marble top above an ormolu scroll mounted frieze, c1810, 20½ in (57 cm). **$3,000-4,000**

satinwood low bookcase, of reakfront form with galleried p, the frieze with 3 drawers laid to simulate fluting, c1880, 2 in (183 cm). **$3,000-4,500**

Library Bookcases

An unusual George III mahogany bookcase with moulded cornice, fluted frieze and 2 geometrically and gothic pattern glazed cupboard doors, 78 in (198 cm). **$10,500-14,000**

A George II mahogany and crossbanded mahogany cabinet bookcase, restored, c1740, 45 in (115 cm). **$4,000-5,000**

A George III mahogany bookcase, the upper section deepened, the backboards replaced, 73 in (185.5 cm). **$8,500-10,500**

A George III mahogany bookcase, 61 in (152.5 cm). **$4,000-5,000**

A large George III architectural library bookcase, the moulded cornice above three reeded pilasters opening to reveal internal book compartments, 144 in (366 cm). **$5,500-7,000**

A George III mahogany cabinet
bookcase, with later brass grille
doors, c1800, 66½ in (169 cm).
$4,000-5,000

A fine George III Sheraton
mahogany bookcase cabinet,
inlaid with boxwood edging,
37½ in (93.5 cm).
$6,000-8,000

An unusual George III mahogany
bookcase, the moulded cornice
with Grecian key decoration, the
fluted frieze with applied carved
paterae, the lower section fitted 2
drawers with 2 sliding tambour
doors under, 57 in (142.5 cm).
$1,500-2,200

A pair of George IV mahogany
cabinet bookcases, with frieze
drawers on a plinth base, restored,
c1825, 44 in (112 cm).
$7,500-10,500

A Georgian mahogany bookcase.
$3,000-4,500

A William IV mahogany cabinet
bookcase, c1825, 46 in (117 cm).
$2,000-3,000

A pair of Regency mahogany and
parcel gilt bookcases, the base
with marble tops, on ring turned
tapering feet, one lacking marble,
minor variations, 46 in (117 cm).
$15,000-20,500

A William IV Gothic mahogany
bookcase, 75 in (187.5 cm).
$3,500-5,000

A Regency mahogany bookcase,
the top section with a classical
moulded pediment inlaid with
brass lines and applied with a
central anthemion, the bowed
base fitted with drawers between
simulated bamboo pilaster
columns, 45½ in (114 cm).
$2,000-3,000

A Regency mahogany bookcase, the later moulded cornice above 2 pairs of geometrically glazed doors, with a secretaire drawer 91 in (232 cm). **$4,000-5,000**

A Regency mahogany bookcase on reinforced splayed feet, 50½ in (128 cm). **$4,000-5,000**

A Regency mahogany Gothic Revival library bookcase, the 4 lancet shaped glazed doors with Gothic tracery and painted glass in medieval style at the top and divided and flanked by crocketted pilasters, 123 in (312 cm). **$22,500-30,600**

A pair of early Victorian walnut bookcases, 39 in (97.5 cm). **$4,000-5,000**

An early Victorian mahogany bookcase, with inverted breakfront upper section, 63 in (158 cm). **$1,700-2,500**

A Victorian burr walnut cabinet bookcase, the terminals with scroll corbels, the moulded cornice above triple glazed doors, c1850, 72 in (183 cm). **$7,500-10,500**

A mahogany bookcase cabinet, with brass ring handles, raised on bracket feet, 42 in (105 cm). **$1,700-2,500**

A Victorian mahogany Georgian style breakfront library bookcase, 65 in (162.5 cm). **$6,000-8,000**

A mahogany bookcase, 19thC, 79 in (197.5 cm) high. **$600-800**

A carved oak library bookcase, mid-19thC, 127 in (323 cm). **$2,000-3,000**

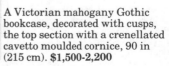

A Victorian mahogany Gothic bookcase, decorated with cusps, the top section with a crenellated cavetto moulded cornice, 90 in (215 cm). **$1,500-2,200**

A mahogany bookcase, early 19thC, 40 in (100 cm). $700-1,000

A mahogany bookcase, the astragal glazed doors, cross banded in satinwood and strung with ebony and box, the lower section similarly crossbanded, 19thC, 35 in (88 cm). $3,000-4,000

A Victorian mahogany bookcase, inlaid with satinwood bands and boxwood geometric lines, 62 in (155 cm). $3,000-4,000

A mahogany two part bookcase, 19thC, 49½ in (123 cm). $3,000-4,000

A Victorian mahogany bookcase, 84 in (200 cm). $3,000-4,500

A late Victorian walnut bookcase, 59 in (148 cm). $1,400-1,700

An Edwardian satinwood bookcase, inlaid with rosewood bands and chequered and ebonised lines, 40 in (100 cm). $3,000-4,500

A George III style mahogany and satinwood banded bookcase, bearing trade label of Bowman Bros, Camden Town, London, c1910, 48 in (122 cm). $2,000-3,000

A veneered walnut bookcase, inlaid in bone with masks, urns and floral tendrils, late 19thC, 39½ in (100 cm). $1,500-2,200

Use the Index!
Because certain items might fit easily into any of a number of categories, the quickest and surest method of locating any entry is by reference to the index at the back of the book.
This has been fully cross-referenced for absolute simplicity.

A mahogany astragal glazed bookcase, on cupboard base, c1930, 35 in (87.5 cm). $1,000-1,400

Secretaire Bookcases

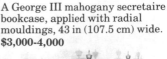

A George III mahogany secretaire bookcase, applied with radial mouldings, 43 in (107.5 cm) wide. **$3,000-4,000**

A George III padoukwood and parcel gilt secretaire bookcase, the broken pediment cornice with fluted vase finial above a pair of shaped glazed cupboard doors, carrying handles, some restoration, 42 in (107 cm). **$6,000-8,000**

A Georgian mahogany secretaire bookcase, with canted corners inlaid with crossbanding and stringing, pierced brass handles, 49 in (122 cm). **$3,000-4,500**

A secretaire bookcase, with satinwood veneers of exceptional quality, c1785, 100 in (253 cm) high. **$34,500-44,200**

A George III mahogany and crossbanded secretaire bookcase, inlaid with stringing, c1800, 47 in (120 cm). **$2,500-3,500**

A George III mahogany and crossbanded secretaire bookcase, c1790, 54 in (137 cm). **$4,000-5,000**

A George III mahogany, tulipwood and mahogany crossbanded secretaire bookcase, 45 in (112 cm). **$25,500-32,500**

MAKE THE MOST OF MILLER'S

Price ranges in this book reflect what one should expect to pay for a similar example. When selling one can obviously expect a figure below. This will fluctuate according to a dealer's stock, saleability at a particular time, etc. It is always advisable to approach a reputable specialist dealer or an auction house which has specialist sales.

A George III mahogany secretaire bookcase, with pear drop cornice, the kingwood banded writing drawer enclosing a fitted interior, c1790, 40 in (102 cm). **$5,500-7,000**

A George III mahogany secretaire bookcase, c1800, 36 in (91.5 cm). **$4,000-5,000**

A George III mahogany secretaire bookcase, inlaid with chequered bands and boxwood and ebony lines, associated, 37 in (92 cm). **$3,500-5,000**

A George III Sheraton secretaire bookcase, the dentil inlaid cornice with shell motif, all inlaid with boxwood and ebony chequer line and sunbursts to the corners, 48 in (120 cm). **$3,000-4,000**

A George III inlaid mahogany secretaire bookcase, the whole outlined with boxwood stringing and having brass loop handles on oval embossed back plates, 43 in (107 cm). **$6,000-8,500**

A good Georgian mahogany secretaire bookcase, the upper section with moulded and key pattern cornice, 43½ in (108 cm) **$3,000-4,000**

A George III mahogany secretaire bookcase, inlaid with satinwood and stringing around all doors and drawers, c1815. **$4,500-7,000**

A late George III mahogany secretaire bookcase, 44 in (110 cm). **$2,500-3,500**

A late George III mahogany secretaire bookcase, inlaid with ebonised lines, the top converted to a gun cupboard, 49½ in (123 cm). **$4,000-5,000**

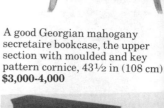

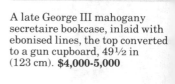

A late Georgian mahogany secretaire bookcase, the secretaire drawer with satinwood facings above 2 doors enclosing sliding tray shelves and faced with rectangular panels with projecting rounded corners, the drawer stamped 'Kentluck & Kent's London', 45 in (115 cm). **$7,500-10,500**

A late George III mahogany secretaire bookcase, 39 in (98 cm). **$4,000-5,000**

A Regency mahogany secretaire
bookcase, the adjustable shelves
enclosed by brass grille panel
doors, 52 in (133 cm).
$4,000-5,000

A carved oak secretaire bookcase,
c1900, 48 in (122 cm).
$1,700-2,500

A late Regency mahogany
secretaire library bookcase, glass
missing, 61 in (153 cm).
$1,300-1,700

A mahogany secretaire bookcase,
on later turned feet, c1830, 43 in
(108 cm). $2,000-3,000

A Regency mahogany secretaire
bookcase, with later broken
swan-neck pediment and two
Gothic arched glazed doors,
42½ in (106 cm).
$3,000-4,000

A fine inlaid mahogany secretaire
bookcase, early 19thC, 46 in
(115 cm). $4,500-5,000

A George IV mahogany secretaire
bookcase, the secretaire drawer
with moulded panels enclosing
pigeonholes and rosewood faced
small drawers, 44½ in (111 cm).
$3,000-4,000

A Regency mahogany secretaire
bookcase, inlaid with boxwood and
ebonised lines, the later top
section with a cavetto cornice and
blind fret frieze, 42½ in (106 cm).
$3,000-4,000

An early Victorian mahogany
secretaire bookcase, on later bun
feet, 42 in (105 cm).
$1,700-2,500

A Victorian mahogany secretaire
bookcase, with scrolling foliate
carved brackets and foliate carved
bookcase doors, the secretaire
drawer with bird's-eye maple
veneered interior fittings, 53 in
(135 cm). $1,700-2,500

Bureaux

A Queen Anne chinoiserie bureau, decorated in gilt and scarlet on a black ground, c1710, 35½ in (90 cm). **$4,000-5,000**

A Queen Anne walnut bureau, the sloping front enclosing a fitted interior including a well, on later bracket feet, 36 in (91 cm). **$5,500-7,000**

A George I walnut and chevron banded bureau, the fall enclosing small drawers, on reduced bracket feet, c1720, 36 in (91 cm). **$4,500-7,000**

A walnut and herringbone banded bureau, early 18thC, 36 in (91 cm). **$5,500-7,000**

A rare and exceptionally small Queen Anne burr mulberry bureau, the top, sides and front with walnut herringbone crossbanding, the slope fall enclosing a fitted interior, 23½ in (60 cm). **$7,500-10,500**

A Queen Anne walnut veneered bureau, in cross- and chevron-banded wood and outlined with a double moulding, the flap with a book-support and enclosing a fitted interior with a well, on bracket feet, feet replaced, c1710, 37 in (94 cm). **$9,000-13,000**

An early Georgian walnut bureau, with crossbanded top, the fall-flap enclosing a fitted interior with a well and secret compartment, on later bracket feet, with carrying handles, 37½ in (95 cm). **$10,000-13,000**

A George II walnut bureau, crossbanded, the fall front revealing a fitted interior, 38 in (95 cm). **$3,000-4,000**

A Queen Anne walnut and crossbanded bureau, inlaid with featherbanding, the fall revealing a stepped and fitted interior, c1710, 38 in (96 cm). **$2,500-3,500**

A George I walnut, crossbanded and herringbone inlaid bureau, with reeded edged fall-front, fully fitted interior with lower compartment, brass drop handles and escutcheons and bracket feet, 36 in (91 cm). **$5,500-7,000**

An early Georgian walnut bureau, with sloping crossbanded flap enclosing a later fitted interior with small drawers and a cupboard door, 38½ in (98 cm). **$4,500-7,000**

A Georgian mahogany bureau, the fall front enclosing drawers and pigeonholes. **$4,000-5,000**

A crossbanded, figured walnut bureau, in two sections, early 18thC. **$4,500-7,000**

An early Georgian figured walnut bureau, the whole crossbanded and with herringbone stringing, the fall front opening to reveal a leather writing surface, pigeonholes, 3 small drawers and 2 semi secret drawers, 30½ in (76 cm). **$7,000-9,000**

An inlaid mahogany bureau, crossbanded in satinwood, having a fall front with clover and ribbon inlay, 42 in (105 cm). **$1,500-2,200**

A George III mahogany bureau, the sloping flap enclosing a fitted interior, 36½ in (91 cm). **$1,700-2,500**

An early George III red walnut bureau, the sloping flap enclosing a fitted interior, on later bracket feet, 31½ in (80 cm). **$3,000-4,500**

A George III mahogany bureau, the fall enclosing a blind fret interior of drawers and pigeonholes, blind fret decoration of later date, 36 in (90 cm). **$1,400-1,700**

A George III mahogany bureau, with well fitted and inlaid interior. **$2,000-3,000**

A Georgian mahogany fall front bureau, the fitted interior inlaid with shell patera. **$600-900**

A George III mahogany bureau, with an interior of various small drawers and pigeonholes, an open recess, lacking cupboard door, 37½ in (94 cm). **$1,400-1,700**

An early George III mahogany bureau, with small drawers and pigeonholes and central cupboard enclosed by the fall, 36 in (91 cm). **$1,700-2,500**

A small George III mahogany bureau, with sloping flap enclosing a fitted interior, on bracket feet, 27 in (69 cm). **$3,000-4,000**

A George III mahogany bureau, with wide mahogany crossbandings, with fitted interior on bracket feet, 36 in (90 cm). **$1,300-1,700**

A George III walnut and mahogany fall front bureau, having fruitwood crossbanding fitted interior with rosewood drawer fronts, c1780, 36 in (90 cm). **$1,500-2,200**

A George III mahogany bureau, constructed with finely figured veneer, good colour and patination, original brasses, c1785. **$2,000-3,000**

A George III mahogany bureau, the sloping fall front enclosing a fitted interior with drawers, pigeonholes and a central cupboard, c1800, 42 by 43½ in (107 by 110 cm). **$1,700-2,500**

A late George III mahogany bureau, with flame pattern veneers crossbanded slope front, enclosing well fitted interior with shell, satinwood and boxwood inlays, 43 in (107.5 cm). **$1,500-2,200**

A George III mahogany bureau, c1810. **$1,500-2,200**

A George III applewood bureau, c1810. **$1,500-2,200**

A mahogany inlaid bureau, the fall flap crossbanded, inlaid with stringing, leafage spandrels and central shell motif, the fitted interior also inlaid, 19thC, 42 in (107 cm). **$2,000-3,000**

A mahogany bureau, having a fall front enclosing a fitted interior, early 19thC, 36 in (90 cm). **$1,500-2,200**

A late Victorian oak bureau, with a fitted interior and a lock mechanism for the 6 small drawers below, 32 in (95 cm). **$500-700**

MAKE THE MOST OF MILLER'S

Price ranges in this book reflect what one should expect to pay for a similar example. When selling one can obviously expect a figure below. This will fluctuate according to a dealer's stock, saleability at a particular time, etc. It is always advisable to approach a reputable specialist dealer or an auction house which has specialist sales.

An early Georgian style walnut bureau, inlaid with feather banding, the sloping flap enclosing a fitted interior, 30 in (75 cm). **$2,500-3,500**

Cylinder Bureaux

George III mahogany cylinder bureau, in the French style, crossbanded in rosewood and with purpleheart Greek key stringing, with shallow frieze drawer and the cylinder opening in conjunction with a leather lined slide, on cabriole legs, c1770, 38½ in (98 cm). **$7,500-10,500**

A Sheraton mahogany cylinder bureau, inlaid with satinwood bands, the interior with pigeonholes, drawers and pull out leather lined panel with pen compartments, 43 in (107.5 cm). **$3,000-4,000**

An Edwardian inlaid mahogany cylinder top bureau. **$1,000-1,200**

An Edwardian mahogany inlaid bureau à cylindre, in satinwood and boxwood lined borders, stamped Jas.Shoolbred & Company, 30 in (75 cm). **$2,000-3,000**

mahogany cylinder rolltop bureau, inlaid with ribboned bell flower festoons and geometric boxwood lines, basically early 19thC, 39 in (97.5 cm). **$4,000-5,000**

An Edwardian mahogany cylinder bureau, inlaid with satinwood and various woods, the tambour shutter enclosing a fitted interior and writing slide, 36½ in (91 cm). **$2,500-3,500**

An Edwardian inlaid rosewood cylinder top bureau, 28 in (70 cm). **$2,000-3,000**

Bureau de dame

A Victorian inlaid burr walnut ladies bureau, 32 in (80 cm). **$2,000-3,000**

A Victorian walnut bureau de dame, c1870, 41½ in by 31 in (105.5 cm by 79 cm). **$1,200-1,500**

MAKE THE MOST OF MILLER'S

Miller's is completely different each year. Each edition contains completely NEW photographs. This is not an updated publication. We never repeat the same photograph.

An Edwardian mahogany inlaid satinwood and boxwood escritoire, 28 in (70 cm). **$700-1,000**

Continental Bureaux

A Dutch mahogany and floral marquetry cylinder bureau, of bombé outlines, the rolled shutter enclosing a fitted interior and writing slide, late 18thC, 48 in (120 cm). **$5,500-7,000**

A good Dutch marquetry bureau, the fall front enclosing stepped small drawers, pigeonholes and a well, the interior and exterior profusely inlaid with urns of flowers, birds, floral sprays and chains, string lines and an ebony band, early 18thC, 42 in (105 cm). **$5,500-7,000**

A good Dutch Colonial hardwood bureau, outlined with dark wood mouldings, the waved fall enclosing a similarly fitted interior of drawers and pigeonholes above a well, mid-18thC, 41½ in (104 cm). **$3,000-4,500**

A Dutch oak floral marquetry cylinder bureau, the roll shutter enclosing a writing slide and fitted interior, 19thC, 41 in (102.5 cm). **$3,000-4,500**

A Dutch rosewood bureau, of bombé outlines inlaid with urns, birds and foliate marquetry in chequered and chevron satinwood banded borders, early 19thC, 38 in (95 cm). **$3,000-4,500**

A Second Empire burr walnut bureau, the shaped panelled fla[p] enclosing a leather lined writi[ng] surface bordered with tulipwo[od] inlaid with brass lines, 55 in (137.5 cm). **$2,000-3,000**

A Dutch mahogany cylinder bureau, with ebonised lines, the roll shutter enclosing a thuyawood interior and writing slide, 19thC, 35½ in (90 cm). **$4,500-5,000**

A Louis XV ormolu mounted kingwood bureau de dame, the sloping flap inlaid à quatre faces enclosing a fitted interior, re-mounted, twice stamped A. Fleury, 31 in (78.5 cm). **$2,500-3,500**
Adrien Fleury-Nicolay records this maître but not his date of maîtrise.

A Second Empire mahogany bureau, the sliding and telescopic coffered top with a fitted interior, 31 in (77.5 cm). **$1,400-1,700**

A Louis XV style kingwood marquetry bureau de dame, c1840, 33 in (83 cm). **$4,500-5,000**

A French provincial walnut bureau de dame, with sloping fla[p] enclosing a fitted interior, one drawer inscribed in ink 'fait à Sablé par Jean Baptiste Sn marti[n] fils 1789', late 18thC, 25 in (84 cm). **$1,500-2,200**

A Louix XVI style mahogany cylinder bureau de dame, inlaid with satinwood banded and boxwood lined borders, the roll shutter fall enclosing a pen compartment and 3 small drawers, late 19thC, 27½ in (70 cm). **$1,500-2,200**

A Louix XV-style kingwood bureau de dame, with crossbanding and floral spray inlay, c1890, 26 in (66 cm). **$1,000-1,200**

Louis Quinze style kingwood d inlaid bombé shaped bureau dame, with ormolu galleried o, 27½ in (68 cm). **00-900**

A French mahogany cylinder bureau, the interior with lined writing slide and small drawers, c1835, 51 in (130 cm). **$1,500-2,200**

A Louis XVI style cylinder bureau de dame, inlaid with urns, acanthus scrolls and ribboned bellflower festoons in boxwood line borders, 27 in (67 cm). **$1,300-1,700**

French mahogany bureau à ylindre, the cylinder shutter and ull-out writing slide with three rawers below, late 19thC, 3½ in (96 cm). **2,500-3,500**

A Louis XVI style ormolu-mounted mahogany bureau à cylindre, with vernis Martin panelled front, the fitted interior with inset leather pull-out writing surface, 30½ in (76 cm). **$1,300-1,700**

An Italian walnut bureau, inlaid with finely etched ivory, late 17thC, 46 in (115 cm). **$8,500-10,500**

late Biedermeier mahogany ylinder bureau, the tambour hutter enclosing a fitted interior nd writing slide, 52½ in 31 cm). **$1,000-1,400**

An Austrian lightwood and marquetry bureau de dame, inlaid with floral sprays and strapwork, the fall inlaid with an armorial shield flanked by demi-human figures, 24 in (60 cm). **$1,200-1,500**

A North Italian walnut and ebonised bureau, with stepped shaped hinged top, mid-18thC, 49 in (149.5 cm). **$8,500-10,500**

Cabinets – Bureau cabinets

A William and Mary walnut bureau cabinet, the base with a flap enclosing a fitted interior with drawers and pigeon holes surrounding a central cupboard and above a well, restored and with later feet and handles, 38 in (95 cm). $18,000-24,000

A Queen Anne burr walnut bureau cabinet, the associated base with sloping flap enclosing a fitted interior with a well, on later bun feet, 40 in (101.5 cm). $7,500-10,500

A William and Mary burr walnut double dome bureau cabinet, with fully fitted interior with internal secret drawer, 39 in (97.5 cm). $15,000-20,500

A walnut bureau cabinet, on later bracket feet, crossbanded, early 18thC, 36 in (90 cm). $15,000-20,500

A rare Queen Anne walnut and burr ash miniature bureau cabinet, the arched crossbanded upper section enclosing an interior of six drawers flanking a niche, 19 in (48 cm). $2,000-3,000

A walnut crossbanded and inlaid bureau cabinet, bordered with boxwood lines, fully fitted interior with secret compartments, with restorations, early 18thC, 40½ in (101 cm). $10,500-14,000

A George III mahogany secretaire cabinet, the associated dentilled cornice with later tablet cresting, the base with a fitted secretaire drawer, feet with restorations, 37 in (94 cm). $10,500-14,000

A George II mahogany bureau cabinet, with giltwood slip and fall flap enclosing a fitted interior, 35 in (89 cm). $8,500-10,500

A George II rosewood veneered bureau cabinet, the crossbanded baize lined sloping fall enclosing graduated fitted interior, with drawers and pigeon holes about a central enclosed compartment flanked by fluted pilaster secret compartments, 41 in (102 cm). $7,500-10,500

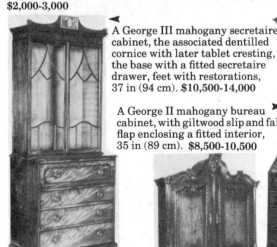

A Dutch mahogany bureau cabinet, carved in relief with husks and medallions, late 18thC, 48 in (122 cm). $6,000-8,000

A George III mahogany bureau cabinet, a crossbanded sloping fall front enclosing a fitted interior, 42½ in (106 cm). $2,000-3,000

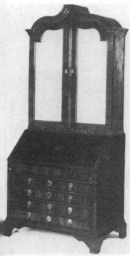

An Anglo Dutch walnut bureau
cabinet, the later glazed cupboard
doors enclosing an elaborate
interior, on later bracket feet,
early 18thC, 39 in (99 cm).
$8,500-10,500

An Italian black and gold lacquer
bureau cabinet, 18thC, 40 in
(102 cm). $15,000-20,500

A Dutch mahogany breakfront
cabinet, 18thC, 72 in (180 cm).
$4,500-5,000

Cabinets on stand

A black and gold lacquer cabinet
on stand, the later stand with
shaped apron and cabriole legs
and pad feet, the cabinet early
18thC, 45 in (114.5 cm).
$4,500-5,000

A Charles II black lacquer
cabinet, the carcase inscribed
Richard Caton, on a mid-Georgian
black and gold lacquer stand,
42½ in (108 cm).
$6,000-8,000

A William and Mary rosewood and
crossbanded marquetry cabinet,
on a later stand, c1700, stand
c1880, 42 in (107 cm).
$3,000-4,500

A Charles II black lacquer
cabinet on silvered wood
stand, 36 in (90 cm).
$3,000-4,500

A William and Mary Japanned
cabinet on a silvered wood stand,
the green-black exterior painted
with chinoiserie figures, cabinet
distressed, c1680, 43 in (110 cm).
$6,000-8,000

A Queen Anne black and gold
lacquer cabinet on stand, on later
ebonised turned legs and moulded
stretchers, redecorated, 43½ in
(110.5 cm). $5,500-7,000

A George III rosewood, kingwood
crossbanded and boxwood strung
cabinet on stand, in the French
taste, with brass mouldings, 33 in
(82 cm). $4,500-5,000

271

A mahogany and parcel gilt free standing corner cabinet, 19thC, 42 in (105 cm). $1,700-2,500

An Edwardian 'Sheraton' satinwood side cabinet, late 19thC, 36 in (92 cm). $4,500-5,000

A George III mahogany and sabicu lady's writing cabinet, with ebonised strung borders, the hinged top on a ratchet support, the side with a drawer, c1800, 15 in (38 cm). $1,000-1,400

An ebonised and pietra dura mounted side cabinet, applied throughout with gilt metal mounts, stamped 'Edwards & Roberts, Wardour Street', c1860, 35 in (89 cm). $3,000-4,000

A George III style satinwood and rosewood cabinet on stand, c1910, 26 in (66 cm). $4,500-5,000

A satinwood inlaid and painted cylinder top desk cabinet, c1880, 30 in (75 cm). $2,000-3,000

A fine Dutch rosewood, oyster veneered walnut, ivory and ebony cabinet on stand, the stand rebuilt at a later date, late 17thC, 72 in (183 cm). $4,500-5,000

A Flemish ormolu mounted tortoiseshell and ebony cabinet on stand, the Regency stand with entrelac mounted frieze on chamfered tapering legs, the cabinet 17thC, 39 in (99 cm). $4,500-7,000

A Georgian style black and gilt lacquered cabinet, 36 in (90 cm). $1,400-1,700

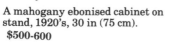

A mahogany ebonised cabinet on stand, 1920's, 30 in (75 cm). $500-600

A Louis XVI ebony, mahogany and marquetry secretaire, surmounted by a later top, 44½ in (111 cm). $5,500-7,000
The marquetry suggests a foreign artisan, possibly German or Swedish working in France.

A fine Louis XIV boulle cabinet on stand, of slight breakfront form, the central cupboard enclosing a mirrored perspective interior, the whole finely inlaid in pewter and brass with foliate scrolls, strapwork and urns of flowers, 38 in (95 cm).
$28,500-36,000

A Portuguese ebony contador, inlaid with pierced brass strapwork flanked by spirally turned pilasters, possibly Colonial, 17thC, 54 in (137 cm).
$4,500-5,000

An Anglo-Indian hardwood cabinet, in the late Regency taste, mid-19thC, 39½ in (100 cm).
$1,400-1,700

A Florentine pietra dura ebony and walnut cabinet on stand, 17thC, the stand later, 36 in (91.5 cm). **$10,500-14,000**

Collector's Cabinets

A rosewood ship's cabinet, 19thC.
$500-600

A Regency satinwood and mahogany collector's cabinet, the stand with square tapering legs branded CR, stamped 3395, minor restorations, 27 in (68 cm).
$1,500-2,200

A pair of Victorian mahogany specimen cabinets, decorated with inlaid ebony stringing, 62 in (155 cm). **$1,400-1,700**

A George III mahogany collector's cabinet, containing a collection of shells, on a later stand with tapering legs inlaid with stringing, c1780, 24 in (61 cm).
$2,500-3,500

A rosewood specimen cabinet, two drawers with a collection of shells, four containing a collection of mounted butterflies, second quarter of the 19thC, 18 in (46 cm).
$1,200-1,500

A doctors American walnut cabinet, 19thC. **$1,700-2,500**

An Edwardian mahogany collector's cabinet, the rectangular moulded top above an arrangement of eight graduated drawers on plinth base, 26 in (65 cm). **$60-100**

Display Cabinets

A Victorian walnut and ormolu mounted display cabinet, the whole crossbanded in tulipwood, 43 in (107 cm). **$1,400-1,700**

A Victorian walnut display cabinet, with marquetry inlay an gilt brass mounts, 30 in (75 cm). **$500-600**

A pair of Victorian ormolu mounted burr maple and burr walnut display cabinets, 27 in (68 cm). **$4,500-7,000**

A rosewood breakfront dwarf cabinet, with a walnut and marquetry cupboard door, partially 17thC, 106 in (268 cm) high. **$2,500-3,500**

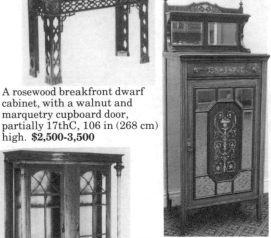

A Victorian rosewood music cabinet, inlaid in ivory and satinwood, 22 in (55 cm). **$600-700**

A late Victorian rosewood and ivory and marquetry inlaid sid cabinet, 65 in (162.5 cm). **$1,200-1,500**

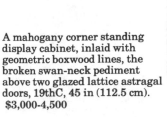

A late Victorian satinwood display cabinet, inlaid with ribboned harewood marquetry and bellflower trails, 51 in (127.5 cm). **$1,500-2,200**

A mahogany corner standing display cabinet, inlaid with geometric boxwood lines, the broken swan-neck pediment above two glazed lattice astragal doors, 19thC, 45 in (112.5 cm). **$3,000-4,500**

A late Victorian satinwood inlai demi-lune display cabinet on stand, c1890, 32 in (81 cm). **$2,500-3,500**

An Adam style mahogany and marquetry cabinet on stand, inlaid in satinwood and harewood, 19thC, 30 in (75 cm).
$2,000-3,000

A Victorian inlaid rosewood cabinet, 18 in (45 cm).
$300-500

A late Victorian mahogany display cabinet, fruitwood inlaid and satinwood crossbanded, with brass finials, 55 in (140 cm).
$2,000-3,000

A George III style mahogany display cabinet, 53 in (132.5 cm).
$1,400-1,700

An Edwardian 'Sheraton' painted satinwood corner cabinet, 25 in (63 cm). **$2,000-3,000**

A mahogany display cabinet, 60 in (150 cm). **$2,000-3,000**

An Edwardian mahogany serpentine fronted corner cabinet, the upper section with inlaid dentil cornice, the lower section with a pair of satinwood banded cupboards, 32 in (80 cm).
$1,400-1,700

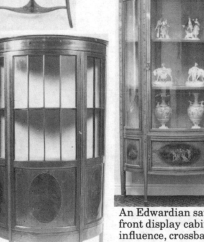

An Edwardian satinwood bow front display cabinet, of Sheraton influence, crossbanded in rosewood and painted with panels of cherubs, 42 in (105 cm).
$1,500-2,200

n Edwardian mahogany emi-lune display cabinet, inlaid ith satinwood and chequered ringing, c1910, 35½ in (90 cm).
,000-1,400

An Edwardian mahogany display cabinet, inlaid with geometric boxwood lines, 72 in (180 cm).
$3,000-4,000

An Edwardian inlaid mahogany display cabinet, 48 in (120 cm).
$1,000-1,400

An Edwardian mahogany and satinwood banded display cabinet, inlaid with arabesques and swags, c1910, 46½ in (118 cm).
$1,200-1,500

275

An Edwardian satinwood standing corner display cabinet, inlaid with chequered and ebonised lines, labelled Druce & Company, Upholsterers and Cabinet Makers, Baker Street, London, W, 34 in (85 cm). $1,700-2,500

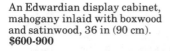

An Edwardian display cabinet, mahogany inlaid with boxwood and satinwood, 36 in (90 cm). $600-900

An inlaid mahogany display cabinet, the upper part have Dutch top, early 20thC, 39½ in (99 cm). $1,300-1,700

An Edwardian inlaid mahogany display cabinet, 26 in (65 cm). $1,000-1,200

An Edwardian rosewood cabinet with boxwood stringing and fine inlays, the lower part having a centre cupboard enclosed by bow front door inlaid with swags and musical instruments, 44 in (110 cm). $1,000-1,200

An Edwardian mahogany and inlaid display cabinet, 51 in (127.5 cm). $1,700-2,500

An Edwardian mahogany and mother of pearl inlaid display cabinet, 45 in (112.5 cm). $2,500-3,500

An Edwardian satinwood line inlaid china cabinet, 27 in (67.5 cm). $300-500

An Edwardian inlaid mahogany bow front display cabinet. $500-600

An Edwardian mahogany serpentine front salon cabinet, the panelled doors quarter veneered and with central oval panels of flame veneer, the whole banded with satinwood, strung with ebony and box, 54 in (135 cm). $4,500-7,000

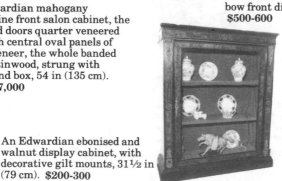

An Edwardian ebonised and walnut display cabinet, with decorative gilt mounts, 31½ in (79 cm). $200-300

An Edwardian mahogany inlaid display case, 23 in (57.5 cm). $500-600

◄ A mahogany display cabinet, 1920's, 27 in (67.5 cm). **$300-500**

A Dutch burr walnut standing vitrine, 19thC, 75 in (187.5 cm). **$3,500-5,000**

A Napoleon III kingwood and floral marquetry secretaire vitrine cabinet, mounted with gilt metal, 32 in (80 cm). **$3,500-5,000**

A French kingwood and ormolu moulded demi-lune hanging display cabinet, c1850, 36 in (92 cm). **$2,000-3,000**

A pair of French ormolu mounted kingwood vitrines, signed H. Martin, 25½ in (64 cm). **$2,500-3,500**

A French ormolu mounted kingwood display cabinet, late 19thC, 26 in (65 cm). **$1,500-2,200**

A French rosewood vitrine, in the vernis Martin manner, the whole profusely mounted with ormolu, signed Paoli, 19thC, 48 in (112.5 cm). **$3,500-5,000**

French vitrine, embellished with ormolu scrolls and inlaid with a marquetry panel of flowers, 19thC, 34 in (85 cm). **$2,500-3,500**

A French rosewood, vernis Martin and bronze mounted vitrine, late 19thC, 41½ in (104 cm). **$2,000-3,000**

A French rosewood and inlaid vitrine, with gilt metal mounts, c1890, 63 in (160 cm). **$2,000-3,000**

A Louis XVI design ormolu mounted marquetry vitrine, 44 in (110 cm). $3,000-4,500

A continental carved giltwood display cabinet, in the 18thC style, c1900, 43 in (109 cm). $1,500-2,200

A Louis XV style mahogany and ormolu mounted vitrine, the painted panels signed 'D. Prat', c1900, 34 in (84 cm). $2,000-3,000

A French rosewood vitrine, with gilt metal mounts, 19thC, 35 in (89 cm). $1,700-2,500

A Louis XVI style mahogany standing vitrine, applied with gilt metal volutes and foliate mounts, 31½ in (79 cm). $4,500-7,000

A German walnut and crossbanded corner display cabinet in the 18thC style, with geometric banding and burr segmented veneers, c1900, 36 in (90 cm). $1,000-1,200

A black and gilt lacquered secretaire cabinet, early 18thC, 44 in (110 cm). $9,000-13,000

An unusual Sheraton mahogany writing cabinet, on twin ring turned tapered supports terminating in brass cappings and castors, 35½ in (89 cm). $4,000-5,000

Secretaire Cabinets

A William and Mary walnut secretaire cabinet, the cornice with a drawer above a cross and feather banded fall front enclosing a fitted interior, with later bracket feet, c1690, 44 in (112 cm). $8,500-11,000

A painted secretaire cabinet, the fall front enclosing drawers and pigeon holes made-up, c1920, 41 in (104 cm). $1,300-1,700

A William and Mary walnut and floral marquetry cabinet on chest with later moulded cornice, a convex frieze drawer and fall flap inlaid with shaped panels of floral marquetry enclosing a fitted interior, restorations, 42 in (107 cm). $4,000-5,000

Side Cabinets

A George III mahogany serpentine fronted cabinet, with satinwood strung borders to the top, c1780, 24 in (61 cm).
$3,000-4,000

A pair of late Georgian mahogany folio cabinets, each with leather lined easel and ratchet top, adapted, 34 in (86 cm).
$3,500-5,000

Regency mahogany side cabinet th brass grilles with claw feet, the style of Thomas Hope, 310. **$3,500-5,000**

A Regency mahogany dwarf cabinet, with later onyx top, 37 in (94 cm). **$2,000-3,000**

A Regency brass inlaid mahogany breakfront side cabinet, in the manner of George Bullock, with later inset veined grey marble top, the doors enclosing three drawers inlaid with parquetry in ebony, amaranth, walnut, satinwood and other specimen woods, 65½ in (166.5 cm). **$6,000-8,000**

Regency rosewood cabinet, the rde antico marble top, c1815, in (153 cm). ,400-1,700

A Regency side cabinet.
$800-1,200

A Regency mahogany cabinet, with gilt metal mounts and brass stringing, with grey marble top, c1815, 38 in (97 cm).
$3,000-4,500

William IV mahogany ffonier, 36 in (90 cm). 00-700

An early Victorian rosewood side cabinet, 81 in (206 cm).
$3,500-5,000

A late Regency rosewood side cabinet, 78 in (198 cm).
$4,500-7,000

A rare papier-mache side cabinet, the top painted with a view of the Doge's Palace, Venice, all in tones of gilt on a green bronze ground on ball feet, originally with a superstructure and probably with drawers, 1840's, 41½ in (104 cm). $2,500-3,500

A painted and parcel gilt wood and gesso library cabinet, with hinged leather covered panel with satinwood and gilt bronze borders, decorated overall with scrolling foliage, the ends each with a monogram JRA and a leather lined slide, distressed, 1840's, 62 in (157.5 cm). $4,500-7,000

A pair of Victorian walnut and marquetry pier cabinets, inlaid with a marquetry urn of flowers on an ebony ground, the pilasters, with gilt metal mounts, 32 in (80 cm). $3,500-5,000

A pair of boulle brass inlaid side cabinets, c1850, 17 in (43 cm). $3,000-4,000

A red boulle breakfront credenza, the ebonised top, with brass line inlaid and cast brass rosette, mid-19thC, 77 in (192.5 cm). $1,300-1,700

A Victorian walnut breakfront credenza, with marquetry panels, kingwood, rosewood and figwood banded, 64 in (160 cm). $2,000-3,000

A walnut and gilt bronze side cabinet, with a reddish marble top, mid-19thC, 28 in (71 cm). $800-1,200

An ebonised and boulle serpentine side cabinet, inlaid with cut brass and red tortoiseshell foliate panels, mid-19thC, 79½ in (197.5 cm). $1,200-1,500

A Victorian walnut and ormolu mounted breakfront cabinet, c1860, 75 in (191 cm). $4,000-5,000

A Victorian walnut and ormolu mounted credenza, inlaid with satinwood arabesques and stringing, the amboyna decorated frieze above a panelled door with a Sevres style porcelain plaque, c1860, 60 in (152 cm). $2,000-3,000

Miller's is a price GUIDE not a price LIST

The price ranges given reflect the average price a purchaser should pay for similar items. Condition, rarity of design or pattern, size, colour, provenance, restoration and many other factors must be taken into account when assessing values. When buying or selling, it must always be remembered that prices can be greatly affected by the condition of any piece. Unless otherwise stated, all goods shown in Miller's are of good merchantable quality, and the valuations given reflect this fact. Pieces offered for sale in exceptionally fine condition or in poor condition may reasonably be expected to be priced considerably higher or lower respectively than the estimates given herein.

A Victorian inlaid walnut bow front credenza, with ormolu embellishments, 65 in (165 cm). $1,700-2,500

Victorian inlaid figured walnut edenza, with ormolu decoration, in (150 cm). **$1,500-2,200**

A Victorian ebonised and walnut crossbanded credenza, with ormolu mounts, 78 in (198 cm). **$1,300-1,700**

A Victorian inlaid ebonised credenza, inset with blue Wedgwood jasperware plaque, crack to curved side door. **$700-900**

Victorian kingwood grained, molu mounted and porcelain set side cabinet, 76 in (192 cm). ,500-3,500

A George III style painted mahogany side cabinet, the top with satinwood crossbanding painted with a continuous ribbon and flower design, 48 in (120 cm). **$2,500-3,500**

An ebonised cabinet, with ormolu mounts and Sèvres panels, 19thC. **$1,300-1,700**

satinwood marquetry and poker rked side cabinet, in the Dutch 'le, stamped Maple & Co., early .hC, 38 in (94 cm). ,000-3,000

A satinwood and marquetry demi-lune side cabinet, in George III style, and crossbanded in rosewood, inlaid throughout with ovals and swags partly in green stained wood, c1880, 59 in (150 cm). **$4,000-5,000**

A satinwood, mahogany and marquetry side cabinet, late 18thC style, 37 in (92.5 cm). **$2,000-3,000**

A French ebonised small meuble d'appui, mounted with gilt metal, 19thC, 33½ in (84 cm). **$1,300-1,700**

pair of Regency style rosewood arf side cabinets enclosed by ick lacquered panel doors corated with chinoiserie, 24 in cm). **$2,500-3,500**

pair of Dutch mahogany bow nt encoignures, inset with rquetry panels, late 18thC, ½ in (64 cm). ,500-7,000

A Dutch satinwood and fruitwood side cabinet, late 18th/early 19thC, 42 in (107 cm). **$4,000-5,000**

A pair of French ebonised meubles
d'appui, with applied ormolu
mounts and porcelain plaques,
c1860, 49 in (122 cm).
$1,500-2,200

A French kingwood and vernis
Martin cabinet, the grey and
purple breche marble slab above a
frieze decorated with musical
instruments and flowers, late
19thC, 36 in (89 cm).
$2,500-3,500

Side Cabinets – Chiffoniers

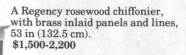

A Regency rosewood chiffonier,
with brass inlaid panels and lines,
53 in (132.5 cm).
$1,500-2,200

A pair of Regency chiffoniers, with
rosewood veneers, in the style of
McLean, c1805, 49 in (122.5 cm)
high. $34,500-44,200

A Regency rosewood chiffonier,
with reeded mouldings and
brocade panels, back partially
replaced, c1810, 60 in (152 cm).
$1,200-1,500

A Regency rosewood chiffonier,
stamped Gillows, Lancaster, in
need of some restoration, early
19thC, 36 in (92 cm).
$2,500-3,500

A Regency brass inlaid rosewood
chiffonier, the superstructure
with three quarter pierced
gallery, the shaped angles inlaid
with stylised flowerheads, on
shaped feet, 36 in (91.5 cm).
$3,500-5,000

A late Regency mahogany
chiffonier, the rectangular top
with a folding writing panel, 27 i
(67.5 cm). $1,300-1,700

A Regency rosewood secretaire
chiffonier, inlaid with
anthemions, vitruvian scrolls and
brass lines, applied with ormolu
mounts, 29 in (72.5 cm).
$3,500-5,000

◄ A William IV rosewood chiffonier,
c1835, 30 in (76 cm).
$1,500-2,200

William IV flame mahogany
chiffonier, enclosing a cellaret
compartment, 35 in (87.5 cm).
$500-600

An early Victorian chiffonier,
36½ in (91 cm). $700-1,000

An early Victorian chiffonier,
with a drawer carved with Prince
of Wales feathers, 39 in (97.5 cm).
$500-600

A Victorian walnut side cabinet,
inlaid with stringing, floral sprays
and gilt metal mounts, 41 in
(108 cm). $1,700-2,500

Victorian mahogany chiffonier,
enclosing a cellaret compartment,
½ in (116 cm). $300-500

A Victorian combined whatnot
and table leaf cabinet, bearing
reg. no. 28395 and indistinctly
stamped 'Wylie and...., Glasgow',
c1860, 25 in (64 cm).
$1,000-1,200

A pair of burrwood and ebony
cabinets, in the French style,
19thC, 53 in (132.5 cm).
$7,000-9,000

French walnut buffet, late
9thC, 56 in (140 cm).
800-1,200

Canterburies

n unusual Regency rosewood
anterbury, 30½ in (76 cm).
,400-1,700

A Regency mahogany canterbury,
on turned feet, drawer missing,
32 in (81 cm). $4,000-5,000

A Regency rosewood canterbury,
19½ in (49.5 cm). $2,000-3,000

A rosewood canterbury, early 19thC, 19 in (47.5 cm). **$1,700-2,500**

A rosewood canterbury, c1840, 24 in (61 cm). **$800-1,200**

A Victorian walnut serpentine fronted music canterbury, with a pierced fret gallery and spiral twist supports, c1850, 24 in (61 cm). **$800-1,200**

A Victorian walnut canterbury, the fret panelled sides and graduating four divisioned top with a central carrying handle, 19 in (47.5 cm). **$1,000-1,400**

A mahogany canterbury, with carved laurel wreath decoration, 19thC, 21 in (52.5 cm). **$800-1,200**

A Victorian walnut music canterbury, the open tier with pierced fret gallery, on pierced lyre-shaped end supports, c1850, 24 in (61 cm). **$1,300-1,700**

A walnut music canterbury, 24 in (60 cm). **$400-600**

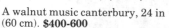

A satinwood music canterbury, late 19thC, 20 in (51 cm). **$2,000-3,000**

Chairs –

A George I walnut wing armchair, on cabriole legs headed by carved shells and suspending bell flowers and ending in claw and ball feet, upholstered in contemporary needlework, added later, restorations to frame. **$7,500-10,500**

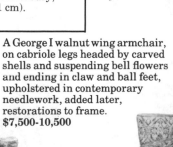

A Queen Anne provincial walnut wing armchair, with restorations, c1710. **$4,000-5,000**

A Queen Anne walnut wing armchair, covered in late 17thC Flemish tapestry on walnut hipped cabriole legs, elmwood cabriole back legs, c1710. **$9,000-13,000**

An Empire grain-painted upholstered rocking chair, with added crest rail over 9 curved spindles supporting a padded back, over scrolling arms with added arm rests and leaf-carved grips over 3 spindles over a plank seat with a pad, Massachusetts, 1825-1835, 44½in (111cm) high. **1,100-1,500**

A Chippendale walnut easy chair, with serpentine crested canted back, flanked by shaped wings continuing to vertically rolled arms above a seat with loose cushion on cabriole legs with ball and claw feet, joined by block and arrow-turned stretchers, upholstered in old flame stitch crewel fabric, Massachusetts, 1750-1780, 46in (115cm) high. **$45,000-55,000**

A Federal mahogany lolling chair, the upholstered back with serpentine crest above shaped open arms over a trapezoidal upholstered seat, on square tapering inlaid legs joined by an H-stretcher, Salem, Massachusetts, 1790-1810, 47in (118cm) high. **$7,500-8,500**

A Federal mahogany easy chair, with bowed crest above shaped wings over outwardly scrolling armrests over a trapezoidal seat, on molded Marlborough legs, New England, 1780-1800, 44in (110cm) high. **$3,000-3,500**

A fine Chippendale mahogany easy chair, the serpentine crest over scrolled wings continuing to flaring horizontally-scrolled arms above a straight rail, on cabriole legs with squared knees and ball and claw feet with raking talons, one rear leg pieced, Massachusetts, 1750-1780, 46½in (116cm) high. **$27,000-32,000**

A Federal mahogany easy chair, with shaped crest flanked by S-shaped wings continuing to scroll arms, New York, 1790-1810, 46in (115cm) high. **$2,500-3,000**

A Federal mahogany lolling chair, the serpentine crest above straight stiles with curved armrests over sloping arm supports, on Marlborough legs with quarter-round molded edges, probably Pennsylvania, 1790-1810, 46½in (116cm) high. **$3,500-4,000**

An early Georgian walnut, elm and oak wing armchair, one foot restored. $2,000-3,000

A George II mahogany wing armchair, on cabriole legs headed by acanthus and claw and ball feet. $2,500-3,500

A George II walnut wing chair, c1750, 47 in (117.5 cm). $15,000-20,500

A George III grey painted bergere, in the Louis XVI style, the moulded frame carved with beading and fluting. $2,000-3,000

A George III mahogany tub bergère. $2,000-3,000

A Federal carved mahogany armchair, the molded square back centering an arch with a pierced vase surmounted with a Prince-of-Wales plume, minor old repairs, New York, 1790-1810, 36in (90cm) high. $4,000-5,000

A Regency bergère chair, c1800, 35½ in (89 cm) high. $7,000-9,000

A George III mahogany musician's chair of Louis XV style. $3,000-4,500

A chair of identical form is illustrated in P. Macquoid, The Age of Satinwood, 1908, fig. 195.

Chairs

★ Bear in mind the environment of the 17th century chair: washed-down stone or earth floors, hence all but the finest might be prone to wear at the feet.

★ Stretcher rails close to the ground are evidence of this, but quality restoration need not be detrimental. Most yew-wood Windsor chairs available today are 19th century but look out for the cabriole leg 18th century model. The best turned leg type will have yew-wood legs, certainly to the front if not back as well and the bow or crinoline stretcher is a big plus.

★ 18th century corner braces to the seat frames were let into the rails from the top before the upholstery was applied, creating an open triangle in each corner: Curvilinear shaped solid corner block fixed with screws is 19th century.

★ Mahogany dining chairs with upholstered 'stuff-over' seats usually have beech rails.

★ Woodworm and successive upholsteries may have caused deterioration; sympathetic replacement of these is essential if the chairs are to be used, but the old original rails should be kept, sealed up, for future reference.

★ Look out for sets of chairs, each one of which has one or more new members; it may indicate a set of, say, five being taken apart and rebuilt as six.

★ The 'carver' to a set of dining chairs will always be wider across the seat than the 'singles'.

★ Check for damage at leg-seat rail junctions to 'drop-in' seat dining chairs. Additional coverings can make the seat bigger and when dropped-in force the frames apart.

★ The best sabre leg to the front of a chair will have the toe forward of the seat rail when viewed from the side.

A pair of late Regency mahogany bergères. $2,500-3,500

Regency mahogany tub
mchair, on ring turned tapering
ɹs stamped MB, one back foot
placed. $3,000-4,500

A mahogany club armchair,
probably by Gillows of Lancaster,
early 19thC. $600-900

A Regency mahogany framed
bergère. $1,500-2,200

William IV mahogany
mchair, on reeded legs with
ass caps and casters.
,500-2,200

A William IV mahogany bergère,
the reeded and foliate carved
showframe with anthemion
decoration. $1,000-1,400

An early Victorian mahogany
bergère, the casters stamped T.W.
Lewty's Patent. $1,300-1,700

vo saloon chairs, framed in
rved mahogany with balloon
cks, 19thC. $1,300-1,700

A pair of lady's and gentleman's
Victorian mahogany armchairs.
$1,500-2,200

A pair of Edwardian satinwood
bergères, decorated with painted
bellhusks, foliage and swags, both
stamped O.M.5226. (2)
$4,500-5,000

mahogany invalid's bergère
tent, the winged back
justable in rake by a handle,
880. $1,000-1,400

A Victorian walnut slipper chair,
in need of renovation.
$400-600

A Victorian mahogany folding
campaign chair. $800-1,200

A late Victorian walnut Foot's Patent adjustable armchair, mounted with a brass arm with writing tray, reading support and turned top, labelled J. Foot & Son, Patentees and Manufacturers, 171, New Bond Street, London, W. **$1,400-1,700**

An American bath chair, the cream painted wickerwork back, arms and footrest with a split cane seat, labelled Knauth Brothers, New York. **$600-900**

An oak invalid's chair by John Ward patentee, with detachab book rest tray, c1905. **$1,200-1,500**

A fine Louis XV giltwood bergère chair. **$1,500-2,200**

A Louis XV beechwood bergèr **$4,500-5,000**

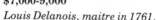

A pair of Louis XV beechwood bergères, by L. Delanois. **$7,000-9,000**

Louis Delanois, maitre in 1761.

A Louis XVI beechwood bergère, by J.R. Nadal, stamped I. Nadal. **$4,000-5,000**

Jean-Rene Nadal, maitre in 1756.

An unusual South German horr chair, constructed of elk horn antlers, 19thC. **$2,500-3,500**

Chairs – Armchair, open

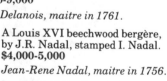

A Louis XVI bergère, by P. Bernard, c1780. **$800-1,200**

A George II red walnut armchair, c1740. **$2,000-3,000**

A Queen Anne walnut and oak armchair, with shepherd's croo arms, on cabriole legs and pad feet. **$1,700-2,500**

A Charles II walnut open armchair, the seat rails replaced. $2,000-3,000

A George II carved mahogany elbow chair. $1,300-1,700

A George II mahogany open armchair. $4,000-5,000

A George III mahogany open armchair, in the manner of Robert Manwaring, some of the carving of a later date. $2,000-3,000

George III mahogany armchair, 1760. $800-1,200

A George III mahogany elbow chair. $800-1,200

A George III mahogany elbow chair. $500-600

George III mahogany open armchair later blocks. $5,500-7,000

A carved mahogany Hepplewhite period armchair, c1785, 37½ in (94 cm) high. $3,000-4,000

MAKE THE MOST OF MILLERS

When buying or selling, it must always be remembered that prices can be greatly affected by the condition of any piece. Unless otherwise stated, all goods shown in Miller's are of good merchantable quality, and the valuations given reflect this fact. Pieces offered for sale in exceptionally fine condition or in poor condition may reasonably be expected to be priced considerably higher or lower respectively than the estimates given herein.

A set of four George III mahogany open armchairs, with moulded shield shaped backs and pierced partially carved splats, and a pair en suite of later date.
$7,500-10,500

A George III mahogany scroll armchair, c1770.
$2,000-3,000

A George III carved mahogany elbow chair, in the Hepplewhite taste, the interlaced trefoil shield shaped back with palm spray and drapery ornament.
$1,500-2,200

A pair of George III mahogany cockpen open armchairs, with pierced trelliswork backs, one with later blocks and largely re-railed, the other with later blocks and reinforced backrail.
$6,000-8,000

A George III mahogany open armchair, in the French taste.
$1,700-2,500

A pair of George III mahogany library armchairs.
$10,500-14,000

A George III mahogany open armchair, in the Louis XV style, later blocks. $4,000-5,000

A George III mahogany open armchair, new blocks and partly re-railed. $6,000-8,500

A George III mahogany upholstered armchair.
$1,300-1,700

A William Kent carved mahogany elbow chair, on square tapered cabriole legs with guilloche trailing decoration terminating in block feet. $1,400-1,700

An Adam period later gilt elbow chair, in the Louis XVI taste, with an interlaced guilloche frame.
$1,700-2,500

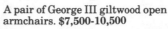

A pair of George III giltwood open armchairs. $7,500-10,500

A George III white painted and gilded open armchair.
$1,200-1,500

A George III black painted and gilt armchair, c1800. $1,300-1,700

A pair of ebonised Regency elbow chairs, with lattice backs.
1,700-2,500

A pair of Regency mahogany armchairs, the rail backs with carved and pierced scroll mid-bars, c1815.
$1,700-2,500

A fine Regency parcel gilt and simulated rosewood open armchair, the lyre shaped splat centred with a muse roundel.
$5,500-7,000

A Regency rosewood and brass inlaid armchair, the top rail inlaid with brass. $1,500-2,200

Regency cream and terracotta painted open armchair, in the manner of C. Tatham.
5,500-7,000

pair of Regency ebonised open rmchairs, with ring turned tablet prails. $2,000-3,000

A set of four Regency style ebonised and parcel gilt armchairs, with en grisaille panels painted with classical scenes. $4,500-5,000

A pair of Regency mahogany rail back elbow chairs.
$5,500-7,000

An unusual George IV mahogany library armchair, lacking reading slide. $2,500-3,500

A late Regency mahogany open armchair, the toprail carved with entwined dolphins, possibly Irish. $1,500-2,200

A Regency mahogany library armchair, in the manner of George Bullock, the scrolled arms inlaid in ebony and brass with anthemions and mounted with ormolu plaques on S-scroll legs. $7,000-9,000

A mid-Victorian carved walnut elbow chair. $1,000-1,400

An early Victorian mahogany reclining open armchair, fitted with a sliding footrest. $1,000-1,400

A Victorian rosewood frame armchair, colonial, c1860. $400-600

A mid-Victorian brass mounted walnut armchair, c1870. $1,000-1,400

A mahogany frame open arm elbow library chair, in the early Georgian manner by Howard & Sons of Berners Street. $14,000-17,000

A Victorain walnut scroll armchair, with padded arms c1870. $700-900

A set of twenty Victorian mahogany armchairs, in the style of Henry Holland, inlaid with brass lines, bellflowers and anthemions in Grecian key pattern borders, and three similar armchairs, lacking brass inlay, stamped Z. & R.P. $14,000-17,000

A pair of Victorian rosewood and upholstered chairs in the French Hepplewhite style, c1880. $1,500-2,200

A continental walnut armchair, with shaped stretchers, early 18thC. $2,500-3,500

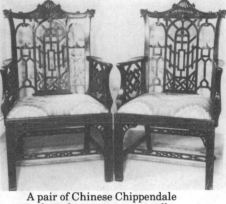

A pair of Chinese Chippendale style mahogany open arm elbow chairs. $4,500-7,000

A Dutch mahogany 'birds and foliage' inlaid elbow chair, 18thC. $1,500-2,200

A set of four early Biedermeier walnut open armchairs, on gilt metal mounted square tapering splayed legs. $4,000-5,000

A continental walnut and upholstered armchair, French or Flemish, c1680. $600-900

A Louis XVI beechwood fauteuil, the seat rail indistinctly stamped FRO...(?). $1,300-1,700

A Regence walnut fauteuil, c1730. $4,000-5,000

A fine pair of Dutch Colonial rosewood and walnut Burgomeister chairs, inlaid with ivory bellflowers, minor variations. $7,500-10,500

A pair of Flemish walnut open armchairs, 17thC. $2,000-3,000

An Italian giltwood open armchair, 19thC. $600-900

Two French gilt framed open armchairs, in 18thC style, 19thC. $1,500-2,200

A set of four Empire white painted and parcel gilt Fauteuils, and a matching stool of a later date. $8,500-11,000

A green painted and parcel gilt armchair, possibly Russian, early 19thC. $1,300-1,700

A pair of Empire mahogany and parcel gilt fauteuils, on foliate sabre legs, upholstery on one distressed, later blocks and minor restoration. $2,500-3,500

Chairs – Corner

A mahogany corner chair, 18thC. $300-500

A George I walnut corner chair, c1725. $2,500-3,500

An Edwardian mahogany corner chair, the backrest inlaid with a floral spray. $80-150

—— Chairs – Dining ——

◄

A pair of George II carved mahogany dining chairs, the backs with scroll top rails, centred by C-scroll, rocaille and foliate cresting, having pierced interlaced vase splats, carved at the knees with foliage, salmon spawn and pendant tassel ornament, terminating in scaly ball-and-claw feet. $1,700-2,500

A set of 6 George II mahogany dining chairs. $3,000-4,500

Stamped WS on the reverse of each back leg.

A pair of early Georgian red walnut dining chairs, with scrolled top rails. $6,000-8,000

A set of 4 mid-Georgian red walnut dining chairs, carved with grotesque masks. $7,000-9,000

A set of 8 late George II walnut dining chairs, minor restorations. $25,500-32,500

A matched set of 9 George II mahogany dining chairs, including 2 armchairs. $5,500-7,000

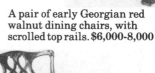

A pair of William and Mary maple side chairs, on block and baluster-turned front legs joined by an elaborately turned front stretcher and rectangular side stretchers, with turned feet, Boston, 1700-1720, 43½in (109cm) high. **$4,500-5,000**

A pair of Queen Anne walnut side chairs, each with a yoked crest rail continuing to curved stiles centering a vase-shaped splat, on cabriole legs with pad feet joined by block-and-turned stretchers, one with restored crest, one with restored splat, various repairs, Boston, 1740-1760, 40in (100cm) high. **$5,000-6,000**

A set of 4 Chippendale mahogany side chairs, each with a serpentine crest rail with rounded ears above a Gothic fretwork splat, on molded Marlborough legs joined by an H-stretcher, severe damage to one splat, other damages and repairs, Philadelphia, 1760-1790, 39in (99cm) high. **$3,500-5,000**

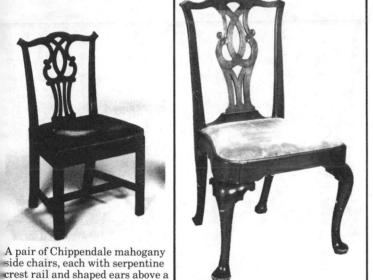

A pair of Chippendale mahogany side chairs, each with serpentine crest rail and shaped ears above a pierced and strapwork splat flanked by tapering stiles over a trapezoidal slip seat, Massachusetts, 1760-1780, 37in (92.5cm) high. **$1,500-2,000**

A Queen Anne walnut side chair, with molded serpentine crest over a pierced splat with scrolled volutes flanked by molded stiles above a balloon-shaped slip seat, Massachusetts, 1745-1765, 37½in (94cm). **$4,000-5,000**

A pair of Chippendale cherrywood side chairs, each with serpentine crest rail with slightly scrolled ears above a pierced strapwork splat, flanked by tapering stiles over a trapezoidal slip seat, one with restored seat rails, Massachusetts, 1760-1790, 37in (92.5cm) high. **$1,500-2,000**

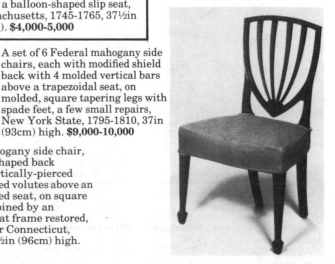

A set of 6 Federal mahogany side chairs, each with modified shield back with 4 molded vertical bars above a trapezoidal seat, on molded, square tapering legs with spade feet, a few small repairs, New York State, 1795-1810, 37in (93cm) high. **$9,000-10,000**

A Federal mahogany side chair, with a shield-shaped back centering a vertically-pierced splat with carved volutes above an over-upholstered seat, on square tapering legs joined by an H-stretcher, seat frame restored, Rhode Island or Connecticut, 1790-1810, 38½in (96cm) high. **$300-400**

A pair of late Federal carved mahogany side chairs, each with shaped crest rail centering a stylized acanthus-carved tablet above another horizontal acanthus-carved tripartite splat, flanked by reeded and scrolled stiles continuing to a trapezoidal slip seat, old repair to one stile at juncture with seat rail, Boston, 1810-1820, 35in (89cm) high. **$2,500-3,500**

These chairs are of a design associated with Boston and are similar to an example illustrated in Berry B. Traçey, et.al. Nineteenth Century America (New York: 1970), no.30.

A pair of Federal mahogany Klismos side chairs, each with figured veneer panelled table crest between reeded scrolled sides, continuing to a reeded swag back, Boston, 1810-1820, 32in (80cm) high. **$900-1,000**

A set of 5 late Federal mahogany side chairs, each with a tablet crest rail veneered with a figured panel outlined by stringing, over a carved stylized foliate splat, above a trapezoidal slip seat, on sabre legs, Philadelphia, 1800-1815, 31½in (78.5cm) high. **$2,500-3,000**

An assembled set of 8 Federal carved mahogany dining chairs, comprising a set of 4 side and 2 armchairs and a matched pair of side chairs, each with a square back centering a Prince-of-Wales plume over a pierced urn with a swag, New York, 1800-1850, armchairs 36in (90cm) high. **$21,000-25,000**

A set of 5 figured maple side chairs, each with tablet crest with scrolled central plinth over a vasiform plinth above a caned seat, on sabre legs, one with repair to crest, American, 1830-1845, each 34in (85cm) high. **$900-1,100**

A set of 8 grain-painted and gilt fancy chairs, each with a cylindrical crest rail above a shaped splat stencilled with cornucopiae, the surface painted in imitation of rosewood and with gilt foliate decoration, New England, 1825-1835, 34in (85cm) high. **$3,000-4,000**

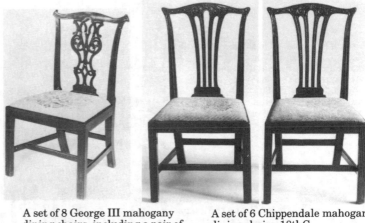

A set of 8 George III mahogany dining chairs, including a pair of armchairs with waved pierced top rails carved with foliage and shell crestings, with pierced interlaced Gothic patterned splats, 5 partly re-railed and another 2 with later blocks. $42,000-54,000

A set of 8 George III mahogany dining chairs, including a pair of armchairs, on chamfered square legs joined by stretchers, some with later blocks. $6,000-8,500

A set of 6 Chippendale mahogany dining chairs, 18thC. $1,500-2,200

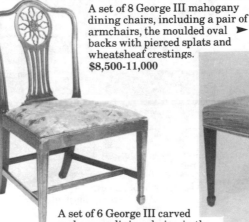

A set of 8 George III mahogany dining chairs, including a pair of armchairs, the moulded oval backs with pierced splats and wheatsheaf crestings. ➤ $8,500-11,000

set of 8 mahogany Chippendale period dining chairs, including 2 arvers. $8,500-10,500

A set of 6 George III carved mahogany dining chairs, in the Hepplewhite taste, with serpentine arched top rails and pierced wheel splats, with radiating Gothic cusp ornament, stamped 'P.H.'. $8,500-11,000

A set of 6 George III carved mahogany chairs, of Hepplewhite design, c1780. $3,000-4,500

A set of 5 Georgian mahogany dining chairs. $1,300-1,700

A pair of Hepplewhite period 'wheat-ear' shield back side chairs, c1785. $1,700-2,500

set of 8 black and gold lacquer ning chairs, including a pair of rmchairs of cockpen type, the acks filled with Chinese paling corated in raised gilt with owerheads and trellis pattern. 22,500-34,000

A pair of George III mahogany pierced ladderback dining chairs. $1,000-1,200

A set of 6 George III mahogany ► dining chairs, including a pair of armchairs, the rectangular backs with tablet top rails above moulded vertical splats with overlapping leaf carved capitals, and another chair of very similar design. $3,000-4,500

Six Georgian mahogany square frame dining chairs, backs inlaid with ebony stringing. $2,000-3,000

A set of 6 George III mahogany dining chairs, the cartouche-shaped backs with pierced waved splats, minor variations, and 6 en suite of late date. $7,500-10,500

A set of 6 country Georgian chairs. $2,000-3,000

A set of 6 mahogany dining chairs, including 2 with arms, one of later date. $3,000-4,500

A set of 7 George III mahogany dining chairs, including an armchair, new blocks. $6,000-8,000

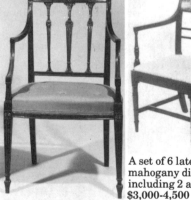

A set of 8 George III mahoga; shield back chairs, including carvers, with reeded and leaf carved splats, c1780. $3,000-4,500

A set of 6 late George III mahogany dining chairs, including 2 armchairs. $3,000-4,500

Four mahogany chairs and 2 armchairs, Hepplewhite period, c1785. $15,000-20,500

A set of 6 George III mahogany dining chairs, including a pair of armchairs, inlaid with satinwood banding, 2 with later blocks. $7,500-10,500

A set of 4 mahogany dining chairs, of Chippendale design. ► $3,000-4,500

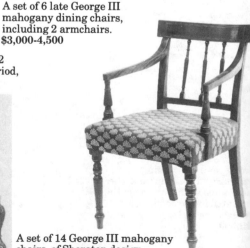

A set of 14 George III mahogany chairs, of Sheraton design, including 2 armchairs, c1800. $7,500-10,500

A set of 6 ropeback mahogany dining chairs, on turned legs, c1810. $4,500-7,000

A set of 9 George IV mahogany dining chairs, including 2 armchairs. $3,000-4,500

A set of 6 George III mahogany chairs, including 2 armchairs, the reeded back supports with banded top rails, c1800. $3,000-4,500

A set of 6 George IV oak and parcel gilt dining chairs. $1,300-1,700

A set of 8 George IV rosewood dining chairs. $3,000-4,500

A set of 7 George IV carved mahogany rail back chairs, including an armchair, with pierced clasp-shaped mid-bars and Trafalgar seats, c1825. $2,000-3,000

Four Regency mahogany sabre-leg dining chairs. $1,000-1,200

A set of 6 Regency mahogany dining chairs, with panel inlaid and bar backs. $1,700-2,500

A set of 8 Regency mahogany dining chairs, the panelled splats with rope-twist brass borders, the later drop-in and caned seats on panelled sabre legs. $10,000-13,000

A set of 10 Regency mahogany dining chairs, including a pair of armchairs with spirally-turned shaped top rails. $14,000-17,000

A set of 7 Regency mahogany and brass inlaid chairs, including one armchair with overscrolled arms, the figures and reeded top rails above horizontal splats, inlaid with fleur-de-lys motifs, with one replaced leg. $3,000-4,500

A set of 6 late Regency mahogany dining chairs. $2,500-3,500

A set of 8 Regency mahogany dining chairs, comprising 6 single and 2 elbow chairs. $4,000-5,000

Six Regency chairs, including 2 armchairs. $2,500-3,500

◄ A set of 6 Regency mahogany dining chairs, with shaped anthemion and foliate carved top rails and joined by rope-twist turned columns. $2,000-3,000

Five Regency mahogany dining chairs, including one armchair. $1,500-2,200

A set of 8 Regency mahogany dining chairs, including a pair of elbow chairs. $6,000-8,000

A set of 5 Regency mahogany dining chairs. $1,300-1,700

A set of 8 Regency mahogany dining chairs, with brass inlaid bar and rope carved rail backs, including 2 armchairs, one adapted. $4,500-7,000

A set of 8 late Regency mahogany dining chairs, including 2 open armchairs. $4,500-7,000

A set of 6 Regency colonial ebony chairs. $1,700-2,500

A set of 10 mahogany dining chairs, including 2 armchairs, each with a reeded rail and pierced latticed back, flanking a central amaranth banded satinwood tablet, early 19thC. $14,000-17,000 ►

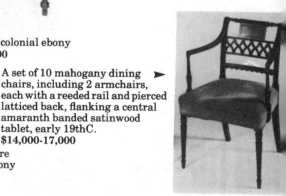

Six Regency mahogany square frame dining chairs, with ebony line inlay to cresting rails. $3,000-4,500

A set of 10 Regency mahogany dining chairs, including a pair of armchairs, with anthemion carved top rails above lobed and scroll carved horizontal splats. $4,500-7,000

A set of 10 Regency mahogany dining chairs, including a pair of armchairs, the top rails with figured panels flanked by reeding above a rope-twist horizontal splat. $6,000-8,000

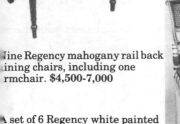

A set of 8 Regency mahogany dining chairs, including a pair of armchairs, with curved panelled top rails centred by ebony compass-medallions and pierced triple arrow splats. $15,000-20,500

Iine Regency mahogany rail back ining chairs, including one rmchair. $4,500-7,000

A set of 6 Regency white painted nd parcel gilt chairs, including 3 rmchairs, re-decorated. ➤ ₹6,000-8,500

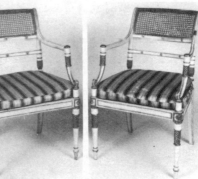

A set of 6 Regency brass inlaid mahogany dining chairs. $5,500-7,000

set of 8 Regency rope-back ahogany dining chairs, on sabre egs, c1810. $14,000-17,000

A William IV mahogany dining chair. $60-100

A set of 6 William IV rosewood dining chairs, the buckle backs with stylised dolphins' tails. $2,000-3,000

set of 11 William IV mahogany ining chairs, including a pair of arver armchairs and 9 side hairs. $3,500-5,000

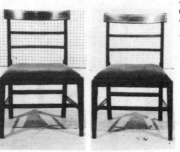

A set of 6 mahogany satinwood, boxwood and ebony line inlaid rail-back dining chairs, 19thC. $2,500-3,500

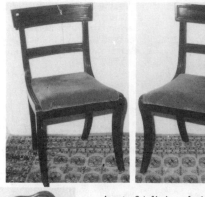

A set of 8 Victorian mahogany dining chairs, including 2 armchairs. $600-700

A set of 4 dining chairs, on sabr legs with bar backs, 19thC. $600-800

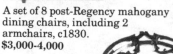

A set of 6 Victorian rosewood chairs. $1,400-1,700

A set of 8 post-Regency mahogany dining chairs, including 2 armchairs, c1830. $3,000-4,000

A set of 6 Victorian mahogany balloon back dining chairs, c1865. $1,500-2,200

A set of 6 Victorian mahogan balloon back dining chairs. $1,500-2,200

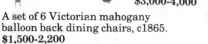

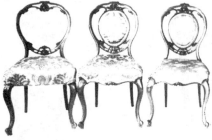

A set of 6 Victorian walnut dining chairs. $1,400-1,700

A set of Victorian dining chairs. $2,500-3,500

Eight Victorian walnut cabriol leg chairs. $2,500-3,500

A set of 6 Victorian ornate carved rosewood spoon-back chairs, c1850. $1,700-2,500

A set of 6 Victorian small mahogany chairs. $1,400-1,700

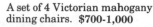

A set of 6 Victorian walnut dining chairs. $1,000-1,400

A set of 4 Victorian mahogany dining chairs. $700-1,000

A set of 4 Victorian mahogany dining chairs. $600-900

A set of 6 Gothic Revival oak dining chairs, by Constantine & Co., with original trade labels. $800-1,200

set of 10 Victorian oak framed airs, in the French taste, cluding a pair of armchairs. ,500-7,000

A set of 14 Victorian oak dining chairs, in the manner of Gillows, the arched moulded top rails with eagle crestings. $4,500-7,000

set of 8 George I style mahogany ning chairs, including 2 open mchairs. $4,500-7,000

Eight Victorian Chippendale style ladderback chairs. $3,500-5,000

A set of 8 Queen Anne style chairs, including 2 armchairs, c1920. $7,000-9,000

set of 10 George III-style ahogany chairs, including 2 mchairs, c1900. ,500-2,200

A set of 8 Chippendale style mahogany dining chairs. $3,000-4,500

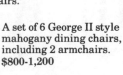

A set of 6 George II style mahogany dining chairs, including 2 armchairs. $800-1,200

A set of 8 Chippendale style dining chairs, including 2 armchairs, 20thC. $4,000-5,000

A set of 8 Chippendale style mahogany dining chairs, including 2 armchairs, c1915. $4,000-5,000

A set of 10 George III style carved mahogany chairs, including 2 armchairs, bearing the trade plate of 'James Shoolbred & Co.', stamped with pattern number c1920. $4,500-7,000

A set of 12 Chippendale style dining chairs. $1,500-2,200

Eight Victorian Chippendale style chairs. $4,500-7,000

A set of 8 Chippendale style mahogany dining chairs, including 2 armchairs. $2,500-3,500

A set of 6 Hepplewhite design mahogany dining chairs, stamped 'Gillows'. $1,500-2,200

Eight Sheraton style mahogany shield-back dining chairs. $1,300-1,700

Six mahogany framed dining chairs, of Hepplewhite design, the shield back with pierced 'heart' splats, entwined foliates and inset Prince of Wales feathers. $1,000-1,400

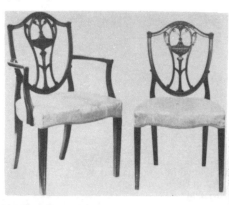

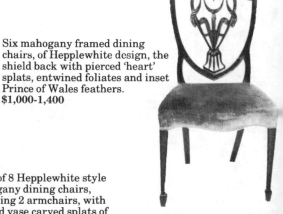

A set of 8 Hepplewhite style mahogany dining chairs, including 2 armchairs, with pierced vase carved splats of neo-classical design to the frames. $6,000-8,000

A set of 14 George III style mahogany dining chairs, including 2 open armchairs, some labelled 'Supplied by the Furniture and Fine Art Depositories Ltd., Islington'. $7,000-9,000

A set of 6 George III style mahogany shield-back chairs, c1890. $1,700-2,500

A set of 6 Austrian cherrywood chairs, the balloon backs with carved anthemion, distressed, c1840. $3,000-4,500

set of 6 Dutch carved mahogany and chequer strung dining chairs, late 18th/early 19thC. $3,000-4,000

A set of 7 Dutch carved mahogany neo-classical dining chairs, late 18thC/early 19thC. $4,000-5,000

A set of 7 Dutch marquetry and walnut chairs, including 2 armchairs, on hoof feet, c1880. $7,500-10,500

A pair of Dutch carved mahogany and floral marquetry dining chairs, in the Queen Anne taste, 18thC. $1,500-2,200

A pair of Portuguese carved rosewood dining chairs, in the rococo taste, 18thC. $3,500-5,000

A set of 4 North Italian painted and gilded dining chairs, with later blocks, mid-18thC. $3,000-4,500

pair of Portuguese rosewood le chairs, the seat rails inforced, mid-18thC. $5,500-7,000

A pair of George II mahogany hall chairs, c1750. $1,500-2,200

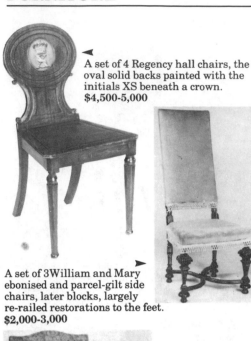

A set of 4 Regency hall chairs, the oval solid backs painted with the initials XS beneath a crown. $4,500-5,000

A set of 4 William IV Irish hall chairs, stamped H.H., c1830. $2,000-3,000

A set of 3 William and Mary ebonised and parcel-gilt side chairs, later blocks, largely re-railed restorations to the feet. $2,000-3,000

A Queen Anne walnut side chair, c1720. $15,000-20,500

A pair of early George III walnut side chairs, stamped WF. $14,000-17,000

A pair of salon chairs, in red lacquer with gilt decoration and cane seats, early 19thC. $400-600

A set of 6 late George II mahogany chairs, with blind Chinese fret, c1755. $7,000-9,000

A Victorian rosewood show frame nursing chair. $600-900

A Victorian rosewood nursing chair, c1850. $700-900

An early Victorian carved giltwood high oval back chair. $400-600

A Victorian mahogany nursing chair. $600-700

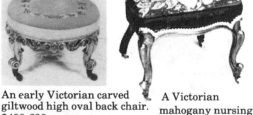
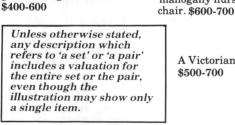

Unless otherwise stated, any description which refers to 'a set' or 'a pair' includes a valuation for the entire set or the pair, even though the illustration may show only a single item.

A Victorian walnut chair. $500-700

A rosewood prie-dieu chair. $300-400

Settees

An unusual giltwood side chair, carved as a swan. $1,500-2,200

A Queen Anne walnut settee, with scrolled handles and shaped supports, the seat raised on acanthus-leaf carved cabriole legs with pad feet and joined by turned stretchers, c1715, 60 in (152 cm). $10,000-13,000

A George III parcel gilt and cream painted sofa, in Louis XVI style, partly redecorated, 78½ in (200 cm). $2,000-3,000

A Regency simulated rosewood on beechwood sofa, on sabre legs with brass block terminals and flowerhead headings, 79 in (201 cm). $1,500-2,200

A George III giltwood window-seat, attributed to William Fell and Lawrence Turton, the seat rail centred by foliate lunettes on panelled tapering legs carved with overlapping guilloches and tassels, 52 in (132 cm). $6,000-8,500

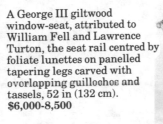

A Regency mahogany settee, c1820. $1,500-2,200

. Federal carved mahogany sofa, he carved tablet crest rail entering 2 crossed sheaves of heat, flanked by bow knots above eeded outcurving arms with ownward scrolling grips above canthus-carved baluster arm upports, casters now removed, lew York, 1800-1815, 80in 203cm) long. $4,000-5,000

An unusual William IV maplewood day bed, the frame carved with foliage and roundels on shaped tapering legs, 86 in (218 cm). $4,500-7,000

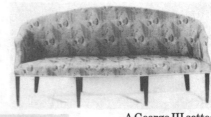

A George III settee, 78 in (198 cm). $4,000-5,000

. Federal carved mahogany ettee, with scrolling tablet crest anked by water leaf-carved iles, the molded sloping rmrests terminating in osette-carved volutes and reeded rn-shaped arm supports, with iinor repairs to armrests, hiladelphia, 1800-1820, 75½in 192cm) wide. $4,500-5,000

A Regency ebonised and gilt settee, with a scroll terminal showframe, on sabre legs with brass caps and casters, 84 in (215 cm). $1,700-2,500

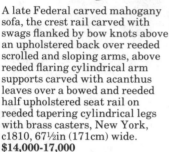

A late Federal carved mahogany sofa, the crest rail carved with swags flanked by bow knots above an upholstered back over reeded scrolled and sloping arms, above reeded flaring cylindrical arm supports carved with acanthus leaves over a bowed and reeded half upholstered seat rail on reeded tapering cylindrical legs with brass casters, New York, c1810, 67½in (171cm) wide. **$14,000-17,000**

A Regency mahogany triple cha back settee, inlaid with satinwo bands, boxwood and ebonised lines, on reeded tapering baluste legs with brass casters, 59 in (150 cm). **$2,000-3,000**

A Regency brass-mounted rosewood chaise longue, 74 in (188 cm). **$4,500-7,000**

An Empire carved mahogany sofa, the scrolled tablet crest rail above a padded back continuing to padded S-scrolled arms with carved dolphin arm supports, above a straight half-upholstered veneered seat rail, on carved dolphin feet, on casters, New York, 1820-1830, 94in (244cm) wide. **$5,500-7,500**

An Empire mahogany veneer recamier, the scrolled and padded back with a leaf-carved terminus over the half-upholstered seat flanked by 2 S-scrolled armrests, on leaf and volute-carved hairy paw feet, on casters, probably Boston, 1825-1835, 81in (206cm) long. **$3,000-4,000**

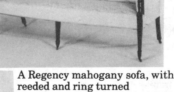

A Regency mahogany sofa, with reeded and ring turned showframe, 76½ in (194 cm). **$1,500-2,200**

A pair of colonial rosewood settees, c1840, 78 in (198 cm). **$3,000-4,500**

A Regency ebonised settee, the front rail replaced, 77 in (195.5 cm). **$3,500-5,000**

A pair of George IV rosewood chaise longues, one distressed, the other in need of restoration, c1830, 72 in (183 cm). **$1,500-2,200**

A William IV mahogany chaise longue, second quarter of the 19thC, 60 in (152 cm). **$1,300-1,700**

A Victorian carved walnut settee the back with a floral scroll carve cresting rail and twin corners wit scroll arms, c1850, 77 in (196 cm **$1,700-2,500**

A Victorian harlequin suite of seat furniture, comprising: a mahogany framed armchair and occasional chair, and ornate rosewood framed settee with vine carved cresting rail, c1850, 84 in (214 cm). $2,000-3,000

A Victorian walnut framed sofa, with scroll arms, carved shaped seat rail and cabriole legs. $700-1,000

A Victorian walnut framed settee. $800-1,200

A Victorian suite of seat furniture, in rosewood and walnut, all with buttoned upholstery, the frames carved with flowers, scrolls, foliage and formal designs, all with cabriole legs, together with 3 rosewood balloon-back side chairs with cabriole legs. $3,500-5,000

A Victorian maple sofa, 55 in (140 cm). $1,000-1,400

A Victorian carved walnut cameo-back settee. $2,000-3,000

A Victorian walnut three piece drawing room suite, including a two-seater settee, c1860, 67 in (170 cm), and a pair of side chairs. $3,000-4,500

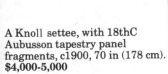

A Knoll settee, with 18thC Aubusson tapestry panel fragments, c1900, 70 in (178 cm). $4,000-5,000

A walnut conversation chair, c1860, 36 in (92 cm) high. $1,500-2,200

A mahogany bergere cane settee, of Hepplewhite design, on 8 fluted square taper legs, on spade feet. $1,000-1,200

An Edwardian rosewood and ivory inlaid two-seat settee. $800-1,200

A Biedermeier mahogany window seat, 54 in (137 cm). $1,500-2,200

An Edwardian seven-piece inlaid rosewood suite, including a canapé, two fauteuils and four chaises. **$1,200-1,500**

A Louis XV cream painted duchesse brisee, by Etienne Meunier. **$4,000-5,000**

A George III sedan chair. **$1,300-1,700**

Chests

A Queen Anne walnut chest, the quarter veneered top above 2 short and 3 long graduated drawers, the sides in pine, on later shaped bracket feet, c1710, 38 in (97 cm). **$2,000-3,000**

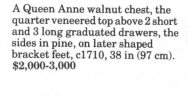

A William and Mary seaweed marquetry chest of drawers, c1690. **$9,000-13,000**

A William and Mary oak chest of drawers, on original bun feet, veneered with yew wood and crossbanded with pearwood, c1695. **$4,000-5,000**

A Queen Anne maple tall chest drawers, the 5 graduated thumb-molded long drawers above a molded base on cabriole legs, with shaped brackets and pad-and-disc feet, New England, 1730-1760, 38½in (96cm) wide. **$11,000-13,000**

A William and Mary oyster walnut and crossbanded chest, inlaid with satinwood stringing, and having segmented top, c1700, 37 in (94 cm). **$4,000-5,000**

An oyster-veneered walnut rectangular chest, inlaid with broad lines and anthemions, mounted with later patterned brass handles and oak feet, early 18thC, 39 in (99 cm). **$3,000-4,500**

A Queen Anne walnut bachelor's chest, with crossbanded folding top, bordered with herringbone lines with gateleg support, on later turned feet, 28 in (72 cm). **$18,000-24,000**

A George I walnut and herringbone crossbanded bachelor's chest, 30 in (75 cm).
$4,000-5,000

A George I walnut chest, with crossbanded quartered top, the sides mounted with brass carrying handles, the upper drawer adapted, 32 in (81 cm).
$4,500-7,000

A walnut bachelor's chest, the hinged crossbanded top inlaid with herringbone bandings, on turned feet, early 18thC, 26 in (64 cm). $6,000-8,500

An Australian walnut and cedar military chest, labelled 'H.T. Jones & Son, Cabinet Makers, Old Racecourse, Parramatta' late 19thC, 34 in (85 cm).
$800-1,200

George II mahogany chest, 1750, 29 in (72.5 cm).
$2,500-3,500

A George II mahogany chest, c1755, 35 in (88 cm).
$1,700-2,500

A George II mahogany chest, 1750, 34 in (87 cm).
$1,700-2,500

A George II mahogany chest, c1755, 37 in (94 cm).
$1,500-2,200

A George II mahogany chest, 30 in (75 cm). $2,000-3,000

Chests

★ 17th century oak coffers were made in sufficient numbers to allow a reasonable supply today.

★ Still expect to find original wire or plate hinges; original lock and hasp; original candle box; reasonably tall feet.

★ The *best* English chest of drawers of the walnut period will be veneered on to pine or other cheaper timber; the drawer linings will be oak, but the interior of the drawer front will not be; only the top surface visible when the drawer is open will have a slip of oak attached.

★ An oak drawer front veneered with walnut suggests either Continental provenance or an early oak chest veneered at a later date; check that holes for handles are compatible inside and out for further evidence of this.

★ Feet on William and Mary chests were either formed by the stile continuing down to the floor or by large turned 'buns'. The former were often retained and used as blocks to be encased by the later more fashionable bracket feet; the 'buns' were often removed in the same cause. To ascertain this, remove the bottom drawer and a hole in each front corner will be present, if bun feet were originally used.

★ By the end of the 18th century, turned wood knobs were fashionable. They were at first fine and small, but soon became the flat bulbous mushrooms so popular on most bedroom and staff quarters furniture. If these are original, it is better to resist the temptation of removing them and applying reproduction brass handles.

★ Accept proper restoration, but avoid improvements.

A fine Chippendale mahogany reverse serpentine chest of drawers, the rectangular and molded top with reverse-serpentine front above 4 graduated drawers with incised molding over a conforming base, on ogee bracket feet, Massachusetts, 1760-1780, 38½in (96cm) wide. **$18,000-20,000**

A Chippendale cherrywood reverse serpentine-front chest of drawers, on shaped bracket feet, feet restored, Connecticut or Massachusetts, 1760-1790, 42in (106cm) wide. **$2,800-3,600**

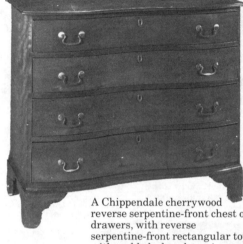

A Chippendale mahogany reverse serpentine chest of drawers, the molded rectangular top with an oxbow front above a conforming base with 4 graduated drawers with scratch-beaded edges, Connecticut, 1760-1780, 42½in (106cm) wide. **$8,000-10,000**

A Chippendale cherrywood reverse serpentine-front chest of drawers, with reverse serpentine-front rectangular top with molded edge above 4 graduated long drawers over a molded base, on shaped bracket feet, feet restored, Connecticut or Massachusetts, 1760-1790, 42½in (106cm) wide. **$4,000-5,000**

A Chippendale mahogany chest of drawers, the top with applied molding, the thumb-molded drawers flanked by fluted quarter columns over a molded base, minor patches to drawer fronts, patch to rear foot, Pennsylvania, 1760-1780, 39in (99cm) wide. **$2,200-2,800**

A Chippendale birch chest with drawers, with a molded top over rows of 13 short drawers centering one deep drawer, the drawer dividers cockbeaded, above a molded skirt centering a carved pendant fan, Massachusetts, 1760-1800, 56½in (141cm) wide. **$3,000-4,000**

A Chippendale maple tall chest of drawers, 35½in (89cm) wide. **$1,400-1,800**

A Chippendale mahogany chest of drawers, with molded edge rectangular top with canted corners above 2 short thumb-molded drawers over a slide above 3 graduated thumb-molded long drawers, flanked by fluted quarter columns, restorations to feet and interior, Pennsylvania, 1760-1790, 43in (107.5cm) wide. **$1,600-2,000**

A Chippendale cherrywood chest of drawers, the rectangular top with molded edge above 4 graduated thumb-molded long drawers on straight bracket feet, Pennsylvania, 1760-1790, 37½in (94cm) wide. **$1,000-1,500**

A Chippendale maple tall chest of drawers, on scalloped bracket feet, New England, 1760-1800, 39½in (100cm) wide. **$2,500-3,000**

. Chippendale mahogany tall hest of drawers, on French feet, 4in (110cm) wide. **$2,500-3,000**

A Federal mahogany banded birchwood bowfront chest of drawers, the bowfront top with banded front edge above a conforming case with 4 graduated banded long drawers over a valanced skirt, New England, 1785-1815, 42½in (106cm) wide. **$4,000-5,000**

A Chippendale mahogany chest of drawers, on ogee bracket feet, restoration to feet, Pennsylvania, 1760-1800, 38½in (98cm) wide. **$1,500-2,000**

A Federal inlaid mahogany bowfront chest of drawers, the centre drawer with an inlaid urn within an inverted-rectangle above 3 long drawers, each with a triple-line inlaid astragal and with eagle embossed brasses, inlay missing from edge of top, New York, 1790-1810, 44in (110cm) wide. **$3,500-5,500**

A Federal cherrywood miniature chest of drawers, the rectangular top with a molded cornice above 3 graduated bead-molded drawers, each with an inlaid diamond-shaped lock escutcheon, small patch to top, Pennsylvania, 1780-1800, 19¾in (49cm) wide. **$4,000-5,000**

A late Federal mahogany bowfront chest of drawers, with graduated veneered and cockbeaded bowed drawers, flanked by reeded outset columns, on turned tapering legs, small patch to one side, Massachusetts, 1800-1820, 40½in (101cm) wide. **$650-850**

A Federal inlaid cherrywood chest of drawers, the rectangular top with a tiger maple banded and line-inlaid edge, New England, 1790-1815, 44in (110cm) wide. **$1,500-2,000**

A Federal cherrywood and mahogany bowfront chest of drawers, the top with bowfront with a checker-inlaid edge above a conforming case, feet pieced, New England, 1790-1810, 40½in (101cm) wide. **$2,500-3,000**

A Federal mahogany veneered
miniature chest of drawers,
19thC, 12in (30cm) wide. $400-500

A George III mahogany
serpentine chest, 29 in (74 cm).
$14,000-17,000

A Federal mahogany and birch
veneered bowfront chest of
drawers, the bowed drawers with
paired flame-figured veneer
panels with rosewood banding,
some restoration to feet, North
Eastern Massachusetts or
Southern New Hampshire,
1790-1815, 4½in (104cm) wide.
$4,000-5,000

Federal mahogany veneer
bowfront chest of drawers, the
bowed rectangular top over 4
conforming cockbeaded drawers
over a shaped skirt, on French
feet, New England, 1790-1810,
2in (105cm) wide. $1,800-2,200

A Federal inlaid walnut tall chest
of drawers, restorations to base,
Pennsylvania, 1800-1815, 40in
(101cm) wide. $1,200-1,500

A George III mahogany bow front
chest of drawers, 31 in (78 cm).
$2,000-3,000

◄

A Federal mahogany and inlaid
maple chest of drawers, with
bowfront top with outset-rounded
corners front and back above a
conforming case of 4 maple and
mahogany veneered and
cockbeaded drawers, flanked by
reeded and ring-turned posts,
Portsmouth area, 1790-1810, 45in
(112.5cm) wide. $1,000-1,500

A George III mahogany
serpentine chest, the top with
moulded edge above a brushing
slide, the drawers flanked by blind
fret corners, 39 in (98 cm).
$3,500-5,000

◄

A Federal figured walnut chest of
drawers, the top over 4
cockbead-molded drawers flanked
by chamfered stiles above a
molded base, on French feet,
drawers insides, feet restored,
Pennsylvania, 1790-1810, 39½in
(100cm) wide. $800-1,000

George III mahogany
pentine fronted chest of
wers, the canted corners
ved with pendant husks, 45 in
2 cm). $2,500-3,500

315

A George III mahogany and kingwood crossbanded serpentine fronted chest, inlaid with stringing, c1790, 41 in (104 cm). $7,000-9,000

A George III satinwood secretaire, the sliding superstructure with one open shelf and pierced Gothic arcaded gallery, the base with a well-fitted leather-lined secretaire drawer enclosing 7 pigeonholes and 5 drawers, 28 in (71 cm). $16,500-22,000

A George III mahogany chest of drawers, c1785. $2,000-3,000

A Victorian teak military secretaire chest, with inset brass corners and handles, the secretaire fitted with a central cupboard with secret pillar drawers, 42 in (105 cm). $1,400-1,700

A George III mahogany chest, the serpentine top, possibly later carved, with egg-and-dart border above a slide, 40 in (102 cm). $3,500-5,000

A George III mahogany serpentine fronted chest, c1790, 38 in (97 cm). $4,000-5,000

A George III mahogany serpentine fronted chest, the chamfered corners with fluted and brass mounted pilasters, on later shaped bracket feet, restored, c1800, 44 in (112 cm). $4,000-5,000

A late Georgian flame mahogany chest, 41 in (102 cm). $300-400

A George III mahogany bow-front chest, inlaid with satinwood and chevron stringing, c1800, 39 in (99 cm). $1,500-2,200

A late Georgian mahogany serpentine front chest, with kingwood crossbanding and satinwood stringing, 37½ in (94 cm). $8,500-10,500

A mahogany chest, early 19thC, 35 in (88 cm). $600-900

A George IV mahogany small bow front chest, with rosewood crossbanded top, c1825, 28 in (71 cm). $1,700-2,500

A Regence walnut and inlaid bow front chest, crossbanded in rosewood and decorated with geometric panels, bordered with stringing, possibly German, 38 in (95 cm). **$5,500-7,000**

An Italian walnut and bone-inlaid chest of drawers, bearing the trade label of Giovanni Bacci Fabbricante E Negiotiante Di Mobili Intagliati Firenze Via della Vigna Nuova N6, on later bracket feet, 34 in (86 cm). **$4,000-5,000**

A Swedish mahogany secretaire chest, the fall front writing drawer enclosing a maple interior, one drawer signed 'Calle Svanlund Ronneby' 39 in (100 cm). **$1,400-1,700**

Wellington Chests

An early Victorian faded mahogany wellington chest, 24 in (60 cm). **$1,500-2,200**

A Victorian bird's-eye maple wellington chest, c1860, 23 in (58 cm). **$1,500-2,200**

A Victorian satin walnut and walnut banded upright escritoire, inlaid with geometric boxwood lines, stamped 'Howard & Sons, Berners Street', 27½ in (68 cm). **$2,500-3,500**

A pair of ebonised and boulle wellington chests, the drawers inlaid with cut brass and tortoiseshell, applied with gilt metal mounts, in need of restoration, c1860, 25½ in (65 cm). **$1,700-2,500**

Chests on Chests

An Edwardian oak wellington chest, 16 in (40 cm). **$200-300**

good marquetry wellington est, stamped 'Edwards & oberts, Wardour St., London', in onised wood with burr maple nding and green-stained arewood strapwork, c1875, 25 in 2 cm). **$2,000-3,000**

An early Georgian walnut chest on stand, the upper section with canted corners, c1720. **$7,500-10,500**

317

A Queen Anne walnut and oak tallboy, with arched broken cornice and compass-medallion frieze, on later bracket feet, 43 in (110 cm). **$5,500-7,000**

A William and Mary walnut cabinet on chest, the feather-banded cupboard doors enclosing an arrangement of drawers, handles and feet replaced, c1695, 43 in (110 cm). **$6,000-8,500**

A George I walnut tallboy, with moulded cavetto cornice, the drawers between chamfered flute angles headed by giltwood capitals, 45 in (114 cm). **$7,500-10,500**

A George II burr-elm tallboy, c1755, 40 in (100 cm). **$4,500-7,000**

A George III mahogany tallboy, with moulded key pattern cornice, on later bracket feet, 39 in (99 cm). **$1,700-2,500**

A walnut tallboy, with later brass bale handles, bracket feet, early 18thC, 39½ in (100 cm). **$3,000-4,000**

A George I walnut tallboy, 42 in (105 cm). **$15,000-20,500**

◄ A crossbanded mahogany chest on chest, early 18thC, 41 in (102 cm). **$7,500-10,500**

A yew-wood tallboy, with chamfered cavetto cornice, with crossbanded drawers mounted with pierced foliate giltmetal handles and lockplates, 40 in (102 cm). **$10,500-14,000**

A Georgian mahogany tallboy, 41 in (102 cm). **$2,000-3,000**

A George II walnut chest on ches secretaire, with slide, half moon sunburst in bottom drawer, 42 in (105 cm). **$14,000-17,000**

A Chippendale maple chest-on-chest, with molded bonnet top terminating in pinwheel-carved volutes and centering a flame-carved finial above 2 short drawers, centering a fan-carved drawer over 4 thumb-molded graduated drawers, Connecticut, 1760-1790, 38in (96cm) wide. **$10,000-12,000**

A Chippendale cherrywood chest-on-chest, in 2 sections: the upper with 3 flame-turned finials above a molded broken arch pediment terminating in leaf-carved volutes above a fan carving over 4 graduated long drawers; the lower part with molded mid-band above 3 graduated long drawers and molded base, on ball and claw feet, 42in (105cm) wide. **$3,500-4,000**

A rare and important Chippendale mahogany chest-on-chest, in 2 sections: the upper case with a closed bonnet pediment with a cove-molded cornice supporting 3 fluted flame finials above 2 shaped thumb-molded panels, over 2 short and 3 long graduated thumb-molded drawers flanked by fluted quarter columns over a mid molding; the lower case with 4 graduated thumb-molded long drawers flanked by fluted quarter columns above a molded base, on ogee bracket feet, lower edges of drawer fronts pieced, interior foot blocks restored, attributed to Thomas Townsend, Newport, Rhode Island, 1760-1780, 85in (217cm) high by 44in (110cm) wide. **$50,000-70,000**

While a half dozen related chest-on-chests are known, the basis for an attribution to Thomas Townsend (1742-1827) of this example is a similar chest-on-chest, originally owned by David Gardiner of Gardiner's Island, bearing the label of Thomas Townsend. A comparison of details of the 2 chest-on-chests reveals that finials, brasses, quarter columns and dimensions are virtually identical. For an illustration of the labelled example, see Dean F. Failey, Long Island Is My Nation (Society for the Preservation of Long Island Antiquities, Setauket, New York: 1976) p.162, no.188.

A Chippendale carved birch high chest of drawers, traces of old red stain, small patches to rear of mid-body molding and several knee brackets restored, top old but not original to bottom, New Hampshire, 1780-1800, 41in (103cm) wide. **$2,000-3,000**

A Chippendale carved maple and birch high chest of drawers, in 2 sections: the upper with cove-molded cornice over 5 thumb-molded and graduated long drawers; the lower section with single long drawer over a deep double fan-carved long drawer above an elaborately scrolled skirt, several knee brackets restored, some slight interior restorations, New Hampshire, 1780-1800, 41in (103cm) wide. **$4,000-6,000**

Use the Index!

Because certain items might fit easily into any of a number of categories, the quickest and surest method of locating any entry is by reference to the index at the back of the book.
This has been fully cross-referenced for absolute simplicity.

A George III mahogany tallboy, the upper section with turned ivory acorn drop cornice, 44 in (110 cm). **$1,500-2,200**

A George III mahogany chest on chest, c1760, 44 in (112 cm). **$3,000-4,000**

A George III flame mahogany tallboy, c1770. **$2,000-3,000**

A George III mahogany chest on chest, c1780, 44 in (112 cm). **$1,500-2,200**

A George III mahogany bow front chest on chest, c1800, 43½ in (108 cm). **$1,200-1,500**

A George III mahogany chest on chest, with blind fret carving and brushing slide below, c1765. **$4,500-7,000**

◄ A George III faded mahogany chest on chest, with fluted and reeded chamfered corners, c1770, 51 in (130 cm). **$3,000-4,000**

A George III mahogany tallboy, with broken dentilled pediment, the drawers flanked by Corinthian pilaster angles, the bottom drawer fitted as a secretaire with pigeonholes and cedar-lined small drawers, around a central cupboard door, the base with 3 drawers on bracket feet, back partly replaced, 44½ in (113 cm). **$7,000-9,000**

A Sheraton period mahogany bow front tallboy chest, having chequered line inlaid cornice and brass anthemion motif mounted frieze, replacement bracket feet, 46 in (115 cm). **$2,500-3,500**

A George III mahogany tallboy, the rosewood banded tablet classical pediment with an arcaded and dentilled frieze, 46 in (115 cm). **$2,500-3,500**

George III Sheraton period chest [?] chest, the cornice with [?]tinwood inlay, 42 in (105 cm). [?],000-1,400

A George III style mahogany chest on chest, the fluted frieze with carved roundels, made-up, 46 in (116 cm). **$1,200-1,500**

Chests on Stands

Queen Anne maple high chest of [?]awers, in 2 parts: the upper case [w]ith a coved cornice over 5 long [gr]aduated thumb-molded [dr]awers; the lower case with one [lo]ng narrow drawer over 3 short [dr]awers above a scalloped skirt, [on] cabriole legs with pad-and-disc [fe]et, minor patches, knee blocks [re]stored, Connecticut, 1740-1760, ['in (93cm) wide. **$10,000-13,000**

A William and Mary walnut chest on later stand, inlaid with satinwood stringing, the sides of stained pine, restored, c1690, 35 in (88 cm). **$1,700-2,500**

[G]eorge I walnut chest on stand, [?]later bracket feet, 40½ in [? c]m). **$2,000-3,000**

A Queen Anne walnut high chest of drawers, New England, 40in (101cm) wide. **$4,000-5,000**

The important Hollingsworth family Chippendale carved walnut high chest of drawers, in 2 sections: the upper with molded swan's neck pediment with carved rosette terminals centering a naturalistically carved cartouche flanked by flame finials on fluted plinths above 5 thumb-molded short drawers; the lower section with applied molding above a case with single thumb-molded long drawer over 3 similar short drawers, the centre drawer with carved concave shell and trailing tendrils above a shaped skirt centering a pendant cockle shell flanked by fluted quarter columns, on acanthus-carved cabriole legs, with ball and claw feet, the brasses appear to be original, Thomas Affleck, Philadelphia, c1779, 94in by 42in (240 by 105cm). **$350,000-400,000**

A chalk cypher on the back of the upper case appears to be a conjoined 'TA'.
The importance of this high chest lies not only in its highly successful design but also in the documentation regarding its provenance. One of a matching pair of high chests and dressing tables made for Philadelphia merchant Levi Hollingsworth by Thomas Affleck, one set is now in the Philadelphia Museum of Art. Various business transactions between Levi Hollingsworth and Affleck are documented in the Paschall-Hollingsworth Papers in the Historical Society of Pennsylvania, including the purchase of a set of 8 mahogany chairs in 1779. The knee carving on these chairs is identical to that on the high chests.

A Queen Anne walnut high chest of drawers, in 2 sections: the upper with a coved cornice above 3 short drawers over 2 short drawers above 3 long thumb-molded drawers; the lower section with a molding over a long drawer above a scalloped skirt, on cabriole legs with stocking-carved trifid feet, skirt re-shaped, Pennsylvania, 1740-1770, 40in (101cm) wide.
$4,500-5,500

A crossbanded walnut chest on stand, some damage, early 18thC, 41 in (102.5 cm).
$2,500-3,500

A walnut chest on stand, wi original handles, early 18th
$7,000-9,000

MAKE THE MOST OF MILLER'S

CONDITION is absolutely vital when assessing the value of an antique. Damaged pieces on the whole appreciate much less than perfect examples. However a rare desirable piece may command a high price even when damaged.

An Austrian fruitwood chest on stand, the rectangular top inlaid with the portrait of a Queen, enclosing a fitted interior, the later stand with spirally turned ebonised legs, the chest late 17thC, 28 in (71 cm).
$8,500-11,000

A George III mahogany chest o stand, with later carved cabrio legs ending in claw and ball fee c1760, 43 in (109 cm).
$1,400-1,700

A George III mahogany commode, outlined throughout with rosewood crossbanding and boxwood stringing, top drawer altered, 42½ in (106 cm).
$5,500-7,000

Commodes

A George III mahogany demi-lun commode, inlaid with stringing, the associated top above doors with oval segmented veneers, flanked by a pair of cupboards in the form of dummy drawers, c1780, 48 in (122 cm).
$7,000-9,000

A George II mahogany serpentine fronted commode, the frieze drawer enclosing compartments and small drawers, 58½ in (145 cm). **$6,000-8,500**

A George III satinwood commode, with serpentine front, crossbanded with rosewood, inlaid with a shell, oval cartouche with a vase of flowers, urns and flowering branches, 44 in (110 cm).
$42,000-54,000

A George III mahogany serpentine fronted commode, c1770, 48 in (122 cm).
$7,500-10,500

A French provincial oak serpentine commode, mid-18thC, 52 in (130 cm). **$1,700-2,500**

A Régence kingwood commode, the top veneered in a geometrically banded design, the sides veneered in a banded lozenge design, 46½ in (116 cm). **$5,500-7,000**

A fine Louis XV provincial beechwood commode, 49½ in (126 cm). **$6,000-8,500**

A Louis XV style kingwood bombé commode, inlaid with panels of marquetry and parquetry, and with gilt-metal mounts, with serpentine marble top, 19thC, 49 in (123 cm). **$2,500-3,500**

A French mahogany and brass mounted commode, in Empire style, with a white marble top, 19thC, 44½ in (111 cm). **$5,500-7,000**

A Louis XV style mahogany and gilt metal mounted commode, c1900. **$1,400-1,700**

A German oak serpentine commode, the top inlaid with star within tulip and scroll border, 18thC, 51 in (128 cm). **$1,700-2,500**

A Régence style carved walnut commode, c1900, 44 in (110 cm). **$1,700-2,500**

A South German walnut serpentine commode, the moulded top with geometric inlay, on later bun feet, 18thC, 40 in (100 cm). **$3,000-4,500**

A South Italian rosewood and ebonised commode, with crossbanded and serpentine moulded top, on later bun feet, mid-18thC, 64 in (163 cm). **$3,000-4,000**

An Italian serpentine walnut commode, with crossbanded and curvilinear veneered panel top, late 18thC, 50½ in (126 cm). **$2,000-3,000**

An Italian kingwood petite commode, the sides and drawer fronts veneered in a goemetrical pattern, 18thC, 24 in (60 cm). **$4,000-5,000**

An Italian walnut commode, the top crossbanded in olivewood and inlaid with a lozenge of mulberry, late 18thC, 51½ in (128 cm). **$1,500-2,200**

An Italian tulipwood commode, of bombé outlines, inlaid with laburnum oyster panels, with gilt metal mounts, late 18thC, 50 in (125 cm). **$4,500-7,000**

An Italian mahogany and kingwood banded marquetry commode, in the Louis XV style, signed 'P. Sermani', early 20thC, 56 in (140 cm). **$7,500-10,500**

Cupboards – Armoires

A mahogany cupboard unit, in the manner of William Vile, the painted panelled interior with shaped shelves, the painted arch fielded panel doors, flanked by carved Corinthian column pilasters, mid-18thC, 55 in (137.5 cm). **$3,000-4,500**

A good North Italian rosewood, walnut and ivory inlaid small commode, the top inlaid with a cherub within a pillared portico, in pewter and ivory, the 3 crossbanded drawers similarly inlaid, with later drawer linings, mid-18thC, 26 in (65 cm). **$2,500-3,500**

An Empire mahogany veneer marble-top secretaire a abattant, the double panelled fall-front writing surface opening to a fitted interior, over 2 Gothic-arch panelled cupboard doors, flanked by columns, feet restored, Boston, 1825-1835, 42in (105cm) wide. **$3,000-5,000**

A burr walnut hanging cupboard, the 2 adapted cupboard doors with arched bevelled mirrored panels above false drawer fronts, on later bracket feet, 51 in (130 cm). **$3,000-4,500**

A Dutch walnut and marquetry armoire, enclosing a later fitted interior, 73 in (185.5 cm). **$7,500-10,500**

A Louis XV provincial oak armoire, missing one back foot, 54 in (137 cm). **$2,500-3,500**

Cupboards – Bedside

A Louis XV style mahogany pedestal cupboard, with rouge marble top, with parquetry inlay in exotic woods and ormolu mounts, 19 in (47.5 cm). **$300-600**

A pair of Regency mahogany bedside cupboards, the hinged flaps between turned columns above commode drawers on bracket feet, 22½ in (57 cm). **$3,000-4,000**

A pair of Regency mahogany pedestal cupboards, each with later grey marble top, the backs with tambour shutters and cupboard doors, 16 in (41 cm). **$5,500-7,000**

A Georgian pot cupboard, 18thC. **$300-400**

A Dutch parquetry walnut bedside cupboard, early 19thC, 19½ in (49 cm). **$1,000-1,400**

A walnut bedside cupboard, with tambour front and tray top, c1760. **$2,000-3,000**

An Edwardian pot cupboard, in mahogany inlaid with satinwood, 15 in (37.5 cm). **$200-300**

Cupboards – Corner

A Queen Anne walnut and featherbanded standing corner cupboard, the moulded cornice above a pair of crossbanded fielded panelled doors enclosing serpentine fronted shelves, fitted for electric light, restored, c1710, 46 in (117 cm). **$8,500-11,000**

A George III inlaid mahogany bow front corner cupboard, 29 in (72.5 cm). **$1,500-2,200**

A George II lacquered hanging corner cupboard, restored, second quarter of the 18thC, 24 in (61 cm). **$800-1,200**

George III mahogany standing corner cupboard, the canted corners with Gothic style boxwood lines, 44 in (110 cm). **$1,700-2,500**

A George III mahogany standing corner cupboard, c1780. **$2,000-3,000**

A late Federal sponge-painted poplar corner cupboard, the whole elaborately sponge-decorated, retaining original white enamel pulls and hardware, by William Rupp, York, Pennsylvania, 51in (128cm) wide. **$5,000-6,000**

A George III mahogany bow fronted hanging corner cupboard. **$700-1,000**

A George III lacquered bow front corner cupboard, decorated with chinoiserie figures in red and gold on a black ground. **$700-1,000**

A Federal walnut corner cupboard, with an elaborately molded cornice above 2 glazed cupboard doors opening to 3 shelves over a mid-molding above 2 panelled cupboard doors, each with applied quarter-round panels, cornice and feet restored, North Carolina, 1790-1820, 55in (138cm) wide. **$2,000-2,500**

An early Victorian inlaid and mahogany crossbanded oak standing corner cupboard, 48 in (122 cm). **$1,500-2,200**

A Dutch mahogany bow front standing corner cupboard, c1770 46 in (117 cm). **$4,500-7,000**

A Dutch walnut standing corner cabinet, with a domed cornice and ogee shaped corners, the pair of panelled doors enclosing a painted interior with later shaped shelves, c1740, 51 in (130 cm). **$4,000-5,000**

A mahogany corner cupboard, with fine flame veneers, early 19thC. **$4,000-5,000**

A pair of painted satinwood standing corner cupboards, painted throughout with ribbons, flowers and foliage, modern, 42 in (107 cm). **$4,500-7,000**

A Dutch mahogany and marquetry standing corner cupboard, inlaid with urn, bird flowers and foliage, 19thC, 33 in (82.5 cm). **$1,400-1,700**

A Queen Anne burr walnut press cupboard, on later shaped bracket feet, c1710, 60 in (153 cm). $14,000-17,000

A French mahogany and boulle bow front encoignure, c1880, 30½ in (77 cm). $1,300-1,700

A George III mahogany linen press, 78 in (195 cm) high. $1,700-2,500

Cupboards – Linen Press

A George III mahogany clothes press, the broken scrolled pediment pierced with Gothic fretwork centred by a tablet inlaid with paterae and dentilled Gothic arcaded cornice, the cupboard doors crossbanded with yew-wood and rosewood enclosing slides, 51 in (130 cm). $9,000-13,000

A good Georgian mahogany linen press, the front with satinwood crossbands, circular and quadrant in inlay, bracket feet, 48 in (120 cm). $2,500-3,500

A George III figured mahogany secretaire linen press, the secretaire drawer faced with oval and cut corner reserves, and enclosing a well fitted interior of drawers and shelves flanking a cupboard door, 51 in (128 cm). $2,500-3,500

A Chippendale flame clothes press, c1770. $2,000-3,000

A Federal inlaid mahogany linen press, in 2 sections: the upper with molded cornice over line-inlaid panelled double doors opening to sliding shelves; the lower section with molded edge over 2 short and 2 long cockbeaded and line-inlaid drawers, front feet restored, molding losses, Pennsylvania, 1790-1810, 50in (125cm) wide. $3,500-4,000

Cupboards – Wardrobe

A George III mahogany and
satinwood crossbanded
gentleman's wardrobe, formerly a
linen press, c1780, 48 in (122 cm).
$1,700-2,500

A large Georgian mahogany
sectional fitted wardrobe, 80 in
(203 cm). **$1,200-1,500**

A Dutch figured walnut wardrobe
18thC, 75 in (190 cm).
$4,500-7,000

A North German cabinet,
veneered on an oak carcase with
panels of burr mulberry with
geometric strapwork in walnut,
and crossbanded in elm, probably
Brunswick, mid 18thC, c1740.
$6,000-8,000

A Georgian mahogany wardrobe,
with inlaid decoration to cornice,
51 in (127.5 cm). **$800-1,200**

A Victorian walnut
wardrobe,
39 in (97.5 cm).
$300-500

A painted poplar step-back
cupboard, 52½in (131cm) wide.
$1,000-1,300

A mahogany gent's wardrobe, late
18thC, 50 in (125 cm).
$800-1,200

A Federal maple step-back
cupboard, top possibly not original
to base, probably Pennsylvania,
early 19thC, 43in (108cm) wide.
$1,100-1,500

Davenports

A Victorian figured walnut davenport, the sliding boxed top with a spindled three-quarter gallery, stamped T. Wilson, 68 Great Queen Street, London, 23½ in (59 cm). $2,500-3,500

A Victorian inlaid walnut davenport, with maple lined interior and a raised stationery compartment. $600-900

A Regency mahogany davenport, 20 in (50 cm). $3,000-4,000

A davenport, veneered in walnut with stringing and inlay, the interior lined with ash, 21 in (52.5 cm). $1,000-1,400

A Victorian walnut serpentine fronted davenport, with a rear hinged stationery compartment, c1850, 21 in (55 cm). $1,300-1,700

A davenport desk, with rosewood veneering, 19thC, 22 in (55 cm). $2,000-3,000

Victorian walnut serpentine fronted davenport, on carved 'dolphin' supports, 21 in (52.5 cm). $1,200-1,500

A Victorian rosewood harlequin davenport, the piano style cover revealing an inset and adjustable writing slide operating in conjunction with the rear rising stationery compartment, c1850, 23½ in (60 cm). $1,700-2,500

A Victorian figured walnut davenport, the hinged sloping writing surface rising to reveal a well fitted with 4 small drawers, 22 in (54 cm). $800-1,200

A Victorian walnut piano top davenport, with fully fitted interior, 24 in (60 cm). $1,000-1,400

A Victorian rosewood davenport, the rising stationery compartment with a pierced brass gallery, drawers and pigeon holes, 22 in (55 cm). $2,000-3,000

Desks – Kneehole

A Victorian burr walnut davenport, in the Louis XV style, inlaid with marquetry and tulipwood bands, applied with gilt metal borders, 26½ in (66 cm). **$7,000-9,000**

A Victorian burr walnut harlequin davenport, the rear with a rising stationery compartment and hinged pierced fret cover, c1850, 23 in (58 cm). **$2,500-3,500**

A Victorian burr walnut and ebonised harlequin davenport, inlaid with boxwood medallions and stringing, c1870, 23 in (59 cm). **$2,500-3,500**

A late Victorian figured walnut davenport, inlaid with boxwood arabesques, the sprung stationery compartment with fretwork interior, 25 in (63 cm). **$3,000-4,500**

Desks

★ Desk correctly describes a piece of furniture on which to read or write and which has the top sloping at an angle. In this form it has medieval origins, but the term now embraces various types, such as bureaux, secretaires and the flat top 'knee-hole'.

★ The Davenport desk is highly sought after. Found after the 1790's, the earliest have the upper desk part sliding forward or swivelling to accommodate the knees of the sitter.

★ Later Regency and Victorian models have column supports to the desk and look out for the rising nest of drawers that works on weights and pulleys, when a secret button is depressed. After the 1840's, the 'piano front' became fashionable and is still most in demand. While it matters not if the price is right and the description fair, remember that single sided knee-hole desks have been made out of Victorian washstands.

★ Knee-hole desks have also been made out of 18th century chests of drawers. Because of cost these are rare and can be detected by incompatible drawer sides.

★ An original leather top in good condition is desirable, but a fine new one is better than a bad old one.

★ A bureau made to take a bookcase on top will have a steeper angle to the fall front to accommodate the case or cabinet.

A Regency mahogany cylinder top desk, with ebony stringing and fitted interior with pull-out writing section, 42 in (105 cm). **$1,500-2,200**

Desks – Cylinder/ Roll-Top

A George III mahogany and crossbanded tambour top kneehole writing desk, with satinwood strung borders, the interior with an inset writing slide, small drawers and a recess, c1800, 45 in (114 cm). **$15,000-20,500**

A Victorian mahogany cylinder rolltop kneehole pedestal desk, 60 in (150 cm). **$1,700-2,500**

A mahogany cylinder top writing desk, early 19thC. **$1,700-2,500**

A Victorian mahogany cylinder desk, with writing slide and maple faced interior drawers, 52 in (130 cm). **$800-1,200**

A George III mahogany kneehole
desk, on panelled bracket feet,
48½ in (121 cm).
$28,500-36,000

A George I walnut kneehole desk,
the quarter veneered top
crossbanded and inlaid with
herringbone lines, on later
bracket feet, 31½ in (80 cm).
$6,000-8,000

n oyster veneered walnut
neehole desk, with crossbanded
p, on later bracket feet, partly
rly 18thC, 36½ in (93.5 cm).
,000-4,500

An early Georgian walnut
kneehole desk, the burr walnut
quarter veneered top, crossbanded
and with herringbone stringing,
30 in (75 cm). $3,000-4,500

mahogany kneehole desk in the
yle of William Kent, 48 in
20cm). $7,000-9,000

George III kneehole desk, 39 in
7 cm). $2,500-3,500

A Georgian fruitwood kneehole
desk, c1750. $4,500-7,000

A George I black and gold lacquer
kneehole desk, some restoration to
the feet, 33 in (82.5 cm).
$7,500-10,500

A late George III mahogany
kneehole desk, original brass
handles, 49½ in (124 cm).
$2,000-3,000

A Regency mahogany library
desk, 46 in (114 cm).
$7,500-10,500

A Queen Anne walnut kneehole
desk, with crossbanded quartered
top, on later bracket feet, 29½ in
(75 cm). $6,000-8,000

Georgian design mahogany
neehole desk, with fluted canted
ners, 32 in (81.5 cm).
300-1,700

An Edwardian kidney shaped
inlaid mahogany kneehole desk,
49 in (122.5 cm). $1,300-1,700

A mid Georgian mahogany
serpentine kneehole desk, with
divided and lidded frieze drawer
with easel mirror, the top formerly
galleried, 45 in (115 cm).
$7,500-10,500

A Queen Anne maple slant-front desk, the thumb-molded slant lid opening to a fitted interior with 4 open shelves flanked by 4 small drawers on each side, New Hampshire or Massachusetts, 1740-1760, 41in (103cm) wide. **$6,000-8,000**

A Federal mahogany slant-front desk, the thumb-molded lid opening to a fitted interior with 5 small drawers above 7 valanced pigeonholes, over a shaped skirt with a pattern-inlaid band, on flaring French feet, few scratches to top, New England, 1790-1810, 39in (99cm) wide. **$1,800-2,600**

A small Chippendale cherrywood slant-front desk, of rare small size with thumb-molded slant lid opening to a fitted interior of 8 valanced pigeonholes centering a drawer with a carved pinwheel above a compartment flanked by drawers, minor repair to feet, Connecticut, 1760-1800, 32in (80cm) wide. **$7,500-8,500**

A Queen Anne maple desk on frame, in 2 sections: the upper with thumb-molded slant lid opening to an elaborately fitted interior of blocked drawers and valanced pigeonholes, centering a fan-carved drawer, 37½in (94cm) wide. **$5,000-6,000**

A Chippendale mahogany reverse-serpentine slant-front desk, with a thumb-molded slant front opening to a fitted interior with 6 pigeonholes centering a prospect door with an inlaid patera concealing small drawers over 3 short drawers, restoration to knee brackets, North Eastern Massachusetts, 1760-1790, 43in (107.5cm) wide. **$3,500-4,500**

A Chippendale mahogany reverse-serpentine slant-front desk, with a thumb-molded slant lid opening to a line-inlaid fitted interior with small drawers over pigeonholes centering a prospect door, concealing small drawers flanked by document drawers, slant lid restored, North Eastern Massachusetts, 1760-1790, 46in (115cm) wide. **$6,000-7,000**

A Chippendale mahogany reverse-serpentine slant-front desk, the thumb-molded lid opening to a fitted interior with valanced pigeonholes between 3 short drawers, each carved with paterae, lid possibly re-veneered, writing surface pieced at hinges, Massachusetts, 1760-1780, 44in (110cm) high. **$4,000-5,000**

A Chippendale mahogany kneehole desk, the drawers cockbeaded, centering a shaped apron drawer over a recess with a hinged cupboard door, base molding and feet restored, New England, 1750-1780, 32½in (81cm) wide. **$1,700-2,200**

A Chippendale walnut slant-front desk, with slant lid opening to a fitted interior of 6 valanced pigeonholes over 2 rows of short drawers centering an inlaid prospect door, flanked by 2 inlaid document drawers, 42in (105cm) wide. **$1,400-1,800**

A Chippendale mahogany slant-front desk, with thumb-molded slant lid opening a fitted interior, feet restored, New York of Pennsylvania, 1760-180 41½in (104cm) wide. **$3,000-4,00**

A Chippendale mahogany slant-front desk, with thumb-molded slant lid opening to a fitted interior of valanced pigeonholes and blocked drawers centering a fan-carved drawer, feet and interior restored, lid pieced, Massachusetts, 1760-1790, 38½in (96cm) wide. **$3,000-3,500**

A Federal mahogany slant-front desk, with thumb-molded slant lid opening to an interior of 12 long drawers centering pigeonholes, on French feet, interior drawer bottoms replaced, repairs to lid at hinges, probably Pennsylvania, 1790-1810, 41½in (103cm) wide. **$2,000-3,000**

A Chippendale mahogany reverse-serpentine slant-front desk, with thumb-molded slant lid enclosing a compartmented interior comprising an inlaid central prospect door, flanked by 2 long over 4 short drawers over 6 valanced pigeonholes, small repair to one foot, Massachusetts, 1780-1800, 43½in (109cm) wide. **$4,000-5,000**

A Federal inlaid cherrywood slant-front desk, with thumb-molded slant lid opening to a fitted interior of 4 short and 2 long drawers over 2 recesses with scalloped valances and centering a short drawer with scalloped skirt, crack to left side of o repairs to feet, New Engl. 1790-1810, 37in (93cm) w **$3,000-4,000**

Desk – Partners

George III mahogany partners' esk, 60 in (152.5 cm).
15,000-20,500

A George III mahogany partners' desk, 54 in (127.5 cm).
$7,000-9,000

A George III mahogany architect's pedestal writing desk, 18thC, 49 in (122.5 cm).
$7,000-9,000

A Victorian carved oak partners' esk decorated with biblical cenes and saints, 80 in (203 cm). 2,500-3,500

An unusually large double sided pedestal desk, 19thC, c1870.
$7,500-10,500

A late Georgian mahogany kneehole pedestal desk, stamped Gillows, Lancaster, 50 in (125 cm).
$3,500-5,000

George III style mahogany artners' desk, c1910, 60 in 50 cm). **$3,000-4,500**

Desks – Pedestal

A mahogany library secretaire by Gillows, early 19thC.
$9,000-13,000

A walnut partners' desk, the crossbanded veneered top of slightly bowed outline, c1900, 56 in (140 cm). **$4,000-5,000**

mahogany pedestal desk, the ylinder front enclosing green oled leather inset, stationery rawers and arched ompartments, 19thC, 48 in 20 cm). **$1,400-1,700**

A mahogany kneehole pedestal desk, early 19thC, 48 in (120 cm).
$2,500-3,500

A Victorian mahogany pedestal desk, third quarter of the 19thC, 60 in (153 cm). **$3,000-4,000**

George III style walnut pedestal sk, c1880, 48 in (122 cm). 500-5,000

A mahogany pedestal desk, third quarter of the 19thC, 79 in (201 cm). **$1,700-2,500**

A Georgian style mahogany kneehole pedestal desk, 43 in (107.5 cm). **$1,300-1,700**

335

A George II style walnut kneehole pedestal desk, 53½ in (134 cm). **$1,700-2,500**

An Edwardian walnut single pedestal desk, 39 in (97.5 cm). **$600-700**

A 'Renaissance' walnut pedestal desk, Italian, third quarter of the 19thC, 55 in (140 cm). **$1,000-1,200**

Desks – Writing

A George III satinwood kneehole desk, branded LL below a coronet, 41 in (104 cm). **$4,500-5,000**

An artist's mid Victorian figured walnut writing desk, 31 in (79 cm). **$3,000-4,000**

A George III mahogany kneehole writing desk, on later shaped bracket feet, restored, c1770, 44 in (112 cm). **$3,500-5,000**

A lady's mid Victorian mahogany writing desk, 47½ in (119 cm). **$1,300-1,700**

A satinwood and marquetry writing desk, the whole inlaid with neo-classical foliage and putti, c1890, 48 in (122 cm). **$4,000-5,000**

A walnut kneehole pedestal desk, 54 in (135 cm). **$1,500-2,200**

A mahogany Sheraton style desk, 46 in (115 cm). **$1,700-2,500**

An Edwardian Carlton House design mahogany desk, painted with swagged foliage, wreaths and scrolls, 42 in (105 cm). **$2,000-3,000**

A mahogany Carlton House desk, 54 in (136 cm). **$3,000-4,000**

A Wooton Desk Co. mahogany travelling desk, of typical form, c1874, 45½ in (116 cm). **$4,500-5,000**

A Louis XV style walnut veneered writing desk, applied throughout with gilt brass foliate mouldings and crossbanded with kingwood, mid-19thC, 44 in (110 cm). **$3,000-4,000**

A Federal inlaid mahogany
tambour desk, in 2 sections: the
upper with triple line-inlaid
rectangular top edged with
pattern inlay above 2 tambour
doors opening to a fitted interior of
triple line-inlaid drawers over 6
balanced pigeonholes, the whole
flanked by checker inlay plinths;
the lower section with hinged
line-inlaid writing surface over 3
graduated checker-inlaid
drawers, one pigeonhole valance
restored, damage to one drawer
pull, Massachusetts, c1790, 41½in
(103cm) wide. **$3,000-4,000**

A Federal inlaid mahogany
tambour desk, in 2 sections; the
upper with banded-edge top over 2
sliding tambour doors enclosing a
fitted interior and centering a
veneered prospect door; the lower
section with banded hinged
writing surface over 2 lightwood
veneered cockbeaded drawers,
34in (85cm) wide. **$1,500-2,000**

A Federal inlaid mahogany
secretary, in 2 parts: the upper
with a shaped pediment over
glazed Gothic arch doors revealing
bookshelves over 2 short drawers;
the lower with a folding writing
surface over 2 long drawers,
Massachusetts, 34in (85cm) wide.
$2,500-3,000

Federal inlaid mahogany
tambour writing bureau, in 2
parts; the upper with a
rectangular top with
pattern-inlaid edge, over 2
tambour doors opening to 2 rows of
small drawers over valanced
pigeonholes; the lower part with a
bowed top over a conforming case,
with a brush slide, above 3
drawers, probably Connecticut,
1790-1815, 39in (99cm) wide.
2,500-3,000

An Empire mahogany secretary
desk, in 2 parts: the upper section
with 2 glazed doors opening to 2
shelves over a roll-top desk,
opening to a fitted interior with 3
short drawers centering 8
pigeonholes; the lower section
with a single long drawer on
baluster and ring-turned tapering
legs on ball feet, bearing the
stamp 'JOHN MEEKS AND SON,
NEW YORK', 1830-1850, 37½in
(94cm) wide. **$2,200-3,000**

337

Dumb Waiters

A George III mahogany three-tier dumb waiter, on spirally turned shaft and arched tripartite base, 24 in (61 cm). **$2,000-3,000**

A George III mahogany three-tier dumb waiter, the graduated revolving shelves with everted gadrooned galleries, 25½ in (63 cm). **$5,500-7,000**

A George III mahogany dumb waiter, 57 in (143 cm). **$1,500-2,200**

◄ A George III mahogany two-tier dumb waiter, with turned tray top, 21½in (56 cm). **$1,500-2,200**

A Louis XVI ormolu-mounted mahogany two-tier dumb waiter, adapted, 32 in (81 cm). **$2,500-3,500**

A George III mahogany two-tier dumb waiter, early 19thC, 25 in (64 cm). **$1,500-2,200**

A Directoire style mahogany dumb waiter, the tiers inset with rosewood and walnut bands with pierced brass galleries, 37½ in (93 cm). **$600-900**

Fireplaces

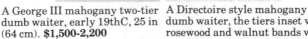

A William IV column chimneypiece, in Sienna marble. **$2,500-3,500**

A Victorian carved Hornton stone chimneypiece, in the Gothic style. **$4,500-7,000**

A Federal pine mantelpiece, the molded cornice with a bowed centre section over a reeded and chip-carved frieze, 1790-1810, mantel 84in (210cm) wide. **$1,500-2,000**

A Victorian carved marble chimneypiece, with Sienna and Verona marble decoration. **$3,000-4,000**

Globes

A Regency mahogany terrestrial globe, by Cary, dated March 1 1815 and plotting the tracks and discoveries made by Captain Cook, Captain Vancouver and M. de la Perouse, 27 in (68 cm) wide. **$7,500-10,500**

J & W Cary 12-inch terrestrial library globe, the sphere applied with hand coloured gores, printed with calendar and zodiac scales, 1800, 36 in (91 cm) high. **$4,000-5,000**

A Regency mahogany celestial globe, dedicated to the Rev. Nevil Maskelyne, D. D. frs. Astronomer Royal...by W & J M Bardin, with calibrated brass horizon, 41 in (104 cm) high. **$4,500-5,000**

A William IV terrestrial globe, by C. Smith & Son, 172 Strand, containing 'The Latest Discoveries and Geographical Improvements to 1830', bearing the name 'John Smith London', 18 in (46 cm) diam. **$3,000-4,000**

A Lothians' new celestial table globe, corrected to 1828, second quarter of the 19thC, 14½ in (37 cm) high. **$700-1,000**

A pair of William IV globes, one terrestrial and one celestial, by A. Hilger, London, c1825, 37 in (93 cm). **$15,000-20,500**

A terrestrial 18-inch globe, by W. & A.K. Johnston, dated 1879, the coloured gores bearing relevant topographical information, 48 in (122 cm) high overall. **$1,500-2,200**

Lowboys

walnut lowboy, with original ndles and replacement legs, 710, 32 in (80 cm). ,000-5,000

A walnut lowboy, with herringbone banding, early 18thC, 31 in (77.5 cm). **$10,000-13,000**

A 'Hepplewhite' mahogany lowboy, 29 in (72.5 cm). **$1,500-2,200**

A Queen Anne style walnut lowboy, inlaid with boxwood lines, the crossbanded moulded top above an arcaded frieze, 29 in (72.5 cm). **$1,200-1,500**

Mirrors – Cheval

A giltmetal mounted mahogany cheval mirror, early 19thC, 40½ in (103 cm). **$1,500-2,200**

A Victorian walnut cheval mirror, third quarter of the 19thC, 37 in (94 cm). **$500-700**

A Victorian oak cheval mirror, the pierced frieze with rectangular plate and moulded slip, 35 in (89 cm). **$1,400-1,700**

A Victorian cheval mirror, the supports carved in the form of cranes, after the town of Cranbrook, Kent, 69½ in (176 cm) high. **$1,200-1,500**

Mirrors – Toilet

A Hepplewhite style mahogany swivel toilet mirror, 19thC, 17½ in (43.5 cm). **$300-500**

A Hepplewhite style swivel toilet mirror, the oval mirror frame crossbanded in walnut and raised on a serpentine satinwood three-drawer base, crossbanded in tulipwood, 19thC, 18 in (45 cm). **$500-600**

A William and Mary style walnut swivel mirror, c1900, 17 in (42 cm). **$600-800**

Mirrors

★ Until 1773, 18th century English looking glass plates were produced from blown cylinders of glass. This restricted the size and so large mirrors of the period were made up of more than one plate. In 1773, a new process enabled the production of the large single piece mirrors which became fashionable thereafter.

★ 18th century carved and gilded mirror frames will be of wood covered with gesso, or occasionally of carton pierre.

★ In the 19th century, cheaper and greater production was achieved by the use of plaster 'stucco' or composition 'carved' decoration built up on a wire frame. This has tended to crack and is thus detectable. Stucco work cannot be pierced with a needle. Carved wood can.

★ Do not have the old mirror plate re-silvered if it has deteriorated, carefully remove and store; replace it with a new specialist made plate. This particularly applies to toilet and dressing mirrors.

★ Store original mirror upright, never flat, using eight batons slightly larger than the plate – six upright and two across to crate the mirror around bubble paper.

The price ranges given reflect the average price a purchaser should pay for similar items. Condition, rarity of design or pattern, size, colour, pedigree, restoration and many other factors must be taken into account when assessing values.

Mirrors – Wall

Charles II walnut mirror, the riginal bevelled mirror plate thin a carved moulded frame, ne gilding, c1680, 20½ in (51). **$2,500-3,500**

A fine William and Mary walnut and marquetry cushion mirror, the frame inlaid with a vase of flowers in stained ivory and fruitwoods, with ink label inscribed 'This marquetrie mirror was the property of Richard Graham, Viscount Preston...', 31 in (79 cm). **$7,000-9,000**

A fine William and Mary ebony, ivory and stained wood marquetry mirror, surmounted by a shaped arched crest inlaid with sprays of jasmine, other flowers and birds in various woods and natural and green stained ivory, 30½ in (76 cm), **$14,000-17,000**

William and Mary oyster walnut shion-framed wall mirror, the er rectangular bevelled plate thin an ovolo border, c1700, in (41 cm). **$1,000-1,200**

A William and Mary oyster veneered mirror, c1680, 26 in (66 cm). **$3,000-4,000**

A Queen Anne giltwood small wall mirror, with gesso strapwork on a pitted ground and with a cresting carved with a shell and leaf scrolls, gesso restored and lower plate replaced, c1705, 18½ in (47 cm). **$1,500-2,200**

A pair of Queen Anne carved giltwood and gesso girandole mirrors, applied with lacquered brass holders from which spring 2 glass branches with candle sconces and drip-pans, 24½ in (61 cm). **$33,000-42,600**

A giltwood pier glass, with divided bevelled arched plates within a bevelled border mirror panel, late 17thC, 36 in (92 cm). **$15,000-20,500**

An early Georgian looking glass, with finely carved detail, c1720. **$7,000-9,000**

A George I gilt mirror, 20½ in (51 cm). **$2,000-3,000**

A gilt-gesso mirror, with candle arms, c1725, 22 in (55 cm). **$14,000-17,000**

A George II carved and gilt gesso wall mirror, with a broken arch pediment, plate later, c1735, 24 in (61 cm). **$4,500-7,000**

An early George II carved giltwood and gesso looking glass, c1730, 33 in (84 cm). **$15,000-20,500**

A George II gilt gesso looking glass, the swan neck pediment centred by a scallop-shell, later plate, c1735, 29 in (74 cm). **$4,000-5,000**

A walnut and parcel-gilt mirror, c1735, 28½ in (71 cm). **$7,500-10,500**

A George II mahogany and parcel-gilt wall mirror, 25 in (63 cm). **$1,500-2,200**

A George II giltwood wall mirror, c1740, 40 in (102 cm). **$19,500-25,500**

A George II carved giltwood and gesso rectangular wall mirror, 25 in (62 cm). **$7,500-10,500**

A George II giltwood wall mirror, 19 in (48 cm). **$3,000-4,000**

A George II giltwood mirror, the bevelled rectangular plate in a re-entrant foliate moulded gesso frame, below a fleur-de-lys Palladian style cresting, 23 in (58 cm). **$3,000-4,000**

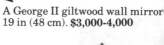

A George II gilt wood mirror, with scroll cornice with carved flowers and leaf decoration and central cartouche, 33½ in (84 cm). **$7,000-9,000**

A George II walnut and giltwood mirror, c1745, 30½ in (76 cm). **$9,000-13,000**

A George II giltwood overmantel, with contemporary but associated bevelled plate, the frame carved with overlapping bulrushes, 66 in (168 cm). **$5,500-7,000**

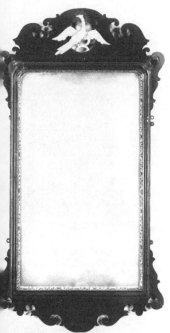

A Chippendale mahogany mirror, repairs to scrolls, American, 1760-1790, 46½in (116cm) high. **$1,500-2,000**

Chippendale mahogany and rcel-gilt mirror, 1760-1790, in (105cm) high. **$2,000-2,500**

A small Chippendale mahogany mirror, the scrolled pediment centering a gold-painted eagle, eagle possibly later, minor repairs to scrolls, American, 1760-1790, 25in (63cm) high. **$800-1,000**

A late Federal mahogany cheval glass, the top rail spirally-reeded, between straight and spirally-reeded posts with turned finials and carved with floral paterae, Philadelphia, 1810-1820, 69in (173cm) high. **$3,000-3,500**

Chippendale mahogany mirror, inor repairs to scrolls, merican, 1760-1790, 35½in 9cm) high. **$1,100-1,500**

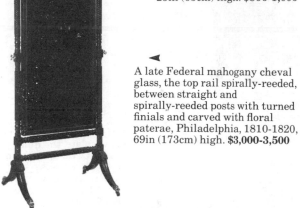

A gilt convex mirror, the crest with a carved spread-wing eagle standing on a rocky plinth flanked by foliate scrolls, re-gilt, glass plate replaced, wing cracked, American, 1820-1830, 43in (108cm) high. **$1,400-1,800**

A pair of late Federal carved giltwood mirrors, American, 1825-1830, 44in (110cm) high. **$14,000-18,000**

A George III carved giltwood wall mirror, with pierced scrolling leaf frame, c1760, 24 in (61 cm). **$3,000-4,000**

An early George III giltwood mirror, with later rectangular plate framed by colonnettes, 29½ in (74 cm). **$8,500-11,000**

A George III carved giltwood looking glass, 27½ in (68 cm) **$1,700-2,500**

A George III giltwood mirror, in ribbed frame pierced and carved with pendant fruit and foliage with a displayed bird cresting, 23 in (58.5 cm). **$3,000-4,500**

A George III giltwood mirror, with later oval plate, the frame pierced and carved with upspringing foliage and C-scrolls rising to a cabochon cresting surmounted by foliage, 32 in (81 cm). **$4,500-5,000**

A George III carved and gilt framed girandole, the pierced triple pagoda surmount above a cartouche-shaped plate with flor scroll surround, c1770, 24 in (61 cm). **$1,500-2,200**

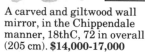

A carved and giltwood wall mirror, in the Chippendale manner, 18thC, 72 in overall (205 cm). **$14,000-17,000**

Make the most of Miller's

Unless otherwise stated, any description which refers to 'a set' or 'a pair' includes a valuation for the entire set or the pair, even though the illustration may show only a single item.

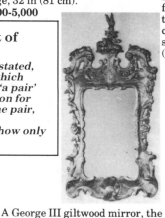

A George III giltwood mirror, the curvilinear rectangular plate in a C-scrolled carved cushion frame, with flower festooned borders below a Palladian style swan-neck cresting, 31½ in (78 cm). **$3,000-4,500**

A George III mahogany wa mirror, late 18thC, 39 in hi (99 cm). **$1,000-1,200**

A George III giltwood mirror, the frame pierced and carved with rockwork, foliate C-and S-scrolls and flowerspray cresting, 23½ in (60 cm). **$3,500-5,000**

A George III giltwood overmantel, with triple bevelled divided plate, 58 in (147.5 cm). **$14,000-17,000**

A carved giltwood Landscape wall mirror, early Chippendale, 57 in (143 cm). **$5,500-7,000**

George III neo-classical ltwood oval wall mirror, with n surmount, and acanthus leaf d husk decoration, 45½ in high 3 cm). **$4,500-7,000**

A George III giltwood mirror, frame carved with scrolling foliage and flowerheads with displayed eagle cresting, 25 in (63.5 cm). **$10,000-13,000**

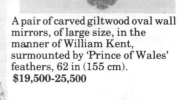

A pair of carved giltwood oval wall mirrors, of large size, in the manner of William Kent, surmounted by 'Prince of Wales' feathers, 62 in (155 cm). **$19,500-25,500**

A George III gilt mirror, the plate with gadrooned and bead carved frame surmounted by an urn and wheatear crest with trailing ivy leaves, 21 in (51 cm). **$1,700-2,500**

Regency giltwood oval mirror, corated with swags and doves, in (82.5 cm). **$800-1,200**

A Regency giltwood mirror, with circular convex plate, the moulded ball-encrusted frame with ebonised slip, displayed eagle cresting, regilded, 41 in (104 cm). **$7,000-9,000**

A carved mahogany wall mirror, in the style of William Kent, late 19thC, 50 in (132 cm). **$5,500-7,000**

vrought-iron mirror frame, by arles Hancock of Cheltenham, in (69 cm). **$2,500-3,500**

Dutch painted and gilded rmantel, early 18thC, 41 in 4 cm). **$1,500-2,200**

A Chippendale style wall mirror, having chequer board string inlay. **$300-500**

A continental mirror, representing wine growing, c1780, 25 in wide (62.5 cm). **$700-900**

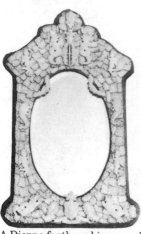

A Swedish mahogany and parcel-gilt pier glass, with divide plate, broken triangular pedimer and lion-mask and thunderbolt cresting, bearing the trade label of P.G. Bylanders/Spegelfabrik/ Hasel No. 77 & 78/vid hörnet af Kyrkooch Fredsgatorne/1 Götheborg,' early 19thC, 35 in (89 cm). **$1,500-2,200**

A Dieppe feathered ivory wall mirror, inscribed in Latin 'Sgotorvm', 18thC, 20 in (50 cm). **$600-700**

A Scandinavian ormolu and cut-glass mirror, the mirrored slip decorated with geometric foliage, the shaped cresting with a vase of flowers, lacking apron, 39½ in (75 cm). **$4,000-5,000**

Screens

A George II mahogany pole screen, embroidered in gros and petit point, the tripod stand with fluted stem and leafy carved knop, the leaf-carved cabriole legs with claw-and-ball feet, c1750, 61 in high (155 cm). **$2,000-3,000**

A Regency black painted and gilt pole screen, 57 in (150 cm) high. **$600-900**

A Victorian rosewood pole screen, with a circular wool worked panel, mid-19thC, 59 in high (150 cm). **$300-500**

A rare William and Mary giltwo fire screen, in the manner of Jol Pelletier, formerly with a panel c1700, 34 in (86.5 cm). **$4,500-7,000**

The name of John Pelletier appears from about 1690-1710 i the Royal Accounts for supplyin table frames, stands, screens an mirror-frames for Hampton Cou and several pieces there can be ascribed to him with some certainty. His origins were presumably in France which would explain the strong French influence in his work.

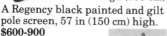

A mid-Georgian mahogany pole screen, faded and holed, 61 in high (155 cm). **$500-600**

A pair of black lacquered fire screens, lacquered in gold and polychrome, on turned column and concave sided base with bun feet, c1850, 57½ in (146 cm). **$1,000-1,200**

An Empire mahogany fire screen, mounted with gilt-metal, on bar feet with castors applied with palmettes united by a turned stretcher, 27½ in (68 cm). **$800-1,200**

A pair of Victorian carved walnut pole screens, c1875. **$1,000-1,200**

Shelves

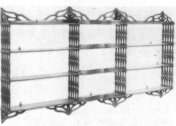

An unusual George III satinwood hanging shelf, each shelf with gilt-decorated edge, c1780, 25 in wide (63.5 cm). **$2,500-3,500**

A set of mahogany hanging shelves, of Chippendale style, 78 in wide (198 cm). **$2,500-3,500**

mahogany firescreen, the silk oestry showing sign of wear, thC. **$100-150**

A George III style mahogany wall bracket, with fretted galleried sides, late 19thC, 36½ in wide (93 cm). **$800-1,200**

A George III style mahogany wall bracket, 19thC, 34 in (86 cm). **$1,500-2,200**

giltwood and vernis Martin ree-fold screen, c1900, 68½ in gh (171 cm). **$1,500-2,200**

A Regency rosewood desk canterbury, the top divided by a bobbin turned gallery with scrolling end supports and rope-twist handles, 16 in wide (40 cm). **$2,000-3,000**

alnut-veneered and Chinese uer three-fold screen, the entine-topped panels outlined an ebonised banding and aining 3 folds from a Chinese en decorated in shades of gilt, lacquer c1800 and from a er screen, the screen -19thC, each fold 85½ in by 33 17 by 84 cm). **$3,000-4,500**

A Dutch polychrome leather four-leaf screen, decorated with exotic birds among flowering foliage in an imitation of coromandel lacquer, 84½ in high (215 cm). **$6,000-8,500**

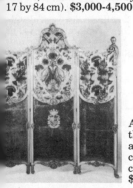

A Victorian gilt and gesso three-leaf screen, the acanthus and shell moulded frame with a central high arched mask cresting, 89½ in high (222.5 cm). **$1,400-1,700**

PRICES

The never-ending problem of fixing prices for antiques! A price can be affected by so many factors, for example:
- *condition*
- *desirability*
- *rarity*
- *size*
- *colour*
- *provenance*
- *restoration*
- *the sale of a prestigious collection*
- *collection label*
- *appearance of a new reference book*
- *new specialist sale at major auction house*
- *mentioned on television*
- *the fact that two people present at auction are determined to have the piece*
- *where you buy it*

One also has to contend with the fact that an antique is not only a 'thing of beauty' but a commodity. The price can again be affected by:–
- *supply and demand*
- *international finance – currency fluctuation*
- *fashion*
- *inflation*
- *the fact that a museum has vast sums of money to spend*

Sideboards

A George III mahogany bowfront sideboard, inlaid with burr elm panels, satinwood bands and boxwood lines, 54 in (135 cm). **$4,500-7,000**

A George III mahogany and crossbanded sideboard, inlaid with boxwood stringing, c1790 71 in (181 cm). **$14,000-17,000**

A George III mahogany sideboard, inlaid with leaf spandrels and geometric boxwood lines, with brass galleried surmount, 72 in (180 cm). **$6,000-8,000**

A George III small sideboard, on square tapering legs with spade feet, the whole outlined in boxwood stringing with tulipwood crossbanding, c1790, 45½ in (113 cm). **$1,700-2,500**

A George III mahogany bowfront sideboard, inlaid with boxwood lines and banded with satinwood, 60 in (150 cm). **$2,000-3,000**

A George III small mahogany sideboard, inlaid with kingwo and satinwood banding and fa decoration, c1790, 41 in (104 c **$7,500-10,500**

A George III mahogany sideboard, of bowfronted form, 55½ in (138 cm). **$3,500-5,000**

A George III mahogany bow-fron sideboard, with satinwood crossbanding and stringing and fan decorated ovals, c1790, 60 in (152 cm). **$8,500-10,500**

A George III mahogany sideboard, the bowed top formerly with a gallery, later back, 78 in (196 cm). **$3,500-5,000**

A George III mahogany demi-lune sideboard, with satinwood stringing, flanked by two deep drawers and end cupboards, 80 in (200 cm). **$4,500-7,000**

A George III mahogany apsidal sideboard, inlaid with satinwood strung borders, c1790, 65½ in (166 cm). **$1,500-2,200**

A small Hepplewhite period mahogany bow-front sideboard with 2 cellaret drawers (divide interiors), replacement oval br plate handles, 44 in (110 cm). **$4,000-5,000**

A George III mahogany and satinwood crossbanded bow-front sideboard, c1790, 69 in (175 cm). **$3,000-4,500**

George III mahogany sideboard,
the manner of Gillows of
ncaster, the raised
perstructure with 3 secret
wers, the incurving centre
h a frieze drawer, 52 in
2 cm). **$4,500-7,000**

A George III mahogany and
crossbanded breakfront
sideboard, inlaid with satinwood
stringing, formerly with a rear
brass gallery, c1800, 72 in
(183 cm). **$4,500-5,000**

A George III mahogany sideboard,
with crossbanded rectangular top
and fluted border, on fluted
tapering legs, 72 in (183 cm).
$3,000-4,500

A George III mahogany and
crossbanded sideboard, on 6
tapering square supports with line
inlay and crossbanding, 72 in
(183 cm). **$3,000-4,000**

A George III mahogany
serpentine fronted sideboard,
decorated with inlaid ebony and
boxwood stringing, 66 in (165 cm).
$4,500-7,000

A Georgian bowfront mahogany
sideboard, with central drawer
over a tambour shutter flanked by
a pair of crossbanded cupboards,
48 in (120 cm). **$1,000-1,200**

Regency mahogany twin
destal sideboard, crossbanded
d lined with chequers and inlaid
th classical urns, 78 in (195 cm).
,000-1,400

A late Georgian small mahogany
dressing table or sideboard, with
wide crossbanded top, all inlaid
with stringing and narrow bands
of conjoined X motifs, 39 in
(100 cm). **$4,500-5,000**

A Regency mahogany breakfront
sideboard, with ebonised strung
borders and mouldings, the rear
with a brass gallery, 72 in
(183 cm). **$2,500-3,500**

Regency mahogany sweep front
eboard, inlaid with ebony
inging and on 6 turned and
ged supports, 54 in (137 cm).
,700-2,500

A Regency mahogany breakfront
sideboard, the bowed crossbanded
top above one frieze drawer and a
swivelling cupboard in the arched
centre, enclosing a lead-lined
cellaret, 54½ in (138 cm).
$3,500-5,000

An unusual Regency mahogany
corner sideboard, the shaped top
and concave kneehole flanked by 2
deep drawers, one lead-lined, 53 in
(135 cm). **$2,000-3,000**

A pair of Irish Regency mahogany
sideboards, the bowed tops with
rope-twist borders and brass
galleried backs surmounted by
finials, 59 in (157 cm).
$14,000-17,000

A Regency brass-inlaid and
mahogany pedestal sideboard,
86 in (219 cm). **$4,000-5,000**

A Regency mahogany bowfront sideboard, inlaid with boxwood lines and satinwood banded borders, 53½ in (133 cm). **$3,000-4,500**

A late Regency mahogany bowfront sideboard, inlaid with chequered boxwood lines and rosewood banded borders, labelled 'S. & H. Jewell, 29-31 Little Queen Street, Holborn, West Central', 42 in (105 cm). **$1,700-2,500**

A Victorian carved mahogany sideboard. **$800-1,200**

A large Jacobean style oak sideboard, by Maples & Co., 90 in (200 cm). **$500-700**

A Victorian mahogany sideboard, 59 in (147.5 cm). **$600-800**

A Regency mahogany bowfront sideboard, inlaid with ebonised lines, 46 in (115 cm). **$1,700-2,500**

A William IV mahogany sideboard, the raised back with carved decoration, 58 in (145 cm). **$1,500-2,200**

A mid Victorian oak sideboard, with a castellated Gothic arched panel back with plumed finials flanking a central shield surmounted by a coronet, the drawers stamped A.J. Owen & Co., New Bond Street, 60 in (150 cm). **$800-1,200**

A.J. Owen moved from Oxford Street to 116-117 New Bond Street in 1869 and from there to Brook Street in 1883.

An Edwardian mahogany sideboard, decorated with satinwood crossbanding and stringing, 76 in (190 cm). **$1,200-1,500**

A good 'Adam' style mahogany sideboard, c1900, 84 in (214 cm). **$1,700-2,500**

A Regency mahogany bowfront sideboard, inlaid with ebonised stringing, on associated reeded and turned tapering legs, 57 in (142.5 cm). **$3,000-4,000**

A mahogany Sheraton style sideboard, having crossbanded border decoration, 66 in (165 cm). **$3,000-4,000**

A Victorian mahogany in sideboard, with satinwood banding. **$1,300-1,700**

A mahogany pedestal sideboard late 19thC, 90 in (200 cm). **$600-900**

A George III-style satinwood a crossbanded demi-lune sideboa with ebonised stringing and segmented veneers, c1890, 42 (107 cm). **$1,000-1,200**

A Federal mahogany veneer sideboard, probably Virginia, 1780-1800, 68in (170cm) wide. **$3,600-4,000**

A Federal inlaid mahogany sideboard, the D-shaped top with pattern-inlaid edge, on square tapering legs with inlaid bellflowers, the entire surface with pattern stringing, restorations, New England, 1790-1810, 68in (170cm) wide. **$4,000-5,000**

A Federal mahogany veneer sideboard, with banded-edge rectangular top with D-shaped center section above a conforming case of 2 veneered cockbead-molded doors centering a cockbead-molded drawer, above double doors, Maryland, 1790-1810, 72in (183cm) wide. **$3,500-4,500**

The taper of the legs and turning of the feet are virtually identical to a pair of Maryland chairs now in the White House, Washington, D.C. and illustrated in American Antiques from the Israel Sack Collection 1957-1964, Vol.1, p.126, no.355.

A Federal mahogany veneer sideboard, with serpentine top over a conforming case of one long cockbeaded and veneered drawer, flanked by 2 short ones over cockbeaded bottle drawers, 46in (115cm) wide. **$1,500-2,000**

An Empire mahogany sideboard, the broken pediment backsplash centering a carved eagle finial, flanked by 2 carved pineapple finials and a brass gallery, New York, 1810-1830, 61in (153cm) wide. **$1,800-2,400**

A Federal inlaid mahogany sideboard, with a bowed serpentine top above a conforming case with a bowed long drawer centering an inlaid foliate paterae flanked by 2 short drawers, each over a deep drawer inlaid with quarter fans flanking 2 cupboard doors, each inlaid with a seashell, Connecticut, 1790-1818, 70½in (179cm) wide. **$25,000-30,000**

351

A late Federal mahogany veneer sideboard, on reeded tapering legs with brass ball feet, New York, 1810-1830, 72½in (184cm) wide. **$650-1,000**

A Federal style inlaid mahogany sideboard, the top edged with banding and lightwood stringing over a conforming case of one triple line-inlaid long drawer flanked by 2 short drawers, above 2 doors with fan-inlaid spandrels and centering similarly inlaid recessed double doors, by Kensington Company, New York City, N.Y., bearing the label of Kensington Furniture, 41 West 45th Street, New York, on the back, 72in (183cm) wide. **$1,800-2,200**

Stands

A South German carved and painted bear hallstand, late 19thC, 79 in (201 cm). **$3,000-4,000**

A mahogany adjustable music stand, c1870, 48 in (120 cm). **$700-900**

A Victorian mahogany spindle circular umbrella stand, with brass base and brass decoration **$200-300**

A rosewood and brass combined pole screen, wine and games table, 19thC. **$800-1,200**

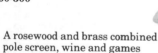

A South German carved wood bear and cub hat stand, the infant climbing a gnarled tree above its standing parent, both beasts with glass eyes, c1890, 82 in (208 cm). **$2,500-3,500**

A Victorian beechwood hat and coat stand. **$200-300**

A Victorian walnut music stand, c1860. **$1,000-1,400**

An unusual George III mahogany lectern, 30 in (75 cm). **$1,500-2,200**

A Victorian calamanderwood and ebony folio stand, with 2 pierced racks bordered with partridgewood and satinwood 34 in (86.5 cm). **$7,500-10,500**

A pair of Regency Lac Burgante jardinières on stands, inlaid with figures in landscapes and blossoming foliage, having brass carrying handles and metal liners. **$8,500-10,500**

A George II style brass bound oval mahogany jardinière. **$1,300-1,700**

Sheraton Revival mahogany
nd marquetry music stand,
900, 53 in (135 cm).
00-1,200

A Federal style figured maple stand, 17in (43cm) wide. **$350-400**

An Empire grain-painted and stencilled washstand, New England, 1825-1835, 17in (43cm) wide. **$200-300**

A George III mahogany and
atinwood two tier etagère, each
atinwood veneered tier
rossbanded in kingwood, c1790,
4 in (112 cm). **$4,000-5,000**

A pair of Venetian giltwood torchères, 34 in (86 cm). **$4,000-5,000**

A Federal mahogany two-drawer stand, New England, 1790-1820, top split, 16in (40cm) wide. **$500-600**

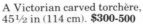

A Federal cherrywood two-drawer stand, New England, 1790-1820, 18in (45cm) wide. **$1,100-1,400**

A Victorian carved torchère, 45½ in (114 cm). **$300-500**

A mahogany shaving stand, early
20thC, 36 in (90 cm).
$300-500

A pair of scagliola pedestals,
simulating Siena marble, late
18thC, 18 in (46 cm).
$5,500-7,000

Stools

A George I walnut stool, some
restorations, 20 in (50 cm).
$1,700-2,500

A George II mahogany stool,
upholstered in needlework to a
Soho design on cabriole legs, one
foot partially replaced, with a
handwritten label inscribed 'stool
one of a pair recovered in
needlework by the late Lady
Chute the design taken from the
Vanderbank tapestries made at
Soho in 1720', 36 in (66 cm).
$3,000-4,500

A George III mahogany stool one
seat rail possibly replaced, 21½ in
(54.5 cm). **$3,000-4,500**

A George I walnut stool, the
rectangular padded needlework
seat on cabriole legs and pad feet
$5,500-7,000

A walnut stool, with burr walnut
seat rail, cabriole legs headed by
masks and hairy paw feet, 24½ in
(62 cm). **$2,000-3,000**

A mahogany stool, with plain
frame, cabriole legs headed by
shells and foliage and claw
and ball feet, 22 in (58 cm).
$4,000-5,000

A fine ebony and ivory inlaid
mahogany stool, with stringing of
lighter wood and detailing with
ivory and ebony, an additional
filet of ebony between upholstered
seat and frame, branded 'Sumner
Greene His True Mark' on one leg
and with an upholsterer's paper
label THE CHEESEWRIGHT
STUDIOS, INC, 1030 EAST
GREEN ST., PASADENA,
CALIFORNIA, designed by
Greene & Greene, executed in the
workshop of Peter Hall for the
Cordelia A. Culbertson House
living room, Pasadena, California,
c1911, 25in (64cm) wide.
$2,800-3,500

A fine late Federal carved
mahogany stool, Boston,
Massachusetts, 1810-1820, 25in
(63cm) wide. **$9,000-10,000**

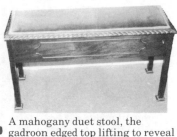

A piano stool, with circular adjustable top, 19thC.
$150-200

An Edwardian piano stool.
$200-300

A mahogany duet stool, the gadroon edged top lifting to reveal a storage compartment.
$150-200

Tables – Architects

An unusual George III mahogany architects portable table, the top with double ratchet support, 25 in (62.5 cm). **$600-900**

A George III mahogany library desk, in the manner of Gillows, with moulded baize lined top and double ratchet frame above a fitted secretaire drawer, the 3 right hand drawers adapted and re-lined, later back, 50½ in (128 cm). **$3,500-5,000**

An early George III mahogany architects table, 44 in (110 cm).
$2,000-3,000

Tables – Breakfast

A George III mahogany breakfast table, the crossbanded oval top with satinwood band, 56 in (142 cm). **$14,000-17,000**

A George III mahogany breakfast table, with moulded tip-up top, on ring turned spreading shaft, 65½ in (166 cm).
$8,500-10,500

A George III mahogany breakfast table, by Gillows, the top inlaid with boxwood and ebony lines, stamped 'Gillows Lancaster', 41½ in (105,5 cm).
$15,000-20,500

A fine George III rosewood breakfast table, the tip-up crossbanded top bordered with satinwood, 53 in (134.5 cm). **$4,500-7,000**

A George III satinwood, rosewood and mahogany breakfast table, the crossbanded top on ring-turned vase-shaped shaft and splayed quadripartite base inlaid with boxwood lines, 55½ in (139 cm). **$7,500-10,500**

A George III satinwood crossbanded mahogany breakfast table, c1800, 43 in (107 cm).
$1,700-2,500

A George III mahogany breakfast table, 54 in (135 cm).
$2,000-3,000

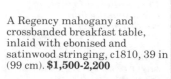

A Regency mahogany and crossbanded breakfast table, inlaid with ebonised and satinwood stringing, c1810, 39 in (99 cm). **$1,500-2,200**

A George III mahogany breakfast table, the top with a reeded border, c1800, 55 in (140 cm).
$2,500-3,500

A Regency satinwood mahogany and rosewood breakfast table, the crossbanded tip-up top with ring turned shaft, fluted splayed quadripartite base and claw feet, adapted, 65½ in (166 cm).
$4,500-7,000

A Regency mahogany breakfast table, with crossbanded tip-up top, on baluster shaft and reeded splayed quadripartite base, 60 in (152 cm). **$1,700-2,500**

A Regency rosewood breakfast table, c1820, 42 in (107 cm).
$1,700-2,500

A William IV mahogany pedestal breakfast table, the crossbanded and flame segmented veneered top with beaded borders, 59½ in (149 cm). **$7,000-9,000**

A late George III mahogany breakfast table, the top with yew-wood crossbanding and fluted edge, 58½ in (148 cm).
$1,700-2,500

A Regency satinwood and mahogany breakfast table, the top crossbanded in rosewood, c1810, 35½ in (89 cm).
$1,500-2,200

A Regency mahogany breakfast table, 53½ in (136 cm).
$1,400-1,700

A Regency mahogany snap-top breakfast table, 54 in (135 cm).
$2,500-3,500

MAKE THE MOST OF MILLERS

When buying or selling, it must always be remembered that prices can be greatly affected by the condition of any piece. Unless otherwise stated, all goods shown in Miller's are of good merchantable quality, and the valuations given reflect this fact. Pieces offered for sale in exceptionally fine condition or in poor condition may reasonably be expected to be priced considerably higher or lower respectively than the estimates given herein.

A Regency mahogany and rosewood crossbanded rectangular drop-leaf breakfast table, c1810, 36 in (91 cm).
$1,700-2,500

A Regency mahogany breakfast table, with line inlay, the crossbanded moulded tilt top with rounded ends on a tapering column, 66 in (188 cm).
$15,000-20,500

A Regency mahogany breakfast table, c1815. **$4,000-5,000**

A late Regency mahogany breakfast table, 53 in (132.5 cm).
$1,000-1,400

An early Victoria rosewood breakfast table, the circular tilt-top with banded edge inlaid with brass arabesques, 50 in (125 cm). **$2,500-3,500**

An early Victorian rosewood breakfast table, 54 in (137 cm). **$1,200-1,500**

A Victorian walnut breakfast table, mid-19thC, 56 in (142 cm). **$1,300-1,700**

A Victorian burr walnut oval breakfast table, c1860, 54 in (135 cm). **$1,500-2,200**

A Victorian rosewood breakfast table, third quarter of the 19thC, 29 in (72.5 cm). **$2,000-3,000**

A Regency style mahogany and inlaid snap top breakfast table, the top inlaid with geometrical string lines and star motifs, stamped 'Edwards & Roberts', 33 in (82.5 cm). **$1,200-1,500**

A mahogany tilt top breakfast table, with crossbanded top, 58 in (145 cm). **$800-1,200**

Tables – Card

A George II mahogany card table, the baize lined interior with projecting corners and counter wells, 31 in (79 cm). **$3,000-4,500**

A George II mahogany card table, the eared baize lined folding top with counter wells, 32 in (81 cm). **$4,000-5,000**

A George II shaped padoukwood card table, with concertina action, with 4 sunken counter holders inside, top split, 35 in (87.5 cm). **$3,000-4,500**

A William and Mary black and gold japanned gateleg card table, the baize lined top decorated with raised Chinese figures and temples with 2 frieze drawers opening to the sides, restorations, 32 in (81 cm). **$3,000-4,500**

A George II mahogany card table, the top with outset rounded corners and guinea wells, feet replaced, 35 in (87 cm). **$1,300-1,700**

A George II mahogany card table, of small size, the top with rounded outset corners enclosing candlestands and guinea wells, 32½ in (81 cm). **$2,000-3,000**

357

A Chippendale mahogany card table, the serpentine top with a fluted edge folding above a conforming skirt with a coved cornice molding and a chip-carved edge molding, on square tapering legs with pierced fretwork brackets, patches to hinge areas of top, Newport, Rhode Island, 1770-1790, 31in (77.5cm) wide. **$7,000-8,000**

A Federal inlaid mahogany card table, the D-shaped top with a serpentine front edge with double line inlay, top detached, old repair to rear legs, Pennsylvania or Maryland, 1790-1810, 35in (87.5cm) wide. **$1,000-1,300**

A Federal mahogany and birch veneer card table, the bowed rectangular top with outset-rounded corners and banded edges above a conforming skirt with flame-figured birch veneer panels above rosewood banding, over reeded tapering cylindrical legs, Northeastern Massachusetts, 1800-1815, 36in (90cm) wide. **$4,000-5,000**

A Federal mahogany card table, the hinged serpentine top above a conforming apron with cockbeaded edge, Philadelphia, 1790-1810, 35½in (88.5cm) wide. **$1,000-1,300**

A Federal inlaid mahogany card table, on 4 inlaid square tapering legs with inlaid cuffs, Middle Atlantic States, 1790-1815, 29in (72.5cm) high. **$1,400-1,800**

A Federal inlaid mahogany card table, the top with a line-inlaid edge folding above a conforming veneered and line-inlaid skirt, on square tapering legs inlaid with icicles and stringing, small crack to one leaf, Rhode Island, 1790-1810, 28½in (71cm) high. **$3,000-4,000**

A Chippendale mahogany card table, the folding top with astragal-molded edge above a flame-figured veneered skirt with an applied astragal-molded edge, on Marlborough legs with beaded centre molding and pierced brackets, Philadelphia, 1760-1790, 36in (90cm) wide. **$4,000-5,000**

Provenance: John S. Walton, Inc.

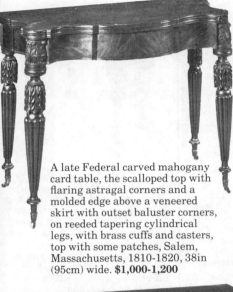

A late Federal carved mahogany card table, the scalloped top with flaring astragal corners and a molded edge above a veneered skirt with outset baluster corners, on reeded tapering cylindrical legs, with brass cuffs and casters, top with some patches, Salem, Massachusetts, 1810-1820, 38in (95cm) wide. **$1,000-1,200**

A Federal mahogany and figured maple veneer card table, the rectangular top with bowed front and banded edges folding above a conforming veneered skirt, on a double lyre-shaped partially-veneered base with brass wire strings, New York, 1800-1815, 36in (90cm) wide. **$20,000-25,000**

A late Federal carved mahogany card table, the shaped hinged top with canted outset-rounded corners and reeded edge above a conforming veneered apron with bead-molded skirt, the legs headed by carved cornucopiae on a star-punched ground on ball-turned feet, Salem, Massachusetts, 1810-1820, 36in (90cm) wide. **$1,600-2,000**

A late Federal mahogany veneer card table, with hinged top revolving over a compartment above a conforming veneered apron centering a raised panel and flanked by 2 corner panels, the whole edged with banding above an enclosed carved double-lyre pedestal, on molded sabre legs with applied ring-turned bosses at the knees with stylised brass paw feet and casters, minor veneer repairs to base, by Cornelius Briggs, Boston, 1825, 36½in (91cm) wide. **$2,200-3,000**

A pencil inscription under the top reads'....1825/C. Briggs 578 Washington Street.'

A Federal inlaid mahogany and birch veneer card table, with a reeded serpentine top folding above a conforming skirt veneered with figured birch panels framed by pattern stringing, on reeded tapering cylindrical legs with brass cuffs, some restoration to inlay and veneer, Northeastern Massachusetts, 1800-1815, 39in (97.5cm) wide. **$4,000-5,000**

A George II red walnut card table, the projecting square corners with candle stands, the cabriole legs carved with cabochons and frilled scroll brackets and ending in claw and ball feet, the 2 back legs opening with concertina action, c1740, 33 in (84 cm).
$6,000-8,500

A pair of early George III mahogany card tables, the baize lined hinged tops with a moulded edge, 35 in (87 cm).
$2,500-3,500

A fine Federal inlaid mahogany card table, with bowfront hinged top edged with patterned banding above a conforming apron veneered with 3 rectangular birch panels on the front and 2 panels on the side over diamond-pattern edging, on square tapering line-inlaid legs headed with inlaid broken columns and with diamond-patterned cuffs, attributed to Levi Bartlett, Concord, New Hampshire, 1800-1810, 36in (90cm) wide.
$9,000-11,000

Provenance: Peter Eaton Antiques A table of similar form, with broken pilaster inlay, in a private collection bears the label of Levi Bartlett (1784-1864). See Benjamin Hewitt, 'Regional Characteristics of Inlay on American Federal Card Tables,' The Magazine Antiques, May, 1982, p.1168, pl. IV.

An Irish mid-Georgian walnut combined tea, card and games table, with eared hinged triple flap top, the baize lined games top with guinea wells and candle sconces, the games top inlaid in fruitwood with chess squares and backgammon enclosing a hinged compartment with an easel top and sliding dice tray, 35½ in (90 cm). **$6,000-8,500**

A George III satinwood, crossbanded and painted card table, 39 in (97.5 cm).
$4,500-7,000

A mid-Georgian mahogany card table, 36 in (91.5 cm).
$3,500-5,000

A late Federal carved mahogany card table, the scalloped top with molded edges folding above a conforming veneered skirt, the outset-rounded corners with carved acanthus leaves against a star-punched ground, with ring and ball-turned feet, Salem, Massachusetts, 1810-1825, 39½in (98.5cm) wide. **$1,400-1,800**

This table is very similar to 2 tables attributed to Nathaniel Appleton, Jr., with carving probably by Samuel Field McIntire. The tables and a group of related furniture by Appleton and McIntire are illustrated and discussed by Fiske Kimball, 'Salem Furniture Makers', Antiques, vol 24, no. 3 (September, 1933), p.90.

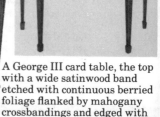

A George III card table, the top with a wide satinwood band etched with continuous berried foliage flanked by mahogany crossbandings and edged with stringing, restored, 36 in (90 cm)
$3,500-5,000

A George III satinwood demi-lune card table, the figured top inlaid with a broad mahogany banding above a kingwood banded frieze, 36½ in (91 cm).
$2,500-3,500

A George III satinwood card table, with kingwood crossbandings edged with stringing, 38 in (95 cm). **$4,500-7,000**

A George III satinwood and mahogany card table, crossbanded with rosewood and inlaid with boxwood and ebonised lines, above an inlaid frieze on square tapering legs, associated, 38 in (95 cm). $5,500-7,000

A George III mahogany card table, with rectangular baize lined folding top edged with entrelac and rosette, the plain frieze with concertina action, 36 in (91.5 cm). $2,000-3,000

A fine George III mahogany card table, in the French manner, the serpentine top with 'entrelac' carved rim, the rear support extending on a concertina action, 36½ in (91 cm). $9,000-13,000

A George III mahogany card table, with crossbanded baize lined serpentine top, one leg replaced, 39 in (99 cm). $3,000-4,500

A pair of Federal mahogany card tables, each with hinged, shaped serpentine top with reeded edge above a conforming veneered apron centering 2 sunburst-carved panels and edged with cockbeading, old repair to one leg, Philadelphia, 1800-1815, 35½in (88.5cm) wide. $4,000-5,000

A pair of Regency brass inlaid rosewood veneered card tables, each raised on a pair of lyre supports with downscrolled legs and arched stretcher, inlaid throughout with stringing, brass work distressed and some veneer detached, c1805, 36 in (91 cm). $15,000-20,500

A Regency calamander and brass inlaid card table, the rosewood crossbanded top inlaid with a border of stylised foliate designs and paterae, 36 in (90 cm). $2,000-3,000

A Regency calamander wood veneered card table, inlaid with stringing and small panels of pearwood, c1805, 36 in (91 cm). $3,000-4,500

pair of Regency satinwood card tables, each with rosewood crossbanded top inlaid with a half shell medallion, 34 in (86.5 cm). $7,000-9,000

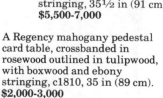

A pair of Regency rosewood card tables, inlaid with cut brass and stringing, 35½ in (91 cm). $5,500-7,000

A Regency mahogany pedestal card table, crossbanded in rosewood outlined in tulipwood, with boxwood and ebony stringing, c1810, 35 in (89 cm). $2,000-3,000

A Regency calamanderwood and satinwood card table, bearing the trade label 'George Simpson Upholder Cabinet Maker & Undertaker no 19 South Side of St. Pauls Churchyard London', 36 in (91.5 cm). $2,500-3,500

361

A Regency rosewood veneered swivel top card table, with brass marquetry and line inlay, the top crossbanded and lined with baize, on casters, top repaired, 35 in (87.5 cm). **$1,000-1,400**

A Regency rosewood and coromandel banded card table, with gilt mounts, c1815, 36½ in (92.5 cm). **$1,300-1,700**

A pair of Regency rosewood and brass marquetry card tables, the tooled leather lined crossbanded hinged swivel tops bordered with brass lines, 36 in (90 cm). **$6,000-8,000**

A Regency crossbanded mahogany and line inlaid card table, a few small pieces of veneer missing, 36 in (90 cm). **$400-600**

A Regency rosewood card table, inlaid with brass lines, 36 in (90 cm). **$1,700-2,500**

A Regency rosewood card table, 36 in (90 cm). **$600-900**

A William IV mahogany card table, the fold over top on acanthus carved baluster column, second quarter of the 19thC. **$1,400-1,700**

A Victorian burr walnut and tulipwood banded card table, 37 in (92.5 cm). **$1,400-1,700**

A fine Federal inlaid mahogany and bird's eye maple card table, the serpentine top with a band of lunette inlay on the edge folding above a conforming skirt with rosewood banding, on reeded tapering cylindrical legs, attributed to John and Thomas Seymour, Boston, c1800, 38½in (96cm) wide. **$8,000-10,000**

A Victorian walnut card table, the rectangular top with rounded ends inlaid with ebony and boxwood motifs, 38 in (95 cm). **$600-900**

An Edwardian inlaid amboyna envelope top card table, 22 in (55 cm). **$800-1,200**

A pair of ebonised and burr chestnut card tables, the moulded bow ended swivelling tops each with an ivory inlaid lozenge and a frieze with a Wedgwood-type plaque, c1870, 36 in (91 cm). **$1,700-2,500**

An early Georgian style walnut card table, the crossbanded shaped folding top enclosing a floral tapestry lining, 34½ in (86 cm). **$1,300-1,700**

A Louis Philippe ormolu mounted figured walnut card table, the swivelling top inlaid in stained woods with floral marquetry, 36½ in (91 cm).
$1,500-2,200

A George II mahogany centre table, mid-18thC, 35 in (84 cm).
$2,500-3,500

n ormolu mounted kingwood arquetry and marquetry card able, inlaid with a floral spray nd flowerhead trellis work, 28 in 71 cm). **$2,500-3,500**

A boulle serpentine card table, mounted with ormolu Grecian face masks, inlaid with classical scrolls, birds and flowers, 19thC, 35 in (87.5 cm). **$800-1,200**

A George III mahogany tilt-top pedestal table, c1800, 53 in (135 cm). **$1,400-1,700**

id-Georgian red walnut centre le, with rectangular top and 3 s swivelling to form a agonal top, 32 in (83 cm).
500-10,500

A giltwood centre table, with moulded Carrara marble top, inlaid in brightly coloured scagliola, 82 in (205.5 cm).
$10,500-14,000

A cream and pale blue painted centre table, with moulded serpentine marble top, 95½ in (242.5 cm). **$4,500-7,000**

giltwood centre table, with ulded verde antico marble top, in (119 cm). **$15,000-20,500**

A Regency mahogany centre table, the crossbanded top inlaid with ebony stringing, on a gunbarrel turned column and outswept tripod support, 29½ in (74 cm). **$800-1,200**

A Regency faded rosewood centre table, with gilt metal mounts and crossbanded top, c1815, 50 in (125 cm). **$6,000-8,500**

egency pollard oak centre le, in the manner of George lock, with tip-up top ssbanded with rosewood and l's-eye maple and inlaid with ss and ebony lines interrupted leur-de-lys on spirally reeded -wood shaft, with ebonised green painted collars, 41 in 2.5 cm). **$6,000-8,500**

A Regency rosewood centre table, with 2 frieze drawers and 2 slides mounted with star pattern handles, 30 in (75 cm).
$4,500-7,000

A Regency ormolu, parcel gilt and rosewood centre table, with tip-up top, the frieze with a foliate band on fluted spreading shaft, 48 in (120 cm). **$3,500-5,000**

A mahogany centre table, with gadrooned, riband and flowerhead borders, the envelope folding top above a simulated frieze applied with patera, with acanthus scrolled feet, 19thC, 29 in (72.5 cm). **$1,300-1,700**

A mahogany and burr walnut centre table, the crossbanded top supported on 5 bronze greyhounds, and shaped plinth base, 73 in (185.5 cm). **$6,000-8,500**

A mahogany centre table, the top with a crenellated border, stamped 104 452, c.1845, 52 in (130 cm). **$2,500-3,500**

A figured walnut centre table, the waved hinged top veneered in segments, c1850, 51 in (127.5 cm). **$1,700-2,500**

A William IV brass inlaid parcel gilt and rosewood centre table, with banded tip-up top, the frieze with gadrooned ormolu border, 48 in (120 cm). **$8,500-10,500**

An early Victorian oak centre table, with chamfered moulded top and one panelled frieze drawer flanked by carved foliate bosses on pierced trestle ends, 48 in (122 cm). **$1,500-2,200**

An ormolu-mounted marble-topped kingwood centre table, the top inset with a panel of chequered fluorspar, bluejohn and white marble within a slate border and a moulding, c1840, 30 in (75 cm). **$1,700-2,500**

A walnut centre table, the top inset with a chequer board specimen marble panel, mid-19thC, 32 in (81 cm). **$3,500-5,000**

A Victorian amboyna, pollard oak and ebonised centre table, in the Gothic taste, the inlaid border with stylised foliage alternating with lozenge and flower head design, with pierced tracery centred by an inlaid roundel, 46 in (115 cm). **$3,500-5,000**

A William IV mahogany centre table, second quarter of 19thC, 39 in (97.5 cm). **$1,000-1,200**

A pollard oak centre table, c1830, 57 in (150 cm). **$2,500-3,500**

An early Victorian rosewood centre table, the sixteen-sided gadrooned tip up top on massive spreading foliate shaft, 54 in (135 cm). **$3,500-5,000**

An inlaid walnut table, the moulded hinged top veneered with walnut and with 6 wedge-shaped harewood panels, inlaid with peasant figures, and enclosed by a rococo scrollwork in a variety of woods, c.1850, 51 in high (127.5 cm). **$3,500-5,000**

A Victorian walnut centre table, the quarter veneered serpentine top on cabriole legs carved and pierced with cabochons and C-scrolls, 64 in (188 cm). **$2,500-3,500**

circular burr walnut and
onised centre table, c1870, 40 in
00 cm). **$1,400-1,700**

late Victorian rosewood and
laid centre table, the top with a
oad satinwood banded border,
e frieze inlaid with satinwood
edallions, the tapered square
gs joined by an X-shaped
retcher, c1900, 44 in (110 cm).
,000-1,200

Dutch walnut and ebony
arquetry centre table, the
ossbanded top decorated with an
rangement of geometrical
arquetry panels, the later base
th an inlaid frieze drawer, 50 in
25 cm). **$2,500-3,500**

A French boulle and ebonised
entre table, 19thC.
1,400-1,700

A Victorian burr walnut centre
table, c1870, 48 in (122 cm).
$1,000-1,200

A Louis XV style kingwood and
ormolu mounted bureau plat, the
crossbanded leather inset top with
brass edge above 3 similarly
crossbanded drawers, c1870, 69 in
(175 cm). **$4,500-7,000**

A Victorian walnut centre table,
inlaid with foliate marquetry, the
serpentine top centred by a
butterfly, with rosewood banding,
41 in (102.5 cm). **$1,000-1,200**

A Louis XV style kingwood centre
table, with gilt metal mounts, one
mounted engraved 'F. Linke', the
carcass stamped with the number
7444. **$4,000-5,000**
Francois Linke (fl. 1882-1935).

A French ebonised and satinwood
marquetry centre drop-leaf table,
with ormolu mounts, the waved
frieze with a drawer and masks,
with plate glass top, c1870, 58 in
(145 cm). **$1,000-1,200**

A late Victorian inlaid rosewood
centre table, by Edwards and
Roberts, with floral marquetry
decoration, 32 in (80 cm).
$1,000-1,200

A Dutch marquetry inlaid
tray-top centre table, the inlay
depicts birds, an urn of flowers,
and floral and foliate sprays, some
damage, late 18thC, 22 in (55 cm).
$1,000-1,200

An ormolu-mounted amaranth,
bois satiné and stained fruitwood
centre table, after the model by
J.-H. Riesener, the frieze with 2
drawers, one spring loaded,
decorated with putti engaged in
various astrological and other
pursuits, 43 in (107.5 cm).
$15,000-20,500

A Louis XV Transitional style
mahogany table ambulante,
applied with ormolu mounts, the
segmented veneered curvilinear
top with crossbanding and brass
outlined borders, 34 in (85 cm).
$1,400-1,700

A fine Empire mahogany marble-top centre table, with a white marble top over a veneered skirt and gilt stencilling, on 3 leaf-carved and reeded turned feet with casters, New York, 1825-1835, 29½in (73.5cm) high. **$9,000-11,000**

An Italian pietra dura marble specimen table, raised on an English rosewood triple column stem, the top inset with various coloured marbles, mala chite, lapis lazuli, the centre inlaid with various shells, all on a slate base, early 19thC, 28 in (70 cm). **$1,000-1,200**

A Swedish white painted centre table, with shaped moulded breccia marble top, the pierced frieze carved with a shell cresting, flowerheads and foliage, 71½ in (181.5 cm). **$6,000-8,500**

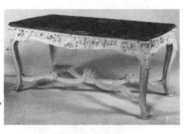

An unusual mahogany ebony an rosewood centre table, the top inlaid with a mother-of-pearl panel of flowers, flanked by animals and butterflies, possibly Russian, 2 legs distressed, 19thC 33½ in (84 cm). **$4,500-7,000**

A Portuguese rosewood centre table, the top with ropetwist border above 4 fielded frieze drawers each side, 77½ in (197 cm). **$7,500-10,500**

A Louis XV style kingwood and satinwood parquetry serpentined centre table, with floral scroll inlay, the frieze with a drawer, stamped and bearing trade plate of James Schoolbred & Co, No.2992, c1910, 30 in (75 cm). **$1,700-2,500**

Tables – Console

A Regency parcel gilt and mahogany console table, 26 (66 cm). **$2,500-3,500**

An unusual Regency rosewood and ebonised console table, with pale green marble slab, 43 in (108 cm). **$2,000-3,000**

A corner console table, with variegated marble top, 19thC, 37 in (92 cm). **$4,500-7,000**

A painted console table, part early 18thC, 35½ in (89 cm). **$1,700-2,500**

Tables – Dining

A good Victorian mahogany extending dining table, the rectangular top on 5 large fluted tapering supports, with casters, third quarter of the 19thC, 192 in (488 cm), extended. **$2,500-3,500**

A George IV mahogany rectangular extending dining table, with 5 leaves and telescopic action, c1825, 159 in (404 cm), extended. **$3,000-4,500**

A George III mahogany 'D' end dining table, the twin pedestals with columnar stems and quadruple moulded splayed legs on casters, c1790, 114 in (243 cm). **15,000-20,000**

A George III mahogany twin pedestal dining table, resupported, 89 in (226 cm), including one extra leaf. **$6,000-8,500**

A Regency mahogany twin pedestal 'D' end dining table, c1810, 99 in (252 cm), extended. **10,500-14,000**

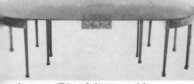

mahogany 'D' end dining table, with 2 lap central section and 2 'D' ds, early 20thC, 102 in (259 cm). **,500-3,500**

A good early Victorian Jupe's patent expanding mahogany table, by Johnstone, Jupe and Co., the centre bearing a brass boss engraved 'Jupe's Patent' and the frame stamped 'Johnstone, Jupe & Co., New Bond St., London, No. 10506', 82 in (178 cm), extended. **$19,500-25,500**

A mahogany 'D' end dining table, c1770. **$8,500-10,000**

A George III mahogany triple pedestal dining table, the rectangular top with rounded corners, now without leaves, pedestals made up, c1800, 143 in (363 cm). **$6,000-8,500**

A George III mahogany extending dining table, comprising 2 'D' shape ends, a rectangular centre portion and 2 extra leaves, restored, 110½ in (281 cm), extended. **$6,000-8,500**

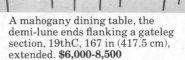

A mahogany dining table, the demi-lune ends flanking a gateleg section, 19thC, 167 in (417.5 cm), extended. **$6,000-8,500**

A Georgian figured mahogany twin pedestal dining table, with dropleaf centre. **$3,500-5,000**

A fine Regency mahogany patent extending dining table, by B.P. Titter, Norwich, bearing the maker's plaque 'B.P. Titter & Co., Inventors and Manufacturers, Norwich', 118 in (299 cm), extended. **$9,000-13,000**

B.P. Titter is recorded as living at St. Symonds Street, Norwich, in 1811.

A fine Regency mahogany twin pedestal dining table, 131 in (333 cm), extended. **$10,500-14,000**

A Regency mahogany three pedestal dining table, including 2 extra leaves of a later date, 152 in (390 cm). **$8,500-10,500**

A George III mahogany 3 pillar dining table, with 2 loose leaves, 145 in (369 cm). **$15,000-20,500**

A William IV mahogany 'D' end extending dining table, with 3 leaves, c1835, 119 in (320 cm), extended. **$4,500-7,000**

A George III mahogany dining table, late 18th/early 19thC, 48 in (122 cm). **$1,400-1,700**

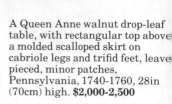

A Queen Anne maple drop-leaf table, the molded top with 2 drop leaves above a double ogee-carved skirt on cabriole legs with pad-and-disc feet, repair to one foot, New England, 1740-1760, 27½in by 40½in (68.5 by 101cm). **$5,000-6,000**

A Queen Anne walnut drop-leaf table, with rectangular top above a molded scalloped skirt on cabriole legs and trifid feet, leaves pieced, minor patches, Pennsylvania, 1740-1760, 28in (70cm) high. **$2,000-2,500**

A Queen Anne walnut drop-leaf dining table, the oval top over an arched skirt on cabriole legs with stocking-carved trifid feet, Pennsylvania, 28in by 62in (70 by 155cm). **$2,200-2,500**

A Queen Anne maple drop-leaf table, the oval top above an ogee-arched skirt, on reel-turned tapering cylindrical legs with pad feet, New England, 28in (70cm) high. **$1,500-2,000**

A Chippendale mahogany drop-leaf table, with oval top over an ogee-arched apron, on cabriole legs with ball-and-claw feet, 27in (67.5cm) high. **$1,000-1,500**

HOW TO USE MILLER'S

Unless otherwise stated, any description which refers to 'a set' or 'a pair' includes a valuation for the entire set or the pair, even though the illustration may show only a single item.

A Queen Anne cherrywood drop-leaf table, with oval top above a convex ogee-shaped apron, on cabriole legs with pad feet, repairs to top, Massachusetts, 1740-1760. **$2,000-2,500**

A Queen Anne walnut drop-leaf table, the top over a straight skirt, on tapering cylindrical legs with pad feet, one leaf slightly warped, American, 1740-1770, 28in (70cm) high. **$1,200-1,600**

A Queen Anne walnut drop-leaf dining table, on cabriole legs with thumb-molded posts and stocking-carved pad feet, few minor repairs, Pennsylvania, 1740-1770, 27in (67.5cm) high. **$3,500-4,500**

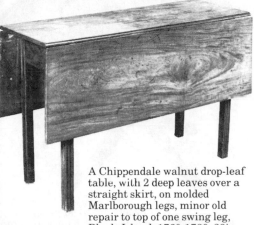

A Chippendale walnut drop-leaf table, with 2 deep leaves over a straight skirt, on molded Marlborough legs, minor old repair to top of one swing leg, Rhode Island, 1760-1780, 28in (70cm) high. **$1,100-1,400**

A Federal inlaid cherrywood drop-leaf table, the drop leaves with inlaid quarter fans on square tapering line-inlaid legs, one leaf pieced at edge, inlay restored, New England, 1790-1820, 27½in (68.5cm). **$700-900**

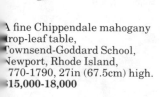

A fine Chippendale mahogany drop-leaf table, Townsend-Goddard School, Newport, Rhode Island, 1770-1790, 27in (67.5cm) high. **$15,000-18,000**

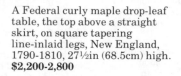

A Federal curly maple drop-leaf table, the top above a straight skirt, on square tapering line-inlaid legs, New England, 1790-1810, 27½in (68.5cm) high. **$2,200-2,800**

A Federal mahogany drop-leaf table, with rectangular top on square tapering legs with spade feet, feet restored, 1790-1810, 29½in (73.5cm) high. **$600-800**

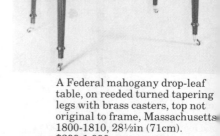

A Federal mahogany drop-leaf table, on reeded turned tapering legs with brass casters, top not original to frame, Massachusetts 1800-1810, 28½in (71cm). **$800-1,000**

A mahogany 3 pillar dining table, early 19thC, 152 in (286 cm), extended. **$15,000-20,500**

A mahogany extending dining table, the centre portion with twin flaps and the whole raised on ten square section and fluted legs, 112 in (285 cm), extended. **$1,500-2,200**

A Federal mahogany drop-leaf table, the molded top with canted corners and 2 drop leaves above a panelled and veneered skirt, on 4 baluster-turned and acanthus-carved supports, and legs with brass paw feet and casters, restoration to edge of top New York, 1800-1820, 28½in (71cm). **$1,800-2,200**

A fine William IV mahogany extending dining table, with 2 extra leaves, 86 in (188 cm), capable of extending to 118 in (299 cm) but lacking the necessary leaves. **$7,500-10,500**

A Victorian oak extending dining table, the rounded rectangular top with egg-and-dart border on ribbed baluster legs, 210 in (533 cm), including 6 extra leaves. **$2,500-3,500**

A George III mahogany dining table, in 2 sections, including a extra leaf, 71 in (180 cm). **$2,500-3,500**

A George III style mahogany 2 pillar dining table, with brass toe casters, c1900, 83½ in (214 cm). **$3,500-5,000**

A William IV rosewood pedestal dining table, oval top, reeded edge and beaded frieze, 54 in (135 cm). **$2,500-3,500**

A George III mahogany 'D' end twin pedestal dining table, inlaid with boxwood lines, including an extra leaf and 2 heat resistant pads, adapted, 74 in (188 cm). **$2,500-3,500**

A mahogany dining table, including 3 extra leaves, 164 in (416 cm). **$2,500-3,500**

A George IV mahogany extending dining table, 54 in (135 cm). **$1,300-1,700**

A Victorian mahogany extending dining table, on cabriole legs with ball and claw feet, with 3 extra leaves, 120 in (305 cm), extended. **$1,300-1,700**

Tables – Display

A French boulle bijouterie table, the serpentine outline with cherub ormolu shoulders and cabriole legs, 19thC, 31 in (77.5 cm). **$600-900**

A Louis XVI style cherrywood vitrine table, inlaid with boxwood lines and applied with ormolu mounts, 25 in (62.5 cm). **$2,500-3,500**

A Louis XVI Transitional style tulipwood vitrine table, 25½ in (64 cm). **$2,500-3,500**

Tables – Dressing

A George III mahogany and inlaid dressing table, restored, 35 in (87.5 cm). **$800-1,200**

A George III mahogany bow front dressing table, inlaid with satinwood strung borders, with a frieze drawer and an arched apron flanked by 2 short drawers, c1790, 36 in (91.5 cm). **$1,700-2,500**

A fine George III satinwood and rosewood dressing table, the well fitted interior with a mirror and various compartments, the frieze with a false drawer front, 30½ in (77.5 cm). **$8,500-10,000**

A George I walnut veneered dressing table, with later top, 29½ in (74 cm). **$2,500-3,500**

A George III marquetry dressing table, with divided hinged lid inlaid with satinwood ovals and banded with tulipwood, enclosing a later glass-lidded interior, 21 in (53 cm). **$3,500-5,000**

A George III mahogany bow fronted kneehole dressing table, with satinwood strung borders, c1790, 37 in (94 cm). **$2,500-3,500**

A George III mahogany enclosed dressing table, the hinged divided top opening to reveal a rising panel, the front with one long and two short mock drawers, alterations, 33 in (83 cm). **$600-900**

A Queen Anne carved cherrywood dressing table, with molded top above thumb-molded drawers, one carved with 2 half-pinwheels over a deeply scalloped skirt carved with a beaded ogee flanked by geometric molded carving, the sides ogee-shaped, top reset minor repairs to drawer fronts, possible re-carving of the skirt, Eastern Connecticut, 1740-1760, 30½in (76cm) high. **$15,000-18,000**

A Chippendale walnut dressing table, the molded top with shaped corners, above thumb-molded long drawer over 3 short drawers above a scalloped skirt wth scalloped sides, Philadelphia, 35in (87.5cm) wide. **$4,000-5,000**

A Queen Anne birch and pine dressing table, the molded top above 5 drawers, one fan-carved above an elaborately scrolled apron on cabriole legs with pad feet, crack to surface, old small repairs to 3 feet, attributed to the Dunlap Family, New Hampshire, 1740-1760, 37½in (93.5cm) high. **$11,000-13,000**

A Queen Anne cherrywood dressing table, with thumb molded-edge top above one long over 3 short thumb-molded drawers above a scalloped skirt with acorn pendants, 31in (77.5cm) high. **$15,000-18,000**

A Queen Anne cherrywood dressing table, with dished top with cusped corners above a cockbeaded drawer over a scalloped apron, on cabriole legs with pad feet, 28½in (71cm) high. **$1,000-1,200**

A Queen Anne walnut dressing table, the molded top with cusped corners above 4 drawers, one drawer with carved fan above a blocked and shaped skirt on cabriole legs with pad feet, 30in (75cm) high. **$4,000-5,000**

A Chippendale style mahogany dressing table, with molded-edge top above thumb-molded drawers centering an elaborately carved drawer flanked by fluted quarter columns above a shell-carved scalloped skirt, on cabriole legs with acanthus-carved knees and ball-and-claw feet, Philadelphia, 34in (85cm) wide. **$3,000-4,000**

A Chippendale inlaid maple dressing table, the top over one long and 4 short drawers centering a pinwheel inlaid drawer, on cabriole legs with ball and claw feet, formerly the base to a high chest, 38in (95cm) high. **$1,500-1,800**

A kneehole satinwood enclosed dressing table, with geometrical boxwood line inlay, the interior with triple bevelled folding mirror plates and glazed sliding compartments, fitted with a part silver mounted hobnail cut-glass suite, ivory backed brush and manicure set, labelled 'Maple & Co., London, Registered No. 541491' 32 in (80 cm). **$2,500-3,500**

An unusual satinwood dressing table, the hinged divided top opening to reveal an arrangement of compartments, faced with black chinoiserie paper decorated in gilt with sprays of bamboo and waterlilies, 46 in (115 cm). **$1,700-2,500**

An Edwardian satinwood bedroom suite, with oval segmented veneers and kingwood banding and stringing, comprising: a kidney shaped dressing table, 54 in (137 cm); a large wardrobe, 90 in (229 cm); a bow front bedside cupboard, 17 in (43 cm); and a satinwood framed dressing table mirror, c1910. **$1,700-2,500**

An Anglo Dutch corner dressing chest, veneered on oak, the top with a rising central portion with hinged mirror and 3 small wedge shape drawers, 18thC, 36 in (90 cm). **$1,400-1,700**

A walnut kneehole dressing table, in the Queen Anne manner, crossbanded and herringbone inlaid, 19thC, 32 in (80 cm). **$1,700-2,500**

A French kingwood parquetry and ormolu mounted table à ouvrage, the serpentine hinged top enclosing a tulipwood veneered interior with a tray and a mirror panel, indistinctly stencilled 'L' Homme Jeune, Fabricant, Benisteuil..... No. 30', c1880, 25 in (64 cm). **$1,700-2,500**

A Louis XV kingwood poudreuse, quarter veneered and banded, 29 in (72.5 cm). **$1,000-1,400**

A Louis XVI style mahogany and kingwood crossbanded parquetry table à ouvrage, the hinged top revealing a mirror and a drawer with compartments, below is a shallow well, 26 in (66 cm). **$1,400-1,700**

Tables – Dropleaf

A George II oval faded red walnut drop leaf dining table, c1740, 54 in (137 cm). **$1,700-2,500**

A mid Georgian mahogany drop leaf table, on club legs and pad feet, 54½ in (136 cm). **$2,000-3,000**

A mahogany drop leaf table, 18thC, 29 in (72.5 cm). **$1,400-1,700**

Tables – Drum

A George III mahogany drum top table of small size, the crossbanded top inset with a tooled green leather writing surface, c1810, 36 in (90 cm). **$2,500-3,500**

A George III mahogany drum table, with leather lined top and 4 frieze drawers divided by 4 dummy drawers, 35 in (87.5 cm). **$3,500-5,000**

A late George III mahogany drum table, the circular leather lined top with alternate real and dummy drawers, c1800, 39 in (99 cm). **$3,500-5,000**

A William IV mahogany drum table, with 6 real and dummy convex drawers, second quarter of the 19thC, 47 in (117.5 cm). **$1,400-1,700**

A fine Regency mahogany drum table, the circular revolving top inset with green tooled leather, fitted with 4 frieze drawers, 2 fitted angle drawers and 2 dummy drawers, with brass handles, 42 in (105 cm). **$4,500-7,000**

A Victorian drum library table, the revolving top with inset leather panel and the frieze fitted with two deep drawers, 2 smaller drawers and 4 quadrant drawers, 48 in (120 cm). **$1,400-1,700**

Tables – en chiffoniere

A Louis XV kingwood and amaranth table en chiffoniere, with white marble top, mid-18thC, 15 in (37.5 cm). **$1,700-2,500**

A French kingwood and parquetry table en chiffoniere, with oval brass gallery, 2 small drawers, on cabriole supports, with ormolu mounts and sabots and kidney-shaped under platform, 15½ in (38 cm). **$1,000-1,400**

Tables – games

A Directoire mahogany tric-trac table, with rectangular reversible baize lined tray top enclosing a backgammon board with 2 small drawers, 45 in (112.5 cm). **$5,500-7,000**

French kingwood games table, e baize lined swivel folding top th bird, urn and floral arquetry inlays in various oods, 19thC, 24½ in (61 cm). ,400-1,700

A Regency inlaid rosewood fold over top games table, with parquetry border decoration, 35½ in (88 cm). **$3,000-4,500**

Dutch walnut and marquetry ames table, with triangular old-over top, inlaid with a central rn of flowers and trailing owering foliage, late 18thC, 9½ in (100 cm). **$1,400-1,700**

A mahogany games table, crossbanded in rosewood, late 18thC. **$10,500-14,000**

A mahogany framed 'Nina' table, the dished top inlaid with various woods depicting horse racing, on faceted square tapering legs, labelled 'Grands Prix, G. Caro, 8 Rue du Grand Prieux, Paris.' 72 in (183 cm). **$4,500-7,000**

Card tables

★ The commonest 18th century form has the foldover top supported on one back leg hinged to swing out at 90 degrees. Better is the model with both back legs hinged, each opening to 45 degrees from the frame.

★ Best of all is the 'concertina' or folding frame.

★ Popular during the early 19th century and thereafter was the swivel top allowing use of the central column support.

★ The swivel top was also used on French Revival models after 1827, particularly those decorated with Boulle marquetry.

★ 19th century Boulle work, revived in 1815 in London by Le Gaigneur, was thinner than the 18th century original. Can be spotted by the brass being prone to lift and the tortoiseshell to bubble. Presence of this plus a swivel top eliminates 18th century origin. The four flap 'envelope' or bridge table was a development of the Edwardian period Sheraton Revival. The best examples are of rosewood with a degree of fine inlay. In view of comparatively recent age, condition should be excellent to command a high price.

★ Many plain Sheraton period card tables were inlaid during the Edwardian period. To spot, view obliquely against the light; original inlays will conform perfectly with the rest of the surface; new inlay will not, unless completely resurfaced, when shallow colour and high polish will be evidence.

★ All carving to English cabriole legs should stand proud of the outline of the curve; such decoration within the outline indicates recarving.

A George III rosewood games table, the rectangular fold-over top on square tapering supports, c1800, 36 in (90 cm). **$1,400-1,700**

A George III rosewood games table, with reversible slide inlaid for chess and cribbage, opening to reveal a well fitted for backgammon, above a frieze drawer fitted with a writing slide, the sides with candleslides, 18½ in (47 cm). **$4,500-7,000**

A George III fiddle-back mahogany Pembroke games table, the reversible top inlaid with a chessboard, 27½ in (69 cm). **$1,500-2,200**

A late George II/early George I walnut games table, the rectangular top with outset corners, dished inside for counters, 35 in (87.5 cm). **$2,500-3,500**

A George II red walnut triple top tea or games table, c1730, 32 in (80 cm). **$4,500-7,000**

A Damascan fruitwood and inlai games table, inset with mother-of-pearl, 33 in (82.5 cm). **$1,500-2,200**

A Damascan olivewood games table, inlaid with geometric lozenges of mother-of-pearl and various fruitwoods, 35 in (87.5 cm). **$3,000-4,500**

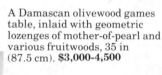

A late Victorian figured walnut games table, stamped 'Bros.', 42 in open (105 cm). **$1,700-2,500**

A Victorian walnut games table, the top with marquetry inlay. **$1,300-1,700**

An ebonised games table, with registration mark for 11th Ma 1882, 23½ in (60 cm). **$400-600**

A Victorian games and work table, in walnut, c1870. **$1,500-2,200**

A Victorian pedestal games table, 24 in (60 cm). **$600-800**

USE THE INDEX!

Because certain items might fit easily into any of a number of categories, the quickest and surest method of locating any entry is by reference to the fully cross-referenced index at the back of the book. This is particularly true this year when certain sections, e.g. Liverpool Porcelain and Oak Furniture have been featured in isolation.

Tables – Library

A George III mahogany library able, the crossbanded top with a oulded edge, the frieze with arewood lines, 55 in (137 cm). **4,500-7,000**

A Regency mahogany drum library table, the top lined in tooled green leather and with 4 real and 4 dummy drawers on a reeded pillar, 44 in (110 cm). **$6,000-8,500**

A Regency mahogany octagonal library table, c1810, 45 in (112.5 cm). **$2,500-3,500**

A George IV brass inlaid rosewood eneered library table, inlaid roughout with simple brass otifs, c1820, 46 in (115 cm). **4,500-7,000**

A rosewood library table, early 19thC, 30 in (75 cm). **$1,200-1,500**

An early Victorian mahogany library table, the top with a lotus leaf carved edge, 59 in (147.5 cm). **$1,400-1,700**

A Victorian rectangular ahogany library table, the top ossbanded with rosewood, 840, 49 in (122.5 cm). **,400-1,700**

A Victorian burr walnut pedestal library table, in the style of Gillow, 52 in (130 cm). **$4,000-5,000**

A Victorian mahogany library table, in the Gothic taste, 50 in (127 cm). **$2,500-3,500**

Tables – Loo

A Victorian oval walnut loo table, crossbanded in bird's-eye maple, 47 in (117.5 cm). **$600-900**

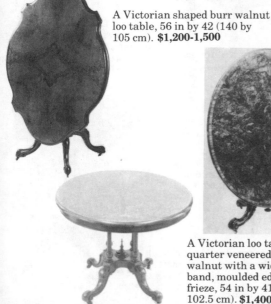

A Victorian shaped burr walnut loo table, 56 in by 42 (140 by 105 cm). **$1,200-1,500**

A Victorian loo table, the top quarter veneered in figured walnut with a wide tulipwood band, moulded edge and wavy frieze, 54 in by 41 in (135 by 102.5 cm). **$1,400-1,700**

A Victorian walnut oval snap-top loo table, 48 in (120 cm). **$800-1,200**

MAKE THE MOST OF MILLER'S

Every care has been taken to ensure the accuracy of descriptions and estimated valuations. Price ranges in this book reflect what one should expect to pay for a similar example. When selling one can obviously expect a figure below. This will fluctuate according to a dealer's stock, saleability at a particular time, etc. It is always advisable to approach a reputable specialist dealer or an auction house which has specialist sales.

Tables – Nest of

A set of 3 George IV rosewood quartetto tables, labelled 'W. Constantine & Company, Leeds.' 22 in (55 cm). **$1,300-1,700**

A set of 4 mahogany, satinwood and rosewood quartetto tables, with crossbanded tops, from 12 in (30 cm) to 19 in (47.5 cm). **$4,500-7,000**

A set of 4 William IV rosewood quartetto tables, 19 in (47.5 cm). **$1,700-2,500**

A set of William IV rosewood quartetto tables, possibly French, c1835, 22 in (55 cm). **$2,500-3,500**

A quartetto of George III style mahogany tables, late 19thC/early 20thC the largest 29 in (72.5 cm). **$1,300-1,700**

A set of 4 George III style satinwood quartetto tables, each with an ebonised rimmed and tulipwood banded rectangular to with a painted central oval, on simulated bamboo twin column end standards, 20 in (50 cm). **$1,700-2,500**

Tables – Occasional

A George III satinwood occasional table, the oval top inlaid with scrolling foliate arabesques with central harewood panel, 23 in (57.5 cm). **$3,500-5,000**

A George II mahogany occasional table, the rectangular tray top with carrying handles above one frieze drawer, 20 in (51 cm). **$14,000-17,000**

A pair of Georgian satinwood occasional tables, with oval tops and plain friezes edged with chequered lines on tapering legs 20½ in (52 cm). **$1,700-2,500**

A George IV rosewood table, the rectangular top with rounded corners and scrollwork trestle supports, c1820, 31½ in (80 cm). **$1,000-1,400**

A Regency rosewood occasional table, the grey and pink mottled marble top with pierced brass three-quarter gallery above a drawer inlaid with brass stringing, 18 in (44 cm). **$4,500-7,000**

A tulipwood table, the crossbanded top veneered in segments and centred by a Sèvres-type plaque, with gilt brass mounts throughout, c1850, 8 in (45 cm). **$1,500-2,200**

n occasional table, inlaid in arious woods, 21 in (52.5 cm). 00-700

n Edwardian mahogany table, th line inlay on kick out feet, in (60 cm). **$100-200**

Louis XVI style rosewood and arquetry table de lit, inlaid with oral bouquets, with a brass allery, 19 in (47.5 cm). 1,500-2,200

A small kidney shaped walnut table, inlaid with satinwood marquetry, c1850, 26 in (65 cm). **$600-700**

A Victorian Chippendale style mahogany lamp table, c1860. **$600-700**

A Victorian rosewood table, 48 in (120 cm). **$700-900**

An Edwardian mahogany kidney shaped table, with satinwood line inlay on kick out feet, 27 in (67.5 cm). **$200-300**

A Victorian walnut revolving occasional table, with original candle holder, c1860, 20 in (50 cm). **$700-1,000**

A walnut, rosewood and satinwood drop table, in the French manner, c1880, 41 in (102.5 cm), extended. **$1,500-2,200**

A Louis Phillipe mahogany and kingwood table à rognon, with gilt metal mounts, 30 in (76 cm). **$1,700-2,500**

A French table, with coloured marble top fitted with a shallow frieze drawer and applied gilt ormolu mounts, 19thC, 24 in (60 cm). **$800-1,200**

379

A George III mahogany pedestal table, 29 in (72.5 cm).
$1,200-1,500

Tables – Pedestal

A mid Georgian mahogany pedestal table, 31 in (77.5 cm).
$600-800

A Regency simulated rosewood and parcel gilt pedestal table, the top inset with grey marble, labelled 'COLE, Carver and Gilder, print seller, 273 High Street, Exeter', 21 in (52.5 cm).
$1,200-1,500

A William IV ebonised and parcel gilt pietra dura pedestal table, the top inlaid with coloured stones, within a broad slate border, mid 19thC, 29 in (74 cm).
$1,300-1,700

A mahogany pedestal table, the tilt top with pie-crust borders mounted on a bird cage and fluted tapering column, late 18thC, 28 in (70 cm). **$1,300-1,700**

A pair of Indo-Portuguese ebony pedestal tables, each with an ivory and wood specimen segmented top inlaid with chevrons and geometric white metal lines, mid 19thC, 23½ in (58 cm).
$3,000-4,500

A Victorian papier mâché and ebonised pedestal table, the tilt top decorated with a harbour scene, inlaid with mother-of-pearl, 26 in (65 cm).
$1,500-2,200

A George III satinwood and tulipwood crossbanded Pembroke table, containing a drawer in the frieze, on square legs headed with oval paterae, 38½ in (96 cm).
$7,000-9,000

A George III mahogany Pembroke table, with rounded rectangular twin flap top and frieze drawer on chamfered square legs joined by a pierced X-shaped stretcher, one leg spliced, 39 in (99 cm).
$2,000-3,000

Tables – Pembroke

A George III mahogany and rosewood crossbanded Pembroke table, c1810, 32½ in (83 cm).
$1,500-2,200

A George III rosewood and mahogany Pembroke reading table, with a central circular marquetry panel, with ribbon tied swags in ebony, box and fruitwood, 43 in (108 cm).
$2,000-3,000

A George III mahogany Pembroke
table, brass drop handles, on
square taper legs with brass
terminals and casters, 32 in
(80 cm). **$1,200-1,500**

A George III satinwood Pembroke
table, the oval twin flap top
crossbanded in rosewood with one
frieze drawer, on square tapering
legs, 38 in (96.5 cm), open.
$7,000-9,000

A George III mahogany Pembroke
table, the twin flap top
crossbanded with rosewood and
satinwood, 39 in (99.5 cm).
$2,000-3,000

A George III mahogany Pembroke
table, with two-flap top with a
wide satinwood band outline with
stringing, inlaid with stringing
and headed by oval panels and
ending in brass casters, 41½ in
(105 cm). **$4,500-7,000**

A mid Georgian mahogany
Pembroke table, 24 in (60 cm).
$2,000-3,000

A George III mahogany Pembroke
table, the crossframe stretchers
centred by wheel shaped panel,
c1800, 33 in (84 cm).
$1,200-1,500

A George III mahogany and
satinwood Pembroke table, the
crossbanded oval twin flap top
inlaid with trailing flowerheads,
37 in (94 cm). **$14,000-17,000**

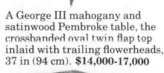

George III painted satinwood
Pembroke table, distressed,
1785, 40½ in (101 cm).
10,000-13,000

A George III mahogany Pembroke
table, 35½ in (90 cm), extended.
$1,200-1,500

A George III satinwood Pembroke
table, the twin flap top
crossbanded in mahogany and
later painted with a band of ribbon
tied peacock feathers, 37½ in
(95 cm), open. **$14,000-17,000**

Regency brass and ebony inlaid
mahogany Pembroke table, with a
burr wood veneered drawer and a
pair of flat pilasters with sabre
legs, c1805, 40½ in (103 cm).
4,500-7,000

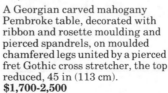

A Georgian carved mahogany
Pembroke table, decorated with
ribbon and rosette moulding and
pierced spandrels, on moulded
chamfered legs united by a pierced
fret Gothic cross stretcher, the top
reduced, 45 in (113 cm).
$1,700-2,500

A fine Federal inlaid mahogany Pembroke table, the top with 2 drop leaves above a line-inlaid skirt with a single drawer flanked by bookend inlay, on legs with icicle inlay, line inlay and inlaid cuffs, attributed to the Townsend or Goddard Shops, Newport, Rhode Island, 1785-1810, 27½in (68.5cm) high. **$34,000-38,000**

A Federal inlaid mahogany Pembroke table, the top with 2 drop leaves above a bowed skirt with a single drawer flanked by stiles with bookend inlay, restorations to inlay and possibly to leaves, New England, 1790 - 1810, 29in (72.5cm) high. **$2,000-2,500**

A Federal inlaid mahogany Pembroke table, the top with 2 drop leaves above a line-inlaid skirt with one cockbeaded drawer, cuffs, interior restorations, American, 1790-1810, 28½in (71cm) high. **$650-750**

A Federal inlaid mahogany Pembroke table, with 2 drop leaves above a thumb-molded drawer, on square tapering legs with inlaid cuffs, repair to top, American, 1790-1810, 28½in (71cm) high. **$900-1,000**

A pair of Federal inlaid mahogany Pembroke tables, each with an oval top with 2 drop leaves and a triple line-inlaid border above a bowed skirt with a drawer centering on oval veneer panel, surrounded by triple line-inlay and flanked by inlaid paterea on each stile, one table with top edge slightly chamfered, New York, 1790-1810, 29in (72.5cm) high. **$23,000-26,000**

George III mahogany Pembroke
ble, broadly crossbanded in
atinwood, on square tapered legs
laid with satinwood panels,
0½ in (76 cm).
1,500-2,200

Sheraton mahogany Pembroke
ble, the figured top with a
rrow mahogany crossbanding
d boxwood line inlay, late
thC, 31 in (77.5 cm).
,200-1,500

ate George III satinwood
mbroke table, inlaid with
wood and ebony lines, the top
ssbanded with kingwood, 43 in
7.5 cm). $5,500-7,000

satinwood pier table, with
molu bordered top decorated
d inlaid later with foliate scrolls
d paterae, 40 in (101 cm).
,000-3,000

A good George III mahogany
Pembroke table, the top with
rounded rectangular leaves and
crossbanded in satinwood and
kingwood, above a frieze drawer
inlaid with geometric ebony
stringing, 35 in (88 cm).
$800-1,200

A Georgian mahogany pedestal
Pembroke table, having a
satinwood crossbanded top and
boxwood stringing.
$1,000-1,400

A mahogany pedestal Pembroke
table, 19thC, 36 in (90 cm).
$500-600

Tables – Pier

A George II mahogany pier table,
with later marble top, now fitted
with a side drawer, 45½ in
(114 cm). **$4,500-5,000**

A George III mahogany Pembroke
table, by Gillows of Lancaster, the
top with canted corners and
crossbanded in satinwood, banded
in ebony and with square tapering
legs inlaid with boxwood
stringing, c1795, 40 in (101 cm).
$4,500-5,000

A George III mahogany Pembroke
table, inlaid with chequered
boxwood lines, with crossbanded
folding oval top, 33 in (82.5 cm).
$1,300-1,700

A small Edwardian satinwood
Pembroke table, painted with
garlands of flowers and ribbons,
27 in (67.5 cm). **$1,300-1,700**

A Dutch mahogany and
marquetry pier table, 26½ in
(67 cm). **$1,000-1,200**

A Regency ormolu mounted pier
table, with white marble top,
57½ in (146 cm). **$2,500-3,500**

A pair of George III pine pier tables, the Vitruvian scroll frieze centred by a mask and floral swags, formerly gilt, tops modern restored, c1730, 70 in (178 cm). **$8,500-11,000**

A French Empire walnut pier table, with gilt metal and engine turned mounts, the top Italian, in parquetry specimen marble, c1810, 36 in (92 cm). **$8,500-11,000**

Tables – Reading

A Regency brass inlaid rosewood veneered library book table, the top and sides inlaid with brass stringing, 24 in (60 cm). **$4,000-5,000**

A George III mahogany drawing room reading or writing table, c1800, 24 in (60 cm). **$4,500-7,000**

An early George III mahogany reading table, 28 in (71 cm). **$10,000-13,000**

Tables – Serving

A pair of Regency mahogany serving tables, by Gillows of Lancaster, on foliate ribbed tapering legs, one stamped 'Gillows Lancaster', 76 in (193 cm). **$8,500-11,000**

A George III mahogany and crossbanded breakfront serving table, 57 in (142.5 cm). **$1,300-1,700**

◄ A Regency mahogany serving table, the top reduced at the back with 3 panelled frieze drawers, 77½ in (197 cm). **$14,000-17,000**

A George III mahogany serving table, with serpentine top, formerly with a gallery, 107½ in (272 cm). **$4,500-7,000**

A Regency mahogany serving table, 90 in (225 cm). **$1,300-1,700**

Tables – Side

A Victorian mahogany three-tier dinner wagon, 47 in (117.5 cm). **$300-500**

A George I Anglo Dutch walnut side table, the serpentine cross- and feather-banded top above 2 conforming drawers and shaped apron, on cabriole legs with pad feet, c1720, 32 in (81 cm). **$7,500-10,500**

A George I giltwood and gesso side able, c1725, possibly Irish, 39 in 97.5 cm). **$5,500-7,000**

A pair of George II mahogany side tables, the later tops crossbanded with walnut, 44½ in (113 cm). **$1,400-1,700**

pair of George II mahogany side ables, in the manner of Gillows, ancaster, shaped aprons fitted ith 3 drawers and centred by pplied carved scallop shell, 32 in 1 cm). **$22,500-25,500**

An unusual mid Georgian walnut side table, with lappeted knees terminating in club feet, c1750. **$5,500-7,000**

A George II later white painted and carved side table, in the manner of William Kent, having an egg-and-dart edge and frieze decorated in relief with Vitruvian scrolls centred by a pierced foliate scroll cartouche, 55 in (138 cm). **$10,500-14,000**

A late George II mahogany side table, with yellow veined black marble top, the frieze edged with ribbon ornament, 44 in (110 cm). **$10,500-14,000**

n early Georgian mahogany side ble, 33½ in (83 cm). ,500-2,200

A George III satinwood, rosewood and marquetry side table, with crossbanded serpentine top inlaid with an oval centred by a rosette framed by trellis and rosette pattern parquetry, 30½ in (75 cm). **$22,500-25,500**

pair of Georgian decorated alf-round side tables, in the truscan taste', ebonised and ainted en grisaille with gilt, 48 in 21 cm). **$6,000-8,000**

A black and gilt lacquered side table, 43½ in (108 cm). **$1,500-2,200**

A George III mahogany side table, 58 in (145 cm). **$3,500-5,000**

A pair of Regency mahogany marble topped side tables, the friezes with brass stringing at the front, probably Irish, one with marble broken, c1820, 69 in (176 cm). **$9,000-13,000**

An early George III mahogany side table, the crossbanded top veneered in triangles and with canted corners, c1765, 69 in (176 cm). **$9,000-13,000**

A Regency rosewood side table, with brass line inlaid top, one piece of veneer missing, 42 in (105 cm). **$1,300-1,700**

A Dutch marquetry side table, inlaid overall with flowers and birds and butterflies, 19thC, 32 in (81 cm). **$1,500-2,200**

A grained and parcel gilt hall table, of early Georgian style, with massive black fossil marble top, traces of gilding, second quarter 19thC, 96 in (244 cm). **$10,500-14,000**

A George II style mahogany side table, with rectangular verde antico marble slab above a vitruvian scroll carved frieze, 50 in (125 cm). **$2,500-3,500**

A Victorian amboyna table. **$1,500-2,200**

A French Empire mahogany side table, with black marble top, the front supports with cast metal female head terminals tapering to feet, 39 in (99 cm). **$1,500-2,200**

An Italian ebonised walnut and marquetry side table, the top inlaid with strapwork above 2 frieze drawers. **$6,000-8,000**

A North Italian walnut side table, the shaped bow top crossbanded with rope twist carved edge above a guilloche carved frieze, centred by an oval medallion with a classical portrait bust, on turned and fluted tapered legs headed by carved patera panels, late 18thC, 56 in (141 cm). **$1,500-2,200**

A Portuguese rosewood side table, the pierced apron carved with foliage and rockwork, on cabriole legs headed by cartouche clasps and claw-and-ball feet, mid-18thC, 43 in (109 cm). **$9,000-13,000**

Tables – Silver

A mahogany silver or centre table, possibly Cork, c1740, 31 in (79 cm). **$3,000-4,000**

A mahogany silver table, of George III style, with pierced rectangular tray top, the frieze carved with geometric blind fretwork on pierced divided legs, 29 in (73 cm). **$5,500-7,000**

MAKE THE MOST OF MILLER'S

Every care has been taken to ensure the accuracy of descriptions and estimated valuations. Where an attribution is made within inverted commas (e.g. 'Chippendale') or is followed by the word 'style' (e.g. early Georgian style) it is intended to convey that, in the opinion of the publishers, the piece concerned is a later – though probably still antique – reproduction of the style so designated. Unless otherwise stated, any description which refers to 'a set', or 'a pair' includes a valuation for the entire set or the pair, even though the illustration may show only a single item.

Tables – Sofa

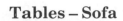

A George III rosewood and
crossbanded sofa table, inlaid with
satinwood stringing, c1800, 35 in
(88 cm), when closed.
3,000-4,500

A small George III mahogany
ship's sofa table, the top
crossbanded in satinwood, above a
pair of frieze drawers inlaid with
sectionalised Greek key pattern
stringing, c1800, 40 in (101 cm),
open. **$4,500-7,000**

A late George III mahogany sofa
table, the drawers edged in ebony
and downswept trestle supports
with ebony stringing and brass
casters, c1805, 56 in (140 cm),
open. **$8,500-10,500**

A Regency satinwood veneered
sofa table, crossbanded in
kingwood with rounded corners,
1810, 59½ in (152 cm).
$7,500-10,500

A Regency rosewood and
satinwood inlaid sofa table, 60 in
(150 cm), open. **$7,000-9,000**

An amboyna small sofa table,
painted in the style of Angelica
Kauffman, early 19thC, 36 in
(90 cm). **$4,500-7,000**

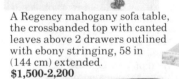

Regency mahogany sofa table,
2½ in (159 cm), open.
2,500-3,500

A Regency mahogany sofa table,
the crossbanded top with canted
leaves above 2 drawers outlined
with ebony stringing, 58 in
(144 cm) extended.
$1,500-2,200

A Regency brass inlaid ebony and
pollard oak sofa table, in the
manner of George Bullock, the
chamfered twin flap inlaid with a
foliate border, 69 in (175 cm),
open. **$14,000-17,000**

Regency rosewood sofa table,
inlaid with brass lines and foliate
motifs, 60 in (150 cm).
5,500-7,000

A mahogany sofa table, the
crossbanded folding top with 2
frieze drawers, on turned tapering
end standards, the reeded down
curved legs with foliate brass
block feet, part 19thC, 37 in
(92.5 cm). **$4,500-5,000**

A Regency mahogany sofa table,
with fall ends, broad crossbanded
borders with boxwood and ebony
stringing, on twin bamboo pattern
columns and stretcher on reeded
cheval feet, brass paw terminals
and casters, 64 in (163 cm).
$6,000-8,000

A Regency rosewood sofa table,
with twin flap top inlaid in
satinwood, with a band of
bellflowers, 58½ in (148 cm),
open. **$4,500-5,000**

A Regency faded rosewood and mahogany sofa table, with crossbanded twin flap top, the frame possibly later, 59 in (150 cm), open. **$3,500-5,000**

A Regency rosewood sofa table, the rounded rectangular twin flap top with 2 ebonised and beaded panelled frieze drawers, 58 in (145 cm). **$4,500-5,000**

A Regency rosewood sofa table, with 'D' end leaves and beaded edging, 57 in (142 cm). **$2,000-3,000**

A Regency mahogany sofa table, 66 in (168 cm) open. **$5,500-7,000**

A Regency rosewood sofa table, with rounded rectangular twin flap top inlaid with a broad band of cut brass, fitted with a cedar lined drawer each side, 60 in (152.5 cm) open. **$7,000-9,000**

A Regency brass inlaid rosewood sofa table, 36 in (90 cm). **$1,300-1,700**

A Regency sofa table in rosewood some damage. **$15,000-20,500**

A Regency rosewood sofa table, the top crossbanded with pollard oak, the frieze with 2 cedar lined drawers, with later stretcher, 51 in (130 cm). **$7,500-10,500**

A William IV sofa table, veneered in faded figured rosewood with satinwood banding, 36 in (90 cm) closed. **$1,300-1,700**

A George IV carved rosewood sofa table, with bead moulded borders. c1825, 37 in (94 cm) closed. **$2,000-3,000**

A William IV small rosewood sofa table, with rope moulded top, a pair of bead moulded drawers, c1830, 54 in (137 cm). **$2,000-3,000**

A William IV faded mahogany sofa table, 37 in (92.5 cm). **$3,000-4,500**

Tables – Sutherlan

A George III mahogany Sutherland table, 35 in (87.5 cr open. **$1,300-1,700**

A burr walnut Sutherland table, early 19thC, 36 in (90 cm). **$800-1,200**

Tables – Tea

George III mahogany tea table, Hepplewhite style, the knuckle int defective and replaced with etal hinge, c1775, 37 in (93 cm) en. **$400-600**

mahogany fold-over emi-circular tea table, on abriole legs, 18thC, 33 in 2.5 cm). **$500-600**

pair of Regency mahogany tea ables, with rounded folding tops laid with lines, 36 in (90 cm). 5,500-7,000

William IV rosewood tea table, 6 in (90 cm). **$1,300-1,700**

A Georgian inlaid mahogany folding tea table, crossbanded to the top and with swivel action opening to tea table. **$1,500-2,200**

A mahogany pillar tea table, with piecrust rim and birdcage support, 18thC, 24 in (60 cm). **$8,500-10,000**

A William IV rosewood tea table, 36 in (90 cm). **$400-600**

A mahogany rosewood banded 'D' shaped fold-over swivel-top tea table, 1820-1830. **$1,000-1,400**

A William IV tea table, with fold-over swivel top, the front fitted with 3 drawers edged with ebony and on trestle supports, probably padoukwood, 44½ in (110 cm). **$1,700-2,500**

A Sheraton period mahogany and line inlaid tea table, 36 in (90 cm). **$1,200-1,500**

A late Chippendale period oblong folding tea table, with carved frieze, 32 in (80 cm). **$800-1,200**

A George IV mahogany tea table, Scottish, second quarter of the 19thC, 36 in (91.5 cm). **$1,300-1,700**

Tables – Tip Top

A Georgian mahogany table, 30 in (75 cm). **$600-700**

A figured mahogany tip-top table, with moulded edge and shaped frieze, early 19thC, 42 in (105 cm). **$1,200-1,500**

Tables – Tray

A mahogany butler's tray, on later stand, 19thC, 26 in (65 cm). **$400-600**

A pair of mahogany tray-top tables, each with waved crossbanded chamfered top inlaid with a musical trophy, 24 in (60 cm). **$3,000-4,000**

Tables – Tripod

A good George II mahogany tripod table, with birdcage support and a solid, tapering ringed columnar support, c1755, 39 in (97.5 cm). **$3,500-5,000**

An early George III mahogany tripod table, with tip-up pie-crust top, open birdcage and spreading fluted shaft, 33 in (84 cm). **$5,500-7,000**

A mid-Georgian mahogany tray top tripod table, c1770. **$7,000-9,000**

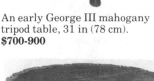

An early George III mahogany tripod table, 31 in (78 cm). **$700-900**

A mahogany tripod table, the waved circular top with pierced fretwork gallery, 27 in (67.5 cm). **$3,000-4,000**

A George III mahogany tripod table, the circular tip-up top with later pierced gallery, 29 in (73 cm) **$5,500-7,000**

A George III mahogany tripod table, with waved tray top, the fluted shaft carved with foliage and spiral turning on tripartite base, 11 in (28 cm). **$7,000-9,000**

A George III mahogany pie-crust bird cage table, the later tilt-top above a baluster pillar and tripod supports, c1760, 29 in (73 cm). **$1,300-1,700**

A Chippendale walnut tilt-top candlestand, on arched cabriole legs with shod slipper feet, plugs to 2 cleats missing, New England, 1760-1780, 29in (72.5cm) high. **$1,800-2,200**

A Chippendale mahogany tilt-top tea table, Massachusetts, 1760-1780, 27in (67.5cm) high. **$1,000-1,200**

A Federal mahogany tilt-top tea table, Massachusetts, 1790-1810, 28in (70cm) high. **$800-1,000**

A Federal mahogany stand, New England, 1800-1815, 27in (67.5cm) high. **$600-700**

A Chippendale mahogany birdcage tea table, the top tilting above a birdcage with baluster supports over a baluster-turned pedestal with a fluted base, now on casters, the 2-board top reglued, Pennsylvania, 1760-1780, 27½in (68.5cm) high. **$1,800-2,200**

A Chippendale carved mahogany scallop-top tea table, with scalloped edge top tilting and revolving above a birdcage support between shaped maple cleats over a baluster-turned pedestal, on acanthus and flower carved tripod cabriole legs with shod pad feet, crack in top, New York or Connecticut, 1770-1800, 29in (72.5cm) high. **$18,000-20,000**

Two similar Federal mahogany stands, each with oval top tilting above a tapering columnar and urn-turned pedestal, on 3 arched square, tapering legs with spade feet, Massachusetts, 1790-1810, 27½in (68.5cm) high. **$4,700-5,000**

A George III red walnut tripod table, 11 in (28 cm). **$1,400-1,700**

A George III mahogany tea table, with birdcage swivelling mount on baluster column and tripod pad feet, 30 in (75 cm). **$600-700**

A George III mahogany tripod table, 26 in (65 cm). **$700-900**

A Regency tripod table, the tip-up top with slightly raised and moulded edge, 31 in (78 cm). **$1,500-2,200**

A Regency rosewood tripod table, 23½ in (60 cm). **$1,700-2,500**

A pair of William IV burr walnut and oak tripod tables, 17 in (42.5 cm). **$6,000-8,000**

A walnut tripod table, the top with a wavy border on a pierced stem and downswept supports, 26 in (65 cm). **$1,000-1,200**

A mahogany snap-top table, 19thC. **$300-400**

A mahogany table, 19thC. **$80-150**

A Louis XVI mahogany gueridon, with ormolu bordered circular white marble top, 31 in (78 cm). **$3,500-5,000**

Tables – Wake

An Irish George III mahogany wake table, with twin flap top, gateleg action, shell and foliate cabriole legs on claw-and-ball feet, 89 in (226 cm). **$14,000-17,000**

Tables – Wine

A mahogany wine table, having a reeded border, 18thC, 18½ in (46 cm). **$700-900**

A late Regency mahogany drinking table, with brass backrail and hinged flaps with later adjustable paddle, with two later coasters, the casters stamped 'Copes Patent', 72 in (183 cm). **$4,500-7,000**

A mahogany wine table, c1900, 12 in (30 cm). **$150-200**

Tables – Work

A George III amboyna work table, in the French taste, with a rising screen lined with 19th century Chinese embroidered silk, fitted with a leather lined slide and a drawer at the side, 17 in (43 cm). **5,500-7,000**

A Sheraton period rosewood and inlaid combined work and writing table, with a pull-out screen, 2 slides, a drawer, and a pouch, a few pieces of veneer missing, 14½ in (36 cm). **$3,000-4,500**

A late Federal mahogany sewing table, the top above 2 narrow drawers over a pleated and striped silk work bag, acanthus-carved and spirally-reeded turned tapering legs with ball feet, Salem, Massachusetts, 1810-1820, 28in (70cm) high. **$1,000-1,200**

late George III mahogany work ble, 19½ in (49 cm). **1,200-1,500**

A rosewood work table, with panelled mirror frieze, with gilt metal winged claw feet, early 19thC, 19 in (48 cm). **$2,000-3,000**

A late Regency rosewood work table, 21 in (53 cm). **$1,400-1,700**

A Regency rosewood and coromandel crossbanded combined games and work table, inlaid with brass stringing, 2 pen drawers and a reversible section with chessboard inset, 24 in (61 cm) when closed. **$2,000-3,000**

A Federal mahogany work table, the astragal-end hinged top with reeded edge opening to a 4 compartment tray flanked by deep demi-lune compartments, Philadelphia, 1800-1815, 26½in (66cm) high. **$2,200-2,800**

A Federal mahogany sewing table, with hinged, molded-edge oblong top opening to a centre well flanked by 2 candleslides over 2 deep wells, bears an old repair label on underside: 'C.F. Meiser-/19 sey St. Bost/Fine Furniture/and Artistic Decoration', New York or Boston, 1800-1815, 29in (72.5cm) high. **$3,500-4,000**

A fine Empire mahogany work table, with 2 drop leaves with rounded corners above fitted drawers, with hinged work surface above a sliding frame for a workbag, on a trestle base with acanthus-carved lyre-shaped supports, attributed to Rufus Pierce, Boston, 1820-1830, 28in (70cm) high. **$2,600-3,000**

A late Federal mahogany worktable, the top with outset-rounded corners and a double bead-molded edge above veneered and cockbeaded drawers flanked by leaf-carved colonettes above ring-turned and reeded tapering cylindrical legs, Salem, Massachusetts, 1800-1820, 31in (77.5cm) high. **$2,500-3,000**

A Federal mahogany and birch veneer work table, the top above fitted birch veneer drawers flanked by reeded outset three quarter columns over a pedestal of 4 urn- and baluster-turned columns over a rectangular base, on 4 water leaf and incised vine-carved legs with carved paw feet, Massachusetts, 1790-1815, 30½in (76cm) high. **$1,300-1,600**

Peter Semus Antiques

Just 3 miles to the west of Brighton, Sussex are the warehouses of Peter Semus. A wide range of stock is carried along with the following services.

- **CONTAINER SALES SERVICE:** Full container loads to any destination: merchandise can be either totally refinished or just clean.

- **CUSTOM FURNITURE MAKING:** Conversion furniture such as Bureau Bookcases, Breakfront Bookcases, Desks, Chests, Cabinets. Individual "One off" items undertaken.

- **INDIVIDUAL SALES:** There is no obligation to buy entire shipments; customers for one or two pieces are very welcome.

- **REFINISHING SERVICE:** Any item bought here can be restored in our own extensive workshops. Loose leathers for desk tops available.

- **LONDON AND SOUTHERN SHIPPING:**
  This separate division specialises in Overseas Packing and Shipping; collections made anywhere nationwide; one piece or whole container; Antiques or Household.

Please give Peter the chance to discuss your exact requirements so hopefully the best all round package can be put together for you.

Contact Peter at the Warehouse, Gladstone Road, Portslade Sussex BN4 1LJ
Showroom address: 379 The Kingsway, Hove, Sussex, England
Telephone 011442 73 420154

A late Regency mahogany pedestal work table, inlaid with ebonised lines, 21 in (53 cm). **$1,000-1,400**

A Regency mahogany pedestal work table, inlaid with ebonised lines, with simulated drawer frieze, the reverse with a brushing slide and 2 small drawers, 16 in (40 cm). **$1,300-1,700**

An Anglo Indian rosewood work table, early 19thC, 30 in (75 cm). **$600-800**

A Regency Tunbridge-ware work table, inlaid with a central cube pattern within a wide kingwood border and 'Vandyke' pattern outer border in various woods, and with fitted interior, legs cut, c1825, 15 in (38 cm). **$2,000-3,000**

A late Regency rosewood games/work table, the top inlaid with backgammon and cribbage boards, c1830, 22 in (55 cm). **$800-1,200**

A William IV mahogany work table, stamped 'James Winter, 101 Wardour Street', 24 in (60 cm). **$800-1,200**

A Victorian inlaid walnut work and games table, requiring restoration, 24 in (60 cm). **$800-1,200**

l. A Victorian walnut work table, the stand with quadruple cabriole supports joined by a stretcher. **$600-700**
r. A William IV drop flap work table, in rosewood with satin clad needlework drawer. **$800-1,200**

An early Victorian rosewood games/work table, the hinged swivel top inlaid with a chessboard, 21 in (53 cm). **$500-600**

A papier mâché and mother-of-pearl work table, the top opening to reveal a fitted interior, inlaid throughout with mother-of-pearl designs and gilt lines, silk bag perished, mid 19thC, 18 in (45 cm). **$800-1,200**

A marquetry and brass mounted ladies work table, with a fitted interior, with mirror, 19thC, 21 in (53 cm). **$300-400**

A rare olivewood work table, mid 19thC, 19 in (47.5 cm). **$2,000-3,000**

A Victorian walnut games/work table, 16 in (40 cm). **$1,000-1,400**

A carved oak Victorian work table, 20 in (50 cm). **$500-600**

A Georgian style mahogany sewing table, late 19thC, 14 in (35 cm). **$300-500**

A late Victorian walnut chess-top work table, the lid lifting to reveal a fitted interior, 17 in (42.5 cm). **$300-500**

A French marquetry and ormolu drum work table, 19thC. **$1,700-2,500**

A French boulle and ebonised work table, the interior with a mirror and rosewood tray above a rosewood veneered well, the apron with a shallow sliding well, c1870, 23½ in (60 cm). **$1,000-1,200**

Tables – Writing

A George II mahogany partners writing table, possibly Irish, 75 in (190 cm). **$3,500-5,000**

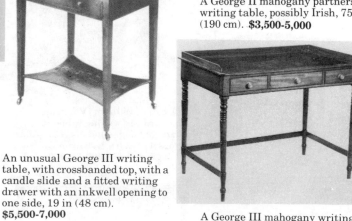

A late George III mahogany double sided writing table, altered, c1780, 54 in (137 cm). **$6,000-8,000**

An unusual George III writing table, with crossbanded top, with a candle slide and a fitted writing drawer with an inkwell opening to one side, 19 in (48 cm). **$5,500-7,000**

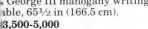

A George III mahogany writing table, 65½ in (166.5 cm). **$3,500-5,000**

A George III mahogany writing table, in the manner of Gillows of Lancaster, with ebonised strung borders, c1800, 42 in (105 cm). **$1,000-1,200**

A George III mahogany partners writing table, the ends fitted with 2 slides above a central frieze drawer, 49 in (122 cm).
$16,500-22,500

A Regency mahogany writing table, with pencil inscription underneath 'this table was made by Chippendale and Haigh. It was in the library at Ashburnham Park, Sussex and was part of a suite of writing tables, reading tables, etc. sold by Lady Catherine Ashburnham', 48 in (122 cm).
$5,500-7,000

A Regency mahogany writing table, with crossbanded top framed by boxwood lines, 38 in (95 cm). **$6,000-8,000**

A mahogany partners writing table, very early 19thC.
$7,500-10,500

A mahogany writing table, with an inlaid boxwood frieze fitted with 6 small drawers, early 19thC, 53½ in (133 cm).
$5,500-7,000

A Regency parcel gilt and pollard oak writing table, the rectangular top with re-entrant corners, the pierced trestle ends with turned shaped spindles, 44 in (110 cm).
$14,000-17,000

A Regency rosewood writing table, in the manner of John McClean, with crossbanded top above 2 slides and a fitted drawer, 19 in (48 cm). **$4,500-7,000**

A pair of William IV oak and pollard oak writing tables, the crossbanded rounded rectangular tops with 2 frieze drawers, 57 in (142.5 cm). **$10,000-13,000**

A Regency mahogany rent table, with a secretaire fitted with a hinged writing slide, revealing alphabetically labelled lidded compartments and a pair of secret drawers, 43 in (109 cm).
$1,300-1,700

A pair of Regency pollard oak writing tables, with crossbanded tops, on scrolled solid trestle ends, joined by platform stretchers, 48 in (122 cm). **$7,000-9,000**

A Regency rosewood writing table, 37 in (93 cm).
$14,000-17,000

A Regency mahogany writing table, in the manner of Gillows of Lancaster, the eared crossbanded top with recessed centre, 60 in (150 cm). **$5,500-7,000**

A William IV rosewood writing table, inlaid with a panel of specimen marbles including porphyry, onyx and alabaster, 56 in (142 cm).
$7,500-10,500

A pollard oak writing table, 1830's, 54 in (135 cm). $1,300-1,700

A mahogany writing table, of Chippendale style, 19thC, 54 in (135 cm). $2,500-3,500

A walnut writing table, mid-19thC, 39 in (98 cm). $1,700-2,500

A Victorian walnut and marquetry writing table, the shaped kingwood crossbanded top inlaid with bulrushes and trellis panels in various stained woods, 2 in (81 cm). $3,000-4,000

A walnut writing table, in the French taste, inlaid with floral marquetry borders, mid 19thC, 47½ in (118 cm). $2,500-3,500

A Victorian ormolu mounted ebony, kingwood and burr-yew bureau plat, the top inlaid with foliate strapwork with a frieze drawer, 54 in (107 cm). $5,500-7,000

A Victorian figured walnut writing table, in the Louis XV style, 34 in (85 cm). $1,200-1,500

A Victorian burr walnut writing table, the inlaid marquetry and inset leather lined curvilinear top with flowered lunette borders centering an octagonal lidded casket pen compartment, 48 in (120 cm). $1,200-1,500

A Victorian ormolu mounted walnut and kingwood writing table, of Louis XV style, 38½ in (98 cm). $1,500-2,200

A late Victorian kingwood writing table, in the Louis XVI style, inlaid with parquetry panels, rosewood bands and boxwood lines, 43 in (107.5 cm). $3,000-4,000

A Chippendale style mahogany writing table, applied with cabochons, foliate C-scrolls and flowerhead mouldings in lunette and gadrooned borders, 54 in (135 cm). $1,700-2,500

A George III style mahogany small writing table, the tambour top, inlaid with satinwood stringing, the tambour with floral spray inlay, c1910, 23 in (58 cm). $1,200-1,500

An Edwardian satinwood and crossbanded kidney-shaped writing table, 48 in (120 cm). $1,300-1,700

A Louis XV style tulipwood writing table, applied with ormolu mounts and brass mounted borders, 50½ in (126 cm). $4,500-7,000

A Louis XVI Transitional style kingwood bureau plat, applied with gilt metal mounts, 52 in (130 cm). **$3,000-4,500**

An ormolu mounted kingwood and tulipwood bureau plat, of Louis XV style, 43½ in (111 cm). **$3,000-4,500**

A Louis Phillipe writing table, in kingwood, with crossbanding and brass surround, porcelain panels of fruit and birds and monogram within ormolu mounts to the frieze, stamped 'E.H.B.', c1840, 26 in (65 cm). **$3,500-5,000**

A late Regency rosewood teapoy, inlaid with satinwood shell medallions and spandrels, 14½ in (36 cm). **$600-900**

Teapoys

An inlaid mahogany teapoy, early 19thC, 30½ in (76 cm) high. **$500-600**

Washstands

A Victorian rosewood teapoy, the circular hinged top revealing a pair of lidded canisters and a pair of apertures, c1850, 20 in (50 cm). **$800-1,200**

A late Georgian III mahogany enclosed washstand, the interior with an adjustable rising mirror and a concave fronted water container with brass tap, contemporary brass bowl and soap container, 26 in (66 cm). **$1,700-2,500**

A Regency mahogany corner washstand, c1820. **$600-700**

Whatnots

A late Georgian mahogany miniature three-tier etagère, 16 in (40 cm). **$600-900**

A George III mahogany whatnot, with original brass cup casters. **$2,500-3,500**

◄ A Victorian mahogany whatnot, 16½ in (41 cm). **$400-600**

A George III mahogany whatnot, 18 in (45 cm). **$600-900**

A Regency mahogany four-tier whatnot, on brass cappings and casters, c1810, 17 in (43 cm). **$1,300-1,700**

A Victorian mahogany corner whatnot, 32 in (80 cm). **$1,000-1,200**

A Victorian thuyawood serpentine two-tier whatnot, inlaid with boxwood lines and applied with gilt metal mounts, the top applied with amaranth and satinwood radial bands, 28½ in (71 cm). **$1,700-2,500**

Wine Coolers

A Continental satinwood three-tier etagère, French or Belgian, c1825, 30½ in (76 cm). **$1,700-2,500**

A George III mahogany cellaret, 22 in (56 cm). **$2,000-3,000**

A pair of painted leather fire buckets, painted with a rim border and the inscription George Burdick 1838, American, dated 1838, 17in (42.5cm) high. **900-1,200**

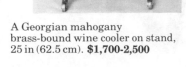

A Georgian mahogany brass-bound wine cooler on stand, 25 in (62.5 cm). **$1,700-2,500**

A Chippendale mahogany cellaret on stand, with hinged top opening to a fitted interior, the case with 2 bail handles, the stand with thumb-molded rim and square tapering legs, stand restored, probably Southern, 1760-1800, 33in (82.5cm) high. **$1,600-1,900**

Wine Coolers

★ Cisterns for cooling wines were noted back in the 15th century and as objects of furniture became popular after about 1730. The cellaret is basically a cooler with a lid and fitted with a lock.

★ There are two main types: those made to stand on a pedestal or sideboard and those with legs or separate stands to stand on the floor.

★ Octagonal, hexagonal, round or oval, the commonest form is of coopered construction with a number of brass bands.

★ A cooler made to stand on a pedestal will often have the lowest brass band as near to the base as possible; a cooler made to fit into a stand will have the band slightly up the body to allow a snug fit.

★ It is important that all mounts are original and condition should be good, but the absence of the old lead lining is not serious. An octagonal cooler or cellaret on stand may command a slightly higher price than a hexagonal model, but both are much in demand.

★ After 1800, the sarcophagus shape became popular and later Regency models were made with highly figured mahogany veneers and large carved paw feet.

★ There were not many new designs after the 1850's.

A George III mahogany and brass-bound wine cooler on stand with leather casters, 24 in (60 cm)
$3,000-4,500

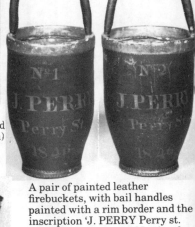

A pair of painted leather firebuckets, with bail handles painted with a rim border and the inscription 'J. PERRY Perry st. 1846', and numbered 'No 1' and 'No 2', Newport, Rhode Island, dated 1846, 18½in (46cm) high.
$1,200-1,600

A George IV mahogany sarcophagus cellaret, with stepped chamfered rectangular top, 25½ in (65 cm). **$1,000-1,200**

A fine pair of Regency mahogany sarcophagus wine coolers, with lead-lined interiors, one with a lift-out shelf, 30 in (76 cm).
$8,500-10,000

An ormolu mounted mahogany wine cooler, the brass liner mounted with entrelac-and-rosette border and patera carrying handles on moulded supports centred by beading, headed by rams' masks and ending in hoof feet, 20 in (50 cm). **$5,500-7,000**

A Regency mahogany sarcophagus shaped cellaret, the interior with a later metal liner for coal, 26 in (65 cm).
$1,200-1,500

A Regency small mahogany wine cooler, 14 in (36 cm).
$3,000-4,500

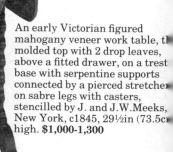

An early Victorian figured mahogany veneer work table, the molded top with 2 drop leaves, above a fitted drawer, on a trestle base with serpentine supports connected by a pierced stretcher, on sabre legs with casters, stencilled by J. and J.W.Meeks, New York, c1845, 29½in (73.5cm) high. **$1,000-1,300**

Miscellaneous

late Victorian yellow oak
rcophagus shaped wine cooler,
amped Wilkinson & Son, 8, Old
ond Street. **$1,000-1,200**

A George III brass mounted
mahogany peat bucket, with
detachable liner, 15 in (38 cm).
$7,000-9,000

A good George III mahogany and
brass-bound plate bucket, 19½ in
(49 cm). **$1,300-1,700**

◄ A fine pair of brass-bound
mahogany buckets,
the octagonal
bodies pierced with fluted
arcading, 13 in (32 cm).
$9,000-13,000

George III mahogany and
ass-bound plate bucket, 18 in
cm). **$600-900**

A pair of George III mahogany
bottle carriers, 12½ in (32 cm).
$5,500-7,000

► A mahogany pail, inlaid with
bands of foliate motifs, and
bound with brass, early
19thC, 13 in (33 cm).
$600-700

A pail, made up of bands of
mahogany and fruit wood,
brass-bound, with galvanised
liner, early 19thC, 11 in (29 cm).
$800-1,200

Victorian leather fire bucket.
00-500

A pair of painted canvas and
pinewood dummy board figures,
each of a Scots Guard, 19thC, 81 in
(206 cm) high. **$6,000-8,500**

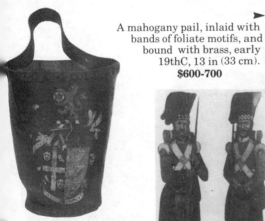

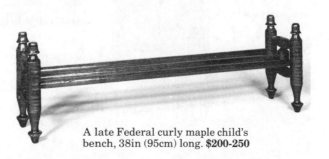

pair of dummy board figures,
th a boy and a girl in late 16thC
ess, 36 and 32 in (91.5 and
cm) high. **$1,500-2,200**

A late Federal curly maple child's
bench, 38in (95cm) long. **$200-250**

A set of George III mahogany library steps, late 18thC, 102½ in (259 cm) high. **$7,500-10,500**

A set of Regency mahogany bedside steps, the lower 2 lined with green leather with a drawer fitted with a bidet with impressed Wedgwood mark on turned tapering feet, 18½ in (47 cm). **$7,000-9,000**

A metamorphic set of mahogany folding library steps, the 6 treads in 2 parts folding into the top of an upholstered stool, early 19thC, 36 in (90 cm). **$7,500-10,500**

A set of figured walnut bed steps, early 19thC. **$400-600**

A rare Victorian John Hughes patent walnut nursery yacht, in need of restoration, c1850, 66½ in (169 cm). **$1,700-2,500**

A George III mahogany jardinière, with massive lead lined gadrooned body on spreading fluted socle and later square plinth, 27½ in (70 cm). **$8,500-10,000**

A George III satinwood and mahogany tray, with crossbanded waved oval top, 29 in (73.5 cm). **$2,000-3,000**

Bookcases

A pine glazed bookcase, 39 in (97.5 cm). **$300-400**

A late Georgian pine bookcase, 42 in (105 cm). **$1,000-1,200**

A pine bookcase, early 18thC, 90 in (229 cm). **$1,700-2,500**

A pine glazed top bookcase, 19thC, 43 in (107.5 cm). **$600-800**

Country Chairs

A pine bed settle, c1740, 72 in (183 cm). **$1,000-1,200**

An elm bobbin back farmhouse armchair, c1840. **$150-200**

An elm slat back cottage armchair, c1880, 26 in (65 cm). **$100-200**

A 'Busby Stoop' rocker, c1880. **$300-500**

A pair of beech Thonet dining chairs, c1910. **$80-150**

A set of 6 wheelback chairs, with cabriole legs and crinoline stretchers, c1950. **$400-600**

Chests

A folding chair. **$50-70**

An Irish Georgian two-piece mule chest, with new knobs, c1830. **$300-500**

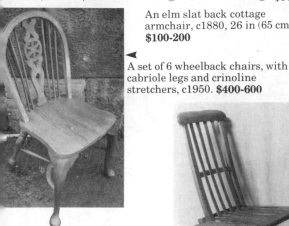

Georgian specimen chest, with 4 drawers at each side, panelled front and back. **$300-500**

A late Georgian chest, 34 in (85 cm). **$300-500**

A chest of drawers, recently painted floral theme, no handles or knobs, 1860-1880. **$400-600**

Pine Scottish chest, c1850, 48 in (120 cm). **$400-600**

A Victorian pine chest of drawers. **$300-400**

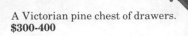

A Victorian painted chest of drawers, with bun feet, c1875. **$400-600**

Commodes

A pine commode, 19thC, 17 in (42.5 cm). **$50-70**

A Victorian commode, recently painted. **$300-400**

Cupboards

A panel side bonnet drawer cupboard, c1780, 54 in (135 cm). **$1,300-1,700**

An Irish corner cupboard, c1800, 52 in (130 cm). **$1,300-1,700**

An Irish food cupboard, c1800. **$1,500-2,200**

A pitch pine cupboard, c180 71 in (180 cm). **$400-600**

An Irish fielded food cupboard, c1800, 50 in (125 cm). **$1,000-1,400**

A pine press, c1840, 51 in (127.5 cm). **$1,000-1,400**

A pine linen press, by Heal & Co., London, porcelain handles, c1850, 43 in (107.5 cm). **$700-1,000**

A pine chiffonier, with bra escutcheons, c1850, 34½ i (86 cm). **$400-600**

A linen press, 19thC, 49 in (122.5 cm). **$700-1,000**

A pine unit, the centre cupboard with 2 shelves, 19thC, 55½ in (139 cm). **$200-300**

A wall cupboard, c1860, 29 in (72.5 cm). **$60-90**

Dressers

A fiddle front dresser, c1780, 54 in (135 cm). **$1,000-1,200**

A two-piece pine dresser, c1780, 90 in (229 cm). **$1,700-2,500**

A George III pine dresser, the later raised open shelved back with a moulded cornice, c1790, 66 in (168 cm). **$2,000-3,000**

A pitch pine glazed top dresser, 44 in (110 cm). **$500-600**

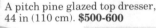

A scratch carved pine dresser, c1780. **$1,000-1,200**

A pine pot board dresser, with new base, 83½ in (212 cm). **$700-1,000**

An Irish pine dresser, 18thC, 54 in (135 cm). **$1,000-1,200**

A pine dresser, with new drawers and back boarding, 19thC, 84½ in (216 cm). **$700-900**

An Irish dresser, c1880, 50 i (125 cm). **$700-1,000**

Mirrors

A pine cheval mirror, 19thC, 31 in (77.5 cm). **$700-900**

A pine swing mirror, 23½ in (59 cm). **$100-150**

MAKE THE MOST OF MILLER'S

Price ranges in this book reflect what one should expect to pay for a similar example. When selling one can obviously expect a figure below. This will fluctuate according to a dealer's stock, saleability at a particular time, etc. It is always advisable to approach a reputable specialist dealer or an auction house which has specialist sales.

Sideboards

A serpentine fronted pine sideboard, with original handles, c1840. **$400-600**

A Regency pine sideboard, 54 in (135 cm). **$600-700**

Stools

Tables

An Irish wine table, with an unusual carved Celtic design, 1820-1840, 21 in (52.5 cm). **$150-200**

pine round stool, 9½ in (24 cm).
5-30

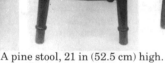

pine stool, 18 in (45 cm).
0-45

A pine stool, 21 in (52.5 cm) high. **$30-45**

A cricket table, c1840, 24 in (60 cm) high. **$100-150**

A cricket table, c1850, 30 in (75 cm) high. **$200-300**

A cricket table, c1850, 27 in (67.5 cm) high. **$200-300**

A pine plant stand, 24 in (60 cm) high. **$30-60**

pine side table, 25 in (62.5 cm).
00-200

A pine side table, 33 in (82.5 cm).
$100-150

n Irish double stretcher table,
850, 84 in (215 cm). **$500-600**

A pine side table, 30½ in (76 cm).
$100-150

An adjustable bed table, 23½ in (59 cm). **$80-150**

Washstands

A pine washstand, c1850, 21 in (52.5 cm). **$80-150**

A pine towel rail, 19thC, 26 i (65 cm). **$60-100**

Miscellaneous

A set of pine hanging shelves, 23 in (57.5 cm). **$60-100**

A set of pine hanging shelves, 39 in (97.5 cm). **$200-300**

A set of pine shelves, 19thC, 27 in (67.5 cm). **$80-150**

A plate rack, with drain hole in bottom, c1840, 36 in (90 cm). **$200-300**

A small pine stand, 19thC, 18 in (45 cm). **$50-70**

A set of pine pigeonholes, 37 i (92.5 cm). **$80-150**

A pine door, with brass letter box, handle and finger plate, 26 in (65 cm). **$300-400**

A pine umbrella stand, 23 in (57.5 cm). **$50-70**

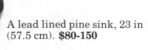

A pine fireplace, 38 in (95 cm **$80-150**

A lead lined pine sink, 23 in (57.5 cm). **$80-150**

Drinking Vessels

Scandinavian birchwood ankard, with brass trim, 18thC, in (12.5 cm). **$300-400**

A silver mounted blackjack tankard, the rim edged with foliage, with spreading body, another similar but smaller, both 18thC, 6 and 4½ in (15 and 11 cm). **$1,300-1,700**

A sycamore goblet, c1850, 11½ in (29 cm). **$300-400**

A pair of oak goblets, c1850, 11 in (27.5 cm). **$400-600** ►

pair of mahogany goblets, 840, 6½ in (16 cm). 400-600

A Scotch whisky jug, in alder wood, copper lid and trim, c1800, 9½ in (24 cm) high. **$400-600**
The dark stripes are caused by the soaking of the wood in peat.

A pair of oak wine coasters, 18thC, 5 in (12.5 cm) diam. **$300-400**

n unusual sailorwork seed cup, e turned wood vessel applied verall with various coloured eds in designs of architecture, llicks and hearts, dated 1870, 0½ in (37 cm) high. **$400-600**

Dining Room

A set of peat bellows, the cylindrical drum mounted with the figures of a leaping horse and a fox, 19thC, 31 in (77 cm). **$700-1,000**

A set of rosewood and brass mechanical bellows, c1820, 25 in (62.5 cm). **$600-800**

A set of rosewood and brass mechanical bellows, with a beech body and brass mounted funnel, wheel lacking, c1830, 27 in (68.5 cm). **$60-100**

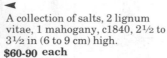

A collection of salts, 2 lignum vitae, 1 mahogany, c1840, 2½ to 3½ in (6 to 9 cm) high. **$60-90 each**

A mahogany salt, 18thC. **$100-150**

411

A lignum vitae salt, 18thC, 3½ in (9 cm). **$150-200**

A lignum vitae coffee grinder, in two parts with detachable cover, with acorn shaped finial and steel folding handle, 18thC, 8 in (20 cm). **$400-600**

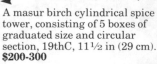

A sycamore spice grinder, 17thC, 10 in (25 cm). **$800-1,200**

A masur birch cylindrical spice tower, consisting of 5 boxes of graduated size and circular section, 19thC, 11½ in (29 cm). **$200-300**

A small oak butter tub, the oval body with 2 plain brass bands, 8 in (20 cm). **$300-400**

A George III coopered mahogany bread dish, the sides bound in brass, c1790, 14½ in (37 cm). **$1,000-1,400**

A pair of mahogany platters, 18thC, 8½ in (21 cm). **$200-300**

A walnut cheese coaster, c1810, 17 in (43 cm). **$400-600**

A lignum vitae Gothic style pricket candlestick, 20 in (50 cm). **$600-700**

Needlework

A fruitwood spinning wheel, with acanthus leaf-carved moulded platform, possibly Austrian or Swiss, 28 in (71 cm) high. **$1,200-1,500**

An egg cup stand, in laburnum and mahogany, c1820, 14½ in (36 cm) high. **$600-900**

It is unusual to find an egg stand for 10 egg cups.

A pine ewer, painted to simulate terracotta, c1800, 26 in (65 cm). **$1,200-1,500**

A spinning wheel, 19thC. **$300-500**

A spinning wheel, with bobbin turned spokes and turned legs, 19thC. **$300-600**

Treen

For a larger section on Treen see Miller's Antiques Price Guide 1985, Volume VI.

Miscellaneous

A rosewood vanity bottle, 11 in (27.5 cm) high. **$300-500**

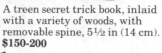

A French hazelnut wood cigar box, lined with tortoiseshell, c1840, 5 in (12.5 cm). **$100-200**

A treen secret trick book, inlaid with a variety of woods, with removable spine, 5½ in (14 cm). **$150-200**

A carved oak ship's figurehead, English, 19thC, 43 in (109 cm) high. **$1,000-1,200**

An acorn string holder, in lignum vitae, c1775, 6½ in (16 cm) high. **$300-400**

An unusual treen bucket, on ebonised turned stem, with brass swing handle, constructed in bands of various woods with ripple exterior and ebonised bands, 14½ in (37 cm) high. **$800-1,200**

A sycamore mortar, 18thC, 6½ in (16 cm) high. **$300-400**

A rosewood pot and cover, c1820, 5½ in (14 cm) high. **$300-400**

A mahogany watch stand, c1840, 12½ in (31 cm). **$300-400**

A pair of emu/ostrich egg stands, in oak, c1850, 7 in (17.5 cm) high. **$300-500**

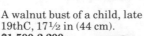

A walnut cup and cover, c1800, 9½ in (24 cm) high. **$400-600**

A walnut posy bowl, c1860, 7½ in (19 cm) high. **$300-500**

A walnut bust of a child, late 19thC, 17½ in (44 cm). **$1,500-2,200**

An unusual tôle peinte post box, in the form of a post office counter, 19thC. **$800-1,200**

A walnut ram's head with curly horns, c1750, 8½ in (21 cm). **$700-900**

An oak bust, of Rabbie Burns, c1796, 12 in (30 cm) high. **$700-900**

413

Clocks – Longcase

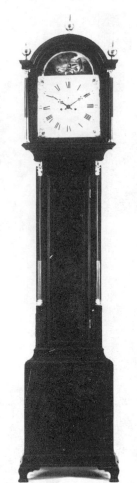

A William and Mary 8-day longcase clock, with silvered chapter ring, seconds dial and ormolu cherub spandrels, inscribed Mich. Shields, London, 91 in (232 cm). **$6,000-8,000**

A William and Mary marquetry inlaid longcase clock, with later movement. **$3,500-5,000**

A walnut marquetry longcase clock, the 11 in (27.5 cm) square brass dial plate inscribed Thos. Taylor in Holborn, London, with an 8-day pillar movement, 17thC, 85 in (216 cm). **$7,000-9,000**

Clocks

All clock measurements refer to height unless otherwise stated.

A Federal inlaid mahogany tall case clock, on ogee bracket feet, together with a new reproduction dial of the original, some veneer missing, some peeling on original dial, dial signed by Aaron Willard, Boston, 1800-1815, 92in (234cm) high. **$15,000-18,000**

A walnut marquetry longcase clock, of month duration, by Robert Dingley, London, the 10 in (25 cm) brass dial with silvered chapter ring, the movement with 6 ringed pillars, anchor escapement and striking locking plate on the backplate, with later bottom moulding and bun feet, with Equation of Time table inside the door, late 19thC, 83 in (211 cm). **$25,500-32,500**

A Queen Anne walnut longcase clock, of month duration, by Edw. Speakman London, the month-going movement with 5 ringed pillars, rack strike and anchor escapement, restorations, 108 in (275 cm). **$9,000-13,000**

A walnut parquetry longcase clock, the 10 in (25 cm) brass dial signed on the chapter ring William Bates, Leicester Fecit, the 5 pillar movement latched to the centre pillar, anchor escapement 'inside' locking plate striking, plinth with restoration, c1700, 81 in (206 cm). **$7,000-9,000**

An arabesque marquetry longcase clock, the 11½ in (29 cm) square brass dial inscribed Robert Alexander Edr, the ringed pillared movement with inside countwheel strike and anchor escapement, early 18thC, 82½ in (209 cm). **$5,500-7,000**

A George I simulated tortoiseshell longcase clock, the dial signed Richard Purratt Newport Pagnell, 88 in (224 cm). ~~$30,000~~ **1,500**

A mahogany longcase clock, London. **$6,000-8,000**

Federal painted tall case clock, e deep red painted hood with olled pediment, the cupboard r painted with blue, orange d yellow tulips on a brown vine r a brown vase with an incised scription, the base similarly corated, on French feet, repairs dial, some paint restoration to e, feet and upper back board h restorations, Pennsylvania, 80-1800, 94in (240cm) high. **000-6,000**

Federal mahogany inlaid and inted dwarf tall case clock, the hed glazed door painted with low and black stringing and nked by 2 Doric columns, the nted dial flanked by 4 ndrels painted with American elds, over a valanced skirt on cket feet, works possibly by hua Wilder, Hingham, ssachusetts, 1810-1820, 46in 5cm) high. **$12,000-15,000**

A George II 8-day longcase clock, by Samuel Lee, London, with 12 in (30 cm) dial, the movement with anchor escapement and rack striking mechanism, in walnut veneered case with feather crossbanding movement and case damaged, 87 in (222 cm). **$3,500-5,000**

A seaweed panel marquetry longcase clock, on a replaced base, and containing a later twin-train movement with anchor escapement, 18thC, 85 in (216 cm). **$3,000-4,500**

415

An early George III oak longcase clock, the 12 in (30 cm) brass dial inscribed Richd. Corless, Stockport, the movement with anchor escapement and rack striking on a bell, restored, mid-18thC, 88 in (224 cm).
$1,500-2,200

A fine Chippendale walnut tall case clock, the base with an elaborately scalloped panel flanked by fluted quarter columns, on ogee bracket feet, with pendulum, key and winder, without weights, damage to pendulum, feet reduced, by Adam Brant, New Hanover Township, Montgomery County, Pennsylvania, 1770-1800, 97in (246cm) high. **$13,000-15,000**

Provenance
This clock was owned by Adam Brant and appears in an inventory dated July 17, 1804, now in the Norristown Historical Society. The clock is also listed in Brant's will as an '8-day clock'.

A Georgian 8-day longcase clock, in walnut case with arched brass dial and pierced spandrels, by William Tomlinson.
$2,500-3,500

A Georgian japanned longcase clock, now containing a dial signed John Dewe Monde Lane Southwark, the 5 pillar rack striking movement with anchor escapement, 102 in (259 cm).
$1,500-2,200

A Federal mahogany tall case clock, the hood with scrolled pediment and 3 wooden finials, the white-painted dial with a moon dial, a seconds dial and a chapter ring, the spandrels painted with the Four Seasons, on turned tapering feet, with 2 weights, works not original to case, works by E. Francis, Leesburg, Virginia, c1815, 94in (240cm) high.
$2,000-2,500

A walnut and mulberry longcase clock, the 12 in (30 cm) brass dial inscribed Joseph Rasher, London, the 5 ringed pillared movement with anchor escapement, 18thC, 99 in 251 cm).
$5,500-7,000

A George III 8-day longcase clock, with 12 in (30 cm) brass dial, signed 'Heny Hawkins, Plymouth', the arch showing 'High Water at Plymouth' and phases of the moon, the movement with anchor escapement, rack striking on one bell, 87 in (222 cm).
$2,000-3,000

An inlaid mahogany longcase clock, with satinwood crossbanding, the 8-day movement with inside countwheel, signed on the chapter ring Peter Walker, London, 92 in (234 cm).
$3,000-4,500

A George III mahogany longcase clock, the brass dial with moving ship in the arch, and signed Wm. Howell Bristol, the 8-day movement with anchor escapement and rack strike, 92 in (235 cm).
$6,000-8,000

A mahogany George III longcase clock, the 12 in (30 cm) brass break-arch dial plate inscribed Robert Hood, London, the 8-day 5-pillar 3-train movement with rack striking on an hour bell and quarter hour chiming on 8 bells, late 18thC, 94 in (239 cm).
$15,000-20,500

A George III longcase clock, plaque inscribed Jno. Williams, London, 91 in (233 cm).
$2,000-3,000

Georgian mahogany longcase clock, the 12 in (30 cm) silvered dial signed Trail, Edgware Road, Paddington, the twin train movement with anchor escapement, 90 in (229 cm).
$2,500-3,500

An inlaid mahogany longcase clock, with 3-train movement, quarter chiming and playing 7 named tunes, late 18thC, 96 in (244 cm).
$2,000-3,000

A George III mahogany longcase clock, c1800.
$2,000-3,000

A Scottish mahogany longcase clock, the 8-day movement with anchor escapement and rack striking, by Wm. Thomson, Perth, c1770, 84 in (215 cm).
$1,500-2,200

A George III mahogany and inlaid longcase clock, signed indistinctly Norwich, the 8-day movement with anchor escapement and rack striking on a bell, 89 in (227 cm).
$2,000-3,000

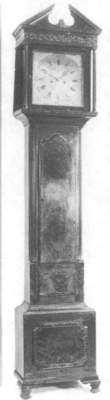

An oak longcase clock, 30-hour striking movement by J. Horsnaile, 18thC, 74 in (188 cm).
$1,000-1,200

A George III mahogany longcase clock, the 8-day movement with anchor escapement and striking on a single bell, arch inscribed Thos. Conley, Whitby.
$1,200-1,500

A longcase clock, by Joel Ettry of Horton, Dorset, the 8-day striking movement fronted by a brass dial, in original oak case, c1760.
$800-1,200

An Irish George III mahogany longcase clock, with brass face signed Adam Somervill, Dublin, the case labelled P.J. Walsh & Son, 20 Batchelors Walk, Dublin, 95 in (272 cm).
$1,700-2,500

A George III Lancashire style longcase clock, dial signed Hadwen Liverpool on the chapter ring with cherub and scroll spandrels, rack striking movement with anchor escapement, 93 in (237 cm).
$3,500-5,000

A late Georgian mahogany longcase clock, the brass dial signed around moon phase in the arch Samuel Shepley Stockport, the 8-day movement with anchor escapement and rack strike, 96 in (245 cm).
$3,500-5,000

An inlaid mahogany longcase clock, strung in ebony and box, the 8-day 2-train movement striking on a bell, the brass dial inscribed Wenham, Deerham, late 18thC, 90½ in (231 cm).
$2,500-3,500

An oak longcase clock, the 13 in (32.5 cm) brass dial signed Winstanley, Holywell, the movement with anchor escapement and rack striking on a bell, c1800, 83 in (211 cm).
$1,200-1,500

A walnut longcase clock, with 8-day striking movement, by William Clarke, Stalybridge, 18thC, 96 in (244 cm).
$3,500-5,000

A mahogany longcase clock, brass dial with rolling moon, 8-day movement striking on single bell, early 19thC.
$3,000-4,500

A late George III longcase clock, in mahogany case, by John Criddle, Bridgewater, 96½ in (244 cm). $2,000-3,000

A Sheraton inlaid figured mahogany longcase clock, by Richardson of Paisley, 8-day duration, c1805. $1,500-2,200

A longcase clock, by William B. Marsh, London, the black and gilt softwood case decorated with painted paper panels, having 8-day striking movement, the 12 in (30 cm) steel face with calendar and chapter rings, and brass spandrels, early 19thC. $1,300-1,700

An oak longcase clock, with 14 in (35 cm) diameter brass dial, the movement with anchor escapement and rack striking on a bell, c1820, 88 in (224 cm). $800-1,200

A fruitwood longcase clock, by George Lassiter, Wisbech, 8-day rack striking movement, c1830, 84 in (215 cm). $1,400-1,700

An 8-day mahogany longcase clock, by T. Massey, London, rack striking date and second hands, c1840, 76 in (193 cm). $1,500-2,200

An 8-day Scottish longcase clock, by Thos. Taylor of Anstruther, rack striking, c1840, 85 in (217 cm). $1,300-1,700

A Scottish mahogany longcase clock, the 12 in (30 cm) arch painted dial signed W. Alexander Aberdeen, 19thC, 85 in (217 cm). $1,500-2,200

An oak longcase clock, inscribed Courter, Ruthin, enclosing an 8-day mechanism, 87 in (222 cm). $600-800

A Scottish mahogany longcase clock, the dial signed Christie of Perth, 19thC, 88 in (224 cm). $800-1,200

A late Victorian mahogany chiming longcase clock, the movement with massive plates, deadbeat escapement chiming on a series of 8 tubular gongs, late 19th/early 20thC, 110 in (280 cm). **$3,000-4,000**

A mahogany and oak longcase clock, with painted dial. **$500-600**

A carved oak longcase clock, with brass face flanked b barley twist columns, on fielded and carved plinth, 84 in (215 cm). **$200-300**

A Federal birch tall case clock, the door revealing a painted brass dial inscribed 'SAMUEL RANLET, MONMOUTH', the case with coved mid molding above a rectangular thumb-molded cupboard door, flanked by quarter columns over a coved molding, above a rectangular base on straight bracket feet, some restoration to dial seat, no key, by Samuel Ranlet, Monmouth District, Maine, 1790-1810, 92½in (236cm) high. **$6,500-7,500**

A fine Federal inlaid mahogany tall case clock, the hood with pierced fretwork and 3 line-inlaid plinths with brass finials, the spandrels painted with polychrome and gilt fans, with curly maple inlaid panels, the base with curly maple and mahogany banding and pattern stringing above a scalloped skirt, on flaring French feet, with weights and a pendulum, without key or winder, by Aaron Willard, Junior, Boston, 1800-1820, 91in (232cm) high. **$16,000-20,000**

An Edwardian painted satinwood longcase clock, the engraved silvered dial with a Star of David and calendar sector to the centre within the chapter ring, signed Wm. Eastwood, the 4 pillar movement with rack strike and anchor escapement, 98 in (249 cm). **$3,000-4,500**

An Edwardian inla mahogany longcase clock, with 8-day movement striking and chiming on tubular gongs. **$1,500-2,200**

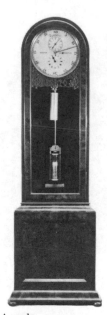

A mahogany longcase chiming regulator, the 13 in (32.5 cm) diameter enamel dial signed C & T. Hammond, Manchester, the movement with deadbeat escapement, rack striking on a gong and chiming on 8 overhead bells, 4 spoke work, with 3 brass cased weights, second quarter of the 19thC, 82½ in (210 cm).
$1,500-2,200

A mahogany longcase regulator, the 8-day movement with steel cased weight, mercury compensated pendulum and deadbeat escapement by Harper, Wolverhampton, 19thC, 83 in (211 cm).
$1,500-2,200

A Regency mahogany regulator, the 12 in (30 cm) circular silvered dial signed Hamley, London, the 6-pillared movement with deadbeat escapement and maintaining power, 75 in (192 cm).
$3,500-5,000

Clocks – Bracket

An ebonised bracket clock, engraved and signed above 'Jasper Taylor in Grayes Inn', the ringed pillared movement with verge escapement and pull quarter repeating on 4 bells, early 18thC, 16½ in (41 cm).
2,500-3,500

An 8-day striking bracket clock, engraved on chapter ring, Windmills, London, in 19thC ebonised case, with brass finials and carrying handle.
$1,500-2,200

An ebonised quarter-repeating bracket clock, the 7 in (17.5 cm) dial signed J. Windmills, London, the movement with 5 ringed pillars, pull quarter repeat with 5 hammers, verge escapement with bob pendulum and inside rack, with restoration, 15½ in (39.5 cm). **$3,500-5,000**

Joseph Windmills was Free of the Clockmakers' Company in 1671 and Master 1702-23. This clock may be dated c1700. Note that the verge is pivoted in the back of the dial plate.

A George II fruitwood striking bracket clock, the dial signed Tyler London, the twin fusee movement with verge escapement, pull quarter-repeat on 6 bells, 16 in (40 cm). **$3,500-5,000**
Reminiscent of the work of the Delander Family.

A George II walnut striking bracket clock, by John Ellicott London, now converted to anchor escapement, a pull quarter-repeat train removed, case with some restoration, 19 in (48 cm). **$4,500-7,000**

A Georgian walnut bracket clock, signed Sam Whichcote, London, the 6-pillared movement with verge escapement, 19 in (48 cm). **$2,000-3,000**

An ebonised bracket clock, the dial inscribed Robert Henderson, London, with automata in the arch, the painted landscape with 4 blacksmiths having moving arms, with verge movement, 18thC, 18½ in (46 cm). **$3,500-5,000**

A small and rare ebony-veneered grande sonnerie bracket clock, the 7 in dial signed Joseph Knibb London, the 3-train movement with latched dial, triple divided front plate, 10 vase-shaped pillars, 2 now pinned, verge escapement with bob pendulum, the backplate signed Joseph Knibb Londini Fecit, with restoration, 13 in (33 cm). **$22,500-34,000**

An ebonised bracket clock, by Christopher Pinchbeck, the dial inscribed Chris Pinchbeck Senior, London, with automata in the arch, the 6-pillar hour striking fusee movement with original verge escapement and 6 bell pull quarter repeat, 18thC, 21½ in (54 cm). **$7,000-9,000**

◄ A bracket clock, in burr walnut case, by Jos. Kirk, Harstoft, 18thC, 16 in (40 cm). **$3,000-4,500**

A George III ebonised striking ► bracket clock, the movement with 6 baluster pillars to the arched plates, inverted chain fusees, rack strike and, now incomplete, quarter repeat on 2 bells, anchor escapement, signed Hindley York, some alterations, 21 in (53.5 cm). **$4,500-7,000**

A Georgian mahogany bracket clock, the enamelled dial signed Gardner, London, the fusee movement converted to anchor escapement, 15 in (38 cm). **$1,200-1,500**

A walnut bracket timepiece, signed Smallwood, Litchfield, the ringed pillared movement with verge escapement and pull quarter repeat, now missing, 18thC, 18 in (46 cm). **$1,300-1,700**

An early George III mahogany striking bracket clock, of Elicott type, the dial signed Ellicott London, with later hour hand, the twin fusee movement, ringed pillars, converted to wire lines and anchor escapement, later additions to feet, 16 in (40 cm). **$2,000-3,000**

A George III inlaid mahogany striking bracket clock, the enamel dial signed 'Wright in the Poultry Watchmaker ot the King', the twin fusee movement now with wire lines and converted to anchor escapement, 16 in (41 cm). **$2,500-3,500**

A red lacquered and chinoiserie decorated bracket clock, inscribed Wm. Page, London, the 5-pillared fusee movement converted to anchor escapement, 18thC, 18 in (45.7 cm). **$3,500-5,000**

A George III ebonised quarter striking bracket clock, by Justin Vulliamy London, triple chain fusee movement with verge escapement, rise-and-fall regulation to spring suspended pendulum, quarter strike on 6 bells, 14½ in (37 cm). **$7,500-10,500**

◄ A George III ebonised quarter chiming bracket clock, the brass dial signed Perigal, London, the fusee movement with verge escapement, striking the quarters on 8 bells, 21 in (53.5 cm). **$3,000-4,500**

A Georgian mahogany bracket clock, signed Joseph Wynn, Windsor, the movement with alarm, anchor escapement, 18½ in (47 cm). **$2,000-3,000**

A George III mahogany striking bracket clock, now with a twin fusee movement with verge escapement, the dial signed Thos. Wagstaffe, London, 19 in (48 cm). **$3,000-4,500**

An ebonised quarter chiming bracket clock, the 3-train 5-pillar fusee movement now with anchor escapement, bell striking, chiming the quarters on 6 bells actuated by a pin drum, and with pull repeat, signed on an inset plaque Danl. Catlin, Lynn, 20 in (50 cm). **$1,500-2,200**

Daniel Catlin, Kings Lynn, 1784.

A George III mahogany bracket clock, by Benjamin Dunkley, Tooting, with anchor escapement, 22 in (55 cm). **$400-600**

A George III mahogany striking bracket clock, the silvered dial signed James Wild, London, the twin fusee movement with trip repeat, now converted to wire lines and anchor escapement, 16 in (41 cm). **$3,000-4,500**

A George III mahogany striking bracket clock, the silvered dial signed Francis Dorell, London, twin fusee movement with verge escapement, 19 in (48 cm). **$4,500-5,000**

An ebonised balloon bracket clock, the fusee movement with verge escapement, the bell striking, the dial signed J. Leroux, London, 19 in (48 cm). **$1,200-1,500**

John Leroux, Charing Cross, London, free in 1781, worked until 1808.

◄

A small Regency walnut bracket clock, the chipped 4½ in (11 cm) enamel dial signed Barraud, London, the movement with arched plates, chain fusees and anchor escapement, the backplate signed Barraud Cornhill, London, 12 in (30 cm). **$2,500-3,500**

A Regency walnut cased bracket clock, with double chain fusée movement, maker Raw Brothers, 31 Duke Street, Grosvenor Square, London. **$600-900**

An ebonised bracket clock, with brass mounts, striking on a gong, y Winterhalder & Hoffmier, 1900, 15½ in (39 cm). 300-400

A large green painted and gilt bronze bracket clock, the dial signed Guiot A Paris, the movement with narrow anchor escapement and outside numbered countwheel, c1720, 39 in (99 cm). $2,500-3,500

A German oak bracket clock, 3-train fusee movement, Westminster chimes, by Winterhalter & Hoffmier, late 19thC, 17 in (42.5 cm). $1,000-1,200

A Louis XIV French ormolu mounted boulle bracket clock, the movement with vase shaped pillars, verge escapement, silk suspension, outside numbered locking plate, and signed Gribelin a Paris, 49½ in (126 cm). $4,500-5,000

Probably Nicolas Gribelin, born 1637, died 1719 aged 82 years.

French Louis XV boulle bracket ock and bracket, the dial signed egnault a Paris, with outside cking plate striking, now with nchor escapement, and a atching bracket, c1750, 34 in 7 cm). $3,000-4,500

Clocks – Carriage

Victorian miniature carriage ock, contained in a decorated se, maker's mark J.B. London 90, 3½ in (9 cm). 00-900

A very small and rare enamel mounted carriage timepiece, the movement numbered 921, with cylinder escapement, the top dated 1898, with leather travelling case from J.W. Benson, London, 2 in (5 cm). $1,500-2,200

A good English carriage clock, the enamel dial signed Dent 33 Cockspur St, London, the repeating movement with spotted plates, chain fusees, maintaining power, the lever escapement with gilt platform and free-sprung compensation balance and gong striking, the back plate signed M.F. Dent, 8 in (21 cm). $7,500-10,500

This clock may be dated to the late 1850's shortly after Richard Edward Dent's widow Marianna Frederica changed the style of the firm to M.F. Dent following her husband's death in 1856.

A lacquered brass striking carriage clock, with uncut compensated balance to lever platform, stamp of Drocourt, 6 in (14.5 cm). **$1,300-1,700**

A carriage timepiece, the movement with lever escapement in gilt brass case, 5 in (12.5 cm). **$1,000-1,200**

A French repeating carriage clock, by Francois-Arsene Margaine, the 8-day movement with lever escapement and compensated balance wheel, the back numbered 12658, 8 in (20 cm). **$800-1,200**

A gilt metal striking carriage clock, with uncut compensated balance to silvered lever platform, travelling case, stamp of Drocourt, 7 in (7.5 cm). **$1,300-1,700**

A gilt metal porcelain mounted carriage clock, with lever platform, strike on bell, with stamp of Japy Freres, 9½ in (24 cm). **$5,500-7,000**

A Champleve enamelled brass carriage clock, with cut compensated balance to lever platform, lacking one pivoting block for the handle, travelling case, 7 in (18 cm). **$4,500-7,000**

A gilt metal striking carriage clock, with bridge to lever balance, outside countwheel strike on bell on backplate stamped Lucien Paris, 6 in (16 cm). **$1,000-1,200**

An ormolu quarter striking Pendule d'Officier, the fusee movement with lever escapement, alarm and pull quarter repeating, signed Robert & Courvoisier, early 19thC, 8½ in (21.5 cm). **$4,500-7,000**

A French brass carriage clock, the movement striking on a bell, with Jules type lever escapement, signed Jules, Paris, 827, 19thC, 6½ in (16.5 cm). **$1,000-1,400**

Clocks – Mantel

A walnut mantel clock, the 4½ in (11 cm) silvered dial signed Dent, 61 Strand, London, 1711, the movement with chain fusees and anchor escapement, minute hand lacking, 10 in (25.5 cm). $1,500-2,200

A Regency rosewood mantel clock the dial signed Wm. Wilson, outhampton Street, Strand, the ve pillared fusee movement with nchor escapement, 12 in (30 cm). 1,700-2,500

mantel timepiece, the silvered al signed Arnold, 84 Strand, ndon, 544, the fusee movement th anchor escapement, 19thC, ½ in (29 cm). $800-1,200

A fine and rare mahogany veneer lighthouse clock, the original blown clear glass dome with a knop finial above a white porcelain dial inscribed 'Simon Willard's Patient', with an ormolu laurel wreath finial, over a chased brass collar above a tapering cylindrical case with a brass collar with chased foliage, scrolls and flowerheads, on an octagonal base with molded foot, by Simon Willard, Roxbury, Massachusetts, 1825-1830, 26in (65cm) high. $65,000-85,000

This clock is reported to have descended in the Slater family and was obtained in 1971 from the Samuel Slater house in Webster, Massachusetts.
The clock was originally trimmed by approximately 2 inches in the back to accommodate its location on a mantel shelf in the Slater house. This original alteration has been carefully restored.

A satinwood mantel timepiece, the 4 in (10 cm) silvered dial signed Bunyan & Gardner, Manchester, the single train fusee movement with anchor escapement, 9.5 in (24 cm). $800-1,200

A small George III gilt metal mantel clock, by Ellicott, the movement now with chain fusees and lever escapement, 12 in (30 cm). $2,000-3,000
An interesting example of the neo-classical taste in case making, this clock may be dated c1780.

A late Georgian inlaid mahogany striking mantel clock, the enamel dial signed Arnold London, the chain fusee movement with anchor escapement, 13 in (33 cm). $3,000-4,500

A rosewood mantel clock, the twin fusee movement with lever platform escapement striking on a gong and signed on the backplate, Viner, London, 19thC, 9 in (23 cm). **$3,000-4,500**

A Victorian repeating 8-day mantel clock, the 8-day movement with anchor escapement, chain fusee going, striking and chiming trains, 36½ in (91 cm). **$1,000-1,200**

An ebonised and brass inlaid mantel timepiece, the fusee movement inscribed on the backplate, D & W. Morice, 86 Cornhill, 19thC, 7½ in (19 cm). **$1,500-2,200**

A Victorian mahogany mantel clock, the movement with anchor escapement and striking on a bell, 19thC, 23½ in (59.5 cm). **$300-600**

A fine Elkington mantel clock, 11 in (27.5 cm). **$2,000-3,000**

A Victorian rosewood four glass mantel clock, the silvered dial signed Brockbank and Atkins, London, Number 2291, the twin chain and fusee movement with anchor escapement striking on a gong, 11½ in (29 cm). **$1,200-1,500**

A gilt bronze and alabaster nautical mantel timepiece, French movement with cylinder escapement, bearing an E. Bertaux label, 19thC, 15½ in (39 cm). **$700-1,000**

An English ormolu mantel timepiece, the timepiece chain and fusee movement with verge escapement, signed James Lesley, Strand, London, Number 81, 12 in (30 cm). **$800-1,200**

An ebony clock with ivory inlay, late 19thC. **$300-400**

A French porcelain mantel clock, the dial signed Felix Sandoz, London, with striking movement, late 18thC, 11 in (28 cm). **$1,500-2,200**

An Edwardian inlaid mahogany mantel clock, c1900, 13 in (32.5 cm). **$300-400**

A French bronze and ormolu mounted clock, the movement with silk suspension and countwheel strike, signed Galle a Paris, early 19thC, 27½ in (70 cm). **$1,300-1,700**

A small bronze and gilt bronze mantel timepiece, the enamel dial signed Louis Habram a Montbrison, the similarly signed verge watch movement numbered 377, watch replaced, early 19thC, 4 in (9.5 cm). **$2,500-3,500**

A French gilt brass mantel clock, the enamel dial, and visible desfontaines deadbeat escapement, inscribed Brevete, Le Roy & Fils, Pals Royal Gie Montpensier, 13-15 Paris, with twin train movement, 19thC, 21 in (53.5 cm). **$3,000-4,500**

A French four glass mantel clock, the movement inscribed Klaftenberger, Paris, 19thC, 11 in (28.5 cm). **$600-900**

A quarter chiming tortoiseshell and cut brass inlaid mantel clock, with Louis XIV style case, the triple fusee movement with anchor escapement, striking the hours on a gong, 19thC, 23 in (58 cm). **$3,000-4,000**

An ormolu and Sevres pattern mantel clock, the dial signed Bourdin a Paris, 17 in (43 cm). **$1,500-2,200**

An ormolu mantel clock, with jewelled Sèvres pattern porcelain dial, striking movement, 15 in (38 cm). **$1,500-2,200**

A French white marble and ormolu mounted mantel clock, the enamel dial signed F. Barbedienne a Paris, the case also signed, 19thC, 16½ in (42 cm). **$1,000-1,200**

Lantern

A brass lantern clock, the dial signed Peter Closon Neere Holburne Bridge Londini Fecit, the posted framed movement with balance wheel and verge escapement, countwheel and alarm on bell, with restorations, 15 in (38 cm). $3,000-4,500

A brass striking lantern clock, the dial signed Gerardus Brand, Fecit, Amstelodamj, the 2-train movement with verge escapement and bob pendulum, 9½ in (24 cm). $6,000-8,000

A small and rare alarum lantern timepiece, the 2½ in (6 cm) dial signed Tho. Tamkin de Bedforde fecit, the movement with verge escapement, the alarum arm pivoted above I, pendulum lacking, 8½ in (21.5 cm). $9,000-13,000

A brass lantern clock, the dial inscribed, J. Windmills, London and single steel hand, the 30-hour movement with anchor escapement and countwheel strike, 15 in (38 cm). $1,500-2,200

USE THE INDEX!
Because certain items might fit easily into any of a number of categories, the quickest and surest method of locating any entry is by reference to the fully cross-referenced index at the back of the book. This is particularly true this year when certain sections, e.g. Liverpool Porcelain and Oak Furniture have been featured in isolation.

A brass lantern clock, with a double chain fusee movement, with striking on 2 bells, c1860, 16 in (40 cm). $800-1,200

Skeleton

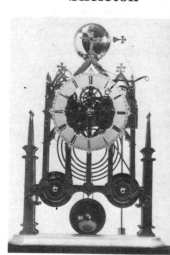

A skeleton clock, the movement with chain fusees, anchor escapement, a gong for the hours and striking the half hours on a bell, with a glass dome, 19 in (48 cm). $1,500-2,200

A brass lantern clock, with 17thC posted frame, the dial engraved R.L. beneath the alarm disc, now fixed, containing a 19thC twin fusee movement, 13 in (33 cm). $1,000-1,200

An unusual skeleton clock, the dial signed John Carr Swaffham, the fusee movement with anchor escapement, with a cracked glass dome, 9½ in (24 cm). $1,300-1,700

skeleton clock, the movement
ith anchor escapement and pull
peat striking on an overhead
ell, with a cracked glass dome,
850, 24 in (61 cm).
1,400-1,700

A brass skeleton clock, with dial
inscribed, Hry. Marc a Paris, the
movement with outside
countwheel and bell strike, c1860,
18 in (46 cm). **$500-700**

A fine pierced brass repeating
cathedral skeleton clock, the
movement having chain fusee,
anchor escapement, striking
hourly on gong, half hourly on
central bell, glass dome, 19thC,
21½ in (54 cm).
$1,500-2,200

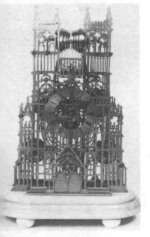

Wall

Victorian brass chiming
eleton clock, of York Minster
pe with triple chain fusees,
chor escapement and mercury
ndulum, with inscription and
ted 1881, 25 in (62.5 cm).
,500-5,000

A brass skeleton clock, with twin
fusee six pillared movement, with
anchor escapement, 19thC,
17½ in (44.5 cm). **$1,000-1,200**

A Federal giltwood gallery clock,
the circular giltwood case
surmounted by a scrolled
pediment and alternating
flowerheads and barley motifs in
relief, surrounding a circular
white painted wooden dial with
Roman numerals and the
inscription 'A. WILLARD JR.
BOSTON', dial partly repainted,
case partially re-gilt, door and
églomisé panel restored, probably
Simon Willard, Roxbury,
Massachusetts, 1800-1820, 30½in
(76cm) wide. **$14,000-18,000**

*A similar clock, by Simon Willard,
is at Greenfield Village, Henry
Ford Museum.
See The American Clock by
William H. Distin and Robert
Bishop (New York, 1976) illus.52.*

Georgian mahogany wall dial
ck, signed Robt. Mawley,
ndon, fusee timepiece
vement reconverted to verge
apement, 13½ in (34 cm).
500-2,200

A Georgian mahogany wall
timepiece, the dial signed Joseph
Newman, London, the fusee
movement with engraved tapered
backplate and verge escapement,
18 in (46 cm). **$1,000-1,200**

431

A black forest postman's alarm wall clock, c1870. **$200-300**

A French tole-peinte wall clock, 19thC, 18 in (46 cm). **$1,300-1,700**

A late Victorian oak drop dial wall clock, with white painted dial inscribed, G.W.R. the single fusee movement with anchor escapement, labelled G.W.R. 1362, 27½ in (70 cm). **$200-300**

A two weight Vienna walnut wall clock, by Gustav Becker, c1890, 48 in (120 cm). **$600-900**

An American regulator striking wall clock, in a walnut case, c1890 26 in (65 cm). **$300-400**

A double weight Vienna regulator wall clock, in walnut case, rack striking, by Gustav Becker, c1890. **$700-1,000**

A gilt cartel clock, by Mynuel, Paris, 19thC. **$2,000-3,000**

A walnut wall regulator, signed M Schonberger, Vienna, the movement striking on a gong with wood rod pendulum, 45 in (112.5 cm). **$1,500-2,200**

A walnut cased German wall clock, striking on a gong, c1900, 34 in (85 cm). **$300-400**

A French ormolu cased cartel clock, in the Louis XV style, the movement striking on a bell, inscribed G.D.S. M.Sins du Louvre, early 20thC, 21½ in (54 cm). **$1,000-1,200**

A Japanese wall clock, the bracket lacquered in red and black, the brass movement with double verge foliot escapement countwheel strike and alarm, 14½ in (37 cm). **$1,400-1,700**

Garnitures

A Friesian Stoelkiok, the movement with vertical verge escapement and outside rack striking, 18thC, 29 in (74 cm). $1,500-2,200

A French gilt brass clock garniture, the 2-train movement with Brocot type suspension, outside locking plate, bell striking, numbered 1022, and signed Rollin a Paris, 21 in (53 cm). **$2,000-3,000**

A Louis XV style ormolu wall clock, 38 in (95 cm). **$1,300-1,700**

A French clock garniture, the dial inscribed Maple & Co. Ltd., Paris, the 8-day movement striking on one bell, some damage, 30 in (75 cm). **$3,500-5,000**

A French white marble, bronze and ormolu clock garniture, the 2-train movement with dial signed N. Crouille, Amiena, 12 in (31 cm), flanked by a pair of matching 2-light candelabra, 11 in (28 cm). **$700-1,000**

An ormolu and porcelain mounted timepiece, with a French verge watch movement, c1820, 20½ in (51.5 cm). **$700-1,000**

A French gilt brass clock garniture, 19thC, 15 in (38 cm). **700-900**

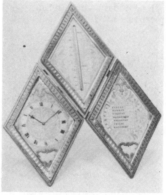

A gilt brass Strut timepiece, the 3 segments containing the movement, a thermometer and a manual calendar, 19thC, 6 in (15 cm). **$3,000-4,500**

Misc – clocks

A gilt metal calendar Sedan timepiece, the 4 in (10 cm) cracked enamel dial signed Cuthbert, London, the movement with a bright cut and engraved cock, c1770. **$1,000-1,200**

◄

A French pink porcelain and ormolu clock garniture, 2-train movement with decorated dial, 13 in (33 cm), flanked by a pair of 2-light candelabra, 12 in (31 cm). **$1,500-2,200**

gilt metal Strut timepiece, the al inscribed Finnigans, 5 in (3 cm). **$1,000-1,400**

A gold half quarter dumb repeating duplex watch, the full plate movement signed Reid & Auld, Edinburgh, 1266, lacking dust cover, London 1811, 5.6 cm. **$1,500-2,200**

A plunge quarter repeating silver cased pocket watch, by James Tregent, hallmarked London 1781. **$700-900**

James Tregent was watch maker to the Prince of Wales.

A William IV gentleman's key wound pocket watch, the 18ct gold case hallmarked Chester, 1830 maker T.E & H.F. incise, the movement with cylinder escapement, signed Thomas and Jno Ollivant, Manchester, No. 7206, 1830. **$1,000-1,200**

A Victorian 18ct gold quarter repeating hunter pocket watch, the case diamond set on green enamel, the white enamel dial with Roman numerals, the keyless lever movement signed J.W. Benson, 62 & 64 Ludgate Hill, London, No. 9486, dated 1890. **$1,000-1,200**

A Swiss gold and enamelled half hunter cylinder watch, together with a pendant set with an amethyst. **$300-400**

An 18ct yellow gold demi hunting cased keyless lever stop watch, by Charles Frodsham, No. 07635, hallmarked London, 1889. **$1,000-1,200**

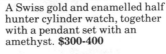

A repousse gold pair cased verge watch, no. 2769 by John Dowson of Grays Inn, London, the case hallmarked 1757, 4.9 cm. **$2,000-3,000**

A Swiss silver sector watch, the shaped movement marked Record Watch Co., Tramelan. **$1,500-2,200**

A Swiss gold and enamel open faced key wind watch, the bridge type movement with cylinder escapement, the gold cuvette numbered 21042, and signed D.F. Aubert a Geneve, 3.5 cm. **$1,400-1,700**

D.F. Aubert, Geneva is recorded as working in the early part of the 19thC.

A Swiss gold half hunter cased keyless cylinder watch, the gilt bar movement with wolf's tooth winding, the dial signed Lecomte, Geneve, 3.7 cm together with a gold guard chain. **$1,000-1,200**

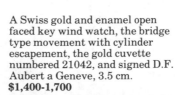

Barometers – wheel

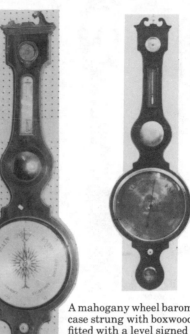

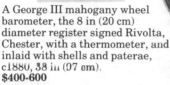

A George III mahogany wheel barometer, the 8 in (20 cm) diameter register signed Rivolta, Chester, with a thermometer, and inlaid with shells and paterae, c1880, 38 in (97 cm). **$400-600**

A mahogany wheel barometer, the case strung with boxwood and fitted with a level signed E. Cetti & Co., No. 11 Brook Strt., Holbn, London, a mirror, a thermometer, a hygrometer, 19thC, 49 in (123.8 cm). **$1,000-1,200**

mahogany wheel barometer, ith an 8 in (20 cm) diameter gister, with a hygrometer, nvex thermometer and level, gned J. Pini, 23 Brook Street, olbn, London, restored, c1840, in (102 cm). **$500-600**

A five dial banjo barometer, contained in a mahogany case, boxwood strung, by P. Soldini, Hull, early 19thC. **$300-400**

◄ A George III inlaid mahogany framed banjo barometer and thermometer, by Tacchi, Bedford. **$400-600**

r. A rosewood wheel barometer timepiece, with 12 in (30 cm) silvered scales inscribed D. Fagioli & Son, 3 Gt. Warner St, Clerkenwell, mercury thermometer, hygrometer, spirit level and timepiece, 51 in (127.5 cm). **$2,000-3,000**

l. An inlaid mahogany wheel barometer timepiece, with 12 in (30 cm) silvered scales, mercury thermometer, hygrometer and spirit level, inscribed V. Zanetti, Manchester, 50½ in (128 cm). **$3,500-5,000**

A Georgian inlaid mahogany framed wheel barometer and thermometer in banjo case, inscribed G.C. Ross, York, 39 in (97 cm). **$500-600**

A barometer and thermometer with inset small convex mirror, with ivory turning handle, 19thC. **$500-600**

Stick

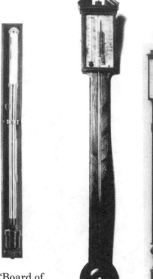

A brass 'Board of Trade' marine standard barometer, signed Adie & Son, Edinburgh, with thermometer, gimbal mount and iron cistern, 19thC, 39 in (97 cm).
$600-700

A George III mahogany stick barometer, signed P. Caminada, Taunton, with engraved scale and thermometer, c1820, 38 in (95 cm).
$600-800

A mahogany ship's barometer, with ebony stringing, ivory plates engraved J. Bassnett, Liverpool, with thermometer, gimbal mounting, ivory adjustment knob, 19thC, 37 in (94 cm).
$2,000-3,000

A Georgian mahogany stick barometer, signed Cetti & Co., London, with a thermometer, 38 in (95 cm).
$700-900

A George III walnut stick barometer, by Jno. Corti, the concave pediment flanked by the original brass finials, with paper dial and chevron veneered moulded shaft, c1800, 38 in (98 cm).
$2,000-3,000

C.f. Nicholas Goodison, English Barometers 1680-1860, page 176, plate 115.

A Victorian stick barometer/ thermometer by Chadburn Brothers, Sheffield, in a walnut case, 37 in (93 cm).
$400-600

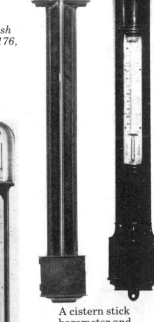

A mahogany stick barometer, the scale engraved G & G. Dixey, Opticians to the King, 3 New Bond Street, London, with thermometer, early 19thC, 36½ in (91 cm).
$1,000-1,200

A Georgian barometer, signed G & G. Dixey, Opticians to the King 3 New Bond Street, London, with vernier, bowed glazing, thermometer, 39 in (99 cm).
$1,700-2,500

A mahogany stick barometer, engraved J. Cuff, London, with thermometer, restored, reconstituted, 36½ in (91 cm).
$1,000-1,200

A cistern stick barometer and thermometer, by Dollond, London, the bow front mahogany case with ebony stringing, with turned bone adjusting knob, early 19thC, 41 in (102 cm).
$2,500-3,500

A mahogany stick barometer with silvered brass plate, signed H. Gregory, Near the India House, London, with diagonal thermometer cistern guard, 18thC, 40½ in (102.8 cm).
$2,000-3,000

Georgian ossbanded ahogany veneer ick barometer, graved arometer, Knie, ecit, the case with corative ebony and xwood stringing, ½ in (94 cm). ,000-1,200

A Victorian mahogany stick barometer, by Marratt & Short, 63 King William Street, London, c1860, 36 in (90 cm). **$600-800**

A Georgian mahogany stick barometer, engraved Nairne, London, mounted with a Fahrenheit thermometer, with pierced brass reservoir cover, 39 in (97 cm). **$2,500-3,500**

A mahogany stick barometer, the silvered plate signed P. Riva, Fecit, the case boxwood and ebony strung, with ivory ball finial, early 19thC, 37½ in (95.2 cm). **$800-1,200**

A late Georgian stick barometer by Roncketi, Manchester, with a thermometer in mahogany case with rope pattern line inlay, broken arch pediment with bronze eagle finial, 38 in (95 cm). **$500-600**

MAKE THE MOST OF MILLER'S

Every care has been taken to ensure the accuracy of descriptions and estimated valuations. Where an attribution is made within inverted commas (e.g. 'Chippendale') or is followed by the word 'style' (e.g. early Georgian style) it is intended to convey that, in the opinion of the publishers, the piece concerned is a later – though probably still antique – reproduction of the style so designated. Unless otherwise stated, any description which refers to 'a set', or 'a pair' includes a valuation for the entire set or the pair, even though the illustration may show only a single item.

A Georgian mahogany stick barometer, the silvered plate signed P. Tarone, fecit, fitted with a thermometer, the case strung with boxwood and ebony, 37 in (94 cm). **$700-900**

stick barometer in ewood case, inlaid mother of pearl, h thermometer d ivory register te by Russ, ndon, 19thC. 0-900

◄ A George III mahogany stick barometer, with a thermometer signed Torre & Co., London, c1800, 37½ in (95 cm). **$600-800**

A mahogany and brass mounted marine barometer, signed George Stebbing, Portsmouth, lacks gimbal, with ivory thermometer and suspension ring, mid-19thC, 38½ in (96 cm). **$1,000-1,400**

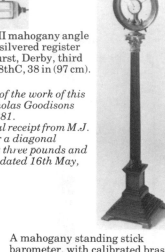

A rare George III mahogany angle barometer, the silvered register signed Whitehurst, Derby, third quarter of the 18thC, 38 in (97 cm). **$7,000-9,000**

For an account of the work of this maker, see Nicholas Goodisons Barometers, p.281.
With the original receipt from M.J. Whitehurst 'For a diagonal barometer', cost three pounds and three shillings, dated 16th May, 1789.

A walnut case combined timepiece, barograph, aneroid barometer and thermometer, the timepiece chain fusee movement with anchor escapement, signed Chadburn & Son, Liverpool, 27 by 14 in (67.9 by 35.6 cm). **$700-1,000**

The Chadburn family were important makers and retailers of optical, mathematical instruments, barometers, etc, with a factory at Sheffield and later a branch at Liverpool.

A mahogany standing stick barometer, with calibrated brass dial framing a clock, 46½ in (118 cm). **$2,000-3,000**

A desk aneroid barometer, signed R & J. Beck, 31 Cornhill, London, gilt brass case, late 19thC, 4 in (10.2 cm). **$400-600**

The Royal Polytechnic Mercury barometer, in carved hardwood case. **$400-600**

Chronometers

An eight day marine chronometer, by Hatton & Harris, No. 570, the movement with Earnshaw spring detent escapement, compensation balance, in brass box in mahogany case, diam. of bezel 1.33 cm. **$8,500-11,000**

A two day marine chronometer, the movement with, replaced, spring detent escapement, numbered 4250, inscribed, D. McGregor & Co. Ltd., Liverpool, Glasgow, Greenock, No. L/8024. **$1,200-1,500**

A two day marine chronometer, the movement with Earnshaw type spring detent escapement, the dial inscribed Thomas Adams Maker to H.R.H. Prince Albert, 36 Lombard St, London, numbered 3986, with inset ivory disc inscribed Adjusted By W.F.Price, 3986. **$1,500-2,200**

A two day marine chronometer, the movement with Earnshaw type spring detent escapement, free sprung bi-metallic balance and helical spring, impressed 21853, inscribed W.F. McDonnell, Central Chambers, Liverpool 1702. **$1,200-1,500**

An eight day marine chronometer by John Roger Arnold, the movement with Arnold type spring detent escapement, free sprung compensated balance with helical spring, c1813. **$4,500-7,000**

A coromandel and brass inlaid marine chronometer, late 19thC. **$1,300-1,700**

n eight day marine chronometer, he movement with Earnshaw pe spring detent escapement, e plate signed Parkinson & rodsham, Change Alley, London, 3. **$3,000-4,500**

A two day marine chronometer, the movement with Earnshaw type spring detent escapement, signed Charles Shepherd, Maker to the Royal Navy, 53 Leadenhall Street, London, 503, the detent missing, the balance damaged. **$800-1,200**

Scientific instruments – dials

French silver Butterfield type al, signed Delure A Paris, 8thC, 3 in (8 cm). 00-1,200

An English brass Butterfield type dial, unsigned, the base with the latitudes of English and Irish cities, the spring-loaded gnomon engraved with a degree scale for latitudes 45°-60°m, late 17thC, 3 in (7.5 cm). **$1,000-1,200**

A silvered brass compass dial, engraved with the cardinal points and signed J. Gilbert, Maker, Tower Hill, London, early 19thC, 5 in (12.7 cm) diam. **$300-500**

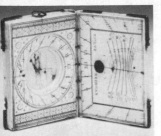

A brass and silver English perpetual calendar, unsigned, one volvelle engraved 'A Perpetuall Almanack', late 17thC, 2 in (5 cm). **$800-1,200**

A German diptych dial, unsigned, the lid pasted with a label of latitudes for 46 continental cities, 18thC, 4 in (10 cm). **$400-600**

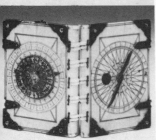

A silver and ivory Dieppe diptych dial, the lid engraved with equinoctial ring, the paper dial listing towns and their latitudes, 17thC, 2 in (5.3 cm). **$700-1,000**

A rare Paul Reinmann ivory book-form diptych dial, Nuremberg, dated 1602, needle missing, 3 by 2¼ by ½ in when closed (7.6 by 5.5 by 1.3 cm). **$5,500-7,000**

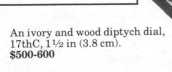

An ivory and wood diptych dial, 17thC, 1½ in (3.8 cm). **$500-600**

A brass equinoctial dial, the hinged equinoctial plate silvered and signed Mackenzie, London, 19thC, 5½ in (14 cm). **$1,300-1,700**

An Augsberg-type gilt brass universal equinoctial dial, by Ludians Theodor Muller, 18thC, 3 in (7.3 cm). **$400-600**

A brass equinoctial dial, the hinged equinoctial plate silvered and signed Watkins & Hill, London, 19thC, 3 in (7.6 cm). **$600-800**

A brass miner's dial, the silvered brass compass dial engraved 'J. Casartelli's Patent, Manchester, No.333', 2 × 0°-60°, contained in a mahogany case, late 19thC, 13¼ in (33.7 cm). **$400-600**

A brass universal equinoctial ring dial, unsigned, the bridge with sliding pinhole sight and engraved with Zodiac and calendar scales, late 18thC, 6 in (15 cm). **$1,500-2,200**

A horizontal brass sundial, dated 1596, 4¼ in (11 cm) square. **$1,000-1,200**

A brass octagonal sundial, signed George Adams, London, mounted with a gnomon, 15 in (37 cm). **$500-600**

Globes

A fine English patent star finder, the globe 5¾ in (14.6 cm) diam., inscribed Cary & Co., Makers to the Admiralty, 7 Pall Mall, London, mahogany case 8½ in (21.9 cm). **$800-1,200**

A star globe, by H. Hughes & Son Ltd., London, 10½ in diam. (26.7 cm), the lid applied with an instruction label. **$400-600**

A pocket globe, by Kenton, 19thC, 3¼ in (8 cm) diam., contained in the original associated mahogany case, 4 in (10 cm) high. **$600-800**
◄

A Xela star globe, 8 in (21 cm) diam., the gores decorated with the constellations and label inscribed Navisphere de Mr. de Magnac, Bte, E. Bertaux, Editeur, Paris, the meridian half circle H. Hughes & Son Ltd., London, No.502, case 10¾ in (27.3 cm). **$300-500**

A pocket globe, by Lane, London, dated 1818, 3¼ in (8 cm) diam. **$800-1,200**

terrestrial globe, 1¾ in (4 cm), he hand-coloured gores decorated ith the Continents, entitled Model of the Earth by J. Manning, a card box, with a trade label for ulman's of Greenwich, 19thC. **200-300**

A miniature terrestrial globe, 1½ in (3.5 cm), by Newton & Sons, dated 1842, in case 2½ in (6 cm) high. **$400-600**

A Malby celestial globe, 3 in (7.5 cm), with a trade label inscribed Malby Celestial Globe, Manufactured for the Commissioners of Irish National Education, Dublin, 1857. **$600-900**

Malby's terrestrial globe, on ooden stand with square rround. **$1,200-1,500**

Surveying

A terrestrial globe, 1¾ in (4 cm), by C. Smith & Son, 63 Charing Cross, 19thC, on base 4¼ in (10.5 cm). **$200-300**

An ebony octant, no. 2003, inscribed C. Johansson, in shaped mahogany case with two telescopes, Continental mid-19thC, 10 in (25 cm), **$800-1,200**

ebony octant, signed T. emsley, Tower Hill, London, in aped oak case, c1800, 10½ in 5.7 cm). **$500-700**

A German sextant, by Bernh. Bunge, Berlin, S.O. No. 740, the telescope with 2 shades and electrical attachment, with accessories and trade label, 10 in (26 cm). **$800-1,200**

A Georgian double frame brass sextant, indistinctly signed on the arc Berge, London, the frame with adjustable telescope socket, 7 shades and mirrors, radius 8 in (21 cm). **$1,200-1,500**

A Cary brass sextant with gold scale, numbered 3856, the 'T' frame with 2 sets of coloured filters, with sleeved aperture for pillar mounting, in fitted mahogany case containing two telescopes and 2 filters, 12 by 11 in (29.8 by 28.6 cm). **$2,500-3,500**

ebony framed octant, signed hard Rowland, fitted with 2 -hole sights, 2 shades, mirrors, hC, the index arm radius 16 in cm). **$1,500-2,200**

441

A double sextant, by W & S. Jones, c1800. **$2,500-3,500**

A brass transit theodolite, by A.T. Cooke & Sons, the sighting telescope focusing by rack and pinion, 15½ in (39 cm). **$600-900**

A brass theodolite, with 1 in (2.5 cm) telescope with rack and pinion focusing and located by twin clamps on the half vertical circle, signed M. Gardner & Sons, Opticians & C, Glasgow, early 19thC, 4 in (9.6 cm). **$600-800**

An anodised and lacquered brass 6 in (15 cm) theodolite, signed Stanley Gt. Turnstile, Holborn, London, No. 8557, and associated staff and tripod, late 19thC, 14 in (36.5 cm). **$1,000-1,400**

A late Victorian brass transit theodolite, by Troughton & Simms, London, with associated vernier mechanism, telescope with adjustable focusing arrangement with accessories, 14 in (35 cm). **$600-900**

A brass protractor, signed Adams, Fleet Street, London, 18thC, 18 in (45.7 cm). **$600-800**

A brass military pattern theodolite, signed Troughton and Simms, London, No. 131, with a number of attachments, 19thC, 11 in (29 cm). **$500-700**

A lacquered brass English dual purpose miners theodolite, by William Wilton, early 19thC, 9 in (22.9 cm) with accessories. **$1,400-1,700**

A brass sector, signed Butterfield Paris, with 6 scales Le Cordes, Les Solides, Les Paries Egales, Porigones, Les Plans, Poids des Boulets and Calibre des Pieces, 18thC, 7 in (17.2 cm). **$500-700**

A lacquered brass circular protractor, by Elliott Bros, London, 19thC, 7½ in (19 cm) **$200-300**

A brass circular protractor with drawing cursor, signed J. Gargovey, 5, Bull St, Birm^m. **$200-300**

An anodised brass French pattern semi circumferentor, by Stanley, London, 11 in (27.5 cm). **$200-300**

A brass surveyor's level the telescope 19 in (48.5 cm) long, the silver brass dial signed W & S. Jones, London, 19thC. **$300-500**

elescopes

A brass sector by John Rowley, signed I. Rowley Fecit, 18thC, 12 in (30.5 cm). **$600-900**

A waywiser, the silvered brass dial signed Elliott Bros, London, 19thC, 44 in **$600-800**

2½ in (6 cm) brass Gregorian reflecting telescope, on stand, signed T. Blunt, 22 Cornhill, ondon, length of tube 14 in (35.5 cm), English, late 18thC. **$1,000-1,400**

A lacquered brass transit telescope, by T. Cooke & Sons Ltd. London, York & Capetown, having a 2½ in (6.3 cm) diam. lens, the body tube 23 in (58.4 cm) long, 19thC. **$1,400-1,700**

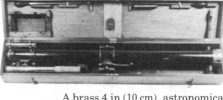

A brass 4 in (10 cm), astronomical refracting telescope, by John Browning, London, having a 56 in (139 cm) long black lacquered body tube, with a prismatic eyepiece mount and a John Browning McClean's Star Spectroscope eyepiece, late 19thC, case 59 in (147 cm) wide. **$600-900**

rare brass double-draw o-power telescope, the hogany covered two section ly tube 25 in (63 cm) long, fitted th a draw tube either end, the epiece with a dust slide, signed scough, London, Inv^t et Fecit, 559/360, 18thC. **700-2,500**

A 2½ in (6 cm) J.H. Dallmeyer brass two-draw telescope, 2 (ex 3) eyepieces, pine case 35½ in (89 cm). **$300-500**

A 4½ in (10.5 cm) brass reflecting telescope, signed W. & S. JONES, Holborn, London, late 18thC, with later tripod stand. **$700-1,000**

A lacquered brass and iron astronomical refracting 5 in (12.5 cm) telescope, by T. Cooke & Sons Ltd., London and York, the 67 in (170 cm) long body tube with rack and pinion focusing and mounted with a telescopic sight, the clockwork mechanism controlled by a governor within a cage, mounted on a webbed iron pillar, 58¼ in (148 cm) high with circular platform base, late 19thC. **$5,500-7,000**

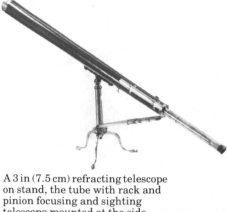

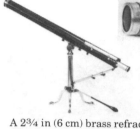

A four-draw Sheffield plated telescope, signed Ebsworth, 54 Fleet Street, London, early 19thC 28¼ in (71 cm) long fully extended, in a leather case. **$500-600**

A 2¾ in (6 cm) brass refracting telescope, signed FRASER & SON, LONDON, the 43¼ in (110 cm) long body tube (re-finished) with rack and pinion focusing, 19thC, with accessories in mahogany case 45¼ in (114 cm) long. **$1,500-2,200**

A 3 in (7.5 cm) refracting telescope on stand, the tube with rack and pinion focusing and sighting telescope mounted at the side, signed around the eyepiece aperture Dollond, London, tube 43 in (109 cm) long. **$1,300-1,700**

A refracting telescope, signed Ramsden, London, late 19thC, 9½ in (24 cm) long. **$300-500**

A 7½ in (18.5 cm) Newtonian reflecting telescope, having a 55 in (138 cm) long grey-painted tinned-iron body tube, with brass sighting telescope. **$500-600**

A rare silver and shagreen pocket telescope necessaire, signed Ribright,Optician, Fecit, London, the body engraved * BY Ye KINGS ROYAL PATENT and containing a knife, tweezers and other items, 18thC, 4 in (10 cm) long. **$2,500-3,500**

A telescope, by James Show c1750. **$3,500-5,000**

A single-draw brass 2 in (5 cm) refracting telescope, unsigned, the tube 36½ in (91.5 cm) long, with accessories, case 38½ in (96 cm) wide. **$500-600**

A brass 2½ in (6 cm) reflecting telescope, unsigned, having 13 in (33 cm) long body tube, early 19thC. **$500-600**

Microscopes

A lacquered brass compound binocular petrological microscope, signed R. & J. Beck, 31 Cornhill, London, 19thC, with range of accessories. **$1,500-2,200**

A lacquered brass compound binocular microscope, engraved Baker, 244 High Holborn, London, 19thC, 15½ in (39 cm) high, with accessories, including a bull's-eye condenser. **$500-600**

A lacquered brass compound monocular microscope, signed Adie & Son, Edinburgh, 19thC, 11 in (28 cm) wide, with one objective and bull's-eye condense **$200-300**

provincial lacquered brass
binocular simple microscope,
signed Britton, Barnstaple,
thC,
00-1,200

A lacquered brass compound
binocular microscope, by
Carpenter & Westley, 24 Regent
Street, London, mid-19thC,
with accessories.
$1,200-1,500

A botanical microscope, the pillar
signed Cary, London, late 18thC,
5 in (12.7 cm) wide, with
accessories. **$500-600**

acquered brass compound
ocular microscope, signed C
llins, Optician, 157 Gt.
·tland St., London,
h accessories.
700-2,500

A brass binocular microscope,
signed H. Crouch, 54 London
Wall, London, and numbered 354,
with accessories. **$500-600**

An unusual lacquered brass
travelling microscope, by J.B.
Dancer, Manchester, 19thC,
$600-800

A John Cuthbert brass reflecting
microscope, dated 1828, lacking
all reflecting optics, 11 in (28 cm)
high. **$2,500-3,500**

acquered brass compound
nocular microscope, signed J.B.
ncer, Optician, Manchester,
hC, 16¼ in (41 cm) high, with
aduated drawers containing
es and accessories.
0-900

A brass 'Culpeper' type
microscope, signed Lincoln,
London, early 19thC, 12¾ in
(32 cm) high, with a drawer of
accessories. **$1,200-1,500**

A lacquered brass and iron
compound binocular microscope,
signed H. Crouch, 51 London
Wall, London, 574, 19thC,
with accessories,
dated June 16th 1871.
$600-700

445

A brass binocular microscope, No. 5064, signed Ross, London, with bar-limb construction, with full set of accessories, c1880, 15 in (38 cm) high. **$1,700-2,500**

A brass compound binocular microscope, signed Smith & Beck, 6 Coleman St., London, 19thC, in a mahogany cabinet, 19¼ in (49 cm) high, with a bull's-eye condenser. **$1,200-1,500**

A lacquered brass compound monocular microscope, signed Watkins, Charing Cross, Lond with disc of 6 objectives, with accessories including a set of 6 ivory slides and fish plate, earl 19thC, **$1,200-1,500**

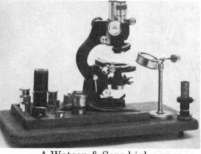

A lacquered brass compound binocular microscope, signed Watson & Son, 313 High Holborn, London, 912, 19thC, 19 in (47 cm) high, with a wide range of contemporary accessories, and a collection of glass slides, and some 1920's accessories. **$1,400-1,700**

A Watson & Sons high power binocular microscope, numbered 79995, a Flatters & Garnett precision micro-projector, a case of slides, transformers, condensers and other accessories. **$300-500**

A Greenough stereoscopic biobjective binocular microscope by Carl Zeiss, Jena, mounted on later stand, with glass stages an plated frame, with 2 objectives, c1930. **$100-200**

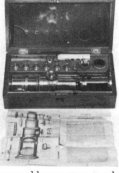

A lacquered brass compound monocular microscope, unsigned, early 19thC, 11 in (27.5 cm) wide, with accessories and original instructions. **$300-600**

A Victorian brass microscope, with spare lenses, 12½ in (31 cm **$200-300**

A lacquered brass botanical microscope, unsigned, early 19thC, with accessories including forceps and slides, 3¾ in (9.8 cm) wide. **$300-600**

Medical Instruments

A set of Charrierre amputation instruments, French, with a saw with interchangeable blade, 3 Liston-type knives, scalpels, retractor, tourniquet, needles and silk-ligature thread, mid 19thC, case 16 by 6 in (40 by 15 cm). **$1,200-1,500**

The firm of Charrierre are France's best known 19th century Surgical Instrument Makers.

Miller's is a price GUIDE not a price LIST

The price ranges given reflect the average price a purchaser should pay for similar items. Condition, rarity of design or pattern, size, colour, pedigree, restoration and many other factors must be taken into account when assessing values.

A set of Down Brothers operating instruments, with 24 assorted chrome-plated instruments for minor operations, early 20thC, case 10¼ by 7 in (26 by 18 cm). $300-500

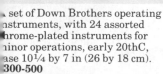

A set of William Smith field surgeons instruments, English, including long and short amputation knives, large and small saws, tourniquet, needles, Keys Saw, retractor, double-ended elevator and bone cutters, early 19thC, case 19 by 6 in (48 by 15 cm). $1,400-1,700

William Smith is recorded as working in London between 1803 and 1831.

A post mortem set, containing 2 trephines, an elevator, lenticulars, an Itley's saw, cranium forceps and brush, 19thC, 9½ in (24 cm) wide. $800-1,200

A large set of Down Brothers naval surgeon instruments, English, containing 60 assorted instruments for amputation, dentistry, drainage, trepanning, bullet extraction and tracheotomy, late 19thC, the case 18 by 9½ by 5 in (46 by 24 by 12.5 cm). $1,300-1,700

A post mortem set, containing a saw, chisel, a Liston knife, universal handle and 4 scalpels, early 19thC. $300-500

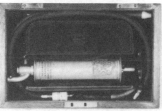

A lacquered brass medical syringe, by Viss, 62 Strand, London, 19thC, with a set of 4 ivory tubes and other accessories. $200-300

A Royal Navy pattern surgeon's general operation set, by William Fr. Durroch, 28 St. Thomas's St. East, with 2 amputation saws, 5 Liston's amputating knives, metacarpal saw, bullet forceps, bone forceps, trocar and cannulae, bistouries, Bowman's scissors, Hey's skull saw, 2 Petit's screw tourniquets, lenticular, toothkey, 2 tooth forceps, catheters, 7 scalpels, trephine handle with 2 blades, (one lacking), thread, etc. with 2 pessaries, c1860. $1,700-2,500

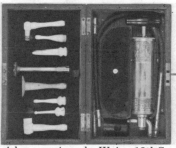

A brass syringe, by Weiss, 19thC, with an extensive range of ivory accessories. $300-500

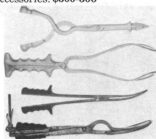

Gynaecological instruments, English, including a Smellies perforator, a pair of Simpsons' obstetrics forceps, 2 Crainiotomy forceps, late 19thC. $600-800

A pair of steel nasal polyps forceps, with silver handles, 19thC. $200-300

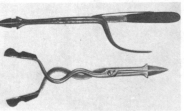

A decapitation hook, by Mayor & Meltzer, with an unusual 19thC Curtis with burnished steel shank, the ebony handle incorporating a screw attachment and a scoop by Maw, London. $300-500

A burnished steel basilyst, with spring assisted curve cutting blades and chequered ebony handle, by Mathews, London, 19thC, 14¼ in (36.2 cm) long, and a pair of perforators, signed Portsea Island Union. $600-700

A pair of razors, by G. Deakin, 18thC, in leather covered carrying case, 6¼ in (16 cm) long. $200-300

A silver and shagreen etui, containing 6 steel lancets with tortoiseshell guards, by Evans, Old Change, London, 19thC, 2½ in (6 cm) high. **$300-500**

A single-bladed brass and iron scarificator, Continental, with compartment for housing alternate blades, early 18thC, 4¼ in (11 cm) high. **$500-700**

A scarificator set, including brass scarificator, engraved Wood York with 3 spare blades, 19thC, in fitted case, 3¼ in (8 cm) wide. **$300-500**

A William IV silver lancet case, the 4 lancets with tortoiseshell guards, 2½ in (6 cm) high. **$200-300**

A mahogany and brass mounted domestic medicine chest, most bottles with labels of Bewley & Evans, Lower Sackville St., Dublin, the drawer below containing 6 further bottles, scales, pestle and mortar, 19thC, 12 in (30.5 cm) wide. **$1,400-1,700**

An unusual parcel gilt and horn linctus dropper, English, the tail section removing to reveal the dropper with pierced tongue, hallmarked W.G. London 1884, 6 in (15 cm). **$1,500-2,200**

A George III mahogany and brass fitted domestic medicine chest, 23 in (58 cm) high. **$1,500-2,200**

Scientific instruments : dental instruments

An apothecary's chest, 10¾ in (27.5 cm). **$1,000-1,200**

A ceramic phrenological bust, by L.N. Fowler, 337 Strand, London, mid-19thC, 12 in (30 cm) high. **$1,400-1,700**

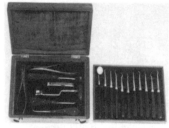

A set of dental instruments, English, containing a set of 10 probes and scalers, a mirror, a key with dog-leg shank, 3 elevators, 2 pairs of extractors and a gum lancet, c1880, the case 9 by 7½ in (23 by 19 cm). **$1,400-1,700**

A set of dental hygiene instruments, Continental, the 9 steel instruments for scraping and filing, late 18thC, in case 3 by 2½ in (7.5 by 6.5 cm). **$700-900**

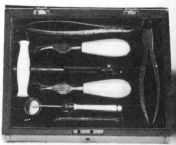

A set of Ash dental instruments, English, third quarter of the 19thC, case 10 by 8 in (25.5 by 20 cm). **$1,400-1,700**

Claudius Ash & Sons, Dental Instrument Manufacturers, Broad St., Soho, and later at Kentish Town, c1859-1875.

A set of dental scaling instruments, c1800, in case 3 in (7.5 cm) long. **$800-1,200**

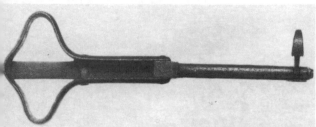

An unusual folding iron tooth key, pitted overall with corrosion, mid-18thC, 6 in (15 cm) high. **$1,300-1,700**

A coloured wax instructional model of the development of the human teeth in glazed case, 15¾ in (40 cm) wide, and a moulded simulated ivory model of a tooth in case. **$500-700**

Scientific instruments : miscellaneous

A collection of 4 brass and one ivory drawing instruments, one signed 'á pouces de Paris'. **$400-600**

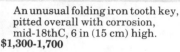

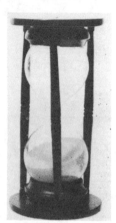

A presentation walnut-veneered drawing instrument case, bound with nickel plate, by Adie, Broadway Works, Westminster, with numerous nickel-plated and ivory instruments, and water-colour paints and brushes, late 19thC, 13½ in (36.5 cm) wide. **$800-1,200**

A ship's hour glass, English, early 19thC, 9¼ in (23 cm) high. **$300-400**

A set of brass drawing instruments, comprising: folding square, ruler, parallel ruler, pens, dividers and charcoal holder, the ruler inscribed Made by Tho. Wright – Instrument Maker to His Majesty, one instrument missing, 18thC, the case 6¾ in (17 cm). **$1,500-2,200**

A French alloy and nickel-plated brass anemometer, by Jules Richard, 25 Rue Melingue, Paris (XIXe). **$300-400**

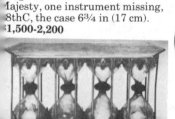

A brass sand clock, one glass now lacking sand, late 18thC, 8½ in (21.5 cm) wide. **$1,500-2,200**

A lacquered brass and mahogany galvanometer, by Siemens Bros. & Co. London, late 19thC, 18 in (46 cm) high. **$500-700**

A miner's brass air-flow meter, 6 in (15 cm) diam., in leather case. **$300-400**

An electrostatic friction generator, by W. & J. George Ltd., Birmingham & London, late 19thC, 18 in (45 cm) high, with 4 static electricity demonstration devices. **$200-300**

A chondrometer, by De Grave, Short & Fanner, 19thC, 12¼ in (31 cm) long. **$400-600**

An electrical induction coil, by Harry W. Cox Ltd., early 20thC, 21½ in (54 cm) long, with brass terminals and switch, 28 in (71 cm) long overall. **$400-600**

A Sullivan's galvanometer, engraved H.W. Sullivan, 19 Great Winchester St., London E.C., 14½ in (37 cm) high. **$300-500**

A Melloni's thermo electric/optical bench apparatus, by Société Genevoise, Geneva, supplied by Queen & Co. Philadelphia PA, 29 in (73 cm) long. **$1,400-1,700**

A Kentotometer, by Brady & Martin Ltd., Newcastle-on-Tyne, 17 in (42.5 cm) high. **$300-400**

A lacquered gyroscope, the base signed T. Cooke & Sons, York & London, late 19thC, 10½ in (25.5 cm) high, with accessories. **$600-800**

A brass set of scales, 19thC, 4½ in (11.5 cm) wide. **$600-700**

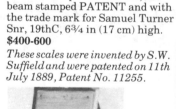

A rare brass postal balance, the beam stamped PATENT and with the trade mark for Samuel Turner Snr, 19thC, 6¾ in (17 cm) high. **$400-600**

These scales were invented by S.W. Suffield and were patented on 11th July 1889, Patent No. 11255.

A lacquered brass and mahogany double-barrelled air pump, identical to type produced by Benjamin Messer, Minories, London, c1820, with Magdeburg sphere, some damage, 14 in (35 cm) high. **$700-1,000**

cameras

A rare 4.5 cm by 6 cm Voigtlander Bijou single-lens reflex camera, with Heliar 10 cm. f4.5 lens, with photographer's manuscript exposure diary. **$2,000-3,000**

An Ensign roll-film Reflex Tropical model camera, 4.25 in. f7.7 lens. **$300-400**

A brass chondrometer, signed Corcoran & Co. London, early 19thC, 10 in (24 cm) wide, with instructions and weights table inside lid. **$300-400**

A brass Builoscope, stamped Universal Scala Centesimale No. 15075, 10½ in (26 cm) wide. **$300-400**

A quarter plate sliding box wet-plate camera, with Petzval-type portrait lens. **$700-1,000**

A wet-plate camera, probably English, with Petzval-type lens, 2 plate holders and ground glass focusing screen, 1870's, 6 by 6 in (15 by 15 cm). **$600-700**

l. A 4.5 cm by 6 cm Tropical Sonnet miniature folding plate camera, by Contessa-Nettel. **$1,200-1,500**

r. A 2 by 2 Marion's Metal Miniature camera, with 100 mm f.7 Petzval-type lens, with 13 plate holders and pack of unexposed Britannia Dry Plates. **$1,700-2,500**

A quarter-plate Duplex Ruby tropical reflex camera, by Thornton Pickard, with Ross Xpres 6½ in. f4.5 lens. **$1,700-2,500**

A rare whole plate Marion's mahogany sliding box twin-lens reflex camera, with pair of Voigtlander Euryscop IV No.3 brass-bound lenses – Nos. 35633 and 35634, with set of Waterhouse stops, rack focusing and detachable exterior reflex viewing mirror, 14½ in (36 cm) high. **$1,700-2,500**

A rare quarter-plate Adams Hand Camera, with pull-out lens/shutter housing, rack focussing Wray 5½ in. lens with iris diaphragm. **$200-300**

A Zeiss Contaflex 35 mm twin-lens reflex camera, No.Z42828, with Sonnar 5 cm. f5 taking-lens No. 1754370 - and integral exposure meter. **$800-1,200**

An Alpha Reflex camera, Swiss, model 7b, with Heinz Kilfitt Makro-Kilar 90 mm f/2.8 lens, shutter 1 1/1000 sec. and rangefinder, 1950's. **$600-700**

A fine Biokam 17.5 mm hand-cranked cinematograph camera and projector, by Alfred Darling, Brighton No. 190 in polished mahogany casing with Voigtlander: Euryscop 38 mm f7.7 and Projection Lenses, with 3 unopened tins of 17.5 mm film. **$3,000-4,500**

A lacquered brass Camera Lucida, unsigned, fitted with an adjustable prism, 19thC, 9 in (23 cm) long. **$100-200**

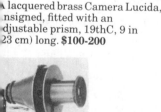

A rare 3¼ by 3¼ Demon Detective Camera, No. 2 size, invented by Walter O'Reilly, London and manufactured by W. Phillips, for the American Camera Co, with maker's instructions. **$1,300-1,700**

A rare Photoret Magazine Snap Shot Watch Camera, by the Magic Introduction Co. New York. **$600-800**

rare Brins Patent Miniature Detective Camera, English, no. 7143, missing parts, c1891, 6 in (15 cm) high. **$2,500-3,500**

A black painted Thornton Pickard gun camera, with revolving film magazine and trigger operated shutter release, 38½ (99 cm) long. **$600-700**

451

A rare Claudet's Patent hand-held stereoscope, with bifocal separation body design and stamped gilt credit Claudet 107 Regent St., patented March 1855. **$600-900**

Scientific instruments : viewers

A Kaleidoscope, probably German, for viewing opaque objects, with a revolving drum mounted with artificial flowers, mirrors in need of re-silvering, c1860, 12½ in (32 cm) high. **$800-1,200**

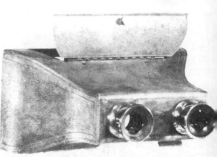

A Claudet's Patent Brewster-pattern stereoscope, with stamp Claudet 107 Regent Street. **$300-400**

A Brewster Patent Kaleidoscope, English, tube 10 in (25 cm) long, the side with small drawer containing a variety of coloured glass chips and glass slips for making kaleidoscope discs, 11¼ in (28 cm) long. **$1,700-2,500**

Sir David Brewster published his Treatise on the Kaleidoscope in 1816 and patented his design the following year.

l. An early mahogany taper-bodied diapositive viewer, with box-form slide chamber, with one doped tissue hand-coloured diapositive view of the interior of the Thames Tunnel, viewer 20½ in (51 cm) long overall, together with various printed illustrations and plans of the '...projected Thames Tunnel...' one dated 1827. **$500-700**
r. A cardboard-barrelled zoetrope optical toy, drum 7 in (17.5 cm) diam. in wood box. **$300-500**

An Emil Reynaud Praxinoscope, French, the painted metal drum containing coloured lithographic cartoons, with candle illuminant above, with 25 cartoon strips, late 19thC, 8 in (20 cm) high. **$800-1,200**

A Wrench Triple Focusing Magic Lantern, English, the three-jet burner illuminant with reflector, late 19thC, 26 in (66 cm) long. **$500-700**

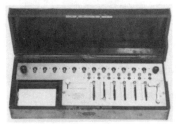

A rare Thomas De Colmar Arithomometer, the brass mechanism with capacity of 6 by 7 by 12 figures, mid 19thC, 18 in (46 cm) wide. **$1,700-2,500**

A Carpenter & Westley Phantasmagoria lantern, English, complete with Argand lamp and glass chimney, c1830, 25 in (64 cm). **$400-600**

PRICES

The never-ending problem of fixing prices for antiques! A price can be affected by so many factors, for example:
- *condition*
- *desirability*
- *rarity*
- *size*
- *colour*
- *provenance*
- *restoration*
- *the sale of a prestigious collection*
- *collection label*
- *appearance of a new reference book*
- *new specialist sale at major auction house*
- *mentioned on television*
- *the fact that two people present at auction are determined to have the piece*
- *where you buy it*

One also has to contend with the fact that an antique is not only a 'thing of beauty' but a commodity. The price can again be affected by:–
- *supply and demand*
- *international finance – currency fluctuation*
- *fashion*
- *inflation*
- *the fact that a museum has vast sums of money to spend*

A pair of oval dishes, with diamond and flute cutting, scalloped rims and cut bases, c1830, 7 in (17.5 cm).
$100-150

Candelabra

A pair of air-twist tapersticks, each with cylindrical nozzle with everted rim over a stem enclosing an air corkscrew flanked by collars, c1750, 6 in (14.7 cm).
$3,000-4,500

A Bohemian cut and coloured sweetmeat bowl and cover, the ruby glass bowl with turnover shaped rim with gilt palisade flutes round the base, c1830, 7½ in (19 cm). **$600-700**

A Venetian standing bowl, the border with traces of gilding between 2 applied blue bands, c1500, 10 in (25.5 cm).
$1,500-2,200

A cut candlestick, 1760-1770, 7 in (18 cm). **$300-500**

A baluster candlestick, c1720, 8½ in (21.5 cm). **$1,400-1,700**

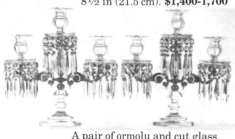

A pair of ormolu and cut glass three light candelabra, 16 in (40 cm). **$2,500-3,500**

A pair of sulphide candlesticks, probably by Apsley Pellatt, on octagonal diamond panelled stem enclosing a sulphide statuette of La Frileuse, after Houdon, one foot chipped, c1820, 8 in (20.3 cm).
$1,200-1,500

A pair of cylindrical candlesticks, facet cut, the stems with faceted knops, 15 in (37.5 cm).
$600-700

A giltmetal and cut glass hanging dish-light, 43 in (107.5 cm).
$3,000-4,500

Chandeliers

A George III style cut glass chandelier, with repairs, 58½ in (146 cm). **$9,000-13,000**

A good eight arm cut glass chandelier, having a gilt corona, the bag with 6 tiers of buttons and icicles terminating in a glass ball, English, c1810, 48 in (120 cm).
$22,000-42,000

The colour of the glass is particularly fine and the cutting of fine quality.

Decanters

A set of six early Georgian engraved decanters, with ringed stoppers, 9½ in (23.5 cm), and six matching glasses. **$800-1,200**

A hexagonal moulded decanter, with string ring, c1730, 11½ in (29 cm). **$100-150**

l. A pair of ovoid spirit decanters, with flute cut shoulders and neck rings, cut hexagonal stoppers, c1730, 8½ in (21 cm). **$100-150**
r. A pair of ovoid spirit decanters, with knife edge neck rings and lozenge stoppers, c1800, 8½ in (21.5 cm). **$300-400**

A pair of Cork decanters, the half fluted bodies with etched decoration and triple ring necks, later dissimilar stoppers, marked to base Cork Glass Co., c1810. **$700-1,000**

A rare marked Irish 'Union' decanter and stopper, made for Mary Carter and Son, engraved with a ribbon inscribed The Land We Live In, above the initials M.P., the reverse with a spray of shamrock flanked by a rose and a thistle, 10½ in (26.5 cm). **$1,700-2,500**

Mary Carter and Son had a retail shop at 80 Grafton St., Dublin in about 1800. The firm is listed in Dublin directories although no advertisements are known. For a pair of unmarked decanters similarly engraved see Phelps Warren, Irish Glass, pl. 107.

A decanter of club shape, the base and neck flute cut, with 2 bands of egg and tulip engraving, with cut lozenge stopper, c1780, 10 in (25 cm). **$300-500**

A pair of dark heavy Irish decanters, the fluted bodies cut with stars and diamonds, c1790, 9 in (23 cm). **$700-900**

A good pair of ovoid spirit decanters, with fluted and blaze cutting, annulated neck rings, with target stoppers, c1810, 7 in (18 cm). **$300-500**

A pair of oval ribbed spirit bottles, with band of small diamonds round shoulders, 7 in (16 cm). **$100-200**

A Cork Rodney decanter, the squat mallet body with moulded base fluting and engraved Vesica pattern, with 3 feathered neck rings, loose moulded disc stopper, embossed on base Cork Glass Co., c1800, 8½ in (21.3 cm). **$700-900**

A pair of Irish cut decanters, with band of alternate square and oval diamond panels, annulated neck rings, mushroom stoppers, c1820, 8 in (20 cm). **$500-600**

A Victorian wine decanter, bell shaped and heavily ribbed, some damage, 10 in (25 cm).
$30-60

A pair of ovoid decanters,, the bodies with broad flute cutting, c1830, 9 in (22 cm).
$600-800

A large heavy cut decanter, with base and strawberry diamond cutting round the ovoid body, prism cut neck, diamond cut hollow mushroom stopper, c1825, 9½ in (23.5 cm). **$100-150**

A pair of straight sided decanters, with relief strawberry cut diamonds, moulded neck rings, c1840, 8½ in (21 cm).
$600-800

Drinking glasses

A Victorian oak tantalus, with 3 cut glass decanters.
$600-800

A pair of spirit decanters, the ovoid bodies with flute cut bases and slanting bands of cut diamonds, c1825, 7½ in (18.5 cm).
$400-600

A baluster goblet, the bell bowl with a tear to the solid lower part, supported on a triple annulated knop above an inverted baluster section, c1710, 9 in (22 cm).
$800-1,200

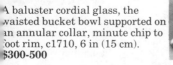

A baluster deceptive wine glass, on a ball knop enclosing a tear above a short plain section, c1700, 4 in (10.5 cm). **$300-500**

A baluster cordial glass, the waisted bucket bowl supported on an annular collar, minute chip to foot rim, c1710, 6 in (15 cm).
$300-500

A deceptive wine glass, on an inverted baluster stem with elongated tear, 5½ in (13.2 cm).
$300-400

A baluster wine glass, of drawn trumpet shape, the stem with an angular waist knop, c1730, 7½ in (18.5 cm). **$300-400**

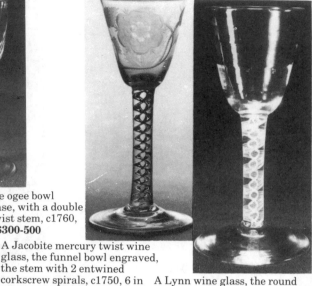

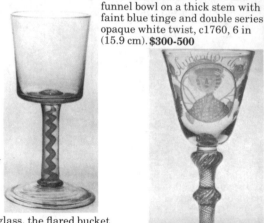

A wine glass, the ogee bowl reticulated at base, with a double series opaque twist stem, c1760, 6½ in (16 cm). **$300-500**

A Jacobite mercury twist wine glass, the funnel bowl engraved, the stem with 2 entwined corkscrew spirals, c1750, 6 in (15.7 cm). **$500-600**

A Lynn wine glass, the round funnel bowl with 3 horizontal corrugations, on a double series opaque twist stem, c1760, 6 in (15.5 cm). **$500-600**

An unusual cordial, the round funnel bowl on a thick stem with faint blue tinge and double series opaque white twist, c1760, 6 in (15.9 cm). **$300-500**

A Ratafia glass, the short narrow round funnel bowl fluted and engraved with a basket of roses and floral sprays, c1760, 7 in (17.5 cm). **$700-1,000**

A wine glass, the pan top bowl with multi spiral air twist stem, c1750, 6 in (15 cm). **$300-400**

A wine glass, the flared bucket bowl set on a stem enclosing an opaque gauze corkscrew, folded conical foot, c1760, 7 in (17.8 cm). **$500-600**

A rare air twist Jacobite portrait goblet, the funnel bowl engraved with a portrait of Prince Charles Edward in Highland dress within a cartouche inscribed Audentior ibo and flanked by oak and thistle sprays, very slight chip to foot rim c1750, 8 in (20 cm). **$5,500-7,000**

A colour twist wine glass, with a funnel bowl, the stem with a brick red core entwined within 2 thick opaque spiral threads, c1765, 6 in (15 cm). **$700-1,000**

An air twist wine glass, with trumpet shaped bowl, c1750, 7 in (17 cm). **$300-400**

A rare Lynn ale glass, the extended funnel bowl with horizontal rings and initial 'T'M', double series opaque twist stem, c1760, 7 in (17.5 cm). **$1,200-1,500**

A Beilby enamelled wine glass, foot chipped, c1770, 6 in (14.5 cm). **$700-900**

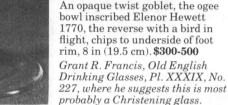

A rare Irish volunteer glass, of drawn funnel form, inscribed Newry Rangers 1779 flanking a royal crown, the reverse with ears of corn, mercury twist stem, conical foot, chip on foot rim, 1779, 8 in (20.3 cm). **$2,500-3,500**

◄

An opaque twist goblet, the ogee bowl inscribed Elenor Hewett 1770, the reverse with a bird in flight, chips to underside of foot rim, 8 in (19.5 cm). **$300-500**
Grant R. Francis, Old English Drinking Glasses, Pl. XXXIX, No. 227, where he suggests this is most probably a Christening glass.

A fine colour twist wine glass, the ogee bowl on a stem with a double series opaque twist and outer spiralling translucent blue twist, 7 in (17.2 cm) **$1,500-2,200**

A political mixed twist goblet, the rounded bowl inscribed Wilkes and Liberty, the reverse with a bird in flight, c1775, 7 in (17.3 cm). **$600-700**

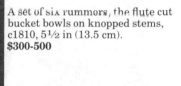

A set of six rummers, the flute cut bucket bowls on knopped stems, c1810, 5½ in (13.5 cm). **$300-500**

A bucket rummer, with base fluting and band of blaze cutting, band of thistle engraving, radially cut underneath, c1820, 8½ in (21.5 cm). **$200-300**

A rummer, the fluted ogee bowl engraved with band of wriggle and star decoration, floral sprays, and a peasant woman, domed square lemon squeezer foot, c1800, 5½ in (13.6 cm). **$200-300**

A bucket bowl rummer, engraved with Sunderland Bridge, Span 276 feet, Height 100 feet, the reverse with monogram 'EB', c1820, ½ in (13.5 cm). **$300-500**

A blown three-mold flip glass, American, early 19thC, 5¾in (14cm) high. **$100-150**

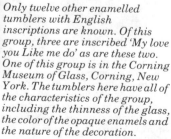

Two rare enamelled blown clear glass tumblers, each enamelled in polychrome with bands of decoration over the inscription in white 'My love you Like me do', possibly by Henry William Stiegel's American Flint Glass Works, Manheim, Pennsylvania, 1772-1774, approx. 4½in (11cm) high. **$4,000-5,000**
Only twelve other enamelled tumblers with English inscriptions are known. Of this group, three are inscribed 'My love you Like me do' as are these two. One of this group is in the Corning Museum of Glass, Corning, New York. The tumblers here have all of the characteristics of the group, including the thinness of the glass, the color of the opaque enamels and the nature of the decoration.

457

A set of four jelly glasses, the trumpet bowls diamond cut, on short knopped stems, c1800, 4½ in (11.7 cm). **$80-150**

Four jelly glasses:-
l. With a trumpet bowl and geometric cutting, solid cut feet, c1780, 4 in (9.8 cm). **$30-45**
l.c. A similar larger glass, c1790, 4½ in (11.5 cm). **$50-70**
r.c. A trumpet bowl, with lower half diamond cut, c1790, 4½ in (11.2 cm). **$30-45**
r. With a trumpet bowl and geometric cutting, c1800, 4½ in (11 cm). **$30-60**

A pair of jelly glasses, with flute prism and diamond cutting, c1825, 4½ in (11 cm). **$50-70**

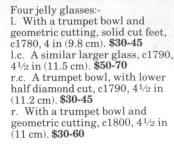

A good sweetmeat/champagne, the double ogee bowl with flared rim on an 8 sided star studded pedestal stem, c1750, 7 in (18 cm). **$400-600**

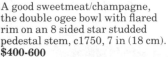

A sweetmeat, the double ogee bowl with dentillated rim, knopped opaque twist stem, c1760, 3½ in (8.5 cm). **$300-50**

Four jelly glasses:-
1. A trumpet bowl with geometric cutting, cut circular foot, c1800, 4 in (10.5 cm). **$200-300**
l.c. A syllabub, with pan top bowl, plain conical foot, c1750, 5 in (12 cm). **$80-150**
r.c. A ribbed trumpet bowl, air beaded knop, c1800, 4½ in (11 cm). **$30-45**
r. A closely ribbed trumpet bowl, cut round rim, c1800, 3½ in (9 cm). **$30-60**

A sweetmeat, the double ogee rib moulded bowl with everted rim, moulded Silesian stem with coile base collar, domed moulded foot, c1760, 6½ in (16 cm). **$300-400**

Glass : flasks

Three pitkin-type flasks, two double pattern molded with ribbing and swirling, one single pattern molded with swirling, two olive green and one amber, Ohio and New England, early 19thC, approx. 5½in (14cm) high. **$500-600**

A Bohemian enamelled 'Milchglas' flask, in the form of a pistol, small chips, mid-18thC, 11½ in (28.5 cm). **$1,200-1,500**

A blue-tinted flask, decorated ➤ with light moulded vertical ribbing and 2 applied spiral milled trails, pewter neck mount, Alpenland, 17th/18thC, 5 in (13 cm). **$1,300-1,700**

Glass : jugs

n extremely rare and important
avenscroft lead glass
canter-jug, with vermicular
llar, cable trailing to the
oulders, looped handle with
umb-rest and rib-fluted lower
dy, Ravenscroft, London, c1685,
n (22.5 cm) high.
,000-8,500

A blown glass creamer, baluster
shaped with molded lip and
threaded body, with a crimped
handle and stepped foot, probably
Mid Western, mid-19thC, 4in
(10cm) high. **$100-150**

An unusually small Nailsea jug,
the olive green body with opaque
white splashes, c1800, 5¼ in
(13 cm). **$400-600**

l. A blue cream jug, diamond facet
cut overall, with gilt rim, c1800,
3½ in (9 cm). **$300-400**
r. A brown amethyst cream jug,
c1800, 3 in (7 cm). **$200-300**

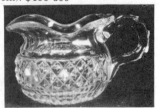

A cream jug, of bellied shape, cut
with base and neck fluting and
band of diamonds, c1825, 3¼ in
(7.8 cm). **$200-300**

claret jug, the body flute and
ism cut, c1830, 11 in (28 cm).
00-300

A claret jug, with base fluting,
band of strawberry cut diamonds
and prism cutting, c1825, 10 in
(24.5 cm). **$400-600**

A claret jug, with tapered flute cut
body, c1840, 11 in (28 cm) high less
stopper. **$200-300**

◄ A good claret jug, with flute and
prism cutting, with cut pouring
neck, c1840, 10½ in (26 cm).
$300-400

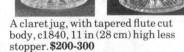

amber glass claret jug, with
wter mounts, 19thC, 13 in
2.5 cm). **$400-600**

◄ A cut glass and
silver mounted
claret jug,
Birmingham, 1871.
$1,300-1,700

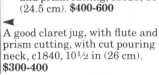

A pair of Victorian
trumpet-shaped glass claret jugs,
the mounts cast and chased with
satyrs masks, Elkington & Co.,
10¾ in (27 cm). **$1,000-1,200**

A Victorian silver mounted glass claret jug, maker's mark WH, London, 1875 11¾ in (30 cm). **$600-900**

An Edwardian engraved glass claret jug, with plated mount. **$400-600**

A hand-engraved claret jug, Paw & Co., 1895. **$1,300-1,700**

A late Victorian claret jug, the ovoid pink glass body cut with a rayed design, Birmingham 1897 by E.S. Jones, 12 in (30 cm). **$800-1,200**

Glass : Paperweights

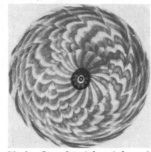

A Baccarat faceted white double-clematis weight, with a yellow honeycomb centre and 4 green leaves, with allover facet cutting and on star-cut base, 2½ in (6.2 cm) diam. **$600-900**

A Baccarat dated scattered millefiori weight, the brightly-coloured canes including silhouettes of a monkey, a dog, a pigeon, a cockerel, an elephant, a deer, a pony and a cane inscribed 'B 1848', 3¼ in (8 cm) diam. **$1,000-1,200**

A Baccarat flower weight, with star-cut base, 2½ in (6.5 cm). **$2,500-3,500**

A Baccarat miniature garden paperweight, set with blue and red flowers, on a ground of stiff green leaves, the exterior facet-cut, 1½ in (3.5 cm). **$300-400**

A Baccarat paperweight, the flower with blue and white petals, with yellow stamens and green leaves, star-cut base, 2 in (5 cm). **$1,500-2,200**

A Clichy fluted swirl weight, with alternate turquoise and white spiral staves radiating from a central dark pink and white cane 3 in (7.2 cm) diam. **$1,300-1,700**

Because certain items might fit easily into any of a number of categories, the quickest and surest method of locating any entry is by reference to the index at the back of the book.
This has been fully cross-referenced for absolute simplicity.

A Clichy patterned millefiori weight, with 6 circles of canes including one of pink and white roses, radiating from a central pink circle enclosing a cobalt blue cane, 3¼ in (8 cm) diam. **$600-900**

A Clichy close millefiori weight, the large brightly coloured canes including 2 pink roses and a white rose in predominant shades of moss-green, blue and purple, 2¼ in (5.7 cm) diam. **$600-700**

A blue tinted shaped rectangular scent bottle and stopper, with yellow metal mounts, with engine turned bands, 4 in (10 cm). $30-45

A clear double ended scent bottle, with embossed silver mounts, c1860, 6 in (14.8 cm). **$100-200**
A round cut scent bottle, with silver mount, hallmarked London 1871, 3½ in (8.5 cm). **$80-150**
A clear flute cut double ended scent bottle, with chased silver gilt mounts by Samson Mordan, c1870, 6 in (14.5 cm). **$100-200**

Three blown glass perfume bottles, two Steigel types, amethyst, cylindrical with tapering necks and applied collars, the ribbing swirled to the right at the neck, the stopper spherical with ribbing, 6½in (16cm) high, the third cobalt blue with a ribbed body, 5¾in (14cm) high, early 19thC. **$1,100-1,300**

A faceted shaped rectangular amber stained scent bottle and stopper, with white metal mounts chased with foliage, 24 in (60 cm). $30-45

A Victorian faceted ruby glass double ended scent bottle, with silver gilt mounts, in original fitted case, S. Mordan, London 1875, 5 in (12.5 cm). **$300-400**

A Stourbridge cameo scent bottle, white cased on turquoise, with repousse silver mount and top, Birmingham 1897, late 19thC, 3 in (7.5 cm). **$400-600**

A Webbs cameo glass scent flask, the opaque red glass overlaid with opaque white, silver gilt screw cap, marked rd11109, c1880, 6 in (14.3 cm). **$2,000-3,000**

A cameo scent bottle, the pale amber ground overlaid in white, with silver mount and hinged ball stopper, clear glass inner stopper, the silver London, 1885, fitted leather case, c1885, 6 in (15.5 cm). **$600-900**

Tankards

A Bohemian waisted cylindrical blue tinted faceted scent bottle and stopper with gilt borders, 2½ in (6 cm). **$15-30**

A cameo frosted cone shaped scent bottle, combed in turquoise and white, with silver mounts, 5 in (12.5 cm). **$200-300**

German blue tinted pewter mounted tankard, probably Bohemia, early 17thC, 6½ in (16.5 cm). **$4,500-7,000**

A Milchglas tankard, with combed decoration in iron red, applied scroll handle, Siebenburgen, Hungary, 18thC, 6 in (14.5 cm). **$500-700**

A Bohemian enamelled Milchglas tankard, painted in colours, enriched with gilding, mid-18thC, 6½ in (16.5 cm). **$800-1,200**

A German clear glass stein, with annular moulding, the pewter mount engraved round rim, 'G Mulenthal S/C CV Raulenfeld D, 25/"/1884', 8½ in (21.6 cm). **$100-200**

Vases

A German engraved tankard, with domed pewter cover with urn thumbpiece engraved FH, possibly the Master 'W', Winbach, late 18thC, 10 in (24.5 cm). **$1,300-1,700**

A celery vase, the body with flute and blaze cutting with a band of diamonds in between serrated cut rim, star cut foot, c1830, 6½ in (16.3 cm). **$300-400**

An over painted pink and white satin glass vase, 19thC, 12 in (30 cm). **$80-150**

An enamelled and gilt Bohemian overlay glass vase, the cranberry coloured body overlaid with panels alternately of criss crossed white trelliswork and of flowers on a solid gilt ground, c1860, 12 in (31 cm). **$700-1,000**

A Victorian opaline glass vase, 6 in (15 cm). **$80-150**

A green glass vase, with an overlap opaque white glass pan on a baluster stem and domed circular foot, the whole gilt with branches, French, 19thC, 14½ (36 cm). **$200-300**

A white opaline vase, painted with sprays of brightly coloured flowers between a gilt lined rim, 11½ in (29 cm). **$300-400**

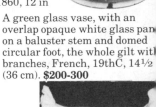

A green glass footed vase, Southern New Jersey, late 19thC, 10in (25cm) high, damaged. **$200-250**

A pair of Victorian frilled top opaline glass vases, hand pain with rare orchids, 16 in (40 cm **$400-600**

A pair of Bohemian ruby glass
vases, printed and painted in
colours, all-over decorated with
leaf sprays in gilt, 18 in (45.5 cm).
$1,500-2,200

A Bohemian ruby stained and
white overlay vase, gilt with
bands of C-scrolls and vines
between a gilt lined rim, 11½ in
(29 cm). **$300-400**

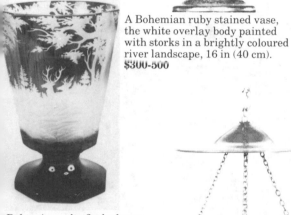

A Bohemian ruby stained vase,
the white overlay body painted
with storks in a brightly coloured
river landscape, 16 in (40 cm).
$300-500

A Bohemian ruby stained vase,
enamelled and gilt with panels of
flower sprays between C-scrolls,
16 in (40 cm). **$300-400**

Bohemian ruby flashed vase,
the bowl deeply engraved with
deer, c1870, 6½ in (16.8 cm).
$200-300

A group of 4 blown clear glass
'Bride's' banks, possibly Boston &
Sandwich Glass Company,
mid-19thC, 6½in (16cm) high.
$130-200

A blown glass hanging lamp, of
blown rose-coloured glass, with a
domed circular lid above a
tapering cylindrical shade, with a
tripartite candleholder,
electrified, late 18th-early 19thC,
shade 11in (27.5cm) deep.
$1,500-2,000

A blown glass hanging lamp, of
blown colourless glass engraved
with wreaths and flowers, the
domed circular lid above a
tapering cylindrical shade, with
foliate ormolu gallery and
pendant, the tripartite
candleholder electrified, 19thC,
14½in (36cm) high. **$2,500-3,000**

A pair of cut glass vases, engraved
by William Fritsche, signed with
WF monogram, c1900, 10 in
(25 cm). **$1,700-2,500**

463

An Art Nouveau inlaid mahogany armchair. **$300-400**

An Arts and Crafts oak armchair. **$100-200**

A pair of upright metal chairs, of almost Gothic style. **$300-500**

A set of 6 mahogany dining chairs, the central splat carved with an elaborate dragon motif. **$600-900**

An English Art Nouveau mahogany and marquetry settle, inlaid in various fruitwoods, c1890, 73 in (185 cm). **$1,200-1,500**

A Kohn beech settle, the design attributed to Joseph Hoffmann, 48½ in (121.5 cm). **$400-600**

A Louis Majorelle Art Nouveau mahogany and walnut armoire Les Clematites, carved with fr of clematis blossom, c1900, 73½ in (187 cm). **$3,500-5,000**

A French walnut Art Nouveau buffet, attributed to Maison Diot, 54 in (135 cm) wide. **$800-1,200**

An Art Nouveau oak vitrine, c1900, 25 in (62.3 cm). **$1,700-2,500**

A Peter Waals walnut library bookcase, with ebony and boxwood stringing, early 20thC, 76 in (193 cm) wide. **$14,000-17,000**

Provenance: The bookcase bears a label which reads: 'No. L.392 in the Catalogue of C.H. St. J. Hornby' – a patron of the Arts and Crafts movement.

An Aesthetic movement ebonised mahogany side cabinet, 34 in (85.5 cm). **$600-700**

An Aesthetic movement ash combination wardrobe, 51 in (127.5 cm) wide, and a similar dressing table, 43 in (107.5 cm wide. **$600-700**

A late Victorian ebonised side cabinet, in the Arts and Crafts style, inset with blue and cream glazed pottery tiles, 37 in (93 cm). **$1,000-1,200**

A glazed cabinet, c1910, 63 in (160 cm) wide. **$1,700-2,500**

An Edwardian inlaid mahogany display cabinet, inlaid with stylised peacock in various woods, 48 in (120 cm) wide. **$800-1,200**

An Aesthetic movement mahogany corner desk, 30 in (75 cm). **$300-500**

An Aesthetic movement bedroom suite by Gillows & Co., with wardrobe, dressing table, washstand and bedside cabinet in simulated satinwood, stamped Gillow & Co., on door stiles. **$600-900**

A late Victorian Arts and Crafts pollard oak and ebonised sideboard, 90 in (229 cm) wide. **$500-600**

A late Victorian Arts and Crafts oak kneehole pedestal desk, 57½ in (144 cm). **$2,000-3,000**

An Arts and Crafts oak desk, attributed to the workshops of L. & J.G. Stickley, 38½ in (96 cm) wide. **$500-600**

An Aesthetic movement ebonised occasional table, after a design by E.W. Godwin, 26½ in (66.5 cm). **$300-500**

A Galle two-tiered marquetry tea table, the satinwood top inlaid with fruitwoods, with bronze handles, the top inlaid Galle, 31 in (79 cm) at widest. **$1,200-1,500**

Glass

A Daum enamelled glass vase, decorated in coloured enamels, against an acid etched ground of spirals heightened in gold and silver, signed Daum Nancy on base, 3½ in (8.50 cm). **$400-600**

An oak and copper combined hall seat and chest, embellished in copper with plant form panels and studded edging, 30½ in (76 cm) long. **$400-600**

An earthenware vase, in a brown and blue-green streaked glaze with copper crystalline highlights on the neck, molded FULPER, by Fulper, c1915, 9¾in (24cm) high. **$400-500**

An earthenware vase, with a textured light olive glaze, with dark green crystalline highlights, ink-stamped FULPER, by Fulper c1915, 11¾in (31cm) high. **$400-500**

An earthenware mug, decorated by Marie Rauchfuss, with a black boy in a 'Standard' glaze, impressed with firm's marks and 837, and inscribed with artist's monogram, minor flake to rim, by Rookwood, 1897, 5¼in (13cm) high. **$800-900**

An earthenware cream pitcher, created by Joseph Meyer and Anna F. Simpson, the body sculpted with pale blue tulips and blue-green leaves on a matt blue ground, impressed NC B JM AFS and painted ED.13, by Newcomb College, 1910, 4¾in (12cm) high. **$700-800**

An earthenware mug, decorated by Sadie Markland, with an Indian in a 'Standard' glaze, impressed with firm's marks and 587C and inscribed with artist's monogram, by Rookwood, 1897, 5in (12.5cm) high. **$1,000-1,300**

A silver-plated copper-overlaid earthenware jug, decorated by Edward Diers, with blue grapes and olive-blue leaves in a 'sea green' glaze, the reverse with a thick silver-plated copper vine, artist's monogram and 906D G, by Rookwood, 1900, 4¾in (12cm) high. **$3,500-4,000**

An earthenware teapot, decorated by Kataro Shirayamadani, in yellow and green in a 'Standard' glaze, impressed with firm's marks and 615W and inscribed with artist's signature, by Rookwood, 1892, 6½in (16.5cm) high. **$450-550**

An earthenware vase, with a streaked dark mustard, coffee, brown and sky-blue glaze, inscribed FULPER, by Fulper, c1915, 10in (25cm) high. **$450-500**

An earthenware vase, the tan ground decorated with a black rabbit riding a fox outlined in gil, impressed ROOKWOOD 1882, b Rookwood, 1882, 10¼in (26cm) high. **$550-650**

A large cylindrical earthenware vase, the tan body, divided by 3 gilt impressed columns, decorated with pink and blue, impressed ROOKWOOD 1883 Y WA and with a kiln, by Rookwood, 1883, 16½in (42cm) high. **$1,100-1,400**

An earthenware vase, decorated by Edward Diers, with pink and light blue hydrangeas in a 'Vellum' glaze, impressed with firm's marks and 950C V, inscribed V and with artist's monogram, by Rookwood, 1908, 10¼in (26cm) high. **$700-800**

An earthenware vase, decorated by Harriet Wilcox, with blue-tinged pink-centered white chrysanthemums on a matt green ground, impressed with firm's marks and 381Z, painted with artist's monogram, by Rookwood, 1903, 7¾in (19cm) high. **$2,000-2,500**

An earthenware lamp base, decorated by Albert R. Valentien, the squat spherical body on a tan ground bordered by gilded impressed bands, impressed ROOKWOOD 1882 Y 95 with an anchor and artist's monogram, by Rookwood, 1882, 9¾in (24cm) diam. **$2,300-2,600**

A porcelain vase, decorated by Katherine Cherry, with a banded white and brown matt glaze, painted TD and inscribed KEC with indistinct marks, by University City, 2¼in (5.5cm) high. **$200-300**

An earthenware vase, decorated by Fred Rothenbusch, with purple-brown and olive trees in the foreground and a distant valley in the background in a 'Vellum' glaze, impressed with firm's marks and 30D V and inscribed with artist's monogram, by Rookwood, 1919, 10in (25.5cm) high. **$1,000-1,400**

A porcelain covered vase, decorated by Taxile Doat, in a textured pale olive and tan glaze, the fitted cover walnut, ink-stamped UNIVERSITY CITY MO 1914 PORCELAIN WORKS TD and inscribed Ps-P, 3in (7.5cm) high. **$200-300**

A porcelain vase, by Edward G. Lewis, the ovoid body with blue-speckled ochre glaze and streaked ox-blood, separated by a central band of dark brown waves, inscribed EGL, by University City, 4¾in (12cm) high. **$900-1,000**

A Daum enamelled glass vase, the amethyst body acid etched with thistles heightened with gilding and colours, signed on base Daum Nancy, and the foot with French poincons in original fitted case for Polak Aine, Sucr. de F. Gast Paris, 4½ in (11 cm). **$1,000-1,200**

This piece was given by Queen Victoria to the controller of her household, Lord Clinton-Pelham.

A Favrile glass vase, by Tiffany Studios, the white lustre pearshape body with frieze of gold pulls at top and base, inscribed L.C.T., F280, 7¼in (18cm) high. **$700-800**

A Favrile glass bud vase, by Tiffany Studios, the marbled green and blue glass ground with brown iridescent feather pull design, inscribed X 1265, 7¼in (18cm) high. **$600-700**

**DAUM BROTHERS,
Auguste (1853-1909),
Antonin (1864-1930)**

Makers of decorative domestic glassware, the Daum Brothers turned to art glass production following the Paris Exhibition in 1889. Since they worked in Nancy, it is not unnatural that they should have been greatly influenced by Gallé – with whom they are invariably unfavourably compared. Inevitable as such comparison is, it is unfortunate, because their work is highly competent and frequently displays a high standard of artistic merit.

A Daum cameo glass vase, the streaked matt amber glass etched with a winter landscape, heightened with dark brown and white enamel, painted signature Daum Nancy, c1900, 21 in (52 cm). **$2,000-3,000** ➤

A calyx floriform Favrile glass vase, by Tiffany Studios, the transparent amber foot with green leaf pulls with triangular vase in ivory with green leaf pulls, inscribed LCT T5332, 11½in (29cm) high. **$1,600-2,000**

A Daum cameo glass vase, the ➤ opalescent and translucent body having faint ruby veining and overlaid with deep ruby glass acid etched with honeysuckle against a martelé ground, signed on base Daum Nancy, 17 in (42.25 cm). **$4,000-5,000**

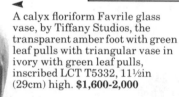

A Daum winter landscape vase lamp, the mottled orange and yellow body acid etched and naturalistically painted, with gilt metal fitments, signed on base Daum Nancy, the mounts stamped Jed. Robj Bte. G.G.D.G., Paris 3120, 6½ in (16.50 cm). **$1,200-1,500**

A Favrile glass jack-in-the-pulpit vase, by Tiffany Studios, in gold iridescence, the flattened circular base raised by slender stem to wide brim with peaked top, in blue-pink lustre, inscribed 1422H., L.C.T., 14in (35cm) high. **$1,900-2,200**

A Favrile glass cordial set, by Tiffany Studios, the gold iridescent bulbous dimpled body raised to slender neck with dimpled stopper, and 6 matching dimpled cordial cups, inscribed L.C.T., 11in (28cm) high. **$1,400-1,600**

A Favrile glass and bronze counterbalance table lamp, by Tiffany Studios, the damascene glass shade in green with greenish gold waves, inscribed L.C.T., D, 10in (25cm), and a counterbalance base with adjustable shade fixture, impressed Tiffany Studios, No.415, 16in (40cm) high. **$2,800-3,200**

1906 price list describes this model as No.415 – balance lamp for 10in shade.

A 'Black-Eyed Susan' leaded glass and bronze table lamp, by Tiffany Studios, the green and white mottled ground surrounding yellow flowerheads with black centres on light and dark green stems, impressed tag, 16in (40cm) diam., on a three-light base with squat ribbed standard on ball feet, impressed Tiffany Studios, D805, 22in (55cm) high. **$7,500-8,500**

1906 price list describes this model as No.1447 – 16in. Black Eyed Susan, dome.

A Favrile glass and bronze candle-lamp, by Tiffany Studios, the dish-shaped base supporting 9 cabochon jewel turtlebacks encircling boubache orb, impressed Tiffany Studios 485, with large gold iridescent ribbed glass shade, inscribed L.C.T., 16in (40cm) high. **$1,700-2,000**

1906 price list describes this model as No.485 – one light, like No.1210, plain base, large tripod, jewels.

A Lotus leaded glass and bronze table lamp, by Tiffany Studios, in green glass shading to white at the undulating lower rim, impressed tag, 25½in (64cm) diam., on a ribbed base raised on 5 ball feet, impressed Tiffany Studios and No.28622, 26¾in (67cm) high. **$12,500-14,000**

1906 price list describes the shade as 'No.1524 – 25in. Lotus Pagoda'. It is today generally referred to as a 'Mandarin Lotus'. The 1906 price list describes the base as 'No.370, Library Standard mushroom design'.

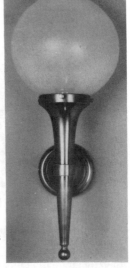

A pair of brass and glass wall sconces, designed by Frank Lloyd Wright for the B. Harley Bradley House, Kankakee, Illinois, c1900, executed by Willy H. Lau, the spherical opalescent glass globes on trumpet-turned brass supports extended on bell-form wall mounts, unsigned, 18in (45cm) high. **$2,500-3,000**

c.f. David A. Hanks, The Decorative Designs of Frank Lloyd Wright, E.P. Dutton, New York, 1977, p.45, for a contemporary (c1900) illustration of the model in situ in the living room of the Bradley House.

A Gallé cameo glass soli-fleur vase, the matt white and pale yellow glass overlaid in pale purple, cameo signature Gallé, c1900, 12 in (30.8 cm). **$1,200-1,500**

A Gallé cameo glass and fire polished vase, the pale green and russet mottled glass overlaid in russet, cameo signature Gallé, c1900, 8 in (19.9 cm). **$800-1,200**

A Gallé cameo glass landscape ➤ vase, the greyish body tinted amber at the neck and base, overlaid with 2 tones of brown glass, signed in cameo Gallé, 16 in (40 cm). **$1,700-2,500**

A large Gallé cameo glass ceiling dome, well carved and polished around the rim in deep red against a frosted ground of pale lemon, gilt bronze foliate ceiling rose mount, cameo signature, 21 in (52 cm). **$4,000-5,000**

GALLÉ, Emile
(1846-1904)

If not the father, certainly one of the foremost figures of the French Art Nouveau movement, Emile Gallé was the founder of the Nancy school. After a liberal education, he began his working life as apprentice to his father, a studio glassmaker. The development of his unique Art Nouveau style is considered to have dated from about 1884, and within six years he was running a factory supplying large quantities of studio glass to, among others, the Parisian shop of Sebastian Bing, the international entrepreneur. The shop was called l'Art Nouveau.

Gallé was widely imitated by other glass workers, but few, if any, could match his technical skill or artistic feeling. In 1880 he began to produce Art Nouveau furniture of extremely high quality, often embellishing his products with inlays – notably mother of pearl – and characteristically delicate marquetry designs.

Following his death in 1904, articles produced by his factories continued to be signed 'Gallé', but all were marked with a star from that time onward.

A good Gallé cameo glass vase, of ▲ baluster form, the greyish body tinted pale amber and overlaid with mottled pink and lemon glass beneath a further overlay of brown and acid etched with delicate blooms and buds of incarvillea on brown stems with leaves, signed in cameo Gallé, 15 in (37 cm). **$1,700-2,500**

A Gallé cameo glass vase, the milky ground shading to amber and mottled with amethyst, the partly hammered body overlaid in brown and engraved foliage, Galle cameo signature, c1900, 8 in (20.5 cm). **$1,500-2,200**

A Gallé moulded blown and cameo glass vase, the matt translucent pinkish amber glass overlaid in sepia and pale green cameo signature Gallé, c1900, 12 in (29.2 cm) **$8,500-11,000**

HOW TO USE MILLER'S

Unless otherwise stated, any description which refers to 'a set' or 'a pair' includes a valuation for the entire set or the pair, even though the illustration may show only a single item.

A Gallé cameo glass landscape bowl and cover, the latter overlaid in green against a frosted pink ground, the outer rim and base cut with scattered tumbling autumnal leaves, signed in cameo, 6 in (14.5 cm). **$800-1,200**

A small Loetz iridescent glass vase, decorated with bright blue horizontal feathering on a ground of random splashes of golden iridescence, 4 in (10 cm). **$500-600**

Gallé cameo glass vase, the eyish body tinted pink and erlaid with olive green and dark own, acid etched with fern onds, signed in cameo Gallé, 14 (35.50 cm). ,200-1,500

A fine quality cameo glass vase by Gallé, dog roses overlaid on an amber ground, signed Gallé, 12 in (30 cm). **$1,500-2,200**

A Gallé double overlay cameo glass vase, decorated with violets, in green and violet over a frosted base, signed in cameo Gallé and a star, c1910, 6 in (15 cm). **$600-900**

CAMEO GLASS

The body is overlaid with a 'skin' of coloured glass, sometimes in several layers and reduced by various methods to produce a relief image. The processes for this reduction are acid-etching, the most general form, using bitumen of Judea as an acid-resistant agent, or carving with a wheel or both processes together. Sometimes a piece may be painted or stencilled with coloured decoration which superficially may resemble cameo decoration.

Kosta cameo glass vase, esigned by Gunnar Wenneberg, e mottled lilac body overlaid ith carved lilac violets, engraved osta 310 G. Wenneberg, A.E. Bn, 900, 7 in (17 cm). **$500-600**

A Gallé cameo vase, in shades of brown and blue on a frosted light amber ground, 8 in (19.8 cm). **$600-900**

A Loetz iridescent glass vase, exhibiting a feathered peacock blue iridescence and applied with a sinuous foliate silver overlay, signed Loetz, Austria, 9½ in (23.50 cm). **$600-700**

small Loetz iridescent glass ase, the green glass body xhibiting a pale peacock blue idescence and webbing, with a lver appliqué of sinuous iterwoven tendrils, 4½ in 1.50 cm). **$300-400**

A small Loetz iridescent glass vase, with silver appliqué, the pale green glass covered with random splashes of cobalt blue and green iridescence, and decorated in silver appliqué, 4 in (10 cm). **$300-500**

A Muller Freres cameo glass vase, overlaid in brown and etched with a lakeland scene on a yellow ground, cameo mark, Mullers Freres, 11 in (27.5 cm). **$800-1,200**

471

A Tiffany iridescent rosewater vase, incised L.C.T. R5638, 12 in (30 cm). **$1,700-2,500**

A porcelain vase, decorated by Taxile Doat, the green glazed ovoid border with a blue crystalline glaze around the rim, painted UC 19TD14, by University City, 1914, 2¼in (5.5cm) high. **$350-450**

A Walter pâte-de-verre dish, the glass of honey tone with dark brown streaks, signed A. Walter, Nancy and Bergé Sc, for Henri Bergé as modeller, 7 in (17.5 cm). **$1,200-1,500**

An experimental Favrile glass paperweight vase, by Tiffany Studios, the clear body with trailing green foliage and purple blossoms at the shoulder, unsigned and incomplete, 7 in (18 cm). **$800-1,200**

Provenance Purchased from the Tiffany Studio liquidation sale.

A porcelain vase, decorated by Edward G. Lewis, in a rose-streaked pale yellow, tan and green glaze with green crystalline highlights around the base and dark green rectangles around the rim, impressed EGL, by University City, 3in (7.5cm) high. **$350-450**

A porcelain vase, in a textured black-streaked matt cucumber glaze, inscribed UP, by University City, 3¾in (9cm) high. **$200-250**

A sea blue frosted and bubbled glass figure, of Pierrot with his lover's lute, on a hexagonal glass base, made in France signed Walter of Nancy, 9½ in (24.5 cm). **$1,700-2,500**

Lamps

A bronze and Favrile glass candlestick, by Tiffany Studios, with 8 openings with green blown glass inserts on tripod support with leaf feet and suspended snuffer, and an insert supporting a 'Grape Leaf' pattern filigree shade, impressed Tiffany Studios, No.1212, 10½in (26cm) high. **$800-1,000**

1906 price list describes this model as No.1212 – one light, 3-legged, extinguisher.

A leaded glass and copper table lamp, by Roycroft, of yellow-streaked green glass with a checkered band of green and pink, raised on a hammered copper base with 2 riveted bands and rectangular handles, stamped with firm's mark, 18½in (47 cm) high. **$4,500-5,000**

c.f. the model illustrated in Nancy Hubbard Brady, The Book of Roycrofters, House of Hubbard, East Aurora, New York, 1977, p.23.

◄ A copper and mica table lamp, by Dirk Van Erp, c1912, the hammered copper base with tapered cylindrical neck and spherical body, stamped with a windmill and DIRK VAN ERP in a box, 18in (46cm) high. **$5,500-6,000**

A copper and mica table lamp, by Dirk Van Erp, c1915, the conical shade of 4 mica panels encasing a copper floral design and separated by riveted hammered copper columns, raised on a sherical hammered copper base, stamped with a windmill, SAN FRANCISCO and DIRK VAN ERP in a broken box, 11¾in (29cm) high. **$1,600-2,000**

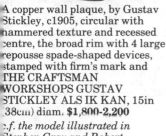

A copper vase, by Dirk Van Erp, stamped with a windmill and DIRK VAN ERP in a closed box, 10in (25cm) high. **$1,000-1,200**

A copper wall plaque, by Gustav Stickley, c1905, circular with hammered texture and recessed centre, the broad rim with 4 large repousse spade-shaped devices, stamped with firm's mark and THE CRAFTSMAN WORKSHOPS GUSTAV STICKLEY ALS IK KAN, 15in (38cm) diam. **$1,800-2,200**

c.f. the model illustrated in Stephen Gray and Robert Edwards, Collected Works of Gustav Stickley, Turn of the Century Editions, New York, 1983, p.159, no.344.

A copper table lamp base, by Gustav Stickley, of elongated oviform with heavily hammered texture, stamped with firm's mark and ALS IK KAN, 25½in (65cm) high, with woven cane shade. **$1,700-2,000**

◄

A copper umbrella stand, by Gustav Stickley, c1905, finely worked with repousse foliate design on either side applied handles and riveted down the side and at the base, stamped with firm's logo, model no.382, 25in (63cm) high. **$1,800-2,200**

A copper jardiniere, by Gustav Stickley, c1905, with repousse spade-shaped devices on obverse and reverse, stamped with firm's mark and THE CRAFTSMAN WORKSHOPS GUSTAV STICKLEY ALS IK KAN, 19in (48cm) high. **$3,000-3,500**

c.f. the model illustrated in Stephen Gray and Robert Edwards, Collected Works of Gustav Stickley, Turn of the Century Editions, New York, 1981, p.156, no.275.

An Art Nouveau bronze lamp, 14 in (35 cm). **$1,000-1,200**

An Agate Favrile glass and bronze table lamp, by Tiffany Studios, the deep amber baluster body vertically banded in blue and ochre shading to blue and lavender between opalescent ribs, impressed Tiffany Studios New York, 14½ in (37 cm). **$1,400-1,700**

A Favrile glass and bronze desk lamp, by Tiffany Studios, the shade in iridescent peacock blue glass with radiating bands of silver dots, inscribed L.C.T. Favrile, the bronze impressed Tiffany Studios New York 327 11413, 15 in (39.5 cm). **$1,400-1,700**

A laburnum leaded glass and bronze floor lamp, by Tiffany Studios, with yellow flower clusters amongst green leaves on a sky blue ground, impressed Tiffany Studios New York, 63 in (159.5 cm). **$30,000-42,500**

A large spelter figure, Libellule, designed as a lamp cast after a model by Auguste Moreau, printed metal tag Libellule par Aug, Moreau, c1900, 46 in (115 cm). **$3,000-4,000**

A German silvered pewter and nautilus shell desk lamp, designed as either a wall or table lamp, monogram MH and maker's symbol, c1900, 11 in (28 cm). **$2,000-3,000**

A gilt bronze table lamp, inscribed Raoul Larche and impressed with the Siot Deceaville foundry seal, cast from a model by Raoul Francois Larche, French, wired for electricity, early 20thC, 17 in (43.8 cm). **$14,000-17,000**

The present model is one of several models by Raoul Larche of 'La Loie' which were wired as table lamps. Known for her dramatic use of lighting and swirling scarves in her stage performances, Loie Fuller (1862-1928) was a great inspiration to artists in all media at the turn of the century. cf. Alastair Duncan. Art Nouveau Lighting (1978), pp.81, 112-113, figs. 55-57 for a further discussion of Larche's work in lighting specifically his 'Loie Fuller' lamps which were also marketed in a smaller size.

Jewellery

An American gold and turquoise necklace, set with teardrop-shaped cabochons of turquoise matrix, stamped with 'Im' monogram and '14k', 16 in (40.5 cm). **$700-900**

A Danish Art Nouveau hammered silver brooch, set with lapis lazuli, Continental silver marks, c1910, 4½ in (12 cm). **$300-400**

A Murrle Bennett navette shaped gold wirework brooch, with turquoise matrix and 3 seed pearls, stamped MB monogram and 15ct. on the pin, c1900, 4 cm wide. **$300-400**

A William Hutton & Son hammered silver and turquoise and blue enamel belt, each plaque with hallmarks and the buckle with full hallmarks for 1904 and maker's monogram W.H. & S.Ld within shaped surround, 28 in (69 cm). **$1,000-1,200**

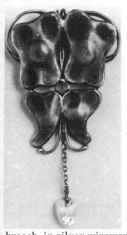

A brooch, in silver wirework, turquoise enamel and with a seed-pearl drop on silver chain, attributed to C.R. Ashbee, c1900, 2½ in (7 cm). **$500-600**

An Art Nouveau silver, enamel and plique à jour pendant, stamped Deposé and with a 900 continental silver mark, c1900, 3 in (7.5 cm). **$800-1,200**

A Horta gold double locket, set with a sapphire and 14 small diamonds, stamped Horta y Cie, c1900, 3.5 cm diam. **$1,700-2,500**

A Murrle Bennett silver and green and red enamel pendant and chain, stamped MB&Co. silver, c1910, pendant, 1½ in (4 cm) long. **$300-500**

An Artificers Guild Ltd., hair comb, in tortoiseshell, applied with silver tendrils centred with moonstone and amethyst cabochons, 12 cm long, in original fitted case for their premises at Maddox St. **$300-400**

A large Art Nouveau bronze and brass centrepiece, 17 in (43 cm) high. **$600-700**

Metal

A pair of Arts & Craft Movement silver bowls, with handles set with green cabochon stones, by Guild of Handicrafts Ltd., after the design by C.R. Ashbee, 12 in (30 cm) overall, 22 ozs. **$2,500-3,500**

An Art Nouveau pewter fruit bowl, stamped WMF. **$500-600**

A Liberty Tudric rose bowl, decorated in relief with the legend 'And the musk of the rose is blown and the woodbine spices are wafted abroad', stamped 'Tudric 011', 9½ in (24 cm) diam. **$500-600**

A silver Guild of Handicrafts porringer, the loop handle set with a cabochon amethyst, clear glass liner, London hallmarks for 1900 and maker's mark, 7½ in (19 cm), 3 oz 12 dwt gross weight. **$1,000-1,200**

A Guild of Handicrafts silver tazza, c1900. **$3,000-4,500**

A large Continental centrepiece, embossed and chased overall in rococo style, import marks for 1906, 19 in (47 cm) over handles, 49 ozs. **$8,500-11,000**

A Wiener Werkstätte plated fish knife, designed by Josef Hoffmann, stamped with registered trademark, 'WW' monogram, Hoffmann's monogram and 'JF' in circle, 7½ in (19 cm) long. **$300-500**

Josef Hoffman (1870-1956)
* born in Austria
* founder of the Vienna secession in 1899
* influenced by Charles Rennie Mackintosh
* very functional style
* founder of the Wiener Werkstätte in 1903.

An eight-light bronze chandelier, cast after a design by Carlo Bugatti, c1910, 65 in (165 cm) high. **$2,500-3,500**

A pair of Kayserzinn pewter candlesticks, stamped Kayserzinn 4521, c1900, 12 in (30.5 cm) high. **$600-700**

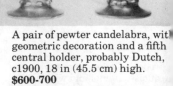

A pair of pewter candelabra, with geometric decoration and a fifth central holder, probably Dutch, c1900, 18 in (45.5 cm) high. **$600-700**

An Arts and Crafts brass hanging chandelier, glass shades wanting 25 in (62 cm) wide. **$300-500**

A silver Liberty Coronation spoon. **$300-400**

A German forty-eight piece part canteen of cutlery, comprising: 1 forks, 12 spoons and 12 fish knive and forks, silver coloured metal stamped with '800' and maker's mark for A.C. Franck of Hambur **$1,200-1,500**

A set of six Liberty & Co., silver and enamelled coffee spoons, with shaded blue green enamels, marked 'L & Co' with Birmingham marks for 1937, in original fitted case, 4½ in (11.25 cm) long. **$500-600**

A dressing table set, of lignum vitae, with decorative Art Nouveau silver mounts and the initials MH in monogram with red enamelled background, 1926-1927. **$1,000-1,200**

A silver caddy spoon, marked 'R. for Robert Stebbings, London 1903, 4½ in (11.75 cm) long, 1.50 ozs. **$80-150**

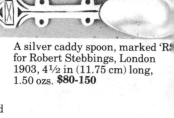

A silver mounted dressing table set, in the Art Nouveau style, 1903, 1904 and 1905 maker's mark CD and with P.O.D.R. number 374815/7. **$300-500**

A bronze figure of 'Circe' by Bertram Mackennal, incised on the base with the artist's signature and the foundry mark of Gruet Jeune, verdigris patches, 23 in (57 cm). **$19,500-25,500**

A large bronze statuette of 'Daphne' by Raoul Larche, signe 'Raoul Larche', 37½ in (93.5 cm **$3,000-4,500**

water pitcher, by Dominick & ...aff, Newark, New Jersey, 1882, ...e body and handle ...ammer-faceted, the body ...epousse and chased with a bird ...mong foliage in the Japanese ...aste, engraved with inscription ... the bottom, marked and dated, ...n (20cm) high. **$4,500-5,000**

A bronze figure of 'Truth' by Bertram Mackennal, the shaped base incise cast above the rim with the title 'Truth' and also 'Mackennal, June 12 1894, London', foundry mark Gruet Jeune, 25 in (62 cm). **$18,000-24,000**

A bronze figure cast as a naked Andromeda by J. Herbert Hart, incise cast signature and dated 98, 12 in (30.5 cm). **$1,200-1,500**

A large bronzed metal figural lamp, after Moreau, inscribed Math Moreau, Hors. Concoiouf. 46 in high (115 cm). **$3,000-4,500**

Walker and Hall silver mounted ...aret jug, after a design by ...hristopher Dresser, maker's ...arks for Sheffield 1904. 9½ in ...4 cm). **$400-600**

A sauce boat, by Gorham Manufacturing Company, Providence, 1905, the sides repousse with ocean waves and decorated with cast applied fish and seaweed, the handle chased with monogram 'AGS', marked on bottom, 8in (20cm) long, 15 oz. **$900-1,000**

A WMF silver plated pewter mounted green glass decanter, stamped WMF and other usual marks, c1900, 15½ in (38.5 cm). **$600-700**

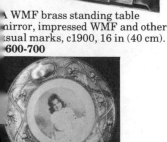

A WMF brass standing table ...irror, impressed WMF and other ...sual marks, c1900, 16 in (40 cm). ...600-700

A WMF silvered metal dressing mirror, 14 in high (35 cm). **$600-700**

A pewter and coloured enamel dressing mirror, in the Art Nouveau style, attributed to the March Brothers, 20 in (50 cm). **$400-600**

...n Art Nouveau silver photo ...ame, Birmingham 1902. ...300-400

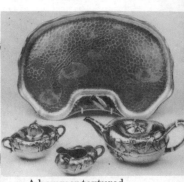

A hammer textured silver-coloured metal four piece tea service, by Tiffany & Co., the leaf modelled tray inlaid in green yellow and red coloured metals, makers marks and 5176M1781, 5291/2633 (tray) c1890, tray 15 in (37.5 cm) wide, 70 ozs gross. **$4,000-5,000**

A Guild of Handicrafts Ltd., silver beaker base, designed by Charles Robert Ashbee, set with seven oval garnet cabochons, marked 'CRA' in shield and London hallmarks for 1900, 4½ in (11.75 cm), 6.50 ozs. **$3,000-4,000**

An English silver Art Nouveau frame. **$600-700**

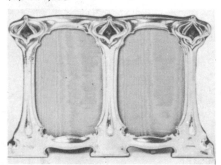

A William Hutton & Sons silver and enamelled double picture frame, maker's marks for London 1903, 8 in (19.75 cm) high. **$1,300-1,700**

A Liberty Tudric hammered pewter teaset, designed by Archibald Knox, stamped Tudri 0231 Rd. 420290 and other mar c1900, tray 18½ in (48 cm) wid **$700-1,000**

A H. Meinhardt silver coloured metal vase, 25½ in (63 cm) high. **$800-1,200**

A Hukin & Heath plated letter rack, designed by Christopher Dresser, marked 'H & H', numbered '2555' and 'registration mark for 9th May 1881', 5 in (12.25 cm). **$400-600**

An Arts and Crafts movement toast rack, set with turquoise stones, by the Guild of Handicrafts, one end split, London 1904, 5 in (12.5 cm), 7½ ozs. **$600-700**

A pocket flask, by Tiffany & Company, New York, 1891-19 marked, 5in (12.5cm) long, 4o 10dwt. **$850-950**

A Victorian three piece Aesthetic movement teaset, inscribed, by Messrs Barnard, 1877, height of teapot 8 in (20 cm), 39.5 ozs. **$800-1,200**

An Omar Ramsden hammered silver tankard, engraved Omar Ramsden me fecit, London hallmarks for 1914, 5 in (12.5 cm) high, 16 ozs. **$1,000-1,400**

A pewter oil lamp, made by Henck, designed by Allin Muller. **$300-500**

An Art Nouveau French gold case fob watch. **$400-600**

An Austrian enamelled box and cover, by Georg Anton Scheidt, silver coloured metal with Austrian poinçons and 'G.A.S.' maker's mark, 2 in (5 cm) diam. **$600-700**

A bronze plaque of a Greek classical maiden's head, by James Pittendrigh Macgilluray, signed 'Macgilluray 1908', all set in an architectural wooden frame, frame height 35 in (88 cm). **$800-1,200**

A Bergman bronze vessel, stamped with Vase and 'B' mark, 6½ in (16 cm). **$800-1,200**

A Tiffany Studios bronze and Favrile glass inkwell, with original glass liner, impressed Tiffany Studios New York, c1910, 15½ in (16.5 cm) diam. **$800-1,200**

A pair of English Arts and Crafts silver plated wall sconces, with enamel plaques, unmarked, c1900, 16 in (40.5 cm) high. **$1,300-1,700**

An Art Nouveau WMF white metal dish, with stamped marks, 15½ in (38 cm) high. **$400-600**

A pair of Elsley brass fire dogs, designed by C.F.A. Voysey, the base shaped like a Greek Omega, stamped Elsley & Co., c1900, 18 in (44.3 cm) high. **$4,000-5,000**

A Goldscheider pottery butterfly girl, by Lorenzl, glazed in claret, yellow and blue, incised Goldscheider, Wien, Lorenzl, 10½ in (26.5 cm) high. **$1,200-1,500**

Art Nouveau: ceramics

A Goldscheider pottery figure, by Dakon, impressed Dakon and Goldscheider, 15½ in (38.5 cm). **$600-700**

A Goldscheider porcelain head of a young woman, with red lips and brown hair, wearing a blue lace head scarf, printed Goldscheider U.S.A., 11½ in (29 cm) high. **$300-500**

A William De Morgan art pottery dish, decoration with a dragon in ruby copper lustre on a white ground, slight discolouration, 14½ in (36 cm). **$500-600**

A Minton 'Secessionist' jardiniere and stand, with tube-lined decoration of stylised pink flowers outlined in black and a shaded blue background, printed and impressed marks Minton Ltd., 41½ in (103.5 cm) high, c1910. **$1,500-2,200**

A Mintons Secessionist jardiniere, with pale green ground, the peacocks outlined in relief green transfer and impressed mark to base, early 20thC, 17 in (43 cm) diam. **$600-800**

A Minton moon flask, painted by W.S. Coleman, signed, neck damaged, 17 in (42.5 cm). **$300-500**

A William De Morgan tile, painted in turquoise, blue and green, impressed DM98 in circle, 6¼ by 6¼ in (15.5 by 15.5 cm), and a De Morgan tile painted in beige, yellow and shades of green with stylised carnations and leaves, impressed 'Sand's End Pottery' mark, 6¼ by 6¼ in (15.5 by 15.5 cm). **$300-400**

A Pilkington's Royal Lancastrian vase, decorated by Gordon M. Forsyth, with lions in silver mottled lustre against a bright blue ground, printed marks, artists monogram on base, c1905, 11½ in (29 cm) high. **$500-600**

Pilkington's Royal Lancastrian wares Pottery

The pottery department of Pilkington's Royal Lancastrian wares was established in 1898. Much of the early work was influenced by Lewis Day. Though not the exclusive production of the factory it was the range of hand painted lustre wares which attracted most attention. Some superb pieces were produced by artists Charles Cundall, Gordon Forsyth, Richard Joyce, Annie Burton, Gladys Rogers and W.S. Mycock. As these artists monogrammed their work it can be readily identified. After 1918 both the quantity and quality of wares declined due to the gradual break-up of the team of artists. Production finally ceased in 1937 though two further periods of production took place from 1948 to 1957 and from 1972 to 1975.

A Pilkinton's 'Royal Lancastrian' wall plaque, possibly by Gwladys Rodgers, impressed 'Royal Lancastrian, Made in England', 10½ in (26 cm) diam. **$200-300**

A Pilkington's Royal Lancastrian ware vase, in yellow, blue and ruby lustre, decorated by Gordon M. Forsyth for Pilkington's, impressed Bee mark, VIII, England 218, 8 in (20 cm) high. **$500-700**

A Royal Dux centrepiece, picked out in pale colours and brushed gilding, applied triangle mark and stencil mark in green, 1920's, 16½ in (41 cm). $500-600

Pilkington's Royal Lancastrian marks

* lustre wares and tiles are particularly collectable
* early wares are marked with a P (and tiles with the company name)
* between 1903 and 1916 the mark includes a P and two bees
* from 1916 to 1938 the mark includes a P within a complex rosette and the wording Royal Lancastrian, England (1914-1923)
* from 1924 to 1929 the word Royal appears above the rosette
* between 1930 and 38 the words Made in England are used
* later wares are marked Handmade in England (1948-1957) or Lancastrian Pottery, England (1972).

A Royal Dux porcelain bottle vase, with pink patch marks, some damage, 18 in (45 cm) high. $400-600

A Royal Dux classical style group, the bracket base clad with water lilies, 11 in (27,5 cm) high. $300-500

A Royal Dux Art Nouveau table centrepiece, 17 in (42.5 cm) high. $500-700

A Royal Dux glazed polychrome figure, modelled as 2 Arabian dancers, raised triangle mark, 12½ in (31 cm) high. $400-600

A Royal Dux pottery group, with the raised triangular mark, 13½ in (33 cm) high. $500-600

A Villeroy & Boch 'Mettlach' stoneware wall plaque, decorated in browns, putty grey, blue and lemon, impressed factory marks, numbered 2645, 18½ in (46 cm) diam. $1,000-1,200

A large Villeroy & Boch Mettlach' wall plaque, decorated in vivid colours, in he Persian manner, Mettlach mark on back and numbered 1294 and 27, 18 in 45 cm) diam. $300-400

A pair of Carters & Co. Poole pottery vases, probably by Lily Gillam, green matt glaze running into buff, Carters, Poole, faintly incised, remains of Liberty & Co. label, 9½ in (23.8 cm) high. $300-400

A Rozenburg pottery vase, painted Rozenburg den Haag marks, c1910, 7½ in (18 cm) high. $200-300

A Foley 'Pastello' earthenware vase, with painted underglaze decoration of a house, in a purple landscape against a yellow sky, printed marks The Foley 'Pastello' England, c1900, 6½ in (16.5 cm) high. $400-600

A pair of Villeroy & Boch 'Mettlach' stoneware vases, in muted tones of browns, red, greys, pale blue and lemon, factory marks and each numbered 2598/99, 10½ in (26 cm) high. $400-600

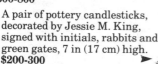

A large Ault pottery vase, designed by Christopher Dresser, covered with liver-red glaze, impressed facsimile signature on base, 20 in (50 cm) high. $800-1,200

A Robert Anning Bell painted relief plaster panel, emblematic of honeysuckle, heightened with gilding against a dark turquoise ground, signed R. An. Bell and dated '99', 16 by 12 in (40 by 30 cm), in contemporary ebonised frame with remains of Fine Art Society Exhibition label. $2,000-3,000

A Foley 'Intarsio' pottery vase, painted in vivid colours. $600-800

A pair of pottery candlesticks, decorated by Jessie M. King, signed with initials, rabbits and green gates, 7 in (17 cm) high. $200-300

A Shelley enamelled porcelain figure, the white circular base with the words in black, printed marks, 12 in (30 cm) high. $600-900

An unusual Shelley child's beaker, decorated in colours with a design by Linda Edgerton, inscribed with the nursery rhyme 'Mary, Mary Quite Contrary', printed marks and signature on side, 4 in (9.8 cm) high $200-300

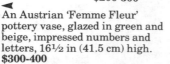

An Austrian 'Femme Fleur' pottery vase, glazed in green and beige, impressed numbers and letters, 16½ in (41.5 cm) high. $300-400

An unusual Continental pottery vase, painted in dark blue and yellow on a shaded lemon and beige ground with blue, green and brown banding, unmarked, 13 in (32.5 cm) high. $100-200

An unusual Burmantofts faience plaque, painted by William Neatby, impressed Burmantofts 'Faience' and signed Wm. Neatby and dated 1887, 16 in (40 cm) diam. **$300-400**

A Riessner, Stellmacher and Kessel Art Nouveau porcelain vase, coloured in green, yellow and gilding against a shaded yellow and white ground, impressed crown mark Amphora, Austria, 15024-46, 15 in (37.5 cm) high. **$100-200**

A French stoneware figural vase, by James Vibert, glazed shaded turquoise and brick red, signed J. Vibert and on the handle E. Muller as maker, 6½ in (16 cm) high. **$400-600**

James Vibert was born in Switzerland in 1872 and in 1892 was employed in the workshops of Rodin.

A large Theodore Deck faience circular wall plate, 'Phryne', impressed T.H. Deck and signed R. Collin(?), 24½ in (61 cm) diam. **$800-1,200**

A rare Della Robbia clockcase, designed by Ruth Bare and decorated by Alice Jones, painted ship mark flanked by DR above the artist's monogram LJ and 57, c1904, 18¼ in (46 cm). **$1,200-1,500**

The inscription is linked with Ruth Bare's involvement with the Positivist Movement.

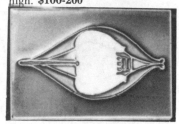

A tube lined Art Nouveau tile, with a blue background. **$25-30**

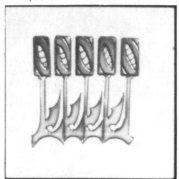

A tube lined Art Nouveau tile, with a cream background, c1900. **$30-60**

An Austrian lustre glazed porcelain pitcher, by Ernst Wallis, c1900. **$600-700**

A small Art Nouveau furniture tile. **$25-30**

A Morris-ware vase, by Hancock, signed Partridge. **$200-300**

An English tube lined Art Nouveau tile, with a green background. **$25-30**

Art nouveau : Doulton

An early Doulton Lambeth stoneware jug, decorated by Hannah B Barlow, with silver collar and cover, o.u.m. artist's monogram and London hallmarks for 1872, 11½ in (28 cm). **$600-700**

A Doulton stoneware jug, of tapering form with skirted base, and a pair of beakers, incised by Hannah Barlow, impressed mark Doulton Lambeth 1878 and signed BHB, with silver mounts, London 1878, the jug 9½ in (24 cm). **$800-1,200**

A Doulton Lambeth biscuit barrel, with plated hinged top, decorated with a sheepdog and sheep by Hannah Barlow, impressed mark and date 1873 and incised marks, 8½ in (21 cm). **$400-600**

An early Doulton Lambeth three-handled loving cup, decorated by Hannah B. Barlow, c.m., dated 1876, artist's monogram numbered 558, also signed on side, 6½ in (16 cm). **$500-600**

A vase, by Hannah Barlow, incised with a band of donkeys and 2 young children feeding rabbits, impressed Doulton Lambeth, 10½ in (26 cm). **$300-500**

A Royal Doulton pottery vase, decorated by Hannah Barlow, with fox attacking sheep, 12 in (30 cm). **$600-700**

A Royal Doulton stoneware vase, by Frank A. Butler, incised with dark green and brown spiky bulbs with mottled green and light blue centres, c.m.l. & c., incised artist's monogram, number 996, 13 in (33 cm). **$500-600**

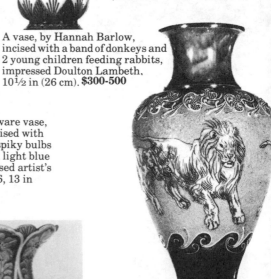

A pair of baluster vases, by Hannah Barlow, incised with lions, impressed Doulton Lambeth England marks, 14 in (35 cm). **$1,500-2,200**

A large Doulton Lambeth faience jardiniere, painted by Florence E. Lewis, with a shaded green and lemon ground, i.c.f.m., artist's monogram and numbered 317, 13 in (33 cm). **$600-700**

A large pair of Doulton Lambeth vases, decorated by Frank A. Butler and Mary Ann Thomson, all in olive greens, blues, russet, brown, green and white, r.m. dated 1885, with F.A.B. monogram, numbered 532 and MT monogram on inner necks, 21½ in (53.5 cm). **$2,500-3,500**

A set of 3 Doulton Lambeth faience tiles, painted by Florence E. Lewis, framed, c.m., painted artist monogram, Minton and Hollins, 8¼ by 8¼ in (20.5 by 20.5 cm). **$600-800**

A pair of Doulton Lambeth stoneware and brass candlesticks, by Frank A. Butler, in olive greens, blues, brown and russet, r.m., and artist's monogram and numbered 550, 10 in (25 cm). **$400-600**

A Doulton stoneware vase, decorated by Edith Lupton, in dark coloured glazes, impressed and incised marks including the date 1888, 13 in (33 cm). **$600-900**

A pair of Doulton Lambeth stoneware jardinières, by Edith D. Lupton, incised with olive green foliate scrolls against deep blue, c.m., dated 1877 with artist's initials, numbered 512 and 513, and assistant's initials for Eliza J Hubert, 8 in (20 cm). **$800-1,200**

A Royal Doulton oviform stoneware vase, by Mark V. Marshall, c.m.l. & c., incised with artist's initials, 685, assistant's mark for Emily Partington, date shield for 1907, 12 in (30 cm) **$500-600** ►

A Doulton Lambeth jug, by Mark V. Marshall, r.m. incised artist's initials 105 and assistant's initials MH & JBH, 9 in (23 cm). **$1,500-2,200**

This piece is illustrated in Doulton Stoneware Pottery 1870-1925, Richard Dennis, 1971, No. 388.

DOULTON WARES

Doulton marks – abbreviations

o.u.m.	– oval undated mark
o.m.	– oval mark, dated
c.m.	– circular mark
r.m.	– rosette mark
r.m. & e.	– rosette mark and England
d.l.e.	– Doulton Lambeth England
d.s.l.	– Doulton Silicon Lambeth
d.s.p.	– Doulton & Slaters Patent
c.m.l. & c.	– circle mark, lion & crown
c.m. & l.	– circle mark and lion
r.d.e.	– Royal Doulton England
s.c.m.	– slip-cast mark
i.c.f.m.	– impressed circular faience mark
r.d.f.	– Royal Doulton Flambé
b.r.m. & c.	– Burslem rosette mark & crown

A cylindrical jug, modelled with a band of blue and brown foliage outlined in white on a stoneware ground, by M.V. Marshall, impressed Doulton Lambeth England mark, 10½ in (26 cm). **$400-600**

A pair of Doulton stoneware vases, by Eliza Simmance, with stylised lily motifs on a streaked pale green ground, impressed mark, incised artist's initials, 1900's, 9 in (23 cm). **$500-600**

A Doulton Lambeth stoneware exhibition ewer, shown at the 1893 Chicago Columbian World Fair, modelled by Mark V. Marshall, in ochre, cobalt and green, 72 in (183 cm). **$15,000-20,500**

A pair of Doulton Lambeth green and blue decorated tankards, 6 in (15 cm) high. **$100-150**

A Doulton Burslem vase, painted by W. Slater, signed, with chrysanthemums in shades of yellow, blue, mauve and green on a mottled turquoise ground, printed marks, 1890's, 19½ in (48.5 cm). **$700-900**

A Doulton Lambeth stoneware model of a carpenter's bag, attributed to George Tinworth, d.l. and Rd.162583, 3 in (8 cm) high. **$300-400**

A vase, by G.H. Tabar, incised with blue flowerheads and dark green leaves and foliage on a green ground, impressed Doulton Lambeth 1881, 10½ in (26 cm). **$300-400**

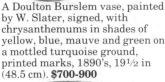

A Doulton Lambeth stoneware globular vase, by Eliza Simmance, glazed olive against a ground of slip-decorated petals, r.m., dated 1886, with artist's monogram numbered 875, 10½ in (26 cm). **$600-700**

A George Tinworth stoneware figure, of a Merry Musician, inscribed with the monogram T.G., 4 in (10 cm). **$300-500**

An unusual Doulton Lambeth stoneware group, modelled by George Tinworth, signed on base Doulton's Lambeth and with GT monogram, 7 in (17.5 cm). **$1,300-1,700**

A Royal Doulton stoneware jardinière and stand, in muted colours on a moss green ground, hair crack to rim, 37 in (92 cm) high. **$700-900**

Martin Bros

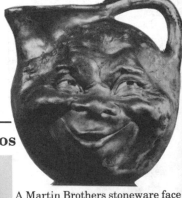

A Martin Brothers stoneware face jug, covered in an orange brown glaze, the eyes detailed in white, incised 'Martin Bros. London and Southall 10. 1896', 8½ in (21 cm) high. **$2,500-3,500**

A stoneware Martin Brothers bird tobacco jar and cover, incised and modelled decoration in shades of grey and brown on a stone coloured ground, body and head incised 'R.W. Martin & Bros. London and Southall 15.4.1903', 11 in (28 cm). **$5,500-7,000**

A tall Martin Brothers bird, the detachable head robustly modelled with the eyes humorously laughing above the prominent open beak, the body in brown glazing, the wings spattered in blue, signed and dated 'Martin Brothers, London and Southall 9, 1898', 13 in (32.5 cm). **$7,500-10,500**

A stoneware Martin Brothers grotesque double face jug, in pale grey glaze mottled with brown, the hair and handle in a darker brown, incised 'R W Martin & Bros, London and Southall', c1900, 6 in (17 cm) high. **$1,400-1,700**

A large Martin Brothers stoneware vase, signed 'Martin Bros., London and Southall' and dated '8-1894', 14 in (34.50 cm). **$1,000-1,200**

A Martin ware imp musician 'Tambourine player' modelled as a grotesque creature with exaggerated ears and grinning expression, signed on tambourine 'Martin Bros, London and Southall', 4½ in (11.25 cm). **$1,300-1,700**

An early Martinware jug, in blues, browns and greens, signed 'R. W. Martin' and 'E9' 8½ in (21.50 cm) high. **$300-400**

The form this decoration takes shows the obvious influence of the designs of Christopher Dresser, perhaps from 'The Art of Decorative Design' of 1862.

An unusual Martinware globular pouring vessel, decorated with a sunburst centred in shallow relief with a grotesque face, creased in anguish, all against a dark brown ground, signed 'Martin, London', 9 in (23 cm) high. **$700-900**

MAKE THE MOST OF MILLER'S

Price ranges in this book reflect what one should expect to pay for a similar example. When selling one can obviously expect a figure below. This will fluctuate according to a dealer's stock, saleability at a particular time, etc. It is always advisable to approach a reputable specialist dealer or an auction house which has specialist sales.

A Martinware vase, incised with white flowerheads and green foliage with dragonflies and a butterfly in flight on a brown ground, incised 'Martin Brothers, London, Southall', 7 in (17.5 cm). **$500-600**

A Martin Bros. stoneware flower vase, with blue, grey and brown glazes on a pricked surface, incised marks, 12½ in (31 cm) high. **$300-500**

A stoneware Martin Brothers vase, incised 'Martin Bros. London & Southall 3-1894' 9½ in (24 cm). **$300-600**

A stoneware Martin Brothers jardinière, glazed in blues and greys on a stone coloured ground, incised 'Martin Brothers, London & Southall 10-1892', 11 in (27 cm) high. **$1,400-1,700**

Moorcroft

William Moorcroft Wares

William Moorcroft was born in Burslem in 1872. He studied at the Burslem School of Art, the National Art School (now the Royal College) and in Paris. In 1897 he joined James Macintyre and Co as a designer in their new Art Pottery department. In 1898 Moorcroft designed and produced a range known as Florian Ware. Moorcroft had total control of production and was able to experiment with a variety of glazes and decorating methods. Moorcroft used a white porcellaneous body of great strength. Wares were generally thrown rather than moulded and Moorcroft drew the original designs for every shape and size of pot himself. These were generally taken from nature, particularly plant forms, and were outlined on the pot using a thick slip which also served to prevent the metallic infill glazes from merging during firing.

Macintyre's Art Pottery closed in 1913 and Moorcroft established his own company at Cobridge, continuing with designs produced at Macintyre's as well as developing new ones.

In 1928 Moorcroft gained the Royal Warrant and his company flourished on an international reputation built on the foundations of quality and style. During the late 1930's many Art Potteries were forced to close but Moorcroft soldiered on thanks to the continued support of a thriving American market.

In 1945 William's son Walter took over the Cobridge works and continued to produce a wide range of designs mostly sold to an appreciative American public.

A Macintyre Moorcroft pottery vase, decorated in red, yellow, green and blue glazes, printed mark in brown and signed in green, retailed by John Walsh Limited of Sheffield, 12½ in (31 cm). **$600-900**

A good Moorcroft Macintyre 'Florian' ware vase, with slip-trailed decoration of dark blue flowers within panels on a paler blue ground, green painted 'W. Moorcroft' signature and printed mark 'Florian ware Jas. Macintyre & Co. Ltd., Burslem, England', c1900, 12½ in (31 cm). **$600-800**

A Moorcroft Florian vase, painted in lilac pattern in shades of blue, printed marks and inscribed 'W.M' 7 in (17.5 cm) high. **$400-600**

A Moorcroft-Tudric 'Hazeldene' bowl, decorated internally and externally with stylised trees in the eventide palette, raised on a 'Tudric' pewter base, stamped on pewter 'Tudric Moorcroft' '01311'; 10½ in (26 cm) **$500-600**

A Macintyre Aurelian ware tazza and cover, attributed to William Moorcroft, dark blue ground, blue scale panels, and gilded panels with orange flowers and leaves, printed 'Macintyre Burslem England' mark and monogram and printed retailer's mark 'Made for Ward & Son, Doncaster', c1898, 12 in (30 cm). **$300-600**

A Moorcroft vase, painted with a fish in yellow and green on a green to blue ground, impressed marks, signed in green, 12 in (30 cm) high. **$800-1,200**

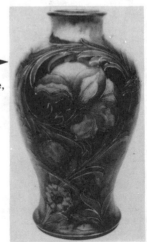

A pair of Moorcroft vases, ► trailed in white slip with scrolling flowers and foliage, picked out in dark coloured glazes, green script signature, impressed Burslem mark, c1920, 12½ in (32 cm). **$1,700-2,500**

A large Moorcroft 'Hazeldene' baluster vase, decorated in the 'moonlit blue' palette, impressed 'Moorcroft, Made in England' signed 'W. Moorcroft', 10½ in (26 cm) high. **$500-600**

A large and deep flared bowl, by Moorcroft, painted in the Claremont design with pink, yellow and blue toadstools on a mottled bluish green ground, the border inscribed 'Facta non verba vincit omnia veritas', impressed 'Moorcroft, Made in England', and green painted signature, 14 in (35 cm). **$1,200-1,500**

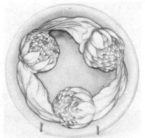

A Moorcroft 'Waratah' plate, decorated with 3 large white and red flower blooms and green leaves against a green ground, impressed facsimile signature, 'Potter to H.M. The Queen, Made in England', 9 in (22.5 cm). **$500-600**

A Moorcroft box and cover, painted with the Toad Stool pattern on a green ground, painted mark 'W. Moorcroft, 1913', 6½ in (16 cm). **$400-600**

An unusual enamelled cigarette box, in vivid colours, some foil backed and with gilt detailing, cedar wood lined, unmarked but possibly Austrian, 5 by 3½ in (13 cm by 9 cm). **$500-600**

Macintyre/Moorcroft

* first Art Pottery produced in 1897. Early wares marked Macintyre and/or W. Moorcroft des.
* William Moorcroft established his own works in 1913.
* 1913-21 wares impressed MOORCROFT BURSLEM with painted W.Moorcroft signature
* after 1916 impressed ENGLAND
* 1921-1930 impressed MADE IN ENGLAND
* 1930-1949 paper label, BY APPOINTMENT, POTTER TO H.M. THE QUEEN used
* 1949-1973 label states BY APPOINTMENT TO THE LATE QUEEN MARY
* rivals copied patterns and colours

A William Moorcroft 'Claremont' pattern bowl, slip trailed with red flushed toadstools on a mottled green/blue ground, facsimile signature, Liberty mark, early 20thC, 10½ in (26 cm). **$600-800**

A Moorcroft tobacco jar and cover, painted with the Cornflower pattern, purple flowers amongst green scrolling foliage on a creamware ground, impressed mark and signed 'W. Moorcroft' in green, 5½ in (13 cm) diam. **$600-800**

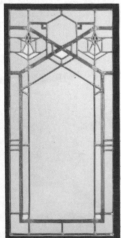

A leaded glass window, designed by Frank Lloyd Wright for the B. Harley Bradley House, Kankakee, Illinois, c1900. **$2,500-3,000**

A large Moorcroft pottery vase, decorated with poppies on a dark blue ground, impressed marks 'made in England' Potter to H.M. Queen, inside script signature W. Moorcroft and factory paper label, 15 in (37.5 cm) high. **$300-500**

A Martin Bros. stoneware vase, brown and buff glazed, with decoration of flowering tendrils, mark to base 'R.W. Martin & Bros., London and Southall. 8/84'. **$300-400**

489

A Mission oak fall-front desk, by Gustav Stickley, with brass hardware on sloped square sides joined by undershelf, opening to reveal a pigeonholed interior, model 706, marked, 30in (75cm) wide. **$1,700-2,000**

A Mission oak daybed, by Gustav Stickley, model 216, unsigned, 80in (203cm) long. **$1,200-1,500**

An Arts and Crafts oak chair, in the style of Frank Lloyd Wright, unsigned, 45in (113cm) high. **$800-900**

An oak writing desk, by Gustav Stickley, with letter racks in the back both vertical and horizontal, each drawer with triangular bails, with red decal, model no. 708, c1910, 40in (102cm) wide. **$900-1,000**

An oak 'Chalet' desk, with wicker basket, by Gustav Stickley, model no. 505, unsigned, c1902, 22½in (57cm) wide. **$1,800-2,000**

An oak bow-arm Morris chair, by Gustav Stickley, red decal, the logo outlined, model no. 2340, c1902, 24in (61cm) high to arm. **$4,500-5,000**

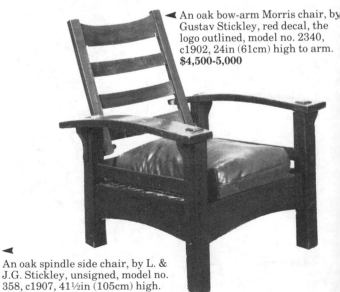

An oak spindle side chair, by L. & J.G. Stickley, unsigned, model no. 358, c1907, 41½in (105cm) high. **$800-1,000**

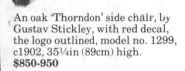

An oak and rush armchair, by
Gustav Stickley, unsigned, model
no.1289A, c1902, 40½in (103cm)
high. **$350-450**

An oak 'Thorndon' side chair, by
Gustav Stickley, with red decal,
the logo outlined, model no. 1299,
c1902, 35¼in (89cm) high.
$850-950

◄ A pair of oak and leather side
chairs, by Gustav Stickley, with
red decal, model no. 380, c1905,
40in (101cm) high. **$350-450**

An oak buffet, by Gustav Stickley,
the apron featuring a gentle
inverted V, with red decal
'Stickley' outlined, model no. 955,
c1902, 59in (149cm) wide.
$2,000-2,400

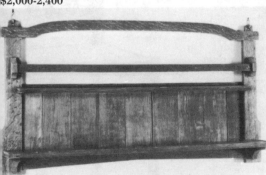

An oak plate rack, by Gustav
Stickley, with red decal 'Stickley'
outlined, model no. 903, c1901,
45½in (114cm) wide. **$2,000-2,500**

An oak library table, by Gustav
Stickley, with original leather top
and tacks, the two-drawer pulls
with oval bailed copper hardware,
branded signature and paper
label, model no. 615, c1912, 48½in
(122cm) wide. **$3,500-4,000**

491

An oak side table, by L. & J.G.
Stickley, with single drawer with
'Shaker' knob, unsigned, model
no. 550, c1912, 29in (74cm) high.
$400-600

An oak vanity and mirror, by
Gustav Stickley, unsigned, mode
no. 907, c1910, 48in (120cm) wide
$2,000-2,500

◄

An inlaid curly maple side chair,
designed by Harvey Ellis,
executed by Gustav Stickley, wit
branded signature, model no. 353
c1912, 39¾in (101cm) high.
$1,800-2,000

An oak 'Spindle' side chair, by
Gustav Stickley, black decal,
model no. 378, c1910, 40in
(101cm) high. **$1,000-1,200**

An inlaid curly maple rocking
chair, designed by Harvey Ellis,
executed by Gustav Stickley,
branded signature, model no. 337,
◄ c1912, 32½in (82cm) high.
$2,000-2,500

An inlaid curly maple side chair,
designed by Harvey Ellis,
executed by Gustav Stickley,
unsigned, model no. 353, c1912,
39½in (100cm) high. **$1,500-2,000** ►

An unusual Clement Heaton cloisonné enamelled panel, stamped 'Clement Heaton et Co., Neuchâtel', dated '1898' and numbered 'N134B', 18 by 14 in (45 by 35.50 cm). **$500-600**

Clement J. Heaton studied stained glass and metalwork techniques in his father's firm, Heaton, Butler and Bayre and set up his own firm 'Heaton's Cloisonné Mosaics Ltd.', moving to Neuchâtel, Switzerland in the early 1890's. He emigrated to America in 1912.

An Arts and Crafts enamelled plaque, decorated with a gentleman connoisseur examining a figural statuette, with embossed and shaped copper frame, indistinct signature 13 by 15 in (32 by 37 cm) overall. **$1,200-1,500**

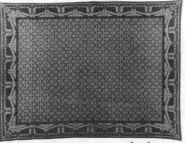

An Art Nouveau cover, of red, white and pale blue wool, 61½ by 83½ in (156 by 212 cm). **$500-600**

A silver and ivory mounted stoneware chocolatière, by Jean Pointu and Cardelilhac, 'marbled' green, brown, blue and tan glaze, with carved ivory handle, incised 'Jean U' and numerals 137 on body, the mounts impressed with French poinçons, c1900, 8¼ in (20 cm). **$2,500-3,500**

Art deco Furniture

A Robert Thompson Mouseman oak bed, signed with a carved mouse, 61 in (152.2 cm). **$1,200-1,500**

A pair of Robert Thompson Mouseman oak armchairs, carved with the letters F.W.R. and date 1928, each signed with a carved mouse. **$800-1,200**

An Art Deco burr maple veneer cocktail cabinet, 43 in (107.2 cm) wide. **$1,300-1,700**

A palissandre, ivory and gilt bronze coiffeuse, by Sadier, unsigned, 64in (162.5 cm) wide. **$6,000-8,000**

For an illustration of an identical model set with a slightly larger mirror, see Paul Frankl, Form and Re-Form, Hacker, New York, 1972, .p.62.

A pair of Thebes stools, 14 in (35 cm). **$1,000-1,200**

An Art Deco screen, 66 in (188 cm) high. **$500-600**

A Reflectone Corporation low ▶ backed perspex revolving stool, printed paper labels, Unilevel, the Reflectone Corporation (U.S), c1940, 26 in (64 cm). **$300-500**

493

A 1950's painted Formica cocktail cabinet, in the form of a fireplace, 40 in (100 cm). **$600-800**

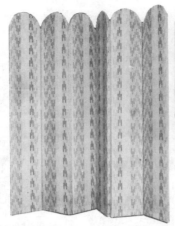

An Art Deco screen, 66 in (188 cm) high. **$300-500**

A blonde mahogany and burr walnut bedroom suite, by Esse American, comprising: a three-drawer chest of drawers, glass-shelves vanity with roun mirror, single headboard, footboard and rails, all asymmetrically designed, with horizontal pulls, chest 48in (120cm) wide. **$2,100-2,500**

Art Deco
Glass

◄

A Kosta vase, 'Autumn Sonata designed by Vicke Lindstrand, c1955. **$1,500-2,200**

A Barovier and Toso 'patchwork' glass vase, with a red and smoked glass patchwork design, inscribed Barovier and Toso Murano, 9½ in (24 cm). **$600-900**

A large Fulvio Bianconi vase, the amber coloured body overlaid with applied asymmetric trailed blue circles, engraved signature Fulvio Bianconi 1957, 15½ in (39 cm). **$2,500-3,500**

A black enamelled frosted glass vase, 'Dahlias', intaglio moulde R. Lalique, 5½ in (14 cm). **$600-900**

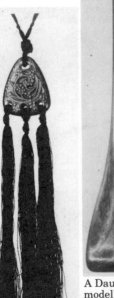

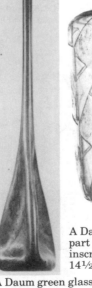

A Daum etched green glass vase, part polished, part frosted, inscribed Daum Nancy France, 14½ in (36 cm). **$600-900**

A Daum green glass vase, modelled with brown streaks, signed Daum Nancy, 24 in (60 cm). **$400-600**

A Lalique jade green pendant, with silk cord and tassels, engraved mark, 2 in (5 cm). **$400-600**

A large clear and grey stained glass vase, of geometric form, engraved in script Lalique, 13 (33 cm). **$2,000-3,000**

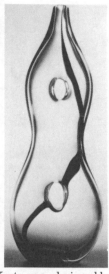

Kosta vase, designed by Vicke Lindstrand, internally decorated with a swirling dark amethyst stripe, signed, c1955, 12 in (30.5 cm). **$1,000-1,200**

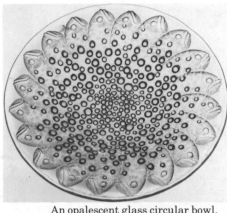

An opalescent glass circular bowl, 'Roscof', engraved R. Lalique France, 14 in (35 cm). **$500-600**

A frosted polished and blue stained mantel clock, 'Muguet', stencilled R. Lalique, France, 8½ in (21.5 cm). **$1,000-1,400**

A cased set of 6 Lalique scent bottles and stoppers, designed for Coty, with original embossed gilt Coty labels, one bottle with rim chips. **$800-1,200**

A Lalique clock, 'Inseparables', moulded signature, 1930's 4½ in (11.5 cm). **$1,000-1,200**

A frosted and clear glass seal, 'Papillon Ailes Fermées', engraved script mark R. Lalique, in (7 cm). **$400-600**

A frosted and grey stained glass paperweight, 'Aigle', engraved in script R. Lalique. **$600-900**

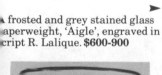

A Lalique glass opal tinted frosted glass vase, 'Saint Francois', 7 in (17.7 cm). **$300-400**

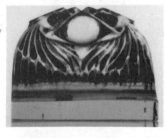

A polished and blue stained glass paperweight, 'Deux Aigles', intaglio moulded R. Lalique engraved France, 3 in (8 cm). **$600-900**

An opalescent floral engraved and blue stained 'Reflets' vase, by R. Lalique, c1928, 5 in (12.5 cm). **$400-600**

A frosted and opalescent glass vase, 'Raisins', heightened with strong blue staining, stencilled R. Lalique France, 6 in (15.75 cm). **$600-800**

A large frosted and clear glass ceiling globe, 'Grande boule de Gui', lower bowl engraved script Lalique, one side panel cracked, 22 in (55 cm). **$2,000-3,000**

An intaglio moulded vase, 'Coupe Herone', with frosted doves perched on stylised boughs, stencilled Lalique Crystal France, 1950, 7½ in (19 cm). **$300-800**

An opalescent frosted and blue stained glass vase, stencilled R. Lalique, 9 in (22 cm). **$600-900**

A glass vase, moulded with a frieze of stylised antelopes, heightened with blue staining, stencilled mark R. Lalique France, 5 in (12.5 cm). **$600-700**

A Lalique opalescent glass vase, 'Chandon', modelled with thistles and with brown staining, etched marks, 8½ in (21 cm). **$500-600**

An electric blue glass vase, 'Epines', intaglio moulded R. Lalique, 9½ in (23.75 cm). **$1,400-1,700**

A frosted and opalescent glass vase, 'Oleron', engraved script R. Lalique, France, No. 1008, 3½ in (9.25 cm). **$300-500**

A Lalique opalescent vase, 'Avalon', signed R. Lalique, France, 6 in (15 cm). **$600-700**

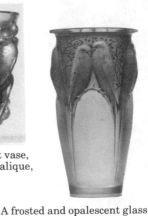

A frosted and opalescent glass vase, 'Ceylan', heightened with blue stain, wheel cut R. Lalique France, and engraved No. 906, 9½ in (24 cm). **$1,000-1,200**

A large Lalique opalescent glass vase, 'Salmonides', heightened with matt blue staining, impressed R. Lalique, France, and engraved R. Lalique, France, No. 1015, 11½ in (29 cm). **$3,000-4,500**

A Lalique frosted glass oviform vase, 'Aigrettes', heightened with traces of blue staining, signed R. Lalique, France, No. 988, 10 in (25.30 cm). **$2,500-3,500**

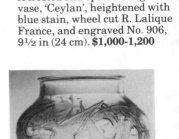

A Lalique vase, in clear and satin finished glass, decorated with swallows in flight, moulded Lalique signature and engraved France, c1930, 9½ in (24 cm). **$400-600**

A Lalique glass circular hand mirror, 'Deux Oiseaux', with a reflecting inner surface with grey staining, moulded Lalique, 6½ in (16 cm). **$600-700**

A Lalique frosted glass oviform vase, 'Archers', with traces of brown staining, signed R. Lalique, France, No. 893, 11 in (27 cm). **$1,400-1,700**

A Lalique opalescent bowl, with blue staining, acid stamped R. Lalique, France, c1930, 9½ in (23.5 cm). **$2,500-3,500**

A Lalique frosted glass figure, 'Suzanne', signed R. Lalique, France on base, 9 in (22.5 cm). **2,500-3,500**

A frosted glass statuette, 'Source de la Fontaine', wheel cut R. Lalique France, mounted upon polished stone plinth of square section, 22 in (55 cm). **$4,000-5,000**

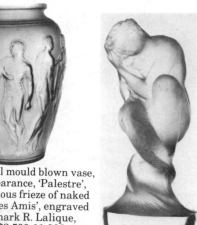

A monumental mould blown vase, of frosted appearance, 'Palestre', with a continuous frieze of naked Olympians, 'Les Amis', engraved block capital mark R. Lalique, 17 in (42 cm). **$8,500-11,000**

A frosted and opalescent glass statuette, 'Sirene', relief moulded mark, R. Lalique, and engraved on the base R. Lalique France, 4 in (10.5 cm). **$700-900**

A Lalique drinking set, 'Bahia' comprising a jug and 6 tumblers in clear and satin finished amber glass, small bruise to rim of one of the glasses, acid stamped marks R. Lalique, c1930, jug 9 in (23 cm) glasses 5 in (13 cm). **$700-900**

A frosted and clear glass vase, 'Danaides', 7 in (18 cm). **$700-900**

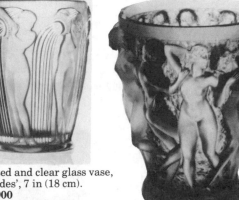

A Lalique moulded glass vase, 'Bacchantes', in satin finished glass with blue staining, incised signature R. Lalique France, c1930, 10 in (25 cm). **$4,000-5,000**

An amber glass shallow bowl, 'Martigues', relief moulded mark R. Lalique, and wheel cut France, 14½ in (36.5 cm). **$1,300-1,700**

A Lalique glass bowl, decorated with 5 opalescent milky swirling mermaids, marked R. Lalique France, 12 in (30 cm). **$1,300-1,700**

A Lalique opalescent glass circular box and cover, 'Deux Sirenes', relief moulded mark, engraved marks France No. 43, 10½ in (26 cm). **$1,400-1,700**

A frosted glass vase, 'Bacchantes', engraved mark in script Lalique, 1950, 10 in (25 cm). **1,300-1,700**

Note the higher price of the earlier piece. This price differential is also due to the blue staining.

A frosted glass box, 'Paon', the top with a peacock perched on a bough, all heightened with blue, engraved in script R. Lalique, 5 in (12 cm). **$500-600**

An opalescent glass box and cover, 'Libellules', moulded R. Lalique, 7 in (17 cm). **$500-600**

A Nemours Lalique blue stained bowl, moulded R. Lalique France, 10 in (25 cm). **$400-600**

A clear and frosted glass car mascot, 'Archer' intaglio moulded R. Lalique, wheel cut France, 5 in (12.5 cm). **$700-900**

A frosted glass powder box, 'Degas', engraved mark in script on box, R. Lalique France No. 66, and moulded Lalique on cover, 2½ in (6.5 cm). **$300-500**

A Lalique car mascot, 'Faucon', in clear and satin finished glass, moulded signature R. Lalique France, c1930, 6 in (15.7 cm). **$1,000-1,400**

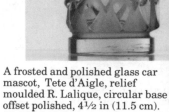

A frosted and polished glass car mascot, Tete d'Aigle, relief moulded R. Lalique, circular base offset polished, 4½ in (11.5 cm). **$1,400-1,700**

A glass car mascot, 'Hirondelle', the polished glass with pale amethyst tint, relief moulded mark, R. Lalique France, rim chip to circular base underside, 6 in (14.5 cm). **$700-900**

A Lalique frosted glass car mascot, 'Longchamps', moulded R. Lalique France, 5 in (12.5 cm). **$2,500-3,500**

A Lalique frosted glass car mascot, 'Vitesse', moulded R. Lalique France, and having original Breves Galleries, Knightsbridge chromed mount with coloured filter, 7 in (17.5 cm). **$2,500-3,500**

A clear and polished glass car mascot, 'Cinq Chevaux', in Breves Galleries plated mount, relief moulded R. Lalique and wheel cut France, 6 in (15 cm). **$2,500-3,500**

A frosted and clear glass car mascot, of pale amethyst tint, 'Victoire', the spirit of the wind well modelled with open mouth and stylised hair streaming behind, relief moulded R. Lalique, Breves Gallery chromed light mount, 10 in (25.5 cm). **$7,000-9,000**

A Leerdam heavy pale yellow tinted glass vase, designed by A.D. Copier, acid stamped CL, Copier Leerdam, monogram, c1935, 9 in (22 cm). **$700-900**

A Lalique frosted glass car mascot, 'Petite Libellule', with moulded veining, moulded Lalique France, and engraved R. Lalique France, 6½ in (16 cm). **$1,400-1,700**

A Muller vase, in clear and frosted glass, signed Muller Luneville France, c1930, 8 in (20 cm). **300-500**

An Orrefors clear glass decanter and stopper, 'Susanna och gubbarna', designed by Edward Hald, engraved signature Orrefors Hald 1230 C9T, c1935, 9½ in (23.5 cm). **$600-700**

An Orrefors glass vase, designed by Vicke Lindstrand, engraved with the figure of a golfer, signed Orrefors, LA and numbered 1823, 6 in (15.5 cm). **$600-700**

An Orrefors clear glass vase, ► signed in diamond point Orrefors 3746 C.7.A.R., c1940, 11 in (28 cm). **$400-600**

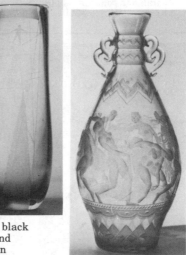

An Art Deco glass decanter, of alique style and 6 glasses. **200-300**

An Art Deco glass decanter, black enamelled with geometric and starburst designs, five tots en suite, 10 in (25 cm). **$400-600**

An Orrefors grey tinted vase, designed by Simon Gate, engraved Orrefors S. Gate 234.27 A.D., c1930, 9½ in (23.5 cm). **$1,200-1,500**

A cut glass decanter and stopper, modelled with geometric patterns in black and frosted glass, 7½ in (19 cm), and 6 liqueur glasses en suite, 2½ in (6 cm). **$400-600**

Verlys moulded glass vase, moulded signature A. Verlys rance, c1930, 11½ in (28.5 cm). **300-500**

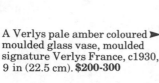

A Verlys pale amber coloured ► moulded glass vase, moulded signature Verlys France, c1930, 9 in (22.5 cm). **$200-300**

A set of 6 Art Deco glass goblets, enamelled with peacocks in green and blue, and nude female figures against a black enamelled ground, some signed Vedar, one with slight chip, 8 in (20 cm). **$800-1,200**

Six Art Deco glass scent bottles.
$300-400
Front – An Argy Rousseau
pâté-de-verre cube paperweight,
modelled with moths, 2 in (5 cm).
$700-1,000

An Orrefors clear glass decanter,
signed in diamond point LA 409/6,
c1950, 11 in (28 cm). **$200-300**

Art Deco Jewellery

A Mexican Art Deco silver brooch,
signed 'Rebajes', c1930.
$300-500

A Theodor Fahrner Art Deco
brooch, with a central triangle of
amazonite flanked by bands of
marcasite, silver coloured metal
stamped '935' and 'TF' monogram,
1½ in (3.75 cm) square.
$600-700

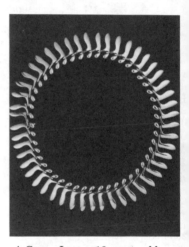

A Georg Jensen 18 carat gold
necklace, designed by Bent
Gabriel Petersen, composed of 49
interlocking articulated pieces of
abstract design, with gold safety
catch, gold marks and stamped
'Georg Jensen', design introduced
1959. **$5,500-7,000**

Art deco – metal

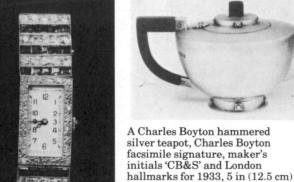

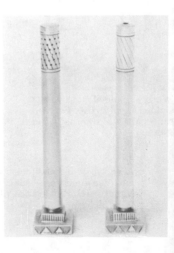

A French Art Deco sapphire and
diamond dress watch, in platinum
setting. **$1,700-2,500**

A Charles Boyton hammered
silver teapot, Charles Boyton
facsimile signature, maker's
initials 'CB&S' and London
hallmarks for 1933, 5 in (12.5 cm)
high, 21 oz 19 dwt. gross weight.
$800-1,200

An unusual Georg Jensen silver
salt and pepper pot, designed by
Jergen Jensen, maker's marks,
designers initials 'JJ' numbered
'793' and with London import
marks for 1938, 5 in (12 cm) high.
$800-1,200

A pair of Hagenauer two-branch chromed metal candlesticks, impressed marks 'Hagenauer Wien, Made in Austria' and maker's monogram, c1925, 17 in high (43 cm). **$1,400-1,700**

A Friedrich Jornik Viennese bronze casket, stamped mark 'AT Austria', signed in the bronze 'Fried. Jornik', c1925, 12½ by 7½ in (31.5 by 18.5 cm). **$800-1,200**

A Viner & Co., four piece silver and ivory tea service, each piece with Sheffield hallmarks for 1936 and stamped maker's initials 'E.V', 55 oz 15 dwt. gross weight. **$1,500-2,200**

An Austrian hammered silver and silver-gilt box, with carved ivory finial, Austrian silver marks, c1925, 3½ in (8.2 cm high), 12 oz 10 dwt. gross weight. **$800-1,200**

A pair of Dora Gordine four-branch chandeliers, inscribed Dora Gordine 7/10/1932, 29 in (73 cm) to top of column. **$2,500-3,500**

An Emmy Roth hammered silver and ivory teaset, with German silver marks and engraved signature 'Emmy Roth', except sugar tongs marked with 800 mark only, c1930, tray 18 in (44.5 cm long), 93 oz 5 dwt gross weight. **$7,000-9,000**

Emmy Roth had her own silver workshops in Berlin during the 1920's and 1930's. Her work is illustrated in Deutsche Kunst und Dekoration and was included in many exhibitions, notably in the Ausstellung Europäisches Kunstgewerbe (Leipzig), 1927.

An Art Deco silver mirror, c1920. **$600-800**

An unusual plated picnic set, stamped 'AGRA' in oval, 'Sonder Lall P.S.' with stag's head. **$400-600**

◄

A pair of Omar Ramsden silver and enamelled oval picture frames, with shaded blue and green enamelling, backed in blue fabric, maker's mark 'OR' for London 1925, 5¾ in (14.25 cm high). **$800-1,200**

A pair of bakelite table lamps, unsigned, c1935, 19½ in (49.5 cm). **$1,500-2,200**

An Art Deco cigarette case, the design attributed to Paul Brandt, in red and black enamels, silver coloured metal stamped 'Made in France' and maker's mark 'R.A.S.' and anchor in square, 3½ by 3 in (8.5 by 7.5 cm). **$400-600**

A silver teaset, with bakelite handles, made in India. **$1,400-1,700**

Art deco figures

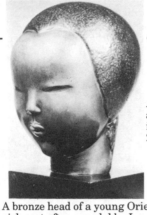

A bronze and alabaster lamp, cast after a model by A. Kelety, signed in the bronze 'A. Kelety' c1925, 22 in (55 cm). **$4,500-7,000**

'The Red Shawl', a Richard Garbe lacquered Japanese ash statue, cracked, some flaking, c1930, 55 in (138 cm). **$7,000-9,000**

A bronze head of a young Oriental girl, cast after a model by I. Codreano, signed in the bronze 'I. Codreano 1927', 13 in (32 cm). **$1,500-2,200**

A large bronze figure of a dancer, by Charles d'Orville Pilkington Jackson, signed 'Pilkington Jackson' and dated 1922?, 32 in high (80 cm). **$4,500-7,000**

A carved marble figure, by Thomas Brock, 'Eve', repaired at ankles, 35½ in (89 cm). **$2,000-3,000**

A gilded bronze figure, entitled Nenette, by Juan Clara, signed, 8½ in (21 cm). **$600-800**

A German bronze group by Jager, signed Jager, 13½ in (34 cm). **$500-600**

A bronze and gilt bronze figure, cast from a model by A. Gory, signed 'A. Gory', c1920, 21 in (52 cm). **$2,000-3,000**

A Damascened silvered and gilt bronze figure of a scarf dancer, cast from a model by Raymond Guerbe, French, inscribed 42 Raymond Guerbe, early 20thC, 30½ in (77.5 cm). **$4,500-7,000**

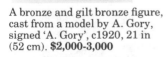

A bronze group of 2 men, on a marble base, by Nepa, 27½ in long (67.5 cm). **$600-900**

◄ A bronze figure of a girl, by S. Molselsio, signed S. Molselsio and dated 1919, 12½ in (31.75 cm). **$500-600**

A small Art Deco gilt metal figure,
amber onyx base, 8 in (20 cm).
$150-200

A Lorenzl Art Deco spelter figure,
silvered, 11½ in (29 cm).
$300-400

A Lorenzl gilt and painted bronze
figure, inscribed Lorenzl, 10 in
(25 cm). **$800-1,200**

Limousin spelter Art Deco table
lamp, 16½ in (41 cm). **$300-400**

Art deco : bronze and ivory figures

An Art Deco figure group
'Friends', by Demetre Chiparus,
on a shaped rectangular brown
onyx base, signed, 16½ in (41 cm)
high. **$4,500-7,000**

A bronze and ivory figure by
Chiparus, 'Innocence', wearing
turquoise cold-painted dress, the
marble base inscribed D.
Chiparus, 9½ in (23 cm).
$1,000-1,200

An Art Deco bronze and ivory
figure, of a woman in Elizabethan
costume, on a stepped onyx base,
signed Chiparus, defect. 10 in
(25 cm) high. **$1,000-1,200**

gilded bronze and ivory figure,
a girl feeding poultry, by D.
lonzo, signed, 9½ in (24 cm).
,000-1,400

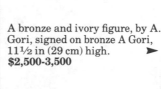

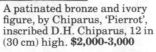

A bronze and ivory figure, by A.
Gori, signed on bronze A Gori,
11½ in (29 cm) high.   ➤
$2,500-3,500

A patinated bronze and ivory
figure, by Chiparus, 'Pierrot',
inscribed D.H. Chiparus, 12 in
(30 cm) high. **$2,000-3,000**

A gilt bronze and ivory group, by
Chiparus, signed, onyx plinth, 6 in
(15 cm) high. **$1,400-1,700**

503

A cold-painted silvered bronze and marble bust of a young lady in a turban, French, cast and carved from a model by A. Gory, inscribed A. Gory, early 20thC, 15 in (38 cm) high, including white alabaster base. **$2,500-3,500**

A Preiss bronze and ivory figure of Beach Ball Girl, inscribed F. Preiss, 15 in (37.5 cm) high. **$4,500-7,000**

A gilded bronze and ivory figure of a girl on stepping stones, by C.H. Monginot, signed, 8 in (20 cm). **$600-900**

A F. Preiss cold painted bronze, ivory and marble figure of 'Ecstasy', raised on a walnut stand, signed on the marble base, 51 in (128 cm) high overall. **$3,000-4,500**

A F. Preiss cold painted bronze and ivory figure of The Archer, signed on the base, 10 in (25 cm) high. **$2,500-3,500**

An Austrian gilt bronze and ivory figure, signed Brandel Wien, 19 in (47 cm) high. **$1,700-2,500**

A bronze and ivory figure of an ► elegantly dressed young lady, cast after the model by Quenard, and so signed, 13 in (32.5 cm) high, raised on a marble cut corner base. **$1,000-1,200**

◄
An ivory figure of a naked girl, slight damage, 20thC, 6 in (15 cm). **$300-400**

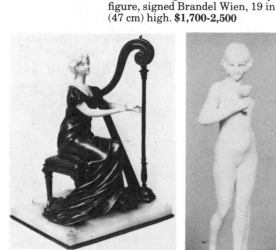

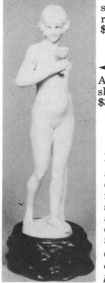

A French part gilded bronze and ivory figure of a young lady playing a harp, signed Gregoire, fitting for electric light and original lamp shade, 13½ in (34 cm) high. **$1,500-2,200**

A bronze and ivory figure, 'Girl with a Cigarette', cast and carved after a model by Bruno Zack, ivory cracked at face, small piece missing from cigarette butt, signed in the bronze Bruno Zack and monogram within a square, c1925, 29 in (72.5 cm) high. **$9,000-13,000**
Cf. Bryan Catley, Art Deco and other Figures, London, 1978, p.305, similar example illustrated.

Clarice Cliff Wares c1925-1963

Clarice Cliff worked as a decorator at A. J. Wilkinson Ltd., Royal Staffordshire Pottery. Between 1924 and 1925 she attended evening classes at the Burslem School of Art under Gordon Forsyth. Wilkinson's took over the nearby Newport Pottery and Clarice Cliff was encouraged to apply her designs to the warehouse stock. In 1928 some 720 pieces were produced to test the market and by 1929 the whole production of the Newport Pottery was turned to the range of Bizarre wares by Clarice Cliff.

Early designs were of simple geometric patterns outlined in black and filled in with bright oranges, reds, blues and yellows to remain within the compass of inexperienced decorators. By 1931, 150 decorators were employed directly supervised by Cliff.

Some difficulty was experienced in moulding and firing Cliff's pottery designs, particularly where angular shapes were used. Though Clarice Cliff continued to work at the factory until 1963 her active involvement in design ended in the early 1950's.

Art deco : ceramics

A Clarice Cliff Bizarre seven piece cabaret set, with yellow and green geometric decoration on a cream ground, printed marks Bizarre by Clarice Cliff, Wilkinson Ltd., England, c1930, 9 in (23 cm). **$1,000-1,400**

A Clarice Cliff wall plate. **$300-400**

A Bizarre Lotus vase, with a geometric band between wide yellow and iron red bands, printed and impressed marks, Newport, late 1930's, 12 in (29.3 cm). **$600-900**

A Clarice Cliff mug, designed by Laura Knight, with female heads and an abstract design in orange, brown, blue and black on a cream ground, many printed marks including Bizarre by Clarice Cliff Wilkinson Ltd., and artist's facsimile signature, c1930, 6½ in (16 cm). **$300-500**

A Clarice Cliff Bizarre Inspiration vase, painted in the Blue Pines design with dark blue and russet, printed marks, painted Inspiration, 10 in (25 cm). **$1,400-1,700**

A Clarice Cliff Bizarre ewer and basin wash set, painted in strong bright colours, detailed with black, printed marks, ewer 10 in (25 cm), basin 15 in (37.5 cm). **$2,500-3,500**

A Clarice Cliff twin handled Bizarre pottery vase, painted in orange, black, rust red and mauve, printed factory marks, Newport Pottery, 12 in (29.5 cm). **$600-900**

A Clarice Cliff jar and cover, painted in blue, purple, yellow, pink, grey and black with a Forticist pattern, black printed marks and facsimile signature, 1930's, 10 in (24.5 cm). **$600-900**

A Newport pottery Clarice Cliff 'Applique' teapot and cover, 6 in (15 cm). **$600-900**

A large Clarice Cliff Bizarre wall charger, in shades of yellow, red and green rim, printed marks, 18 in (45 cm). **$1,000-1,400**

A Clarice Cliff Bizarre jug and basin set, painted in bright red, green and blue stylised flowering plants, outlined in black and having yellow, blue and red banding, factory marks, 8 in (19.5 cm). **$1,400-1,700**

A Clarice Cliff Bizarre single handled Isis vase, painted in russet, grey and shades of green with white blossoms, printed marks, 12 in (30 cm). **$800-1,200**

A Clarice Cliff Bizarre part tea service, with blue, orange and yellow flowers with green leaves, comprising a D-shaped teapot and cover, a cream jug and a sugar bowl, all with printed marks. **$200-300**

A Clarice Cliff Bizarre jardinière, painted with a band of yellow and mauve diamond shapes outlined in green on a blue ground, printed marks, 9½ in (24 cm). **$500-600**

A Clarice Cliff Bizarre Fantasque tea service, painted in the Summer House design in red, black and yellow, comprising a teapot, milk jug, sugar castor, slop bowl, a biscuit barrel, one cake plate, 6 teacups and saucers, 6 side plates, all with printed marks. **$4,000-5,000**

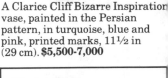

A Clarice Cliff Bizarre Inspiration vase, painted in the Persian pattern, in turquoise, blue and pink, printed marks, 11½ in (29 cm). **$5,500-7,000**

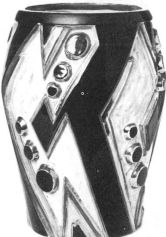

A Clarice Cliff 'Sgraffito' Bizarre vase, painted in black, royal blue, silver and pale blue, printed mark, Newport, painted 5995 Sgraffito, 9 in (23 cm). **$700-900**

A Clarice Cliff 'Fantasque' pottery jardiniere, painted in bright colours, the lower body painted in orange, 8 in (20 cm). **$800-1,200**

Clarice Cliff

* marked wares produced between 1925 and 1963
* it would be very unusual to find unmarked examples
* marks are nearly always black though gilt was occasionally used
* a variety of markings are found but usually include: hand painted Bizarre by Clarice Cliff the name of the pattern the maker, either Newport Pottery or Wilkinson Ltd
* pre-1935 wares in unusual shapes or rare patterns are particularly collectable

A Clarice Cliff Bizarre crocus pattern individual tea set, 7 pieces, 1935. **$100-200**

earthenware vase, designed by ie Irvine, sculpted with pale ow flowers and green leaves on atte blue ground, impressed 80 SF 26 and with designer's rk, Newcomb College, 1930, in (19cm) high. **$500-600**

An amusing Clarice Cliff 'Age of Jazz' two sided plaque, modelled as 2 girls, one in an apple green ball gown, the other dressed in orange, dancing the tango with their respective escorts, facsimile signature Bizarre and factory marks, 7 in (17.5 cm). **$6,000-8,500**

An earthenware vase, decorated by Margaret H. MacDonald, with light blue, blue and olive trees on a white ground, impressed with firm's marks and 892B and painted with artist's monogram, by Rookwood, 1940 10½in (26cm) high. **$1,000-1,300**

MAKE THE MOST OF MILLER'S

When a large specialist well-publicised collection comes on the market, it tends to increase prices. Immediately after this, prices can fall slightly due to the main buyers having large stocks and the market being 'flooded'. This is usually temporary and does not affect very high quality items·

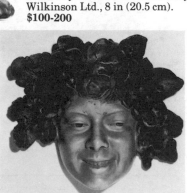

n earthenware vase, decorated Jane L. Sacksteder, with rple-centered brown and tan ack-eyed susans on a grey and hite ground, impressed with m's marks and 778, painted th artist's monogram and 573B, Rookwood, 1946, 9½in (24cm) gh. **$250-350**

A Clarice Cliff moulded lotus blossom vase, with pinkish petals, with base decorated with green leaves on a blue ground, printed marks, 8½ in (21 cm). **$60-90**

A Wilkinson Ltd., pottery figure, possibly by Clarice Cliff, printed mark Royal Staffordshire Pottery, Wilkinson Ltd., 8 in (20.5 cm). **$100-200**

Clarice Cliff pottery te-a-tête. **$300-400**

A 'Bacchus' Goldscheider mask, signed Lorenzac. **$300-400**

A Shelley teaset, comprising: a teapot, sugar bowl and milk jug, 2 square sandwich platters, 12 cups and saucers, 9 side plates, in yellow and black on a white ground, all pieces with printed Shelley England mark and registered no. 723404, c1930, teapot 5 in (13 cm) high. **$600-700**

A rare panda teapot, by Beswick c1930. **$100-200**

An earthenware vase, created by Anna F. Simpson and Joseph Meyer, sculpted with blue oak trees and hanging moss on a matte light blue ground with a white moon, impressed NC SB48 JM AFS 250, Newcomb College, 1930, 8in (20cm) high. **$900-1,000**

A Shelley Art Deco part teaset, comprising: 6 cups and 5 saucers, 5 side plates and a sugar bowl, decorated in black, orange and beige with sunburst motifs against a white ground, printed factory marks, Rd. no. 756533. **$600-700**

A Louis Wain model of a cat, with a lemon, green, yellow and red coloured body, printed and painted marks, 6½ in (16 cm) high. **$300-500**

A Shelley 'Mode' shape teaset, comprising: a milk jug, a sugar bowl, 6 cups and saucers, 6 side plates, decorated in grey and acid green on a white ground, all pieces with printed Shelley England mark and registered no. 756533, c1930. **$800-1,200**

Art Deco : Royal Doulton

A Shelley three-piece pottery nursery teaset, in bright colours on a white ground, designed by Mabel Lucie Atwell and painted artist's signature on each piece, c1925, 4, 5 and 7½ in (10, 13 and 19.5 cm) high. **$600-800**

A Royal Doulton table lamp, The Balloon Seller, HN583, withdrawn 1949. **$600-700**

A Royal Doulton figure of 'Crinoline', by George Lambert, HN2, figure number 253, painted Doulton and Co., and printed Royal Doulton England mark, 6¼ in (15.5 cm) high. **$2,000-3,000**

A Royal Doulton figure, 'Butterfly', HN720, withdrawn 1938. **$600-900**

A Royal Doulton figure of 'The Poke Bonnet', HN612, withdrawn 1938, (23.5 cm) high. **$600-700**

A Royal Doulton figure, 'Mephistopheles & Marguerite', HN775, designer C.J. Noke, withdrawn 1949, 7¾ in (19.5 cm) high. **$1,300-1,700**

A Royal Doulton figure, 'MISS 1928', HN1205, designer L. Harradine, withdrawn before 1938, 7 in (17.5 cm) high, 'MISS 1926' wrongly marked as 'MISS 1928', HN1205, designer L. Harradine, withdrawn before 1938, 7 in (17.5 cm) high. **$1,500-2,200**

A small Royal Doulton figure, 'Bluebird', HN1280, green printed and red painted marks, indistinct impressed date (19)28(?), 4½ in (1.5 cm). **$300-500**

A Royal Doulton figure, 'Cassin', HN1232, designer L. Harradine, withdrawn 1938, 3 ¾in (9 cm) high. **$600-700**

A Royal Doulton figure, 'Phyllis', HN1420, designed L. Harradine, withdrawn 1949, 9 in (22.5 cm) high. **$200-300**

A Royal Doulton figure, 'Marietta', HN1341, printed and painted marks, impressed date (19)33, 8½ in (21 cm). **$600-800**

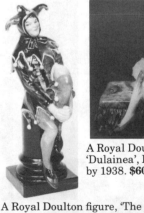

A Royal Doulton figure, 'Dulainea', HN1419, withdrawn by 1938. **$600-900**

A Royal Doulton figure, 'The Jester', HN1295, withdrawn 1949, signed C.J. Noke, 10 in (25 cm) high. **$500-600**

A Royal Doulton wall mask of 'Sweet Anne', in pink and blue, HN1590, printed Royal Doulton England marks. **$600-700**

A Royal Doulton figure, 'The Alchemist', designed by L. Harradine, unmarked but HN1282, date code for 1937, introduced 1928, withdrawn 1938, 11½ in (29 cm) high. **$1,200-1,500**

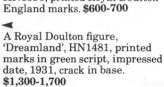

◀

A Royal Doulton figure, 'Dreamland', HN1481, printed marks in green script, impressed date, 1931, crack in base. **$1,300-1,700**

A Royal Doulton figure, 'June', HN1691, designer L. Harradine, withdrawn 1949, 7½ in (18.5 cm) high. **$300-400**

A Royal Doulton figure, 'Daffy Down Dilly', HN1712, designed by L. Harradine, introduced 1935, withdrawn 1975, 8in (20 cm) high. **$300-400**

A Royal Doulton figure, 'Romany Sue', HN1758, 1936-1949, hairline in shawl, 9½ in (23.5 cm). **$400-600**

A Royal Doulton figure, 'Matilda' HN2011, printed and painted marks, 'COPR 1947', 10 in (25 cm) **$400-600**

This figure apparently pre-dates the 1948 date of introduction listed in Eyles & Dennis 'Royal Doulton Figures', p.322.

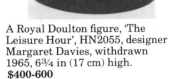

A Royal Doulton figure, 'The Leisure Hour', HN2055, designer Margaret Davies, withdrawn 1965, 6¾ in (17 cm) high. **$400-600**

A Royal Doulton figure, 'Spring Flowers', HN1807, designer L. Harradine, withdrawn 1959, 7¼ in (18 cm) high. **$300-400**

An unissued porcelain figure of a young girl seated in a chair wearing a blue dress feeding a baby, printed Royal Doulton England marks HN 2252, 5 in (12.5 cm). **$800-1,200**

A Royal Doulton figure, 'Sir Walter Raleigh', HN2015, withdrawn 1955. **$400-600**

A Royal Doulton seated figure 'Linda', HN2106, withdrawn 1976. **$150-200**

A Royal Doulton figure, 'Sleepy Head', HN2114, printed Royal Doulton England marks, 4¾ in (12 cm) high. **$700-900**

A Royal Doulton figure, from the Seasons series, 'Winter', HN2088, introduced 1952, withdrawn 1959. **$300-400**

A Royal Doulton figure, 'Masquerade', HN 2251, circle mark, lion and crown, c1960, 8½ in (21 cm). **$400-600**

A Royal Doulton figure, 'Fortune Teller', HN2159, introduced 1955, withdrawn 1967. **$300-400**

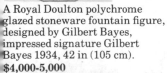

A Royal Doulton polychrome glazed stoneware fountain figure, designed by Gilbert Bayes, impressed signature Gilbert Bayes 1934, 42 in (105 cm). **$4,000-5,000**
Cf. The Doulton Story. A Catalogue of the Exhibition held at the Victoria and Albert Museum, 1979, p.29 for an article on Gilbert Bayes Polychrome Stoneware.

A Royal Doulton miniature 'Spook', red cloak, badly damaged, 4 in (10 cm). **$700-900**

A Royal Doulton figure, 'The Puppetmaker', HN 2253, 1962-1973, 8 in (20.9 cm). **$300-500**

A Royal Doulton figure, 'The Shepherd', M.17, miniature, withdrawn 1938, 4 in (10 cm). **$600-800**

A Royal Doulton character jug, 'The Clown', the red haired version, modelled by H. Fenton, printed mark and title in green, c1940, 6½ in (16.2 cm). **$1,500-2,200**

A Royal Doulton character jug, 'The White Haired Clown', D 6322, large, designer L. Harradine, withdrawn 1955. **$1,000-1,200**

A Royal Doulton character mug, 'The Poacher'. **$500-600**

A Royal Doulton character mug, 'Friar Tuck'. **$300-600**

A Royal Doulton character jug, 'Punch & Judy Man', D 6590, designed by D. Biggs, introduced 1964, withdrawn 1969, 7 in (17.5 cm). **$600-700**

A Royal Doulton character jug, 'Dick Whittington', designed by M. Henk, c.m.l. & c., introduced 1953, withdrawn 1960, 6½ in (16 cm). **$400-600**

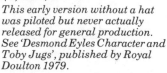

A rare Royal Doulton character jug, 'Drake', hatless version, date code for 1940, 6 in (15 cm). **$4,000-5,000**
This early version without a hat was piloted but never actually released for general production. See 'Desmond Eyles Character and Toby Jugs', published by Royal Doulton 1979.

A Royal Doulton character jug, 'Jarge', D 6288, large, designer H. Fenton, withdrawn 1960. **$300-500**

A Royal Doulton character jug, 'Field Marshall, the Rt. Hon. J.C. Smuts', 7 in (17.5 cm). **$1,500-2,200**

A Royal Doulton character jug, 'The Jockey', D 6625, large, designer, D. Biggs, withdrawn 1975. **$200-300**

A Royal Doulton character mug, 'The Vicar of Bray'. **$150-200**

A Royal Doulton character jug, "Arry' (Brown with Buttons), designed by H. Fenton, introduced 1947, withdrawn 1960, 6½ in (16.25 cm). **$1,500-2,200**

A Royal Doulton character jug, 'Gondolier', D 6589, designed by D. Biggs, introduced 1964, withdrawn 1969, 8 in (20 cm). **$600-700**

A Royal Doulton character jug, 'Captain Hook', D 6597, designed by M. Henk and D. Biggs, introduced 1965, withdrawn 1971, 7 in (17.5 cm). **$400-600**

Silver – Baskets

A Georgian silver cake basket, maker R. Wallam, c1771, 12½ in (31 cm), 21.5 ozs. **$800-1,200**

A fine George II cake basket, engraved with a coat-of-arms, the handle engraved later with a crest, by David Willaume II, 1730, 15 in (38.8 cm), 86 ozs. **$28,500-36,000**

A George II silver basket, by Thomas Parr, London 1743. **$7,000-9,000**

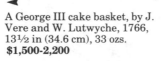

A George III cake basket, by J. Vere and W. Lutwyche, 1766, 13½ in (34.6 cm), 33 ozs. **$1,500-2,200**

A George III swing handle cake basket, with bright cut rim and beaded border, with contemporary monogram, the underbase with later inscription, by William Plummer, 1778, 13 in (33 cm), 25 ozs. **$1,300-1,700**

A George III swing handled cake basket, chased with oval tassies and drape festooning, by Burrage Davenport, 1779, 14½ in (36 cm), 39 ozs. **$2,500-3,500**

A George III sugar basket, by William Abdy, London, 1788. **$500-600**

A George III swing handle sugar basket, gilt interior, by William Vincent, 1772, 4 in (10.5 cm), 10.5 ozs. **$600-800**

A George III cake basket, by Burrage Davenport, London 1782, 14 in (35 cm), 25 ozs. **$1,500-2,200**

A Victorian cake basket, by John Figg, London, 1840, 12 in (30 cm), 44 ozs. **$1,500-2,200**

A George III cake basket, chased with fluting and pierced above with trelliswork, engraved with a crest by Paul Storr, 1801, 15 in (37.7 cm), 30 ozs. **$5,500-7,000**

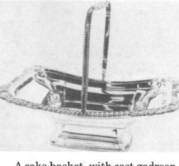

A cake basket, with cast gadroon and shell border, shallow foot folding handle, Sheffield 1898, 32 ozs. **$400-600**

An Edward VII cake basket, crested, Goldsmiths and Silversmiths Company Ltd., London 1905, 1154 gms, 37.1 ozs. **$2,000-3,000**

A Dutch basket, maker's mark only IB, 14 in (35 cm), 39½ ozs. **$1,200-1,500**

A Victorian pedestal sugar basket, with a blue glass liner and a Victorian sifting spoon, Sheffield 1853, basket 4½ in (11 cm), 8 ozs. **$500-600**

A pedestal cake stand, the edge finely pierced with scrolling foliage in the Art Nouveau taste and with 4 vacant oval panels, Sheffield 1917, 5½ in (14 cm), 8.5 ozs. **$400-600**

A Victorian pierced silver basket, London 1898, 47 ozs. **$2,000-3,000**

513

A fine two-handled bowl, shaped circular, with 2 S-scroll twisted wire handles, on a molded circular foot, the lobed sides divided into 6 panels of deeply-chased stylised foliate decoration, marked on the bottom, by Bartholomew Schaats, New York, 1690-1700, 8in (20cm) wide overall, 6oz. **$36,000-40,000**

A punch bowl, circular, with lobed serpentine rim on a circular foot, the hammered surfaces with relief gilt flowers, the foot with 4 chased pinwheels, the interior gilt, marked on bottom, by Tiffany & Company, New York, 1880-1891, 10in (25cm) diam., 36oz. **$2,800-3,000**

A pair of beakers, each cylindrical, with an applied molded strap handle, the body engraved with an oval cartouche surrounding script initials 'BW' on one and 'LB' on another, both engraved with swags at the rim, with roulette-work details, one with engraved inscription on the bottom 'Bathsheba Whiting Born 17 April 1755', the other 'Luke Baker born 14 Jany 1750-51', unmarked, some solder repairs to bottom, Boston, 1790-1810, 3in (8cm) high, 8oz. **$600-800**

A Dutch beaker, with strapwork and lozenge ornament, by Hindrick Sluiter, Groningen, 1682, 6 in (15 cm), 5 oz 16 dwts. **$3,500-5,000**

A German beaker, by Tobias Jansen Kremer, Emden 1660 12¾ oz. **$10,500-14,000**

Silver – Beakers

A beaker by Hugh Wishart, New York, 1784-1825, 7½ in (20 cm), 16 oz. 10 dwt. **$3,500-5,000**

According to family tradition, this beaker was copied by Wishart from a virtually identical Dutch beaker of the 17thC belonging to the same family.

A beaker, barrel-shaped, with reeded borders at shoulder and base, the body engraved with foliate script initials, 'SSL', marked on bottom, by Alexander S. Gordon, New York, 1795-1803 3½in (9cm) high, 4oz. **$400-500**

A beaker, tapering cylindrical, with everted rim and molded footrim, engraved with script initials 'SF to AFD 8th Decr. 1793', unmarked, American, dated 1793, 3¼in (8cm) high, 3oz. **$250-350**

Silver – Bowls

A Victorian bowl, inscribed 'Tarporley Hunt 1871', by Robert Hennell, London, 1838, 9½ in diam. (24 cm), 36 oz. **$1,000-1,200**

A waste bowl, London 1792, by Michael Plummer. **$600-900**

A George III silver bowl, later embossed, gilt interior, London 1812, 10 in diam. (25 cm), 20 oz **$300-400**

A Victorian parcel gilt card case, by Wallington & Deakin, Birmingham, 1854, cased. **$700-900**

An Edwardian cigarette case, cover enamelled in sepia with a photograph of a lady, by H.C. Davis, Birmingham, 1907. **$200-300**

A Victorian card case, by Roberts and Belk, Sheffield, engraved with an Egyptian slave, 1872, cased. **$200-300**

The silver section is ordered chronologically in alphabetical category order. In each section the Continental silver follows the British silver.

A Victorian card case, die-stamped with the Scott Memorial, Edinburgh, engraved with a name, H.T. Birmingham, 1850, 3½ in (8 cm). **$300-500**

A combined card case and carnet-de-bal, of book shape, inscribed 'S.S. "Arequipa" launched by Miss Graves Barrow 28 Sept. 1889', Birmingham, 1890. **$200-300**

A late Victorian card case, by George Unite, Birmingham, 1894, cased, 4 in (10 cm). **$200-300**

An American card case, unmarked, c1870. **$300-400**

A German cigarette case, bearing English import marks. **$400-600**

A Russian cigarette case, decorated in relief with a 17thC Russian boyar lecherously embracing a young girl, apparently unmarked, c1910 metalwares, 4½ in long (11.5 cm), 5.75 gross weight. **$600-700**

A Queen Anne silver tobacco box, maker: probably Benjamin Bentley, 3½ in (8 cm). **$800-1,200**

A Continental cigarette case, with concealed enamelled cover depicting a posed nude, with English marks for Birmingham 1911. **$1,000-1,200**

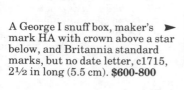

A George I snuff box, maker's mark HA with crown above a star below, and Britannia standard marks, but no date letter, c1715, 2½ in long (5.5 cm). **$600-800**

A George III snuff box in the form of a purse, the interior engraved with a contemporary inscription, 1814 maker's mark RB incuse. **$400-600**

A George III reproduction of a George II armorial snuff box, by Phipps & Robinson, 1806, 3 in long (7 cm). **$400-600**

A George III silver gilt snuff box, in original case, with cast classical scene, by A.J. Strachen, London, 1812, 3 in (7.5 cm). **$2,000-3,000**

A George III commemorative snuff box, of Horatio, Viscount Nelson, by Simpson & Son, Birmingham, 1809, 2½ in long (5 cm). **$400-600**

A George III Scottish snuff mull, modelled after a horn example with inscription, by Robert Haxton, Edinburgh, 1813, 2 in high (5 cm). **$500-600**

A George III vinaigrette, by Richard Lockwood, 1804, 1½ in (3 cm). **$150-200**

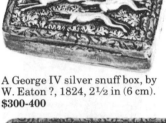

A George IV silver snuff box, by W. Eaton ?, 1824, 2½ in (6 cm). **$300-400**

A George III silver gilt musical snuff box, by John Linnett of London, c1817 with gold rim, 3½ by 2 in (8 by 5 cm). **$6,000-8,500**

A George IV silver gilt snuff box, decorated with a medieval battle scene in relief, marked on base and lid, Thomas Shaw Birmingham, 1829, 3½ in (9 cm). **$1,200-1,500**

A William IV engine turned snuff box, chased in low relief with view of Abbotsford, by Gervase Wheeler, Birmingham, 1836, 2½ in long (6.5 cm). **$600-900**

A George IV silver gilt snuff box, by Charles Rawlings, decorated in relief with two boxers fighting bare fisted and naked to the waist, 1824, 3 in (7.8 cm). **$1,700-2,500**

An Edwardian vesta case, Chester, 1906. **$150-200**

A William IV hunting scene snuff box, by Nathaniel Mills, Birmingham 1835, 3 in (7.5 cm). **$1,000-1,400**

A Turkish snuff box, enamelled in blue and green, unmarked, 19thC, 2½ in (5 cm). **$300-400**

A George IV silver gilt vinaigrette, gilt worn and hinges defective, Birmingham 1821 with maker's marks of Thomas and Samuel Pemberton, 1½ in (3.4 cm). **$150-200**

Even with a good maker, small collectables such as vinaigrettes must be in good condition to achieve good prices.

◄ A French niello work snuff box, 3 in (8 cm). **$600-700**

A late Victorian vesta case, enamelled with a Jack Russell terrier, by Sampson Mordan, 1887. **$300-400**

A late Victorian vesta case, modelled as an envelope enamelled with a mauve stamp and postmark 'Halifax Oct. 16 "97" ', Birmingham, 1897. **$500-600**

An American vesta case, c1900. **$100-150**

A continental pomander, formed from six segments, the interior gilded and crudely decorated, probably German, c1600, 2 in (5.5 cm). **$3,500-5,000**

A George IV vinaigrette, by Joseph Willmore, Birmingham 1827, 1½ in (3.4 cm). **$150-200**

A George III silver gilt vinaigrette, with internal pierced grille, Samuel Penbeton, Sheffield, 1814, 1½ in long (4 cm). **$400-600**

A Victorian silver vinaigrette, with tartan engraving, by perhaps Edward Turnpenny 1847. **$150-200**

An unusual George III vinaigrette, the cover engraved with an eagle, the base formed as a shell, by Matthew Linwood, Birmingham 1817, 1 in (2.6 cm). **$500-600**

 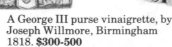

An Edwardian vesta case, chased with three cyclists, Birmingham, 1906, 2½ in (4.5 cm). **$400-600**

A George III purse vinaigrette, by Joseph Willmore, Birmingham 1818. **$300-500**

A George III purse vinaigrette, by John Shaw, Birmingham 1819, 1 in (2.8 cm). **$300-400**

A Victorian vinaigrette, by Nathaniel Mills, Birmingham 1839, 1½ in (3.9 cm). **$300-400**

An early Victorian vinaigrette, by Francis Clarke, Birmingham 1843, 1½ in (4.3 cm). **$300-400**

A Victorian silver gilt vinaigrette, the cover die stamped with a view of Abbotsford, by Nathaniel Mills, Birmingham 1837, 2 in (4.1 cm). **$150-200**

A Victorian silver vinaigrette, by Cocks & Betteridge, 1801, 1 in (2.5 cm). **$150-200**

A Victorian silver vinaigrette, with cast Windsor Castle lid, by Gervase Wheeler, 1843, 1½ in (4 cm). **$400-600**

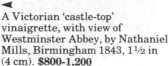

A Victorian 'castle-top' vinaigrette, with view of Westminster Abbey, by Nathaniel Mills, Birmingham 1843, 1½ in (4 cm). **$800-1,200**

A Victorian engine-turned vinaigrette, by Nathaniel Mills, Birmingham 1839, 2 by 1 in (4.6 by 3.1 cm). **$300-500**

A Victorian vinaigrette, by Joseph Willmore, Birmingham, 1837, 2 in (4.7 cm). **$400-600**

A Victorian vinaigrette, engraved with view of the Crystal Palace, by Nathaniel Mills, Birmingham 1850, 2 in (5.3 cm). **$300-500**

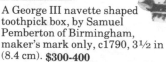

A George III nutmeg grater, by James Phipps, c1780, 2 in (5.3 cm). **$300-500**

A box, with pull off cover, engraved with Charles II and a retainer hiding in the Boscobel oak, with Parliamentarian cavalrymen searching for him below, the base engraved with the armorials of Carlos, unmarked, c1670, 2 in (5.5 cm). **$1,000-1,200**

Charles II wandered as a fugitive for six weeks after the battle of Worcester in 1651, a reward of £1000 on his head, and hid, amongst other places, in an oak tree at Boscobel before finally escaping to France where he began his years of exile before the Restoration of 1660.

A Charles I counterbox, the cover chased with a portrait profile of James I, containing 31 counters with portraits and arms of Kings and Queens of England, possibly by Simon de Passe, 1 in (2.5 cm). **$1,500-2,200**

A Charles II tear-drop shaped nutmeg grater, c1685, 1½ in (3.7 cm). **$400-600**

A Victorian purse vinaigrette, makers initials G.W. Co., 1858, ½ in (1.5 cm). **$300-400**

A Chinese Export nutmeg grater, chased with Chinese scenes, inscribed 'W.N.A. 16-3-1919', by Leeching of Canton, Hong Kong & Shanghai, c1875. **$800-1,200**

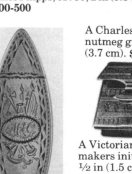

A George III navette shaped toothpick box, by Samuel Pemberton of Birmingham, maker's mark only, c1790, 3½ in (8.4 cm). **$300-400**

An Edward VII silver and tortoiseshell novelty vesta box, London 1903, 3 in (8.5 cm). **$600-700**

A George III patch box, by John Jago, 1791, 1½ in (3.1 cm). **$150-200**

A Dutch box in the form of a cello, import mark for London 1898, 6½ in (16.5 cm), 118 gms (3.7 ozs). **$300-400**

A Victorian cheroot case, F.C. Birmingham 1845, 4½ in (11 cm). **$300-500**

A Chinese Export circular box, on a blue enamelled background, stamped with Chinese characters only, c1880, 2½ in (6.8 cm), 3.75 ozs. **$400-600**

A George III commemorative patch box, with a portrait of Nelson, by Cocks & Bettridge of Birmingham, maker's mark only, c1798, 1 in (2.7 cm). **$300-500**

As this piece appears to bear Cocks & Bettridge's first mark (1773-1801), it was presumably made to celebrate Nelson's victories in Egypt rather than Trafalgar.

Candelabra

A pair of George III candelabra, by V. Tucker & Co., Sheffield 1809, 23 in (57.5 cm). 6,000-8,500

A pair of French four light candelabra, by H. Voisenet, Paris, c1880, 22 in (55 cm), 250 ozs. $10,000-13,000

A George IV four light candelabrum, by Joseph Cradock, 1829, 20½ in (52 cm), 116 ozs. $5,500-7,000

A Victorian candelabrum entrepiece, with an applied coat-of-arms crest, motto and resentation inscription to estock Robert Reid for 32 years n the Bombay Civil Service and ated 1849, by E.J. and W. arnard, 28½ in (71 cm), 291 ozs. 9,000-13,000

Candlesticks

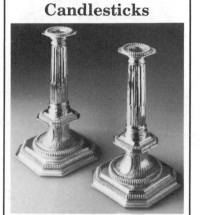

A pair of Queen Anne candlesticks, with fluted stems and gadroon borders, by John Bach, London 1705, 9 in (22.5 cm), 28 oz. **$10,500-14,000**

A Victorian four light candelabrum, T., J., & N., Creswick, Sheffield, 1851, 24½ in (61 cm), weight of branches 70 ozs. **$2,500-3,500**

pair of William III candlesticks, aker's mark IL, a coronet above nd pellet below, c1695, 7 in 7.5 cm), 30 ozs. **$7,500-10,500**

A pair of George I candlesticks, by Peter Courtauld, London, 1719. **$4,000-5,000**

A pair of George II rococo cast silver candlesticks, John Quantock, London, 1754, 49 ozs. **$3,000-4,500**

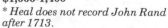

A Queen Anne taperstick, maker's mark only struck four times, John Rand, London, c1710, 4½ in (11 cm), 4 oz 11 dwt. **$1,000-1,400**

Heal does not record John Rand after 1713.

A near matching pair of George II tapersticks, James Gould, London, 1731/32, 4 in (11 cm), 7 oz 13 dwt, excluding later nozzles. **$2,500-3,500**

A pair of late George II table ➤ candlesticks, by William Shaw and William Priest, London 1755, 9½ in (23 cm), 1113 grammes. **$2,000-3,000**

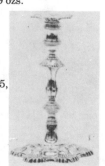

A pair of George III chamber candlesticks, maker's mark A.L., perhaps for Augustin Le Sage, 1766, 26 ozs. **$5,500-7,000**

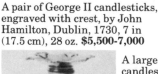

A George III taperstick, William Cafe, London, 1764, 5 in (12.5 cm) 5 oz 10 dwt. **$800-1,200**

A set of four George II candlesticks, engraved with a crest, by George Wickes, 1745, 8½ in (21 cm). **$15,000-20,500**

A pair of George II candlesticks, engraved with crest, by John Hamilton, Dublin, 1730, 7 in (17.5 cm), 28 oz. **$5,500-7,000**

A large pair of George III table ➤ candlesticks, Ker and Dempster, engraved with double headed eagle crest below motto 'I Byde My Time', marked on bases only, Ker and Dempster, Edinburgh 1762, 15 in (38 cm), 1148 gms, 36.9 oz. **$3,000-4,500**

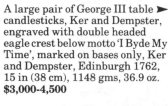

Four George II table candlesticks, William Gould, London 1743/4, 7½ in (18 cm). **$8,500-10,000**

A pair of George III travelling chambersticks, the interior holding the detachable sconces and conical extinguishers, by Samuel Whitford (II), 1815, except one extinguisher by a different maker, 1810, in fluted case, 5 in (12 cm) diam, 16.25 ozs. **$2,000-3,000**

A good pair of George II cast candlesticks, with detachable nozzles, by John Cafe, London 1754, 36 oz. **$3,000-4,500**

A George IV chamber candlestick, with shell thumbpiece and extinguisher, by Matthew Bolton and Plate Co., Birmingham 1821, 5 in (12.5 cm), 4 oz. **$600-800**

A pair of early Victorian silver candlesticks, maker's mark H.W. & Co. (Henry Wilkinson & Co.), Sheffield 1840, one candlestick 1839, 10 in (25 cm). **$800-1,200**

A pair of George IV candlesticks, marked on bases and nozzles, Robert Garrard, London 1825, 12 in (30 cm), 53 oz 16 dwt. **$3,000-4,000**

A pair of Victorian table candlesticks, in late 18thC style, Edinburgh 1897, 11 in (28 cm), loaded. **$1,200-1,500**

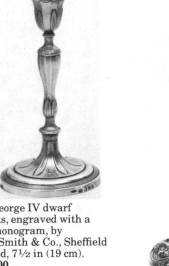

A pair of Edward VII table candlesticks, in 18th century style, Sheffield 1901, 8 in (20 cm), loaded. **$800-1,200**

A pair of George IV dwarf candlesticks, engraved with a crest and monogram, by Nathaniel Smith & Co., Sheffield 1822, loaded, 7½ in (19 cm). **$1,200-1,500**

A pair of late Victorian candlesticks, Sheffield 1895, loaded, 12 in (33.5 cm). **$1,000-1,200**

A pair of French silver gilt travelling chambersticks, c1840, 2 in (4 cm). **$1,300-1,700**

A George III chamber candlestick, having matching nozzle and extinguisher to the scroll handle, crested with initials, fully marked, by John Mewburn, London 1817, 12 oz. **$800-1,200**

A pair of William IV chambersticks, by Robinson Edkins and Aston, 1835. **$2,000-3,000**

A pair of Victorian figurative silver and parcel gilt candlesticks, by George Fox, London 1898, 9 in (23 cm), 30½ oz. **$2,000-3,000**

A pair of Victorian Corinthian column dressing table candlesticks Martin Hall & Co., Sheffield, 1896, loaded, 7 in (17 cm). **$500-600**

A pair of George III round chamber candlesticks, by John Crouch I and Thomas Hannam, London 1793, 18 oz. **$1,300-1,700**

Casters

A George I vase shaped caster, ► engraved with a later crest within rococo cartouche, probably 1721, maker's mark possibly that of Charles Hatfield, 8 in (20 cm), 17 ozs 12 dwts. **$2,500-3,500**

◄ A Queen Anne pear-shaped caster, the domed bayonet fitting cover pierced with stylised foliage and quatrefoils, with baluster finial by John Elston , Exeter 1711, 7½ in (19 cm), 9 ozs 5 dwts. **$5,500-7,000**

A Victorian table garniture, by D and C. Hands, 1869 and C.F. Hancocks, 1877, 18 in (46.3 cm) and 28 in (71.7 cm), 445 ozs. **$30,600-34,000**

A French centrepiece, Paris, c1860. **$3,000-4,000**

A Victorian table centrepiece, the border with four pierced vase holders interchangeable with four petal shaped dish holders, by Stephen Smith, 1872, 19 in (48.1 cm), 135 ozs. **$8,500-11,000**

An unusual circular comport, the rim with 3 applied cast model dragons with outstretched wings, London 1925, 8 in (20 cm), 32.25 ozs. **$600-700**

A Victorian candelabrum centrepiece, with engraved glass dish, Sheffield, 1878, maker's mark TB.JH, 25½ in (64.7 cm), 145 ozs. **$3,000-4,000**

Coffee Pots

A silver coffee pot, decorated with rococo embossing and chasing of scrolls, with floral and tree decorations, maker James Gould, London 1742, 26 ozs. **$2,500-3,500**

A Queen Anne coffee pot, with a coat-of-arms within baroque cartouche, by Joseph Ward, 1705, 11 in (27.8 cm), gross 25 ozs. **$6,000-8,500**

A small George II coffee pot, cover marked with lion passant, by Edward Feline, 1732, 6¾ in (17 cm) scratch weight 13=13=12, 14 ozs. **$1,500-2,200**

A George III coffee pot, maker's mark indistinct, apparently Thomas Whipham and Charles Wright, London 1764, 11 in (27.5 cm), 909 gms (29.2 ozs). **$2,000-3,000**

A George III baluster coffee pot, gadroon edged, the domed hinged cover with pagoda shaped finial, on spreading support, by Walter Brind, 1773, 13 in (32 cm), 30 ozs. $4,000-5,000

An early George III baluster coffee pot, by Daniel Smith and Robert Sharp, London 1766, 11½ in (29 cm). $3,000-4,000

A Queen Anne plain tapering cylindrical coffee pot, engraved with a crest by John Ruslen, 1711, 10 in (25.4 cm), gross 26 ozs. $9,000-13,000

A Queen Anne coffee pot, the swan-neck spout at right angles to the handle, later decorated with baroque style chasing, by Anthony Nelme, 1713, 10 in (25 cm), 23 oz. $3,500-5,000

A Queen Anne plain tapering cylindrical chocolate pot, by John Fawdery 1, 1709, 10 in (26 cm), gross 23 ozs. $6,000-8,500

A George I plain tapering cylindrical coffee pot, engraved with a crest, by Thomas Mason, 1725, 10 in (24.8 cm) gross 27 ozs. $7,500-10,500

A George I plain pear shaped beer jug, engraved with a later coat-of-arms in a scrolling foliage and scalework cartouche, by Paul De Lamerie, 1721, 10 in (25 cm), 36 ozs. $25,500-32,500

A George III coffee pot, in the neo-classical style, with bands of bright cut engraved decoration, beeded girdle and edges, with acanthus terminals, raised on a circular foot, overstuck maker's mark for Thomas Ollivant, London 1792, 13½ in (34 cm), 790 grammes gross. $1,300-1,700

A George III silver pear shaped coffee pot, repousse floral and engraved decorated at a later date, small hole under handle, maker's mark W.C., possibly William Cox, London, 1775, 11 in (27.5 cm), 28 ozs. 10 dwts. $800-1,200

A George III baluster coffee pot, marked on body, base and lid Fuller White, London, 1763, 10½ in (26.5 cm), 30 ozs. $1,700-2,500

A George II coffee pot, with tucked in base on spread circular foot, engraved with lozenge armorials for a lady, by Fuller White, 1751, 9½ in (24 cm), 22 ozs.
$1,700-2,500

A George III coffee pot, William Stephenson, London 1795, 11 in (28 cm), 843 gms, 27.1 ozs.
$1,500-2,200

A George III silver gilt coffee jug, stand and lamp, engraved with a crest, the jug and stand by Paul Storr 1805, the lamp by John Emes 1802, 12 in (29.7 cm), gross 53 ozs. **$7,500-10,500**

A fine William IV melon panelled baluster coffee pot, by E.J. and W. Barnard, leaf chased and with embossing to the shoulders, engraved crest and coat-of-arms, in wood case, London 1834, 9½ in (24 cm) with bag liner, 29 ozs.
$1,000-1,400

Cups

A rare Charles II 'Falconry' tumbler cup, unascribed, Provincial, engraved with the initials I M, maker's mark GDX, mullet below within a shield struck three times underneath base, c1680, 2½ in (6 cm) high, 3.5 ozs. **$3,000-4,500**
* *From the style of engraving and the character of the maker's mark, the cup was probably made in the North of England, possibly in the Hull area. Michael Clayton traces tumbler cups from the middle of the 17thC and notes they were sometimes known as 'Cocking bowls' in the North West of England where they were given in cock fighting contests as prizes.*

A Regency plain tapering cylindrical coffee pot, by Crispin Fuller 1817, 9 in (23.2 cm), 30 ozs.
$2,500-3,500

A late Victorian reproduction porringer, the circular body chased with scroll and fish scale cartouches, by the Barnards, 1890, 5½ in (14 cm), 16 ozs.
$600-700

A Queen Anne porringer, fluted and chased with an initialled scale work cartouche below a corded girdle, beaded spurred handles, Seth Lofthouse, London 1704, 4½ in (11 cm) diam, 7 oz 8 dwt.
$500-600

A James II two handled porringer, engraved with chinoiserie birds, pricked with initials BA, maker's mark PR in monogram, 1685, 3 in (7.5 cm), 6 ozs 10 dwts.
$3,000-4,000

A William and Mary porringer, the underbase engraved with initials, by Robert Timbrell ?, 1691, 4 in (10 cm), 8 ozs.
$1,200-1,500

A set of three silver inscribed trophy cups, the large cup 19 in (47 cm). **$800-1,200**

A footed cup, baluster-form, with a flaring rim, on a spreading circular foot, the rim and footrim with beaded borders, marked on bottom, by William Adams, New York, 1831-1842, 5in (13cm) high, 3oz. 10dwt. **$200-250**

A footed cup, baluster-form, with flaring double bead-molded rim, on a stepped circular foot, body engraved with script initials, marked on bottom, one small bruise, by Jones, Shreve & Brown, Boston, 1854-1857, 5¼in (13cm) high, 5oz. 10dwt. **$200-250**

A presentation cup, baluster form on knopped stem over a spreading circular foot, with 2 scrolled handles, the body and foot repousse and chased with flowers and scrolls, the stem and foot with applied foliate borders, one side engraved in script 'William H. Vanderbilt from his friend Chauncey M. Depew Dec. 21st 1891', marked on bottom, by Tiffany & Co., New York, c1891, 9in (23cm) high, 42oz. **$1,500-2,000**

A trophy cup, cylindrical, with a flaring molded rim etched with seaweed, 2 scrolled handles with acanthus-leaf grips, and a molded footrim, the base with a repousse and chased border of dolphins, cat-tails and scallop shells, one side with engraved inscription for the New York Yacht Club the other side with an etched scene with 2 sailboats, marked on bottom, by Tiffany & Co., New York, c1890, 8in (20cm) high, 37oz. 10dwt. **$1,600-2,000**

A presentation goblet, tapering cylindrical, on a spreading circular foot, the cup repousse and chased with a cartouche and trophies enclosing an engraved inscription '1808, Republican Blues. Are we not Brothers. Presented to Lieut. John E. Davis by his Brother Soldiers... Savannah Jan. 8. 1857', flanked by chased flags, the reverse with a repousse soldier standing before a field of chased tents, unmarked, dent to foot, American, possibly Savannah, c1857, 7½in (19cm) high, 9oz. 10dwt. **$1,400-1,600**

A trophy cup, flaring cylindrical, with an applied mid-band and a C-scroll handle with stylised foliate handle joins, the body engraved with an inscription 'Championship of the Newport Junior Polo Club, Presented by Cornelius Vanderbilt Esq...1887', marked on bottom, by Whiting Manufacturing Co. Providence, c1887, 16oz. 10dwt. **$300-400**

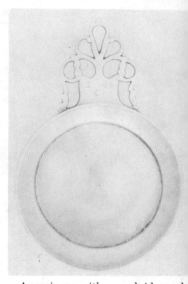

A fine and rare set of 5 goblets, each vase-shaped, on a spreading circular foot, the cup with a bead-molded mid-band over vertical reeding, the side engraved with 3 foliate script initials, marked on edge of foot, by Joseph Lownes, Philadelphia, 1790-1820, 5½in (14cm) high, 38oz. **$10,000-12,000**

A porringer, with curved sides and everted brim, the keyhole type pierced handle with contemporary engraved initials 'TCH', mark struck on back of handle and bottom of bowl, by Elias Pelletreau, New York, 1760-1800, 7in (18cm) long overall, 4oz. 10dwt. **$2,000-2,500**

A pair of George III silver mounted coconut cups, maker's mark S.B. probably for Sarah Buttall, marked on bases, silver gilt liners and rims, one shell damaged, London 1791, 6½ in (16.5 cm). **$1,000-1,200**

A William IV campana shaped cup, cast above with a group of horses and figures and with a laurel wreath enclosing an inscription dated 1836, on silver mounted marble plinth, the foot stamped Storr and Mortimer, by Paul Storr, 1835, in fitted case, 10½ in (26.5 cm), 110 ozs. **$16,500-22,000**

A historical tumbler, by William Anderson, the base with an inserted Spanish coin dated 1741, New York, c1744, 3 in (7.5 cm), 3 oz. **$3,000-4,500**

A porringer, with slightly flared rim and bowed sides, the pierced strapwork handle engraved with owner's initials 'AB', marked inside of bowl, by Jacob Perkins, Newburyport, 1781-1816, 7¾in (19cm) long, 10oz. **$3,600-4,000**

◄

An American plain porringer, engraved with initials D.G.L., by John Coburn, Boston, c1760, 7 ozs 18 dwts. **$2,500-3,500**

A George III Hanoverian pattern basting spoon, engraved J.M., maker James Gilsland 1771. **$500-600**

A fine old English pattern basting spoon, engraved J.G. and J.M., maker Alexander Thompson, c1775. **$600-900**

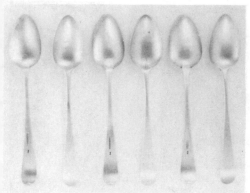

A set of 6 teaspoons, with a pointed oval bowl with a tipped drop and a downturned oval-end handle, with a short mid-rib on the back, each marked 'J. Lownes' in a conforming reserve, and 'WG' incuse, maker's mark of Joseph Lownes, Philadelphia, 1785-1815, retailer's mark of William Gale, New York, 1824-1850, 6in (15cm) long, 3oz. **$500-600**

A numbered set of eleven tapering Old English pattern teaspoons, by William Hannah and another matching by a different maker, early 19thC. **$300-500**

A ladle and 2 serving spoons, ladle in medallion pattern, with a gilt bowl; Gorham server hammer-faceted, the handle applied with copper and brass cherries and leaves; Caldwell server with a foliate handle and a hammer-faceted bowl engraved with a spiderweb, each marked, ladle retailed by William Wilson & Son, Philadelphia, c1882, servers by Gorham Manufacturing Company and J.E. Caldwell, c1882, ladle 13¼in (33cm) long servers 9½in (23cm) long, gross weight 11oz. **$500-700**

Twelve place setting of flatware, comprising silver, all contained in a fitted serpentined George I style walnut canteen, by Viners of Sheffield. **$2,500-3,500**

A William IV fiddle, thread and shell table service, by Samuel Hayne and Dudley Cater, 1836, comprising 18 table-spoons, 18 table-forks, 18 dessert-spoons, 18 dessert-forks, 12 teaspoons, 4 sauce-ladles, 2 gravy spoons, 6 salt-spoons, a mustard spoon, 248 ozs. **$15,000-20,500**

MAKE THE MOST OF MILLER'S

Miller's is completely different each year. Each edition contains completely NEW photographs. This is not an updated publication. We never repeat the same photograph.

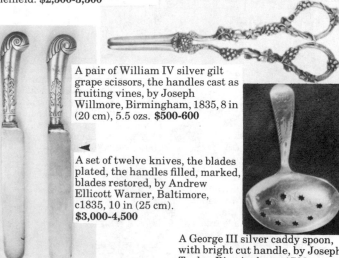

A pair of William IV silver gilt grape scissors, the handles cast as fruiting vines, by Joseph Willmore, Birmingham, 1835, 8 in (20 cm), 5.5 ozs. **$500-600**

◄ A set of twelve knives, the blades plated, the handles filled, marked, blades restored, by Andrew Ellicott Warner, Baltimore, c1835, 10 in (25 cm). **$3,000-4,500**

Four German silver christening spoons, bearing various marks and initials, 6½ ozs. **$300-500**

A George III silver caddy spoon, with bright cut handle, by Joseph Taylor, Birmingham, 1799. **$150-200**

A George III frying pan caddy spoon, by William Pugh of Birmingham, 1807. **$300-400**

A rams horn caddy spoon, by John Lawrence of Birmingham, 1811. **$400-600**

A George III sun-ray shell bowl caddy spoon, by Taylor & Perry Birmingham, 1830. **$60-90**

A William IV shell bowl caddy spoon, by Joseph Wilmore, 1831. **$60-90**

A silver caddy spoon, with eagles wing design, by Joseph Wilmore, Birmingham, c1820. **$1,200-1,500**

Dishes

A George I dish, on rim foot, engraved with a coat-of-arms, coronet and motto, 1719, maker's mark partly worn, probably HO for Edmund Holaday, 5 in (12 cm), 2 ozs 16 dwts. **$2,000-3,000**

Twelve George III shaped circular dinner plates, engraved with a coat-of-arms, motto and coronet, by William Tuite, 1764, 10 in (24.4 cm), 208 ozs. **$10,500-14,000**

A pair of George II dinner plates, engraved with a coat-of-arms, by Paul De Lamerie, 1748, 10 in (24.7 cm), 34 ozs. **$6,000-8,000**

Six George III dinner plates, engraved with coat-of-arms, John Wakelin and William Taylor, London 1777, 10 in (25 cm), 3015 gms (96.9 ozs). **$3,000-4,500**

A George IV meat dish, by Paul Storr 1820, 16 in (41.3 cm), 52 ozs. **$3,000-4,500**

Inkstands

A set of 12 plates, with a gadrooned border, with an engraved inscription on bottom '...From Adrian & Eleanora Iselin', dated 1897, marked, by Howard & Company, New York, 1897, 10½in (26cm) diam., 262oz. 10dwt. **$4,000-6,000**

A serving dish, with cast applied foliate border surrounding a shallow bowl, marked on bottom, by Samuel Kirk & Son, Baltimore, 1880-1890, 14½in (36cm) diam., 52oz. **$1,000-1,200**

A George III inkstand, with foliate shell and egg and dart borders, with 2 silver mounted glass fittings, apparently made into condiments, by John Roberts & Co., Sheffield, 1813, 3½ in (9 cm), 2.5 ozs weighable silver. **$300-400**

A pair of shaped mask small dishes, London 1888, 3½ in (9 cm), 4½ ozs. **$300-400**

Jugs

A covered sugar bowl and a cream pitcher, each vase-shaped, with broadly-fluted sides, a flaring cylindrical neck, and a domed circular foot, the handles S-scrolled with applied foliate thumb grip, the sugar bowl with domed lid with a cast flower finial, each marked on bottom, by Lincoln & Reed, Boston, 1838-1848, sugar bowl 9¾in (24cm) high, 33oz. 10dwt. $600-800

A cream pitcher, vase-shaped, with a foliate S-scrolled handle and a stepped circular foot, the shoulder with a band of die-rolled scallop shells and acanthus leaves, the stem and foot with die-rolled bands of grapes and leaves, the body with presentation inscription and date 1835 in script, marked on bottom, by Peter Thompson, Boston, c1835, 6½in (16cm) high, 9oz. $300-500

A George III hot-water jug, engraved with bands of bright-cut foliage and floral swags, maker's mark RG, 1787, possibly Richard Gardner, 13 in (32.5 cm), 25 oz. $2,500-3,500

A cream pitcher and covered sugar bowl, each globular, with a partly reeded body, a die-rolled oak leaf and acorn band at the shoulder, a die-rolled band of shells at the rim and foot, on a spreading circular foot, the strap handles squared and molded, the sugar bowl with a domed lid with finial, each engraved with later initial 'H', marked, by Ebenezer Cole, New York, c1825, sugar bowl 8¼in (21cm) high, 28oz. $800-1,000

A pair of Victorian wine decanters, by Rawlings & Sumner, London 1838. $1,300-1,700

A George IV cream jug, cast and chased with cherubic musicians in a rural landscape, by Edward Farrell, 1822, 5 in (12.5 cm), 11.5 oz. $700-900

A cream pitcher, pyriform, with double scroll handle, scalloped rim and 3 scroll feet, the knees and feet of scallop shell form, engraved with owner's initials 'MO' on bottom, marked twice on bottom, 2 small bruises, repair to one foot, by Otto Paul de Parisen, New York, 1765-1785, 4in (10cm) high, 3oz. 10dwt. $2,500-3,000

An unusual Victorian silver mounted glass claret jug, in the form of a fish, probably a carp, Alexander Crichton, London, 1881, 14 in (35 cm). $5,500-7,000

A Victorian Scottish hot water jug, makers mark AGW, Edinburgh 1838, 12½ in (31 cm), 31½ oz. $800-1,200

Models

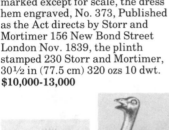

A Victorian model of a goat, marks indistinct, c1875, 5 in (13 cm), 209 gms (6.7 ozs) all in. **$300-400**

A Victorian figure of Justice, fully marked except for scale, the dress hem engraved, No. 373, Published as the Act directs by Storr and Mortimer 156 New Bond Street London Nov. 1839, the plinth stamped 230 Storr and Mortimer, 30½ in (77.5 cm) 320 ozs 10 dwt. **$10,000-13,000**

A Victorian group of a King and Queen, on ebonised wood plinth, by Charles Reily and George Storer, 1846, length of group 14½ in (36.7 cm), 198 ozs. **$8,500-11,000**

The group is probably inspired by Queen Victoria and Prince Albert dressed as King Edward III and his Queen Philippa in which guise they attended the Plantagenet Ball on May 12 1842.

Mugs

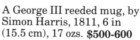

A modern model of a vintage 'Opel' car, import mark for London 1976, 3 in (7.5 cm), 145 gms (4.6 ozs). **$300-400**

A continental model of an ostrich, import marks for 1896, 17 in (43 cm), 47 ozs 10 dwts. **$1,700-2,500**

A German silver and ivory figure, B. Niereshiem of Hanau, imported London, 1926, 9½ in (24 cm), 20 ozs all in. **$1,400-1,700**

A continental model of a ewe and lamb, probably central European, defective, 19thC, 9½ in (24.2 cm), 27 ozs. **$1,200-1,500**

A George II mug, London 1728. **$700-900**

A George III reeded mug, by Simon Harris, 1811, 6 in (15.5 cm), 17 ozs. **$500-600**

A William and Mary small mug, by Thomas Havers, Norwich, 1689, 2 in (5 cm), 1 oz 5 dwts. **$1,700-2,500**

A child's mug, tapering cylindrical with reeded borders at shoulder and base, the squared handle with applied chased acanthus leaves, the body engraved with a presentation inscription dated '1817', marked on bottom, one small bruise, by Anthony Rasch, Philadelphia, c1817, 2¾in (7cm) high, 3oz. 10 dwt. **$500-600**

A George IV mug, the body chased with trailing foliage and berries on matted ground, by Philip Rundell, 1820, 3 in (7.3 cm), 7 ozs. **$1,300-1,700**

A Victorian spool shape christening mug, inscribed and dated, J. & N. Creswick, London 1853, 4½ in (11.5 cm), 173 gms (5.5 ozs). **$300-500**

A George II silver baluster shaped mug, engraved with contemporary coat-of-arms, maker's mark B.C. (Benjamin Cartwright), London 1753, 5 in (12.5 cm), 12 ozs 12 dwts. **$600-700**

A William IV campana shaped christening mug, E.E.J. & W. Barnard, London, 4 in (9.5 cm), 165 gms (5.3 ozs). **$300-400**

A christening mug, raised on silver gilt against a frosted grey background, gilt interior, in fitted velvet case, inscribed with monogram and coronet, by George Fox, 1867, 3½ in (9 cm), 5 ozs. **$600-700**

A cann, marked near rim, some bruises to bottom, by William Homes, Boston, c1750, 5 in (12.5 cm), 12 ozs. **$1,500-2,200**

An Edwardian christening mug, the sides chased in relief with putti and foliage, the foot as 4 dolphin supports, by Francis Higgins, 1901, 5 in (12 cm), 9.5 ozs. **$400-600**

Salts

A set of 4 salts, oval with a gilt bowl, 2 cast stag's-head handles, a beaded rim, and a cast foliate base with 4 scrolled feet, with engraved monogram, one marked on bottom, marked 'K.G. & J.', probably Boston, c1860, 5in (13cm) long overall, 14oz. **$1,000-1,200**

A pair of salts, fluted shell-shaped, with a cast bird handle, on a molded circular foot, with a gilt bowl, marked on bottom, by Whiting Manufacturing Company, c1865, 4in (10cm) long, 3oz. **$300-400**

A pair of salts, with rounded sides, on applied grapevine rim and 4 cast grapevine feet, the body repousse and chased with grapevines, marked 'PURE COIN' and with eagle pseudo-hallmarks on bottom, probably New England, c1845, 3in (7.5cm) diam., 6oz. **$400-500**

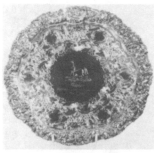

A William IV salver, the centre engraved with a greyhound and with presentation inscription, possibly Robert Gainsford, Sheffield 1836, 10 in (25 cm), 20.75 ozs. **$600-800**

A Regency salver, on cast winged rosette paw feet, by Rebecca Emes and Edward Barnard, London 1817, 12 in (30 cm), 32 ozs. **$1,300-1,700**

A Victorian salver, by John S. Hunt, 1857, 23½ in (59.7 cm), 140 ozs. **$4,500-7,000**

A pair of George II cream boats, on 3 cast stepped feet, by William Justis, 1741, 4 in (10.5 cm), 7 ozs. **$1,200-1,500**

A Victorian circular salver, on 4 acanthus foliage and paw feet, with laurel rim, maker's mark JNM, 1896, 19 in (48.7 cm), 96 ozs. **$2,500-3,500**

Sauce Boats

A George II sauceboat, maker's mark R.I., possibly for Robert Innes, 1751, 7½ in (19 cm), 10.75 ozs. **$600-800**

A George III oval sauceboat, by William Skeen, 1763, 8 in (20.5 cm), 12.5 ozs. **$600-800**

A pair of George II sauceboats, John Swift, London, 1735, 8 in (19.7 cm), 827 gms (26 ozs 12 dwts). **$7,500-10,500**

A pair of George II plain sauceboats, engraved with a crest, by Robert Innes, 1755, 23 ozs. **$1,500-2,200**

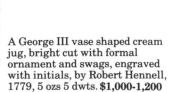

A pair of George III sauceboats, by Smith and Sharp, London, 1765. **$3,000-4,500**

A George III vase shaped cream jug, bright cut with formal ornament and swags, engraved with initials, by Robert Hennell, 1779, 5 ozs 5 dwts. **$1,000-1,200**

A George III compressed brandy saucepan, makers Wakelin and Taylor, London 1782, 13.5 ozs. all in. **$600-700**

Scent Bottles

A George III silver gilt sauceboat, on 3 flower, foliage and scroll feet, engraved with a coat-of-arms, crest and motto, by Paul Storr, 1820, 23 ozs. **$6,000-8,500**

A George III sauceboat, by Peter and Ann Bateman, London, 1792, 5½ in (14.4 cm), 6 ozs. **$800-1,200**

A Victorian earthenware scent bottle, painted in the Imari style in red, gold and blue with the 'Old Witches' pattern, plain silver cap, by Saunders & Shepherd, Birmingham, 1885, 3 in (7.1 cm). **$100-150**

A Victorian parcel gilt scent bottle, interior complete with glass stopper, by Edwin Culver, 1878, 2½ in (6.2 cm). **$300-400**

A Victorian gold mounted ruby glass scent bottle, decorated with turquoise set swags, the cover with cabochon set garnet, c1860, 3½ in (9 cm). **$600-700**

A Victorian silver circular scent bottle, enamelled with mauve and yellow pansies and blue forget-me-nots, by Saunders & Shepherd, c1880, 1½ in (3.3 cm). **$300-400**

A Victorian silver circular scent bottle, enamelled on front with white and yellow roses, by Saunders & Shepherd, 1880, 2 in (4.5 cm). **$300-400**

A Victorian scent flask, Chester, 1898, 3 in (7 cm). **$60-90**

An Edwardian scent bottle, printed in colours with a Japanese lady playing a samisen, the plain silver cap hallmarked Birmingham, 1904, 2 in (5.8 cm). **$80-150**

A Japanese scent bottle, c1900, 6 in (15 cm). **$300-400**

An Edwardian scent bottle, printed in colours, the plain silver cap hallmarked Birmingham, 1905, 1½ in (4 cm). **$80-150**

A painted porcelain scent bottle, with plain silver cap, Birmingham, 1907, 2 in (5.6 cm). **$80-150**

Services

A George III four piece teaset, chased with arched fluting and a matted background, by John Emes, 1800, 40 ozs. **$2,500-3,500**

A four-piece tea and coffee service, comprising: a teapot, a covered sugar bowl, a cream pitcher and a waste bowl; each vase-shaped, on a domed circular foot with a scalloped rim, the domed lids repousse and chased with ocean waves and surmounted by cast sea-shells, above an applied ocean wave border, the handles foliate and scrolled, with ivory insulating rings, the teapot spout repousse with foliage, the bodies and feet repousse with flowers, fruit and scrolls, with an engraved inscription, the waste bowl dated 1855, 3 pieces marked on bottom, by E. Stebbins & Company, New York, c1855, teapot 10½in (26cm) high, gross weight 77oz. 10dwt. **$1,800-2,400**

A six-piece tea and coffee service, comprising: a hot water urn, a coffeepot, a teapot, a covered sugar bowl, a cream pitcher and a waste bowl; each urn-shaped, on a stepped circular foot, with an applied gadrooned border at the shoulder and beaded borders at the rim and footrim, the entire surface bright-cut engraved with neo-classical ornament with roulette-work and stippled details, the handles foliate scrolled, two with ivory insulating rings, the lids domed, with acorn finials, the hot water urn with a burner; each marked on bottom, by Gale & Willis, New York, 1859, hot water urn 17in (43cm) high, gross weight 189oz. **$4,000-5,000**

A six-piece tea and coffee service, comprising: a kettle on stand, a coffeepot, a teapot, a covered two-handled sugar bowl, a cream pitcher and a waste bowl, each urn-shaped, on circular stem and foot, with repousse and chased flowers and scrolls; the handles trefoil-arched, the lids stepped and domed, with acorn finials, coffeepot marked on bottom, coffeepot by William Gale & Son, New York, c1858, other pieces probably New York, c1871, kettle on stand 14½in (36cm) high overall, gross weight 197oz. **$3,000-4,000**

A five-piece tea and coffee service, comprising: a coffeepot, a teapot, a covered sugar bowl, a cream pitcher and a waste bowl; each globular, with etched relief birds and raspberry vines and applied scrolled bands, the lids with spiral reeding, the handles C-scrolled with ivory insulating rings, marked on bottom, by Gorham Manufacturing Company, Providence, 1887, coffeepot 6¾in (17cm) high, gross weight 76oz. 10dwt. **$3,000-3,500**

Make the most of Miller's

Unless otherwise stated, any description which refers to 'a set' or 'a pair' includes a valuation for the entire set or the pair, even though the illustration may show only a single item.

A six-piece tea and coffee service, comprising: two coffeepots, a teapot, a covered sugar bowl, a cream pitcher and a waste bowl; one coffeepot cylindrical, other pieces pyriform; each repousse and chased with flowers and leaves against a foliate-engraved ground, the lids domed, the rims with die-rolled bands of fleur-de-lis, the pots with ivory insulating rings, five pieces marked, cylindrical coffeepot partially marked, by Dominick & Haff, Newark, New Jersey, 1880, coffeepot 8¼in (21cm) high, gross weight 105oz. 10dwt. **$3,000-3,500**

A Victorian silver three piece teaset, with engraved rococo cartouches, scrolling foliage and flowers, Sheffield 1849, maker Hawksworth Eyre & Co., 1849/50, 45 ozs. $800-1,200

A Victorian teaset, by E. and J. Barnard, London 1851. $7,000-9,000

A Victorian pear shaped tea and coffee service, engraved twice with a crest and motto, by Charles Reily and George Storer 1845 and 1846, coffee pot 11 in (28 cm), 74 ozs. $3,000-4,500

A Victorian cabaret set, J.S. Hunt, each piece stamped Hunt & Roskell, late Storr & Mortimer, London, 1857/59, the salver 8½ in (21.8 cm), 33 ozs all in. $1,500-2,200

A three-piece tea service, comprising: a teapot, a covered sugar bowl and a cream pitcher; each compressed baluster form, with broadly-reeded sides, on a lobed foot, the scrolled handles and scalloped rims with applied foliate decoration, the lids domed and chased with acanthus leaves, marked on bottom, wooden finials added, by John B. Jones Jr, for Lows, Ball & Company, Boston, 1840-1846, teapot 7¾in (19cm) high, gross weight 65oz. $800-1,000

A Victorian three piece teaset, by Stephen Smith, London 1866. $1,400-1,700

A Victorian four piece teaset, by T.W., London 1878/9. $2,000-3,000

A late Victorian repousse silver five piece tea and coffee service, Sheffield 1896, 123 ozs. $3,000-4,000

A Victorian silver gilt tea-service, engraved in the Chinese taste with birds and foliage, by Stephen Smith, 1879, gross 18 oz 15 dwts. $1,200-1,500

535

A Victorian four piece tea and
coffee service, in the Indian style
with all-over engraved decoration,
Johnstone and Co., Glasgow
1896/7/8, 1577 gms 50.7 ozs.
$1,700-2,500

A Victorian four piece tea service,
maker Jas. Deakin & Sons,
Sheffield 1899, 59 ozs.
$1,000-1,200

A George V three piece
tea-service, of Barge form,
Sheffield 1916, 980 gms total
gross. **$500-600**

A George V four piece tea-service,
Bradford and Son Ltd., London
1931/3, 2631 gms, 84.5 ozs all in.
$1,400-1,700

A four piece tea and coffee set, by
Messrs Carrington, London 1901,
gross 86 ozs. **$1,700-2,500**

A French four piece teaset,
modelled by Morel Ledeuil, c1880.
$2,500-3,500

Tankards

A Charles II plain cylindrical
tankard, engraved with a later
coat-of-arms, the handle pricked
with initials, maker's mark DG,
between fleurs-de-lys in a lozenge,
1681, 7 in (18.4 cm), 28 ozs.
$4,500-7,000

A baluster cann, with a molded
rim, an S-scroll handle and a
molded circular foot, the body
engraved with script initials 'RL'
to 'EPT', marked on bottom, minor
repair to inside of footrim, by
Rufus Green, Boston, 1760-1777,
5in (13cm) high, 11oz.
$2,200-2,500

A Queen Anne plain cylindrical
tankard, engraved with initials
and date, by Humphrey Payne,
1704, 7 in (17.2 cm), 23 ozs.
$3,000-4,000

A pair of canns, each pyriform,
with an S-scroll handle, molded
rim and molded circular footrim,
engraved on the bottom with
owner's initials 'CST', marked
with crown and cartouche touch
on bottom, repairs at handle joins,
by Samuel Edwards, Boston,
1730-1762, 5½in (13.5cm) high,
22oz. **$3,500-4,500**

*According to family tradition,
these canns were once owned by
Charles and Sarah Tilden,
married c1820. Their initials were
probably engraved on the canns at
that time.*

Tea Caddies

A Danish silver mounted pottery
tankard, c1806, 8 in (20.4 cm).
$1,000-1,200

A Victorian parcel gilt
presentation peg tankard, in the
Scandinavian style, engraved
with the badge of the Royal Scots
Greys, by Frederick Elkington,
1872, 11½ in (29 cm), 49 oz.
$1,500-2,200

A George I octagonal tea caddy,
London, 1714. $1,500-2,200

A George III square tea-caddy, 3
sides engraved with a Chinoiserie
figure, the base patched, by Aaron
Lestourgeon, 1772, 14 oz
5 dwts). $3,000-4,500

A George III tea caddy, with key,
marked on lid and base,
Godbehere & Wigan, London,
1790, 6¼ in (15.7 cm), 19 oz
16 dwt (615 gms).
$2,000-3,000

A set of 3 George II
bombe-tea-caddies, chased with
flowers, foliage, shell ornament
and fluting, engraved with a crest,
by Francis Crump, 1756, in fitted
veneered tortoiseshell case with
silver mounts, 26oz.
$3,000-4,500

tortoiseshell cased set of 3 early
George III tea caddies, by Daniel
mith & Robert Sharp, 1763, the
rger 5½ in (14 cm), the two
naller 5 in (12.5 cm).
10,000-13,000

A set of 3 ivory cased George III
silver gilt caddies, in an
Indo-Colonial domed ivory casket
with stained floral border and
silver handles, on bracket feet,
maker's mark TL, 1771, 5 in
(12.5 cm), 28 oz. $14,000-17,000
*This maker's mark is noted by
Grimwade (No. 3845) as
appearing on caddies dated 1770
and 1771 but remains unidentified.*

wo early George III caddies,
ntained in a Georgian silver
ounted mahogany case, by
ierre J. Gillois, 1776, 6½ in
6 cm) and 6 in (15 cm).
4,500-7,000

A set of three George III caddies,
by Richard Mason & Benjamin
Stephenson, 1773, 8 in (20 cm) and
8½ in (21 cm), 22 oz.
$1,700-2,500

A shagreen cased matched set of George II/III canisters, of ogee form, one by Samuel Taylor, 1758, **the other by** Samuel Herbert & Co., 1763, 5½ in (14 cm), **the covered mixing bowl similarly decorated**, by John Payne , 1769, 6 in (15 cm), maker's mark JW. **$1,700-2,500**

A George III oval gadroon edged part-fluted caddy, the cover with green stained ivory finial, by Richard Cooke, 1801, 6½ in (16 cm), 15 oz. **$1,200-1,500**

A George III tea-caddy, the base engraved with later initial, marked on base and cover, by John Denziloe, London, 1786, 5½ in (13.5 cm), 16 oz. **$2,000-3,000**

A George III oval thread edged caddy, by Peter and Ann Bateman, 1795, 7½ in (19 cm), 12 oz. **$1,200-1,500**

A pair of shagreen cased George III silver gilt caddies, the vase-shaped bodies part swirl fluted, lead lined, in shaped fish-scale case with silver mounts on ball and claw feet, by Emick Romer, 1769. **$2,500-3,500**

A pair of William IV caddies, in a rosewood box, by Robert Hennell III, 1834, 6 in (15 cm), 24 oz. **$3,000-4,500**

A George III tea caddy, by Peter, Ann & William Bateman, London, 1800, marked on base and lid, 7 in (18 cm) 13 oz 18 dwt (432 gms). **$1,500-2,200**

A George III tea caddy, bright cut and wrigglework with pendent tassels, the lid with stained ivory cone finial, by Robert Hennell, London, 1788, 6 in (15 cm), 12 oz (387 gm 9 dwt). **$1,700-2,500**

A fine pair of William IV 'Rococo Revival' caddies, richly embossed chased and applied with foliate sprays between swirling foliate scrolls, by Charles Fox I, 1835, 8 in (20 cm), 43 oz. **$10,000-13,000**

Silver: Tea Kettles

A late Victorian tea kettle, burner and stand, makers mark H.S. Sheffield 1899, 1068 grammes gross. **$500-600**

A George II tea urn and domed cover, the body engraved, the urn shaped lamp and reeded tray by Solomon Hougham, London 1801, 13 in (32 cm), 68 oz. **$2,500-3,500**

A mid Victorian tea kettle and stand, by Stephen Smith, London 1876, 13½ in (34 cm) high, 1388 gms. **$700-1,000**

George III tea-urn, the cover ith fluted cone finial, engraved ith a coat-of-arms, by D. Smith nd R. Sharp, 1785, maker's mark artly worn, in a fitted wood case, 1 in (53 cm) high, 111 oz. 4,500-7,000

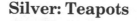

Silver: Teapots

A kettle on stand, the kettle globular, with bail handle and ivory insulating rings, a domed hinged lid, and a curved spout, on a rectangular base with 2 pierced supports and 4 feet, with a cylindrical burner; the kettle repousse and chased with flowers and leaves, the stand flat-chased with flowers, leaves and anthemia, with applied beading, each piece marked on bottom, by Tiffany & Company, New York, 1875-1891, 14¼in (36cm) high, gross weight 63oz. **$1,500-2,000**

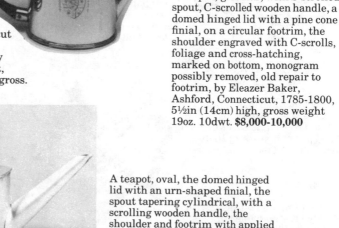

teapot, faceted oval, with bands vertical fluting, the lid domed al, with a wooden finial, the raight spout faceted, the wooden ndle C-scrolled, the body and out with bright-cut engraved rders, garlands, and 2 rtouches, one with an engraved est, marked 'I. SMITH' twice on e bottom, repairs at seams, by hn Smith, Baltimore, c1800, 4in (17cm) high, gross weight oz. **$1,000-1,200**

A George III teapot, bright-cut with border of bellflowers, engraved with contemporary armorial, by Charles Wright, 1772, 5 in (12 cm) high, 13 oz gross. **$800-1,200**

A teapot, globular, with S-scrolled spout, C-scrolled wooden handle, a domed hinged lid with a pine cone finial, on a circular footrim, the shoulder engraved with C-scrolls, foliage and cross-hatching, marked on bottom, monogram possibly removed, old repair to footrim, by Eleazer Baker, Ashford, Connecticut, 1785-1800, 5½in (14cm) high, gross weight 19oz. 10dwt. **$8,000-10,000**

A teapot, oval, the domed hinged lid with an urn-shaped finial, the spout tapering cylindrical, with a scrolling wooden handle, the shoulder and footrim with applied reeded moldings, marked on bottom, by Hugh Wishart, New York, c1810, 7½in (19cm) high, gross weight 22oz. **$2,500-3,000**

A George IV teapot, Phillip Rundell, London, 1821, 7½ in (18.5 cm), 30 oz. **$1,500-2,200**

A Silver bright-cut teapot, with matching stand, London, c1800. **$2,000-3,000**

A George III teapot and stand, with a wreath cartouche, below a bright-cut intertwined frieze, 7 in (17 cm) high, the stand with identical decoration, by Thomas Wallis II, 1800, 6½ in (16 cm) wide, 17.5 oz. **$1,200-1,500**

A George IV teapot, by James Charles Edington, 1829, 10½ in (26.5 cm), 22 oz all in. **$600-900**

A George III oval engraved silver teapot, by Peter Bateman, London, marked 1813, 12 oz. **$600-800**

A William IV teapot, fully marked, Paul Storr, London, 1. 5 in (12 cm) high, 14 oz 3 dwt. **$4,500-7,000**

A Regency compressed spherical teapot, chased with fluting and with central moulded rib, with egg and dart border, by Paul Storr, 1816, 23 oz gross. **$2,000-3,000**

An early Indian Colonial oval teapot, with bright cut swag engraving and crested initialled shield shape cartouches, having a tapering spout, scroll wood handle, maker John Hunt, c1800. **$1,300-1,700**

An Austro-Hungarian teapot, with ivory handle and short sp Vienna 1764, 5 in (12 cm) hig 10.5 oz. **$1,000-1,200**

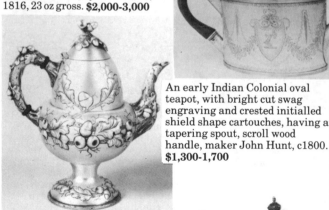

A teapot, marked, monogram removed, a few bruises, by William Brown, Baltimore, c1850, 10 in (25 cm) high, 32 oz 10 dwt gross. **$800-1,200**

A Queen Anne style teapot, with slightly later matching octagonal warming stand, with a burner, Britannia Standard, 8¾ in (22 cm), 41.5 oz gross. **$1,000-1,200**

A Dutch silver-gilt teapot, Adar Loofs, Amsterdam, 1701, 3 in (7.7 cm) high, 166 grm (5 oz 6 dwt **$7,000-9,000**
Adam Loofs was admitted mast of The Hague Guild of Silversmiths in 1682 and died i 1710.

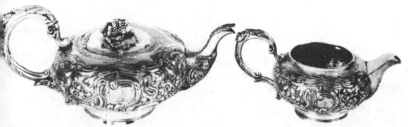

William IV silver teapot, and a
matching cream jug, London 1835,
maker's mark B.S. for Benjamin
Smith III, 34 oz. **$600-700**

A William IV teapot and matching
milk jug, W. Newlan, Dublin,
1832, 34.8 oz. (1085 gms).
$600-800

A Victorian teapot, of
Ashburnham pattern, with
melon-shaped body on pedestal
foot, by Hunt & Roskell, 1875,
33 oz. **$600-800**

A George IV compressed circular
teapot, marked on base, lid,
handle and nut, Paul Storr,
London, 1824, 6 in (14.5 cm), 942
gm (30 oz 6 dwt). **$1,700-2,500**

An Italian teapot, maker's mark
V. Caruso, probably Naples,
c1820, 20 oz. **$600-700**

Silver: Trays

A two-handled tray, with loop
handles, with beaded and leaf
borders and acanthus handle
joins, the molded rim with applied
beaded and leaf borders, the tray
surface with a wide engraved
border of strapwork and foliage,
centering engraved script initials,
marked on bottom with
'TIFFANY & COMPY' in a
serrated rectangle and a single
Gothic 'M', by John C. Moore for
Tiffany & Company, New York,
1848-1852, 30in (75cm) long,
104oz. **$3,500-4,500**

A two-handled tray, with
scalloped rim, a fluted booge, 2
loop handles with cast foliage on
the front and back of handle joins,
an oval footrim with cast leaf
border, the rim with cast applied
chrysanthemums and leaves, the
centre engraved with foliate
monogram, marked on bottom, by
Tiffany & Company, New York,
1891-1902, 16in (40cm) long, 30oz.
$1,500-2,000

A tray, with cast applied shells
and seaweed surrounding a
hammered gilt bowl, with chased
inscription 'J.A.D.W.1882',under
brim, marked on bottom, by
Tiffany & Company, New York,
c1882, 13in (33cm) long, 27oz.
10dwt. **$600-800**

A covered soup tureen, the domed oval lid with a cast stylised anthemion finial, on a spreading oval foot, the tureen with 2 cast stylised anthemion handles, the rim and footrim with an applied die-rolled guilloche, marked, by Whiting Manufacturing Company, c1865, 8½in (21cm) high, 60oz. **$1,200-1,800**

A compote, circular, with flaring sides, a gilt interior and a die-rolled border, on a tapering cylindrical stem with a die-rolled border supported by 3 pierced stylised foliate legs, each terminating with a hoof foot, on a tripartite base, marked on bottom, by Tiffany & Company, New York, 1865-1869, 12¾in (31cm) high, 40oz. **$1,500-2,000**

A covered soup tureen, on a spreading oval foot, with a stylised foliate handle, the body with stylised foliate handles and a die-rolled swag border at rim, one side with an engraved script monogram, marked, by Gorham Manufacturing Company, Providence, 1871, 10¼in (26cm) high, 65oz. **$1,800-2,400**

Three German silver-gilt dishes and covers, by Christianus Drentwett, Augsburg, 1745-1747, circular dishes 10½ in (26 cm) diam, 132 oz. **$15,000-20,500**

A pair of covered vegetable dishes oval, with an everted scallop brim with applied chrysanthemums and leaves, the lid domed, with a applied foliate border and a cast foliate removable handle, the lid rim scalloped with applied foliag on the underside, marked on bottom, by Tiffany & Company, New York, 1891-1902, 3½in (9cm high, 82oz. 10dwt. **$3,000-3,500**

A compote, circular, with 2 cast swallow handles, a circular footrim, on a cast draped female figure stem, over a stepped and domed circular base, the rim, footrim and base with applied die-rolled scroll border, the matte-finished bowl with engraved stylised monogram and a gilt interior, marked on bottom, by J.E. Caldwell & Company, Philadelphia, c1865, 13in (33cm) high, 47oz. 10dwt. **$1,500-2,000**

A George IV soup tureen and cover, the domed cover with detachable scroll handle, engraved twice with a crest, by Robert Garrard, 1828, 11 in (28 cm) high, 124 oz. **$6,000-8,000**

A Queen Anne snuffer-tray and pair of William III snuffers, the snuffer with shaped oblong box and scroll handles engraved with initials ERH, by John Laughton, Jnr, 1698, 10 ozs 13 dwt. **$4,000-5,000**

A Victorian four-cup egg cruet, by John Evans, 1841, 9 in (22.5 cm), 18 oz. **$700-900**

A George III wax-jack, maker's mark indistinct, but possibly for S. Horbort & Co, 1763, 6 oz 6 dwts. **$1,500-2,200**

A Victorian egg frame for six, Joseph Angel, London, 1854, 8¼ in (21 cm), 30 oz. **$1,400-1,700**

A William IV trefoil cruet, two of the three glass bottles with silver mounts, by Joseph and John Angell, 1836, 10 in (25 cm), 19.5 oz. **$1,000-1,200**

A George II oil and vinegar frame, engraved with a crest, by Benjamin Godfrey, 1738, 25 oz. **$3,000-4,500**

A Queen Anne dressing-table mirror, by Benjamin Pyne, 1703, 29¼ in (74.5 cm). **$15,000-20,500**

George III boat-shaped oil and vinegar stand, the stand by Thomas Heming, 1778, the bottle-mounts unmarked, 1 oz. **$1,700-2,500**

A William and Mary dressing-table mirror, the cresting fully marked, each side of the frame struck with the crowned harp and one with the date-letter in addition, by Thomas Bolton, Dublin, 1693, 27½ in (70 cm). **$22,500-25,500**

A George III snuffer tray and snuffers, by William Cripps, London, 1768, 8¼ in (20.5 cm), 10½ oz. **$1,000-1,200**

A Victorian mustard pot, with original green glass liner, by Riley & Storer, 1840, 5 ozs. **$500-600**

A Victorian Dutch cow creamer, import mark for Sheffield 1899, 5½ in (14 cm), 162 gms (5.2 oz). **$700-900**

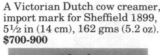

A George III wax-jack by Robertson and Darling of Newcastle, maker's mark mis-stuck, town mark missing, c1795, 8 oz (6 dwts). **$1,000-1,200**

A Highland crest silver menu holder, Edinburgh 1894, 2 by 2½ in (5 by 6 cm). **$100-150**

A George II cow creamer, on later base, the cow John Schuppe, 1758, the base, Charles and George Fox, 1842, both London, 6 in (15 cm), 6 oz 3 dwt. **$4,500-7,000**

A menu holder, with a fox hunting design, by Mappin & Webb, London, 1911, early 20thC, 2½ by 2½ in (6 by 6 cm). **$150-200**

A George V dish ring, Birmingham 1910, 7 in (18 cm), 350 gms (11.2 ozs). **$300-500**

A Victorian large campana shaped vase, by John S. Hunt, 1848, 26½ in (66 cm), approx. 474 ozs. **$14,000-17,000**

A Victorian six division toast rack, by Paul Storr, London 1837, 6 in (15 cm), 12 ozs. **$800-1,200**

A George I sponge box, the hinged cover pierced and engraved with baroque shells, stylised foliage and strapwork, maker's mark only C.R. for Paul Crespin, c1720, 4 in (10.5 cm), 8.75 ozs. **$4,000-5,000**

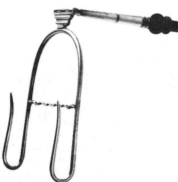

A George III toasting fork, maker's mark W.S., London 1793, 33 in (83 cm). **$600-900**

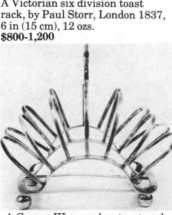

A George III seven bar toast rack, Nathan Smith & Co., Sheffield, 1817, 7 in (17.2 cm), 10 ozs 4 dwts. **$400-600**

An orange strainer, maker's mark H.B., c1720. **$400-600**

A pair of George I or George II silver-mounted fire dogs, engraved with a crest, unmarked, c1725, 19 in (48 cm) high. **$22,500-29,000**

A George IV table bell, engraved with a monogram, John, Henry and Charles Lias, London 1828, 5 in (12.5 cm). **$800-1,200**

An ice bucket and serving spoon, shaped oval, the surface cast and chased in the form of ice crystals, with cast applied icicles, on a similarly-shaped foot, the 2 handles cast in the form of polar bears, one side engraved with the initial 'D' and 'Dec.25.1870'; the spoon with a pierced spade-shaped bowl with a stem handle with a cast polar bear and rope-twist grip; bowl marked on bottom, in original silk-lined box with Starr & Marcus retailer's label, by Gorham Manufacturing Company, Providence, 1870, bowl 6¾in (17cm) high, spoon 11¼in (28cm) long, 30oz. **$8,000-10,000**

A George II cream pail, marked on base, by Walter Brind, London, 1751, 2 in (5 cm) high, 2 oz. **$1,000-1,200**

A Victorian baluster rattle and whistle, with coral teething stick, by Hilliard and Thomason, Birmingham, 1887, 6 in (14.5 cm) long. **$300-500**

A pair of William IV cast grape scissors, by William Traies or William Theobalds, c1835, 5 oz. **$400-600**

A William III medicine funnel, by William Gardner, London, c1700. **$300-400**

A Dutch miniature gaming table, by Willem Van Strant, Amsterdam, 1740, 2½ in (6.3 cm) high. **$500-600**

A rare Charles I Pax, probably English, maker's mark only TB in monogram, c1640, 4 in (10 cm) high, 1 oz 12 dwt. **$1,000-1,200**

In English Church Plate 597-1830 (Oxford 1957), C.C. Oman discounts the possibility of paxes being made in England following the Reformation. However, the engraving on the present example is very close to that on a paten of 1638 from Kingerley Church, Lincolnshire.

A Victorian nurse's buckle, London 1897, 5½ in (14 cm) long, 4 ozs (126 gm). **$200-300**

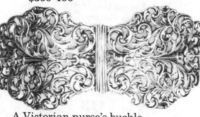

A Victorian parcel gilt pipe, clay lined, c1860, 5 in (12.5 cm) long. **$1,000-1,400**

A George III beehive honey skep, by Thomas Wallis, 1801, 6 in (15 cm) high, 13.5 ozs. **$3,000-4,500**

Wine Antiques

A matched pair of William IV bottle corks, the ivory labels incised 'Brandy' and 'Rum', respectively by John Settle and Henry Williamson, Sheffield, c1830 and by Henry Williamson & Co., Sheffield, 1832. **$300-400**

A George IV hanging nutmeg grater, with steel bow-fronted grater, fully marked, Charles Rawlings, London 1825, 4 in (10.5 cm) high. **$700-900**

A pair of William IV mounted bottle corks, incised 'Brandy' and 'Whiskey', by T. Simpson & Son of Birmingham, but with London hallmarks for 1833. **$400-600**

A Victorian bottle cork, the cast finial modelled as a volunteer artilleryman, by Robert Hennell, c1860. **$200-300**

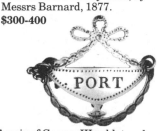

A plated cork, with sweep carrying the tools of his trade. **$80-150**

A George IV mounted bottle cork, the label incised on both sides Hermitage, by Ledsam, Vale & Wheeler, Birmingham, 1829. **$300-500**

A Victorian bottle stopper, modelled as a family crest, by Messrs Barnard, 1877. **$300-400**

A George III bottle ring label, incised 'Benedictine', by Robert Garrard, 2 in (5.5 cm). **$150-200**

A pair of George III wine labels, incised 'Lisbon' and 'Port', maker's mark only I.W. probably Irish, probably for John West, John Wilme or James Wyer of Dublin, c1770, 2 in (4.9 cm). **$200-300**

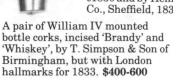

A George III wine label, the title scroll incised 'Claret', by Hester Bateman, c1780. **$300-500**

A pair of George III goblet and festoon wine labels, incised 'Port' and 'Sherry', by John Troby, c1790, 2 in (5 cm). **$300-400**

A George III Scottish wine label, incised 'Claret' by George Fenwick, Edinburgh, 1806, 4 in (9.7 cm). **$200-300**

A George III wine label, incised 'Claret', maker's mark of Thomas Watson overstriking the original maker's mark, 1796, 2 in (5.5. cm). **$80-150**

A George III Provincial crescent shaped wine label, incised 'Brandy', by Hampston & Prince, York, c1780, 1½ in (4.1 cm). **$150-200**

A William IV wine wagon with Victorian coasters, fully marked, by Joseph and John Angell, London, 1835, the coasters, 1839, 13 in (33.2 cm), weight of wagon 35 ozs 10 dwt. **$4,000-5,000**

A pair of George III wine coasters, London hallmark, marks rubbed, 5 in (12.5 cm). **$500-600**

A good George III corkscrew, with bright engraved decoration, by Forrest & Wasdell, Birmingham, 1800, 4 in (10.8 cm). **$600-800**

A French wine taster, the rim engraved A. Baradu, possibly Rennes, maker's mark CD, c1771, 3 in (8 cm), 5 ozs. **$800-1,200**

A Charles I rare York wine taster, the initials RR crudely incised near the rim, by Sem Casson, 1641, 3½ in (9 cm), 1.5 ozs. **$1,700-2,500**

A silver Farrow & Jackson's type open frame corkscrew, impressed Doughty, West Strand, Samuel Horton, Birmingham 1841, 7 in (17 cm). **$3,000-4,500**

An 18thC French wine taster, maker's mark IN with a goblet or chalice, untraced, inscribed around edge I. Bonnaventure, c1750. **$1,700-2,500**

A silver wine cooler, modelled on the Warwick vase, London 1902, maker's Edwd. Barnard & Sons Ltd, 112 ozs. **$3,000-4,500**

A Victorian wine ewer, Charles Reily and George Storer, London 1842, 14 in (36 cm), 952 gms (30.6 ozs). **$1,000-1,400**

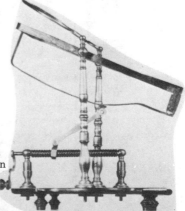

A decanting cradle, on shield shaped mahogany base, the brass vertical columns supporting an iron cradle, 14½ in (36 cm). **$600-800**

A pair of old Sheffield plate wine coolers, c1825. **$3,000-4,000**

A novelty silver plate bottle holder, English, struck with the PODR mark for 1st February, 1868, plating worn, bottle now missing, c1870, 17 in (43 cm). **$1,000-1,200**

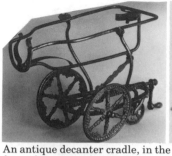

An antique decanter cradle, in the form of a gun carriage, 12½ in (31 cm) long. **$700-900**

A German made 'ladies legs' corkscrew, with two-tone green stockings, c1920. **$150-200**

An Armstrong patent multi-lever corkscrew, c1902, extending to 10 in (25 cm). **$80-150**

A 'scissors' corkscrew, incorporating a wire cutter, c1900. **$80-150**

A Thomason type bronze barrel corkscrew, with bone handle and patent label, c1820. **$200-300**

Prices of corkscrews vary considerably depending on condition and refinements.

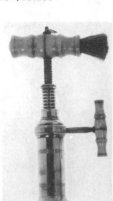

An unusual brass hammer head corkscrew possibly a pipe smoker's companion, 3 in (7.5 cm) long. **$400-600**

A two-pillar bronze cage corkscrew, with ebony handle, English, c1850. **$150-200**

A bone-handled 'king screw' with wide brass rack, c1830. **$200-300**

A George III silver corkscrew, by Joseph Taylor, unusual engraving to sheath and handle, c1790, 3 in (7.5 cm) long. **$600-800**

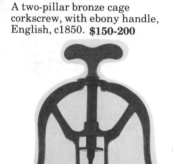

A turned wood handled corkscrew, with brush and auger type helix, early 19thC. **$100-150**

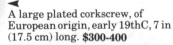

◄ A large plated corkscrew, of European origin, early 19thC, 7 in (17.5 cm) long. **$300-400**

A Heely A1 double lever steel corkscrew, c1880. **$50-70**

A pocket corkscrew, U.S. patent, mid-19thC. **$80-150**

A mahogany port slide, c1820, 8 in (20 cm). **$300-500**

An English mahogany bottle carrier, c1770, 12 by 18 in (30 by 45 cm). **$1,400-1,700**

Misc

A pair of Sheffield plate entree dishes, c1845. **$2,000-3,000**

A pair of late Regency Sheffield plate meat dishes and matching covers, dishes 16 in (40 cm). **$700-900**

A pair of Sheffield plate entree dishes and cover, on heater bases. **$800-1,200**

A pair of Sheffield plate meat dish covers, Matthew Boulton, 11 in (28 cm) long. **$400-600**

A pair of plated warming meat dishes and covers, Henry Wilkinson and Co., Sheffield, c1860, 18½ and 15½ in (47 and 38 cm) long. **$1,000-1,400**

A set of 4 Sheffield plated entree dishes, covers and detachable handles, by Matthew Boulton, struck with the double sun mark of Matthew Boulton and Plate Co., 10 in (25 cm). **$600-700**

A pair of plated Adam style candelabra, 20½ in (51 cm). **$600-800**

A Sheffield plate candlestick, c1825, 9½ in (24 cm). **$30-45**

A pair of silver plated candlesticks, with detachable nozzles, maker's mark J.D. & S., Sheffield 1895, 6 in (15 cm). **$400-600**

A large silver plate centre-piece, with an associated frosted glass holder, by Elkington & Co., c1855, 29½ in (25 cm). **$1,700-2,500**

A pair of Sheffield plated candelabra, stamped Mortons Patent, 14 in (35 cm), extending to 19½ in (49 cm). **$700-900**

A pair of Sheffield plate candelabra, slight repair, 21½ in (54.5 cm). **$500-600**

A set of four George III Sheffield plate candlesticks, with reeded bands and detachable nozzles, loaded, 11 in (27.5 cm). **$700-900**

A pair of Victorian plated candelabra, 20½ in (51 cm). **$1,200-1,500**

A pair of Sheffield plate chamber sticks, c1820, 5 in (12.5 cm). $300-400

Three electroplated Adam style table candlesticks, 11 in (27 cm). $300-500

A large Sheffield plate table centre-piece, 19½ in (49 cm). $800-1,200

A set of four Sheffield plate telescopic table candlesticks, slight damage to nozzles, 11 in (23 cm) extended. $300-400

A plated tea and coffee set, including a large 2 handled tea urn, by Walker & Hall. $1,500-2,200

A gilt Elkington & Co Epergne, in early George III style. $14,000-17,000

A Victorian EPNS tea-service by Elkingtons. $300-400

A Victorian tea and coffee service, by Elkington & Co. $700-1,000

A Victorian electroplated tea and coffee service, Martin Hall & Co., c1875. $800-1,200

A large Victorian plated gallery tea tray, the centre with a presentation inscription dated 29th August 1873, makers Thomas Bradbury & Sons, also marked William Alexander & Son, Glasgow, 24½ by 19 in (61 by 47.5 cm). $800-1,200

An early period oval teapot, the body engraved with foliate borders and festooning, c1785, 4½ in (11 cm). $500-600

A Sheffield plated tea tray, 29½ in (73.5 cm). **$800-1,200**

A set of three Sheffield plate salvers, c1820. **$1,000-1,200**

A Victorian electroplated seven bottle cruet, 2 glass bottles silver topped. **$200-300**

A Sheffield plate tea urn, c1820. **$1,000-1,400**

An electroplated ink stand, with presentation inscription, 13½ in (34.5 cm). **$800-1,200**

A George III rare silver plated key to the Garden at Westminster, with initials GR, the reverse inscribed The Rt. Honble. the Speaker', 3rd quarter 18thC, 4 in (9.5 cm). **$1,200-1,500**

A Sheffield plate candle snuffers and tray, c1824. **$60-90**

A Victorian openwork cake basket, by Henry Wilkinson, London 1860. **$300-600**

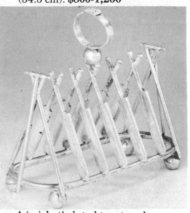

A 'cricket' plated toast rack. **$150-200**

Gold

A George III 18ct gold snuff box, by Alexander James Strachan, 1806, the cover 1807, 3 in (7.5 cm). **$1,700-2,500**

A Swiss gold snuff box, 1802, 3½ in (8.9 cm), approximately 3 ozs. **$1,500-2,200**

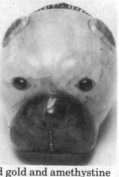

A jewelled gold and amethystine quartz snuff box, rose diamond bands for mouth missing, struck with mark E.T. possible German, c1790. **$1,700-2,500**

A Swiss gold snuff box, the centre set with enamel miniature of a lady, maker's mark CW, c1840, 3½ in (8.5 cm). **$1,500-2,200**

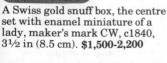

A 9ct gold card case. **$300-400**

An Empire gold snuff box, the glazed cover and base with oiled miniature landscapes including rivers, turreted buildings and rocky outcrops, the sides veneered in tortoiseshell, by Adrien Maximilien Vachette, Paris, with 2nd standard mark 20ct for 1795-97 and warranty mark for 1809-19, 3½ in (9.2 cm). **$5,500-7,000**

Simon Mathuerin Lantara (1728-1778) French painter and engraver, whose modest ambitions led him to dispose of his work through street markets. The figures in his paintings are thought to be the work of other artists, including Joseph Vernet (see Benezit, Dictionnaire des Peintres, Sculpteurs, etc).

A gold box, engraved with posies of flowers, unmarked, 19thC, 3 in (8.3 cm). **$1,500-2,200**

A George III 18ct two colour gold oval engine turned vinaigrette, probably by Artaxerxes Brown, 1810, 1½ in (3.1 cm). **$800-1,200**

A Swiss gold and enamel box, slight enamel damage, maker's initials FJ, 3 in (7.6 cm). **$3,500-5,000**

A gold and agate etui, containing 6 various implements, English, c1780, 4 in (10.5 cm). **$2,500-3,500**

A gold mounted oval seal, inset with a bloodstone, mounted with a shoulder length bust of a negro wearing a carved ivory hat, including swivel, complete in original fitted case, 1 in (2.5 cm). **$1,300-1,700**

A blond tortoiseshell gold mounted circular box, the rim and base with gold pique border, 18th/19thC, 2½ in (6 cm). **$200-300**

A blond tortoiseshell and gold pique snuff box, later gilt metal mounts, probably French, some damage and restoration, c1720, 3 in (7.5 cm). **$800-1,200**

A gold mounted tortoiseshell snuff box, the lid with a gold framed oval cameo, the gold edge with inscription dated 1802, 3½ in (8.1 cm). **$200-300**

A Neopolitan tortoiseshell and mother of pearl casket, 18thC, 5½ in (14 cm). **$2,500-3,500**

A French gold mounted tortoiseshell box, the interior of the lid inscribed Amitie Reconnaissance, in black enamel, with 3rd standard mark for 1819-38 and lozenge maker's initials, illegible, 3 in (7.5 cm). **$2,500-3,500**

A rare Neopolitan tortoiseshell piqué spyglass, inlaid in gold piqué posé et point, some damage and restoration, c1760, 2½ in (6 cm). **$1,000-1,400**

A group of four pique tortoiseshell boxes:
t. Oblong box, c1780. **$1,700-2,500**
l. Circular box, c1800. **$1,700-2,500**
r. Box in the form of a cross, c1760. **$1,500-2,200**
b. Oval box, c1720. **$1,500-2,200**

A gold mounted tortoiseshell box, the cover set with a gilt medallic portrait of George IV, by Rundell, Bridge & Rundell after T. Stothard, the reverse with a view of Windsor Castle, split to side, c1830, 3 in (8.3 cm). **$1,700-2,500**

Metalwork
Brass

A pair of brass candlesticks,
mid-18thC, 9 in (22.5 cm).
$1,700-2,500

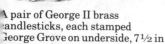

A pair of George II brass
candlesticks, each stamped
George Grove on underside, 7½ in
18.8 cm). **$1,000-1,400**

A pair of petal-base brass
candlesticks, c1720, 8 in (20 cm).
$1,000-1,400

A Georgian brass taperstick,
mid-18thC, 5 in (13 cm).
$800-1,200

A pair of brass candlesticks,
18thC, 9 in (22.5 cm).
$500-700

A pair of brass candlesticks, early
18thC, 7½ in (19 cm).
$700-900

A pair of George II brass table
candlesticks, c1735, 8½ in
(22 cm). **$800-1,200**

17thC style Low Countries
brass pricket candlestick,
2 in (30 cm). **$500-600**

A pair of George I brass
candlesticks, 6 in (15 cm).
$700-900

A Dutch brass foot warmer, No.
178?2, 18thC, 12 in (30 cm).
$400-600

An oxidised ten light chandelier,
20thC, 37 in (94 cm).
$1,000-1,200

n eight branch gilt brass
chandelier, 20thC, 35 by 30 in
?4 by 76 cm). **$800-1,200**

A collection of four brass padlocks,
19thC. **$300-400**

A brass rim lock, the plate finely
engraved with squirrel, wild birds
and dragon's head, the sides and
mortice of bombe section, the
mechanism with typical cut
decoration, the key turned with
baluster shaft, 17thC, 9½ by 5 in
(23.5 by 12.5 cm). **$800-1,200**

A Dutch brass foot warmer, mid-18thC, 11 in (28 cm). **$300-400**

A collection of six miniature brass padlocks, the largest 1 in (3 cm). **$200-300**

A Dutch brass sconce, embossed with putti and foliate fruiting swags, the arms fixed, 17th/18thC, 16½ in (41 cm). **$400-600**

A small German brass and copper gilt casket, with intricate lock and lid stamped MM for Michel Mann, with key, 17thC, 3 in (7.3 cm). **$4,000-5,000**

An unusual brass reliquary circlet, with 4 glazed panels with ink labels containing relics, 17thC, 8 in (20.5 cm). **$600-800**

A brass sundial, 42 in (105 cm). **$700-900**
Provenance:
Formerly at Culuss Lodge, Isle of Wight.

A matched pair of French brass chestnut urns, late 18thC, 13 in (33 cm). **$1,400-1,700**

A brass oval barbers bowl, 18thC, 13½ in (34 cm). **$300-400**

A lacquered brass ember fire kerb, 19thC, 44 in (112 cm). **$300-400**

An Edwardian brass coal scuttle and shovel. **$300-400**

A Barbedienne bronze figure of a classical maiden, green weathered patination, fitted as a fountain, by Jean Alexandre Joseph Falguiere, 66 in (168 cm). **$4,500-7,000**

Bronze

A French bronze figure of a young man carrying a furled flag, by L. Laporte. **$500-700**

A bronze figure of Leda and the Swan, incised F. Righetti F. Romae 1787, weathered, 13 in (33.5 cm). **$800-1,200**

A bronze and cold painted figure of a slave girl, by Emmanuele Villani, early 20thC, 16 in (41 cm). **$1,500-2,200**

A bronze showing a seated young courtship couple in 18thC style dress, 7 in (17.5 cm). **$200-300**

bronze figure, by Hippolyte loreau, inscribed Chant de 'Aloutte. **$1,300-1,700**

An English bronze statuette of a naked girl, known as 'Tribute to Hymen', after Sir Alfred Gilbert, inscribed A. Gilbert 1900, anteros missing from left hand, early 20thC, 11 in (27 cm). **$800-1,200**

A gilt bronze group, on pale green onyx plinth, by Faillot, inscribed Faillot, 19thC, 15 in (38 cm). **$1,000-1,200**

Edme Nicholas Failot, 1810-1849, exhibited at the Salon from 1838.

French bronze statuette of agar, cast from a model by Aime lillet, signed Aime Millet, ooden plinth, 19thC, 12 in 9.5 cm). **$500-600**

A French bronze statuette, of Jason holding aloft the golden fleece, cast from a model by Alfred Desire Lanson, sword bent, late 19thC, 20 in (50 cm). **$700-1,000**

A large French bronze figure of Mercury after Giambologna, with base, drilled, 19thC, 75 in (192 cm). **$7,000-9,000**

A bronze group of a youth and lioness, mid and dark brown patination, by Louis Potet, signed Loye Potet and with Exposition gold medal stamp of 1900, early 20thC, 22 in (56 cm). **$1,000-1,200**

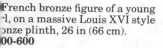

French bronze figure of a young l, on a massive Louis XVI style nze plinth, 26 in (66 cm). 00-600

A painted bronze figure of an Arab boy vendor, cast from the model by Pepin, so signed, and applied with a plaque and foundry mark, 19thC, 15 in (37.5 cm). **$800-1,200**

A French bronze allegorical group of Winter, after Clodion, edge of base slightly bent, 19thC, 32½ in (81 cm). **$1,500-2,200**

A bronzed figure of a camel, being ridden by an Arab boy, rubbed brown patination, late 19thC, 27 in (69 cm). **$2,500-3,500**

A fine English bronze statuette of Teucer, larger version, by Hamo Thornycroft, signed and dated 1881 and inscribed 82, or possibly 88, late 19thC, 26½ in (66 cm). **$14,000-17,000**

A bronze group of Mercury, being taught archery, dark brown patination, 19thC, 15½ in (39 cm). **$700-1,000**

A Bacchanalian bronze group, signed Delafontaine and impressed Schoenewerk, 19thC, 23½ in (59 cm). **$800-1,200**

An English bronze statuette of Charles George Gordon, cast from a model by Hamo Thornycroft, signed and dated 1888 and inscribed Charles George Gordon and published by Arthur Leslie Collie 39^B Old Bond S^t, London May 6 1889 and underneath J.XIII, late 19thC, 15 in (37 cm). **$1,500-2,200**

l. A Bergman cold painted bronze group of camel, carrying 2 women in drape hung panniers and being led by an Arab, Austrian, the base stamped Geschutz and with maker's stamp, c1900, 6 in (15 cm). **$800-1,200**
r. A cold painted bronze group of an Arab, galloping on horseback holding his jezail aloft, on a marble base, Austrian, c1900, 7½ in (19 cm). **$1,000-1,200**

A bronze group of two race horses and jockeys, by Bernard Winskill, 23 by 12 in (57.5 by 30 cm). **$2,500-3,500**

A bronze group of two frolicking putti, after Clodion, on veined marble base, dark brown patination, signed Clodion, c1870. **$1,200-1,500**

A French bronze model of cupid, 19thC, 13 in (32.5 cm). **$500-600**

A bronze group of Una and the Lion, on a shaped slate base, 19thC, 5½ in (14 cm). **$100-200**

A silvered bronze equestrian group of an Arab warrior, 19thC, 6½ in (16 cm). **$300-400**

A bronze group of a little girl, green/brown patination, Italian, by Antonio Giovanni Lanziroti, signed A.G. Lanziroti, c1870, 20 in (51 cm). **$3,000-4,500**

A pair of French bronze busts of Le Pecheur Napolitain and La Rieuse Napolitaine, cast from models by Jean Baptiste Carpeaux, reddish marble plinths, late 19thC, 4 by 4 in (10 by 10.5 cm). **$1,400-1,700**

A South African bronze bust of a kaffir dozing, cast from a model by Anton van Wouw, signed and dated 1907 and inscribed G. Nisini-fuse Roma, early 20thC, 12½ in (31 cm). **$14,000-17,000**

A pair of bronze busts of Vespasian and Vitellus, early 19thC, 11 in (27.5 cm). **$2,500-3,500**

A bronze model of a Medici lion, after the antique, 19thC, 19 in (47.5 cm). **$1,300-1,700**

A pair of bronze figures of Chinese geese, weathered green outdoor patination, late 19th/early 20thC. **$2,500-3,500**

An animalier bronze of a bull, of rich brown patination and crisp detail, by Isidore Bonheur, signed by the artist and stamped PEYROL, mid-XIXC, 15½ in (39 cm). **$5,500-7,000**

See Les Animaliers – Jane Horsewell where it is described as rare. The plaster model was shown at the Salon of 1865 and the bronze ordered for the Sultans Palace, Constantinople.

A French bronze model of a stag cast from a model by Christopher Fratin, 19thC, 14 in (35 cm). **$800-1,200**

A pair of Regency bronze models of sphinxes, on rectangular plinths, 8½ in (22 cm). **$4,000-5,000**

A French bronze group of a pointer and a setter approaching a partridge, cast from a model by Pierre Jules Mene, signed, 19thC, 16½ in (41.5 cm). **$1,500-2,200**

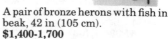

A pair of bronze herons with fish in beak, 42 in (105 cm). **$1,400-1,700**

557

A pair of large bronze Marly horses, after Coustou, 23½ in (60 cm). **$2,000-3,000**

A large bronze Marly horse, after Coustou, brown patination, 22 in (56 cm). **$800-1,200**

A bronze group of terriers, rich brown patination, Pierre Jules Mene, signed P.J. Mene, 8 in (20 cm). **$1,500-2,200**

A French bronze group of two antelopes, cast from a model by Pierre Jules Mene, signed and dated P.-J. Mene 1859, 19thC, 11 in (27 cm). **$4,000-5,000**

A bronze figure of a greyhound, cast from a model by P.J. Mene, 11 in (27.5 cm). **$800-1,200**

A bronze figure of a saddled hunter, 16 in (40 cm). **$2,000-3,000**

A bronze figure of a running elephant, rich dark brown/green patination, by Antoine Louis Barye, signed Barye, c1835, 5½ in (14 cm). **$2,500-3,500**

A bronze figure of a prowling jaguar, by Thomas Francois Cartier, 10in (25 cm). **$800-1,200**

A bronze figure of a lion, rubbed gilt patination, South German, inscribed Leggitime Certanibus late 17thC, 9½ in (24 cm). **$2,000-3,000**

A pair of bronze figures of centaurs, after the antique, on rouge marble bases, 19thC, 8 in (20 cm). **$800-1,200**

A French bronze mortar, 17thC, 4 in (9.6 cm). **$300-400**

A Tuscan bronze mortar, 16thC 4½ in (11.4 cm). **$400-600**

An Italian bronze mortar, 16thC, 7 in (17.3 cm). **$1,000-1,400**

A Flemish mortar, the neck inscribed Nicolavs Boel Me Fieri Fecit Anno 1630, chip to rim, 17thC, 7½ in (19 cm). **$1,300-1,700**

A bronze mortar, Spanish, 15th/16thC, 4 in (10 cm). **$400-600**

A German bronze mortar, 15thC, 7½ in (19 cm). **$2,500-3,500**

A French bronze relief of a Louis XIV General in armour, set within large marblised wooden panelling, inscribed Girardon, 29 in (72 cm). **$2,500-3,500**

A bronze relief panel, by Isidore Bonheur after Rosa Bonheur, 64½ in (164 cm). **$1,500-2,200**

A bronze relief panel, depicting horses, by Isidore Bonheur, after Rosa Bonheur, 64½ in (164 cm). **$4,000-5,000**

A set of twelve bronze bell weights, ranging in size from 56lb to 10 oz, the 56lb Avoir engraved Royal Hospital Greenwich 1826 and Maynott Maker, London. **$2,000-3,000**

A set of five graduated bronze weights, each inscribed County of Meath, Navan Division and dated 1835, 12 to 5½ in (31 to 14 cm). **$1,000-1,400**

An Italian bronze hand bell, the original handle replaced with a Flemish (?) latten figure of Flora, the bell with traces of black lacquer, 16thC, the handle perhaps later, 6 in (15 cm). **$400-600**

A rare Naval bronze picture medal, English, in leather bound case, by T. Webb, opening to twelve coloured aquatints published by Edward Orme, c1820, 3in (7.5 cm). **$1,000-1,400**

A pair of continental bronze ewers, after Clodion, with satyrs seated on the shoulders holding rams horns, 19thC, 17 in (42.5 cm). **$1,000-1,200**

A Venetian bronze inkwell, on 2 colour marble base, perhaps associated, lacking a wing, 15th/16thC, 6 in (15 cm). **$400-600**

A pair of French bronze candelabra, in the form of bear cubs chasing monkeys up trees, cast from models by Christophe Fratin, marble bases, 19thC, 25 in (62 cm). **$4,000-5,000**

A classical bronze ornamental urn, 31 in (77.5 cm). **$500-700**

Three Italian oval bronze medallions of the Roman Emperors, Vitellius, Servius Galba and Domitius VI, 16thC, 4 in (10.5 cm). **$400-600**

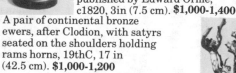

A French gilt bronze oval jardinière, 19thC, 26½ in by 17 in (66 by 42.5 cm). **$2,500-3,500**

A pair of Louis XV style gilt bronze figural chenets, each with a putto holding stalks of grain and seated on a rocaille base, 15 in (37.5 cm). **$700-1,000**

Copper

A pair of brass andirons, with an elaborately-turned standard over an openwork base, with faceted finials, on ball feet, with similar logstop, American, c1830, 22½in (56cm) high. **$500-800**

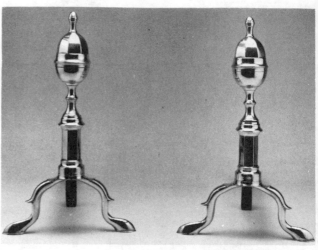

A pair of brass andirons, with acorn terminus above an octagonal faceted turning over a turned stem, above a hexagonal standard, on spurred arched legs with shod slipper feet, with wrought iron logstops and billet bar, American, 1800-1810, 18½in (46cm) high. **$1,800-2,000**

A pair of brass andirons, stamped 'W. HOLMES FOUNDER BOSTON', with 2 ring-turned columns joined by 2 U-shaped horizontal bards and surmounted with a banded ball finial, by W. Holmes, Boston, early 19thC, 10¼in (26cm) high. **$1,500-1,800**

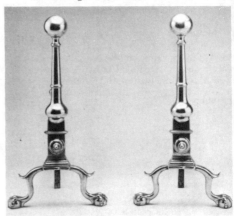

A fine pair of brass andirons, with ball finial above ringed tapering columnar shafts continuing to a ball turning over a plinth with bull's-eye boss, on spurred arched legs with ball and claw feet, the billet bars with conforming log stops, Rhode Island, 1750-1780, 21in (52.5cm) high. **$6,500-7,500**

A pair of brass andirons, the ball finial with a faceted midband on a narrow stem over a hexagonal molding and two ball turnings, on a hexagonal footrim, with curving brass rail and brass logstops, with a wrought iron billet bar, Boston, 1810-1830, 13½in (33.5cm) high. **$800-1,200**

A pair of brass andirons and fire tools, with elaborately turned standards and turned finials, on arched spurred legs on ball feet, the tools comprising: shovel and pair of tongs, with elaborately turned finials, American, early 19thC, 16in (40cm) high. **$400-500**

A copper-applied centerpiece bowl, circular, the flaring sides hammer-faceted and applied with cast silver and copper berries and fruit and two silver-and-copper flies, the domed circular footrim repousse and chased with ferns and foliage and with traces of parcel-gilding; the bowl interior also with traces of gilding, the bottom with an engraved inscription and date '1882', marked on bottom, by Whiting Manufacturing Company, Newark, New Jersey, c1882, 4½in (11cm) high, gross weight 33oz. **$2,000-2,500**

A copper tea kettle, with a strap handle over an ovoid body, a stepped domed cover with turned brass finial and a serpentine spout, early 19thC, 11in (27.5cm) high. **$200-250**

A copper and steel Apothecaries shop sign in the form of a pestle and mortar with 2 red bullseye lenses for illuminating lamp, the cover with chimney vent. **$400-600**

A copper tea kettle, the stepped dome cover with acorn finial over a cylindrical body, with tubular handle and serpentine spout, early 19thC, 13in (32.5cm) high. **$250-300**

Iron and steel

A pair of silver-plated and iron andirons and matching tongs, poker, shovel, broom and stand, each with urn finial above a square tapering support with neo-classical motifs over pierced galleries on similar urn-turned and tapering feet, 25½in (63.5cm) high. **$600-800**

A copper tea kettle, with arched tubular handle above a tapering cylindrical body, domed cover with an acorn finial and a serpentine spout, stamped on underside of cover, by Morris Cohen & Co., Liverpool, 11in (27.5cm) high: together with a nest of six copper and brass pans, Schatz & Bolander, Birmingham, bears stamp on side of body. **$250-300**

A set of 3 cast-iron escutcheons for letter slots, rectangular with scrolled ends, 2 with hinged doors cast LETTERS, each impressed Y & T, designed by Burnham and Root, executed by the Yale and Towne Manufacturing Co. for the Reliance Building, Chicago, c1895, 8in (20cm) long. **$200-250**

Two pairs of escutcheon plates and doorknobs, rectangular, cast with scrolled ends, one cast with RELIANCE; the scalloped doorknobs cast with radiating curved lines, plates cast Y & T 401½, designed by Burnham and Root, executed by the Yale and Towne Manufacturing Co. for the Reliance Building, Chicago, c1895, 10in (25cm) long, with shafts. **$800-1,000**

A cast iron tilting kettle, with a bail handle over a tapering cylindrical body, a stepped domed cover and strap tilter with serpentine spout, 8in (20cm) high. **$200-250**

A cast iron exterior stair baluster, consisting of 2 horizontal bars, with an ornate frieze of stylised leaves and whiplash, connected by 6 railings with upper and lower scrolled shields cast with leaves and whiplash and 3 central rectangular shields cast in an openwork geometric motif, unsigned, designed by Louis H. Sullivan, probably executed by the Yale and Towne Manufacturing Co., for the Guaranty, Buffalo, New York, 1894-1895, 34½in (86cm) high. **$2,500-3,500**

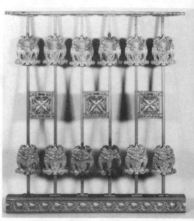

A wrought and cast iron strongbox, early 17thC, 12 in (30 cm). **$1,000-1,200**

A wrought iron strongbox, the iron sheets riveted to a wooden (?) core and reinforced by wrought iron straps, 2 hinges and a hasp, 2 ring handles, late 16th/early 17thC. **$2,000-3,000**

A rare French iron Masterpiece lock, at each side 2 grilles pierced with scrolls, one opening to reveal 2 locking and 1 free bolt, on the reverse the barrel fixed by a turned boss with pierced scalloped edge, the key with fine-toothed bit of triangular section, the bow cast with scrolls, 18thC, 6 by 3 in (15.7 by 7.9 cm). **$4,000-5,000**

An iron Armada chest, mid-17thC, 31½ in (80 cm). **$800-1,200**

A pair of large iron fire-spit dogs, with later log rests, mid-17thC, 25½ in (75 cm). **$1,500-2,200**

A cast iron fire-back, centred by a Tudor rose beneath a bishop's mitre, supported by a lion and a dragon and the initials T K, dated 1571. **$2,000-3,000**

A black painted iron and leather watchman's lantern, the conical top with brass studs, with sliding cylindrical body and carrying handle, early 17thC, 12 in (30.5 cm). **$800-1,200**

This lantern is very similar to that in the Tradescant Room, Ashmolean Museum, which belonged to Guy Fawkes.

A set of twelve octagonal pewter plates, with multiple reeded rims, each engraved with the arms of the Christie Miller family of Dorset, touch marks of the maker Thomas Chamberlain, 1 silvered, 18thC, 9½ in (24 cm). **$4,000-5,000**

A mid-Georgian steel trivet, mid-18thC, 13½ in (34 cm). **$400-600**

A cast-iron group of a boar being attacked by dogs, black patination, Russian, by Pierre Jules Mene, the base signed and dated P.J. Mene, 1846, the underside with cyrillic stamps dated 1895, 10 in (26 cm). **$600-700**

Pewter

A pewter barbers bowl, probably continental, 18thC, 11 in (28 cm). **$300-500**

A very fine and important decorated Charles II broad rimmed pewter charger, the broad rim finely engraved with continuous scenes of the hunt, maker's touch WB with a trotting horse, No. 66 London Touch Plate and Cotterell No. 5485, stamped on reverse, 1660-1665, (71.5 cm). **£33,000-35,000**   *P*

This appears to be the fifth largest recorded English pewter Charger aside from those understood to belong to the Royal Family and located at Glamis Castle, and may well be the largest decorated example in existence. For further information on large chargers see articles by Ian Robinson in the Journal of the Pewter Society (vol. 1, no. 1, Spring 1977, and vol. 4, no. 2, Autumn 1983).

A pewter bleeding bowl, English indistinctly stamped Down London, 19thC, 5½ in (14 cm). **$600-700**

A cylindrical tapering glockenkanne, Swiss, 18th/19thC, 11½ in (29 cm). **$600-700**

A cylindrical tankard, the cover with ureteur, relief medallion, knob thumbpiece, scroll handle, on spreading circular base, Swiss, 18thC, 9 in (22 cm). **$500-600**

A fine tapering flagon, the hinged cover with knob finial and scroll thumbpiece, double scroll handle, on spreading circular base, English, late 18thC, 13½ in (34 cm). **$700-900**

A circular tobacco box, with relief medallion of a gentleman smoking a pipe, 18thC, 6 in (15.5 cm). **$300-400**

A baluster shaped wine flagon with spout, plain thumbpiece to the circular cover, plain handle, Dutch or Flemish, 18th/19thC. 10 in (24 cm). **$600-700**

A baluster shaped wine flagon, with touchmark of Godefriedus Luyben, Dutch or Flemish, 18th/19thC, 9 in (22 cm). **$300-500**

Three French pewter culinary moulds, each hinged, including an elephant and 2 roosters, 9 in (23 cm) each bearing Fabrique stamps, late 19thC. **$600-700**

A large pear shaped coffee urn, with 3 brass taps, bearing touchmarks of G. Hendriks, Alkmaar, Dutch, 19thC, 21 in (54 cm). **$1,400-1,700**

Lead

A pair of lead two-handled garden urns, 22 in (55 cm).
$2,500-3,500

An English lead statue of Mercury, after Giambologna, some repairs, late 18thC. 68 in (172 cm). **$6,000-8,000**

A pair of lead garden figures **$1,000-1,200**

A lead garden figure of a young child, inscribed A.R., 47 in (117.5 cm). **$400-600**

Firemarks

Wiltshire and Western Assurance Society later Salamander Fire Office, lead, raised salamander, enveloped by smoke and flames on oval with beaded border, ribbon above, policy no. 758 impressed on panels below, traces of original gilding, 806/26A, G to E. **$1,400-1,700**

Misc

A pair of green Japanned Pontypool chestnut urns, 12 in (31 cm). **$1,400-1,700**

Bath Fire Office, lead, arms of the City of Bath on a shield, with scrolled border, policy no. 3305 on panel below, 639/11Ai, E. **$1,200-1,500**

Phoenix Assurance Company, Coade stone, rectangular, phoenix rising from flames and 'Protection' raised in concave oval, 'Rebuilt' raised above, '1794' raised below all within border, chip to bottom right corner, 23E, E. **$1,700-2,500**

A pair of black and gold Japanned Pontypool chestnut urns, decorated with chinoiserie landscapes, 12½ in (32 cm). **$2,500-3,500**

A Regency tole ware coal scuttle, decorated with gilt flowers, insects and foliage on rouge ground, 18½ in (46 cm). **$1,200-1,500**

A red and gilt Pontypool coal scuttle, on wheels in form of seashell with porcelain handle, early 19thC. **$1,000-1,200**

London Assurance, lead, seated figure of Britannia with shield, spear and harp, policy no. 8163 on panel below, with incurved top corners, overpainted, 9D, E. **$1,500-2,200**

A good pair of metal campana shaped gardens urns, 24½ in (61 cm). **$600-700**

A large polished steel and brass fire basket, early 20thC, 34 by 48 in (86 by 122 cm). **$1,000-1,200**

A moulded zinc and sheet iron rooster weathervane, late 19thC, 35 in (77.5 cm) long. **$2,000-3,000**

A Louis XV style gilt metal fender, stamped G.G. 53 in (132 cm). **$600-700**

A Japanned tin plate warmer, decorated with gilt foliate scrolls on a red ground, early 19thC, 16 by 27 in (41 by 69 cm). **$2,000-3,000**

A Russian metal figure, c1860, 16 in (40 cm). **$700-1,000**

A lacquered leather fire helmet with gilt metal lion comb, inscribed West of England, 19thC. **$400-600**

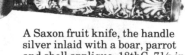

A Saxon fruit knife, the handle silver inlaid with a boar, parrot and shell applique, 18thC, 7½ in (19 cm). **$100-200**

Ivory

A pair of French carved ivory triptych figures, both with a replacement octagonal sectioned wooden base, 8 in (20 cm). **$1,000-1,200**

An ivory carving of Ceres, a sheaf of corn at her sandalled feet, a swatch of hair trailing about her naked breast, 17th/18thC, 7½ in (19 cm). **$700-1,000**

A German carved ivory cup and cover, 19thC, 13½ in (34 cm). **$2,500-3,500**

A pair of carved ivory figures, each showing a 17thC gentleman, the bases veneered in ebony, 19thC, 10½ in (26 cm). **$1,000-1,200**

A continental carved ivory handled knife and fork, the steel knife blade stamped with cutler's mark HOW, 17th/18thC, 7½ and 10 in (19 and 25 cm). **$1,500-2,200**

A French troubadour style bone and ivory coffer, veneered on a pine carcase, early 19thC, 19½ in (48.5 cm). **$3,000-4,500**

A French ivory triptych, depicting Joan of Arc, 19thC, 7 in (17.5 cm). **$1,000-1,200**

A Dieppe carved bone wall mirror, 33½ in (84 cm). **$700-1,000**

A carved ivory hunting horn, bearing the initials GIR and the date 1695, the parcel gilt mounts 19thC with indistinct hallmarks, the whole probably 19thC, 15 in (37 cm). **$1,700-2,500**

An oval ivory portrait medallion, in glazed and gilt frame, by Jean Mancel, inscribed Elius Landey, Aetatis XXXIII a Barcelona, signed I.M.F. 1710, 4 in (9.5 cm). **$1,700-2,500**

A well scrimshawed and polychromed whales tooth, entitled, Recovery off the Falkland Islands, Dec 22nd 1835, and initialed W.N., the reverse scrimshawed with a number of ships attacking a shore battery entitled, An Action, 8 in (20 cm). **$2,500-3,500**

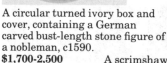

A circular turned ivory box and cover, containing a German carved bust-length stone figure of a nobleman, c1590. **$1,700-2,500**

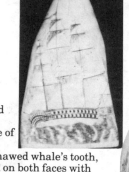

A scrimshawed whale's tooth, decorated on both faces with portrait of a man-of-war, mid 19thC, 7 in (18 cm). **$1,400-1,700**

A pair of scrimshawed walrus tusks, decorated and polychromed with line and dot portraits of Queen Victoria, Prince Albert and allegorical group and 3 other portraits, now mounted on late wooden base as a gong support, English, mid 19thC, 19 in (48 cm). **$1,700-2,500**

A pair of polychromed and scrimshawed whales teeth, decorated by J. Robinson and portraying 2 whalers, one entitled Whaling Barge Lindseys of 'Sydney Leaving the Heads on a Cruise 1845', 6½ in (16.5 cm). **$1,400-1,700**

A large prisoner-of-war bone model of a 84-gun-third-class-ship-of-the-line, 43 in (107 cm) long. **$18,000-24,000**

A Napoleonic prisoner-of-war bone model of the Lapheniz (?). **$2,000-3,000**

A bone prisoner-of-war ship model, of a 90 gun ship-of-the-line, carved polychrome figurehead, standing on a straw work plinth, now in a later glazed case, 9 in (22 cm) long. **$5,500-7,000**

A prisoner-of-war bone model of a three-masted ship, supporting wooden stand, early 19thC, 28½ by 24 in (71 by 60 cm). **$1,700-2,500**

A prisoner-of-war bone model of a guillotine, with sliding guillotine blade, prisoner with detachable head, some pieces missing, early 19thC, 9½ in (24 cm). **$600-900**

An Anglo Indian bone carving, of a traditional North Indian Fort/Residence, some slight damage, 19thC, 10 in (25 cm). **$1,000-1,400**

Marble

An English marble bust of Flora/Diana, by Henry Garland, 19thC, 22 in (55.5 cm). **$1,400-1,700**

A North European marble head of John the Baptist, probably French, 15thC, 11 in (27.5 cm). **$1,700-2,500**

A white carrara marble bust, by J.C. Lough, 19thC, 27 in (67.5 cm). **$600-900**

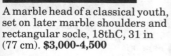

A marble head of a classical youth, set on later marble shoulders and rectangular socle, 18thC, 31 in (77 cm). **$3,000-4,500**

An Italian marble statue of Mercury Lulling Argus, after Thorwaldsen, parcel gilt wood pedestal, feather on petasus restored, 19thC, 40½ in (101 cm). **$5,500-7,000**

Meerschaum

A rare Austro Hungarian portrait meerschaum cheroot holder, carved in full relief with 'La Famille Elbin', in contemporary fitted case, c1875, 8 in (20.8 cm). **$600-700**

A rare Austro Hungarian portrait meerschaum cheroot holder, with amber stem, carved in full relief with 'La Famille Elbin', in contemporary fitted case, c1875, 8 in (20.8 cm). **$1,000-1,200**

The Elbin Family of acrobats, the subject of the group on this interesting pipe, was formed by Jim Elbin whose real name was Thomas E. Pritchard. Elbin was born in Birmingham where he trained as a silversmith before commencing his gymnastic activities in the 1860's or early '70's. The troupe travelled successfully all over Europe during the 1870's and early '80's, appearing at many theatres and also privately before such as the Tzar of Russia. He retired as an acrobat, probably before 1890, and settled in Worcester where he kept the Falcon, a public house in Broad Street.

A marble bust, c1800, 20 in
(50 cm). **$1,000-1,200**

A Scottish marble bust of Sir John
Rennie, the sculptor's cousin, by
George Rennie, with drapery over
his left shoulder, signed and dated
on the reverse G.Rennie Sculptor
1831 and inscribed Sir John
Rennie, on a turned marble socle,
29 in (73 cm). **$1,400-1,700**

*Sir John Rennie (1794-1874)
succeeded his father John Rennie
as a civil engineer and was
knighted in 1831 for supervising
the construction of London Bridge,
a rare distinction for a civil
engineer at that time. The bust
must have been commissioned to
record this honour.*

*As well as being a sculptor, George
Rennie (1802-60) was active as a
politician and served as Governor
of the Falkland Islands from
1841-1855.*

A pair of French marble statuettes
of dancing bacchanti, slightly
weathered, one arm missing, by P.
Charlier, 19thC, 34½ in
(86.5 cm).**$1,000-1,400**

A Carrara marble statue of Venus,
signed L. MacDonald fecit, Roma
1837, 55 in (140 cm) high
excluding plinth.
$16,500-22,500

A white marble figure of a lady,
signed Flamand, 32½ in (81 cm).
$1,000-1,400

A marble bust of a lady fawn, 23 in
(57.5 cm). **$600-900**

A fawn and grey flecked marble
bust, depicting a girl in mob cap,
signed Pugi, 18½ in (46 cm).
$600-700

An Italian marble bust of Dante,
19thC, 22 in (55.5 cm).
$500-600

A pair of marble urns and covers,
applied with gilt bronze
decoration, by Susse Freres,
stamped on the lid Susse Fres,
19thC, 9½ in (24 cm).
$1,000-1,200

An Italian white marble bust, on
pedestal, signed Lombardi, Roma
1878, late 19thC, 69 in (175 cm)
overall. **$3,000-4,500**

A Regency marble bath, discoloured surface, 24 by 60 by 29 in (60 by 150 by 73 cm). **$3,000-4,500**

An early Georgian Breccia marble cistern, the mid-Georgian walnut stand with frieze centred by lion masks on splayed cabriole legs headed by shells and foliage ending in paw feet, 24 in (61 cm). **$14,000-17,000**

A pair of ormolu and siena marble columns, 68½ in (174 cm). **$4,000-5,000**

A pair of imitation porphry columns, on a plaster socle, c1820, each 12 in (30 cm). **$1,500-2,200**

A George III blue-john vase, with red, purple and honey coloured markings, c1800, 16 in (40 cm). **$3,000-4,500**

An Italian porphry bust of a Roman Emperor after Tadda, on later serpentine torso and socle, chipped, 16thC, 15 in (37.5 cm). **$1,000-1,200**

A blue-john urn and cover, colour varying from amethyst to honey and on stepped marble base, early 19thC, 12 in (30 cm). **$1,200-1,500**

A Nottingham alabaster figure of an Apostle, possibly St. Jude, an oar damaged, supported with his left hand, polychrome, 14thC, 17 in (43 cm). **$6,000-8,500**

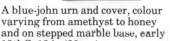

Terracotta

Two terracotta busts of George Washington and Benjamin Franklin, Franklin wearing a waistcoat and overcoat; Washington dressed in Roman garb, both truncated at shoulders, in squared moulded bases, after Houdon, both 25in (62.5cm) high including base. **$700-1,000**

A French terracotta statuette of Cupid with a dove, toe, finger and ends of bow missing, wing repaired with glue, some hairline cracks, late 18thC, 15½ in (39 cm). **$4,000-5,000**

A terracotta group of Venus and Cupid, signed L. Tinant, 14 in (36 cm). **$500-600**

A French terracotta chinoiserie group an Oriental family, gilt wood plinth, by Josse Francois Joseph Leriche, f.ᶜᶜ 1785, mirror in her left hand and tip of his hat and lock of child's hair repaired, finger missing, 14 by 20 in (35.5 by 50 cm). **$14,000-17,000**

Leriche worked from 1757 for the Manufacture of Sevres where he was in charge of the sculpture workshop. Most of his other known works are in biscuit.

Two terracotta garden urns. **$1,000-1,200**

Plaster

A plaster portrait bust of The Hon. Mrs. Maryanna Marten, by Augustus John, 24 in (60 cm). **$1,700-2,500**

A painted terracotta bust of a Nubian lady, after Goldscheider early 20thC, 26 in (65 cm). **$1,000-1,200**

A white glazed terracotta urn early 19thC, 15½ in (39.5 cm **$1,000-1,200**

A French terracotta bust of a bacchante, in the manner of Marin, minor chips, greyish marble socle, 19thC, 25 in (62 cm). **$3,000-4,500**

A set of four matching Regency composition stone basket weave garden urns, some cracks and slight damage, 19½ in (49 cm). **$1,700-2,500**

A fine carved and painted figure of a rooster, carved in the round perched on a domed base, painted yellow with black and red trim, by Wilhelm Schimmel, Cumberland Valley, Pennsylvania, mid-19thC, 5in (12.5cm) high. **$900-1,200**

A French terracotta bust of a young girl, after Caffieri, inscribed J.J. Caffieri 1773, Paris, on a turned marble socle, late 19thC, 27 in (67.5 cm). **$1,500-2,200**

Wood carvings

An Austrian Gothic wood group, of the Virgin and Child, much original colour and gilding, first quarter 15thC, 47½ in (120 cm). **$9,000-13,000**

A large carved pine figure of th Mourning Virgin, probably Spanish, 15thC, 72 in (183 cm) **$4,000-5,000**

A carved and painted wood ship's figurehead, the three-quarters length figure carved in the shape of a maiden with long flowing red hair and with two removable arms, one holding up a wreath of polychrome-painted flowers and wearing a grey-painted dress encircled at the hips by a carved band of flowers and fruits, on a stylised gilt gadrooned base, late 19thC, 35in (87.5cm) wide. **$2,000-4,000**

A carved and painted wood ship's figurehead, the three-quarter length figure carved in the form of a Canadian or English army corporal, wearing a black-painted beret and red jacket with gilt trim and holding a rolled paper in his left hand, on a stylised base, restoration to paint, 18½in (46cm) wide. **$1,000-1,200**

A carved and painted wood ship's figurehead, the three-quarter length figure carved in the shape of a maiden with blond hair, wearing a green-painted dress, over a scrolled base, parts repainted, late 19thC, 16in (40cm) wide. **$1,200-1,500**

A carved pine ship's figurehead, formed as a woman, with late white paint, 18thC, 19in (47.5cm) high. **$1,000-1,500**

A carved and painted cigar store Indian princess, the full length figure with a plumed headdress centering a star and wearing a fringed shawl and dress, the right hand pressing 2 cigar boxes to her chest, on a chamfered rectangular base, late 19thC, 59½in (148.5cm) high. **$4,500-5,500**

A carved and painted wood cigar store Indian princess, the full length figure with a feather headdress and wearing a fringed shawl dress and pants and holding a group of cigars in her raised right hand, on a brown-painted square tapering base inscribed on the front CIGARS, old repainting on headdress, late 19thC, 68in (170cm) high. **$5,000-7,000**

A carved and painted cigar store Indian queen, with plumed headdress and long fringed gown with a feathered belt and red mantle, holding a bunch of cigars in her right hand,, on a green and black-painted plaster of paris rectangular base, restoration to paint, late 19thC, 77in (195cm) high. **$2,000-3,000**

A carved and painted cigar store figure of a Scotsman, the elaborately carved full-length figure wearing traditional Scottish costume of kilt, epaulettes, plaid hat and socks with bow-tied shoes and holding a pipe in his left hand, on a rectangular base, restorations to paint, American, late 19thC, 67½in (168.5cm) high. **$2,000-3,000**

A rare carved and painted pine standing lion, the full bodied figure with black and yellow groove carved mane, red/orange ears, nose and mouth, the tail wrapped around a smooth rear torso, on a green rectangular ground mound, by Wilhelm Schimmel, Cumberland Valley, Pennsylvania, 1865-1890, 9in (22.5cm) long. **$10,000-12,000**

The few Schimmel lions known each have a tail which reaches over the body to the head. This example, with a tail that twists around the body, is extremely rare.

A pair of carved wood gilt and polychrome statuettes, crowns detachable, slight damage and slight restoration only, Spanish, 17thC, 10 in (26 cm). **$700-900**

A carved wood figure of one of the Fates, probably South German, 17th/18thC, 27 in (67 cm). **$500-600**

A French walnut wood carving, mounted on a later stained oak stand, 18thC, 39½ in (100 cm). **$3,000-4,500**

A continental carved wood figure of a youth, 19thC, 68 in (172 cm). **$3,000-4,500**

A pair of carved pine female figures in the style of Clodion, 63½ in (162 cm). **$6,000-8,000**

A pair of carved limewood putti, 40 and 32 in (100 and 80 cm). **$1,400-1,700**

A pair of Italian gilt wood herms of youths, on tapered marbled wood pedestals, fingers damaged, 18thC, 45 in (112 cm). **$4,500-7,000**

A carved wood sandpiper, East Coast States, 20thC, 15 in (37.5 cm). **$1,000-1,200**

A rare walnut frame, containing a plaster relief plaque of the Virgin and Child after Rossellino, 17thC, 29 in (72.5 cm). **$700-900**

CHRONOLOGICAL TABLE FOR THE NEAR EAST

Pottery Neolithic	6th and 5th millennium B.C.
Chalcolithic Period	4th millennium B.C.
The Early Bronze Age	3100-2200 B.C.
The Middle Bronze Age	2200-1550 B.C.
The Late Bronze Age	1550-1200 B.C.
The Iron Age	1200-586 B.C.
The Persian Period	586-332 B.C.
The Hellenistic Period	332-30 B.C.
The Roman Period	30 B.C.-450 A.D.

Antiquities

An Attic black figure amphora, decorated with a warrior with shield and spear, reserved on an overall black ground, restored, 16½ in (41 cm). **$7,500-10,500**

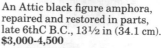

An East Greek black figure neck amphora, mid-6thC B.C, 10 in (25 cm). **$1,500-2,200**

An Attic black figure amphora, second half of 6thC B.C., 11 in (28 cm). **$1,500-2,200**

An Attic black figure amphora, repaired and restored in parts, late 6thC B.C., 13½ in (34.1 cm). **$3,000-4,500**

A green glazed frit ushabti, with nine rows of hieroglyphs, Dynasty XXVI, 7 in (17.5 cm) high. **$600-800**

An Attic red figure oinochoe, 5thC B.C, 7½ in (17.5 cm) high. **$300-500**

A Corinthian aryballos, painted on the buff coloured body with 2 harpies in brown and purple, 3rdC B.C, 2½ in (6.5 cm). **$300-500**

An aryballos, the body with degraded green glaze, 3 in (7 cm). **$500-600**

An Attic black figure hydria, repaired with minor restoration, c500 B.C, 13½ in (34.3 cm). **$7,500-10,500**

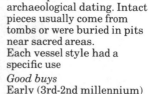

A Tanagra terracotta figure of a draped female, c3rd/2ndC B.C, 11 in (27.5 cm). **$1,000-1,200**

An Attic little master lip cup, late 6thC B.C, 5 in (13 cm). **$3,000-4,500**

A Carthaginian limestone figure of a lion, 6th-5thC B.C., 7½ in (19 cm). **$1,000-1,200**

A red figure squat lekythos, running dog above meander line, early 4thC B.C, 4 in (9.5 cm). **$400-600**

A Greek black glazed askos, Athens, c425 B.C., 5 in (12 cm). **$300-400**

Pottery

Most important artifacts for archaeological dating. Intact pieces usually come from tombs or were buried in pits near sacred areas.
Each vessel style had a specific use

Good buys
Early (3rd-2nd millennium) undecorated pottery was made in beautiful shapes and is very much undervalued. It is well documented and small pieces are still inexpensive. Read: "Archaeology of the Holy Land" by Katherine Kenyon. "Ancient pottery of the Holy Land" by Ruth Amiran.

Watch out for:
Repairs: dip the piece in water – any repairs will show up another colour.
Cleaning: It is dangerous to try and clean pottery without experience. It may be friable. If you use hydrochloric acid, it is difficult to remove from the fabric of the pottery.

Metalware

A Roman bronze of a nude dancing female figure, 3rd/4thC A.D, 3 in (7.5 cm). **$300-400**

A South Italian black glazed Janus-headed flask, early 4thC B.C, 8 in (19.7 cm). **$1,700-2,500**

A Tarentine terracotta figure of a dancing female, left arm missing, neck and hem repaired, 4thC B.C, 10 in (26 cm). **$600-900**

An Egyptian bronze figure of the Moon God, Ptolemaic Period, 5½ in (14 cm). **$600-900**

A Syrian terracotta altar, early 1st Millennium B.C, 7 in (17.8 cm). **$1,500-2,200**

An Etruscan bronze mirror, mounted in modern ivory handle, last quarter of the 4thC B.C, 6 in (16 cm). **$1,000-1,200**

A bronze figure of Harpocrates, wearing an ib heart amulet, Late Period, 4 in (10.3 cm). **$500-700**

An Alexandrian terracotta figure of Harpocrates squatting, 3rd/1stC B.C, 6.3 in high. **$300-400**

A Luristan bronze pendant in the form of a double headed foal, 8th/7thC B.C, 3½ in (9 cm). **$500-700**

A bronze figure of Venus and Cupid, Graeco-Roman, from Egypt, 7 in (18 cm). **$7,500-10,500**

An erotic bronze figure in the form of a lamp, comprising a reclining naked man with enlarged phallus, Graeco-Roman, from Egypt, 4 in (8.3 cm). **$1,700-2,500**

A bronze bust of a young man, fragmentary, Roman, probably from Egypt, 4¼ in (10 cm) high. **$600-800**

An Egyptian gilded bronze figure of Seth, both hands pierced, left arm repaired, mounted, Late New Kingdom, 7 in (17.2 cm). **$7,500-10,500**

A bronze figure of the goddess Fortuna, Roman, 2½ in (6 cm). **$500-600**

Marble

An archaic bronze stamnos, restored, handles and foot additional, c5thC B.C, 16¼ in (41 cm) high. **$600-900**

A Luristan bronze finial, 9th/8thC B.C, 5½ in (14 cm) high. **$1,000-1,200**

A Roman marble head of Apollo, the eyes with unarticulated pupils, nose and part of lips restored, early 2ndC A.D, 10½ in (26.8 cm). **$4,000-5,000**

A marble sarcophagus relief fragment of Cupid, 3rdC A.D, 14 by 12 in (36 by 30.6 cm). **$3,000-4,500**

A marble head of a man, in the style of the Roman Late Republic, top of head and left side flattened for attachments, 14 in (35 cm) high, a marble head of a woman, in the Roman style, possibly Faustina the Younger, 13½ in (34 cm) high. **$1,000-1,200**

A marble lower torso of a dancing child, modelled with one chubby leg flung back, 13½ in (34 cm). **$500-600**

A Roman marble fluted urn, with a human headed crab medallion carved in relief on one side, 1st/2ndC A.D, 15 in (38 cm). **$6,000-8,000**

A late Hellenistic marble sculpture of Eros with dolphin, c1stC B.C, from Crete, 17 in (43.2 cm). **$15,000-20,500**

An Etruscan marble lower half of a sarcophagus, c3rd/2ndC B.C, 19 in (50 cm). **$1,300-1,700**

A marble relief of a male torso, inscribed with the name of Marcus Aurelius Asclepiades, who has made this gift for Sylvanus, c2ndC A.D, 20 in (50.8 cm) high. **$1,500-2,200**

A Roman marble statuette of Jupiter, the base inscribed to Jupiter, the Best, the Greatest, Septimius Pius, soldier of the Legion XIII Gemina, has placed this ex voto/offering, second half of 2ndC A.D/early 3rdC A.D, 12 in (30.5 cm) high. **$1,700-2,500**

A painted mud plaster fragment, New Kingdom, 11 by 8 in (28 by 20.3 cm). **$2,000-3,000**

A Roman green glass bottle, the surface iridescent, 4th/5th century A.D, 3 in (7.5 cm). **$200-300**

A limestone bas-relief of a seated official, in wooden frame, Dynasty VI, 14 in (35.1 cm) high. **$1,700-2,500**

A good and unusually large Celtic sandstone head, 18½ in (46 cm) high. **$2,000-3,000**

Found in the late '50's as part of a dry stone wall at Fewstone. Formerly in the collection of S. Jackson and illustrated as number 47 in his book 'Celtic and other stone heads'.

A manganese purple mould blown glass Janus-headed flask, 2nd century A.D, 2½ in (6 cm). **$200-300**

A Gesso painted wooden falcon, with green painted lattice decoration on the body, detailed brown facial markings, a lid from a sarcophagus, Late Period Ptolemaic, 9 in (23 cm) long. **$600-900**

Persian Works of Art

A silver and copper inlaid brass bowl, probably Egypt, c1900, 5 in (12 cm). **$600-800**

A Fars brass bowl (tas), with incised decoration, engraved with owner's names, 14thC, 7 in (17.9 cm). **$2,000-3,000**

A Coco-de-mer shell kashkul, dated 1255 A.H, – 1839 A.D, 11 in (27.3 cm). **$600-900**

A Qajar moulded polychrome pottery tile, 11½ in (29.3 cm). **$100-200**

An enamelled centrepiece, in the shape of a mosque, all in indigo, madder, green, ivory and saffron, 16½ in (42 cm) sq. **$700-1,000**

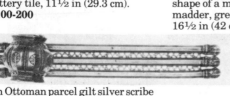

An Ottoman parcel gilt silver scribe set, comprising a pencase and an inkpot, with a tughra mark at the base, 18th-19thC, 8 in (20.7 cm). **$1,200-1,500**

An Indo-Persian steel writing set, 19thC, 8½ in (21.7 cm). **$600-800**

A small silver and copper inlaid brass box, 5 in (13 cm).
$300-500

A Persian underglaze painted pottery cock's head ewer, decorated in black under a turquoise glaze with sketchy scrolls and naturalistic details on the head, 13thC, 10 in (26.1 cm).
$1,700-2,500

A silver and copper inlaid brass jug, of bell shaped form, decorated with inscription cartouches, within strapwork borders and trefoil medallions, probably Egypt, c1900, 8 in (19.5 cm). **$600-800**

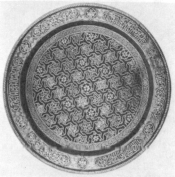

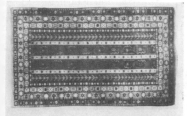

A Qajar lacquer table, 19thC, 24 in (51 cm). **$1,200-1,500**

An Ottoman silver mirror back, 19thC, 10 in (25.2 cm).
$600-800

A silver inlaid brass tray, with a geometric design, probably Egypt, c1900, 15 in (37.4 cm).
$600-800

Rugs & Carpets

A fine Agra rug, with 2 blue panels in the centre, depicting red galloping horses, light brown medallion border, red and camel linked sunburst guards, 82 by 49 in (209 by 125 cm).
$1,400-1,700

An Agra carpet, the light blue field with herati pattern, 164 by 125 in (416 by 312 cm).
$7,500-10,500

An Agra carpet, the burgundy field in a green palmette and vine border between blue and burgundy stripes, areas of corrosion, 137 by 89 in (347 by 226 cm). **$4,000-5,000**

◄

An Antique Bergama rug, with shaded brick-red field, around a large ivory and red gabled stylised floral lozenge medallion, with golden-yellow stylised floral brackets, a short kilim strip at each end, slight overall wear, repaired, 82 by 66 in (208 by 168 cm). **$2,500-3,500**

An antique Bergama rug, with tomato-red field, in a border of hooked stellar panels between ivory and apricot flowering vine stripes, with associated tassels, 70 by 69 in (178 by 175 cm).
$3,500-5,000

►

A large Amritzar carpet, the ivory field with columns of alternate red and blue serrated medallions issuing tendrils, one small repair, 203 by 137 in (516 by 347 cm). **$4,500-7,000**

A fine antique Belouch rug, with royal blue field in a brick red stylised flowering vine border, 60 by 56 in (152 by 142 cm). **$600-900**

A Belouch rug, with ivory field, in a broad burnt-orange border, areas of slight wear, slight damage to sides, 54 by 32 in (137 by 81 cm). **$1,000-1,200**

A fine Beshir Juval, with ox-blood field, in a blue floral border with plain outer stripe containing stylised jewels, 78 by 40 (193 by 102 cm). **$1,300-1,700**

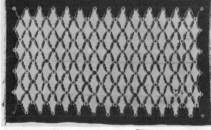

A fine Bessarabian kilim, the ivory field with a blood-red border, 131 by 79 in (330 by 200 cm). **$1,300-1,700**

A fine antique Belouch rug, the camel field with diagonal rows of brick-red and purple floral hexagons, 69 by 38 in (175 by 96.5 cm). **$600-900**

An Antique Bessarabian kilim, with charcoal field, in a raspberry-red border, between ivory serrated flowering vine stripes, areas of slight wear, repaired, 174 by 129 in (442 by 326 cm). **$6,000-8,500**

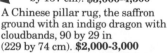

An antique Chinese rug, the beige field with clouds and seed pearls around 9 dragons, 100 by 62 in (253 by 157 cm). **$3,000-4,500**

A Chinese pillar rug, the saffron ground with an indigo dragon with cloudbands, 90 by 29 in (229 by 74 cm). **$2,000-3,000**

An Esfahan prayer rug, the ivory field in a beige border of arabesques, flowerheads and floral ovals, areas of slight wear, 88 by 56 in (224 by 142 cm). **$1,500-2,200**

An Esfahan carpet, the ivory field with an indigo lobed floral medallion, with saffron floral spandrels, with madder border, twin guard stripes, 135 by 87 in (343 by 221 cm). **$15,000-20,500**

A fine antique Chinese carpet, with ivory field in a light blue border between ivory and plain stripes, 140 by 109 in (354 by 276 cm). **$6,000-8,500**

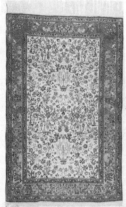

A part silk Esfahan rug, the ivory field in a beige border, with triple light blue floral stripes, 64 by 40 in (163 by 102 cm). **$2,000-3,000**

A part silk Esfahan rug, the ivory field with a pale indigo and ivory lobed medallion and spandrels, with a beige border, 92 by 58 in (234 by 147 cm). **$6,000-8,000**

A Heriz prayer rug, the tan field with blue floral columns supporting a mihrab, in a shaded indigo floral border between multiple tan and ivory floral stripes, 76 by 52 in (193 by 132 cm). **$3,000-4,000**

An antique Heriz carpet, the brick-red field around a stepped ivory medallion, with large floral indigo medallion, in a broad indigo border, with 4 ivory calligraphic panels bearing date AH 1326, areas of slight wear. **$14,000-17,000**

Good Heriz are fetching up to 5 times as much as 4 years ago.

A large Heriz carpet, having a central blue medallion on a red ground, 183 by 225 in (464 by 569 cm). **$19,500-25,500**

Heriz carpets have become increasingly popular over the last 4 years. An uncrowded design, pale madder, pale blue, ivory and saffron all add to the value. Good borders are also important.

A Heriz rug, the brick-red field round a royal blue medallion, in a royal blue border, between golden yellow flowering vine stripes, one tiny hole, 109 by 75 in (276 by 191 cm). **$1,500-2,200**

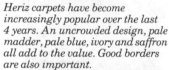

A Heriz carpet, c1870, 158 by 128 in (401 by 325 cm). **$14,000-17,000**

An antique Hila carpet, the indigo field with a central light blue floral medallion and spandrels, in a blood-red border of boteh, areas of slight wear, 151 by 78 in (383 by 198 cm). **$6,000-8,500**

A Gendge runner, a kilim strip at one end, 120 by 42 in (305 by 107 cm). **$1,000-1,400**

Although a strong design runners do not sell well due to the lack of demand for passage floor covering.

A pair of part silk Kashan prayer rugs, with rust-red field, the indigo mihrab with flowering vine and arabesques, in an indigo border, each 83 by 54 in (211 by 137 cm). **$6,000-8,500**

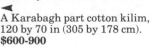

A Gendje rug, the field with 5 madder, ivory and indigo hooked gul medallions, 95 by 40 in (241 by 102 cm). **$2,000-3,000**

A Karabagh part cotton kilim, 120 by 70 in (305 by 178 cm). **$600-900**

A fine Karagashli rug, the shaded indigo field with 3 brick-red floral lozenges, in a mustard-yellow border and outer shaded blue floral lozenge stripe, very slight damage at one end, replaced ends, 57 by 35 in (145 by 89 cm). **$3,000-4,000**

An antique Karabagh prayer rug, with an ice-blue flowering vine border between reciprocal stripes, 62 by 35 in (157 by 89 cm). **$1,400-1,700**

A pair of Kashan rugs, the indigo field of each around a large ivory panel, containing a scalloped burgundy medallion, in an ivory border, each 82 by 57 in (208 by 145 cm). **$5,500-7,000**

A Kashan Mochtasham rug, the royal blue field in a royal blue palmette and boteh vine border, 78 by 53 in (198 by 135 cm). **$3,000-4,000**

Mochtasham (or Mohtasham) was a master weaver in Kashan. Not all the carpets given this name are woven by him but his designs have continued to be used.

A Kashan pictorial rug of prayer design, the mustard mihrab with scenes from the Old Testament story of Joseph, with verses from the Koran and flowers within guard stripes, 93 by 55 in (238 by 140 cm). **$4,500-7,000**

The mihrab (or mehrab) is the arch at the top of the carpet, only appearing in prayer rugs.

An antique Kurk Kashan rug, the rust-red field around a royal blue tracery vine, in a broad indigo palmette between golden yellow flowering vine and reciprocal skittle-pattern stripes, ends and sides slight wear and damage, 81 by 52 in (206 by 132 cm). **$3,000-4,000**

Kurk is the softest wool taken from the chest of the sheep. The products tend to be finely spun and of good weave.

A good Caucasian Kazak runner, with a dark ground medallion central ground and three-banded border, 148 by 66 in (376 by 168 cm). **$1,000-1,400**

A Karatchopf Kazak rug, the tomato-red field around a large chequered panel containing an ivory octagon, in a bottle-green stylised glass and serrated leafy vine border, areas of wear, 85 by 67 in (215 by 170 cm). **$1,500-2,200**

A Kazak double ended prayer rug, with blue field, the red spandrels with hooked diagonal bars, the cream main border with a C-motif, some damage and low in parts, 86 by 58 in (219 by 148 cm). **$500-700**

A fine antique pictorial Kirman rug, with indigo field, 88 by 58 in (224 by 147 cm). **$3,500-5,000**

A fine antique Kuba rug, the indigo field in an indented ivory and beige frame, 63 by 51 in (160 by 130 cm). **$3,000-4,500**

A fine antique Qashqai rug, the brick-red field with herati pattern, with an indigo octagon, in an ivory border with brick-red and blue boteh stripes, 75 by 54 in (191 by 137 cm). **$3,500-5,000**

A silk Qum rug, the salmon pink field around an indented purple medallion, in a royal blue floral border, 81 by 56 in (206 by 142 cm). **$5,500-7,000**

A Samarkand rug, the madder field with 3 slate medallions, an aubergine wave border, 108 by 55 in (274 by 140 cm). **$3,000-4,000**

A Qum fine wool and silk hunting rug, with a floral figured pale brown ground, 82 by 54 in (208 by 137 cm). **$600-800**

A Sarough rug, the black field with a pale indigo shaped medallion containing a madder rosette, madder and indigo spandrels, with a black and madder waved border, 83 by 56 in (211 by 142 cm). **$1,000-1,200**

A Sarouk Central Persia rug, c1890, 82 by 53 in (208 by 135 cm). **$2,000-3,000**

A fine Shirvan rug, the pale blue field scattered with stylised flowerheads and animals around a string of 4 stepped concentric lozenge medallions, in an ivory border with brick-red and blue flowerhead stripes, 124 by 47 in (314 by 119 cm). **$5,500-7,000**
This rug has a well balanced border and good colour.

A Shirvan rug, the indigo field with an ivory hooked vine border between stripes, 67 by 46 in (170 by 117 cm). **$3,000-4,500**

A Shirvan rug, with 6 figured dark blue, red and ivory star shaped medallions on a figured brick-red ground, 2 small repairs, 94 by 53 in (240 by 134 cm). **$1,700-2,500**

► An unusual silk Soumac, the ivory ground with birds and animals in a golden yellow hooked lozenge and stylised animal border between burnt orange stripes, 75 by 53 in (191 by 135 cm). **$5,500-7,000**

A Turkoman carpet, in shades of plum, cream, blue and green, 111 by 63 in (282 by 160 cm). **$1,700-2,500**

581

A Tabriz compartment carpet, all in ivory, saffron and blue, outlined in red and blue, containing palmettes and flowers at intersection, terracotta border with same compartment, with alternate flowerhead, two vine borders, 1930, 103 by 136 in (162 by 346 cm). **$7,000-9,000**

A fine Turkoman Tekke carpet, the brick field with 5 rows of 14 ivory and brick, indigo and red quartered guls, 128 by 86 in (325 by 218 cm). **$1,500-2,200**

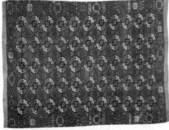

An antique Tekke carpet, the rust-red field with 5 columns of linked Tekke guls, small areas of repair and staining, 114 by 83 in (289 by 211 cm). **$7,000-9,000**

An antique Yomut carpet, the fox-brown field with diagonal rows of kepse guls, 156 by 91 in (396 by 231 cm). **$1,500-2,200**

GLOSSARY

Abrash	Variations of density in a colour seen in a carpet by irregular horizontal washes, can greatly add to the value.
Aniline	Chemical dye, a derivative of coal-tar, first produced in the 1860's, most common in the red-blue-purple range, colours tend to fade (orange-pink, for instance can fade to walnut-brown).
Boteh	Widespread pattern of Persian origin (original meaning 'cluster of leaves'), used in Europe in the Paisley pattern.
Ch'ang	Chinese endless knot, the inextricable knot of destiny.
Chrome dye	A fast synthetic dye now used in all the major rug weaving areas, colours do not fade.
Gol Henai Pattern	Floral pattern associated with Persian rugs, mainly found on Hamadan rugs.
Hejira (or Hijra)	The beginning of the Muhammedan calendar, 16 July, A.D. 622.
Herati Pattern	Also called the mahi or fish pattern. This common pattern originated in East Persia.
Jufti	'False' knot, either Turkish or Persian, whereby the knots are tied to four, not two, warp threads.
Kelim	Also spelled kilim, gilim, gelim. Principally from Anatolia.
Madder	Deep red-brown dye.
Palas	Caucasian name for kelim.
Palmette	A flowerhead of heart-shape with many radiating lobes or petals.
Sileh	A corruption of a now lost Caucasian place name. A form of Soumak, sileh pieces tend to be woven with rows of large S-motifs.
Soumak	Sumak, Summak, Sumacq, Sumakh, thought to be a corruption of Shemaka, town in south east Caucasus.
Spandrels	Architectural term for the space between the curve of an arch and the enclosing mouldings.
Swastika	A hooked cross. Chinese symbol for 10,000 (wan) and happiness.
Tiraz	Official weaving factory usually set up under Royal patronage.

A fine antique Turkoman embroidered tent band, 568 by 9 in (1,431 by 23 cm). **$3,000-4,500** ►

A Tabriz pictorial rug, depicting Napoleon, after a painting by David, within a slate floral border, 46 by 29 in (117 by 74 cm). **$1,400-1,700**

A Tabriz silk carpet, the plain madder field with a pale indigo and rose madder lobed floral medallion and spandrels, 106 by 74 in (269 by 188 cm). **$5,500-7,000**

A Teheran Tree of Life rug, the ivory field with trees, leopards, stags and hares, slight damage, 1930, 57 by 84 in (145 by 215 cm). **$1,400-1,700**

A fine Tekke Turkoman rug, the fox-brown field with 3 columns of linked Tekke guls, 49 by 43 in (124 by 109 cm). **$3,000-4,000**

An antique North-West Persian kilim, the rose-red field with a broad dark blue border, very minor damage, 141 by 74 in (357 by 188 cm). **$1,200-1,500**

MAKE THE MOST OF MILLER'S

The 1986 Miller's has a large section of textiles, embroidery and costume. There has been a tremendous increase in interest, reflected in prices, in early needlework. Hence we have increased the number of illustrations in this section.

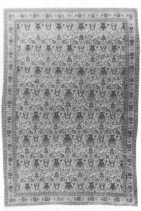

A fine Zelli Sultan rug, the ivory rug with flowering vases with perching birds, 82 by 55 in (208 by 140 cm). **$3,000-4,500**

A fine Central Persian embroidered horse blanket, the royal blue field with rows of boteh, in a butter yellow stylised floral border between similar red and blue stripes, very minor damage to sides, 70 by 53 in (178 by 135 cm). **$2,000-3,000**

Textiles

A Tibetan thanka, depicting a central figure of Guru Rinpoche, wearing blue, red and brown robes and an orange-red hat, some wear, 19thC, 32 by 57 in (80 by 144 cm) overall. **$600-900**

A long sampler of linen, worked in sky blue, lime green and pink and yellow silks, by MH and dated 1650, 20 by 8¼ in (50 by 21 cm), framed and glazed. **$3,000-4,500**

◄

A needlework sampler, by Jane Plowman, 1774, the linen ground embroidered in coloured silks, in eye and cross stitches, designed with the alphabet, a prayer and geometric designs, 17 by 8½ in (42.5 by 21 cm), framed and glazed. **$600-900**

A needlework sampler, by Margaret Liddle Bothell, the linen ground embroidered in coloured silks and wools, worked mainly in cross stitch, early 19thC, 19 by 16 in (48 by 40 cm), framed and glazed. **$600-900**

A needlework sampler, by Ann Maria Dachtler, aged 9 years 1811, worked mainly in pink, blue and brown, in cross and satin stitches, 17 by 12½ in (43 by 30.5 cm), framed and glazed. **$600-800**

A needlework sampler, 'Mary Dunn worked this sampler in the eleventh year of her age, 1724', 21 in (53 cm), in ebonised and gilt frame. **$1,000-1,400**

583

A fine sampler, worked in silk threads on linen, signed Eliza Mary Mason, aged 12 years, 19 in (48 cm) excluding later giltwood frame. **$1,400-1,700**

A needlework sampler, dated 1836, 31 in (77.5 cm). **$1,200-1,500**

A needlework sampler, by Harriot Farrow, aged 12, 1837, worked with numbers, text, flowering plants, animals and birds, 18½ in (46 cm), in walnut veneered frame. **$600-900**

A needlework picture, embroidered in cross, tent and running stitches with coloured wools, worked with initials AM, early 17thC, 8 by 10 in (19.5 by 25.5 cm), framed and glazed. **$600-800**

A needlework sampler, by Hannah Booth, work done in the year 1826, aged 11 years, the linen ground worked with coloured wools in cross and eye stitches, 21½ in by 22 in (53.5 by 55 cm). **$500-600**

A William IV needlework sampler, worked with religious verse and 'Mary Belt, died June the 25th aged 23' and 'Frances Elliot finished this work aged eight years 1833' inside a strawberry border, 24 by 21 in (60 by 53 cm), framed. **$1,500-2,200**

A needlework sampler, by Mary Ann Brooker, aged 10 years, the wool ground worked mainly in brown and green silks, mainly in cross stitch, 17 by 12½ in (43 by 31.5 cm). **$400-600**

A linen worked sampler, by Mary Charlton, aged 15, in 1827, with a practice band and religious inscription, in a contemporary mahogany frame inlaid with boxwood designs, 25 by 20½ in (64 by 52 cm). **$400-600**

A Spanish needlework sampler, by Lucia Izquierdo, Ano de 1837, the linen ground worked in brown and green silks, 15 in (37 cm). **$400-600**

A Charles II embroidery picture, in stumpwork and tentstitch, within a silver filigree wire border, in a later glazed frame, 23 by 18½ in (57 by 46 cm). **$2,000-3,000**

A stumpwork picture, the ivory silk ground embroidered in coloured silks, c1660, 9 by 15 in (23 by 38 cm). **$800-1,200**

◄

A needlework picture, worked in coloured silks and silver thread with some raised work and with some strips of mica and beads for eyes, the grass worked in chenille work, English, mid-17thC, 10 by 14½ in (25 by 36 cm), framed and glazed. **$4,500-7,000**

This was possibly the lid of a casket.

A stumpwork picture, worked with applied blue, green and brown coiled thread and petit point, embroidered mainly in satin stitch with coloured silks, the whole on an ivory silk ground, c1660, 17 by 21 cm (43 by 53 cm). **$2,000-3,000**

A Georgian silk and hairwork landscape picture, within green and gilt coiled paper frame on pearl chip ground, 17 by 14½ in (42 by 36 cm) overall. **$1,200-1,500**

A stumpwork picture, the ivory silk ground embroidered mainly in blue, brown and green silks, worked in needlepoint, satin, French knot and other stitches, late 17thC, 6½ by 9 in (16.5 by 23 cm). **$600-900**

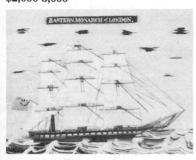

A 'sailor-work' wool picture of the Eastern Monarch of London, 19thC, 14 by 18 in (35 by 45 cm), in maple frame. **$800-1,200**

A needlework panel, embroidered in petit point, early 18thC, 24¾ by 20¾ in (62 by 52 cm), in gilt frame, glazed. **$600-900**

A framed and glazed embroidered picture, worked by Harriet Sloly, aged 12, 1833, 21 by 16½ in (52 by 41 cm) overall. **$600-900**

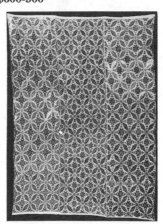

A linen worked picture, early 19thC, 23 by 20½ in (58 by 52 cm). **$500-600**

A George II tent stitch panel, in shades of red and blue, sky and water corroded, c1730, 20¾ by 17¼ in (52 by 44 cm). **$800-1,200**

A Naxos silk embroidery, with blood-red serrated leaves and floral motifs, in 3 joined strips, small areas of slight wear and repair, 79 by 57 in (201 by 145 cm). **$600-900**

A gros and petit point picture, the ground worked in yellow silk and the blooms and leaves in mainly red, green and blue wools, early 18thC, 24 by 19 in (59 by 48 cm). **$1,200-1,500**

A picture of a hunting scene, in Oriental taste, worked in cross and tent stitches with coloured wools, the turn-back border embroidered with Mary Winn 8.6.12.(10) 15.11.12, early 18thC, 41 by 26 in (102 by 65 cm). **$1,400-1,700**

A gros and petit point screen panel, early 18thC, 33 in (83 cm) high, mounted on a pole screen with tripod support. **$1,000-1,200**

An embroidered silk picture, in verre eglomise slip and later giltwood frame, 16 by 20 in (41 by 51 cm). **$600-800**

A petit point picture, worked in mainly blue, green, brown and ivory silks, c1660, 13½ by 18 in (34 by 45 cm). **$1,000-1,200**

The Travellers new guide through the principal direct roads of England and Wales, printed in rose madder on cotton, and embroidered in blue with the initials IM, late 18th/early 19thC, 24 by 26½ in (60 by 66 cm). **$300-400**

A pieced and quilted cotton coverlet, the white ground with green latticework forming diamond reserves, each with red and green grapevines, 3 sides with red and green grapes, the ground quilted in a foliate pattern, signed in ink on reverse: 'To Turner from Mamma', browned, Loudon County, Virginia, 19thC, 87 by 83in, (217.5 by 206cm). **$400-600**

A North West African textile, probably Algerian, woven in cream and blue on a red ground, 52 by 99 in (130 by 252 cm). **$400-600**

A wool and cotton Jacquard coverlet, in a floral and striped pattern, worked in red and olive green wool and natural cotton, signed by G. Baer, Antietam, Fredericks County, Pennyslvania, 1856, 82 by 76in, (205 by 192.5cm). **$300-500**

A pieced and quilted cotton coverlet, in wreath-of-roses pattern, the design worked in red, green and yellow fabric, surrounded by a rosebud and vine border, the ground quilted in a square pattern, American, 19thC, 106 by 81in, (265 by 205cm). **$600-800**

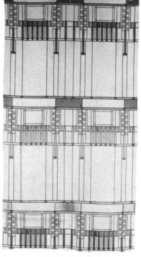

A bolt of 'Taliesin Line' fabric, the white linen printed in a geometric pattern of green, turquoise, blue and black, unsigned designed by Frank Lloyd Wright for F. Schumacher and Co., 1955, 86 by 44in (218.5 by 112cm). **$1,800-2,400**

According to David Hanks, The Decorative Designs of Frank Lloyd Wright, E.P. Dutton Co., New York, 1979, p.198: 'Because of the delicate nature of the fabrics ... few large samples have survived and are considered rare'.

A pieced and quilted cotton coverlet, the white ground with green latticework forming 13 diamond reserves, each with a red geometric design, the border with triangular reserves, with red and green grapes and leaves, the ground quilted in a grapevine and foliage pattern, minor browned spots, Virginia, dated 1853, 87½ by 82in, (218.5 by 205cm). **$900-1,200**

A historical copper-plate printed cotton textile, printed in red ink on natural plain-woven cotton, depicting Liberty seated on an altar surrounded by portrait medallions and America kneeling beside, holding portrait medallion of Washington and Franklin, above inscription: 'AMERICA PRESENTING AT THE ALTAR OF LIBERTY MEDALLIONS OF HER ILLUSTRIOUS SONS', with Washington standing at left receiving a laurel wreath from Victory unframed, fragment, English, c1783, 25 by 27½in (62.5 by 68.5cm), **$500-700**

A historical copper-plate printed cotton double kerchief, printed in brown ink on natural plain-woven cotton; the right panel square, depicting a full-length portrait of Washington flanked by an excerpt from his resignation speech and a eulogy, above an eagle, a merchant ship, and the British lion, the whole beneath a swag with the title, 'THE EFFECT OF PRINCIPLE/BEHOLD THE MAN', the left panel square, depicting a scene of young George Washington and the cherry tree above an explanatory verse, the whole beneath a ribbon with the title, 'THE LOVE OF TRUTH MARK THE BOY', the printed double panel quilted, and backed with a pieced printed cotton portion of a coverlet, with ink inscription and signed 'Mary M. Goldsmith', framed between double glass to expose both sides, by the Germantown Print Works, Germantown, Pennsylvania, c1806, 12 by 24in (30 by 60cm) **$1,000-1,500**

Tapestries

An Aubusson tapestry, woven in wool and silk in verdure tones, signed in the selvedge'.. M.R. Aurucvin .l. Tixier...' 111 by 140½ in (281 by 354 cm). **$4,500-7,000**
The weaver is probably Jean Tixier who is recorded at Aubusson in 1673.

A Brussels Tapestry, woven in silk and wool with the marriage of Thobias, restorations, late 16thC, 169 by 101 in (430 by 256 cm). **$9,000-13,000**

A Beauvais tapestry, woven in silk and wool, early 18thC, 93 by 118 in (236 by 300 cm). **$4,500-7,000**

A Flemish verdure tapestry, cut and rejoined, 17thC, 94 by 102 in (239 by 259 cm). **$4,500-7,000**

A Flemish tapestry panel, depicting Samson fighting a lion, 17thC, 100 by 43 in (257 by 110 cm). **$600-900**

A Brussels verdure tapestry, poor condition, folded, late 17th/early 18thC, 123 by 103 (312 by 261 cm). **$3,000-4,500**

A Flemish verdure tapestry, in associated cut and rejoined foliate border, early 17thC, 118 by 84 in (300 by 213 cm). **$6,000-8,000**

A panel of tapestry, for a large cushion cover, on stretcher, Flemish, early 17thC, 33 by 26 in (82.5 by 65 cm). **$6,000-8,000**

A Teniers tapestry, woven in wool and silk with merry-making rustic figures, lacking border, in later selvedge, possibly Lille, early 18thC, 81 by 156 in (206 by 396 cm). **$5,500-7,000**

A historical painted leather Masonic apron, painted in gilt, red and blue, depicting a variety of Masonic symbols, and with 2 leather drawstrings, signed in ink under flap 'De Witt Clinton', and on back 'Gardiner Conklin', New York State, early 19thC, 14in (35cm) wide. **$1,500-2,000**

Costume

An open robe and petticoat, of pink and white striped silk brocaded with garlands of pink, yellow, red and green flowers, with original stomacher, the silk French, 1774-1775. **$8,500-10,000**

A short apron of ivory silk, worked in coloured silks and raised gold thread enhanced with sequins, c1730. **$1,200-1,500**

A priest's alb of white lawn, with whitework embroidery, the deep hem and cuffs of early 18thC Brabant lace, 19thC. **$300-400**

A Polonaise of black cotton, printed with a design of flowers, trimmed with lace and festooned skirt, c1785. **$4,500-7,000**

A linen smock, the front and back bodice with smocking, 19thC. **$100-200**

A dress of cotton, printed with a chine design in mauve and pale green, with matching pelerine, c1830. **$800-1,200**

A Chinese robe, of terracotta damask silk embroidered with blue, green and ivory silks and gold thread, mid-19thC. **$500-600**

A two-piece gown of black silk ► brocade, woven with flowers in red, blue and green, and a black silk petticoat, c1860. **$600-900**

A two-piece gown of chine silk, the ivory ground printed with brown checks and florets in red and green, and a day bodice with wide sleeves and fringing, c1850. **$600-900**

A dress of printed worsted, the blue ground with lozenges in mainly red, green and ochre, possibly American, c1840. **$600-800**

A man's caped paletot cloak, of brown tweed, c1865. **$800-1,200**

Believed to have belonged to John Brown 'Her Majesty's Highland servant'.

A silk lined red ground Victorian paisley cape with silken tassels. **$400-600**

A Chinese summer robe of brown gauze, embroidered mainly in red, blue and yellow silks and gold thread, altered, early 19thC. **$1,000-1,200**

A beaded dress, embroidered on a cream silk chiffon ground with trailing loops of glass beads, with paste jewels on the midriff, 1920. **$500-600**

A Rajasthan robe of plum silk, embroidered mainly in green, brown and ivory silks, having mirror insets, altered, 19thC. **$400-600**

A dragon robe, blue ground with nine dragons, c1860. **$1,300-1,700**

A ladies semi-formal robe, embroidered with roundels of hydrangea, with navy ground, c1850. **$1,000-1,200**

A pair of shoes of ivory silk brocade in green and pink silk and bound in pink ribbon, linen lined, c1700. **$3,000-4,500**

◄ A Chinese skirt, of midnight blue silk, applied with gold thread, lined, late 19thC. **$400-600**

A Palestinian dress 'Djillayeh', of indigo linen, the yoke with brown, yellow and purple silk embroidery. **$400-600**

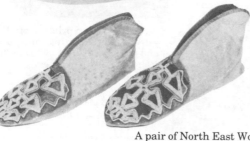

A pair of North East Woodlands Indian moccasins, the front and heel with beadwork decoration. mid 19thC. **$600-700**

A pair of shoes, of ivory silk brocaded in green, red and yellow, bound in green ribbon, with the accompanying clogs of leather and matching brocade, c1730. **$1,500-2,200**

A pair of shoes of black kid decorated with embroidery and blue silk insertion, the sole inscribed Mayer Julien a Paris, mid 19th C. **$300-400**

A pair of shoes of bottle green morocco with low heels, c1790. **$1,000-1,400**

Lace

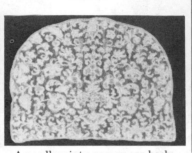

A Flemish cap back, having oeil de perdrix and other fillings, c1700's, 8 in (20.5 cm). **$300-500**

A needlepoint a reseau cap back, possibly point de Sedan, c1700, 7 in (18 cm). **$300-500**

An Alençon cap back, having mainly oeil de perdrix fillings, c1760. **$200-300**

A pair of Valenciennes lappets, c1730's, 20½ in (51 cm) long. **$500-600**

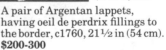

A Cluny lace bedspread, 19thC, 118 by 84 in (300 by 216 cm). **$800-1,200**

A deep flounce of Brussels bobbin lace, another matching, 19thC, each 36 by 99 in (90 by 250 cm) joined. **$600-700**

A pair of Argentan lappets, having oeil de perdrix fillings to the border, c1760, 21½ in (54 cm). **$200-300**

A pair of Brussels lappets, with oeil de perdrix fillings, c1730, 21 in (53 cm). **$300-500**

Textile Printing Blocks

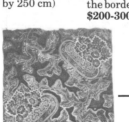

A carved wooden printing block, worked in brass picotage and bar work, by Knight & Son, Brick Lane, No. FIII71, c1850, 8½ in (21 cm) square. **$200-300**

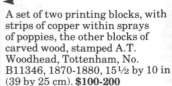

A carved wooden printing block, worked in brass strips, insertions and picotage, No. F10807, c1820, 10 by 7½ in (25 by 19 cm). **$300-400**

◄

A set of two printing blocks, with strips of copper within sprays of poppies, the other blocks of carved wood, stamped A.T. Woodhead, Tottenham, No. B11346, 1870-1880, 15½ by 10 in (39 by 25 cm). **$100-200**

A set of four carved wooden printing blocks, stamped J. Barrett, No. F21904, late 19thC, 12 in (30 cm) square. **$500-600**

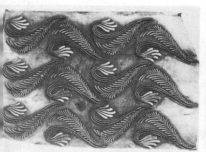

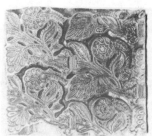

A print block, worked in copper strips with sprigs of snow-drop like flowers, stamped 14558, late 19thC, 16 by 11 in (40 by 27.5 cm). $300-400

A print block, worked with sprays of poppies and other flowers in strips of copper, stamped J. Barrett, No. F21407, c1900, 13 by 11 in (32.5 by 27.5 cm). $100-200

A set of six printing blocks, the print block of carved wood and copper bars worked with a design of exotic flowers and crowns in 17thC style, possibly by Thomas Wardle, No. F12065, c1883, 18 by 16 in (45 by 40 cm). $1,000-1,200

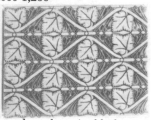

A carved wooden printing block, worked in brass strips and picotage with 2 large sprays of passion flowers, No. F11172, 1860-1870, 8½ in (21 cm). 200-300

A set of two printing blocks, for borders of shawls, the print block of cast pewter, the other block of carved wood, marked 056, stamped Larking, c1870. $300-500

A carved wooden print block, worked with Art Nouveau designs of stylised vines, stamped J.T. Larking, Hackney, continental, No. F12588, c1907, 12½ by 9½ in (31 by 24 cm). $300-400

◄ A printing block, for a border worked in carved wood and strips of brass with an Egyptian frieze, No. NG 54, early 19thC, 3 by 8 in (7.5 by 20 cm). $300-500

A printing block, for a shawl border, worked in brass picotage and bars, No. 01158, mid-19thC, 5 by 9 in (12.5 by 22.5 cm). $100-150 ►

Fans

A fan, the leaf painted with a central vignette of a school-room scene at a Dame school, the guardsticks backed with mother-of-pearl, English, c1760, 10½ in (26 cm). $600-900

A fan, commemorating The Great Exhibition of 1851, with a box labelled LT Piver Parfumeur Rue St. Martin 103 Paris and 160 Regent Street, London, mid 19thC. $300-400

A fan, the chickenskin leaf painted with a trompe d'oeil of prints lying on material, the engravings signed and dated Angelus Albonesi Romanus 1760, the mother-of-pearl sticks painted, silvered and gilt, Italian, the sticks possibly French, 11½ in (29 cm). $1,000-1,200

The artist is presumably the Angelico Albonesi who was working as an engraver in England and Italy during the second half of the 18thC, producing among other things Roman views.

A printed fan, the leaf a hand-coloured etching with riddles and conundrums, published 31 May, 1800 by Lewis Wells, Fanmaker, 26 Leadenhall Street, London, with wooden sticks, 10 in (25 cm). 400-600

A fan, the leaf of Brussels point de gaze, the silvered and gilt mother-of-pearl sticks carved and pierced, signed F. Houghton 1892, 14 in (35 cm). $800-1,200

A Chinese ivory brise fan, with monogram EM, c1750, 10½ in (26 cm). **$300-600**

A lace trimmed gauze fan, having floral gilt and silvered decorated mother-of-pearl sticks, signed J. Patte, late 19thC. **$150-200**

A pair of Canton pierced ivory parasol cockade fans, each with original carved ivory hanging box, 1 box damaged, c1800, the fans 15 in (37.5 cm) radius, the boxes 11 in (27.5 cm) long. **$2,000-3,000**

A Chinese mother-of-pearl brise fan, c1830, 7½ in (18.5 cm). **$600-700**

A Chinese fan, with alternate sticks of enamelled gilt metal filigree, pierced and carved ivory, some stained green or red, sandalwood, tortoiseshell and mother-of-pearl, c1850, 11 in (27.5 cm). **$300-400**

A French fan, with carved, pierced, silvered and gilt tortoiseshell sticks, with painted paper leaf, c1750, 10½ in (26 cm). **$300-500**

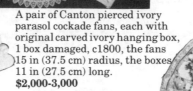

A Canton pierced tortoiseshell brise fan, with 3 gold lacquered vignettes of Chinese figures, the guardsticks also lacquered in gold, c1870, 10½ in (26 cm). **$600-800**

A French fan, with carved, pierced, painted and gilt ivory sticks, the vellum leaf painted with lovers, c1760, 11½ in (29 cm). **$300-500**

A printed fan, 'Entrevue du General Buonaparte et du Prince Charles pour les preliminairs de la paix', a hand coloured etching of the 2 figures, the reserves stencilled in blue and black, with fruit and wheat, with wooden sticks, c1790, 9½ in (24 cm). **$300-400**

A fan, with silk leaf, decorated with sequins, the ivory sticks carved, pierced and gilt set, both guardsticks set with mother-of-pearl painted with flowers, French, c1770, 11 in (27.5 cm). **$500-600**

A double image fan, one leaf painted with a proposal scene, the hidden scene depicts a lady falling into a trap watched by agitated figures, the ivory sticks decorated with red and gold foil and silvered, French, c1770, in 18thC leather fan box. **$800-1,200**

A fan, the leaf painted with lovers, the border inserted with a band of pressed silver paper, the mother-of-pearl sticks carved with putti, pierced and silvered, in glazed fan case, French c1770, 10 in (25 cm). **$800-1,200**

A fan, the leaf painted with little girls watching a peep show, signed H.M. Campes, the ivory sticks carved with children and flowers, painted and gilt, in silk covered Duvelleroy box, French, c1865, 11 in (27.5 cm). **$800-1,200**

A fan, the gauze leaf painted with an allegory of Day and Night, indistinctly signed A. Lafeve, the serpentine wooden sticks lacquered with hours of the day, in box, c1890, 14 in (35 cm). **$300-500**

An Italian fan, with carved and pierced mother-of-pearl sticks, the vellum leaf painted with the contest of Minerva and Neptune, c1710, 11 in (28 cm). **$600-900**

An Italian fan, with ivory sticks carved and pierced, the chicken-skin leaf painted with oval medallions of romantic views, in a box, c1790, 11½ in (29 cm). **$800-1,200**

A Japanese fan, the ivory sticks pierced with medallions, c1870, 12 in (30 cm). **$500-600**

A fan, the mother-of-pearl sticks carved, pierced and gilded, each guard inset with a painted porcelain plaque of a girl, the silk leaf painted with a musical party, in a box labelled Melville & Ziffer Venezia, c1860, 11 in (27 cm). **$500-600**

A fan, the leaf painted with a bunch of pansies and violets and the Royal Arms of Sweden and Denmark signed Mathild, 1878, with tortoiseshell sticks, 1 guard stick set with the initial L crowned, in leather fan box stamped with gilt crown, 11½ in (29 cm). **$500-600**
Queen Louise of Denmark daughter of King Carl XV of Sweden married King Frederik VIII of Denmark.

An Austro-Hungarian ivory brisé fan, the guards applied with enamelled silver gilt decoration, set with garnets, turquoises and pearls, in a box, late 19thC 9 in (23 cm). **$500-600**

A fan, the leaf painted with a classical scene, the mother-of-pearl sticks carved with figures, silvered and gilt and backed with mother-of-pearl, Flemish, c1750, 11½ in (29 cm). **$600-800**

Dolls

A turned and carved painted wooden doll, with inset enamel eyes, the later white kid arms with separated fingers and thumbs, and with later knee joints, with many other clothes, early 19thC, 21 in (52.5 cm). **$3,000-4,000**

A waxed-composition shoulder doll, fabric body, with kid leather hands, dressed in contemporary underclothes, c1840, 24 in (61 cm). **$300-500**

An early English wooden doll, with painted face, black eyes, red mouth and nostrils, the wooden legs string-tied to the hips, the crudely carved forearms and hands joined by material to the torso, in her original silk dress, gesso on head cracked, wig missing, early 18thC, 10 in (25.5 cm). **$1,700-2,500**

A wax-over-papier mâché shoulder-headed doll, c1860, 21 in (52.5 cm). **$300-500**

A fine wooden doll, the carved ➤ wood body with cloth upper arms and painted lower arms with finely carved elongated fingers, late 18thC, 20 in (50 cm). **$2,000-3,000**

l. A bisque shoulder-headed doll, with closed mouth, fixed blue eyes, with stuffed kid and cloth body, in contemporary clothes, 17½ in (43.5 cm) high. **$600-800**
r. A poured wax child doll, with price mark in ink on chest, 18 in (45 cm). **$600-800**

A painted wooden Grodenthal-type doll, wearing contemporary Welsh costume, 14½ in (36 cm). **$600-900**

◄ A wooden doll, with painted features, early 18thC, 11 in (28 cm). **$700-900**

An English poured shoulder-wax doll, with real hair, in original dress and pique cape, left leg broken, c1880, 23½ in (60 cm). **$600-700**

An English poured wax doll, with fixed blue eyes, fabric body with waxed lower limbs, one arm repaired, c1860, 24 in (61 cm). **$400-600**

An English waxed shoulder-composition doll, right leg broken, late 19thC, 16 in (40.5 cm). **$300-400**

A wax over composition shoulder head doll, with open/closed mouth, 35½ in (88 cm). **$800-1,200**

A wax-over-composition shoulder headed doll, with original colouring on the face, with original cream silk frock with lace insertions, 14 in (35 cm). **$400-600**

A cased and glazed waxed composition doll, 17½ in (44 cm). **$400-600**

A German Bahr & Proschild bisque doll, impressed 604 12, c1910, 20½ in (52 cm). **$1,200-1,500**

594

◄ A papier mâché headed doll, the kid body with wooden limbs, in contemporary green and white muslin dress, 10 in (25 cm). **$600-900**

With a hand written note inscribed; this doll was dressed by Miss Aldam of Fawn Castle 1835.

A papier mâché shoulder head doll, possibly dressed as a guard, with cloth body, 14 in (35 cm). **$1,200-1,500**

A papier mâché headed doll, the kid body with painted wooden limbs attached with red paper bands, c1830, 9½ in (23.5 cm). **$300-500**

A German shoulder-papier mâché pedlar doll, the kid body with wooden lower limbs, in original clothes, carrying a tray of wares with paper label of hand-written music 'The Polka' signed J Brocklesh, slight cracking on face, feet glued to stand, c 1830, 10½ in (26.5 cm). **$1,200-1,500**

A French Belton type bisque costume doll, 19thC, 10½ in (27 cm). **$300-500**

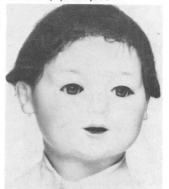

A bisque headed character doll, blue sleeping eyes, jointed composition body, marked 5730 SANTA 12 with a Gebruder Heubach sunburst, 28 in (70 cm). **$1,200-1,500**

A bisque headed character doll, in original spotted frock and straw hat, marked 3 8420, impressed with a Heubach square mark and stamped 74 in green, 9 in (22.5 cm). **$600-900**

A German George Borgfeldt bisque doll with Armand Marseille head, impressed G. 327. B. A. 15. M., c1910, 27½ in (69 cm). **$600-900**

A rare German Gebruder Heubach character doll, no 8420, with original short blonde wig, closed slightly pouting mouth, arms and legs repainted, c1915, 11 in (28 cm). **$600-700**

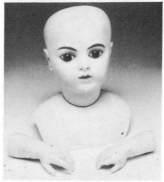

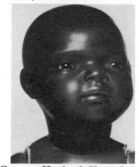

A German Heubach Koppelsdorf black bisque doll, unclothed, impressed 399.3. D. R. G. M., c1910, 18 in (46 cm). **$600-900**

Make the most of Miller's

Unless otherwise stated, any description which refers to 'a set' or 'a pair' includes a valuation for the entire set or the pair, even though the illustration may show only a single item.

A French Bru Jeune bisque shoulder head and bisque hands, the head impressed BRU.Jne 11, one shoulder impressed L, two fingers on one hand missing, c1875, 8 in (20 cm). **$4,500-7,000**

A German Gebruder Heubach ► bisque character doll, unclothed, three tiny hairlines issuing from firing on wig socket, impressed 6970 5, c1910, 15 in (38 cm). **$800-1,200**

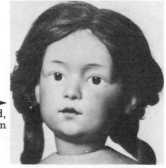

A German Gebruder Heubach bisque headed baby doll, with open mouth and upper teeth, wearing original dress and bonnet, impressed 3 Heubach Germany, 12 in (30.5 cm). **$300-400**

A Jumeau bébé, jointed wood and papier mâché body, dressed in original pink satin dress, marked to the rear of the head in red, 'Depose Tête Jumeau Bth SGDG 8', fingers chipped and cracked, eyes re-set, head cracked and broken above left temple, French, c1890, 19 in (48 cm). **$700-1,000**

A bisque headed automaton standing figure, with remains of original Spanish fancy dress, with bisque arms holding the remains of a tambourine, as the music plays she moves her head and arm, marked Depose Tête Jumeau BP SGBG, 17½ in (43.5 cm). **$2,500-3,500**

A bisque headed bébé, with jointed composition body, marked 8 and stamped on the body Bébé Jumeau Diplome d'Honneur, 19½ in (48.5 cm). **$1,200-1,500**

A Jumeau bisque doll, with jointed wood and composition body, lawn dress, with blue stamp BEBE JUMEAU Bte S.G.D.G. DEPOSE on buttocks, and DEPOSE TETE JUMEAU 14 in red. **$4,500-7,000**

An Emile Jumeau bisque doll, eight ball jointed wood and composition body, with straight wrists and blue stamp on buttocks, JUMEAU Medaille d'Or Paris, impressed DEPOSE E 7 J and E JUMEAU Med Or 1878 Paris Depose, pate replaced, kiln red spotting on face, c1880, 16 in (41 cm). **$3,000-4,000**

A French bisque head doll, by Jumeau, with jointed composition body, marked 10 Paris Deposé, the head stamped Deposé Tête Jumeau Bte S.G.D.F. 10, and the body stamped Bébé Jumeau Diplome d'Honneur, 22 in (55 cm). **$2,000-3,000**

A German Jutta character baby, with an elipse, open mouth revealing two upper teeth and tongue, detached, cracked at rear of head, impressed 1914 11, 18 in (46 cm). **$300-400**

◄ A German bisque doll, probably by J D Kestner, in original wine red dress, impressed 289 Dep 11, c1890, 21 in (53 cm). **$1,200-1,500**

A rare German Kestner bisque character doll, dressed in W.W.1 British infantry uniform, head impressed 142 W, head damaged to the rear with issuing hairline, c1914. **$300-400**

. rare German Kestner bisque
haracter doll, the head marked
y the rim 178, loose stringing,
1910, 11½ in (28 cm).
1,200-1,500

l. Lenci-type walking doll,
wearing original clothes, the key
wound clockwork mechanism
contained in the fabric-covered
torso, mounted on metal rollers,
impressed 'Brevetto, Made in
Italy, 214491 512077' 19 in
(47 cm). **$600-700**
r. A scarce Chad Valley Princess
Elizabeth doll, with a velvet
covered body with jointed limbs,
wearing original dress with a
pearl necklace, bearing 'Chad
Valley' labels and contained in its
original Bambina box, c1930,
17½ in (43 cm). **$800-1,200**

◄

A Lenci fabric boy doll, of
elongated form, in original
clothes, 1925-26, 23½ in (59 cm).
$400-600

An unusual Limoges bisque head
character doll, marked Toto
Limoges, 22 in (55 cm).
$400-600

A Lenci fabric girl doll, no 258
from the 1925-26 catalogue, of
elongated form, dog missing,
26½ in (66 cm). **$600-700**
*See III 68 Lenci Dolls by Dorothy S
Coleman.*

A Lenci fabric boy doll, dressed in
original overshirt of patchwork
felt, together with cardboard tag
marked Prodvzione original
Lenci, attached to the overshirt,
dust soiled, 21 in (53 cm).
$800-1,200

A German Armand Marseille
black 'My Dream Baby', impressed
341/8k, c1920, 22 in (56 cm).
$600-800

◄

An American Schoenhut
all-wooden doll, with original
blonde wig, fully articulated body
with spring joints, in
contemporary clothes, paint
grazed on face, the back impressed
'Schoenhut Doll, 1 Jan 17.11 USA
Foreign Countries', c1920.
$300-500

A French Schmitt et Fils bisque
doll, the papier mâché pate with
central metal pin joint, with
auburn real hair wig, in the
original clothes, with additional
outfits and nightshirts, hairline
crack from left eye to ear,
impressed 2/0 Bte, S. G. D. G.,
c1880, 14 in (35.5 cm).
2,500-3,500

A German Schoenau &
Hoffmeister Porzellanfabrik   ►
Burggrub bisque 'Princess
Elizabeth' doll, impressed 5,
c1930, 20 in (51 cm).
$2,000-3,000

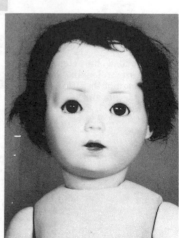

A rare German Schoenau &
Hoffmeister character doll, the
head impressed B 3½, original
spartan brown wig, c1910, 17½ in
(44 cm). **$600-700**

A Bruno Schmidt German bisque character doll, impressed 2048 5, c1910, 18½ in (46 cm). **$1,500-2,200**

An S.F.B.J. bisque head laughing character doll impressed 'S.F.B.J. 235 Paris 10', 18 in (45 cm). **$1,000-1,200**

A good S.F.B.J. French bisque character doll, impressed 226, c1910, 21 in (53 cm). **$1,000-1,200**

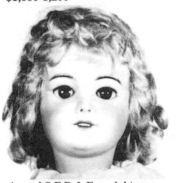

A rare S.F.B.J. French bisque character doll, the head impressed 227 Paris, 4, two fingers missing, c1910, 14½ in (37 cm). **$1,300-1,700**

A good S.F.B.J. French bisque doll, with internal pull-chord voice box, with paper label 'Bébé Vrai Modele Fabrication Jumeau', dressed in original clothes, the head impressed 301 Paris 8, head detached, c1900, 21 in (54 cm). **$500-600**

A French S.F.B.J. Bébé, good jointed wood and composition body, two fingers missing, paintwork damaged on one side, the head impressed 301, c1900, 24 in (61 cm). **$600-800**

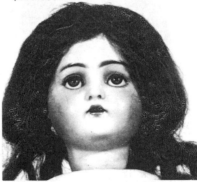

A bisque headed character baby doll, with brown sleeping eyes, open smiling mouth with quivering tongue and two upper teeth, marked K*R Simon and Halbig 116/A 62, 25 in (62.5 cm). **$2,500-3,500**

A bisque headed child doll, marked Simon & Halbig, K*R 73, 28 in (70 cm). **$600-800**

A fine Kammer and Reinhardt bisque head character doll, with sleeping brown eyes, closed mouth and dressed jointed composition body, marked Kammer * Reinhardt Simon & Halbig 117/A 76, 29 in (74 cm). **$8,500-10,000**

A bisque headed child doll, the jointed composition body in original under-clothes, marked Simon & Halbig K*R 43, 17 in (42.5 cm). **$600-700**

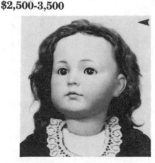

A good bisque doll, on jointed wood and composition French style ➤ chunky toddler body, in original underwear, including red corset, the Simon & Halbig head impressed faintly 1009, head detached, loose stringing, c1905, 26 in (66 cm). **$700-1,000**

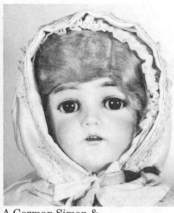

A rare Simon & Halbig bald-headed bisque doll, impressed 919 SH 5, c1880, 13 in (33 cm). **$1,500-2,200**

A German Simon & Halbig/Kammer & Reinhardt bisque doll, with good jointed wood and composition body, dressed in a pink dress with original white lacy underclothes, impressed 66, c1900, 25 in (64 cm). **$700-1,000**

A German bisque doll, the ball jointed wood and composition body in original clothes, impressed S & C 6½ Germany, c1890, 20 in (51 cm). **$600-700**

A bisque headed Bébé Premier Pas, with fixed pale blue yeux fibres outlined in a darker blue and with shaded eyelids, with blond hair wig and composition arms and body portion, the upper legs covered in kid leather with composition from the knee down, 22 in (55 cm). **$1,400-1,700**

A Kammer and Reinhardt bisque head character doll, Peter 101, the jointed composition body with ribboned sailor hat marked H.M.S. Active, marked K*R 101 34, 14 in (34 cm). **$2,500-3,500**

A rare French doll, by Jules Steiner with Simon and Halbig bisque head, the composition lady body stamped in blue on the left hip La Patricienne, dressed in original white laced cotton blouse embroidered La Patricienne, marked 1307 11, 61 in (152.5 cm). **$2,500-3,500**

A French Jules Steiner bisque doll, in pink shift, impressed A15, and stamped in black Le Parisieu Bte, S.G.D.G. A15, with stamp on buttocks Le Petit Parisien BEBE STEINER Medaille d'Or Paris 1889, 22½ in (57.5 cm). **$4,000-5,000**

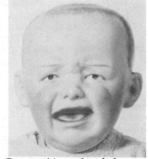

A French walking/talking bisque doll, probably by Jules Steiner, the cardboard body containing the mechanism, and with composition arms and lower legs, one leg detached, movement requires some restoration, late 19thC, 18 in (45 cm). **$1,000-1,400**

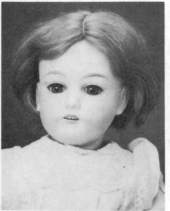

A German bisque doll, impressed C 2½, c1890, 18 in (46 cm). **$600-700**

A Jules Steiner 'C' series French bisque doll, tinted slightly smiling mouth, jointed wood and papier mâché body, the buttocks stamped J (wings) ST, dressed in original christening robe, the head impressed Sie C.O., right index finger repaired, c1880 15 in (38 cm). **$2,000-3,000**

A German bisque headed character doll, of a crying child, marked 8, 16 in (40 cm). **$600-700**

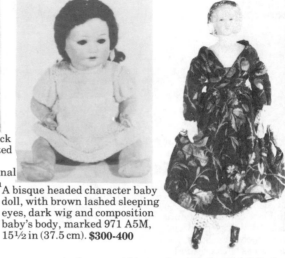

A fine French bisque swivel neck shoulder head doll, with inverted socket joint, the kid body with stitched fingers dressed in original cotton undergarments, 11½ in (29 cm). **$1,000-1,200**

A French bisque swivel headed Parisienne, with original blonde wig, the kid body with separated fingers, in original pink satin dress, c1870, 15 in (37.5 cm). **$1,700-2,500**

A bisque headed character baby doll, with brown lashed sleeping eyes, dark wig and composition baby's body, marked 971 A5M, 15½ in (37.5 cm). **$300-400**

A bisque shoulder headed doll, the head 3 in (7.5 cm) high. **$300-400**

A very rare bisque head character doll, 'Uncle Sam', the jointed composition body dressed in striped trousers, blue felt jacket and top hat, marked S 1, 12½ in (32 cm). **$1,000-1,200**

La Poupée-Modele, a hand coloured printed card doll wearing underclothes, with a quantity of double sided dresses, with wood stand in original box, with label reading 'published by R Ackerman, Jr., 191 Regent St., sold also at 96 The Strand', the doll 8½ in (21 cm). **$1,300-1,700**

1 An Armand Marseille bisque head doll impressed 'Armand Marseille, Germany, 390, A5M', 22 in (55 cm). **$200-300**
2 An Armand Marseille bisque head doll, impressed 'Made in Germany, Floredora A9M', 24 in (60 cm). **$300-500**
3 An Armand Marseille bisque head doll impressed '370, A.M.-5-DEP., Armand Marseille', kid leather body and composition limbs, 23½ in (58.5 cm). **$150-200**
4 An S.F.B.J. bisque head doll impressed 'S.F.B.J. -60-PARIS 5', 20 in (50 cm). **$300-500**
5 An Armand Marseille bisque head doll, impressed 'Armand Marseille 390 Germany A 2/0 M', the jointed wood and composition body marked Schneeglockchen, 16 in (40 cm). **$150-200**
6 An Armand Marseille shoulder bisque doll, impressed '370 A.M. 2/0 DEP made in Germany', 16 in (40 cm). **$100-150**
7 A shoulder bisque doll, impressed '3096', with open mouth and teeth, 17½ in (43.5 cm). **$200-300**

A Scottish boy doll, in Highland dress, bisque lower limbs, sawdust filled body, with small velvet covered case, in glass dome, 11½ in (28 cm). **$200-300**

A bisque headed musical doll, with wired arms and legs with wooden hands and composition legs, wearing original red and cream jester costume, as his tummy is pressed a tune is played and he bangs his cymbals, the head marked 10 1 and with label on the body portion reading D.R. patent nol 56996, 13½ in (33.5 cm). **$1,000-1,200**

An Ideal Novelty Toy Company Shirley Temple doll, dressed in original pink gauze dress with 'The Worlds Darling' badge, in original box, American, c1935, 18 in (46 cm). **$200-300**

A fine French Simonne bisque shoulder headed fashion doll, the gussetted kid body bearing turquoise-blue stamp on chest and separately stitched fingers, c1870, 17½ in (44.5 cm). **$3,000-4,500**

A French automaton, with a Turk sipping a cup of coffee and smoking a hookah, 19thC, 21 in (53 cm). **$6,000-8,500**

A china headed autoperipatetikos, wearing original red wool dress, the mechanism loose, marked 'This doll is only intended to walk on a smooth surface, patented July 15th 1862, also in Europe 20th December 1862', 10½ in (26 cm). **$600-900**

Dolls Houses

A Georgian doll's house, the 2 downstairs rooms each containing fireplaces, one surmounted by the original overmantel mirror, 28 in (70 cm), accompanied by supporting family archive material. **$3,000-4,500**

An unusual painted dog's kennel of doll's house shape, 3 bays and a door with brass plate lettered D. Wadcock, early 19thC, 29 in (74 cm) wide. **$4,500-7,000**

An American Shirley Temple composition doll, with two outfits of clothes, slight crazing to limbs, 15 in (37.5 cm). **$200-300**

A small doll's house, the front with walled garden and the whole with sand finish and decorated with shells and beads, 6½ in (16.6 cm) wide. **$300-400**

A large doll's house, of wooden construction, with cream and brown painted facade, where the paint has peeled the original painted stonework is revealed, lacking all interior decoration, front door needs re-hanging, side door with hole at base, probably English, late 19thC. **$1,000-1,200**

A German doll's 'timber brick' house, the base stamped 'Gesetzlich Geschutz', 24 in (60 cm) high. **$700-900**

A wood, simulated brick, doll's three-storey town house, the six-roomed interior each with fitted fireplace and kitchen with range, 26½ in (66 cm) wide. **$600-800**

A wood, simulated brick doll's town house, with a quantity of furniture, 30 in (75 cm) wide. **$300-500**

An English doll's house, in the form of a three-story town house, with three rooms each with fireplace; 20thC, 39½ in (100 cm) high, together with a large quantity of furniture. **$800-1,200**

A mahogany scale model of an Indian temple, one dome missing, some damage, 58½ in (146 cm) high. **$1,400-1,700**

A printed paper-on-wood doll's house, opening to reveal two rooms with original wall and floor coverings, containing furniture and wool doll's house dolls over wired bodies, 25½ in (63.5 cm) high. **$700-900**

Teddies

A pale cream plush covered Teddy bear, with Steiff button in the ear, 12 in (30 cm) high. **$600-800**

A plush covered Teddy bear, with button eyes, long snout and long felt pads, with Steiff button in ear, 12½ in (31 cm). **$400-600**

An early German black curly plush Teddy bear, probably by Steiff, the straw stuffed body with back hump and swivel joints, pads and plush well worn, c1903, 13½ in (34 cm). **$300-400**

1 A very large pink-brown plush Teddy bear, the head stitched in three parts with pointed brown felt covered snout, the arms each containing a 'growler' when raised, plush worn, c1920, 41 in (104 cm). **$500-700**
2 A blonde long plush Teddy bear, probably Steiff, c1930, 22 in (56 cm). **$300-500**
3 A blonde plush Teddy bear, with straw filled body and swivelling joints, plush worn, 28 in (71 cm). **$200-300**
4 A large fat blonde plush English Teddy bear, with protruding snout black-stitched, straw-filled stitched body with swivelling joints, growler in-operative, pads and feet worn and re-stitched, c1935, 32 in (81 cm). **$300-400**
5 An orange curly plush Teddy bear, with growler, worn on snout, c1935, 24 in (61 cm). **$100-150**

A large straw filled ginger Teddy bear, 30 in (74 cm). **$80-150**

A Teddy bear, probably by Steiff, with long snout, black button eyes, and humped back, stuffed plush covered body, worn, with limp joints and patched paws, c1910, 23½ in (58 cm). **$800-1,200**

A large English gold plush Teddy bear, by Chad Valley Co. Ltd., the straw filled body with swivel joints and suedette pads, with label "By Appointment to Her Majesty Queen Elizabeth the Queen Mother, Toymakers The Chad Valley Co. Ltd", c1955, 40 in (102 cm). **$500-700**
This Teddy bear was called 'Chad' and used to advertise Bear Brand Hosier Co. of Chicago.

A very rare Bing hand enamelled early two-seater Benz racing car, with steerable front wheels, white solid rubber-tyred wheels, clockwork motor with operating hand brake, finished in tan with red lining, German, c1904, 11¼ in (29 cm) long. $14,000-17,000

A rare Bing tinplate and clockwork limousine, handbrake to mechanism, opening doors to rear compartment, finished in dark blue with grey roof, Bing trademark printed to radiator, c1910, 9½ in (23.5 cm). $3,000-4,500

A good Bing tinplate De Dion, German, clockwork mechanism, together with plaster chauffeur, damaged, c1904, 6½ in (16.5 cm). $2,000-3,000

A clockwork ocean liner, by Georges Carette, Nuremburg, c1912, 18 in (45 cm) long. $1,700-2,500

A Carette tinplate and clockwork limousine, opening doors, simple steering with provision for cord operation from rear, sidelamps missing, minor rust and paint defects, c1910, the 12½ in (32 cm) version. $2,500-3,500

This example has a lithographed finish.

A Gunthermann tinplate Vis-A-Vis motorcar, German, the vehicle re-painted, with driver and rubber-tyred wheels, the clockwork mechanism concealed within, side lamps replaced, c1899, 9½ in (24 cm). $1,500-2,200

A tinplate Vis-A-Vis, probably by Gunthermann, including running boards with lamp holders, clockwork mechanism driving rear axle, very poor condition, c1900, 10 in (26 cm). $800-1,200

A Lehmann tinplate saloon car, the chauffeur wearing a blue coat and peak cap, the coachwork in original red and black colours, c1920, 10 in (25 cm) long. $800-1,200

A fine printed and painted tinplate model of a four door limousine, with clockwork mechanism, with operating front headlights and rear number plate, adjustable hand brake, finished in silver and black with red lining, by Tipp & Co, one front light bulb replaced, c1928, 8¼ in (23.8 cm) long. $800-1,200

A C.I.J. tinplate and clockwork Alfa Romeo P2 racing car, rack and pinion steering, external brake to clockwork mechanism, professionally repainted in Italian racing red over French blue, numbers repainted, possibly a factory repaint at time of manufacture, 20½ in (51 cm). $1,000-1,200

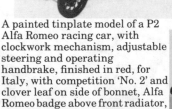

A painted tinplate model of a P2 Alfa Romeo racing car, with clockwork mechanism, adjustable steering and operating handbrake, finished in red, for Italy, with competition 'No. 2' and clover leaf on side of bonnet, Alfa Romeo badge above front radiator, by C.I.J., France, c1926, 21½ in (55 cm). $1,300-1,700

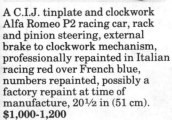

A Jouet de Paris Fiat 501, with clockwork mechanism, c1930. $400-600

A post-war tinplate pedal car 'Austin Devon', with battery operated headlamps, 60 in (150 cm). $300-500

A mechanical toy 'Daredevil', by E.P. Lehmann, German, c1920. **$300-500**

A Lehmann 'Kadi' mechanical toy, German, c1912. **$600-800**

A Lehmann 'Tut-Tut' mechanical toy, German, the driver toots his bugle as car drives erratically along, c1910, 7 in (17.5 cm). **$800-1,200**

A tinplate mechanical toy of a fireman, by F. Martin, French, c1912. **$700-900**

A mechanical celluloid headed Max & Moritz figure, German, c1925, 8 in (20 cm). **$100-200**

A German tinplate figure, 'The Suitor', neck rises and falls as figure moves along, c1925. **$400-600**

Gramophone toys with box, Rastus & the Boxers, manufactured in Boston, Mass., with Gamages original label. **$150-200**

A mechanical toy, the Piano Player, with original box, by F. Martin, French, c1910, 5½ in (13.5 cm). **$1,000-1,200**

The Violinist, by F. Martin, French, c1920. **$300-400**

The Tango Two, the couple will waltz, fox-trot or one-step in correct style to the music, by The Hastings Patent Novelties, Wilton Road, London, SW1. **$60-100**

A German brightly painted tinplate clockwork Merry-Go-Round, one cradle and one passenger missing, 16½ in (41.5 cm). **$1,000-1,200**

A painted tinplate toy of a cat in boots, with clockwork mechanism causing the cat to shuffle forward, swaying from side to side, German, c1903, 6 in (15.5 cm). **$600-800**

The Snooker Player, 6½ by 2½ in (16 by 6 cm). **$300-500**

A printed tinplate toy of Mickey Mouse, operating an Organ Grinder, complete with clockwork mechanism, by Distler, missing left arm and Minnie Mouse, c1936, 6¼ in (16 cm). **$800-1,200**

A J.W.B. tinplate mechanical artist toy, English, c1900, 4½ in (11.5 cm). **$800-1,200**

A rare painted tinplate toy of a monkey, on a four-wheel musical carriage, with simple musical movement, clockwork mechanism, some paint chipped, German, c1903, 7½ in (19.5 cm). **$500-700**

A good and large Marklin tinplate stove, German, with removable chimney at the rear, c1910, 17 in (43 cm) wide. **$1,000-1,200**

A composition-headed clockwork clown cellist, German, not working, late 19thC, 13 in (32.5 cm). **$1,200-1,500**

A rare printed and painted tinplate model of a fair-ground traction engine, with clockwork mechanism, 7 in (18.3 cm), with a four-wheeled car containing a small fair-ground carousel, 5 in (13.2 cm), one rider missing, by Bing, Nuremburg, some rusting, c1906. **$700-1,000**

A fine Ives tricyclist/galloper clockwork toy, in original red and blue outfit, patent date for April 8, 1878, tinplate horse head mounted to the front, the clockwork mechanism causes the rear wheels to rotate, and the boys hands to move backwards and forwards, complete with key, American, c1878, 8½ in (22 cm). **$7,500-10,500**

A Bing tinplate gun boat, German, catalogue no. 10/351/2, clockwork powered, slight damage, slight retouching, c1915, 19¾ in (50 cm) long. **$700-1,000**

An amusing sailor's hornpipe automaton, the two painted figures dressed in sailor's uniform and with articulated legs, dance the hornpipe to the sound of a small cylinder musical movement, English, c1880, **$1,300-1,700**

MAKE THE MOST OF MILLER'S

We are frequently asked why we include damaged lots, multiple lots, lots with unique provenance. The reason is we try to include in Miller's what is available in the market place. It would be a perfect world if all lots were single, perfect and totally representative. This is not the case. Hence we try to reflect what is 'around'.

An Edwardian painted wooden model of a Noah's Ark, containing 120 painted carved wooden animals, 22½ in (56 cm). **$1,200-1,500**

A scarce and early Ernst Plank negro drummer, German, the tinplate base concealing the clockwork movement operating the figure's arms and tinplate musical box, c1890, 14½ in (37 cm). **$2,500-3,500** ►

605

A carved wooden rocking horse, the stand marked Patented Jan. 29, 1880, 49 in (122.5 cm). **$600-900**

A dappled grey rocking horse, English, eyes, mane and reins missing, nylon tail, ears chipped, c1900, 58 in (147.5 cm). **$700-900**

A singing bird automaton, French, modern, the internal clockwork mechanism causes the two birds to warble, move their heads and tails, 20½ in (52 cm) high. **$500-700**

A singing bird automaton, the movement housed in the carved giltwood octagonal base, 19thC, 21 in (52.5 cm). **$2,000-3,000**

An excellent straw-work Noah's Ark, with 180 pieces, comprising 5 figures, 126 beasts and insects, and 49 birds, German, late 19thC, 22 in (56 cm). **$4,500-5,000**

A singing bird automaton, French, the coin-operated mechanism with tail, head and beak movements, with nightingale song, c1880, 20 in (51 cm). **$1,500-2,200**

A Chad Valley gypsy caravan biscuit tin, for W. & R. Jacob & Co., English, c1937, 6¼ in (16 cm), together with a William Crawford & Sons menagerie van, English, c1933, 6¼ in (16 cm). **$300-500**
These were not branded biscuit tins. Had they mentioned 'Jacobs' and 'Crawfords' the price would probably have doubled.

A Bryan's 'clock' amusement machine, with original instruction card, c1930, 31 in (79 cm) high. **$400-600**

A Garretts 'Bijou gold changer' machine, with 3 coin slots with £1, £½, signs cast on each side, English, late 19thC, 11 in (28 cm). **$200-300**

A Cragstan Ford Thunderbird, by Yone Toys, Japan, c1960. **$80-150**

A large plush Mickey Mouse soft toy, English, Reg. No. 750611, ears replaced, 18½ in (47 cm), with smaller plush Mickey Mouse, distressed, 7½ in (18.5 cm), both c1930. **$600-700**

Austrian bronze cats, c1900.

A cat band, comprising a grand piano, 2 choristers and 3 other figures, 2¼ in (5.5 cm). **$800-1,200**

The Tennis Players: a pair of cats, each holding tennis rackets, one about to strike the ball, together with the net, approx. 2¼ in (5.5 cm). **$400-600**

An extremely unusual magician's lamp, tinplate base for candle, English, late 19thC, 7 in (18 cm). **$300-400**

Ring-a-Ring-o'-Roses: a group of 6 cats linking arms and surrounding a kitten, 3 in (7.5 cm). $700-1,000

The Orchestra: a 12-piece group comprising conductor with choral accompaniment, upright piano and other musicians, approx 3 in (6.5 cm). **$1,200-1,500**

A 'Dinah' cast iron money bank, lacking base, 7 in (18 cm); with another in the form of a top-hatted negro, 8 in (20 cm); and 'Little Joe', 5½ in (14 cm), all 3 deposit coins in their mouths and roll their eyes, American, late 19thC. $500-600

A cast iron mechanical money bank, 'Mule and Barn', American, Patented 3rd August 1880, c1885, 8½ in (21 cm). **$300-500**

A painted cast iron 'Jolly Nigger' bank, 6½ in (16 cm). **$100-150**

A rare English 'Giant in the Tower' cast-iron mechanical bank, stamped with Registration no. 196844, paint with wear and chips, late 19thC, 9½ in (24 cm). **$3,000-4,000**

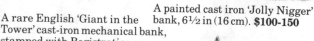

An unusual printed and handpainted mechanical money bank, English, c1860, 14 in (35 cm). **$1,000-1,200**

"The Novelty Bank", the door opens to reveal man with tray, American, Patented 1872, 7 in (17.5 cm). **$600-800**

A cast iron mechanical bank, 'Trick Pony', the horse with articulated head, the stand with food trough hinged to face, with trap key to deposit coin, by Shepard Hardware Co., American, c1890, 7 in (18 cm). **$600-800**

1 'Dinah', cast iron mechanical bank, base replaced, 7 in (17.5 cm). **$200-300**

2 'Stump Speaker', mechanical cast iron bank, 10 in (25 cm). **$100-200**

3 'Jonah and the Whale', mechanical cast iron bank, 10 in (25 cm). **$150-200**

4 'Creedmoor', mechanical cast iron bank, 10½ in (26 cm). **$200-300**

5 'Uncle Sam', cast iron mechanical bank, 11½ in (28 cm). **$200-300**

6 'Trick Dog', mechanical cast iron bank, some damage, 9 in (22.5 cm). **$100-200**

7 'Tammany', mechanical cast iron bank marked Patd. June 8, 1875. **$80-150**

Three S.A. nurses walking and 2 S.A. men helping comrades home after a riot, possibly some retouching, one foot cracked, 1937. **$200-300**

Extremely rare Britains, a set of 12 Paris Office Royal Horse Guards of the British Army, made by painting French Cuirassiers in a different uniform and equipping them with short carbines, presumably issued 1917 when supplies of the real thing impossible to obtain from London, marked underneath 'Wm. Britain, Deposé, Copyright', but undated, paint condition is fair, but only 4 figures are intact, the remaining figures having 5 holes, one missing and one broken arm, 7 horses' legs gone and one plume missing. **$1,700-2,500**

A man in brown uniform exercising, knees bent, rifle held over head, one man waving, one walking, one seated and one at attention, a few cracks, 1939. **$300-400**

Three SS in steel helmets, goose stepping with officer, possibly some retouching, 1939. **$300-400**

Panzer crew in berets, walking, saluting, with binoculars, running with pistol and throwing grenade, two badly cracked, one possibly retouched, 1939. **$150-200**

A recruit at attention and a sentry in snow gear, 1938. **$200-300**

Two riflemen and 2 machine guns on tripods, firing at aircraft, with helper, 1939. **$300-400**

Five men in steel helmets, brown uniform, with an officer in grey, all goose stepping, officer's face possibly retouched, 1939. **$300-500**

Two mountain troops with skis carried over shoulder, some cracks, 1938. **$300-400**

Mounted policeman, some cracks in horse, 1935. **$150-200**

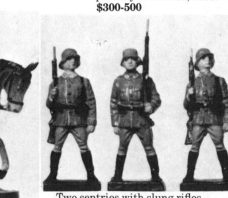

Two sentries with slung rifles, with another at the slope, 1938. **$200-300**

A mounted S.A. figure in coat on walking horse, 1937. **$200-300**

A very fine gauge 1 signals gantry, with 4 signals, oil fired lamps, ladders on both sides, by Bing, c1910, 21 in (53.7 cm). **$700-900**

l. Tippco, no. 194, a scout car with sparking machine gun and panzer man seated in turret, working clockwork motor, 1938, 7 in (17.5 cm). **$300-500**
c.l. Lineol, 2 barbed wire entanglement pieces, no. 5 515. **$150-200**
c.r. Elastolin no. 591/5, motor-cycle machine gun combination with removable machine gun, pillion passenger missing, 1939. **$300-500**
r. Hausser no. 738, a clockwork motor ambulance, with battery lit headlights, interior fitted bunks with stretchers, and electric light, 1938, 12 in (30 cm). **$1,700-2,500**

A well engineered 5 in gauge model of the Great Western Railway 9400 Class 0–6–0 pannier tank locomotive No. 9403, built by J. Cashmore, Halesowen, 34 in (86.5 cm). **$3,000-4,000**

Models

A 3½ in gauge model of the London Midland and Scottish Railway Princess Class 4–6–2 locomotive and tender No. 6200, 'Princess Royal', partially built by H.C. Drummond, Newcastle, c1942 and completed by R. Davis, Cheltenham in 1983, 57 in (145 cm). **$2,500-3,500**

A well engineered 5 in gauge model of the Great Western Railway Dean Single 4–2–2 locomotive and tender No. 3009, 'Flying Dutchman' built by W.C. Godwood, Romsey, Hants, 60 in (152.5 cm). **$4,500-7,000**

A well detailed 5 in gauge model of the British Railways Class 7P6F 4–6–2 Pacific locomotive and tender No 70014, 'Iron Duke' 74 in (188 cm). **$7,000-9,000**

A finely engineered exhibition standard 7¼ in gauge model of the 0–6–0 side tank locomotive No. 1, 'Oliver', based on 'A. S. Harris' built by Hawthorn Leslie & Company 1907 (ex Southern Region) and modelled by R. K. Hall, Louth, 43 in (109 cm). **$6,000-8,500**

A well engineered and presented 5 in gauge model of a Rhodesian Railways Beyer Garratt 2–6–0+0–6–2 locomotive, 82 in (208.5 cm). **$4,000-5,000**

A gauge O clockwork model of the P.L.M. (Paris-Lyons-Mediterranée) 'Pacific' 4–6–2 locomotive and twin bogie tender No. 1020, in original paintwork, by Marklin. **$2,000-3,000**

A well engineered and presented 7¼ in gauge model of the London, Midland and Scottish Railway Class 5P5F 4–6–0 locomotive and tender No.4835, built by D. I. Benham, Bridport, 98 in (249 cm). **$7,500-10,500**

A gauge 1 clockwork model of an 'Atlantic' 4–4–2 locomotive and twin bogie tender, in original paintwork, complete with 3 headlamps and key, in original wood box, by Bing. **$2,000-3,000**

A well engineered and detailed 7¼ in gauge model of the London, Midland and Scottish Railway Class 5P5F 4–6–0 locomotive and tender No. 5157 'The Glasgow Highlander', as built by Armstrong Whitworth and Company and modelled by R. Cogan, North Ferriby and R. Morrell, Brough, 98 in (249 cm). **$7,000-9,000**

An extremely rare 2½ in gauge
live steam spirit fired tin plate
model of the Great Northern
Railway Stirling 'Single' 4–2–2
locomotive and tender No. 776,
complete with all original fittings,
scored and slightly chipped in
places, and a quantity of original
straight and curved track and
points, by Carette, c1902.
$10,000-13,000

A good and scarce German Bing
gauge 2 clockwork 4–4–0
locomotive, No. 2631, finished in
Midland Railway maroon and
black lined yellow, with matching
six-wheeled tender, together with
three near-mint matching fitted
bogie coaches, in original
cardboard box with additional
sections of track and later signals,
c1902. **$6,000-8,500**

A Bing gauge III 4–4–0 spirit fired
'King Edward' locomotive, No.
7098, lacking tender, German,
c1905. **$2,000-3,000**

A fine gauge 0 (3-rail) electric
model of the 0–4–0 electric
locomotive, Ref No. RF66/12920,
with operating front headlamps,
one bulb broken, 2 overhead
pantographs, in original
paintwork, by Marklin.
$400-600

A gauge 0 twin bogie 'Shell' petrol
tanker, ref no. 1954Sh, with side
operating tap, finished in yellow,
by Marklin. **$150-200**

A good Newton & Co, English
brass 2–2–2 locomotive, together
with non-original tender, 12½ in
(32 cm). **$1,300-1,700**

A very fine gauge 0 (3-rail) electric
model of a continental 4–6–2
'Pacific' locomotive and twin bogie
tender, Ref No. HR64/13020, in
original paintwork, with
operating front headlamps, by
Marklin, c1930. **$2,500-3,500**

A Maisie GNR 4–4–2 Atlantic
locomotive and tender, in 3½ in
gauge, with a quantity of
showtrack and coal, designed by
L.B.S.C., numbered 251.
$1,500-2,200

A rare gauge 0 twin bogie
petroleum tanker, ref no. 2928,
Sandiago and Arizona Railway
No. 2928, by Marklin. **$300-500**

A collection of 4 mm scale outside
third rail electric locomotives,
including the L.M.S. 2–8–0 No.
8000, the L.M.S. 4–4–0 No 671,
the L.M.S. Fowler Class 4 F No
4271, the L.M.S. 0–6–0 side tank
locomotive No 7351 and the
British Railways 0–6–2 side tank
locomotive No 46917, and an
inside third rail electric 0–6–0
Continental locomotive
No.E6302, by Marklin.
$300-500

Two gauge 0 C.I.W.L. twin bogie
passenger coaches, including Ref
No 1746/GJ1 restaurant car, with
clerestory roof, Ref No. 1747/GJ1,
sleeping car with clerestory,
opening roofs to reveal
compartment inside, restaurant
car includes 3 people, side opening
doors, both by Marklin.
$500-600

A fine 1:48 scale fully framed and
rigged partially planked model of
the Royal Naval First Rate
Man-of-War, 'The Prince', c1670,
built by C.B. Morris, Louth, 47 by
49 in (120 by 125 cm).
$5,500-7,000

A bone ship model of a second rate
ship-of-the-line, the 94 gun man
o'war presenting 2 retractable
decks above the pinned and
planked hull with baleen strakes,
34½ in (86 cm) long.
$9,000-13,000

A prisoner-of-war bone model of an 88-gun ship-of-the-line, in later glazed oak case, 19thC, 21 in (52.5 cm). **$8,500-10,000**

A prisoner-of-war 98-gun first rate ship-of-the-line, the pinned and planked bone hull with baleine trim below 3 gun decks, on chequer strung bone plinth, 26 in (65 cm). **$14,000-17,000**

An exhibition standard 1/8in: 12 in scale model of the Flower Class Corvette H.M.S. 'Bryony', Pennant No. K192, built by John R. Haynes, Ashdon, Saffron Walden, 10 by 25 in (25 by 62.5 cm). **$5,500-7,000**

A fully planked live steam spirit fired model Thames river launch, of c1870, the hull probably by Steven's Model Dockyard, 16 by 63 in (38 by 160 cm). **$3,000-4,500**

A 1/4in: 12 in scale partially planked unrigged model of the U.S.N. 'Lexington' of c1775, built by R. Cartwright, Plymouth, 1981, 10 by 26 in (25 by 66 cm). **$1,000-1,200**

A model of a paddle steamer 'Caledonian', English, c1900, 56 in (143 cm). **$1,000-1,200**

A ships model of a harbour dredger, with 2 dredging conveyors, winches and wheel house etc, late 19thC, 78 in (168 cm). **$1,500-2,200**

A model of a single vertical cylinder Maudslay Pendulous engine, built by J. Spiller, Battersea, 1815-1825, 16½ by 15½ in (42 by 39.5 cm). **$14,000-17,000**

An exhibition standard 1:24 scale model of the De Havilland No. 1 Biplane of 1909, researched and built by R.A. Burgess, Thornton Dale, wingspan 18½ in (47 cm), 15 in (38 cm) long, overall. **$600-900**

A 1½ in scale model of the traction engine 'Royal Chester', the coal-fired copper boiler silver soldered throughout and currently pressure tested to 180 p.s.i., English, modern, built by T.F. Hamilton, 26 in (66 cm) long. **$3,000-4,500**

This is a precise scale model of Allchin's prototype which was first exhibited at the Chester Royal Agricultural Show, 1926.

A 3 in scale model of a Burrell single cylinder 3 shaft 2 speed general purpose agricultural traction engine, built by A.G. Monday, Gillingham, 30 by 45 in (75.5 by 114 cm). **$4,500-7,000**

An exhibition standard 1:24 scale model of the Airco D.H.2 Serial No. 6011 of c1916, built by R.A. Burgess, Thornton Dale, wingspan 14 in (35.5 cm), 13 in (33 cm) long overall. **$800-1,200**

A working model of a triple expansion marine engine, with reverse, mounted in mahogany frame with glazed case, case 16 in (40 cm) long. **$300-600**

A brass and cast iron model horizontal single cylinder reversing stationary engine, built by H.J. Wood, London, late 19thC, 17 by 9 in (43 by 23 cm). **$700-900**

A scale model of a single vertical cylinder four pillar stationary engine, with parallel motion patented by Mr. Phineas Crowther, Newcastle on Tyne, 1800 and modelled by G. L. Dimelow, Ashton under Lyne, 9 by 6 in (23 by 15 cm). **$400-600**
c.f. 'History & Progress of the Steam Engine' by Eliza Galloway, pp 128/9.

A brass and wrought iron model single vertical oscillating cylinder 4 pillar stationary engine of c1870, 12 by 8 in (30.5 by 21 cm). **$600-700**

Chess Sets

A fine Austrian natural and stained fruitwood chess set, carved as Crusaders and Turks, slight damage to 1 knight and 2 castles, by Johann Rint, 1815-1876, kings 5 in (12 cm) high. **$7,000-9,000**

A model Stuart single cylinder, centre pillar beam engine, with mahogany lagged copper bound cylinder, 1 in bore by 2 in stroke, 10 by 15 in (28.5 by 38 cm). **$400-600**

A Cantonese large ivory chess set, natural and red stained, 1 pawn broken, some wear overall, 19thC, white king 9 in (23 cm) high. **$2,000-3,000**

A French ivory chess set, the bases stained red and green, the king and queen to one side featuring Napoleon and Josephine, the other side featuring Nelson and Emma Hamilton, early 19thC, kings 4 in (10 cm) high. **$10,000-13,000**

A Chinese carved ivory chess set, each piece in the form of emperors, soldiers on horseback and figures riding elephants, one side stained red, late 19thC. **$1,000-1,200**

An English turned boxwood and ebony chess set, late 19thC. **$300-400**

A Chinese red and white ivory chess set, the pieces carved as members of the Chinese Court, with a red and white draughts set. **$600-700**

A rare ivory chess set, with pieces of curving form, one side natural, the other with stained brown detail, 18th/19thC, kings 2 in (5 cm) high. **$8,500-11,000**

An ivory chess set, natural and brown stained, the pieces of bust type with crowned kings and queens, German, probably 19thC, kings 3½ in (9 cm) high. **$4,000-5,000**

A bone chess set, natural and brown stained, the kings and queens with pierced and petalled balconies and turned finials, few chips, German or Austrian, 19thC, kings 4 in (10 cm) high.
$800-1,200

An interesting and early East European ivory chess set, lacks white knight, some damage, early 19thC, the king 3 in (8 cm) high.
$500-700

A German parcel gilt chess set, Johann Heinrich Philipp Schott and his son Johann Martin, Frankfurt a.M, early 19thC, 13 in (33.5 cm) wide, 4200 gr (135 ozs 4 dwt). **$10,500-14,000**

Games

An Anglo Indian ivory and horn mounted folding games box, with chess board, backgammon board and the original ivory and horn chess and backgammon/draughts pieces, Vizagapatam, 19thC, 18 in (45 cm). **$1,500-2,200**

A Delhi ivory chess set, green and natural, a few pieces chipped or repaired, early-mid 19thC, 6 to 2½ in (14.7 to 6.5 cm).
$1,000-1,200

A Victorian grained walnut games compendium, containing a variety of games, the base with spring-loaded secret drawer, by Alex Jones & Co., c1870, 14 in (35 cm). **$2,000-3,000**

An ivory and sandalwood chess and backgammon set, the ivory box board in the form of a double folio volume 'tooled' in black with stylised foliage, probably Mysore, slight lifting of inlay, 19thC.
$2,000-3,000

A Victorian coromandel games compendium, with boxwood and ebony chess pieces, draughts, ivory dominoes, lead part totopoly, with 2 trays and folding gaming board, c1880, 12½ in (32 cm).
$600-700

An Indian ebony and engraved ivory games box, the interior inlaid for backgammon on a sandalwood ground, with 3 contemporary ivory engraved boxes enclosing chess and backgammon pieces, second quarter 19thC, 18½ in (46 cm).
$5,500-7,000

An Indian coromandel games cabinet, with many lidded compartments, drawers and rising section and containing a large quantity of mother-of-pearl counters, 19thC, 17 in (42.5 cm).
$400-600

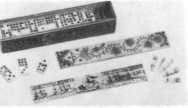

A prisoner-of-war bone dominoes and cribbage casket, with dominoes and cribbage markers, 7 in (17.5 cm). **$800-1,200**

An Anglo Indian ivory and rosewood games box, probably Vizagapatam, opening to form a backgammon board, with English silver hinges, London 1835, 16 in (40 cm). **$2,000-3,000**

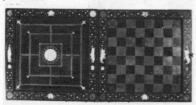

A German marquetry games box, the nine men's morris board centred with a roundel engraved with the Three Graces, the interior with backgammon board, early 17thC, 18 in (45 cm) square.
$8,500-10,000

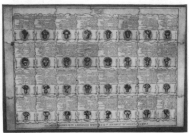

A jigsaw puzzle, titled Chronological Tables of English History for the Instruction of Youth, in the original box with key and trade label, cover missing, published March 25th 1788 by John Wallis. **$200-300**

Musical Instruments

1. A set of English nine-pins, with felt covered wooden ball, late 19thC, 8 in (20 cm) high. **$600-800**
2. German tumbling clowns, with original hinged box, mid-19thC, 11½ in (29 cm). **$500-700**
3. A German game, 'Arabian Geomancy', with hand coloured picture cards with instructions, and mosaic figures and game of geometrical compositions, both contained in original boxes. **$150-200**
4. A peep-show 'The Valley on the Rhein from Bingen to Lurley'. **$300-400**

An Empire brass-mounted rosewood piano, rectangular, with hinged lid opening to keyboard with an engraved brass name plate, the case with 2 short drawers, on baluster-turned and reeded tapering cylindrical legs, on casters, by A. Babcock, Boston, c1825, 67in (167.5cm) wide. **$1,800-2,500**

A George III mahogany and satinwood square piano, by James Henry Houston, London, numbered 1693, 66 in (168 cm) wide. **$3,000-4,000**

An upright pianoforte, 7 octave by Errard Paris, No. 7418, in a walnut banded and ormolu mounted satinwood case. **$3,000-4,500**

An unusual walnut cased upright piano, by Kirkman, London, instrument number 37352, straight strung, c1880, 60 in (150 cm) wide. **$400-600**

A fine Italian violin, by Joannes Florenus Guidantus, bearing the maker's original label; Joannes Florenus Guidantus fecit Bononiae Anno 1731, length of back 14 in (35 cm). **$22,500-29,000**

A violin, by a member of the Fendt Family, with a certificate of Messrs Paul Voigt in London, dated August 1980, stating: The instrument is the work of Bernard Fendt 1775-1832, a characteristic example, etc, c1800, length of back 14 in (35 cm). **$6,000-8,000**

A fine violin, with a bow in case, by John Barrett, bearing the maker's label: Made by John Barrett at Ye Harp & Crown in Piccadilly, London, 1734, L.O.B., 14 in . (35 cm). **$4,500-7,000**

A violin, by W.E. Hill & Sons, labelled William E. Hill & Sons/Makers 140 New Bond Street/London 1915 No. 276, 14 in (35.6 cm), in shaped oak case by W.E. Hill & Sons, with bow. **$5,500-7,000**

An interesting French violin, in case, possibly the work of Claude Pierray, labelled Montagnana, length of back 15 in (36 cm). **$5,500-7,000**

An Italian violin, labelled Joseph et Antonius/Gagliani Filii Nico/Laj...Neap 1803, length of back 14 in (35 cm). **$4,000-5,000**

A violoncello, by Joseph Charotte-Millot, bearing the maker's label, Fabricant Instruments A Mirecourt Vosges, in a shaped brown cloth covered case by Vidoudez in Geneva, c1830, length of back 30 in (75.3 cm). **$9,000-13,000**

A violoncello, by Francois Caussin in Neufchateau, Vosges, c1860, length of back 30 in (75.5 cm). **$8,500-10,000**

A violin, Joseph Rocca in Turin, 1840-1850, bearing a label Joseph Rocca fecit Taurini anno Domini 1845, length of back 14 in (35 cm), upper bouts 6½ in (16.7 cm), lower bouts 8 in (20.8 cm). **$10,500-14,000**

A fine silver mounted violin bow, by E. Sartory, branded E. Sartory à Paris, weight 54 gms. **$2,500-3,500**

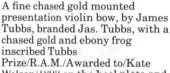

A fine silver and ivory mounted violin bow, by W.E. Hill & Sons, branded W.E. Hill & Sons, weight 62 gms. **$1,700-2,500**

A fine chased gold mounted presentation violin bow, by James Tubbs, branded Jas. Tubbs, with a chased gold and ebony frog inscribed Tubbs Prize/R.A.M./Awarded to/Kate Wilson/1893 on the heel plate and chased gold-sheathed adjuster, weight 58 gms. **$5,500-7,000**

Musical Boxes

A Nicole Frères keywound music box, the cylinder movement stamped with the maker's name and No. 23773, playing 6 tunes, c1840, cylinder 11 in (27 cm). **$1,500-2,200**

A Nicole Frères keywound cylinder musical box, the 28 cm cylinder playing 6 airs, Swiss, c1855. **$1,500-2,200**

Twenty miniature models of brass musical instruments, silver plated, hand made by James Richmond Lloyd in Manchester 1883, 16 in (41 cm). **$1,700-2,500**

A fine Nicole Frères keywound ➤ cylinder musical box, No. 38881, Gamme No. 1603, the 28 cm cylinder playing 6 Scottish airs, replacement winding handle, four teeth missing, Swiss, c1855, the case 18 in (45 cm). **$800-1,200**

A bells-in-sight cylinder musical box, probably by Bremond, the 13 in (33 cm) cylinder playing 8 airs as listed on tune sheet, gamme no. 16078, with 6 graduated bells, applicable at will, Swiss, c1875, 23 in (59 cm) long. **$1,300-1,700**

A large Swiss musical box, by Nicole Frères, No. 51963, playing 8 religious tunes on 19 in (47.5 cm) barrel, with 3-piece comb, 6 bells in sight, 3 teeth missing, 36 in (90 cm). **$3,000-4,000**

A Nicole Frères 'Two Per Turn' keywound cylinder musical box, number 33506, the 12 in (31 cm) cylinder playing 12 airs, with the original instruction card issued by Wales & McCulloch, Ludgate St., London, 21 in (53 cm). **$2,000-3,000**

An Alexandra interchangeable cylinder musical box, with 6 six-air sleeve type cylinders, zither attachment, crank wind motor, the cylinders 6 in (15 cm). **$600-900**

A Ducommun-Girod keywound cylinder musical box, No. 11480, the 10½ in (26.5 cm) cylinder playing 6 operatic airs, Swiss, mid-19thC, 16 in (41 cm) wide. **$1,000-1,200**

A forte-piano musical box, by Bremond, No. 29290, playing 4 operatic airs, Swan's Song, Lohengrin and Marches from Aida, Athalie and Tannhauser, Gamme No. 564, the cylinder 13 by 2 in (33 by 6 cm) diam. **$4,000-5,000**

A bells-in-sight cylinder musical box, the 11 in (28 cm) cylinder playing 20 airs, two-per-turn, Swiss, c1890, case 24 in (61 cm) wide. **$1,000-1,200**

A bells-in-sight cylinder musical box, the 15 in (38 cm) cylinder playing 10 airs, some damage, Swiss, c1875, 26 in (65 cm) long. **$1,000-1,400**

An interchangeable cylinder musical box and stand, by G. Baker-Troll & Co., Geneva, each 13 in (33 cm) cylinder playing 8 airs with an indicator, with 6 further cylinders, 43½ in (109 cm). **$4,500-5,000**

A bells-in-sight interchangeable cylinder musical box, made by the Societe Anonyme de l'Ancienne Maison Billon et Isaac, the three 7 in (17 cm) cylinders playing 4 airs, Swiss, late 19thC, 17 in (43 cm) wide. **$1,500-2,200**

A Stella musical box on stand, 17 in (42.5 cm) disc, with 27 discs and winding handle, c1900. **$3,000-4,000**

An overture music box, the keywound movement stamped Humbert Brollier à Geneve, No. 18777, playing 4 overtures by Weber, Rossini and 2 by Mozart, comb defective, cylinder 11 in (28 cm), case 20½ in (51 cm) wide. **$3,500-5,000**

A forte piccolo musical box, playing 12 airs accompanied by drum and 5 bells, the cylinder 11 in (27.5 cm). **$1,500-2,200**

A continental singing bird automaton box. **$1,500-2,200**

A Swiss gilt metal singing bird box, 19thC, 4 in (10.5 cm) wide. **$1,200-1,500**

A 10½ in (26 cm) symphonion table top disc musical box, complete with 22 discs, 17½in (44 cm) wide. **$1,500-2,200**

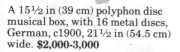

A 15½ in (39 cm) polyphon disc musical box, with 16 metal discs, German, c1900, 21½ in (54.5 cm) wide. **$2,000-3,000**

Phonograph

A 'penny in the slot' upright polyphon disc musical box, with 16 discs, 36½ in (91 cm). **$2,000-3,000**

A 12 in (30 cm) Britannia disc musical box, with double comb movement, with 24 discs, 28½ in (72.5 cm) wide. **$1,400-1,700**

A 12 in (30 cm) disc polyphon long case clock, with 17 discs, winding handles, key and pendulum, German, late 19thC, 80 in (203 cm). **$4,500-5,000**

A coin operated walnut veneered upright polyphon disc musical box, playing 20 in (50 cm) discs, with 14 discs. **$4,000-5,000**

A 25 in (62.5 cm) upright polyphon disc musical box, with 11 discs, 57½ in (144 cm) high. **$3,500-5,000**

◄ An Edison home phonograph, model A with model C reproducer, with 51 cylinders, American, c1900. **$500-600**

A 15½ in (39 cm) polyphon disc musical box, number 84941, with 8 discs, 21½ in (55 cm) wide. **$2,000-3,000**

617

Gramophones

A rare polyphon attachment for an Edison standard phonograph. **$700-900**

The polyphon attachment was marketed by H.B. Babson's Talking Machine Company of Chicago. The principle of 2 soundboxes tracking one behind the other was later used in the Ultraphone in the 1920s.

An H.M.V. oak cased table top wind-up gramophone, having wooden petal horn, c1910. **$500-600**

A Pathe horn gramophone, with Asaphir soundbox, French, c1910. **$500-700**

An HMV model IV horn gramophone 'HBO', with single spring motor, No. 2, originally exhibition, soundbox and large oak horn, c1914, 22 in (55 cm). **$800-1,200**

An Edison bell electron gramophone, picked out in gold, 12 in (30 cm) turntable with Edison bell soundbox, gold plated fittings, winding handle to one side, English, c1920, 45 in (115 cm). **$400-600**

A rare hand driven Kaemmerer and Reinhardt style gramophone, lacking horn and reproducer, together with one E. Berliner record no. 35, German, c1895. **$1,200-1,500**

A Victor 'A'/Gramophone Co. style no. 4 gramophone with style no. 5 type motor in nickel plated iron casing, soundbox, elbow and horn replaced, lacks brake. **$1,200-1,500**

A table gramophone, with 10 in (25 cm) turntable, concert, soundbox, vermillion flared horn, c1910. **$600-800**

A Symphonista horn gramophone, with Symphonista Universal soundbox for lateral cut or hill and dale records, 50 records. **$700-900**

A trade mark gramophone, spring brake and chromium plated fittings, by the Gramophone Company with lacquered brass horn, Clark-Johnson soundbox no. J30730, 1898-1899. **$1,500-2,200**

A trade mark gramophone, with three 7 in Berliner recorders, by the Gramophone Company, Clark-Johnson soundbox no. J3692, spring brake, broken, and bolt brake, 1898. **$1,200-1,500**

Knife Boxes

A pair of Georgian cutlery boxes, veneered in well figured mahogany, interior boxwood strung, 14 in (35 cm) high. **$1,500-2,200**

A George III satinwood cutlery box, crossbanded in olivewood and inlaid with candelabra, original fitted interior, c1790, 15 in (38 cm). **$1,000-1,200**

A figured mahogany and inlaid cutlery box, crossbanded in satinwood with boxwood stringing, the interior with original fittings and star chequered stringing, 18thC, 15 in (37.5 cm). **$400-600**

A pair of George II style mahogany and satinwood banded cutlery urns, inlaid with chequered stringing, c1900, 29½ in (74 cm). **$1,500-2,200**

A figured mahogany knife box, inlaid with white stringing, crossbanded in rosewood, early 18thC, 14½ in (36 cm). **$500-600**

A shagreen slope top knife box, with silver mounts, possibly John Whittington, mid-18thC, c1788. **$800-1,200**

A George III mahogany cutlery box, inlaid with narrow kingwood and wide satinwood bands and stringing, with original interior, together with 71 pieces of steel and stained green ivory table cutlery, 9 in (23 cm). **$1,700-2,500**

Tea Caddies

An unusual early Georgian mahogany caddy, 3 tinned canisters within, by Braithwaite, with original maker's label beneath, 10 in (25 cm) wide. **$600-700**

A George III mahogany tea caddy, inlaid in harewood with shell paterae, 4½ in (11 cm). **$300-400**

A George III rosewood and crossbanded cut-corner tea caddy, inlaid with flower paterae, 7 in (17.5 cm) wide. **$700-900**

A George III satinwood tea caddy, tulipwood crossbanded and satinwood line inlaid, with 2 divisions, 7 in (17.5 cm). **$600-700**

A pair of George III walnut veneered tea caddies, the bodies boxwood strung with frontal mahogany ovals, 4½ in (11 cm). **$1,500-2,200**

A George III amaranth tea caddy, with flat chased silver escutcheons and mounts, 11 in (27.5 cm). **$1,000-1,400**

A good George III oval inlaid tea caddy, veneered in fiddleback mahogany, 5½ in (14 cm) wide. **$700-900**

A George III inlaid tea caddy, the fiddleback mahogany lid and body inlaid with satinwood fan motifs, with Dutch drop handle, 6 in (15 cm). **$600-700**

A George III mahogany tea caddy, the side panels chequer strung and crossbanded, the lid with a border of rosewood between chequered borders of various woods including walnut and sycamore, 7 in (18 cm). **$500-600**

A George III satinwood and crossbanded cut corner tea caddy, with simulated fluting, inlaid in harewood, 7 in (17.5 cm). **$400-600**

A George III hexagon mahogany inlaid caddy, tulipwood crossbanded and chequer strung, 7 in (17 cm). **$1,200-1,500**

A rosewood tea caddy, with 3 gilt decorated ceramic canisters, marked the and sacre, early 19thC, 12 in (30 cm). **$700-900**

An inlaid ebony tea caddy, the veneered lid and sides inlaid with brass stemmed mother-of-pearl stylised foliage, with twin lidded compartments, early 19thC, 8 in (20.5 cm) wide. **$400-600**

A Regency yew-wood caddy, all boxwood strung, twin lidded compartments within, 7½ in (19 cm). **$400-600**

An unusual mahogany and boxwood strung caddy, the interior with 3 lidded compartments, 10 in (25.5 cm). **$300-400**

A George IV rosewood tea caddy, inlaid with continuous satinwood trailing branches, the twin lidded canister similarly decorated, flanking a glass blending bowl, 13 in (32 cm) wide. **$600-700**

A William IV bird's eye maple tea caddy, fitted with twin lidded compartments, 9 in (23 cm) wide. **$300-500**

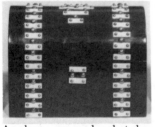

An ebony veneered casket shaped caddy, the interior with twin lidded sections, 8 in (20 cm) wide. **$300-400**

An unusual Stuart tartanware tea caddy, revealing twin lidded divisions with matching plaid, 8½ in (21 cm). **$700-900**

A Victorian coromandel tea caddy, with twin domed compartments with brass plaques, inscribed Black and Green, 9 in (22.5 cm). **$400-600**

A Victorian burr walnut caddy, the sides flanked by ebony baluster pilasters, with twin lidded compartments, 9 in (23 cm). **$300-400**

A Victorian coromandel and brass bound Gothic tea caddy, the twin compartments having spring operated lids marked Black and Green, inscribed Cumming & Son, Edinburgh, 9 in (23 cm) wide. **$500-600**

A silver inlaid tortoiseshell caddy, the silver inlay with engraved details, with single Dutch drop handle, on bracket feet, 18th/19thC, 4½ in (11 cm). **$3,000-4,500**

A tortoiseshell veneered tea caddy, early 19thC, 8 in (20 cm). **$500-600**

A Victorian pewter strung tortoiseshell tea caddy, 8½ in (21 cm). **$1,000-1,200**

A good penwork tea caddy, fitted with twin divisions within, early 19thC, 7½ in (18.5 cm) wide. **$1,000-1,200**

A George III mottled green stained pearwood tea caddy, as a gourd, the hinged cover with stalk finial, and with metal oval lock escutcheon, 5 in (13 cm) high. **$3,000-4,000**

A tortoiseshell bombe caddy, the pagoda roof revealing twin lidded compartments, all pewter strung, on ivory ball feet, 9 in (22 cm). **$1,000-1,200**

A tortoiseshell tea caddy, with ivory stringing and borders, late 18thC, 6½ in (16 cm). **$1,400-1,700**

A penwork caddy, the lid depicting a scene from the 'Lady of the Lake', first half 19thC, 8 in (20.5 cm). **$600-800**

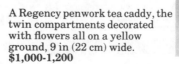

A Regency penwork tea caddy, the twin compartments decorated with flowers all on a yellow ground, 9 in (22 cm) wide. **$1,000-1,200**

A George III boxwood pumpkin tea caddy, painted mottled green, 5½ in (14 cm) high. **$2,000-3,000**

A Regency blonde tortoiseshell tea caddy, ivory strung throughout, the twin canisters with bird's eye maple lids banded in kingwood, 8 in (20 cm). **$1,000-1,200**

A George III tea caddy, in ivory, inlaid with tortoiseshell and with a silver escutcheon and finial, c1790. **$2,500-3,500**

A George III tortoiseshell tea caddy, inlaid with ivory. **$2,000-3,000**

A George III rolled paper caddy, framed by boxwood and ebony strung border, the lid with a central floral medallion, 7 in (18 cm) wide. **$1,000-1,200**

A Tunbridge ware and rosewood tea caddy, the body banded by a girdle of simulated marble, fitted with twin canisters and mixing bowl, 12½ in (31 cm) wide. **$600-900**

A Tunbridge ware and parquetry tea caddy, with rosewood veneered carcase, 6 in (15 cm) wide. **$300-400**

A George III mahogany and scrolled paper work tea caddy, dated 1789, 7 in (17.5 cm) wide. **$700-1,000**

A continental white lacquer caddy, twin lidded compartments within, 18th/19thC, 8½ in (21 cm) wide. **$400-600**

A papier-mache caddy, the black body painted with flowers amongst gilt scrolls, heightened with mother-of-pearl inlay, twin lidded compartments within, 9 in (23 cm). **$600-800**

l. An Indian export horn and ivory casket, the sandalwood interior with 2 ivory lidded compartments, mid-19thC, 10½ in (26 cm). **$700-900**
r. A papier-mache tea caddy, with mother-of-pearl inlay, the interior fitted with twin lidded canisters and a glass mixing bowl, 19thC, 16 in (40 cm). **$400-600**

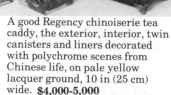

A good Regency chinoiserie tea caddy, the exterior, interior, twin canisters and liners decorated with polychrome scenes from Chinese life, on pale yellow lacquer ground, 10 in (25 cm) wide. **$4,000-5,000**

An unusual painted glass and straw-work caddy, the corners with straw mosaic, with pull-off cap, 18th/19thC, 5½ in (13.5 cm) high. **$300-400**

A Victorian papier-mache tea caddy, with central mother-of-pearl motif, 8 in (20 cm) wide. **$300-500**

A Chinese export lacquer caddy, with lidded pewter canister within, 8½ in (21 cm) wide. **$400-600**

A Regency Japanned caddy, the bombe outline decorated with anglicised oriental scenes, 8½ in (21 cm). **$1,000-1,200**

A black lacquered tea caddy, with gilt chinoiserie decoration, the interior adapted for twin sliding canisters at an early date, 18thC, 11 in (27 cm) wide. **$300-500**

A chinoiserie lacquered tea caddy, 13 in (32.5 cm) wide, early 19thC. **$1,200-1,500**

A fine gold and ivory caddy, trimmed with tortoiseshell border and stringing, late 18thC, 6½ in (16 cm). **$8,500-11,000**

l. A George III walnut tea caddy, the lid enclosing 3 brass canisters, the base with a concealed drawer, c1760, 9 in (22 cm) wide. **$600-800**
c. A Regency red lacquer papier-mache tray, painted with grisaille classical figures and gilt ruiseaux, stamped Howard, London, 18½ in (47 cm) wide. **$1,300-1,700**
r. A George IV Japanned tea caddy, lacquered in cream with chinoiserie figures, the interior with a pair of lidded canisters, c1825, 12 in (30 cm). **$1,200-1,500**

An ivory tea caddy, the edges trimmed with bright cut gold bands, with central dragon, armorial and loop handle, distressed, 4 in (10 cm) wide. **$700-1,000**

A set of three continental enamel caddies in a Vernis Martin case, the satinwood case with rosewood crossbanding to the lid and front, all painted with swags, the lid with Cupid's motifs, 13 in (33 cm) long, the caddies 5 in (12.5 cm) high. **$3,000-4,500**

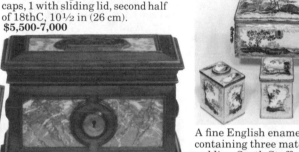

A good Chinese export mother-of-pearl caddy, containing 3 canisters, decorated with panels of birds amongst lotus, 2 with caps, 1 with sliding lid, second half of 18thC, 10½ in (26 cm). **$5,500-7,000**

An Austrian marble caddy, with veined marble panels within walnut borders, on brass bracket feet, a medallion beneath with the monogram F. Ausschl Privilegium Wien 905, 10 in (25 cm). **$300-400**

A Victorian mother-of-pearl tea caddy, opening to reveal a twin lidded interior, on ivory ball feet, 8 in (20 cm). **$600-700**

A fine English enamel tea casket containing three matching caddies, South Staffordshire, c1770, 8½ in (21 cm) long. **$34,500-44,200**

A set of three English enamel caddies in a Chinese export ivory casket, the enamels South Staffordshire, all in wooden travelling case, c1770. **$7,500-10,500**

An inlaid satinwood stationery cabinet, enclosing a fitted interior including postal scales and weights, 13 in (32.5 cm) high. **$500-600**

A large Indian white horn tea caddy, the sandalwood interior with twin ivory lidded canisters and aperture for bowl, first half 19thC, 15 in (37 cm). **$700-900**

A Victorian burr walnut brass bound writing slope. **$150-200**

A Tunbridge ware desk cabinet, with original maker's label, 9 by 6 in (22.5 by 15 cm). **$700-900**

A German Stobwasser lacquered
and painted snuff box, the lid
painted with 'The Village
Politicians after Wilkie', the
interior inscribed Stobwasser's
Fabrik in Braunschweig, 4 in
(10 cm). **$500-600**

A George III style mahogany and
boxwood lined collector's coin
cabinet, 19 in (47.5 cm).
$600-900

A lacquered composition box in
the manner of Stobwasser.
$300-500

A continental horn and bone
casket, 17th/18thC, 7 in (17 cm)
wide. **$600-700**

A mahogany writing pad folder,
9½ in (24 cm) wide. **$150-200**

A pollarded satinwood collector's
cabinet, inlaid throughout with
geometric borders, c1840, 9½ in
(24 cm) wide. **$1,300-1,700**

A George III mahogany
apothecaries cabinet, enclosing a
fitted interior with numerous
drawers and pigeonholes, c1800,
15 in (38 cm). **$1,000-1,400**

A rare George III satinwood and
stained sycamore artists box, the
multiple banded top inlaid with an
oval shell and fan spandrels, fitted
with 2 side drawers, the interior
with a baize hinged and adjustable
surface, above a well fitted with a
lead weight, c1780, 4 by 14 in (10
by 36 cm). **$1,000-1,200**

Eight painted bentwood utility
boxes,, comprising 4 round boxes
and 4 ovoid ones, one with
applique paper covering with
geometric decoration, 19thC, the
largest 13in (32.5cm) diam.
$800-1,000

Enamel

A fine painted and gilt decorated
lady's jewellery box, rectangular,
with a lift-top, decorated with a
river scene with house, a man in a
boat and a man fishing, a Greek
revival home with surrounding
trees, a primitive shanty with
trees, and a street scene with 4
people and over 12 buildings
including a hotel and bank,
possibly Broad Street, New York;
the reserves decorated with gilt
lattice work, minor restoration to
paint and gilt, American, 19thC,
11in (27.5cm) wide. **$3,500-4,500**

An Anglo-Indian ripple effect
coromandel workbox, the lid
inlaid with penwork floral ivory
inlays, fitted with various
compartments and cupboards and
2 matching layers, all with ivory
tortoiseshell, various wood
veneers and silver metal inlaid
facings, 17 in (43 cm) wide.
$300-600

A Staffordshire scent
bottle/bonbonniere, the green
ground with raised gilded
decoration, gilt-metal mounts and
chained scroll stopper, slight
damage, c1765, 4 in (10 cm) high.
$1,000-1,400

A South Staffordshire egg bonbonniere, with milled gilt-metal mounts, the dark blue ground painted with white dots, vertical lavender, yellow and red stripes, restored, 1775-1785, 1½ in (4 cm) high. **$600-700**

A Staffordshire hound's head bonbonniere, the black and white spotted dalmation with pink nostrils and staring yellow eyes, slight damage, 1770-1780, 2 in (5 cm) long. **$1,700-2,500**

A South Staffordshire enamel bonbonniere, formed as a negro's head, c1770. **$3,000-4,500**

A Birmingham snuff box, the underside with a red-breasted robin, the interior of the lid similarly decorated with a stable-boy leading a bay stallion, gilt metal mounts, cracked and chipped, mount loose, 1760-1765, 2¼ in (6 cm) wide. **$1,500-2,200**

An unusual Staffordshire snuff box, reserved on a deep purple ground with raised white scroll and dot decoration, gilt metal mounts with engine-turning, some restoration, c1765, 3 in (8 cm) wide. **$1,000-1,200**

A South Staffordshire enamel snuff box, painted with Frederick the Great, King of Prussia, after the engraving by Antoine Pesne, probably 1757. **$2,000-3,000**

A South Staffordshire table snuff box, with a pastoral subject, c1770. **$1,200-1,500**

A Bilston snuff box, embossed and coloured with flowers on a pale primrose ground, with raised gilt sprays, a few slight cracks, c1770, 2½ in (6 cm) long. **$1,500-2,200**

A South Staffordshire etui, containing a scent bottle, funnel, spoon and other trinkets, c1770. **$2,000-3,000**

A South Staffordshire table snuff box, with a scene from the Commedia dell'Arte, c1770. **$1,500-2,200**

> ## Use the Index!
> *Because certain items might fit easily into any of a number of categories, the quickest and surest method of locating any entry is by reference to the index at the back of the book.*
> *This has been fully cross-referenced for absolute simplicity.*

A South Staffordshire table snuff box, the surrounds richly decorated with raised gold on powder blue, the reserves painted with genre scenes, c1765. **$4,000-5,000**

Three South Staffordshire enamel patch boxes, c1790:-
t. **$400-600**
c. **$300-500**
b. **$300-400**

A 'Wednesbury' scent bottle case, on a deep blue ground, the interior of the lid pink, fitted with a glass scent bottle and stopper, c1780, 2 in (5 cm) wide. **$500-700**

A South Staffordshire etui, c1770. **$1,700-2,500**

A South Staffordshire scent bottle, c1770. **$2,000-3,000**

A South Staffordshire scent bottle, c1770. **$2,000-3,000**

A Staffordshire canister, the borders enriched with raised gilt and yellow scrolls, leaves and dots, the lid with minor cracks and one small chip, 1765-1770, 6 in (15 cm) diam. **$5,500-7,000**

A pair of South Staffordshire enamel candlesticks, painted with river scenes, classical landscapes and figures within reserves, c1770. **$3,500-5,000**

A Staffordshire patch box, with later blue lobed base, some restoration, c1802, 1½ in (4 cm) wide. **$700-900**

A Staffordshire patch box, the lid transfer-printed in black and coloured with Admiral Lord Nelson, the sides dark blue, the interior with steel mirror, restored, 1801-1805, 1½ in (4 cm) wide. **$1,000-1,200**

Nelson was created both Viscount and Vice-Admiral in 1801.

A South Staffordshire travelling inkwell, containing 2 inkpots, an amethyst seal and writing instruments, c1770. **$3,000-4,500**

A rare Birmingham plaque, painted on a white ground with a bouquet of pink yellow and vari-coloured roses, some cracks, 1750-1755, 5 by 4 in (14 by 10 cm). **$1,000-1,200**

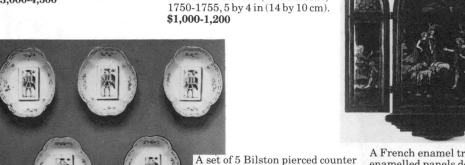

A set of 5 Bilston pierced counter trays, decorated with playing cards, c1780. **$1,000-1,400**

A French enamel triptych, the 6 enamelled panels depicting various Biblical scenes in colours and heightened in gilt, the 3 larger panels signed 'I.R.' in gilt, 19thC. **$700-900**

A pair of tôle peinte verrières, with painted gilt decoration on a mottled red ground, probably French, c1800. **$2,000-3,000**

A rare rectangular Birmingham plaque, transfer printed and painted en grisaille with the Raising of the Cross, two chips, some cracks, 1750-1755, 5 by 4 in (14 by 10 cm). **$600-800**

It would appear that this plaque, which does not form part of the 'Passion' series based on the prints by Sebastian LeClerc, may have been executed experimentally in Birmingham.

An enamel mustard pot and cover, in the form of a knight in armour, probably Birmingham, c1770. **$2,000-3,000**

Ex. Ionides Collection.

A pair of yellow tôle peinte chestnut urns and covers, with paintings of figures with oval reserves, c1790. **$4,500-5,000**

Transport

A 1929 Sunbeam 16 HP four door saloon, engine, 6-cylinder, overhead valve, 2040 cc, 16 hp. 4 speed manual gearbox with right hand change, 4 wheel brakes, artillery wheels, semi-elliptic suspension. **$7,500-10,500**

A 1931 Morris Cowley three-quarter sliding head coupe with dickey, engine, 4-cylinder, side valve, 1550 cc, 11.9 hp, manual 3 forward speed gearbox, 4 wheel brakes, quarter-elliptic suspension. **$4,500-7,000**

Morris was one of the great early success stories of the British Motor Industry. William Morris chose the Cowley Model name in honour of the Oxford suburb where his cars were built.

A 1932 Riley Gamecock special series sports two-seater, engine, 4-cylinder, monobloc, detachable head, 1087, cc, ohv with separate camshafts for inlet and exhaust, manual transmission, semi-elliptic suspension. **$8,500-10,000**

The Riley Gamecock was one of the most attractive versions of the touring Riley Nine range. The first Nine was announced in 1926 at Olympia, and this was to be the model that gave the company real impetus.

A 1932 M.G. Midget 8/33 long chassis type D occasional four-seater, engine, 4-cylinder, single overhead camshaft, 848 cc, 8 hp, 4 speed crash box with remote control gear change, front and rear wheel brakes operated independently for foot pedal and hand lever, suspension semi-elliptic front and rear. **$9,000-13,000**

A 1934 Rolls-Royce 20/25 sports saloon, coachwork by Freestone and Webb, engine, 6-cylinder, overhead valve, 3700 cc, 4 speed synchromesh transmission, 4 wheel mechanical brakes with servo assistance, semi-elliptic suspension. **$15,000-20,500**

A 1947 Lagonda 2.6 litre sports saloon, engine, 6-cylinder, double overhead camshaft, 2580 cc, 4 speed manual gearbox with column change, 4 wheel hydraulic brakes, independent suspension. **$2,000-3,000**

Miller's is a price GUIDE not a price LIST

The price ranges given reflect the average price a purchaser should pay for similar items. Condition, rarity of design or pattern, size, colour, pedigree, restoration and many other factors must be taken into account when assessing values.

A 1947 Jaguar 2½ litre sports saloon, engine, 6-cylinder, pushrod operated overhead valve, 2.6 litres, twin SU carburettors, 4 speed manual gearbox, semi-elliptic suspension at front and rear. **$7,500-10,500**

A 1954 M.G. TF sports two-seater, engine, 4-cylinder, 1250 cc, overhead valve, manual gearbox, 4 wheel hydraulic brakes, independent front and semi-elliptic rear suspension. **$10,000-13,000**

A 1959 Rover 80 four door saloon, engine, 4-cylinder, overhead valve, 2286 cc, 4 speed with overdrive transmission, independent front suspension, semi-elliptic rear, disc front brakes, drums at rear. **$5,500-7,000**

A 1950 Bristol 400 sports saloon, engine, 6-cylinder, 1971 cc, inclined overhead valves, pushrod and rocker operated, 4 wheel hydraulic brakes, independent front suspension, torsion bars rear. **$6,000-8,000**

Introduced in 1946 as an Anglicised version of the pre-war 327 BMW, only some 700 examples of this high quality 4-seat saloon were built.

A 1937 Morris 10-4 four door saloon car no. S2/TN54779. **$300-500**

An early child's pedal car, c1912, overall length 40 in (102 cm). **$600-900**

A rare front wheel drive aluminium Pylon Racer, modelled on a Maserati, c1948, 19 in (48 cm) long. **$600-700**

A 1923 Ariel 498 cc solo motorcycle, engine, single cylinder, 498 cc, 3 speed transmission. **$1,000-1,200**

An Edwardian horse drawn ice cream cart, 141 in (359 cm). **$1,000-1,200**

A 1921 B.S.A. 986 cc solo motorcycle, engine, twin cylinder, adjustable tappets, Mills carburettor, alternatives B.S.A. or Amac, magneto ignition, BSA, sprung frontforks. **$1,700-2,500**

A Victorian dog cart. **$400-600**

A gipsy caravan, Reading style, the panelled sides in green and ribbed blue, 'The Queen' No. 6 by D.F. & Co., by Fennings of Ely, c1895, the whole, c1920. **$3,500-5,000**

A 4-wheel sprung delivery wagon, by Old of Crewkerne, to suit 12.2 hh to 13.2 hh, c1885. **$1,000-1,200**

A Ralli cart, to suit approximately 13.2 hh, by Northover Brothers Bridport and Dorchester, some worm to wings and mudguards but basically sound and in original condition, c1895. **$400-600**

A Romany or showman's late Victorian travelling/living wagon, 'Vardo', by Thomas Tong of Kearsley, Lancashire, c1900, 158 in (401 cm) long. **$5,500-7,000**

An early Velocipede/Boneshaker bicycle, rideable with care, traces of early red enamel to wheels etc, 1860-1870's period, the front wheel approximately 34½ in (86 cm). **$1,000-1,400**

A pair of brass Auterroche opera lights, with bevelled glass and blue filters, 8½ in (22 cm) high. **$300-500**

A hearse, fitted with Warner wheels and lever brake, to suit a single or pair of approximately 15 hh, by Browns of Windsor, although slightly faded all is in original and sound condition, c1895. **$3,000-4,000**

A brass and enamelled Owner Drivers Club badge, stamped 5236, 2½ in (6.5 cm) high. **$300-400**

An exceptionally rare Lucas Motor Luminator, self-generating acetylene central fitting motorcar or fore-car headlamp, 1903-1904 period, 9½ in (23.5 cm) tall overall. **$600-700**

The Motor Luminator was produced in small numbers from about 1902 to 1906 period, and few have survived.

A very rare Ordinary/ Highwheeler bicycle oil powered Hub Lamp, approximately 6½ in (16 cm) tall, stamped Regd. Feb. 14/80. **$400-600**

A motoring picnic hamper, in a brass bound box shaped as a foot rest, 23 in (58 cm) long. **$700-900**

A motoring picnic case, vintage, by Asprey of London. **$600-800**

A pair of brass Lucas King's own sidelights, stamped F141, 8½ in (22 cm) high. **$400-600**

A nickel-plated Royal Automobile Club badge, stamped D4563, 5½ in (14 cm) high. **$100-150**

An electroplated travelling lantern, late 19thC, 9 in (23 cm) high when extended. **$200-300**

A brass Motor Union badge, stamped 1287, 6 in (15 cm) high. **$300-400**

A brass Automobile Association badge, inscribed Stenson Cooke Secretary, stamped 8388, 5 in (13 cm) high. **$100-150**

A brass Royal Automobile Club Associate badge, stamped B40, the centre inscribed Sussex Motor Yacht Club, 5 in (12 cm) high. **$300-400**

A brass and enamelled Royal Automobile Club Associate badge, stamped B2529, the centre inscribed Middlesex County Automobile Club, 4½ in (12 cm) high. **$100-150**

A nickel-plated Royal Automobile Club Associate badge, stamped N35, inscribed Ladies Automobile Club of Great Britain and Ireland, 4½ in (12 cm) high. **$400-600**

A silver-plated figure of a winged nymph, inscribed JNN 1929, 5 in (13 cm) high. **$600-700**

A hollow Royal Automobile Club badge, stamped B1698, 7 in (17 cm) high. **$300-400**

l. A B.A.R.C./Brooklands full member's car badge, numbered 1253 to the reverse. **$300-400**
c. A Selner type late Edwardian silver plated 'Victory' mascot, the base stamped Rd. 669818. **$100-150**
r. A nickelled mascot of a 'Penguin', the base stamped A. Becquerel, rare vintage period. **$150-200**

A white metal figure of a man holding a steering wheel, signed Le Verrier, 3 in (8 cm). **$150-200**

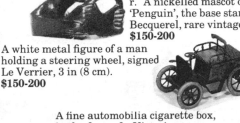

l. A good Rolls Royce 'Kneeling Lady' mascot. **$200-300**
r. A scarce chrome-plated brass Isotta-Fraschini 'Triomphe' type motorcar mascot, 1930's period, 7½ in (18.5 cm) tall. **$100-200**

See 'Motor Mascots of the World', page 118, illustration 455.

A fine automobilia cigarette box, in the form of a Victorian motorcar, approx. 7 in (17 cm) long. **$600-800**

A bronze figure of a seated hare, the base inscribed A. Becquerel and Etling Paris 7543, 7½ in (19 cm) high. **$300-400**

A nickelled 'Spirit of Ecstasy' mascot, for the late Silver Ghost or Phantom One range of Rolls Royce motorcars, approx 6½ in (16.5 cm). **$300-400**

A cast iron centre plate from goods yard gate, possibly Ashford inscribed S.E. & C.R, 11 in (28cm) long. **$60-90**

A brass and red painted number plate, no. 559, 18 by 7 in (46 by 18 cm). **$80-150**

l. The Spirit of Triumph, a chromium-plated stylised figure marked F. Bazin, 6½ in (16.5 cm) high. **$200-300**
r. An Art Deco silver-plated ram, marked G. Poitvin, made in France, no. 21-1777-10, Finnigans of London, 5½ in (14 cm) long. **$400-600**

A brass caricature figure of a grinning cat, 4 in (11 cm) high. **$400-600**

A nickel plated brass caricature figure of a policeman, with painted porcelain head and movable helmet, inscribed Hassall Rd, 611041, 4½ in (11.5 cm) high. **$400-600**

A rare double-sided yellow, red, white, black, blue and grey cnamelled garage advertising and promotional sign for Morris Trucks, early 1920s, approx. 22 by 16 in (55 by 40 cm). **$300-400**

A chrome plated flat type Minerva 'Goddess' mascot on cap, early 1930's, 4 in (10 cm) rare, on correct radiator cap. **$300-500**

l. A top quality chrome plated brass figure of a 'Landing Eagle', crouched on a tree branch, vintage period, the wingspan approx 13 in (33 cm). **$200-300**

A nickel-plated Williamson ticket printer, for tramways, omnibuses, railways, steamboats, stamped 26673, 5 in (13 cm) high, and a quantity of bus tickets. **$50-70**

A set of five Great Western Railway baluster shape pewter tankards. **$500-600**

North British Railway The Home and Haunts of Sir Walter Scott, unframed, colour lithograph, 40 by 25 in (102 by 64 cm). **$300-500**

A black painted South Eastern Railway hand lamp, with red and green filters, internal part missing, 9 in (24 cm) high. **$100-200**

A brass Acme Thunderer Whistle, stamped S.E. & C.R. **$50-70**

Greatstone by the Romney Hythe and Dymchurch Railway, by N. Cramer Roberts, colour lithograph, published by Vincent Brooks Day and Son Ltd., 40 by 25 in (102 by 64 cm). **$100-150**

Sheffield Express leaving St. Pancras 1905, by Richard A. Marshall, signed inscribed and dated 1977, gouache and water colour, 14 by 20 in (36 by 51 cm). **$600-700**

Bradshaw's Continental Railway Steam Navigation and Conveyance Guide and Travellers Manual, no. 1, 6th Mo. June, 1847. **$60-90**

Ravenglass and Eskdale Railway, six whole, 1906 to 1908. **$25-30**

A chronium-plated model of a Hurricane Fighter, mounted on a green marble ashtray, 9½ in (24 cm). **$200-300**

An early padded flying helmet. **$300-500**

North British Railway Extension of West Highland Railway from Fort William to Mallaig for Skye, Lewis and the other Western Islands, unframed, colour lithograph, 43½ by 30 in (110 by 76 cm). **$400-600**

A GWR Railway map of Great Britain, showing routes and connections, laid on cloth, 24½ by 39 in (62 by 99 cm). **$60-100**

The Aerial Derby Sat. May 23rd, 1914, weather permitting at Hendon, with pictorial vignette of air race by Cyrus Cuneo, published by The Dangerfield Printing Co London 1.5.14, on cloth, 30 by 20 in (76 by 51 cm). **$400-600**

A wooden nameplate, from the stern of the British Princess, 34 in (85 cm). **$100-150**

A white metal cigarette lighter, modelled as a standing figure of an airman holding a propeller, 10½ in (27 cm). **$600-700**

631

The "Daily Mail" £5,000 Prize.

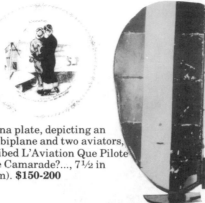

A china plate, depicting an early biplane and two aviators, inscribed L'Aviation Que Pilote Votre Camarade?..., 7½ in (19 cm). **$150-200**

A Hardy 'Uniqua' salmon fly reel, ivorine handle, oval drum latch stamped OIL, c1912, **$50-70**

The 'Daily Mail' £5,000 prize, all about the Waterplane Race Round Britain – August 16, rules and regulations, on card, published by George Phillips and Son, 20 by 12½ in (51 by 32 cm). **$500-600**

A WWI Biplane rudder, with R.F.C. markings and Hickory skid, 49 in (125 cm) high. **$300-500**

Reputed to have crashed in South Tipperary, 1917.

Fishing

A finely carved and painted wooden cast of a large salmon, killed by Admiral Britten on the Namsen River, the Jorum Beat, June 1899, 52 in (130 cm). **$1,300-1,700**

A Hardy Bros. Uniqua fishing reel, 3½ in (9 cm). **$60-90**

A Hardy 'Perfect' all brass fly reel, early transitional model with nickel silver rim and bridges, c1892, 3 in (7.5 cm). **$1,000-1,400**

A good stuffed brown trout, by J. Cooper & Sons, with paper label Caught in Lough Corrib, June 11th, 1912, weight 6 3/4 lbs, the case 31 in (77.5 cm). **$300-400**

J. Cooper & Sons were most prominent and fine experts of this trade.

An Alvey fishing reel, 5 in (12.5 cm). **$50-70**

An American erotic fishing lure, the mermaid, green tail, red head, 36-22-34 mm. **$15-30**

A Hardy 'Sea Silex' sea reel, twin black handles, c1925, 5 in 12.5 cm). **$80-150**

A Pegley-Davies anglers' knife, of nickel silver, 6 tools, knife blade broken. **$15-30**

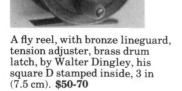

A fly reel, with bronze lineguard, tension adjuster, brass drum latch, by Walter Dingley, his square D stamped inside, 3 in (7.5 cm). **$50-70**

An early brass reel, apparently made from the face of a disused 17thC clock, poor condition, 2 in (5 cm). **$80-150**

A Malloch's patent spinning reel with horn handle, smooth brass foot and line guard arm, c1900, 4 in (10 cm) diam. **$50-70**

A rare 5 in (12.5 cm) 1896-model all brass 'perfect' reel, smooth foot, large ivory knob, bronzing worn on rims, pillars and round handles, but otherwise strong, in leather case, c1896. **$1,500-2,200**

A Hardy Bros 'Bouglé' lightweight fly reel, grooved alloy foot, stand off pillars, including one roller, black handle and Mark II check, finish worn. **$1,000-1,200**

An oblong galvanized zinc live bait can, c1920, 9 in (22.5 cm). **$15-30**

An exceptionally rare Hardy Bros 2½ in (6 cm) 1891-model 'perfect' reel no 231, with ivory handle and Rod-in-Hand mark, retaining much bronzed finish. **$5,500-7,000**

A fine mahogany fly box containing approx 120 gut-eyed salmon flies, 19thC. **$300-400**

Two brown trout by J Cooper & Sons, in bowed glazed case, 33 in (82.5 cm) wide. **$300-400**

Two perch in bowed glazed case caught by H Lord at Dogdyke, August 1903, 34½ in (86 cm) wide. **$300-400**

A stuffed sea trout, in bow fronted case, 27 in (67.5 cm). **$300-400**

A carved wood life size salmon trophy, the fish painted in bluish hues, mounted on mahogany, inscribed upper Glen Tana, April 12th 1907, 46 in (115 cm). **$700-1,000**

A Hardy Bros Ltd 'sea silex' alloy reel with smooth brass foot, ebonite handles and ivorine check handle, brass tension lever, 7 in (15.5 cm) diam. **$300-500**

An Ogden Smith 'exchequer' trout fly reel, brass foot, retaining much original finish, 3½ in (8.5 cm). **$30-45**

A 'carry all' style wicker creel with leather straps, c1910. **$60-100**

A very rare Hardy Bros St George Tournament fly reel of lightweight alloy construction with fully ventilated drum, with black handle and fixed check, c1938, 3 in (7.5 cm). **$800-1,200**

A perforated bait horn, with cork stopper, hardwood base, 19thC, 8 in (20 cm). **$50-70**

A Hans Coper vase, the interior fired dark brown, the exterior mottled and with a spiral band, impressed mark, 5 in (12.5 cm). **$400-600**

A black stoneware vase form, by Hans Coper, covered in a burnished matt manganese glaze, impressed HC seal, c1965, 10½ in (26.5 cm). **$4,500-7,000**

A stoneware handbuilt bust of a man, the 'grogged' surface incised and painted in naturalistic colours, wearing a blue jacket, shirt and green and blue striped tie, incised J.H. Crowley, 20½ in (51 cm) wide. **$700-1,000**

An earthenware slab built vase, by Jacqueline Poncelet, the pale yellow ground striped with white and brown slips and decoration with russet shaped rectangular forms, 12 in (30cm). **$1,700-2,500**

A porcelain rounded bowl, with pierced and cut wide rim, by Eileen Nisbet, covered in a matt blue-green glaze with unglazed outer surface and rim, c1978, 7 in (17.5 cm). **$400-600**

An early and large earthenware slip decorated dish, by Bernard Leach, covered in a golden-brown galena glaze, the centre decorated in dark brown slip, the foot with rectangular slip mark, dated in the border 1920 and enclosing BL script initials, some restoration, 18 in (45 cm). **$1,500-2,200**

A stoneware slab built form, 'Noah's Ark', by Elizabeth Fritsch, matt-glazed in buff and greyish-green, slight restoration to the rim of bowl, c1974, 14 in (35 cm) wide. **$1,500-2,200**

A stoneware flattened rectangular slab bottle, by Bernard Leach, under an iron-brown and hakeme glaze, impressed BL and St. Ives seals, c1959, 8 in (19.5 cm) high. **$3,000-4,000**

A Bernard Leach red pottery dish, decorated with a single oak leaf in cream slip on a dark brown glaze, impressed mark, 8 in (20 cm). **$200-300**

◄ A stoneware thick handbuilt vase, by Ruth Duckworth, the textured surface covered in a dark sepia pigment streaked with green, impressed RWD seal, c1965, 9 in (23 cm) high. **$600-700**

A stoneware oviform vase, by Bernard Leach, made at Dartington Hall, the galena glaze appearing as a metallic black glaze over dark green, impressed BL script seal, c1936, 8 in (20 cm). **$700-1,000**

A stoneware large flattened bowl, by Lucie Rie, covered in a slightly pitted white glaze with a profusion of running manganese specks, impressed LR seal, c1955, 13½ in (34 cm) wide. **$1,500-2,200**

A stoneware vase, by Bernard Leach, covered in a finely mottled blackish-green glaze with traces of iron-brown, impressed BL and St. Ives seals, c1965, 14 in (35 cm). **$1,000-1,200**

A large stoneware bottle, by Janet Leach, covered in a matt dark brown glaze decorated in white slip, impressed JL and St. Ives seals, 19½ in (49 cm). **$600-800**

An inlaid porcelain footed bowl, by Lucie Rie, covered in a matt white glaze and decorated with blue inlaid double linear bands, impressed LR seal, c1982, 9 in (22.5 cm). **$1,300-1,700**

Cf.ed. John Houston, Lucie Rie, Crafts Council, London, 1981, plate 205.

A stoneware footed flared bowl, by Lucie Rie, covered in a lightly pitted cream glaze with a wide copper manganese fluxed and run rim, impressed LR seal, c1980, 10 in (25 cm). **$3,000-4,000**

A stoneware white-glazed bowl, by Lucie Rie, with run matt manganese border and the shiny white glaze flecked with running manganese, impressed LR seal, c1965, 7 in (17.5 cm). **$1,000-1,200**

A porcelain footed large flared bowl, by Lucie Rie, with bronze glazed centre within concentric manganese inlaid rings on a matt white glaze, impressed LR seal, c1980, 10 in (25 cm). **$3,000-4,000**

A stoneware sgraffito bowl, by Lucie Rie, the interior covered in a lightly specked white glaze, the exterior with vertical sgraffito, through a matt manganese glaze, impressed LR seal, c1960, 6 in (15 cm). **$600-800**

An inlaid porcelain and sgraffito bowl, by Lucie Rie, the matt manganese glaze revealing the white body with a thick bronze glaze running from the rim, with purple inlaid white bands alternating with bands of sgraffito through manganese, impressed LR seal, c1980, 9 in (22 cm). **$3,000-4,000**

A stoneware large bowl, by Lucie Rie, covered in a pitted thick white glaze separating to reveal the grey-brown body, impressed LR seal, c1970, 10 in (25 cm). **$4,500-7,000**

Cf.ed. John Houston, Lucie Rie, Crafts Council, London, 1981, plate 163.

A stoneware large bulb bowl and stand, by Lucie Rie, with drainage hole through the foot, the body a medium brown, covered in a white glaze, both pieces impressed with LR seal, restoration to rim of bowl, c1962, 12 in (30 cm) diam. of bowl, 8½ in (21 cm) diam. of stand. **$1,200-1,500**

A porcelain lustre-glazed footed bowl, by Mary Rich, decorated in gold and copper lustres over grey, impressed M seal, 9½ in (24 cm) diam. **$400-600**

A stoneware handbuilt vase, by John Ward, covered in a matt white glaze with traces of pale green, impressed JW seal, 9½ in (24 cm) wide. **$500-600**

An inlaid porcelain white beaker vase, by Lucie Rie, with 4 grey inlaid rings and covered in a matt white glaze with traces of pale pink, impressed LR seal, c1980, 6 in (15 cm) high. **$500-600**

A stoneware black flat thistle form, by Hans Coper, covered in a blistered and pitted matt black manganese glaze, impressed HC seal, restoration to rim, c1962, 8 in (20 cm) high. **$1,000-1,200**

Tribal Art

An Ejagham wood mask, yellow ochre face and black features, probably Nigeria, 13 in (32.5 cm) high. **$400-600**

A pair of Yoruba brass staves, edan Ogboni, each with the finial cast as a head, the conical headgears with pierced loop finials linked by a length of chain, iron spikes, from Ijebu-Ode, 9 in (23 cm) high. **$600-700**

A very fine Yoruba wood horseman, black patina with traces of ochre-coloured pigment on the lips, ears and pectoral pendant, 19thC, 22 in (56 cm) high. **$14,000-17,000**

This is unmistakably by the hand of a sculptor of Ota, 20 miles north of Lagos.
The nobility of the chief who is represented is emphasized by the simple lines of his tunic and by the rod, whip or long flywhisk which he carries over his shoulder. The statue would probably have stood on a shrine, to do honour to an (unidentified) orisha.

A fine Yoruba wood staff, for the Shango cult, two neolithic celts carved in relief, glossy brown patina, formerly at Owu, 23 in (58 cm) high. **$3,000-4,000**

A Yoruba wood staff, for the Shango cult, incised geometric ornament, traces of blue and white pigments, near to Nigeria-Benin border in the region of Keto or Meko, 22½ in (56 cm) high. **$300-500**

A pair of Yoruba wood twin figures, the cheeks with incised scarification marks, slight erosion, from Oshogbo, each 9 in (23.5 cm) high. **$400-600**

A Yoruba wood bowl, with cover, for Ifa divination, crusty black patina, probably from west central Yorubaland, or just possibly from the Igbomina village of Oro, 17½ in (44 cm) diam. **$1,000-1,400**

A Yoruba wood male figure, for Eshu, standing with a large flute, the crescent coiffure carved with another head at the end and a strut for suspension of ornaments, black patina, by Bamgboye, Chief Alaga of Odo-Owa (d.1978), 12½ in (31 cm) high. **$600-700**

An Ibibio wood mask, traces of red, white and yellow pigments, black patina, plaited and knotted fibre headdress, damaged, probably from Ikot Ekpene district, 15 in (37.5 cm) high. **$700-900**

A female Ibeji, metal-stud-inlay eyes, glossy dark reddish brown patina, from Oro, some restoration, 10½ in (26 cm) high. **$300-500**

A Luena wood female figure, with raised coffee-bean eyes below the scorched brows, raised incised headband to the lobed scorched coiffure, minor chips, 20 in (49 cm) high. **$1,400-1,700**

A fine Ogoni wood antelope mask, crusty black patina, 14½ in (36 cm) high. **$1,200-1,500**

An Ogoni wood mask, with articulated lower jaw, crusty black patina, 12½ in (31 cm). **$500-600**

A Lulua wood standing female figure, 10½ in (26 cm) high. **$500-700**

An Ibo wood figure, ikenga, with a sceptre to the right hand, a decapitated head in the left, painted black and white with applied bands of red felt, 21 in (52.5 cm) high. **$400-600**

A Makonde wood mask, with large nose below the protruding brow, gum applied to the eyebrows, glossy reddish brown patina, left ear damaged, 7 in (18 cm) high. **$600-900**

A rare Songo wood male figure, the detachable penis missing, 10¼ in (26 cm) high. **$1,500-2,200**

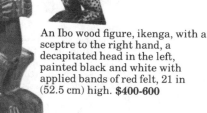

A pair of Naga basketwork bracelets, with bands of cut cowries, 7 in (17 cm) high. **$150-200**

A Benin bronze belt mask, the pupils inlaid with iron, pierced coral-beaded headdress, mid-18thC, 7 in (17 cm) high. **$3,000-4,000**
This appears to have been cast before the introduction of hatching of the eye borders, thought to have been about 1775. The clean neat casting further tends to associate it with the Eresonyen revival of bronze-casting (c1735-1750).

◄

An Ibo wood title stool, incised with chevrons and carved with 4 stylised birds, dark glossy patina, from Awka, Nigeria, 25 in (64 cm) high. **$1,500-2,200**

A Kongo wood figure, with hand-less arms, the eyes inlaid with glass, beaded ear-rings, 7½ in (19 cm) high. **$500-700**

A Benin terracotta head, remains of a beaded collar, a cylindrical hole at the centre, reddish patina, damages to the coiffure and left side of the face, 16thC, 5 in (13 cm) high. **$3,000-4,500**

Terracotta heads in Benin were made for the ancestral altars of the hereditary brass-casters and serve the same purpose as the bronze heads on the Oba's altars and the wooden heads on those of lesser chiefs. These heads are all called uhumwelao.

A large Kongo basket, in buff and dark brown, probably Vili, Zaire, minor damages, 19thC, 13 in (33 cm) high. **$600-900**

A Senufo wood female figure, a twisted brass and copper bracelet to the right wrist, sticky dark brown patina, 7½ in (19 cm) high. **$1,000-1,200**

A Bembe wood seated female figure, the eyes inlaid with white porcelain ovals, some cracks, 10½ in (26 cm) high. **$4,500-7,000**

This is very unusual by virtue of its size (almost twice the usual). It should be noted that the anus has not been pierced, an operation carried out by the doctor (nganga), not the carver. This means that it was used not by the Bembe, but (probably) by the Teke who do not pierce the anus.

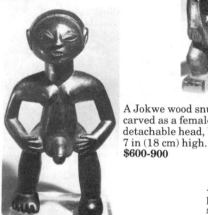

A Jokwe wood snuff container, carved as a female figure, with detachable head, black patina, 7 in (18 cm) high. **$600-900**

A Luba Shankadi wood male figure, black patina, 10½ in (27 cm) high. **$3,000-4,000**

A Baule wood maternity figure, a panel of raised 'latticework' scarification about the navel, blue twisted fibre waistband, pierced at the anus through to the sex for the attachment of a skirt, glossy black patina, cracks, c1920, 21 in (53 cm) high. **$7,000-9,000**

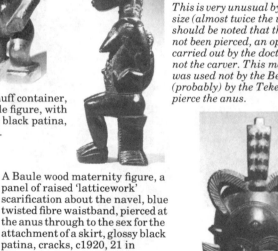

A Senufo wood mask, kpelie, of female form, glossy black patina, 13 in (32 cm) high. **$600-800**

A pair of fine Benin bronze armlets, possibly for the Yoruba Ogboni cult, with loops to retain bells, probably late 19thC, 5 in (12 cm) high. **$2,000-3,000**

A Baule wood mask, probably for the Goli ceremony, 17 in (43 cm). **$1,000-1,200**

A wood helmet mask, for the Sande society, sowei, black patina, probably Sherbro or Temne, 17 in (42 cm) high. **$1,000-1,200**

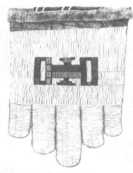

A Sotho beaded hide apron, 21 in (53 cm) long. **$300-500**

A fine Lele-Pende wood cup, the face with Pende features, cross-hatched coiffure, 4 in (9.5 cm) high. **$600-900**

A Mangbetu ivory female figure, with pierced ears, traces of red about the mouth, 14 in (34.5 cm) high. **$1,000-1,200**

An East African wood female figure, white-bead eyes set in gum, gum applied to the eyebrows and coiffure, glossy dark brown patina, 10 in (25 cm) high. **$1,300-1,700**

A fine Pende wood staff, the finial carved with a female figure, with pierced anus, glossy dark brown patina, 21 in (52.5 cm) long, the figure 9 in (22 cm) high. **$3,000-4,000**

A Plains feather war bonnet, the 28 eagle feathers bound with red stroud. **$1,000-1,200**

An Indonesian wood seated male figure, the applied eyes painted gold with black pupils, pierced anus, glossy dark brown patina, 8½ in (21 cm). **$300-600**

An Ojibwa beaded cloth bandolier bag, 63 in long (160 cm). **$600-700**

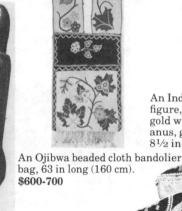

A Kota wood reliquary figure, applied with brass and copper, eroded lozenge base, 13 in (33 cm) high. **$7,500-10,500**

This is in the style of the Obamba sub-tribe, living to the south of Okandja between the rivers Sebe and Lekoni.

A Naga wood group of a male and female in copula, glossy dark brown patina, 11 in (27.5 cm). **$300-400**

A pair of Great Lakes beaded skin moccasins, 9½ in long (24 cm). **$150-200**

A fine Eastern Great Lakes wood 'ball-headed' club, minor damages, early 19thC, 25 in long (62 cm). **$2,000-3,000**

A Navajo silver and turquoise squash-blossom necklace, 24 in long (60 cm). **$400-600**

A Navajo rug, woven in natural brown, white, grey and red handspun yarn with a Third Phase pattern, 60 by 51 in (152 by 130 cm). **$1,500-2,200**

639

A Mochica portrait jar, in red and cream slip, 8 in (20.5 cm). **$500-600**

A Solomon Islands oval wood bowl, crusty black patina, damages, 19thC, 21 in (52 cm). **$400-600**

A Cameroon wood stool, scorched features and ornament to light brown patina, Tikar/Babanki-Kijem, 16 in (41 cm). **$400-600**

A Marquesas Islands basalt poi pounder, the finial carved as a janiform head, a raised panel of linear ornament to each cheek, worn features, reddish grey patina, 8 in (19.5 cm). **$1,500-2,200**

A fine Tairona gold nose ring, Columbia, 1⅓ oz. **$1,000-1,400**

A Solomon Islands wood staff, painted red and black, traces of white pigment, Buka or Bougainville, 61 in long (156 cm). **$300-400**

A rare Nootka whalebone club, the bifurcated finial damaged, old worn patina, stamped with a cannon and the number MA 3548, 19 in (48 cm) long. **$1,500-2,200**

A Peruvian black ware vessel, 7½ in (19 cm). **$150-200**

A Cameroon beaded cloth dance headdress, in the form of a leopard, 78 in (198 cm) long. **$1,000-1,400**

A Tami Island elliptical wood bowl, glossy black patina, 25 in long (62 cm). **$600-800**

A Maori Nephrite figure neck pendant, hei tiki, with some translucent inclusions, with attached bone toggle, 4½ in high (11.5 cm). **$2,000-3,000**

An Australian Aborigine swamp fig fighting shield, painted with asymmetrical motifs in red, yellow and white ochres within black pigment borders, minor damages, north-east Queensland, 19thC, 37 in high (92 cm). **$6,000-8,000**

The irregular form of these shields is due to their being carved from the root of the swamp fig tree. A young man would paint his own shield after initiation with designs associated with protective totems and myths.

A fine Maori wood female figure, the face and lower back with engraved tattooing, moko, the eyes inset with coloured glass, one ear broken, prominent knee joints, feet missing, dark brown patina, first half 19thC, 11 in high (27 cm). **$6,000-8,000**

A Maori wood post, the faces blackened and carved with moko, with shell inlay eyes, 44 in high (111 cm). **$3,500-5,000**

The original painted bass drum skin for 'The Beatles', marked in handpainted black, on aluminium rim, c1964, 20½ in (52 cm). **$7,000-9,000**

An early and interesting 'Quarry Men' calling card, c1958, 2½ by 4 in (6 by 9.3 cm). **$1,000-1,400**

Original Dezo Hoffmann photograph of John Lennon, signed by the photographer, mounted with photographer's label on the reverse, 13 by 12 in (33 by 30 cm). **$300-500**

A 'Presentation' gold disc 'Help', of gold coloured metal mounted above presentation plaque bearing RIAA stamp, framed and glazed, 14 by 11 in (36 by 28 cm). **$8,500-10,000**

Pop Ephemera

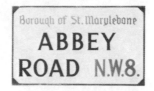

Borough of St. Marylebone 'Abbey Road' Street, sign, 18 by 30 in (46 by 76 cm). **$600-700**

A photographic concert bill and entrance ticket, 'The Beatles for their Fans', the concert April 5th 1962. **$500-600**

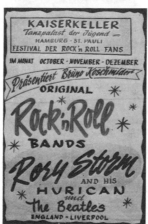

A hand painted poster from the Kaiserkeller, introducing Rory Storm and 'his Hurican und the Beatles', Hamburg, 1960, 43 by 29 in (109 by 74 cm). **$2,000-3,000**

Original Dezo Hoffmann ► photograph of Louis Armstrong, signed by the photographer, 11½ by 15½ in (29 by 39.5 cm). **$200-300**

Beatles 1961-62 fan club card, marked Honorary Member, in blue ink, with a concert card. **$400-600**

Original Harry Hammond photograph of the Beatles, taken in 1963, signed by the photographer, 16 by 20 in (40.5 by 51 cm). **$600-800**

A Beatles 'Presentation' silver disc, to mark the sale of 250,000 copies of their sixth L.P. 'Rubber Soul', February 1966, 18½ in by 16 in (47 by 40.5 cm). **$5,500-7,000**

A Fleetwood Mac 'Presentation' gold disc 'Rumours', framed and glazed, 21 by 17 in (52.5 by 42.5 cm). **$3,000-4,000**

John Lennon's Winebitch 'Professional' harmonica, with sharp/flat lever adjustment, 5 in (12.5 cm) long. **$1,700-2,500**

Used on the 'Walls and Bridges' album.

John Lennon handwritten lyrics 'I'm in Love', in blue ball-point pen, c1963, 7 by 5 in (18 by 13 cm). **$3,000-4,000**

The above lyrics relate to a Lennon/McCartney composition recorded by The Four-most.

Marc Bolan's cane 'Peacock' chair, the woven chair of 2 colour cane, c1972, 58 in (147 cm) high. **$1,000-1,200**

A The Who 'Presentation', platinum disc, 'The Story of the Who', framed and glazed, 1976, 20 by 16 in (51.5 by 41.5 cm). **$1,200-1,500**

A Pink Floyd 'Presentation' gold disc, 'Wish you were here', framed and glazed, 21 by 17 in (52.5 by 42.5 cm). **$1,300-1,700**

An Elton John 'Presentation' gold disc, 'Mama can't buy you Love', framed and glazed, 17 by 13 in (43 by 33 cm). **$1,000-1,200**

Assorted Elvis Presley material, comprising 2 film stills, 10 Werthmeimer photographic reproductions, 4 song sheets and other items. **$300-400**

Woman's Own, January 4th 1936, price 2d, printed by The Sun Engraving Co. Ltd., Southampton St., WC2. **$8**

Magazine Covers

Home Chat, September 28th 1940, price 3d, printed and published by the Amalgamated Press Ltd., Farringdon Street, EC4. **$5**

Picture Post, 4th October 1952, price 4d, publishers Hilton Press Ltd., 43-44, Shoe Lane, EC4. **$5**

Any magazine of special interest, e.g. Churchill is worth more money.

Harper's Bazaar, June 1962, price 3/6d, published by the proprietors The National Magazine Co., 28-30, Grosvenor Gardens, SWI. **$9**

Screen Play, November 1933, ► price 10 cents, published by Fawcett Publications Inc., Broadway at Eleventh, Louisville KY USA. **$15**

Chicago Sunday Tribune, January 15th 1933. **$23**

Picture Plays, December 27th 1919, price 2d, published by Messrs Hutchinson & Co., 34, Paternoster Row, London, EC4. **$8**

The Illustrated London News, September 29th 1923, price 1/-d, publishing Office, 172, The Strand, London, WC2. **$12**

The Queen, March 4th 1922, price 2/-d. **$12**

Picture Goer, November 9th 1946, price 3d, printed and published by Odhams Press Ltd., Long Acre, WC2. **$5**

The Wide World, The Magazine for Men, May 1920, price 1/-d, proprietors George Newnes Ltd., printed by R. Clay & Sons Ltd., Brunswick Street, Stamford Street, London, SE. **$5**

The Queen, September 11th 1915, price 6d, printed and published by Field & Queen (Horace Cox) Ltd., Windsor House, Breams Buildings, EC. **$11**

The Boys Best, November 10th 1911, price 1d, printed and published by George Newnes Ltd., 3-13, Southampton Street, Strand, WC. **$8**

The Illustrated London News, June 21st 1924, price 1/-d, Publishing Office, 172, Strand, London, WC2. **$15**

The Lady, 24th June 1920, price 6d, printed and published by Thomas David Barry, 39-40, Bedford Street and Maiden Lane, WC2. **$9**

The Daily Chronicle four football guides, 1907-1908, 1912-1913, 1913-1914, 1921-1922, price 1d each, printed and published by the Daily Chronicle, Whitefriars Street, London, EC. **$15 each**

The Suffragette, June 13th 1913, price 1d, edited by Christabel Pankhurst, published by Women's Press, Lincolns Inn House, Kingsway. **$6**

Men Only, November 1952, price 1/6d, published by C. Arthur Pearson Ltd., Tower House, Southampton Street, London, WC2. **$5**

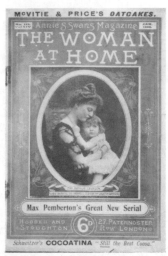

The Woman at Home, January 1903, price 6d, published by Hodder & Stoughton, 27, Paternoster Row, EC4. **$6**

The Bazaar, Exchange & Mart, January 27th 1923, price 2d, printed and published by The Field Press Ltd., Windsor House, Breams Buildings, EC4. **$6**

Woman's Pictorial, May 7th 1921, price 3d, printed and published by the proprietors, The Amalgamated Press Ltd., The Fleetway House, Farringdon Street, EC4. **$9**

The Girls' Own Paper & Woman's Magazine, February 1923, Price 1/-, printed by William Clowes & Sons Ltd., for the Proprietors, 4 Bouverie St. EC4. **$9**

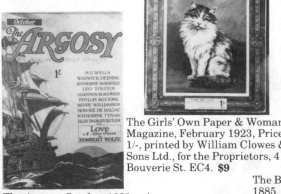

The Argosy, October 1928, price 1/-d, printed and published by The Amalgamated Press Ltd., Fleetway House, Farringdon Street, London, EC4. **$5**

The Boy's Own Paper, August 1885, price 6d, published by Mr. J. Tarn, 56, Paternoster Row.**$6**

The Performer, June 29th, 1939, Price 3d. Published at the offices of the Performer, 18 Charing Cross Road, WC2. **$8**

The Autocar, October 23rd, 1936, Price 6d. Published by Iliffe & Sons Ltd., Dorset House, Stamford St, SE1, show report. **$23**

Vogue pattern book, April 1941. Price 2/6, published by Condé Nast Publications. **$11**

Town & Country Homes, August 1924. Price 1/-. Printed and published by the Amalgamated Press Ltd., The Fleetway House, Farringdon St. EC4, **$15**

The Performer, November 12th, 1936, Price 3d. Published at the offices of the Performer, 18 Charing Cross Road, WC2. **$8**

Popular music, November 10th, 1934. Price 3d. Printed by the Amalgamated Press Ltd., The Fleetway House, Farringdon St, London EC4. **$5**

Vogue, July 20th, 1938. Price 1/-, Published fortnightly by Condé Nast Publications, 112 Fetter Lane, EC4. **$23**

The Motor, November 14th 1933, Price 4d. Printed and published weekly by Temple Press Ltd., 5,7,9,11,13,15 Roseberry Avenue, EC1. **$8**

Theatre World, May 1935. Price 1/-, Published by Practical Press Ltd., 1 Dorset Building, Salisbury Square, Fleet Street, EC4. **$6**

Nash's & Pall Mall Magazine, August 1925, price 1/-, Published by the National Magazine Company, 153 Victoria St, London EC4. **$14**

The Ideal Home, April 1924. Price 1/-, Printed and published monthly by Odhams Press Ltd, Long Acre, London WC2. **$23**

Homes & Gardens, August 1929. Price 1/-, Published by Country Life Ltd., 20 Tavistock Street, Covent Garden, WC2. **$15**

My Weekly, October 26th, 1940. Price 2d. Printed and Published by John Leng & Co. Ltd., 186 Fleet St. EC4. **$3**

Postcards

A fine collection of 103 advertising postcards, 1905-1910. **$700-1,000**

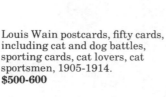

Woven silk C.P.R. Empress Hotel. Victoria, B.C. pub. Thos Plimley. **$300-400**

Louis Wain postcards, fifty cards, including cat and dog battles, sporting cards, cat lovers, cat sportsmen, 1905-1914. **$500-600**

Twenty anti-vivisection and cruelty to animals postcards, many issued by the British Anti-Vivisection Society, Cat Protection League, R.S.P.C.A. c1910. **$50-70**

The Good Old Days, and an untitled Hunting Scene, woven silk, published by W.H. Grant. **$30-60**

Tower Bridge, London. **$60-90**

Comin' thro' the Rye, and The Irish Colleen, woven silk cards. **$50-70**

Queen Victoria's Diamond Jubilee, quart-sized card printed with portrait and inscription, and views of Windsor Castle, Balmoral Castle and Osborne House, 1897. **$50-70**

Cigarette Cards

George V and Mary. **$30-60**

W.H. Newman's Motor Cycle Series 1913, 1/18, No. 12, Bert Yates on his 3½ H.P. Humber. **$30-45**

6 Liebig British Army Uniforms, issued 1889, 6/6. **$80-150**

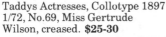

Anonymous Star Girls 1899, 1/25, plain back, No. 14. **$15-30**

Taddys Actresses, Collotype 1897 1/72, No.69, Miss Gertrude Wilson, creased. **$25-30**

7 Taddys Thames Series 1903, 7/25. **$200-300**

Anonymous Trade Issue Military Series approx. 1916, 11/12 (?). **$25-30**

Various Issuers Armies of the World 1900/3, 21/25, Roberts & Sons 15/25, Egyptian Cigarette Manufacturing Co., 5/25, Pezaro (?) 1/25. **$100-200**

18 Carathanassis (Samos, Turkey), Postmen of the World 18/20 (?) and two odds. **$80-150**

12 Faulkner Grenadier Guards 1899, 12/12, some cards with replacement backs. **$60-90**

Ogdens Actresses, no glycerine back, 1895, 1/25, Miss Helen Bruno. **$30-45**

95 Wills Soldiers of the World 1895, 95/100. **$300-500**

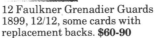

8 Taddys Famous Jockeys, without frame, 1910, 8/25. **$80-150**

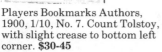

Players Bookmarks Authors, 1900, 1/10, No. 7. Count Tolstoy, with slight crease to bottom left corner. **$30-45**

47 Taddys Russo-Japanese War Series 1904, 47-50, overall F. **$400-600**

American Tobacco Co., Military Uniforms 1900 24/25, tobacco war issue, title error to Royal Horse Artillery, should read Royal Field Artillery, **$80-150**

26 Wills Double Meanings, 1898, 26/50. **$30-60**

Donald's Penguin, 1939, gouache on full celluloid applied to a Walt Disney Productions watercolour background, Producton RM22, Cel 7, scene 21, 7 by 10½ in (17.5 by 26 cm). **$3,000-4,000**

Walt Disney Studio's Mickey Mouse, inscribed Hello Murray! Best Wishes from Walt Disney, signed, pen black ink and body colour, 8 by 6 in (20 by 15 cm). **$1,200-1,500**

Officer Duck, 1939, gouache on full celluloid applied to a Walt Disney Productions watercolour background, Production 2230, Animator: Lounsbery, scene 20, field 5, 7 by 10 in (18 by 25 cm). **$3,000-4,000**

Pluto's kid brother, 1946, gouache on partial celluloid laid down on a Walt Disney Productions watercolour background, Production 2327, 8 by 11 in (20 by 27.5 cm). **$1,700-2,500**

Snow White and the Seven Dwarfs, 1937, The Wicked Queen gasping 'Snow White', gouache on full celluloid applied to a Walt Disney Productions watercolour background, 12½ by 9 in (31 by 22.5 cm). **$3,500-5,000**

Mickey's Birthday, gouache on full celluloids applied to a Walt Disney Productions watercolour background, Production 2264, Cel D30 and 30, scene 4.1, 9 by 10½ in (22.5 by 26 cm). **$10,000-13,000**

Water Babies, 1935, gouache on full celluloid applied to a Walt Disney Productions watercolour background, Production US 26, Animator: Art Babbit, Cels 70 and H5, scene 43, field 5, 8 by 11 in (20 by 27 cm). **$4,000-5,000**

Silly Symphony, Hiawatha, 1937, screenprint in colours printed by the American Display Co. Inc., NYC dated 4-36 in the image, various paper defects, 60 by 40 in (150 by 100 cm). **$3,000-4,500**

The Eyes Have It, 1945, gouache on partial celluloid laid down on a Walt Disney Productions watercolour background, Production 2315. **$1,400-1,700**

I belive in management and workers sitting together, by Donald McGill, signed, watercolour heightened with white, 8 by 6 in (20 by 15 cm), and 3 other watercolours by the same hand. **$1,200-1,500**

In the scrambling trenches of an egg arsenal, by William Heath Robinson, signed and inscribed, pencil, pen, black ink and grey washes, 16 by 11 in (40 by 27.5 cm). **$1,700-2,500**

Nineteen Valentines, 5 hand coloured lithographic designs including the Knot of Love, and 14 others, some printed in silver or gold, 1830-1875. **$400-600**

A collection of Christmas Cards, 500, mainly 1880's-1890's. **$500-600**

L'Armortisseur Haubourdin, coloured lithograph, published by E.T. Gouweloos Fre. & Sr., Bruzells, on linen, 57½ by 37 in (144 by 92.5 cm). **$80-150**

A length of embossed block printed wallpaper, in tones of red on gold background, French, 19thC, approx. 331 in by 20 in (840 by 50 cm). **$80-150**

A collection of approximately 300 lithographed cardboard chemist shop signs, 1910 to 1920, together with an Aspro electric wall clock and a chemists diary for 1891. **$1,000-1,200**

Scripophily

The Mansion House Visitors Book, belonging to the Rt. Honourable John Staples, Lord Mayor of London 1885-1886, containing the signatures of many prominent people of the day, gilt tooled green morocco dust jacket, 1 volume. **$200-300**

£50 14 October 1925, issued at Leeds (Dugg.B.218) several small holes. **$500-600**

£5 1971-78, error with extra paper at left including bars for colour check, Dugg B334. **$80-150**

A log of H.M.S. Bendow, from 1888 to 1891, the script lavishly illustrated with maps, diagrams and illustrations of the ship's voyage through the Mediterranean, quarto. **$600-800**

Martinique 1919 500 francs P.14, heavily restored especially around edges. **$100-150**

Exchequer Bill for £100 issued in April 1811 and overstamped 'Bank of England'. **$500-600**

1862 12 marks (P.A35c) missing right corner tip. **$150-200**

£100 17 January 1938 Dugg B245. **$400-600**

£1 1920 heavy creases. **$80-150**

1777, December 1st, Massachusetts Interest Bearing Certificate for £200, printed by Paul Revere with 'Sword in Hand' vignette at top left. Handwritten details across front of the payment of £12-0-7d. being the interest paid for the first year. **$300-400**

Netherlands, 1943 25 gulden, P.67. **$300-400**

Burundi, 1964 500 francs. **$300-400**

French Equatorial Africa: 1941, 1,000 francs Specimen P.14, with two small spots of foxing therefore. **$200-300**

1861, July 25th, Confederate $5, C.R. Tll-44;P.T. **$700-900**

Costa Rica, 1901 Banco de Costa Rica 5 colones, P.S.173. **$200-300**

1921 $500 Hong Kong & Shanghai Banking Corporation Specimen P.C53, slight damage top left corner, punch cancelled. **$400-600**

Chile: 1876 Banco de Valparaiso 5 pesos P.S488, small tear top centre. **$300-400**

1890 Bank of new South Wales £50 Victoria issue perforated C; Skipper & East". Cut cancelled. **$400-600**

1910 10 kroner P.7. GVF. **$150-200**

Katanga: 1960 set of 10 francs – 1,000 francs all perforated Specimen P1-6 not including 1A, all notes have orthodox serial numbers after a zz prefix but have 00.00.00 in date area. **$600-700**

1930 £1 Bank of Australasia P.S.132. **$300-400**

'Suicidal Melancholy', albumen print, 44 by 30 in (110 by 75 cm). **$1,500-2,200**

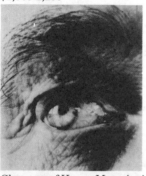

Close-ups of Henry Moore's right eye, silver print, the reverse stamped in ink with photographer's credit Bill Brandt, and titled in ink, 1950's. **$600-700**

Woman in check dress with long hair, albumen print, 7 by 5 in (18.1 by 13.6 cm). **$7,500-10,500**

Transvestite in a police van, glossy Bromide print, signed in ball point 'Weegee', 1941, 11 by 14 in (28.2 by 35.5 cm). **$300-500**

650

Oriental Bamboo

A bamboo group of Shoulao, seated on the back of a deer, the old man holding the beast's horns in one hand and a peach in the other, 2 small boys standing on the rocky ground below, 17thC, 11½ in (29.2 cm). **$600-800**

A well carved bamboo brush pot, unsigned, Meiji period, 5 in (12.7 cm). **$1,000-1,200**

A pair of bamboo figures of Buddhist lions, each with heavily maned head turned, standing on a high rockwork base, several cubs scrambling round the ledges, 19thC, 12½ in (31.3 cm). **$1,000-1,200**

Cloisonné Enamel

A cloisonné enamel dish, of shallow saucer-shape with narrow everted rim, decorated in rich colours on a bright turquoise ground, the reverse with an overall lotus scroll, Wanli, 12 in (29.8 cm). **$4,500-5,000**

A cloisonné enamel circular plaque, minor pitting, 18thC, 20½ in (51 cm). **$2,000-3,000**

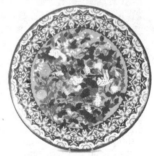

A large cloisonné enamel dish, decorated in colours with 2 kingfishers among foliage, small hole, late 19thC, 23 in (59.5 cm). **$1,200-1,500**

A Japanese cloisonné dish, on a goldstone ground within a border comprising panels of masked birds, with black ground rim, 18½ in (46 cm). **$700-900**

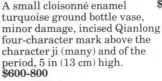

A pair of green ground cloisonné dishes, 19thC. **$300-400**

A decorative cloisonné enamel figure of a prancing horse, decorated with archaistic motifs in colours on a bright turquoise ground, with detachable mane and saddle, 16 in (40 cm). **$1,200-1,500**

A small cloisonné enamel turquoise ground bottle vase, minor damage, incised Qianlong four-character mark above the character ji (many) and of the period, 5 in (13 cm) high. **$600-800**

A garniture of Japanese cloisonné vases, with cranes and pine on a blue ground. **$300-400**

A Japanese bronze and champlevé enamelled figure of a mythical tortoise, with blue and green scale decoration, mid-19thC, 17 in (42 cm). **$1,400-1,700**

A good pair of large Japanese cloisonné enamel vases, each decorated with 2 oblong blue ground panels, the reserves with formal floral and bird designs in colours upon brown grounds. **$1,300-1,700**

A Chinese cloissoné vase, on a sky blue ground reserved with dense scrolling foliage, wood stand, late 18th/early 19thC, 15 in (37.5 cm). **$600-800**

A pair of cloisonné enamel vases, each with a pair of pigeons perched in a gnarled flowering prunus tree, on a midnight blue ground, 14½ in (37 cm) high. **$1,000-1,200**

A cloisonné enamel vase, decorated in colours on a dark blue ground with a cockerel and a hen among flowering chrysanthemums, Meiji period, very slightly scratched, 18½ in (46.1 cm) high. **$1,200-1,500**

A pair of Japanese cloisonné vases, each decorated with a bird of prey amongst branches of pink blossom on a pale turquoise ground, 12 in (30 cm). **$400-600**

A pair of Japanese cloisonné enamel baluster vases, each decorated with chrysanthemums on a dark blue ground, 14 in (35 cm). **$500-600**

A pair of Japanese cloisonné baluster vases, decorated on a grey ground, one with a dove in flight, the other with a pair of doves, c1900, 12 in (30 cm). **$3,000-4,000**

Furniture

A Japanese mother-of-pearl mounted corner display cabinet, lacquered in black overlaid in tones of gilt and red with various stylised devices, 19thC, 51 by 42½ in (130 by 108 cm). **$1,200-1,500**

A pair of fine Chinese rosewood cabinets, 19thC, 82 in (208 cm). **$6,000-8,500**

A pair of Japanese scarlet lacquered cabinets, decorated in gilt and black, within gilt scroll surrounds, the pair of doors enclosing a shelf, c1890, 32 in (81 cm) wide. **$8,500-10,000**

A Japanese lacquered desk cabinet, with Shibayama panels, 10 in (25 cm). **$700-900**

A Japanese hardwood display cabinet on stand, pierced, carved and gilded throughout with motifs and set with ivory and mother-of-pearl inlaid panels, some damage, 81½ in (207 cm) high. **$3,000-4,000**

An Eastern carved hardwood display cabinet, decorated with lacquer panels applied with cold painted cast metal flowerheads, birds and fish, within gilt scroll work, 52 in (130 cm) wide. **$3,000-4,500**

A Chinese hardwood armchair, the back with a glazed embroidered silk panel, the seat inset with a pink marble slab, c1900, 29 in (72 cm) wide. **$600-700**

A Thailand teakwood ceremonial howdah, black lacquered and gilded, with loose seat cushion, 76 in (193 cm) wide. **$600-700**

A Far Eastern carved sideboard, the pierced back with a central peacock, 61 in (152.5 cm). **$600-900**

A Chinese coromandel lacquer eight panel screen, decorated in colours, damaged, 19thC. **$1,300-1,700**

Two hardwood horseshoe armchairs, Qing Dynasty, 39½ and 41½ in (99 and 104 cm) high. **$1,000-1,200**

A carved blackwood 4-post bed frame, late 19thC, 82½ in (210 cm) wide. **$3,000-4,000**

A Japanese Shibayama screen, late 19thC, 74 by 34 in (188 by 85 cm) each fold. **$500-600**

A Chinese porcelain and hardwood fire screen, the panel painted in bright enamel colours, total height 30 in (75 cm). **$1,000-1,200**

A Chinese hardwood and mother-of-pearl inlaid firescreen, with a detachable glazed panel framing a silk embroidered roundel, the solid base on Kylin supports, mid-19thC, 24 in (61 cm). **$600-900**

A hardwood square centre table, Qing Dynasty, 30½ in (76 cm) square. **$600-700**

A pair of Chinese black and gold lacquer low tables, decorated in raised gilt, 19thC, 25½ in (64.5 cm) wide. **$7,500-10,500**

An Oriental carved hardwood occasional table, 19thC. **$1,000-1,200**

A nest of three Chinese hardwood tables. **$500-600**

MAKE THE MOST OF MILLERS

When buying or selling, it must always be remembered that prices can be greatly affected by the condition of any piece. Unless otherwise stated, all goods shown in Miller's are of good merchantable quality, and the valuations given reflect this fact. Pieces offered for sale in exceptionally fine condition or in poor condition may reasonably be expected to be priced considerably higher or lower respectively than the estimates given herein.

A Chinese carved hardwood games table, the top with a sliding satinwood and ebony chessboard, c1870, 39 in (99 cm) wide. **$1,300-1,700**

A Japanese export lacquered pedestal table, with an eagle, and birds in branches, in gilt, c1860, 37 in (94 cm). **$1,000-1,200**

A Chinese hardwood desk, 46 by 33 in (115 by 82.5 cm) wide. **$1,000-1,200**

A Chinese carved hardwood writing table, c1900, 35½ in (90 cm) wide. **$1,300-1,700**

Glass

An overlay glass vase, the bubble-suffused ground decorated in high relief in ruby red with figures representing the 4 noble professions, 11½ in (29.2 cm). **$3,000-4,000**

A Pekin blue glass vase, the metal plain and of even light-blue tone, 4 character mark and period of Qianlong, 7 in (18.3 cm). **$1,000-1,200**

A reverse glass painting, 22 by 30½ in (56.5 by 77.8 cm). **$500-700**

A Chinese mirror painting, the gilt frame carved with strapwork and foliage on a pounced ground, 18½ by 14½ in (47 by 37 cm). **$1,700-2,500**

Use the Index!
Because certain items might fit easily into any of a number of categories, the quickest and surest method of locating any entry is by reference to the index at the back of the book.
This has been fully cross-referenced for absolute simplicity.

Horn

A rhinoceros horn libation cup, the material of rich honey colour, 17thC, 7½ in (19 cm). **$4,500-7,000**

A rhinoceros horn libation cup, the material of rich honey colour deepening towards the tip, wood stand, 18th/19thC, 11 in (28 cm). **$1,500-2,200**

A horn carving of Shou Lao, wood stand, 7½ in (18.5 cm). **$400-600**

An unusual horn brushpot, 19thC, 4½ in (11.4 cm). **$600-700**

Inros

A five-case gold Fundame inro, decorated in takamakie, worn at edges, signed Kajikawa saku, late 18th/early 19thC, with glass ojime, 3½ in (9 cm). **$1,000-1,200**

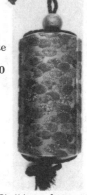

A five-case Kinji inro, decorated in gold and silver hiramakie, signed Kajikawa saku, late 18th/early 19thC, with attached Kaga porcelain bead ojime. **$1,000-1,200**

A four-case inro, decorated in gold, silver, red and black hiramakie, heidatsu and togidashi on a yasuriko ground, nashiji interiors, unsigned, early 19thC. **$1,000-1,400**

A six-case Kinji inro, finely decorated in gold, silver, and red hiramakie, hirame and nashiji, nashiji interiors, slight damage, signed Masayuki saku, early 19thC. **$1,400-1,700**

Ivory

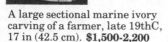

An unusual carved ivory group, engraved and stained detail, some damage, late 19thC. **$1,700-2,500**

A large sectional marine ivory carving of a farmer, late 19thC, 17 in (42.5 cm). **$1,500-2,200**

An ivory figure of a noble fisherman, his robes incised black and applied with engraved mother-of-pearl mon, 5½ in long (13.5 cm). **$400-600**

An ivory figure of Guanyin, wood stand, 18th/19thC, 7 in (18 cm). **$1,000-1,200**

A fine and large carved ivory group of a fisherman, by the Tokyo School, the base in the form of a rock and rippling water, signed on red lacquer tablet, Meiji period, 13½ in (32.5 cm). **$2,000-3,000**

An ivory and Shibayama elephant, inlaid with stained ivory and mother-of-pearl, engraved signature, Meiji period, small pieces of inlay missing, 8½ in (21 cm). **$4,000-5,000**

A fine ivory carving of a girl, signed on the base Michihiro, Tokyo School, Meiji period, 12 in high (30.5 cm). **$1,500-2,200**

A carved ivory junk, with dragon figurehead, pierced and decorated sail, on carved and spangled wood plinth, late 19thC, 22 in high (55 cm). **$700-1,000**

A well carved ivory figure of a nude girl, slightly split, signed on the base Godo above a rectangular red seal, Meiji period, 9½ in (23 cm). **$1,000-1,200**

A Japanese ivory tusk vase, depicting gold lacquer figures and octopus, 19thC. **$1,700-2,500**

A Japanese ivory tusk carving depicting various animals, wood stand, 17½ in long (42.5 cm). **$300-500**

A fine ivory carving of a bijin, partly covered by a silk cloth, the details engraved and lightly stained, signed Gyokuhi to, Meiji period, 5½ in high (15.5 cm). **$600-700**

An ivory and Shibayama nest of boxes, the lid worked in gilt lacquer in low relief with birds, in a landscape, the boxes carved from a solid piece of ivory, 10 in wide (26 cm). **$1,500-2,200**

A good carved ivory okimono, Meiji period, depicting Fukurokoju holding a gnarled staff, with finely engraved robe, engraved signature, 7½ in (19 cm). **$1,300-1,700**

An ivory okimono, depicting Shoki holding a halberd and holding a struggling oni aloft, engraved signature, Meiji period, slight damage, 11½ in (28 cm). **$700-900**

Jade

A white jade screen, flanked by an incised Imperial poem at one end, the stone slightly tinted, 18thC, 9½ by 6 in (24.2 by 15.2 cm). **$3,500-5,000**

A spinach jade ewer and cover, 7 in (18.5 cm). **$2,000-3,000**

A jade group, the figure highlighted by a grey splash in the stone, a spray of lingzhi across one shoulder, 17thC, 3 in (8 cm). **$3,000-4,000**

An amber group of a lion and puppy, the amber of rich reddish brown colour, showing through to yellow in some areas, late 18th/early 19thC, 3½ in (8.5 cm). **$1,000-1,400**

A fine large carnelian agate vase, carved from a milk-white stone with large areas of orange and caramel rich inclusions, and with a lingzhi spray at the bottom right hand side, late Qing Dynasty, 9½ in (23.5 cm). **$3,000-4,000**

A pale celadon seated jade figure of Guanyin, 15 in (37.5 cm). **$6,000-8,000**

A pale celadon jade model, 17th/18thC, 5 in (12.8 cm). **$3,500-5,000**

Lacquer

A Kobako modelled as two overlapping rectangles, finely decorated in gold, silver, green, brown and red hiramakie, hirame, nashiji, togidashi and heidatsu on roironuri and silver fundame grounds, very slight damage, 19thC, 4 in (10.5 cm) wide. **$1,000-1,200**

A lacquer Karabitsu, decorated in gold lacquer on a black ground with Tokugawa mon, cords missing, some damage, Edo period, 20½ in (52.5 cm). **$1,500-2,200**

A Roironuri cabinet, decorated in gold and silver hiramakie with Tomoe mon among scrolling karakusa, engraved copper kanagu, old damage, hinges replaced, 18thC, 19½ in (48.2 cm). **$2,000-3,000**

A Katana Kake for three swords, decorated in aogai with birds and flowering branches against a black lacquer ground, slight damage. **$700-900**

A Japanese black and gold lacquer tray, onlaid in metal and embellished with gilt and silver, 19thC, 23½ in (59 cm). **$3,000-4,000**

A carved cinnabar lacquer panel, with stepped central section and curved indented corners, carved with 3 Daoist Immortals, lattice and key-pattern at the border, minor damage, 18th/early 19thC, 24½ in (61.2 cm) long.
$1,500-2,200

A rare Momoyama period tray, decorated in gold hiramakie and inlaid in aogai on a black lacquer ground, possibly reconstructed, c1600, 16 by 10 in (39.8 by 25.6 cm).
$3,000-4,000

A Shibayama gilt lacquer tray, onlaid in mother-of-pearl, ivory and other materials with finely detailed scene, on 4 short feet, 1 foot missing, 1 glued, signed Shibayama Yasumasa, c1900.
$1,400-1,700

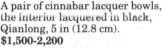

A pair of cinnabar lacquer bowls, the interior lacquered in black, Qianlong, 5 in (12.8 cm).
$1,500-2,200

Metal

A pair of Japanese gold lacquered ostrich eggs, 19thC.
$3,000-4,000

A Chinese bronze group, of a figure of Avalokitesvara, late Ming Dynasty, 12½ in (31.5 cm).
$1,700-2,500

A bronze figure of Guanyin, traces of gilding and polychrome colouring, Ming Dynasty, 15½ in (39 cm). **$1,700-2,500**

A good Seiya bronze, the animal with rush saddle and rope girth, a ring through its nose, wood stand, cast seal, Meiji period, 22 in (55.8 cm). **$2,000-3,000**

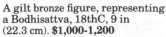

A pair of bronze figures of warriors, their outer garments decorated in gilt nikubori with various mon, one with repaired naginata, maedate missing from kabuto, one signed in a rectangular reserve Yoshimitsu, both late 19thC, 12 in (30 cm) high. **$3,000-4,000**

A Chinese bronze figure of a seated mythological beast, probably late Ming, 11½ in (29 cm). **$300-500**

A gilt bronze figure, representing a Bodhisattva, 18thC, 9 in (22.3 cm). **$1,000-1,200**

A fine large heavily cast bronze model of a snarling tiger, signed in a square reserve Seiya sei, rootwood base, Meiji period, 24 in (60 cm) long. **$4,500-5,000**

A Japanese bronze group of a monkey, the 2 offspring seated on its back, Meiji period, 8½ in (21 cm) long. **$700-900**

A cast iron head of Guanyin, wood stand, Ming Dynasty, 10½ in (16.7 cm). **$1,700-2,500**

A Japanese bronze bird of prey, 22 in (55 cm) high. **$700-900**

A Japanese bronze group, of an elephant being attacked by 2 tigers, Meiji period, 16 by 11 in (40 by 27.5 cm). **$500-700**

A Chinese bronze jardinière, 19thC, 26½ by 17 in (66 by 42.5 cm). **$600-800**

A rare Chinese Shan bronze war drum, 26 in (65 cm). **$1,300-1,700**

Netsuke

A Japanese bronze vase, picked out in coloured patination and gilding, Meiji period, 29½ in (74 cm). **$14,000-17,000**

A boxwood netsuke of an emaciated sage, unsigned, slight old chip, c1800. **$700-900**

A pair of massive Japanese bronze temple lanterns, some corrosion and damage, 19thC, approx. 80 in (203 cm). **$4,500-7,000**

A Tsuishu seal-type netsuke of a karako, with a tsuishu ojime attached, unsigned, 18thC. **$400-600**

An ivory netsuke, of a chubby karako in playful mood, tying a court cap (eboshi) on to his head, engraved and stained detail, signed Gyokuzan, late 19thC. **$300-500**

A bronze koro, the cover surmounted by a figure of Benten, the rim pierced with a reversed swastika (manji) design, signed Somin, late 19thC, 10 in (25 cm). **$1,000-1,200**

A small ivory netsuke of Ashinaga and Tenaga, signed Tomochika, 19thC, 1½ in (3.2 cm) high. **$1,000-1,200**

An ivory netsuke of two karako, pulling along Hotei, engraved and stained detail, unsigned, early 19thC. **$500-600**

A stained ivory okimono style netsuke of Shoki, the Demon Queller, the details engraved, signed on a rectangular red tablet Yoshiaki, late 19thC. **$1,000-1,200**

An ivory netsuke of the Chinese General Choryo, kneeling on the back of a dragon, having rescued Kosekiko's shoe, signed, Kinryusai (Tomotone), Edo School mid-19thC. **$1,000-1,200**

An ivory netsuke, depicting 2 octopuses dressed in human costume, signed in a rectangular seal Masaharu, 19thC, 2 in (4.5 cm). **$1,000-1,400**

A curious subject by this artist, noted for his animal studies and for signing in tensho characters.

An ivory netsuke of Jurojin, a karako holding a staff standing to one side, the details engraved and stained brown, signed Norishige, Edo School, mid-19thC. **$400-600**

An ivory netsuke of a Dutchman, trying to pick up 2 cockerels, the details engraved and stained, inscribed Tomotada, early 19thC. **$1,000-1,200**

A fine Cypress-wood netsuke of a mermaid holding a branch of coral, painted white, red and black in Shuzan style, unsigned, early 19thC. **$1,000-1,200**

A fine ivory netsuke, of a baby asleep, with engraved detail and slight colour on hair, eyes and lips, signed in a rectangular reserve Sosui (Ouchi), 1911-1972, 1½ in (4.3 cm). **$6,000-8,000**

An ivory netsuke of two chonin crouched on a go table, inscribed Okatomo, 19thC, 1½ in (4 cm). **$700-1,000**

A wood netsuke of a hunter pleading for mercy, as a tanuki attempts to smother him beneath its enlarged scrotum, signed Ichimin, mid-19thC, 1 in (2.9 cm) high. **$600-700**

A finely patinated ivory netsuke, of a naked man, inscribed Dozo saku, early 19thC. **$700-900**

An ivory manju netsuke, decorated in shishiaibori with a seated karako, age cracks, unsigned, 19thC. **$600-800**

An ivory netsuke of two quail on a straw mat, inlaid eye pupils, inscribed at a later date Kakuto (?), late 19thC. **$500-600**

An ivory netsuke of a seated sennin, small piece missing from his right hand, unsigned, c1800. **$400-600**

A boxwood netsuke of a seated snarling tiger, with inlaid eye pupils, its fur markings engraved and stained, signed Masanao, Yamada School, 19thC. **$1,000-1,200**

A rare ivory netsuke of a three-clawed dragon, emerging from a pumpkin, the details engraved and stained, signed in a raised rounded rectangular reserve Tadatoshi, early 19thC. **$1,500-2,200**

Neil K. Davey records another example by this artist in his netsuke book and states that he possibly belongs to the Kyoto School.

A finely patinated boxwood netsuke of a seated rat, delicately engraved and eyes inlaid, slightly chipped, signed with a kao, late 18th/early 19thC. **$1,200-1,500**

A boxwood netsuke of a toad, crouching on an overturned well bucket, the details inlaid in ebony, signed Masanao, Yamada School, 19thC. **$500-600**

Cf. Neil K. Davey, Netsuke, pl. 680.

A stained wood netsuke of a coiled serpent, its eyes inlaid in black, unsigned, 19thC. **$600-700**

A boxwood netsuke of a rat, the eyes and other details inlaid, unsigned, style of Masanao, 19thC. **$600-900**

Other examples of the same subject, signed Masanao, are known.

A well painted wood netsuke carved as a no mask, of a demonic man, unsigned, 19thC. **$200-300**

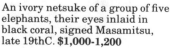

An ivory netsuke of a seated tiger, eating a bamboo shoot, its eye pupils inlaid, inscribed Okakoto, 19thC. **$1,000-1,200**

An ivory netsuke of a group of five elephants, their eyes inlaid in black coral, signed Masamitsu, late 19thC. **$1,000-1,200**

Groups of rats and puppies signed Masamitsu are often seen, but elephants can be considered rare.

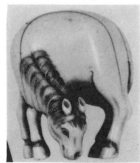

A finely patinated ivory netsuke of a grazing horse, with inlaid black horn eye pupils, its mane and tail engraved, age cracks, inscribed Harutomo, late 18thC. **$1,500-2,200**

Snuff Bottles

A moulded porcelain snuff bottle, enamelled with the Eight Immortals, 3 on a boat, Jiaqing, 26.10.27. **$300-500**

A moulded porcelain snuff bottle, decorated with the Eighteen Lohan, with an ivory tinted glaze, Jiaqing, original stopper. **$700-900**

A hair crystal snuff bottle, stopper. **$400-600**

A glass overlay snuff bottle, decorated in red with figures from the three noble professions, stopper. **$300-400**

A Pekin glass snuff bottle, the opaque ground splashed with flame like orange and red markings, stopper, 1780-1850. **$300-500**

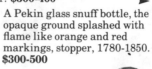

A Yixing snuff bottle, decorated in slip of 2 tones of brown reserved on a dark blue enamel ground. **$600-700**

A carved glass snuff bottle, the upper part of the body decorated in low relief, the metal of pale brown colour, 1800-1860, stopper 16.3.23. **$700-900**

A large purple Chalcedony snuff bottle, carved in deep relief with the Immortal, Hexianggu, stopper, 4.7.19. **$1,000-1,200**

A glass overlay snuff bottle, the opalescent ground dappled with multi coloured splashes beneath a blue overlay prunus in blossom. **$300-400**

Tsuba

A Daisho pair of tsuba, oval shakudo migakiji, each decorated in gilt hirazogan, varnished and with a tiny number stamped on each seppa-dai, unsigned, Kaga school, 3 and 3 in (7.6 and 7.3 cm). **$700-900**

A Mokkogata Kinji presentation tsuba, finely decorated in gold and silver hiramakie, hirame and nashiji and inlaid in Shibayama style, silver seppa-dai and rim, signed on a square red tablet, slightly chipped, late 19thC. **$1,300-1,700**

A Kinji tsuba, decorated in gold and silver hiramakie, hirame and nashiji and inlaid in Shibayama style with Ebisu and Daikoku fishing on the banks of a river, signed Ryoko, late 19thC, 4½ in (11.3 cm). **$1,700-2,500**

A Japanese iron tsuba, pierced with figures, crane, fruiting vines and clouds, detail in gold and copper, signed. **$300-400**

An iron tsuba, pierced and chiselled, with gold, shakudo and copper details, Soten school, 3 in (7.8 cm). **$500-600**

An iron tsuba, pierced and chiselled, gold, shakudo and copper detail, 3 in (7.1 cm). **$400-600**

An iron Soten tsuba, pierced and chiselled, much soft metal detail, signed Goshu Hikone no ju Kaneishi Nomura Kanenori. **$1,300-1,700**

Wood

A carved wood no mask, the eyes inset with gilt-metal, remains of horsehair moustache and beard, old wear, 18th/early 19thC, 8½ in (21.2 cm) long. **$700-900**

A carved and painted wood no mask, of a young woman, probably representing Magojiro, late Edo period, 8½ in (21.3 cm) long. **$1,500-2,200**

A polychrome wood figure of a monk, a rosary held in his left hand, originally coloured in bright blue and showing traces of further colouring and gilding, 27½ in (70 cm). **$3,000-4,000**

Russian Works of Art

A large quarter length wood figure of Guanyin, with traces of red and white pigment, Ming Dynasty, 33 in (83.2 cm). **$1,700-2,500**

A Russian cloisonné enamel snuff box, in pastel shades of blue, green and pink on a yellow background with white bead borders, by Pavel Ovchinnikov, Moscow, c1900, 2 in (5 cm). **$500-600**

A Russian cloisonné enamel and parcel gilt kovsh, in pastel shades of green, dark red, orange, mauve, white and turquoise, by Ivan Klebnikov, c1910, 7 in (17 cm). **$3,000-4,000**

An ebonised hardwood figure of an elephant, c1900, 24 in (61 cm). **$700-1,000**

Two Russian cloisonné enamelled spoons, in red, white, turquoise, dark blue, powder blue and sea green, Moscow, c1890, 6½ in (16.2 cm) long. **$300-400**

A Russian champlevé enamel cigarette case, in dark blue, red and white, maker's mark GK, Moscow, 1889, 3½ in (8.7 cm) long. **$700-900**

A silver gilt niello serving spoon, maker's mark EC, Moscow, 1842, 2 ozs 5 dwts. **$300-500**

A silver gilt and niello box, maker's mark Cyrillic NK, Moscow, c1830, 3½ in (9 cm) long, 4 ozs 4 dwts. **$1,000-1,200**

A silver enamel beaker, on predominantly ivory ground, within white beaded bands, by Grigory Sbitniev, Moscow, minor repair, 1908-1917, 4½ in (11.5 cm) high. **$1,000-1,400**

A silver gilt cloisonné enamel bowl, in blue, green, red and white, within dark blue bands, signed with Imperial warrant mark of Sazikov, Moscow, 1879, 3 in (7 cm). **$600-700**

A jewelled and enamelled silver-gilt kovsh, gem-set by the 26th Artel, Moscow, 1908-1917, 3½ in (8.6 cm). **$700-900**

A bronze group of a horsedrawn cart, signed by Posene, foundry mark of C.S. Woerffel, St. Petersburg, c1900, 22½ in (57 cm) long. **$5,500-7,000**

A bronze equestrian group of the cossack's farewell, inscribed in Cyrillic Gratcheff sculpt, and with the Woerffel foundry mark, 10 in (24.8 cm) high. **$1,500-2,200**

A bronze equestrian group, of charging cossacks, with the foundry mark of Kuznestosv, 17½ in (41.5 cm) long. **$600-900**

A Russian niello cigarette case maker's mark IF (Cyrillics), Moscow, 1883, 3½ in (8.4 cm) long. **$300-400**

A silver ribbed cigarette case, with cabochon sapphire thumb-piece on gold mount, interior dated 1919, maker's mark Cyrillic ID, St. Petersburg, 1908-1917, 4 in (9.5 cm) long. **$500-600**

A silver beaker, maker's mark ?C, assaymaster Andrei Zaitsev, Moscow, 1749, 8 in (21 cm) high, 12 ozs 12 dwts. **$1,500-2,200**

A silver reliquary box, chased with the Virgin, St. George and St. Dimitry, Greek, c1800, 4 in (10.8 cm) high. **$1,000-1,200**

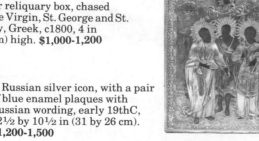

A Russian silver icon, with a pair of blue enamel plaques with Russian wording, early 19thC, 12½ by 10½ in (31 by 26 cm). **$1,200-1,500**

An imperial plain silver chamber pot, engraved with the Imperial crown, signed by F.Z. Genrichsen, workmaster Cyrillic A L, St. Petersburg, late 19thC, 10 in (25 cm). **$4,500-5,000**

663

A rare Prussian Garde du Corps troopers helmet, original leather lining, inside of skull stamped 'C.E. Juncker 1914'. **$3,000-4,500**

A composite Saxony Garde Reiter Officer's helmet, most parts restored. **$1,700-2,500**

A Nazi Police Officer's Shako, printed paper label inside crown 'Erel Tschako' with Nazi helmeted soldier's head. **$300-400**

A Nazi S.A. Kepi, original printed 'R.Z.M.', minor surface moth to dark brown body. **$300-400**

Pistols

A rare 7-barrelled hand rotated boxlock flintlock revolving pepperbox pistol, by Twigg, 8¾ in (22 cm), turn-off barrels 2 in (5 cm), numbered 1 to 6, London proved breech, engraved with 'Twigg' 'London', some light pitting and cleaned bright overall, sides of safety which lock frizzen to fence missing, c1775. **$3,000-4,500**

A scarce Garde du Corps helmet, with silvered Parade Eagle and Garde Star helmet plate, with old hole affixing mounts behind helmet plate plugged, lining restored, a composite piece. **$2,000-3,000**

A rare English silver mounted flintlock holster pistol, maker Tarles of London, full silver hallmark for 1717, some silver wire inlay, early 18thC, 17 in (42 cm). **$1,700-2,500**

A Scottish all steel flintlock belt pistol, 3 stage barrel, one screw lacking, c1750, 8 in (19.5 cm). **$2,000-3,000**

A rare and very fine 7-barrelled hand rotated boxlock flintlock revolving pepperbox pistol, by H. Nock, 8½ in (21 cm), turn-off barrels 2½ in (6 cm), numbered 1 to 6, London proved breech, slab walnut butt, retains approx. 50% faded original finish overall, c1775. **$4,000-5,000**

A good 20 bore flintlock holster pistol, by Burgon, 14 in (35 cm), octagonal barrel 9 in (22.5 cm), Tower proved, engraved 'London', c1780. **$600-700**

A good quality Officer's 20 bore flintlock holster pistol, by Wogdon of London, c1775. **$600-700**
This maker is more famous for his duelling pistols.

A rare single shot 4 barrelled flintlock holster pistol, by Hunt, the barrels and furniture of light coloured brass, 12½ in (31 cm), turn-off integral barrel unit 4½ in (11 cm), Tower proved and London proved, top jaw, screw and cock screw restored, stock fractured across grip and well repaired, c1770. **$1,700-2,500**

An English flintlock 'Queen Anne' cannon barrelled pistol, signed John Hall of London, silver mounts including grotesque lions mask, butt cap, c1730, 12 in (29 cm). **$1,000-1,200**

A rare 4 barrel flintlock turnover pistol, engraved steel frame, signed Segarlis, London, trigger guard operates catch to turnover barrels, 1740/50, 9 in (23 cm). **$1,500-2,200**

A double barrelled flintlock side by side pistol, sighted barrels, signed Simmons, 7 in (17.5 cm). **$1,000-1,200**

A pair of brass barrelled flintlock pistols with cannon barrels, signed 'Perry London', sliding trigger guards, one defective, hallmarks for Birmingham 1780, 18thC, 12 in (30 cm). **$1,700-2,500**

A Scottish all steel flintlock pistol, with rams horn butt and removable pricket, signed MacLeod, early dress type, c1820, 12 in (31 cm). **$1,300-1,700**

A pair of Scottish all steel flintlock belt pistols, three-stage barrels, blued belt hooks and steel ram-rods, c1830, 6 in (15 cm). **$2,000-3,000**

A good brass barrelled flintlock blunderbuss coaching pistol, maker Jackson of London, c1780, 11½ in (29 cm). **$1,000-1,200**

A double bar flintlock tap-action over-and-under pistol, maker Hunt of London, brass frame, steel barrel, c1790, 7 in (18 cm). **$500-600**

An English brass flintlock coaching blunderbuss pistol, fitted under spring bayonet, signed Twigg, London, silver mounts, type used by coach guards, c1785, 15 in (37 cm). **$1,300-1,700**

A brass barrelled flintlock blunderbuss pistol, with brass frame signed Waters & Co. and Patent No.542, 7 in barrel (18 cm). **$1,200-1,500**

A cased pair of English flintlock duelling pistols, maker Patrick of Liverpool, saw handle butts, original case with label and fittings, guns retaining 95% original finish, c1800. **$6,000-8,500**

A silver stocked Balkan/Mediterranean flintlock pistol, known as a 'rat-tail', stock finely chiselled with designs, mechanism and barrel of Italian manufacture, fine condition, 1820-40, 24 in (59 cm). **$1,200-1,500**

A pair of flintlock overcoat pistols, octagonal barrels engraved London, fitted with top spring bayonets, signed Sutherland, top of one cock damaged, 3½ in (8.5 cm). **$1,300-1,700**

A double barrelled Segalas flintlock box-lock pistol, two-stage turn off cannon barrels, inscribed Segalas, London, 4½ in (11 cm). **$700-900**

An 18 bore brass barrelled flintlock Royal Mail coach pistol, by Harding, dated 1836, 15 in (37.5 cm), barrel 9 in (22.5 cm), engraved 'J. Harding & Son, Boro London – (No.) 60', on top, and with '*For His Majesty's Mail Coaches', ramrod restored. **$1,300-1,700**

A four barrel turnover percussion pocket pistol with mahogany butt, inscribed Kavanagh Dublin, early 19thC. **$500-600**

A fine 16 bore New Land pattern flintlock holster pistol, 15½ in (38 cm), browned barrel 9 in (22.5 cm), Tower proved. **$1,300-1,700**

This gun is in almost mint condition.

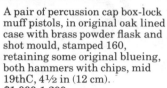

A pair of percussion cap box-lock muff pistols, in original oak lined case with brass powder flask and shot mould, stamped 160, retaining some original blueing, both hammers with chips, mid 19thC, 4½ in (12 cm). **$1,000-1,200**

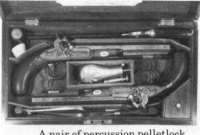

A pair of percussion pelletlock holster pistols, engraved Regent Circus, Piccadilly and inlaid in gold with the maker's mark, C. Moore London Patent, complete with accessories including associated pellet dispenser and maker's trade label, one hammer nose chipped and one ramrod missing, 9 in (22.5 cm). **$4,000-5,000**

A percussion turn-over double barrelled pocket pistol, signed Bond, London, engraved steel frame, c1840, 7 in (17 cm). **$300-500**

A continental pocket percussion pistol, fitted side hammer and fluted ivory butt, Liege proof marks, folding trigger, c1845, 6½ in (16 cm). **$300-400**

A pair of English 17 bore fullstocked percussion travelling pistols, by 'E. Bond, 5, Cornhill, London, Gun Maker to the H.E.I. Compy', crossbolted forends with silver escutcheons, the charcoal blued, c1845. **$1,500-2,200**

A pair of cased continental percussion target or duelling pistols, octagonal twist barrels, unsigned, plain type, 2nd quality, with all fittings, 1850/70. **$1,500-2,200**

A rare cased Model 1913 .38 HV (.38ACP) semi-automatic pistol, serial no.66525, retaining virtually all blueing, with slight marks, by Webley & Scott Ltd. **$1,200-1,500**

A .25 Flobert type combination knife pistol, Unwin & Rogers Patent. **$400-600**

A rare Scottish all steel Snaphaunce pistol, 13½ in (34 cm) sighted ringed barrel, lock plate engraved with initials G.S. and dated 1678, some wear overall. **$6,000-8,500**

G.S. probably stands for Gulielmus Smith who was working between 1672 and 1686.

A .22 (R.F.) model 1911 single shot target pistol by Webley No.135675. **$100-150**

A .41 (R.F.) single action 'cloverleaf' house pistol by Colt No.6231, with nickel plated frame. **$500-600**

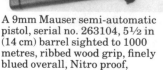

A 9mm Mauser semi-automatic pistol, serial no. 263104, 5½ in (14 cm) barrel sighted to 1000 metres, ribbed wood grip, finely blued overall, Nitro proof, complete with wooden shoulder stock holster no. 345. **$1,000-1,200**

A scarce six shot pinfire apache pistol, 1½ in (3.5 cm) barrels, a German silver frame signed L. Dolne, Inv^or, fitted with 3 in (8 cm) folding blade secured by a catch on the left side, folding trigger and folding German silver knuckleduster butt. **$1,000-1,200**

An unusual double barrelled hand gun, 23 in (27.5 cm) barrels, probably South Eastern Asian, corroded overall. **$1,000-1,200**

A rare 'Volcanic' lever action repeating pistol, 6 in (15 cm) sighted barrel with magazine beneath, faintly engraved Volcanic Arms Co. and Patent date 1854, stamped with serial no. 636, 2-piece wood grip, magazine spring broken. **$2,000-3,000**

A Day's patent truncheon pistol, with blunderbuss barrel, under hammer percussion action bird's head detachable pommel containing three shot, the screw off pommel cap inscribed Day's patent, 16 in (40 cm). **$1,300-1,700**

A Japanese matchlock pistol with gold lacquered stock overlaid with dragonflies etc, barrel inlaid with some silver, signed , c1820, 16 in (40 cm). **$1,300-1,700**

Powder Flasks

A gun sized copper powder flask (R.284), lacquered body embossed with flutes, acanthus and vine foliage, stamped 'G. & J.W. Hawksley', 8¼ in (21 cm). **$100-150**

A carved wood powder flask of 'doughnut' type, for use with a wheel-lock rifle or pistol, German, c1650, 5½ in (14 cm). **$3,000-4,500**

A continental highly embossed copper powder flask, c1800, 7 in (18 cm). **$200-300**

A Scottish horn powder flask, c1830, 16 in (40 cm). **$600-800**

Revolvers

An English percussion transitional revolver, engraved steel frame, unsigned, Birmingham proof, c1845, 11½ in (29 cm). **$400-600**

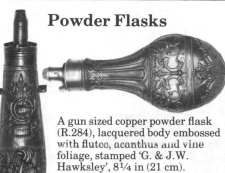

An English percussion pepperbox revolver, 6 shot, unsigned, Birmingham proof, engraved steel frame, 1840-1845, 7½ in (19 cm). **$300-400**

A rare all bronze Budding patent percussion revolver, very few made, c1840. **$1,500-2,200**

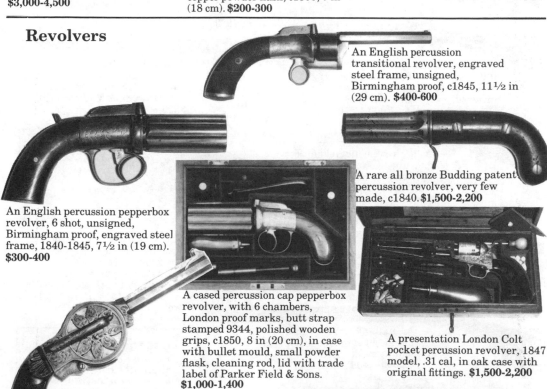

A cased percussion cap pepperbox revolver, with 6 chambers, London proof marks, butt strap stamped 9344, polished wooden grips, c1850, 8 in (20 cm), in case with bullet mould, small powder flask, cleaning rod, lid with trade label of Parker Field & Sons. **$1,000-1,400**

A presentation London Colt pocket percussion revolver, 1847 model, .31 cal, in oak case with original fittings. **$1,500-2,200**

A rare Noel patent ten shot turret revolver, easily removed cylinder, French, c1856, 7 in (18 cm). **$1,500-2,200**

A scarce percussion Colt Paterson revolver, unmarked, this is probably a contemporary continental copy, c1840, 15½ in (39 cm). **$1,500-2,200**

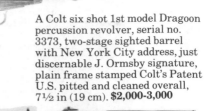

A Colt six shot 1st model Dragoon percussion revolver, serial no. 3373, two-stage sighted barrel with New York City address, just discernable J. Ormsby signature, plain frame stamped Colt's Patent U.S. pitted and cleaned overall, 7½ in (19 cm). **$2,000-3,000**

A .455 Eley single action 'Bisley flat-top target', revolver, by Colt, the 7½ in (19 cm) barrel with Hartford address, serial no. 160865, London black powder proof, retaining about 95% original blueing with slight rust spots, in its oak case with exchange sight blade and oil bottle, the lid with Pall Mall addressed label, 1895. **$6,000-8,000**

A total of approximately 976 Flat-tops were produced, starting in 1894, the lack of the (Bisley Model) marking on the barrel indicates that this is one of the first models, before the adoption of the Bisley name in 1895. See R.L. Sutherland and R.L. Wilson, The Book of Colt Firearms. Kansas City 1971.

A scarce nine shot 'Le Mat' percussion revolver, sighted octagonal barrel, signed Le Mat & Girard's Patent, London. **$3,000-4,500**

A six shot Webley percussion revolver, barrel signed Adams, retaining virtually all its original blueing and colour hardening. **$600-800**

Rifles

A Flintlock gun, by George Wallis of Hull, with a presentation inscription, overall length 48½ in (121 cm). **$1,300-1,700**

George Wallis is recorded working 1753-1803 and in partnership with John Wallis 1804-1822.

A 12 bore 2½ in (6 cm) sidelock 'Imperial Ejector' gun, by Lang & Hussey Ltd., No. 13098(1), 28 in (70 cm) barrels by Gallyon & Sons, I.C. & 3/4 in choke weight, 6 lb 8 ozs, left barrel below recommended thickness. **$1,700-2,500**

A sergeant's India pattern flintlock service musket, stamped WI.167, and original steel ramrod, unsigned, early 19thC, together with socket bayonet. **$1,000-1,200**

A composite percussion Brunswick rifle with 30 in (75 cm) barrel, the lockplate stamped 1864 Tower and V.R. crowned. **$500-600**

A dual system air and flintlock gun, wooden ramrod with brass tip, German, c1800, 52½ in (131 cm), butt plate loose, ramrod associated. **$1,700-2,500**

A London proved 24 bore Lang pattern open frame six shot single action percussion revolver rifle, retailed by Alex Martin, Glasgow, c1845. **$1,000-1,200**

A D.B. 303 sidelock ejector sporting rifle, by George Gibbs, the 26 in (65 cm) barrels with leaf sights to 500 yards, serial no. 17850, 8 lb 14 ozs, black powder proof, stock 14½ in (36 cm), bores worn. **$4,000-5,000**

An Italian Flintlock carbine, with blunderbuss muzzle and hinged folding stock, c1740. **$1,000-1,400**

A wheel-lock hunting rifle, internal wheel, heavy octagonal rifled grooved barrel, brass mounts, some engraving, German or Austrian, c1690, 33 in (83 cm). **$2,000-3,000**

Use the Index!
Because certain items might fit easily into any of a number of categories, the quickest and surest method of locating any entry is by reference to the index at the back of the book.
This has been fully cross-referenced for absolute simplicity.

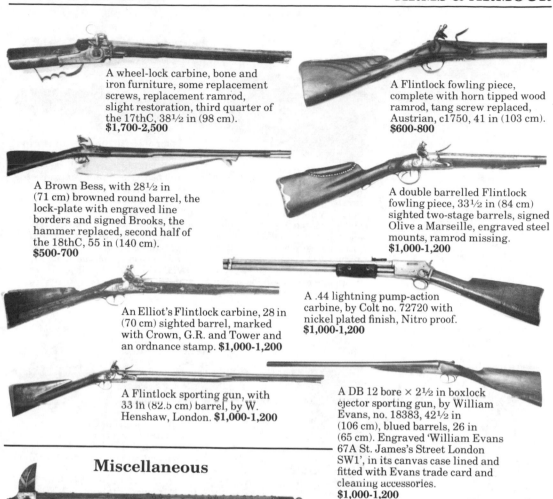

A wheel-lock carbine, bone and iron furniture, some replacement screws, replacement ramrod, slight restoration, third quarter of the 17thC, 38½ in (98 cm). **$1,700-2,500**

A Flintlock fowling piece, complete with horn tipped wood ramrod, tang screw replaced, Austrian, c1750, 41 in (103 cm). **$600-800**

A Brown Bess, with 28½ in (71 cm) browned round barrel, the lock-plate with engraved line borders and signed Brooks, the hammer replaced, second half of the 18thC, 55 in (140 cm). **$500-700**

A double barrelled Flintlock fowling piece, 33½ in (84 cm) sighted two-stage barrels, signed Olive a Marseille, engraved steel mounts, ramrod missing. **$1,000-1,200**

An Elliot's Flintlock carbine, 28 in (70 cm) sighted barrel, marked with Crown, G.R. and Tower and an ordnance stamp. **$1,000-1,200**

A .44 lightning pump-action carbine, by Colt no. 72720 with nickel plated finish, Nitro proof. **$1,000-1,200**

A Flintlock sporting gun, with 33 in (82.5 cm) barrel, by W. Henshaw, London. **$1,000-1,200**

A DB 12 bore × 2½ in boxlock ejector sporting gun, by William Evans, no. 18383, 42½ in (106 cm), blued barrels, 26 in (65 cm). Engraved 'William Evans 67A St. James's Street London SW1', in its canvas case lined and fitted with Evans trade card and cleaning accessories. **$1,000-1,200**

Basically a Webley model 700.

Miscellaneous

A rare German Gothic war-hammer, inlaid with latten bands, on later cloth-covered haft, late 15thC, 24½ in (61 cm). **$3,000-4,000**

A pair of Gothic rowel spurs, of iron, perhaps English, two slightly damaged, late 15thC, 10¼ in (26 cm). **$1,000-1,200**

A Saxon horseman's hammer, early 17thC, 22½ in (56 cm). **$4,500-7,000**

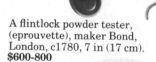

A flintlock powder tester, (eprouvette), maker Bond, London, c1780, 7 in (17 cm). **$600-800**

A Kynoch Limited cartridge display case, removed from the shop of T. Whaley & Son, Ironmongers, Bridge Street, St. Ives (Cambridge), with a comprehensive array of sectioned and inert ammunition in brass and paper cases, case 56 by 45 in (140 by 112.5 cm) overall. **$7,500-10,500**

A rowel spur, of brass, probably English, early 17thC, 6 in (15 cm). **$400-600**

A rare Nazi party brass bugle, oval makers label of 'Meinel and Herold, Musikinstrumentfabrik, Klingenthal i.Sa', N.S.D.A.P. eagle badge, 10½ in (26 cm). **$200-300**

A lady's side-saddle, with wooden frame covered with leather and faced in crimson velvet, worn, on modern wheeled stand, 17thC, 23 in (57.5 cm) long. **$2,000-3,000**

A Gothic rowel spur, for tilting, German, late 15thC, 7¾ in (19 cm). **$500-600**

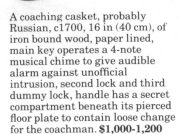

A coaching casket, probably Russian, c1700, 16 in (40 cm), of iron bound wood, paper lined, main key operates a 4-note musical chime to give audible alarm against unofficial intrusion, second lock and third dummy lock, handle has a secret compartment beneath its pierced floor plate to contain loose change for the coachman. **$1,000-1,200**

A pair of ½ pdr. bronze cannon, by R. Gilpin, dated 1764, 33 in (82.5 cm), chiselled with raised crowned 'G' for John, Marquis of Granby, Master General of the Ordnance from 1763-1772. **$7,500-10,500**

The foundry of Richard Gilpin was in the Borough, Southwark, and specialised in smaller pieces – see H.M. Tower of London Armouries, H.M.S.O. 1976, No. 56 for another bronze ½ pdr. by this maker.

Badges

A Victorian Officer's hallmarked silver (Edinburgh 1888) Bonnet Badge of the Argyll and Sutherland Highlanders. **$400-600**

An Officer's gilt and silver fur Cap Badge of the Royal Munster Fusiliers, slight wear to gilt. **$100-150**

A fine Victorian Officer's gilt silver and blue enamelled Busby Grenade Badge of the Royal Marine Artillery, 1866 pattern. **$300-400**

l. A Victorian Officer's 1881 pattern silvered gilt and enamelled Helmet Plate of the Royal Scots Volunteer Battalion. **$300-500**
c. An Officer's gilt Helmet Plate Grenade of the Royal Marine Artillery. **$400-600**
r. A Victorian Officer's 1881 pattern gilt and silvered Helmet Plate of the King's Own Scottish Borderers. **$300-400**

An Officer's gilt and silver fur Cap Badge of the Lancashire Fusiliers. **$100-150**

An Officer's 1874 pattern gilt and enamel Glengarry Badge of the 74th Highlanders. **$300-500**

A Victorian Officer's post-1881 gilt Glengarry Badge of the Gloucestershire Regiment. **$200-300**

l. A Victorian Officer's 1881 pattern gilt silvered and enamelled Helmet Plate of the Border Regiment. **$400-600**
c. A very fine Victorian Officer's silvered Helmet Plate of the 1st Volunteer Battalion, Royal North Lancashire Regiment, 1881 pattern. **$200-300**
r. A Victorian Officer's 1881 pattern gilt and silvered Helmet Plate of the 1st Royal Guernsey Militia. **$300-400**

A Victorian Officer's post-1881 silver gilt and enamel Glengarry Badge of the Dorset Regiment. **$200-300**

An Officer's gilt and silver fur Cap Badge of the Royal Inniskilling Fusiliers. **$200-300**

A Victorian Officer's gilt Shako Badge of the 3rd City of London Regiment. **$400-600**

A good Victorian silver-plated Helmet Plate of the Earl of Chester Yeomanry, 3 of 4 fixing studs missing. **$200-300**

A George V Officer's Helmet Plate of the King's Own Norfolk Imperial Yeomanry. **$300-500**

A Victorian Officer's gilt and blue enamelled Shako Badge of the Royal Marine Light Infantry, 1866 pattern. **$400-600**

A post-1902 Officer's gilt and silvered lance-cap plate of the 17th (Duke of Cambridge's Own) Lancers. **$300-400**

A Georgian Officer's copper gilt rectangular shoulder belt plate of The 8th (The King's) Regiment, c1825. **$600-700**

A Victorian Officer's gilt and silvered lance-cap Plate of the 9th (Queen's Royal) Lancers. **$300-400**

Medals

Five: M.C. George V with bar, 1914-15 star, B.W.M., Victory, I.G.S. 1908 1 bar Afghanistan N.W.F. 1919. (M.C. reverse engraved 2nd Lieut. H.G. Inglis, Oujailah Mesopotamia 8th March, 1916, trio as Lieut 56-Rifles, I.G.S. as 2- 151 Infy) VF, together with relevant group of miniatures, and 2 photographs of recipient. **$600-700**

N.G.S. 1793, 1 bar Victorious with Rivoli, (J.R. Crawford, Midshipman). **$1,000-1,200**

In this action of February 22nd 1812 the 3rd rate Victorious encountered Rivoli, a 74 gun French vessel, off Venic e. The French ship surrendered when the British sloop Weazel joined the action. (Major Gordon states 67 bars issued).

Four: 1914-15 star, B.W.M., Victory, G.S.M. 1918, 1 bar S. Persia (1546 sgt. C. Burrage, 21st Lancers). **$500-600**

See Gordon p.328, 21st Lancers not present as a regt but 'There were, of course, a few European recipients apart from officers'.

l. Three: Military General Service Medal 1793, Waterloo 1815, 71st Regiment Medal for 10 Years' Service (Irwin 3) (James Nisbitt, 71st Foot, Waterloo as Nesbett). **$3,000-4,500**
r, An interesting gold, not hall-marked, medal presented by the President of the United States for saving life at sea, **$1,300-1,700**

President Woodrow Wilson was in office at this time.

A.G.S. 1902, 1 bar Somaliland 1902-04, (7237 Pte. H. Harley, R. Warwick Regt). **$300-500**

Five: D.S.M. Geo V Admiral's bust, 1914-15 star, B.W.M., Victory, R.N. L.S. & G.C., Edward VII (148252 C. Hocken, P.O. Icl. H.M.S. Albion, L.S. & G.C., as Charles Hocken H.M. Coast Guard) VF. D.S.M. awarded 1915, H.M.S. Albion has Dardanelles as a battle honour. **$400-600**

Ashanti War (W.Cook, Asst.Engr., R.N. H.M.S. Druid 73-74). **$100-200**
Afghanistan 1878-80, 1 bar Ali Musjid (12 Bde 281 Pte T. Murphy 81st Foot). **$200-300**
East and West Africa, 1 bar 1893-94, (1263 Cy S.Maj H. Noble 1/W.I.R.). **$200-300**
East and West Africa medal, bar Benin River, 1894 (E. Balsom, Sto. H.M.S. Philomel). **$200-300**
Naval L.S. & G.C. Vic issue, wide suspender (engraved W.Webb Bosns Mte H.M.S. Dasher 26 Years). **$200-300**

D.S.O., Geo V issue. **$300-400**
Military Cross Geo V issue, reverse engraved 'Presented to Capt. W.F. Sheather by H.I.M. King George V Nov 23rd 1918'. **$200-300**
Indian Mutiny 1857-58, 1 bar Central India (Thos Tynan 3rd Madras Eurpn Regt), NEF. **$200-300**
New Zeland Campaign 1863-66, (292 Albert Blogg 43rd lt inftry). **$200-300**
Canada Service Medal, 1 bar Fenian Raid 1866. **$100-150**

Papier Mâché

- made from pulped paper, glue, chalk and sometimes sand
- will take a high polish after painting or japanning
- introduced to England in 1672
- late 18thC Henry Clay of Birmingham patented a way of making strong panels
- avoid chipped or cracked pieces
- good makers include B. Walton & Co., Jennens & Bettridge, Clay
- often plainer earlier pieces worth more
- in 1825 Jennens & Bettridge introduced mother of pearl inlay
- green papier mâché highly desirable.

Papier Mâché

t.l & b.r. A pair of painted papier mâché trays, the scalloped raised edge decorated with trailing gilt rocaille, 19thC, 14½ in (36 cm). **$600-700**

t.r A papier mâché tray, the centre painted with an exotic scene of a peacock on rocks beneath a willow, 12½ in .31 cm). **$400-600**

b.l An unusual blue ground papier mâché tray, 13 in (33 cm) wide. **$400-600**

A papier mâché tray, painted with a pastoral scene of peasants milking by a lakeside, 24½ in (61 cm) wide. **$600-900**

A set of three graduated papier mâché trays, finely painted with a naturalistic spray of garden flowers, 20, 26½ and 33 in (50, 66 and 83 cm). **$4,000-5,000**

A set of four Victorian papier mâché wall plaques, each painted and inlaid mother-of-pearl, 20 in (50 cm). **$2,000-3,000**

MAKE THE MOST OF MILLER'S

Miller's is completely different each year. Each edition contains completely NEW photographs. This is not an updated publication. We never repeat the same photograph.

A papier mâché tray, by Jennens and Bettridge, having gilt and floral pattern with mother-of-pearl inlay, 25 by 18½ in (62.5 by 46 cm). **$1,000-1,200**

A fine George III papier mâché tray, by Alderman and Illidge of Wolverhampton, well lacquered in tones of gilt and green, with a sporting scene, impressed marks on reverse, Illidge, Warranted, rim chip and surface crack, 23 by 31 in (57 by 77 cm). **$3,000-4,000**

Thomas Illidge is recorded as operating in St. James's Square Wolverhampton in c1810.

A risqué papier mâché snuff box, the lid entitled La Precaution Inutile depicting a voyeur at a lady's toilette, the interior with explicit mythological scenes, 19thC, 3½ in (9 cm). **$200-300**

A Continental painted papier mâché snuff box, depicting a young couple embracing intimately, after Fragonard, 19thC, 3½ in (8.5 cm). **$300-400**

A Continental painted snuff box, the lid depicting a pastoral scene of Venus at her toilette, scarcely draped, glazed within gilt border, 3 in (8 cm). **$500-600**

A pair of Regency papier mâché wine coasters, the sides decorated with gilt cornucopia and foliate motifs on a black ground, 5 in (12.5 cm). **$1,000-1,200**

A papier mâché cabinet, rising top enclosing compartments, 6 drawers and central recess, 19thC, 11 by 12½ in (27.5 by 31 cm) **$500-700**

A papier mâché table snuff box, painted with a figure entitled Betende Magdaleine, Nach Guido Beni, the border applied with a silvered metal band inscribed T. Sinister, Manchester, possibly Stobwasser's, 3½ in (9 cm). **$300-400**

Masonic

A fine Masonic punch bowl, the centre of the interior enamelled with an allegorical panel of the sun between 'The pillars at the Entrance to King Solomon's Temple', Qianlong, 15½ in (39.7 cm). **$4,500-7,000**

A Sunderland lustre Masonic Sailors Farewell jug, c1840, 7½ in (19 cm). **$300-400**

A gentleman's masonic open-face pair cased pocket watch, hallmarked London 1807. **$500-600**

A masonic decanter engraved T. Dalzell – 340, c1800, 9 in (22.5 cm). **$600-900**

A burr maple masonic snuff box, 3½ in (8.3 cm). **$300-400**

An oxidised triangular silver cased masonic watch, import mark Edinburgh 1925, with nickel keyless lever 15 jewelled movement. **$1,200-1,500**

An export lacquer masonic box and hinged cover, decorated in gold, silver and red hiramakie and inlaid in aogai on a roironuri ground incorporating a variety of Masonic symbols, metal fittings, old wear and damage, 19thC, 15 by 9½ in (38 by 23.9 cm). **$1,000-1,200**

Judaica

A porcelain dish, with gold transfer printing on white ground with a representation of the Pascal Lamb and legends in Hebrew, possibly Limoges, 19thC, 16 in (39.8 cm). **$600-900**

A silver Menorah on 'Neo-gothic' trefoil base, with acorn finial, Austria Hungary, between 1866 and 1893, 12 in (29.3 cm) high. **$2,000-3,000**

A large bronze Menorah, probably eastern Europe, two drip pans missing, 19thC, 29 in (73 cm) high. **$2,000-3,000**

A silver Menorah, by S. Schefler, St. Petersburg, 1882, 8 by 7 in (19.5 by 17.8 cm) wide, 348 grms. **$3,000-4,000**

A pewter Passover dish, with the seven famous Talmudic scholars at the Seder feast, a modern copy of an 18thC prototype, 14 in (34.4 cm). **$1,700-2,500**

A brass Menorah, probably late 17thC, 4½ by 13 in (11 by 32.7 cm) wide. **$2,000-3,000**

A cloth briefcase, with silver mounts, Touchau Morocco, 20 x 26.5 cm. **$1,400-1,700**

A bronze Sabbath lamp, possibly Holland, 18/19thC, 17 in (42 cm) high. **$400-600**

A four piece brass Sabbath lamp, Holland, early 18thC, 25 in (63 cm) high. **$1,400-1,700**

A gold pressed leather casket, for a circumcision set with wooden frame and brass mounts, probably Dutch, c1800, and 2 leather bound Hebrew booklets. **$2,000-3,000**

A silver Thorah pointer, of tapering form decorated with filigree work, on chain, Israel, 20thC, 13½ in (34 cm) long. **$200-300**

Miller's is a price GUIDE not a price LIST

The price ranges given reflect the average price a purchaser should pay for similar items. Condition, rarity of design or pattern, size, colour, provenance, restoration and many other factors must be taken into account when assessing values.
When buying or selling, it must always be remembered that prices can be greatly affected by the condition of any piece. Unless otherwise stated, all goods shown in Miller's are of good merchantable quality, and the valuations given reflect this fact. Pieces offered for sale in exceptionally fine condition or in poor condition may reasonably be expected to be priced considerably higher or lower respectively than the estimates given herein.

Jewellery Introduction

While collecting jewellery is among the most rewarding of occupations, the road to success is not without pitfalls for the unwary and the inexperienced.

It is essential to develop a good eye. Learn to recognise styles of craftsmanship, of different periods and countries of origin. Learn too, the signs of wear and tear, and indications of poor repair work, the most common of these being the use of lead solder on delicate antique gold work, which can be disastrous.

For investment, look particularly for pieces of exceptional quality and rarity, and even pieces known to be by prestigious jewellery houses of the 20th Century, some of whom are household names (such as Cartier, Van Cleef and Arples, Winstons and Liberty).

There are many makers of fine 'Art Nouveau' and 'Art Deco' too, whose work commands very high prices, but these prices are rarely attained where obvious restoration work has been carried out. Be particularly wary of the very large number of excellent reproductions of this type and style of jewellery which, after it has found its way from the shops dealing only in modern goods, is sometimes very difficult to detect as not being original. Reproductions of Victorian styles however, pose very little difficulty in identification.

In most sections of the jewellery trade, old jewellery is still very good value when compared with its modern counterpart.
There were many exceptional Victorian jewellers (including Hardman of Birmingham, Garrard, Hunt and Roskell, Phillips, Attenborough, Ashbee, Castellani, Giulliano,

Fabergé and the various Hancocks), the work of many being authenticated in the Great Exhibition of 1851.

Naturally, many pieces of jewellery will be bought in states of disrepair. If you wish to enhance the values of such pieces, never attempt 'do-it-yourself' repairs, but seek out a first class jewellery restorer – even though such a one can be hard to find – someone who is sensitive to the very special techniques required when dealing with valuable items from the past.

While reference books will be of value to every collector, remember that, particularly with jewellery, so much depends upon intangibles. However good a photograph may be, it cannot help you to assimilate the additional information necessary when making your own final appraisal. This can only be done by close examination and handling the article yourself.

Jewellery – Rings

A good gold cameo ring, the oval sardonyx carved with bust of Hercules, late 18th/early 19thC, 3 cm. **$1,400-1,700**

A 15ct gold lightweight three stone diamond 'keeper' ring, hallmarked Chester 1895. **$60-100**

An 18ct band ring, set with 5 seed pearls set in a boat shaped setting, dated 1900. **$150-200**

A 9ct gold memoriam ring, set with freshwater pearls with black enamel background to the pearls and also for the engraved shoulders. **$60-100**

An 18ct gold ring, set with 5 brilliant cut diamonds in recessed boat shaped setting, hallmarked London 1905. **$200-300**

These were made between 1860 and the turn of the century. Prices vary greatly according to quality.

A 15ct gold ring, set with 3 garnets and 4 diamond 'chips', hallmarked London 1900. **$150-200**

These rings were mass produced between 1890 and 1920 and were sold when new from £2. 10 s. Od upwards depending upon the size and quality of the stones.

An oval gold cameo ring, the sardonyx cameo carved with a group of Venus, Cupid and Adonis, mid 17thC, the later gold mount with mark, 2.3 cm. **$700-900**

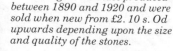

A fine carved white onyx cameo, in contemporary gold setting, the shank restored, 18thC. **$400-600**

It is difficult to find onyx cameos in good condition.

A 15ct gold memoriam ring, set with seed pearls and decorated with black enamel, dated 1876. **$150-200**

A 15ct gold ring set with rose cut diamonds and cabochon turquoise, the stones set in silver, c1890. **$200-300**

An 18ct gold 'belt' or 'buckle' ring, set with a diamond and 2 rubies, Birmingham hallmark 1898. **$200-300**

Most popular between 1885 and 1910.

A late Victorian 9 ct gold hollow, wax filled ring, set with turquoises and pearls, Chester hallmark 1895. **$60-100**

A 15ct gold ring, set with 3 diamonds surrounded by turquoises, pave set with split shoulders, dated 1895. **$200-300**

This ring is typical of the period.

An antique rose-diamond and blue enamel collet and cluster oblong panel ring. **$1,400-1,700**

A single old cut diamond ring. **$400-600**

An antique ruby and diamond circular cluster ring, with carved gold mount. **$1,300-1,700**

An antique diamond cluster ring. **$1,000-1,400**

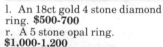

l. An 18ct gold 4 stone diamond ring. **$500-700**
r. A 5 stone opal ring. **$1,000-1,200**

Jewellery – Earrings

A 15ct gold high Victorian style pendant earrings, showing Etruscan influence, c1870. **$400-600**

Fine 15ct gold earrings, of the third quarter of the 19thC, in original condition. **$400-600**

A pair of Indian earrings, with a rosette of flat rose diamonds ringed with natural pearls, clips added later, Jaipur, late 19thC, enamel with minor damage, in fitted case, each 3½ in (9 cm). **$1,700-2,500**

A pair of Art Deco carved emerald ear pendants, with black enamel and diamond chain link mounts. **$4,000-5,000**

A pair of sapphire and diamond ear clips, each set with 3 cut sapphires, 21 brilliant cut diamonds and 5 graduated square cut diamonds, set in white gold. **$1,000-1,200**

A pair of antique blue and white enamel and gem-set marquise panel ear pendants. **$1,400-1,700**

Necklaces/Pendants and Lockets

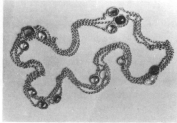

A gold and coral necklace, and a pair of matching earrings, late 19thC. **$600-700**

A rare George III gold and silhouette portrait memorial locket, by John Field, 1771-1841, under rock-crystal, 4.6 cm high, including engraved suspension loop, English, c1810, on a woven hair guard necklace, early 19thC, approximately 50½ in (126 cm) long. **$500-600**

A collar necklace of coral beads, strung and woven into triple rope, with gold fastener set with 3 coral beads, mid-19thC. **$400-600**
This is a traditional design still being produced in Italy to this day.
c. A 15ct gold 'stick' or 'stock' pin, Italian branch coral fixed with entwining gold snake, c1880. **$50-70**

A 15ct gold long guard chain, set with garnets, amethysts, and citrines, the links and settings are as new and show no signs of wear. **$1,000-1,200**

A French gold, ruby and diamond heart shaped pendant locket, the reverse with glazed locket compartment, maker's mark F.L., mid-19thC. **$3,000-4,000**

A Victorian diamond twelve-point star brooch pendant, and a Victorian diamond crescent brooch, in fitted case. **$1,000-1,400**

An enamelled gold and diamond set pendant watch, the chain interspersed with seed pearls and lapis lazuli beads. **$1,700-2,500**

An antique blue enamel, rose cut diamond and half pearl stylised oval cluster pendant. **$3,000-4,000**

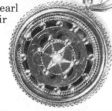

A gold, pink topaz and seed pearl pendant, the reverse with hair compartment, mid-19thC. **$400-600**

An 18ct gold locket, set with turquoises, half pearls and rose cut diamonds, with Etruscan influence, c1860. **$1,000-1,200**

A Victorian circular gold and pearl locket, with applied decoration. **$100-200**

A Victorian cabochon garnet and diamond pendant. **$1,400-1,700**

An enamel and gem set necklace, set with cushion shaped diamond centres interspersed with green enamel ivy leaves and small pearls, gold chain back. **$1,000-1,200**

A Victorian 15ct gold locket, flower spray set with rubies and pearls, c1875. **$400-600**
These are often found badly dented or heavily engraved which drastically reduces the price.

A gold, seed-pearl and diamond brooch pendant, with single star-set diamond centre stone, late 19thC. **$600-700**

An 18ct gold Victorian locket, dated 1875, the monogram set with turquoises, coral and seed pearls, the 9ct gold neck chain is a 20thC replacement. **$500-600**

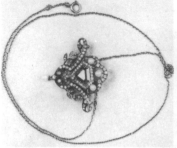

A 15ct gold pendant, set with split 'seed' freshwater pearls and green peridots, typical early 20thC. **$400-600**

Matching 'tear-drop' peridot earrings set in gold with earwires of modern design. **$60-90**

Condition is of the utmost importance for this type of jewellery to attain high prices.

An Edwardian leaf and scrolled shaped pendant, set with central amethyst surrounded by numerous small diamonds, with 4 pearls, and the chain. **$1,700-2,500**

An antique cabochon garnet and rose cut diamond quatrefoil cluster brooch pendant, and a pair of earrings en suite. **$1,400-1,700**

A sapphire and rose diamond ► dragonfly, set with ruby eyes, c1890. **$1,400-1,700**

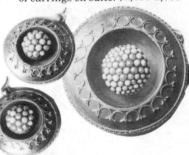

An 18ct gold Victorian brooch and earrings set of classical design, set with turquoises and pearls. **$400-600**

A diamond pendant brooch, with detachable loop, c1890. **$3,500-5,000**

Diamond pieces of this period are still extremely good value.

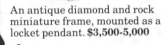

An antique diamond and rock miniature frame, mounted as a locket pendant. **$3,500-5,000**

◄ A Whitby jet bar brooch, hand carved and set with a seed pearl in a gold star and with a gilded brass pin. **$25-30**

A Whitby jet carved cameo, of classical design, with a gilt pin, c1870. **$100-150**

Difficult to find in undamaged condition; this one particularly nice.

A Victorian gold circular tassel brooch, set with pearls and rubies. **$100-200**

A Victorian jet cameo, with hand carved flower spray design, c1870. **$50-70**

An enamelled porcelain plaque brooch, mounted within a gold frame, late 19thC. **$300-500**

Diamonds

The "brillaint cut" for diamonds was invented in the 17th century by a Venetian lapidary named Vincenzo Peruzzi and remained basically much the same for the next 200 years. Most of the diamonds found in Georgian and Victorian jewellery are cut in this way, or if not, the "rose cut" was used. This is a semi-spherical dome shape of triangular facets (usually 24 or 12 in all) culminating in a point. (Even tiny off-cuts of diamonds were made use of, and were commonly known as "chips".) Size was considered of much more importance than colour or quality, and most of the diamonds used in antique jewellery originated in East India or South America. (The stones mined in Brazil sometimes had a definite yellowy tinge, and were commonly known as "Whisky" diamonds for obvious reasons.)

With the discovery of diamonds in South Africa in the mid-19th century there was a shift in the whole world market, and to this day the majority of diamonds come from there.

A carved Victorian shell cameo brooch and earring set, in 9ct gold, c1865. **$300-500**

A 15ct gold mid Victorian shell cameo, of classical design, the mount in the Etruscan style. **$600-700**

An Edwardian diamond brooch, the centre with an old cut diamond collet on a hinged knife bar, the remainder set with small rose cut diamonds. **$1,000-1,200**

A heavy 15 ct gold brooch, set with cabochon onyx in rope twist setting, surrounded by Greek key pattern decoration, with an oval locket space in the back for plaited hair or a miniature. **$200-300**

A gold, diamond, enamel and seed pearl love-token brooch, early 19thC. **$600-800**

A Victorian brooch, of a Swiss landscape on porcelain, in gold frame. **$200-300**

A Victorian silver, flower spray brooch, set with diamonds, gold backed, 1865-1870. **$1,700-2,500**

Most of the diamonds of this period were set in silver to enhance the whiteness and brilliance of the stones. Platinum settings were not generally used until the beginning of this century.

A mourning brooch, made up in unmarked gold, set with garnets around an inset square of plaited hair of the deceased, typical mid-19thC. **$60-90**

A Victorian garnet and gold brooch, with 3 garnet collets, in original case. **$600-700**

A late Victorian 18ct bow brooch, decorated in red enamel and set with 3 brilliant cut diamonds. **$600-700**

The hook on the back to take a fob watch.

A Victorian diamond spray brooch. **$1,300-1,700**

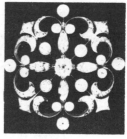

An Edwardian period diamond, emerald and ruby butterfly brooch. **$600-900**

Early examples fetch considerably more.

An Edwardian diamond brooch, centred by an old cut diamond in collet mount, in a case from T & J. Perry, London. **$1,000-1,200**

A continental gold crescent brooch, set with rose cut garnets, c1880. **$100-150**

The quality of the gold is often less than 7ct in this type of garnet jewellery and sometimes it is set in gilded brass.

An Austrian gold and enamel gem set brooch, with ruby eyes, late 19thC. **$1,000-1,200**

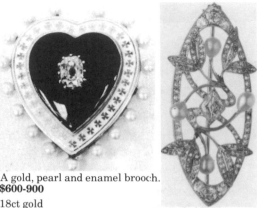

A gold, pearl and enamel brooch.
$600-900

A French mandolin in 18ct gold
and platinum, with rubies and
rose diamond, c1905. **$1,500-2,200**
A platinum mounted diamond
bow brooch, c1925. **$1,300-1,700**

A French gold, diamond and pearl
brooch, pave-set with brilliant cut
diamonds and seed pearls.
$3,000-4,000

A 9ct ruby and diamond bar
brooch, hallmarked 1905.
$60-90

*This type of brooch is still very
plentiful and can be bought for just
a few pounds in poor condition.*

A gold, amethyst and diamond
brooch. **$1,000-1,200**

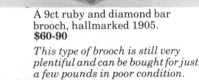

A 15ct gold memoriam set, black
enamel decoration set with seed
pearls, centre stones are cabochon
cut black and white banded onyx,
in the back of the brooch there is a
glass covered recess to take a lock
of hair or a miniature, in original
box. **$600-800**

*Of limited appeal but good
examples fetch high prices.*

A Piqué brooch, in the form of a
Maltese cross, made of
tortoiseshell inlaid with silver and
gold, slightly damaged, late
19thC. **$60-90**

A carved oval cameo, in a gilt
metal mount. **$200-300**

A graduated brilliant cut diamond
crescent brooch, set in silver and
supported by a gold pierced under
gallery. **$1,500-2,200**

A pair of sapphire and diamond
collet and ribbon scroll clip
brooches. **$3,000-4,000**

A diamond panel brooch.
$4,000-5,000

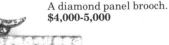

A Victorian moonstone and
diamond bar brooch, diamond bar
mount. **$2,000-3,000**

An eight-pointed Victorian diamond star brooch, with interspersing bars each set with 2 diamonds, set in silver and gold backed. **$700-1,000**

These were often a part of a tiara or a pendant or necklace which was made up in sections and intended to be taken apart in this way when required.

A large cocktail style brooch, gold, sapphire and moonstone, 1940's. **$1,500-2,200**

A lady's Swiss gold and enamel lapel watch. **$600-700**

An Edwardian diamond plaque brooch. **$1,700-2,500**

A square cut emerald and rose cut diamond cluster brooch, with emerald points, mounted in gold. **$4,000-5,000**

An Art Deco period diamond and platinum brooch, of brilliant and baguette cut stones. **$7,500-10,500**

This example has well matched stones. The hand made setting is extremely well constructed and finished.

Bracelets

Price

Prices in jewellery can vary enormously
1. According to age and condition.
2. The basic materials from which it is made.
3. Whether it is hand made or mass produced.
4. The quality of the stones set in the items.
5. Whether the item is at present fashionable.

The last consideration could be the most important of all, because, although fashions go in cycles, it may be many years before an unfashionable item becomes marketable once again. The only value often in these instances is that of the basic materials from which the item is made i.e. Scrap Value.

A diamond panel brooch, the centre with 3 collet-set diamonds, set with cushion and circular cut diamonds. **$6,000-8,000**

A frosted gold hinged bangle, late 19thC. **$700-900**

A Victorian diamond and pearl bangle, with a heavy 18ct gold mount. **$2,000-3,000**

An Edwardian gold hinged bangle, set with moonstone, seed pearls and rubies. **$700-900**

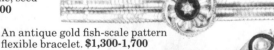

An antique gold multi-link longchain, with amethyst-set barrel clasp. **$3,000-4,000**

An antique gold fish-scale pattern flexible bracelet. **$1,300-1,700**

An antique diamond, half pearl, blue enamel and gold mesh buckle bracelet. **$1,300-1,700**

A cut steel cape buckle, late 18th/early 19thC, 5½ by 2 in (14 by 5 cm). **$30-60**

A Georgian gold slide bracelet frame, 3.5 cm, containing a miniature after Reynolds of a young lady, 2.5 cm, the bracelet formed of twelve gold chain strands. **$2,000-3,000**

A pair of gold bracelets, enamelled in blue, red and white, connected by pin hinges, alternate links set either with 2 pearls or a table-cut paste, early 17thC, some links and pearls replaced, 7 in (18.7 cm). **$5,500-7,000**

◄ A Victorian diamond open-work collet and scroll half hoop bangle. **$1,500-2,200**

Miscellaneous

A selection of old seals and keys, left to right:-
Gold and agate seal, c1880. **$60-90**
Gold swivelling seal, 1895. **$60-90**
Carved agate seal in 15ct gold mount, c1845. **$200-300**
Banded agate seal, intaglio carved 'Jane' 1870. **$30-60**
Pinchbeck key, set with slab cut cornelian, c1860. **$30-60**
Plain pinchbeck key set with onyx, c1855. **$30-60**

An Italian fin de siecle gold and crystal parure, comprising a necklet, earrings with new 9ct gold screw mounts, a two-section cloak clasp, a pin brooch and 2 extension pieces, in all 20 crystals, in morocco case. **$1,000-1,200**

The Mount Edgcumbe platinum and diamond tiara, millegrain and pavé-set with circular, cushion, pear-shaped and rose-cut diamonds, in fitted case by Boucheron, Paris. **$22,500-30,600**

A cultured pearl dragon head, white and yellow gold head encrusted with diamonds and ruby eyes, c1960. **$5,500-7,000**

Coral

The coral most commonly found in Victorian jewellery is of *Mediterranean* origin. It is a secretion of Calcium Carbonate formed by the Coral Polyp and grows on the sea bed rather like a forest of *pink, white* and *orange* coloured trees. The smaller branches of these can be broken into tiny pieces and drilled and strung as necklaces or earrings, but the most desirable pieces are heads and cameos from the trunk of the coral, the latter often set in the Castellani style settings of the time. Fashion dictates the most desirable colour, and at

A coral garniture, 19thC. **$300-500**

the moment it is the most *delicate pink* of the 'Angel Skin' variety which commands the highest price.

The greatest concentration of coral carvers to-day is around *Naples* in Italy where they have been plying their trade for many years if not thousands of years, the only difference now being that much of the coral upon which they work is imported from *Japan*.

There also exists *Black Coral* – this type is found mostly in the waters off *Hawaii*.

DIRECTORY OF INTERNATIONAL AUCTIONEERS

This directory is by no means complete. Any auctioneer who holds frequent sales should contact us for inclusion in the 1987 edition. Entries must be received by April 1986. There is, of course, no charge for this listing.

AMERICA

Associated Appraisers Inc.
915 Industrial Bank
Building
Providence, RI 02906
Tel: (401) 331-9391

Barridoff Galleries
242 Middle Street
Portland, ME 04 101
Tel: (207) 772-5011

Butterfield & Butterfield
1244 Sutter Street
San Francisco, CA 94109
Tel: (415) 673-1362

California Book Auction
Galleries
358 Golden Gate Avenue
San Francisco, CA 94102
Tel: (415) 775-0424

C. B. Charles Galleries, Inc.
825 Woodward Avenue
Pontiac, MI 48053
Tel: (313) 338-9023

Christie's East
219 East 67th Street
New York, NY 10021
Tel: (212) 570-4141

Representative Offices:
California:
9350 Wilshire Boulevard
Beverly Hills, CA 902 12
Tel: (213) 275-5534

Florida:
225 Fern Street
West Palm Beach, FL 33401
Tel: (305) 833-6592

Mid-Atlantic:
638 Morris Avenue
Bryn Mawr, PA 19010
Tel: (215) 525-5493

Washington:
1422 27th Street N.W.
Washington, DC 20007
Tel: (202) 965-2066

Midwest:
46 East Elm Street
Chicago, IL 60611
Tel: (312) 787-2765

DuMochelle Art Galleries
409 East Jefferson
Detroit, MI 48226
Tel: (313) 963-6255

John C. Edelmann
Galleries, Inc.
123 East 77th Street

New York, NY 10021
Tel: (212) 628-1700/1735

Robert C. Eldred Co. Inc.
Box 796
East Dennis, MA 02641
Tel: (617) 385-3116/3377

1808-10 Chestnut Street
Philadelphia, PA 19103
Tel: (215) 563-9275

Garth's Auctions, Inc.
2690 Stratford Road
Delaware, OH 43015
Tel: (614) 362-4771/
369-5085

Kelley's Auction Service
P.O. Box 125
Woburn, MA 01801
Tel: (617) 272-9167

Northgate Gallery
5520 Highway 153
Chattanooga, TN 37443
Tel: (615) 842-4177

O'Gallerie, Inc.
537 S.E. Ash Street
Portland, OR 97214
Tel: (503) 238-0202

Stalker and Boos, Inc.
280 North Woodward
Avenue
Birmingham, MI 48011
Tel: (313) 646-4560

Swann Galleries, Inc.
104 East 26th Street
New York, NY 10021
Tel: (212) 254-4710

Trosby Auction Galleries
81 Peachtree Park Drive
Atlanta, GA 30326
Tel: (404) 351-4400

C. T. Bevensee Auction
Service
P.O. Box 492
Botsford, CT 06404
Tel: (203) 426-6698

Bridges Antiques and
Auctions
Highway 46
P.O. Box 52A
Sanford, FL 32771
Tel: (305) 323-2801/322-
0095

Brookline Auction Gallery
Proctor Hill Road, Route
130
Brookline, NH 03033
Tel: (603) 673-4474/4153

Phillips
867 Madison Avenue
New York, NY 10021
Tel: (212) 570-4830

525 East 72nd Street
New York, NY 10021
Tel: (212) 570-4852

Representative Office:
6 Faneuil Hall
Marketplace
Boston, MA 02109
Tel: (617) 227-6145

Robert W. Skinner, Inc.
Main Street
Bolton, MA 01740
Tel: (617) 779-5528

585 Boylston Street
Boston, MA 02116
Tel: (617) 236-1700

C. G. Sloan & Co.
715 13th Street N.W.
Washington, DC 20005
Tel: (202) 628-1468

Branch Office:
403 North Charles Street
Baltimore, MD 21201
Tel: (301) 547-1177

Sotheby Parke Bernet, Inc.
980 Madison Avenue
New York, NY 10021
Tel: (212) 472-3400

1334 York Avenue
New York, NY 10021

171 East 84th Street
New York, NY 10028

Mid-Atlantic:
1630 Locust Street
Philadelphia, PA 19103
Tel: (215) 735-7886

Washington:
2903 M Street N.W.
Washington, DC 20007
Tel: (202) 298-8400

Southeast:
155 Worth Avenue
Palm Beach, FL 33480
Tel: (305) 658-3555

Midwest:
700 North Michigan
Avenue
Chicago, IL 60611
Tel: (312) 280-0185

Southwest:
Galleria Post Oak
5015 Westheimer Road
Houston, TX 77056
Tel: (713) 623-0010

Northwest:
210 Post Street
San Francisco, CA 94108
Tel: (415) 986-4982

Pacific Area:
Suite 117
850 West Hind Drive
Honolulu, Hawaii 96821
Tel: (808) 373-9166

R. W. Bronstein Corp.
3666 Main Street
Buffalo, NY 14226
Tel: (716) 835-7666/7408

Brzostek's Auction Service
2052 Lamson Road
Phoenix, NY 13135
Tel: (315) 678-2542

Buckingham Galleries, Ltd.
4350 Dawson Street
San Diego, CA 92115
Tel: (714) 283-7286

Bushell's Auction
2006 2nd Avenue
Seattle, WA 98121
Tel: (206) 622-5833

Canton Barn Auctions
79 Old Canton Road
Canton, CT 06019
Tel: (203) 693-4901/379-
0500

Fred Clark Auctioneer, Inc.
P.O. Box 124, Route 14
Scotland, CT 06264
Tel: (203) 423-3939/0594

Cockrum Auctions
2701 North Highway 94
St. Charles, MO 63301
Tel: (314) 723-9511

George Cole, Auctioneers
and Appraisers
14 Green Street
Kingston, NY 12401
Tel: (914) 338-2367

Conestoga Auction
Company, Inc.
P.O. Box 1
Manheim, PA 17545
Tel: (717) 898-7284

Cook's Auction Gallery
Route 58
Halifax, MA 02338
Tel: (617) 293-3445/
866-3243

Douglas Galleries
Route 5
South Deerfield, MA 01373
Tel: (413) 665-2877

The Fine Arts Company of
Philadelphia, Inc.
2317 Chestnut Street
Philadelphia, PA, 19103
Tel: (215) 564-3644

George S. Foster III
Route 28
Epsom, NH 03234
Tel: (603) 736-9240

Fred's Auction House
92 Pleasant Street
Leominster, MA 01453
Tel: (617) 534-9004

Col. K. R. French and Co.
Inc.
166 Bedford Road
Armonk, NY 10504
Tel: (914) 273-3674

Gilbert Auctions
River Road
Garrison, NY 10524
Tel: (914) 424-3657

Grandma's House
4712 Dudley

Wheatridge, CO 80033
Tel: (303) 423-3640/
534-2847

The William Haber Art
Collection, Inc.
139-11 Queens Boulevard
Jamaica, NY 11435
Tel: (212) 739-1000

Charlton Hall Galleries,
Inc.
930 Gervais Street
Columbia, SC 29201
Tel: (803) 252-7927/779-
5678

Harbor Auction Gallery
238 Bank Street
New London, CT 06355
Tel: (203) 443-0868

Harmer's of San Francisco,
Inc.
49 Geary Street
San Francisco, CA 94102
Tel: (415) 391-8244

Harris Auction Galleries
873-875 North Howard
Street
Baltimore, MD 21201
Tel: (301) 728-7040

William F. Hill Auction
Sales
Route 16
East Hardwick, VT 05834
Tel: (802) 472-6308

The House Clinic
P.O. Box 13013A
Orlando, Fl 32859
Tel: (305) 859-1770/
851-2979

Iroquois Auctions
Box 66, Broad Street
Port Henry, NY 12974
Tel: (518) 942-3355

Julia's Auction Service
Route 201, Skowhegan Road
Fairfield, ME 04937
Tel: (207) 453-9725

Kennedy Antique Auction
Galleries, Inc.
1088 Huff Road
Atlanta, GA 30318
Tel: (404) 351-4464

Kinzie Galleries Auction
Service
1002 3rd Avenue
Duncansville, PA 16835
Tel: (814) 695-3479

R. L. Loveless Associates,
Inc.
4223 Clover Street
Honeoye Falls, NY 14472
Tel: (716) 624-1648/1556

Lubin Galleries
30 West 26th Street
New York, NY 10010
Tel: (212) 924-3777

Maison Auction Co., Inc.
128 East Street
Wallingford, CT 06492
Tel: (203) 269-8007

Joel L. Malter and Co., Inc.
Suite 518, 16661 Ventura
Boulevard

Encino, CA 91316
Tel: (213) 784-7772/2181

David W. Mapes, Inc.
82 Front Street
Binghamton, NY 13905
Tel: (607) 724-6741/
862-9365

Mechanical Music Center,
Inc.
25 Kings Highway North
Darien, CT 06820
Tel: (203) 655-9510

Milwaukee Auction
Galleries
4747 West Bradley Road
Milwaukee, Wl 53223
Tel: (414) 355-5054

Wayne Mock, Inc.
Box 37
Tamworth, NH 03886
Tel: (603) 323-8057

William F. Moon and
Company
12 Lewis Road, RFD 1
North Attleboro, MA 02760
Tel: (617) 761-8003

New England Rare Coin
Auctions
89 Devonshire Street
Boston, MA 02109
Tel: (617) 227-8800

Park City Auction Service
925 Wood Street
Bridgeport, CT 06604
Tel: (203) 333-5251

Pennypacker Auction
Centre
1540 New Holland Road
Kenhorst, Reading, PA
19607
Tel: (215) 777-5890/6121

Quickie Auction House
Route 3
Osseo, MN 55369
Tel: (612) 428-4378

R & S Estate Liquidations
Box 205
Newton Center, MA 02159
Tel: (617) 244-6616

Bill Rinaldi Auctions
Bedell Road
Poughkeepsie, NY 12601
Tel: (914) 454-9613

Roan, Inc.
Box 118, RD 3
Logan Station, PA 17728
Tel: (717) 494-0170

Rockland Auction Services,
Inc.
72 Pomona Road
Suffern, NY 10901
Tel: (914) 354-3914/2723

Rose Galleries, Inc.
1123 West County Road B
Roseville, MN 55113
Tel: (612) 484-1415

Rosvall Auction Company
1238 & 1248 South
Broadway
Denver, CO 80210
Tel: (303) 777-2032/
722-4028

Sigmund Rothschild
27 West 67th Street
New York, NY 10023
Tel: (212) 873-5522

Vince Runowich Auctions
2312 4th Street North
St. Petersburg, FL 33704
Tel: (813) 895-3548

Sage Auction Gallery
Route 9A
Chester, CT 06412
Tel: (203) 526-3036

San Antonio Auction
Gallery
5096 Bianco
San Antonio, TX 78216
Tel: (512) 342-3800

San Francisco Auction
Gallery
1217 Sutter Street
San Francisco, CA 94109
Tel: (415) 441-3800

Emory Sanders
New London, NH 03257
Tel: (603) 526-6326

Sandwich Auction House
15 Tupper Road
Sandwich, MA 02563
Tel: (617) 888-1926/5675

Schafer Auction Gallery
82 Bradley Road
Madison, CT 06443
Tel: (203) 245-4173

Schmidt's Antiques
5138 West Michigan
Avenue
Ypsilanti, MI 48 197
Tel: (313) 434-2660

Shore Galleries, Inc.
3318 West Devon
Lincolnwood, IL 60659
Tel: (312) 676-2900

Shute's Auction Gallery
70 Accord Park Drive
Norwell, MA 02061
Tel: (617) 871-3414/
238-0586

Robert A. Siegel Auction
Galleries, Inc.
120 East 56th Street
New York, NY 10022
Tel: (212) 753-6421/2/3

Stack's Rare Coin Auctions
123 West 57th Street
New York, NY 10019
Tel: (212) 583-2580

Sterling Auction Gallery
62 North Second Avenue
Raritan, NJ 08869
Tel: (201) 685-9565/
464-4047

Stremmel Auctions, Inc.
2152 Prater Way
Sparks, NV 89431
Tel: (702) 331-1035

Philip Swedler & Son
850 Grand Avenue
New Haven, CT 06511
Tel: (203) 624-2202/562-
5065

Tepper Galleries
110 East 25th Street
New York, NY 10010
Tel: (212) 677-5300/1/2

Trend Galleries, Inc.
2784 Merrick Road
Bellmore, NY 11710
Tel: (516) 221-5588

Valle-McLeod Gallery
3303 Kirby Drive
Houston, TX 77098
Tel: (713) 523-8309/8310

The Watnot Auction
Box 78
Mellenville, NY 12544
Tel: (518) 672-7576

Adam A. Wechsler & Son
905-9 E Street NW
Washington, DC 20004
Tel: (202) 628-1281

White Plains Auction
Rooms
572 North Broadway
White Plains, NY 10603
Tel: (914) 428-2255

The Wilson Galleries
P.O. Box 102
Fort Defiance, VA 24437
Tel: (703) 885-4292

Helen Winter Associates
355 Farmington Avenue
Plainville, CT 06062
Tel: (203) 747-0714/
677-0848

Richard Withington, Inc.
Hillsboro, NH 03244
Tel: (603) 464-3232

Richard Wolffers, Inc.
127 Kearny Street
San Francisco, CA 94 108
Tel: (415) 781-5127

Samuel Yudkin and
Associates
1125 King Street
Alexandria, VA 22314
Tel: (703) 549-9330

AUSTRALIA

A.S.A. Stamps Co. Pty. Ltd.
138-140 Rundle Mall
National Bank Building
Adelaide,
South Australia 5001
Tel: 223-2951

Associated Auctioneers Pty.
Ltd.
800-810 Parramatta Road
Lewisham, New South
Wales 2049
Tel: 560-5899

G. J. Brain Auctioneers Pty.
Ltd.
122 Harrington Street
Sydney,
New South Wales 2000
Tel: 271701

Bright Slater Pty. Ltd.
Box 205 G.P.O.
Lower Ground Floor
Brisbane Club Building,
Isles Lane
Brisbane, Queensland 4000
Tel: 312415

Christie, Manson & Woods
(Australia) Ltd.
298 New South Head Road,
Double Bay
Sydney,
New South Wales 2028
Tel: 326-1422

William S. Ellenden Pty.
Ltd.
67-73 Wentworth Avenue
Sydney,
New South Wales 2000
Tel: 211-4035/211-4477

Bruce Granger Auctions
10 Hopetoun Street
Huristone Park,
New South Wales 2193
Tel: 559-4767

Johnson Bros. Auctioneers
& Real Estate Agents
328 Main Road
Glenorchy, Tasmania 7011
Tel: 725166 492909

James A. Johnson & Co.
92 Boronia Road
Vermont, Victoria 3133
Tel: 877-2754/874-3632

Jolly Barry Pty. Ltd.
212 Glenmore Road

Paddington,
New South Wales 2021
Tel: 357-4494

James R. Lawson Pty. Ltd.
236 Castlereagh Street
Sydney, New South Wales
Tel: 266408

Mason Greene & Associates
91-101 Leveson Street
North Melbourne,
Victoria 3051
Tel: 329-9911

Mercantile Art Auctions
317 Pacific Highway
North Sydney,
New South Wales 2060
Tel: 922-3610/922-3608

James R. Newall Auctions
Pty. Ltd.
164 Military Road
Neutral Bay,
New South Wales 2089
Tel: 903023/902587
(Sydney ex.)

P. L. Pickles & Co. Pty. Ltd.
655 Pacific Highway
Killara,
New South Wales 2071
Tel: 498-8069/498-2775

Sotheby Parke Bernet
Group Ltd.
115 Collins Street
Melbourne, Victoria 3000
Tel: (03) 63 39 00

H. E. Wells & Sons
326 Rokeby Road
Subiaco, West Australia
Tel: 3819448/3819040

Young Family Estates Pty.
Ltd.
229 Camberwell Road
East Hawthorn,
Melbourne 2123
Tel: 821433

NEW ZEALAND

Devereaux & Culley Ltd.
200 Dominion Road
Mt. Eden, Auckland
Tel: 687429/687112

Alex Harris Ltd.
P.O. Box 510
377 Princes Street, Dunedin
Tel: 773955/740703

Roger Moat Ltd.
College Hill and Beaumont
Street
Auckland
Tel: 37 1588/37 1686/
37 1595

New Zealand Stamp
Auctions
P.O. Box 3496
Queen and Wyndham
Streets
Auckland
Tel: 375490/375498

Alistair Robb Coin Auctions
La Aitken Street, Box 3705
Wellington
Tel: 727-141

Dunbar Sloane Ltd.
32 Waring Taylor Street,
Wellington
Tel: 721-367

Thornton Auctions Ltd.
89 Albert Street,
Auckland 1
Tel: 30888 (3 lines)

Daniel J. Visser
109 and 90 Worchester
Street
Christchurch
Tel: 68853/67297

AUSTRIA

Christie's
Ziehrerplatz 4/22

A-1030 Vienna
Tel: (0222) 73 26 44

BELGIUM

Christie, Manson & Woods
(Belgium) Ltd.
33 Boulevard de Waterloo
B-1000 Brussels
Tel: (02) 512-8765/512-8830
Sotheby Parke Bernet
Belgium
Rue de l'Abbaye 32
1050 Brussels
Tel: 343 50 07

CANADA

A-1 Auctioneer Evaluation
Services Ltd.
P.O. Box 926
Saint John, N.B. E2L 4C3
Tel: (508) 762-0559

Appleton Auctioneers Ltd.
1238 Seymour Street
Vancouver, B.C. V6B 3N9
Tel: (604) 685-1715

Ashton Auction Service
P.O. Box 500
Ashton, Ontario, KOA 180
Tel: (613) 257-1575

Canada Book Auctions
35 Front Street East
Toronto, Ontario M5E 1B3
Tel: (416) 368-4326

Christie's International Ltd.
Suite 2002, 1055 West
Georgia Street
Vancouver, B.C. V6E 3P3
Tel: (604) 685-2126

Miller & Johnson
Auctioneers Ltd.
2882 Gottingen Street
Halifax,
Nova Scotia B3K 3E2
Tel: (902) 425-3366/
425-3606

Phillips Ward-Price Ltd.
76 Davenport Road
Toronto, Ontario M5R 1H3
Tel: (416) 923-9876

Sotheby Parke Bernet
(Canada), Inc.
156 Front Street
Toronto, Ontario M5J 2L6
Tel: (416) 596-0300

Representative:
David Brown
2321 Granville Street
Vancouver, B.C. V6H 3G4
Tel: (604) 736-6363

DENMARK

Kunsthallens
Kunstauktioner A/S
Købmagergade 11
DK 1150 Copenhagen
Tel: (01) 13 85 69
Nellemann & Thomsen
Neilgade 45
DK-8000 Aarhus
Tel: (06) 12 06 66/12 00 02

FRANCE

Ader, Picard, Tajan
12, rue Favart
75002 Paris
Tel: 261.80.07
Artus
15, rue de la Grange-
Batelière
75009 Paris
Tel: 523.12.03
Audap
32, rue Drouot
75009 Paris
Tel: 742.78.01
Bondu
17, rue Drouot
75009 Paris

Tel: 770.36.16
Boscher, Gossart
3, rue d'Amboise
75009 Paris
Tel: 260.87.87
Briest
15, rue Drouot
75009 Paris
Tel: 770.66.29
de Cagny
4, rue Drouot
75009 Paris
Tel: 246.00.07
Charbonneaux
134, rue du Faubourg Saint-
Honoré
75008 Paris
Tel: 359.66.57
Chayette
10, rue Rossini
75009 Paris
Tel: 770.38.89
Delaporte, Rieunier
159, rue Montmartre
75002 Paris
Tel: 508.41.83
Delorme
3, rue Penthièvre
75008 Paris
Tel: 265.57.63
Godeau
32, rue Drouot
75009 Paris
Tel: 770.67.68
Gros
22, rue Drouot
75000 Paris
Tel: 770.83.04
Langlade
12, rue Descombes
75017 Paris
Tel: 227.00.91
Loudmer, Poulain
73, rue de Faubourg Saint-
Honoré
75008 Paris
Tel: 266.90.01
Maignan
6, rue de la Michodière
75002 Paris
Tel: 742.71.52
Maringe
16, rue de Provence
75009 Paris
Tel: 770.61.15
Marlio
7, rue Ernest-Renan
75015 Paris
Tel: 734.81.13

Paul Martin & Jacques
Martin
3, impasse des Chevau-
Legers
78000 Versailles
Tel: 950.58.08
Bonhams
Baron Foran,
Duc de Saint-Bar
2, rue Bellanger
92200 Neuilly sur Seine
Tel: (1) 637-1329
Christie's
Princess Jeanne-Marie de
Broglie
17, rue de Lille
75007 Paris
Tel: (331) 261-1247
Sotheby's
Rear Admiral J. A.
Templeton-Cotill, C.B.
3, rue de Miromesnil
75008 Paris
Tel: (1) 266-4060

MONACO

Sotheby Parke Bernet
Group

P.O. Box 45 Sporting
d'Hiver
Place du Casino,
Monte Carlo
Tel: (93) 30 88 80

HONG KONG

Sotheby Parke Bernet
(Hong Kong) Ltd.
P.O. Box 83
705 Lane Crawford House
64-70 Queen's Road Central
Hong Kong
Tel: 22-5454

ITALY

Christie's (International)
S.A.
Palazzo Massimo
Lancellotti
Piazza Navona 114
00186 Rome
Tel: 6541217

Christie's (Italy) S.R.1.
9 Via Borgogna
20144 Milan
Tel: 794712

Finarte S.P.A.
Piazzetta Bossi 4
20121 Milan
Tel: 877041

Finarte S.P.A.
Via delle Quattro
Fontane 20
Rome
Tel: 463564

Palazzo Internationale delle
Aste ed Esposizioni, S.P.A.
Palazzo Corsini
Il Prato 56
Florence
Tel: 293000

Sotheby Parke Bernet Italia
26 Via Gino Capponi
50121 Florence
Tel: 571410

Sotheby Parke Bernet Italia
Via Montenapoleone 3
20121 Milan
Tel: 783907

Sotheby Parke Bernet Italia
Palazzo Taverna
Via di Monte Giordano 36
00186 Rome
Tel: 656 1670/6547400

THE
NETHERLANDS

Christie, Manson & Woods
Ltd.
Rokin 91
1012 KL Amsterdam
Tel: (020) 23 15 05
Sotheby Mak Van Waay
B.V.
102 Rokin
1012 KZ Amsterdam
Tel: 24 62 15
Van Dieten Stamp Auctions
B.V.
2 Tournooiveld
2511 CX The Hague
Tel: 70-464312/70-648658

SINGAPORE and
MALAYSIA

Victor & Morris Pte. Ltd.
39 Talok Ayer Street
Republic of Singapore
Tel: 94844

SOUTH AFRICA

Ashbey's Galleries
43-47 Church Street
Cape Town 8001
Tel: 22-7527

Claremart Auction Centre
47 Main Road
Claremont, Cape Town 7700
Tel: 66-8826/66-8804

Ford & Van Niekerk Pty.
Ltd.
156 Main Road
P.O. Box 8
Plumstead, Cape Town
Tel: 71-3384

Sotheby Park Bernet South
Africa Pty. Ltd.
Total House, Smit and
Rissik Streets
P.O. Box 310010
Braamfontein 2017
Tel: 39-3726

SPAIN

Juan R. Cayon
41 Fuencarral
Madrid 14
Tel: 221 08 32/221 43 72/222
95 98

Christie's International Ltd.
Casado del Alisal 5
Madrid
Tel: (01) 228-9300

Sotheby Parke Bernet & Co.
Scursal de Espana
Calle del Prado 18
Madrid 14
Tel: 232-6488/232-6572

SWITZERLAND

Daniel Beney
Avenue des Mousquines 2
CH- 1005 Lausanne
Tel: (021) 22 28 64

Blanc
Arcade Hotel Beau-Rivage,
Box 84
CH- 1001 Lausanne
Tel: (021) 27 32 55/26 86 20

Christie's (International)
S.A.
8 Place de la Taconnerie
CH-1204 Geneva
Tel: (022) 28 25 44

Steinwiesplatz
CH-8032 Zurich
Tel: (01) 69 05 05

Auktionshaus
Doblaschofsky AG.
Monbijoustrasse 28/30
CH-3001 Berne
Tel: (031) 25 23 72/73/74

Galerie Fischer
Haldenstrasse 19
CH-6006 Lucerne
Tel: (041) 22 57 72/73

Germann Auktionshaus
Zeitweg 67
CH-8032 Zurich
Tel: (01) 32 83 58/32 01 12

Haus der Bücher AG
Baumleingasse 18
CH-4051 Basel
Tel: (061) 23 30 88

Adolph Hess AG
Haldenstrasse 5
CH-6006 Lucerne
Tel: (041) 22 43 92/22 45 35

Auktionshaus Peter
Ineichen

C.F. Meyerstrasse 14
CH-8002 Zurich
Tel: (01) 201-3017

Galerie Koller AG
Ramistrasse 8
CH-8001 Zurich
Tel: (01) 47 50 40

Koller St. Gallen
St. Gallen
Tel: (071) 23 42 40

Galerie Koller,
New York Office, Inc.
575 Madison Avenue,
Suite 1006
New York, NY 10022
Tel: (212) 486-1484

Kornfeld & Co.
Laupenstrasse 49
CH-3008 Berne
Tel: (031) 25 46 73

Phillips Son & Neale SA
6 Rue de la Cité
CH-1204 Geneva
Tel: (022) 28 68 28

Christian Rosset
Salle des Ventes,
29 Rue du Rhone
CH-1204 Geneva
Tel: (022) 28 96 33/34

Schweizerische Gesellschaft
der Freunde von
Kunstauktionen
11 Werdmühlestrasse
Ch-8001 Zurich
Tel: (01) 211-4789

Sotheby Parke Bernet AG
20 Bleicherweg
CH-8022 Zurich
Tel: (01) 202-0011

24 Rue de la Cité
CH-1024 Geneva
Tel: (022) 21 33 77

Dr. Erich Steinfels,
Auktionen
Rämistrasse 6
CH-8001 Zurich
Tel: (01) 252-1233 (wine)
     (01) 34 1233 (fine art)

Frank Sternberg
Bahnhofstrasse 84
CH-8001 Zurich
Tel: (01) 211-7980

Jürg Stucker Gallery Ltd.
Alter Aargauerstalden 30
CH-3006 Berne
Tel: (031) 44 00 44

Uto Auktions AG
Lavaterstrasse 11
CH-8027 Zurich
Tel: (01) 202-9444

WEST GERMANY

Galerie Gerda Bassenge
Erdener Strasses 5a
D-1000 West Berlin 33
Tel: (030) 892 19 32/
891 29 09

Kunstauktionen Waltraud
Boltz
Bahnhof Strasse 25-27
D-8580 Bayreuth
Tel: (0921) 206 16

Brandes
Wolfenbütteler Strasse 12
D-3300 Braunschweig 1
Tel: (0531) 737 32

Gernot Dorau
Johann-Georg Strasse 2
D-1000 Berlin 31
Tel: (030) 892 61 98

F. Dörling
Neuer Wall 40-41
D-2000 Hamburg 36
Tel: (040) 36 46 70/36 52 82

Roland A. Exner
Kunsthandel-Auktionen
Am Ihmeufer
D-3000 Hannover 91
Tel: (0511) 44 44 84

Hartung & Karl
Karolinenplatz 5a
D-8000 Munich 2
Tel: (089) 28 40 34

Hauswedell & Nolte
Pöseldorfer Weg 1
D-2000 Hamburg 13
Tel: (040) 44 83 66

Karl & Faber
Amiraplatz 3
(Luitpoldblock)
D-8000 Munich 2
Tel: (089) 22 18 65/66

Graf Klenau Ohg Nachf
Maximilian Strasse 32
D-8000 Munich 1
Tel: (089) 22 22 81/82

Numismatik Lanz
München
Promenadeplatz 9
D-8000 Munich 2
Tel: (089) 29 90 70

Kunsthaus Lempertz
Neumarkt 3
D-5000 Cologne 1
Tel: (0221) 21 02 51/52

Stuttgarter
Kunstauktionshaus
Dr. Fritz Nagel
Mörikestrasse 17-19
D-7000 Stuttgart 1
Tel: (0711) 61 33 87/77

Neumeister Münchener
Kunstauktionshaus KG
Barer Strasse 37
D-8000 Munich 40
Tel: (089) 28 30 11

Petzold KG- Photographica
Maximilian Strasse 36
D-8900 Augsburg 11
Tel: (0821) 3 37 25

Reiss & Auvermann
Zum Talblick 2
D-6246 Glashütten im
Taunus 1
Tel: (06174) 69 47/48

Gus Schiele Auktions-
Galerie
Ottostrasse 7 (Neuer
Kunstblock)
D-8000 Munich 2
Tel: (089) 59 41 92

Gus Schiele Auktions-
Galerie
Paulinen Strasse 47
D-7000 Stuttgart 1
Tel: (0711) 61 63 77

J. A. Stargardt
Universitäts Strasse 27
D-3550 Marburg
Tel: (06421) 234 52

AuktionshausTietjen & Co.

Spitaler Strasse 30
D-2000 Hamburg 1
Tel: (040) 33 03 68/69

Aachener Auktionshaus
Crott & Schmelzer
Pont Strasse 21
Aachen
Tel: (0241) 369 00

Kunstauktionen Rainer
Baumann
Obere Woerthstrasse 7-11
Nuremberg
Tel: (0911) 20 48 47

August Bödiger oHG
Oxford Strasse 4
Bonn
Tel: (0228) 63 69 40

Bolland & Marotz
Feldören 19
Bremen
Tel: (0421) 32 18 11

Bongartz Gelgen Auktionen
Münsterplatz 27
Aachen
Tel: (0241) 206 19

Christie's International Ltd.
Düsseldorf:
Alt Pempelfort 11a
D-4000 Düsseldorf
Tel: (0211) 35 05 77

Hamburg:
Wenzelstrasse 21
D-2000 Hamburg 60
Tel: (4940) 279-0866

Munich:
Maximilianstrasse 20
D-8000 Munich 22
Tel: (089) 22 95 39

Württenberg:
Schloss Langenburg
D-7183 Langenburg

Sotheby Parke Bernet
G.m.b.H.
Munich:
Odeonsplatz 16
D-8000 Munich 22
Tel: (089) 22 23 75/6

Kunstauktion Jürgen
Fischer
Alexander Strasse 11
Heilbronn
Tel: (07 131) 785 23

Galerie Göbig
Ritterhaus Strasse 5
(am Thermalbad)
ad Nauheim
Tel: (Frankfurt)
(611) 77 40 80

Knut Günther
Auf der Kömerwiese 19-21
Frankfurt
Tel: (0611) 55 32 92/
55 70 22

Antiquitaeten Lothar
Heubel
Odenthaler Strasse 371
Cologne
Tel: (0221) 60 18 25

Hildener Auktionshaus und
Kunstgalerie
Klusenhof 12
Hilden
Tel: (02103) 602 00

INDEX

692